**This book is to be returned on or before
the last date stamped below.**

13SEP002

THE GREAT MARLBOROUGH
AND HIS DUCHESS

THE
GREAT
MARLBOROUGH
AND HIS
DUCHESS

Virginia Cowles

WEIDENFELD AND NICOLSON
LONDON

For Aidan with love

First published in Great Britain by
George Weidenfeld & Nicolson Limited
91 Clapham High Street, London SW4

ISBN 0 297 78225 8

Text set in 11/12½ pt Linotron 202 Sabon, printed and bound
in Great Britain at the Pitman Press, Bath

Contents

Illustrations and Maps

Portrait of John Churchill, 1st Duke of Marlborough, by John Closterman
(*National Portrait Gallery*)
Miniature of Charles II by Samuel Cooper (*Mauritshuis, The Hague*)
Painting of Barbara Villiers by Sir Peter Lely (*by courtesy of Earl Spencer*)
Louis XIV, the Sun King
(*by courtesy of the Duke of Marlborough, Blenheim Palace*)
James II by an unknown artist, c. 1690 (*National Portrait Gallery*)
Portrait of Arabella Churchill by Mary Beale
(*by courtesy of the Duke of Marlborough, Blenheim Palace*)
The Duke of Berwick painted by Niccolo Cassana (*by courtesy of Earl Spencer*)
Sarah, Duchess of Marlborough, after Sir Godfrey Kneller, c. 1700
(*National Portrait Gallery*)
The burning of the *Royal James*, 1672
(*National Maritime Museum, Greenwich*)
Companion portraits of William and Mary, Prince and Princess of Orange,
by William Wissing, 1685 (*reproduced by gracious permission of
Her Majesty The Queen*)
The Marlborough family, painted by John Closterman, c. 1696
(*by courtesy of the Duke of Marlborough, Blenheim Palace*)
Prince George of Denmark painted by Michael Dahl, 1704
(*reproduced by gracious permission of Her Majesty The Queen*)
Portrait of Anne as a young woman by William Wissing
(*Scottish National Portrait Gallery, Edinburgh*)
Abigail Hill, Lady Masham (*BBC Hulton Picture Library*)
Prince Eugene of Savoy painted by Sir Godfrey Kneller
(*by courtesy of the Duke of Marlborough, Blenheim Palace*)
Engraving of the battle of Blenheim, 13 August 1704
(*National Army Museum*)
Marlborough's note to Sarah giving her news of the victory at Blenheim
(*by courtesy of the Duke of Marlborough, Blenheim Palace*)

Robert Harley, 1st Earl of Oxford, painted by Sir Godfrey Kneller, 1714
   (*National Portrait Gallery*)
Portrait of Sydney, 1st Earl of Godolphin, by Sir Godfrey Kneller, *c.*1705
   (*National Portrait Gallery*)
Henry St John, Viscount Bolingbroke; portrait attributed to J. Richardson
   (*National Portrait Gallery*)
Marshal Villars (*British Museum*)
Marshal Villeroy (*British Museum*)
Marshal Tallard (*British Museum*)
The Duke of Vendôme (*Cliché des Musées Nationaux, Paris*)
Contemporary engraving of the battle of Ramillies, May 1706
   (*National Army Museum*)
The Ramillies playing card (*Royal Library, Windsor, reproduced by gracious
   permission of Her Majesty The Queen*)
Portrait of the 1st Duke of Marlborough by Sir Godfrey Kneller
   (*by courtesy of Hudson's Bay Company, London*)
Sarah, Duchess of Marlborough, by Sir Godfrey Kneller
   (*by courtesy of the Duke of Marlborough, Blenheim Palace*)
Detail from the tapestry showing the battle of Oudenarde, 1708
   (*by courtesy of the Duke of Marlborough, Blenheim Palace*)
Oil sketch of the Duke of Marlborough at the battle of Malplaquet, 1709
   (*by courtesy of the Marquess of Anglesey*)
Detail from the tapestry showing the siege of Bouchain
   (*by courtesy of the Duke of Marlborough, Blenheim Palace*)
Portrait of the Duke of Somerset by Sir Godfrey Kneller, *c.*1703
   (*National Portrait Gallery*)
An engraving of the north face of Blenheim Palace, *c.* 1745 (*British Library*)

MAPS

Acknowledgments

Blenheim Palace is open to the public and visitors can wander through the magnificent rooms and study at leisure the famous tapestries depicting scenes from the great Duke's battles. Some of the windows look upon park and gardens laid out under the supervision of Sir John Vanbrugh, the celebrated architect who was selected by Queen Anne to design the palace as a gift for Marlborough. Not so well known, but with its own fascination, is the Duchess of Marlborough's creation, Marlborough House, which stands on the Mall in London. This edifice sprang into being partly out of spite because Sarah Marlborough was determined to show Vanbrugh that Sir Christopher Wren was a more competent and less expensive architect than himself. Marlborough House is now used by the Commonwealth Relations Office, so I am grateful to Miss Janice Ewan, the curator, for allowing my husband and myself to see the martial frescoes painted by Louis Laguerre. They are crammed with incident and executed with all the verve that the Duchess undoubtedly demanded.

I would also like to thank the publishers who gave me permission to quote from their books: Harrap for Sir Winston Churchill's *Marlborough: His Life and Times*; Longman for G. M. Trevelyan's study of *England under Queen Anne*; Batsford for David Chandler's work on *Marlborough as Military Commander*; Routledge and Kegan Paul for Edward Gregg's *Queen Anne*; W. W. Norton of New York for John Wolf's *Louis XIV*; Macmillan of London and Harper & Row of New York for A. L. Rowse's *The Early Churchills*; and David Green for his biography *Sarah, Duchess of Marlborough*. I thank Mrs Judy Mooney for her unflagging cheerfulness in typing and retyping my manuscript; the staff of the London Library for their courtesy and help; and the librarians in the Manuscript Room of the British Museum for unravelling the mysteries of the Blenheim folders. These papers contain much of the private and official correspondence of the Marlboroughs, and for nearly three centuries were kept at Blenheim Palace, but they are now lodged in the British Library.

I am indebted to Mr Maurice Ashley for reading my manuscript with his usual scrupulous care and saving me from innumerable errors; and to Linda Osband of Weidenfeld's for her expertise as an editor. Finally, I am deeply grateful to my son, Randall Crawley, for his perspicacious criticisms and suggestions, all of which I gladly accepted.

VIRGINIA COWLES
London 1983

Preface

Marlborough could almost be described as England's greatest 'unknown soldier'. Because of the calumnies heaped upon him by political enemies, and believed by subsequent generations of historians, he has never rivalled Wellington as a schoolboy's hero. Yet the fact that in his ten years of campaigning he never lost a battle is a feat unparalleled in military history. He smashed the domination of Louis XIV; ensured the independence and liberty of his country; and opened the gateway for two centuries of English imperial power.

Less surprising is the fact that Marlborough is unknown in France. The French are a chauvinistic people and only too happy to forget a man whose name was once the scourge of her prestigious armies and celebrated generals. The French of today are still familiar with the nursery rhyme, *Malbrouk se va t'en guerre*, but a French schoolteacher recently remarked to the author that she was amazed to discover that 'Malbrouk' was a real man.

This book is a reminder of his service perhaps not to France but to Europe as a whole.

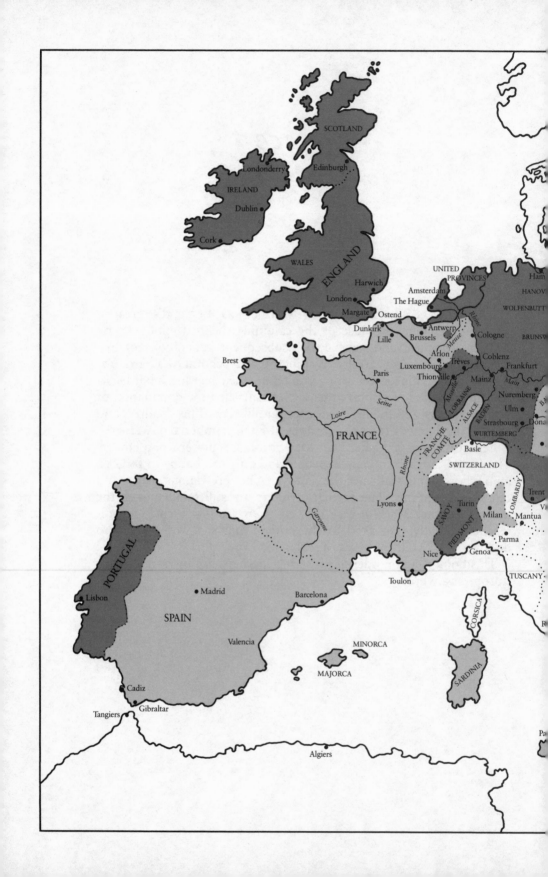

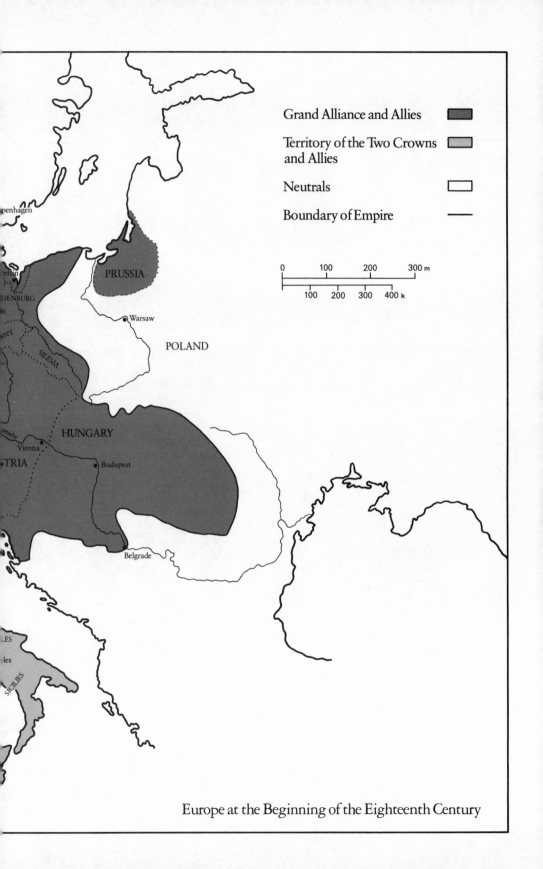

Grand Alliance and Allies

Territory of the Two Crowns and Allies

Neutrals

Boundary of Empire

0   100   200   300 m

100   200   300   400 k

Copenhagen

PRUSSIA

Warsaw

POLAND

BRANDENBURG

SAXONY

SILESIA

HUNGARY

Vienna

AUSTRIA

Budapest

Belgrade

Danube

NAPLES

Naples

SICILIES

Europe at the Beginning of the Eighteenth Century

One

The First Winston Churchill

Winston Churchill, an impoverished gentleman from Dorset, and his ten-year-old son, John, may have been among the dense throng that gathered to greet Charles II when he entered London on 29 May 1660. The date happened to be the King's thirtieth birthday and the occasion was memorable for marking the end of fourteen years of exile. Many people in the noisy, jostling crowd were lucky to have survived the upheavals of the past two decades, but none more so than the triumphant home-comer, Charles himself.

The King's hazardous existence had begun long before the over-throw of the monarchy. At the age of twelve he had seen civil war break out between Cavaliers and Roundheads about the supremacy of the Crown over Parliament. With his nine-year-old brother, James, he was present at the great battle of Edgehill and was allowed to follow further campaigns from the headquarters of his father, Charles I. When he was fourteen he had been placed in nominal command of the army in the west of England, but by this time Oliver Cromwell and his famous 'Ironsides' had entered the struggle and two years later the royalist defeat at Torrington brought the conflict to an end. The Princes succeeded in making their way to France and three years later Charles I was executed.

The exiled Charles II dreamed of freeing England from the rule of the usurper and in 1650 went to Scotland where the Presbyterian oligar-chy, known as 'the Covenanters', were in the process of forming an army. They hailed Charles as King of the Scots, but everything went wrong. The army was no match for Cromwell and suffered two defeats in twelve months – the first at Dunbar, the second at Worcester. In Worcester city the streets ran with blood after hours of hand-to-hand fighting and it was not until his men refused to continue the fight that

Charles agreed to withdraw. He and a few colleagues escaped through the last remaining city gate. He was soon dismayed to find a growing number of stragglers attaching themselves to his party ('Although I could not get them to stand by me against the enemy,' Charles later recalled, 'I could not get rid of them now I had a mind to it.') Eventually he managed to give them the slip by riding off the main road and disappearing into the night. His companions included the Duke of Buckingham and Lord Wilmot. They disguised themselves as humble travellers and, after six precarious weeks as fugitives with a huge price on their heads, reached Brighton and embarked for France. At St Germain Charles invented stories about his experiences in order to protect those who had helped him, but later gave a true account of his adventures: how he had spent the night in an oak tree and at dawn watched Cromwell's soldiers beating through the forest trying to find him; how he had travelled to Bristol as the manservant of a beautiful young royalist lady, Jane Lane; and how he had conversed with a blacksmith and agreed with him that the wicked Charles Stuart ought to be hanged.

Although Charles's mother, Henrietta Maria, was a French princess, a sister of Louis XIII (which made Charles a first cousin of Louis XIV, then a boy of thirteen), Cardinal Mazarin, the ruler of France, was not enthusiastic about offering the royal refugees a permanent home. Nevertheless, he did his duty and even gave Charles a small pension. But the money had to stretch so far that the refugees lived in great need. Indeed, they were so poor that often they could not even afford to buy firewood. Their prospects were so bleak that it is not surprising that Mazarin came to the conclusion that England's Republic might not be as transitory a phase as people predicted. In 1654 the Cardinal made a treaty with Cromwell which, in a secret clause, excluded Charles and his Court from France.

Charles refused to be downcast and departed for Cologne and Brussels in search of new support. 'We pass our lives as well as most people do that have no money,' he wrote from Southern Germany, 'for we dance and play as though we have taken the Plate Fleet.'* Cromwell's spies did not find this cheerfulness in the least commendable. 'I think', one of them reported to England, ' . . . that greater abominations were never practised among people than at this day at Charles Stuart's Court. Fornication, drunkenness and adultery are esteemed no sins among them.'[1] Other agents reported that Charles had taken his 'seventeenth mistress'; and when one of these ladies,

* The Spanish fleet that carried silver to Spain from the River Plate in South America.

Lucy Walter, went to England with her bastard son, Cromwell took pleasure in shipping back 'Charles Stuart's lady of pleasure and the young heir'. As fate would have it, this boy, who in later life became James Scott, Duke of Monmouth and Buccleugh, actually did try to inherit and met his death on the executioner's block. His mother, described by the diarist, John Evelyn, as 'a browne, beautiful, bold but insipid creature', had other lovers after Charles and died in Paris in 1658 'miserably, without anything to bury her'.

The passing years did not seem to improve royalist chances; but just when things looked quite hopeless for Charles, Oliver Cromwell died. His son, Richard, had neither the ability nor the following to keep the reins of government in his hands. Early in 1660 General George Monck, one of Cromwell's most loyal supporters, and now Military Governor of Scotland, set out for London leading four cavalry and six infantry regiments. Ostensibly he was going to England to forestall any potential *coup*, but secretly Monck deplored Richard Cromwell's ineffectual rule and had decided that if England was to be prevented from sliding into chaos, the old order of King and Parliament would have to be re-established.

When Monck arrived in London with the only military force capable of maintaining order, he told the Rump Parliament* that the time had come for new elections. The public was not slow to draw conclusions, and soon Samuel Pepys was noting in his diary that men no longer toasted the King in private but were drinking his health in the taverns. Monck himself was already in touch with Charles II in Holland and advised him to assure the new Constituent Assembly that he would pardon his enemies, uphold the Anglican Church and rule England through the will of a new and free Parliament. When the gracious message, known as the Declaration of Breda, was read to Monck's assembly, members were overcome with gratitude and invited Charles to return to England 'to take the Government of the Kingdom on his shoulders'. A fleet was dispatched to The Hague carrying a chest containing £50,000 as a gift to the King, who could remember nothing but penury. Charles emptied all the coins on his bed and called his sister, Mary, and his brother, James, to look at the staggering sight. In May 1660 the flagship of the fleet, renamed the *Royal Charles*, took the King and his small retinue to Dover, where they were met by General Monck, now Commander-in-Chief of England, Scotland and Ireland, who knelt before him. Charles conferred a knighthood of the Garter on him and a few weeks later made him Duke of Albemarle.

* The surviving members of the Parliament of 1640 which had been purged and finally disbanded by Cromwell.

After two days in Canterbury Charles set out for London. The city gave the royal party a stupendous welcome as though to make up for its deplorable republican lapse. Cannons boomed, flags flew and an immense crowd, laughing and crying, cheered themselves hoarse. John Evelyn the diarist wrote of the

> triumph of above 20,000 horse and foot, brandishing their swords and shouting with inexpressible joy; the ways strewed with flowers, and bells ringing, the streets hung with tapestry, fountains running with wine, the Mayor, Aldermen and all companies in their chains of gold and banners. . . .

The King rode on horseback, bare-headed, dressed in a silver doublet. By the time he reached Whitehall he was nearly deaf from the relentless booming of the cannon and when he arrived at the Palace of Whitehall made a very short 'gracious speech' explaining that he was 'disordered by my journey and with noise still sounding in my ears'. Apparently he soon recovered, for legend has it that he spent his first night as 'a king in possession of a Kingdom' in the arms of his nineteen-year-old mistress, Barbara Villiers. Barbara was a kinswoman of the second Duke of Buckingham and the wife of Roger Palmer, a *complaisant* gentleman who made a point of looking the other way.

If the King thanked the Almighty for his change in fortune many of his subjects, among them Winston Churchill (whom we left in the crowd waiting for the royal procession), also hoped for better times. Churchill was a fervent monarchist who had fought and suffered for the royalist cause. As a Captain of Horse he had taken part in the battles of Lansdowne Hill and Roundway Down and, in 1645, while fighting with the royal garrison at Bristol, had been shot through the arm. With the West Country swarming with victorious Cromwellians, Winston was fortunate to have a mother-in-law who could give him refuge. Lady Drake, a niece of the first Duke of Buckingham, lived at Ashe House near the sleepy Devon village of Axminster and was just as ardent a Roundhead as Winston was a Cavalier. Although she was said to be 'imperious and difficult', family ties apparently proved strong enough for her to overlook Churchill's allegiances which had even led him, while living on her bounty, to write a book on the history of the monarchy and the Divine Right of Kings. Her forbearance was particularly praiseworthy as she had suffered greatly at the hands of royalists who had set fire to Ashe House and driven her out – or so she claimed – half-naked. Her home was a sizeable manor-house built of local stone but, as part of the roof had been destroyed, some of the rooms were open to the sky. Lady Drake had no money for repairs so the family was obliged to huddle together in the undamaged section. Indeed, her daughter, Elizabeth, and her son-in-law Winston spent thirteen years at Ashe House. There, Elizabeth gave birth to most of her twelve children, of whom only five survived infancy and only four became adults. The survivors were the two eldest, Arabella and John, born in 1648 and 1650, and George and Charles, born in 1652 and 1655.

Although little is known of the boyhood of John Churchill, he must have had a happy childhood playing with his brothers in the glorious Devon countryside with its lush meadows and rolling hills. It was a land of wonderful trees and birds, and a trout stream rushed merrily past the house – a godsend when food was short. No doubt the boys played soldiers, their ears ringing with local tales of clashes between Roundheads and Cavaliers. As John was the eldest, he probably made himself general and, perhaps by studying the contours of the countryside for make-believe attacks, he unconsciously trained his eye for future military campaigns.

Other aspects of life in the ruined house were far from easy. Not only was the family deeply divided but hard put to it to make ends meet. It may have been this very impecuniousness that smoothed away the differences. They were a strange household, helping each other to pull in diametrically opposed directions. Lady Drake was using the processes of the law to try and get compensation for royalist damage to her property, while Winston was equally busy trying to avoid the imposition of a fine for having fought against Cromwell. Despite a long drawn-out battle of delaying tactics, Churchill eventually had to pay £446 18s 0d, nearly three times more than his annual income. At Ashe House, John Churchill was forced to tread warily between the conflicting opinions of the grown-ups, and this taught him to guard his tongue and later won him a reputation for secrecy. His deep concern for money also stemmed from those poverty-stricken days, and perhaps it was here, too, that he learned the value of having friends on both sides of a quarrel.

The pendulum swung backwards and forwards between hope and frustration, but now that the Restoration had come, it was Winston Churchill's turn to look for happier circumstances. He did not have to wait long. In 1661, when the Cavalier Parliament was chosen – a Parliament that sat for eighteen years but was only summoned at the King's pleasure – Churchill became Member for Weymouth. Although the King lacked the funds to reimburse impoverished royalists, he did what he could to honour them. In Churchill's case he offered an augmentation of arms to be added to his heraldic propensities. Winston did not regard this as sufficient compensation for the long years of hardship and anxiety, and enblazoned on his new coat-of-arms an uprooted oak tree, below which was the motto '*Fiel pero desdichado*' – 'Faithful but unfortunate'.

No doubt Churchill complained in order to provoke new favours; and in this he was successful, for in 1662 he was appointed one of seven commissioners to assist in working out a land settlement in Ireland. During the Civil War thousands of acres had been confiscated first by one side, then the other, and now scores of owners were asking for restitution and compensation. Winston took his family to Dublin and put his sons in day-schools, but after fifteen tedious months he received permission to return to London on leave. He was rewarded with a knighthood in January 1664 and, as the Commission suffered a temporary eclipse, he was able to spend the rest of the year in London. He took a house in the City and placed his son John in St Paul's School, conveniently close at hand. He occupied himself by taking part in the brief session of Parliament that began in March 1664.

As Parliament only met on the rare occasions when the King summoned it, the duties of an MP were scarcely exacting. Indeed, Churchill was glad to accept another post that summer which made him an official of the royal household. He became a member of the Board of the Green Cloth, a committee whose task was to pay the wages of the Whitehall kitchen staff and to supervise the expenditure of the department as a whole – not an easy task, as the committee soon discovered that the kitchen was the centre of a long-established and profitable enterprise. Churchill's duties commanded an annual salary of £88 13s 4d, and entitled him to free board and lodging at Whitehall. Although he lived with his family in the City, he worked at Court in the day and made use of his lodgings when occasion demanded.

Whitehall, where Winston took up his duties, was not really a palace at all, 'but a heap of houses erected at diverse times and of different models . . . made contiguous . . . in the best manner for the residence of the Court.' The result was a village with a rabbit-warren of streets, squares and gardens and even a lawn for bowls. However, the French visitor who made this observation had to admit that the site was superb, stretching as it did for half a mile along the Thames and reaching back to where No. 10 Downing Street and New Scotland Yard stand today. He granted that it was a 'more commodious habitation than the Louvre, for it contains 2,000 rooms and that between a fine park and a noble river so that 'tis admirably well suited for the conveniency of walking and going about the business of the City.'[2]

The palace was not just a royal residence but the seat of government. There the King consulted his chosen advisers, held his Privy Council meetings, received his ambassadors, even touched for scrofula, known as the King's Evil. The grounds swarmed with royal servants, ranging from humble, below-stairs helpers to aristocrats who served as Gentlemen of the Bedchamber and received anything from £500 to £1,000 a year. As the lower grades were also treated with comparative generosity, it is scarcely surprising that the number of royal retainers snowballed so that before long there were literally hundreds of palace employees whose occupations seemed to be a mystery: 490 Gentlemen of the Privy Chamber in Extraordinary and thirty-two gentlemen of the Chapel, not to mention such anachronisms as a Falconer, a Cross-bow Maker or the fanciful 'Keeper of the Sweet Coffer'.

Unfortunately the King could not manage to run his kingdom on the money granted to him by Parliament: a sum in the region of £1,200,000 (in peacetime), of which nearly half consisted of revenues from the Customs and Excise. The latter was assigned for life and varied according to the volume of the nation's trade. Charles's obligations extended from the maintenance of the Court and innumerable palaces with all their repairs and furnishings, stables and parklands, to the standing cost of the army (about £250,000) and the upkeep of the fleet, a sum that varied from year to year. His expenses always seemed to be a few hundred thousand pounds above his revenue, but he solved his difficulties by borrowing money from the goldsmiths at high rates of interest. Occasionally he was so hard pressed that he could not even pay the servants' wages, which caused near-riots in the palace. On those occasions Charles took drastic steps such as declaring that only the King and Queen and the Duke and Duchess of York should be entitled to ten courses at dinner. However, most of these economies seemed to be unnoticed and on the surface all appeared serene and plentiful. The Court was the scene of 'prodigious plenty', wrote a contemporary observer, which caused foreigners 'to put a high value upon the King and was for the honour of the kingdom'.[3]

Charles II shared these sentiments and was particularly proud of his yeoman guard in scarlet uniforms with black facings, posted at all the palace entrances. Their presence was more ceremonial than authoritative for the public was allowed to wander about the palace grounds at will, and could even go into the gallery of the Banqueting

Hall to watch the King eat his dinner. Seventeenth-century monarchs were expected to live a large part of their private lives in public and in the morning the Gentlemen of the Bedchamber actually handed the King his clothes. Charles disliked ceremonial but he put up with it patiently, although, according to Samuel Pepys (a man more famous for his diary than for the important work he did at the Admiralty), he once referred contemptuously to the Spanish King 'who will not piss but another must hold the chamber-pot.'

Charles II was the most affable monarch ever to sit on the English throne. When he went for his daily walk in St James's Park, his black shoulder-length curls blowing in the wind and his spaniels trying to keep up with his long-legged strides, he often stopped to talk to passers-by. His charming manners, wit and perceptiveness were irresistible, but his unbounded love of pleasure offered such a striking contrast to the tone set by the last incumbent of Whitehall that many onlookers could not accustom themselves to the change. Within a few months of the Restoration, Samuel Pepys was bewailing 'the looseness and the beggary of the Court, which I am feared will bring all to ruin again.'[4] Other observers, such as Anthony Hamilton, who was at the heart of the fashionable world and wrote the memoirs of the Count de Grammont, a Frenchman who had been expelled from Louis XIV's Court for making advances to one of the King's mistresses, took a friendlier view:

> The Court was an entire scene of gallantry and amusements, with all the politeness and magnificence which the inclinations of a prince naturally addicted to tenderness and pleasure could suggest. The beauties were desirous of charming and the men endeavoured to please. All studied to set themselves off to the best advantage: some distinguished themselves by dancing; others by show and magnificence; some by their wit, many by their amours, but none by their constancy.[5]

The King had supper nearly every night with his beautiful mistress, Barbara Villiers. Barbara's husband, Roger Palmer, had faded out of the picture so obligingly (he even went to live abroad) that Charles made him the Earl of Castlemaine. It was an astute move as it also gratified Barbara, who was delighted to be a countess. Barbara had borne the King two children and was destined to produce another three. Charles had given her lodgings in the Cockpit, a Tudor building that was only a stone's throw from his own apartments. Here she entertained for the King several times a week, providing the best company and the best food that she could find. High-spirited and imperious, she never allowed mishaps to baulk her. Once, when the cook appeared and said that he could not roast the beef because the Thames had overflowed and the kitchen was under water, Barbara reacted angrily. 'Zounds! You must set the house on fire, but it shall be roasted!'[6] And roasted it was.

The King hoped that Barbara's new title would placate her over his forthcoming marriage to the Portuguese princess, Catherine of Braganza. He had chosen Catherine not so much for her comely appearance as for her splendid dowry. She promised to bring her husband £360,000 in cash, the island of Bombay and the port of Tangiers, as well as valuable trading privileges for British seamen in the New World. Charles assured Barbara that their relationship would not be altered by his marriage. After the wedding in May 1662 he presented his bride with a list of Ladies of the Bedchamber; but Catherine had been forewarned and when she saw the name of Lady Castlemaine she promptly struck it off. The King was so angry that his chief minister, Lord Clarendon, intervened on the Queen's behalf, but Charles replied hotly: 'Whomsoever I find to be my Lady Castlemaine's enemy in this matter I do promise on my word to be his enemy as long as I live.'[7] Charles sent Catherine's Portuguese Ladies-in-Waiting back to Lisbon and ignored her until she capitulated.

Lady Castlemaine served as a Lady of the Bedchamber for eleven years. For a while everyone speculated as to how she managed to maintain such a firm hold over the susceptible King. Samuel Pepys wrote in his diary that Sir Thomas Crewe had told him that my Lady Castlemaine 'hath all the tricks of Aretine* that are to be practised to give pleasure. . . . '[8] Apparently this information fascinated Pepys for his diary became studded with admiring references to the favourite: 'I glutted myself with looking at her', 'my lady Castlemaine whom I do heartily adore', and about the best dream 'that ever man dreamt, which was that I had my Lady Castlemaine in my arms.'

Many years later, the King turned his charm on Dr Gilbert Burnet, an Anglican bishop, and explained that he did not think that God would damn a man 'for a little irregular pleasure'. If Charles was seeking indulgence for his adultery, he did not get it, but the Bishop was wise enough to keep his opinion of Lady Castlemaine to himself until Charles was dead:

> She was a woman of great beauty but most enormously vicious and ravenous; carrying on intrigues with other men, while yet pretending that she was jealous of him. His passion for her, and her strange behaviour towards him, did so disorder him that often he was not master of himself,

---

* Aretino was an Italian libertine who was painted by Titian.

nor capable of minding business, which in so critical a time required great application.[9]

Despite the fascination that Lady Castlemaine held for the King, he was blatantly unfaithful to her, having dozens of peccadilloes which he declared to be of no account. One of his more serious passions, however, was for a Maid of Honour who refused to respond to his advances. This was Miss Frances Stewart, who was as chaste as she was beautiful. She rebuffed the King repeatedly and, when the Duke of York began to make advances to her, Charles was so angry that he nearly ordered him out of Whitehall. However, the Duke was no more successful than Charles had been and by this time the whole Court was giving advice. The Duke of Buckingham even founded a 'Committee for the Getting of Mistress Stewart for the King', but the young lady was quite unmoved and soon married the Duke of Richmond. Still moping for her, Charles commissioned the goldsmith, Jan Hoettiers, to engrave her in the guise of Britannia so that she could adorn the English coinage, which she still does to this day. Charles then returned to Lady Castlemaine.

Naturally the Duke of York's love affairs did not arouse the same interest as those of the King. Nevertheless, foreign observers could see little to choose between the fecklessness of the brothers. 'This prince', the Venetian envoy reported of James soon after the Restoration, 'applies himself but little to the affairs of the country and attends to nothing but his pleasure; but he is a young man of good spirit, loving and beloved by the King his brother and he discharges the offices of Lord Admiral.'[10]

This early impression of James is misleading, as he had a good deal more on his mind than pleasure. He could be civil, even affable, when he was inclined, but lacked the King's perceptiveness and had not a vestige of humour. Invariably he took wrong decisions by pushing his convictions to extremes. 'He has a strange notion of Government', wrote Bishop Burnet who was well acquainted with him, 'that everything is to be carried on in a high way and that no regard is to be had to the pleasing of the people.' He went on to say that James had an ill opinion of any that proposed soft methods, and 'thinks everyone a rebel who opposes the King in Parliament.'[11] Indeed, James was so obsessed by the doctrine of Divine Right and the sanctity of kings that even when he was alone with Charles and the latter touched on affairs of state, he leapt to his feet and stood respectfully at attention. His passionate loyalty was cherished by Charles, who returned both his trust and affection. However, in later years, when James became a

Catholic, the King found his obstinacy so irritating that he referred to *'la sottise de mon frère'*.

In the early days of the Restoration the brothers were more interested in their romances than in anything else. 'I do not believe there are two men who like women more than you and I do,' Charles once remarked to the French Ambassador, 'but my brother, devout as he is, loves them still more.'[12] Despite James's enthusiasm, his taste was not admired as he seemed to have a penchant for ungainly women. After he became a Roman Catholic, Charles joked that his brother's priests chose his women as a penance.

Even the Duke of York's choice of a wife stimulated controversy. Before the Restoration he had fallen in love with Anne Hyde, the daughter of Sir Edward Hyde, now Lord Clarendon and Charles' chief adviser. Although he had become secretly engaged to her, his sudden leap to grandeur made him reluctant to honour his commitment. Anne was neither beautiful nor well-born and, as James was now Heir Presumptive to the throne, it suddenly seemed to be a poor arrangement. Even Lord Clarendon was angry; he had known nothing of his daughter's intrigue, yet he felt that his enemies would accuse him of trying to promote the union. He judged correctly, for soon one of Charles II's disreputable courtiers was writing scurrilous verses:

> Then the fat scrivenor doth begin to think
> 'Twas time to mix the Royal blood with
> ink.[13]

To make matters worse, Anne let it be known that she was pregnant and it looked as though James was caught. However, several of the Duke's friends, including Lord Falmouth, stepped forward with surprising solutions. One of them offered to swear that Anne had had intercourse with him on many occasions and to claim the child as his own. Word of these suggestions came to Charles's hearing and he angrily sent for his brother. He was not going to allow his relationship with his trusted counsellor, Clarendon, to be ruined by James's caddish friends. He commanded James to marry Anne with no further delay and, as James always complied with the King's wishes, the marriage took place a few weeks later. For a while Anne became more royal than royalty itself, and Samuel Pepys took impish pleasure in going 'to Whitehall and there I showed my cousin Roger the Duchess of York sitting in state while her own mother stands by her.'[14]

The Duchess's pretensions, of course, sprang from an understandable lack of confidence. She was fundamentally kind and sensible and her marriage proved a great success. Although she gave birth to eight children, six of them (including two boys) died in infancy. The only survivors both became Queens of England: Mary, who shared the throne with William of Orange, and Anne, under whose reign John Churchill scored his greatest triumphs. Their succession, of course, was due to the fact that Charles's Queen, Catherine of Braganza, proved barren.

Motherhood was not the Duchess of York's only achievement and she succeeded in making her household famous for 'beauty, brightness and engaging manners'. She became a patron of Sir Peter Lely and introduced the scheme of having the 'handsomest persons at Court painted', resulting in the celebrated portraits whose 'sleepy eye bespoke the melting soul' and were always appropriately *déshabillé*. However, the Duchess demanded beauty in the flesh as well as on canvas and made a point of surrounding herself with Maids of Honour who were prettier than those serving the Queen.

These fifteen-year-old virgins from respectable families were regarded, oddly enough, as fair game for the Court libertines, particularly if the gentleman in question happened to be one of the royal brothers. Apparently the girls were often sent home because they had become pregnant. The Count de Grammont had become a cherished member of Charles's inner circle. In his memoirs he tells of a Miss Warmestre, whose 'consent went along with her eyes to the last degree of indiscretion'; and of a Miss Bellenden, who 'had the prudence to quit the Court before she was obliged to do so'; and of a Miss Wells, 'whose father had faithfully served Charles I and who therefore thought it her duty not to revolt against Charles II.'[15]

The beautiful Frances Jennings, the elder sister of little Sarah who one day would be the Duchess of Marlborough, did not share these amorous inclinations. Frances was the daughter of Richard Jennings, Member of Parliament for St Albans, and became Maid of Honour to the Duchess of York in 1663. Fifteen years old, with brilliant blue eyes, flaxen hair, and a pale, almost translucent skin, the Count de Grammont tells us that nature had given her charms impossible to describe and that the Graces had added the finishing touches. 'La Belle Jenyns', he called her, saying that she suggested 'Aurora or the promise of Spring'.[16] The Duke of York fell in love with her but she took pains not to be alone with him and he finally turned his attention elsewhere. She found her amusement in such escapades as dressing up as an orange girl and crying her wares through the streets. 'What mad freaks the Mayds of Honour at Court have,' commented Samuel Pepys on 1 February 1664, adding that 'few will venture on them [the maids] for wives.' Pepys was proved wrong, for in 1667 Frances Jennings left the Court to marry Captain Sir George Hamilton, a grandson of the Duke of Abercorn, and a nephew of the memoir-writer. However, a year before her departure, another Maid of Honour joined the group who was to prove more amenable to the Duke of York's advances. The newcomer was none other than Arabella Churchill.

Sir Winston Churchill was serving in Whitehall as a member of the Board of the Green Cloth when the invitation from the Duchess of York arrived for sixteen-year-old Arabella. There was great excitement in the family, for these positions were not only coveted by mothers such as Lady Churchill with marriageable daughters, but by all ambitious parents. In the seventeenth century, royal favour was not only the fount of all honours and most riches but, like a magic wand, could open the locked doors of opportunity. Court appointments, therefore, were hotly contested prizes. Who, then, had secured the blue ribbon for Arabella? The good fairy may have been none other than the notorious Lady Castlemaine herself. Not only was Winston's wife, Elizabeth, a kinswoman of Barbara Villiers through her own connections with the Duke of Buckingham, but Elizabeth's sister, Mrs Godfrey, was governess to Barbara's children. Although this lady was many years older than Barbara, she was the latter's friend and confidante and seems to have had the run of the house. Sometimes she asked her nephew, fifteen-year-old John Churchill, to drop into the Cockpit after school hours; both ladies made a fuss of the good-looking boy who sat eating sweets while they gossiped.

Elizabeth knew that Winston was likely to be sent back to Dublin at any moment and was anxious to find Arabella a more rewarding occupation than trailing about after her parents. If only she could launch her into a world that held out some promise! To achieve this end it seems reasonable to suppose that she asked her sister to enlist the help of Lady Castlemaine. The appointment came in the nick of time, for Sir Winston was recalled to Ireland early in 1665. No one could have foreseen the turn Arabella's life would take, for she had no looks and scarcely a head turned when she walked along the polished corridors of Charles II's happy-go-lucky Court. Even the Duke of York, who made a point of appraising the new Maids of Honour, took no interest in the tall, gangling Churchill girl with the pale, unsmiling face.

However, there were other reasons for the Duke's indifference. As Lord High Admiral, James was responsible for the fighting trim of the navy, and trouble was brewing. Holland was England's most formidable competitor in international trade, and Holland was growing increasingly irritated by England's high-handedness. As half the population of the small robust Republic gained its livelihood from commerce and shipping, the Dutch had a huge mercantile marine of over 4,000 ships. The Government had consuls in all the principal sea ports of the world – Africa, America, the Far East, India – to watch over its interests (which probably embraced three-quarters of the world's trade) and a strong navy to protect its merchant ships.

Rivalry with England extended around the globe and included on both sides such high-handed behaviour as taking over a colonial port and confiscating the other's vessels laden with rich manufactures. Sometimes the English went too far. Indeed, the Dutch were still smarting over the Duke of York's outrageous aggression on the other side of the Atlantic barely six months earlier. The King had given his brother a grant of land between Connecticut and Delaware, where-upon James, as Lord High Admiral, dispatched two men-of-war to dispossess the Dutch of their trading-stations on the River Hudson. In August 1664 the expedition seized the Dutch settlement of New Netherlands and its capital, New Amsterdam, and renamed both New York in James's honour.

This incident was one of many clashes that helped to stoke up the naval war that broke out in the spring of 1665. The two fleets joined battle on 3 June off Lowestoft on the east coast of England. The English had ninety-eight ships of forty guns and upwards; the Dutch even more. The Duke of York, who, incidentally, had never received any naval training, nor for that matter had even done a stint at sea, was in command of the flagship, the *Royal Charles*. He was accom-panied by a group of courtiers, among them the Earl of Falmouth who had volunteered to blacken poor Anne Hyde's reputation when James hesitated to marry her. Also aboard was the veteran Captain of the Fleet, Sir William Penn, who, despite the jealousies of James's aristocratic entourage, directed the naval battle with the help of three experienced squadron commanders.

These encounters were very bloody. James's ship engaged the Dutch flagship for four hours until it finally blew up. By this time the Dutch had lost twelve ships and 5,000 men against an English loss of one ship and 1,000 men. The Dutch ordered a general withdrawal and the crews put on sail and made for the Texel. Although the first day had been a resounding victory for England, the Royal Navy failed to overtake the retreating enemy fleet which reached its own waters in safety. The English had lost a vice admiral and a rear-admiral and were lucky to have their royal Duke still with them, for Lord Falmouth had been killed standing next to James on the quarterdeck. The same cannon-ball that carried him off had also killed Lord Muskerry and Richard Boyle, a younger son of Lord Burlington. The Duke was spattered with blood, but unhurt.

England resounded with stories of James's narrow escape and welcomed him home as a hero. Parliament voted him a gift of £120,000 for 'his conduct and bravery in the late engagement', but appealed to the King not to allow James to risk his life again. Charles's Queen had not given him any children, despite three years of marriage, and James was still Heir Presumptive. The King acceded to the request and 'grounded' his brother, although permitting him to retain the title of Lord High Admiral.

While Londoners were acclaiming the Duke for his valour, the Plague, which the Puritans said was the Lord's punishment for the capital's loose living, broke out. In June red crosses began to appear on doors, while the mournful cry 'Bring out your dead' echoed through the deserted streets at night. During the first week a hundred died; by the second, over seven hundred; and by September there was a death toll exceeding a thousand a day. The frightened Court moved to Hampton Court and then to Salisbury, while James, at the King's bidding, went to York, ostensibly on a goodwill tour but in fact because of rumours that the Dutch were trying to stir up a republican rising. Accompanied by the Duchess, he attended innumerable receptions and displays, his exploits aboard the *Royal Charles* meeting with the expected acclaim.

The trip to York, however, became famous for another incident. Once the public festivities were over, James could hunt and shoot to his heart's content. In between his sporting activities he took it upon himself to teach Arabella Churchill, the Duchess's drab little Maid of Honour, to ride. Although he found an exceptionally pretty horse for her, it was too high-spirited, and on the very first day bolted and threw her off. James found her lying half-stunned on the ground, her clothes in disarray. As he leaned over her, he was amazed to discover that a girl so plain could have such alluring legs or, as Anthony Hamilton put it, 'that limbs of such exquisite beauty could belong to Miss Churchill's face.'[17]

James fell in love with Arabella on the spot and before long she became his mistress. She bore him four children and retained her influence for over ten years. Her position could not have been easy as the Count de Grammont claims that the Duchess's jealousy arose from deep chagrin; she could understand her husband's passion for the glamorous Lady Chesterfield or the beautiful Miss Frances Jennings, but she felt that the choice of Miss Churchill 'debased her own merit'.[18] No doubt her annoyance was increased because she usually took a stand against plain girls yet had made Arabella one of her rare exceptions. Nevertheless, in those days married women were obliged to put up with their husbands' infidelities and the Duchess forced herself to re-establish good relations with Miss Churchill.

Shortly after the Duke and Duchess of York returned to the capital, another misfortune took place. This time a great fire, which many Protestants believed had been started by the Catholics, broke out. It destroyed over half the houses in London, almost all made of wood, but miraculously spared Whitehall. Both the King and the Duke rode through the burning areas on horseback directing the army engineers to blow up with gunpowder certain specified houses in order to create voids that might check the flames. They not only exposed themselves to falling debris, but frequently dismounted and laboured with their own hands.

One of the casualties of the conflagration was St Paul's School in the City, where Arabella Churchill's younger brother was a pupil. Although the building was only partially destroyed, it had to be closed and the pupils sent home. As Sir Winston and Lady Churchill were in Ireland, it seems reasonable to suppose that Arabella mentioned her brother's predicament to her new admirer. Apparently the Duke of York had seen the boy about Court on several occasions and remembered him because of his exceptional good looks. In the autumn of 1666 he accepted him as a page.

Sixteen-year-old John Churchill was fortunate to find himself in the household of a prince who understood the art of war, whether on land or sea, more than anything in the world next to his religion. Nevertheless, 1666 was an awkward year for the Duke of York as the Dutch navy scored several spectacular victories over the English. Their famous sailor, Admiral de Ruyter, not only captured a rich merchant convoy in the North Sea flying the Red Ensign, but in June attacked a concentration of English ships off the Nore, and in a four-day engagement sank and captured twenty vessels for the loss of only seven. The toll of life was in the same ratio: 8,000 British seamen lost (many of whom were burned to death when their ships caught fire) as against 2,000 Dutchmen.

This defeat was so unexpected that it could scarcely be believed, but an even greater humiliation was to follow. Charles 11 had run out of funds, an inconvenience that took place with increasing regularity, and, as a result, the Naval Pay Office was unable to honour the pay slips of its naval ratings who were owed for three years' hard service. Several English sailors were so angry that they went to Holland and offered their services. They were employed to guide a handful of Dutch warships past the chain in the Medway to Chatham where they bombarded and burned a number of ships lying at anchor. They left for the open sea towing the pride of the English fleet – the flagship, the *Royal Charles*. It was a disgrace such as England had never before experienced.

Although the Duke of York was still Lord High Admiral, he refused to take responsibility for the outrage because the King had deprived him of his active command. Instead, James turned his attention to military affairs. In the days of his exile he had fought with the French army, serving on the staff of the great Marshal Turenne. He took part in a number of hard-fought campaigns and when Turenne actually praised him for his courage, James's cup overflowed. Ever after he talked of Turenne as 'one of the men in the world I am most obliged to and have the greatest value for.'[19]

When John Churchill joined the Duke's household he had no inkling that one day he, too, would serve under Turenne's watchful eye, but he did his best to please his new master. The Duke liked well-mannered, obedient youths, but he liked them even more if they were interested in the military arts and John Churchill's enthusiasm fulfilled his highest hopes. Often the Duke spent part of the day reviewing and drilling troops and frequently assembled several battalions of the Guards Brigade in Hyde Park and put them through their complicated exercises. The loading and firing of a musket involved twenty-two distinct movements during which the weapon had to be primed, powder inserted, wad and bullet rammed home, and matches lit.

> Very deliberate and stately were the Royal Guards in their round beaver hats and scarlet uniforms as they performed their complicated ritual. All the evolutions to form a front in any direction, or to change into a column, or a square with the steel-helmeted pikemen at the angles, were of the same complex order. But by the long usage of drill and discipline it was hoped that everything would be carried out faultlessly and nothing slurred over in the heart-shaking moments before a whirlwind of horsemen might fall with sabres upon ranks which, their volleys once fired, were for the time being well-nigh defenceless.[20]

John Churchill was thrilled to watch the manœuvres of war, and when the Duke asked him what profession he preferred, John dropped to his knees and said: 'A pair of colours in one of these fine regiments.' His enthusiasm reminded the Duke of his own boyish fervour and John's request was granted. On 14 September 1667, he received a commission as ensign to the King's Own Company of Foot Guards, later known as the 1st Regiment of Foot Guards, still later as the Grenadier Guards. Thus began the connection of England's greatest soldier with one of England's greatest regiments.

While the Duke and his page were attending military exercises in Hyde Park, twenty-nine-year-old Louis XIV of France (Charles II's first cousin) sent an army to invade the Spanish Netherlands, today known as Belgium. Louis regarded war as a sovereign's most agreeable duty. He was strong, athletic and intelligent and revelled in being a king – particularly King of France, which was the greatest power in Europe. He was religious in a superstitious way and believed implicitly in God's passionate interest in his affairs. He loved elegance and was spending huge sums of money building Versailles, but this probably was due less to his respect for the arts than his preoccupation with *gloire*. This strange word meant more than glory, implying status, even respect. It not only explained Louis's insatiable desire to extend his frontiers but was used to describe the awe that his position inspired – or was expected to inspire. In 1661 when the French and Spanish Ambassadors made their initial entry into London in the ostentatious style which etiquette demanded, the Spanish Ambassador stole a march on his French colleague by borrowing as 'servants' several thousand soldiers from the Spanish Netherlands. His splendid retinue completely dwarfed the French Ambassador's entourage of 500 people. When this incident was reported to King Louis he nearly fainted with anger, declaring that it was an insult to his *gloire*. Although the King of Spain, Philip IV, was his father-in-law, Louis broke off relations with him, cancelled all Spanish passports and prepared for war. The Spanish had to submit completely. In May 1662 a Spanish envoy was forced to appear at the Louvre, before the assembled Court and all the foreign ambassadors, and repudiate the behaviour of his colleague in London.

Although Louis had been King of France since the age of four, he did not grasp the reigns of power until 1661 when he was twenty-three and Cardinal Mazarin died. This was because Mazarin, who had ruled France for nine years, was a master of statecraft and Louis was intelligent enough not to interfere. Romantically inclined people insisted, however, that his reluctance was also due to the fact that Mazarin was his mother's lover and the young King was too polite to disturb their way of life. Mazarin left France at peace with her neighbours, but apparently this was not an unqualified blessing, as a prince who came to the throne with no battles to fight was to be pitied. 'It was undoubtedly a little unfortunate', wrote Louis in his memoirs, '. . . to enjoy such tranquillity . . . at a time when my age and the pleasure of being at the head of my armies made me wish for a little more activity abroad.'[21]

However, this state of affairs was not difficult to rectify. Louis's horizon began to open out in 1665 when Philip IV of Spain died, leaving his crown and his vast and scattered empire to his sickly five-year-old son, Carlos II, whom nobody expected to live for more than a few months. Philip had stipulated in his will that when Carlos died, his second daughter, Marguerite – the intended bride of the Habsburg prince, Leopold I, Emperor of the Holy Roman Empire – should be his heir. This was too much for Louis XIV, who reminded the world angrily that his wife, Marie-Thérèse, was Philip's eldest daughter, conveniently overlooking the fact that she had partially renounced the Spanish throne. Nevertheless, he had a claim based on a law of inheritance recognized in several provinces of the Spanish Netherlands. This law declared that a daughter of the first blood could insist on her share of her father's goods even though he had a son by a second bed. Louis decided that his case was so good that there was no need to wait for Carlos to die. As a result, in 1667 the French army, the finest that had been seen since Roman days, began to move towards the Spanish Netherlands under the command of Marshal Turenne to assert the French Queen's 'just claims'.

This territory was ringed by forts, but the Spaniards did not dare to engage mighty France so there was no resistance. The only interference came from God, who opened the skies and sent down torrents of rain which made things precarious for the invaders. The 70,000 troops and miles of horses, mules, carts, carriages and gun-caissons turned the roads into a sea of mud and slowed the invasion to a snail's pace. Apart from the difficulty of transport, there was always the problem of bread for the soldiers and forage for the horses. Special prayers were said in Paris, begging God's forgiveness, and eventually the rain stopped.

The Spanish soldiers were quite ready to surrender their fortresses as there was no prospect of avoiding defeat; and the townspeople begged them not to risk the destruction of their houses by provoking cannon-fire. Nevertheless, etiquette demanded a show of resistance. The Spaniards could not hoist their white flags until the enemy had drawn siege-lines and moved its guns into position. All this took weeks to accomplish. Although one could scarcely describe the

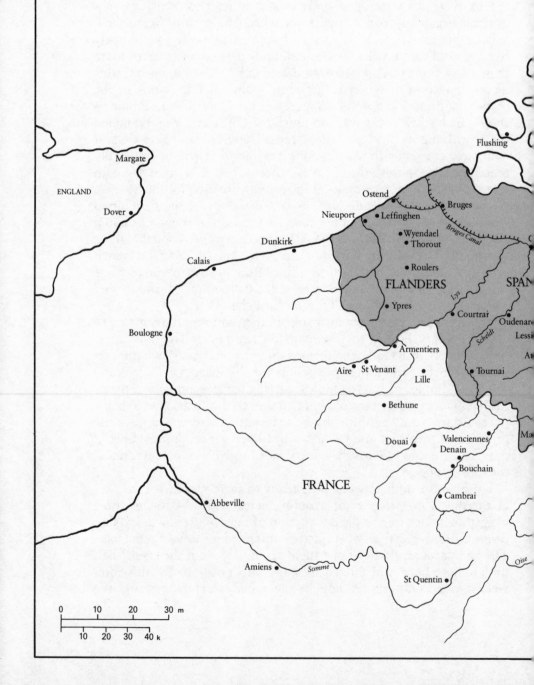

The Netherlands and Flanders,
the territory where the majority of Marlborough's campaigns were fought

Margate

ENGLAND

Dover

Flushing

Ostend

Nieuport ● Leffinghen

● Bruges

Bruges Canal

Calais

Dunkirk

● Wyendael
● Thorout

● Roulers

FLANDERS

SPA

Boulogne

● Ypres

Lys

● Courtrai

Oudenar

Lessi

Scheldt

At

Armentiers

Aire ● St Venant

● Lille

● Tournai

● Bethune

Douai

Valenciennes
Denain

Ma

FRANCE

● Bouchain

● Cambrai

● Abbeville

Amiens ● Somme

St Quentin ●

Oise

0   10   20   30 m

10   20   30   40 k

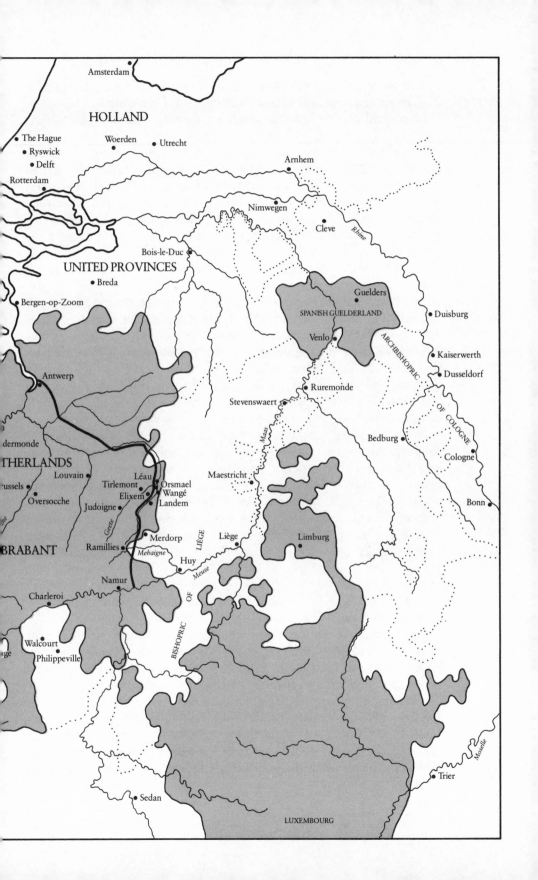

operation as a dangerous undertaking, France was soon ringing with *Te Deums* ordered by the King to thank God for his mercy.

Louis had a superb understanding of public relations. In July he went to Compiègne, picked up his Court and his Queen and took them to Flanders so that the people could see their 'rightful ruler'. The ladies wore their most spectacular dresses and the inhabitants gaped at their silks and satins and diamond-studded combs, at their magnificent carriages and richly embroidered tents. 'All you have seen of the magnificence of Solomon and the grandeur of the King of Persia', wrote one of the courtiers to a friend, 'does not equal the pomp displayed on this trip . . . plumes, gold embroidery, chariots, mules superbly harnessed, parade horses with equipment embossed in gold. . . .'[22]

The many fortifications that fell to the French included Courtrai, Armentiers, Douai, Tournai and Oudenarde. The only difficult operation was the investment of the great fortress of Lille. This was the first important assignment for the brilliant young officer, Sébastien le Prestre de Vauban, who had been discovered by the Minister of War, M. Louvois, and was destined to be the first engineer in history to become a Marshal of France. The success of his assault delighted the King and once again France rang with *Te Deums*.

Not surprisingly, Spain regarded Louis's conquests as outright robbery. Although Louis's campaign had only made small inroads into the disputed territory, the Spanish were not the only people to be disturbed. The Germans were fearful for the fate of the Rhineland, while the Dutch Netherlands saw a direct threat to their homeland. Indeed, the United Provinces had been opposing French expansion in Flanders ever since 1640, as they understood the danger of allowing such a rapacious power to reach their frontiers. England also was concerned at the prospect of Antwerp falling into French hands. Not only would Louis be able to develop the great port as a rival trading-station, but if he established a naval base there he would be able to interfere with the British fleet.

The French occupation of Franche Comté, a province on the border of Switzerland, was the last straw. Although the English and the Dutch had been fighting a naval war off and on for years, and had repeatedly angered and insulted one another, they now buried their differences and formed an alliance which, with the inclusion of Sweden, became known as the famous Triple Alliance. Although Louis had concluded a partition agreement with the Emperor Leopold, there is no doubt that the formation of the Alliance hurried him to the peace table. Two months later, in the summer of 1668, he

signed the Treaty of Aix La Chapelle, which gave him almost everything he wanted. He had to relinquish Franche Comté, but in return
Spain ceded to France all the cities and forts he had captured in the
Spanish Netherlands. Even so, Louis did not regard the settlement as
permanent and secretly set about making new plans for war. His next
target would be Holland itself, a country which deserved to be
castigated for thwarting his 'just pretensions'.

While peace was being negotiated in 1668, John Churchill was on his
way to Tangiers. Who could have imagined that this unknown
subaltern would one day humble the mighty King of France who was
beginning to view the whole of Europe as his private domain?
Churchill had been given leave from his regiment to do a tour of duty
in Africa with whichever branch of the armed services – army or navy
– could make use of his brains and energy. Tangiers had been ceded to
England by Portugal as part of the Queen's dowry and was in a state
of almost perpetual siege by land and sea. The Berber tribes were
fanatical Moslems and the fact that a Christian power was in possession of their biggest sea-port had been a bone of bitter contention
with them for many years. The English garrison defended itself by
digging ditches, preparing redoubts and building high walls. The
Tangiers Horse, as the English regiment was known, was full of
bravado. Every morning they would parade on the desert in full view
of the enemy to remind them that they were ready for a fight. And
when the clash took place, as it always did, a bloody battle developed.
  Churchill served in the garrison for two years but, in 1670, asked to
be transferred to sea duty. He was allowed to join Sir Thomas Allin's
fleet which had been sent out from England to protect merchant
shipping from the pirates and corsairs who swarmed over the
Mediterranean. He was also given the task of ensuring that the ships
that carried provisions from Spain to Tangiers arrived safely. The
corsairs were a serious menace. They emerged from hideaways on the
Algerian coast with astonishing speed and attacked any ship of any
nationality that seemed vulnerable. Sometimes as many as seventy
corsair galleys scanned the sea for victims. Whenever the marauders
succeeded in overpowering a vessel, they auctioned the cargoes and
sold the crews into slavery. Almost all corsair ships were rowed by
these unfortunate captives.
  The year that Churchill joined Sir Thomas, the latter's fleet consisted of ten warships-of-the-line. Furthermore he was supported by a
Dutch sailor, Admiral van Ghent, with another half-dozen ships.
Together, the partnership took a heavy toll of the enemy. In August

the English sank one of the corsair's largest vessels and, in September, an Anglo–Dutch concentration forced a battle near Cape Sparrel in which they sank or burned another seven ships, four of which had forty-four guns each. Altogether the corsairs lost over 2,000 men. There is no record of the part that John Churchill played, but it is unlikely that he failed to find the adventure he was after.

Ensign Churchill did not return to Whitehall until the winter of 1670–71. By this time Charles's Court was famous throughout Europe for its scandalous behaviour. This was partly due to the notor- iety engendered by the group of wild young aristocrats known as 'the Wits' with whom the King surrounded himself. These high-spirited figures, mostly in their twenties, amused the King by their outrageous conversation and madcap escapades, which ranged from imperso- nations to duels and from abductions to drinking bouts which some- times ended with the participants running naked all over the Privy Gardens. The Wits were partial to rhymes and wrote ribald verses about the prominent people at Court. Their favourite targets were the King's mistresses, but they did not spare the King himself, whom they referred to as 'that known enemy to virginity and chastity, the mon- arch of Great Britain'. Lord Rochester went so far as to praise Charles's splendid physical assets:

> Restless he strolls from whore to whore
> A merry monarch scandalous and poor
> Nor are his high desires above his strength
> His sceptre and his — are of a length.[23]

Occasionally Charles banished Rochester from Court, but only for a few weeks. Indeed, he laughed when he learned that the Wits referred to him behind his back as 'Old Rowley' – a Newmarket stallion famous for its potency. One day, when he was walking along a Whitehall corridor, he heard a girl singing a ballad about Old Rowley and knocked at her door. 'Who's that?' she asked, 'Old Rowley himself, Madame,' the King replied with a flourish. 'At your service.'[24] Although twenty-nine-year-old Lady Castlemaine had kept her looks and was still the reigning beauty of the Court, her star was on the wane, for the King's attention was no longer undivided. Charles was enamoured of the little Cockney actress, Nell Gwyn, and in the middle of 1670 also became infatuated with the French beauty, Louise de Kéroualle, whom he persuaded to move to England.

Yet Barbara still had some influence with the King. Four years earlier she had joined her kinsman, the Duke of Buckingham, and played a part in persuading Charles to dismiss his Lord Chancellor, Lord Clarendon. Although in 1671 her importance was greatly diminished, the diarist John Evelyn still referred to her as 'the curse of our nation'. Her hold over the King lay in the fact that she had borne him five children whom he acknowledged as his own. The three boys had been granted dukedoms – Southampton, Grafton and Northumberland – and Barbara herself had recently become the Duchess of Cleveland.* She was every bit as rich as a duchess was expected to be. Charles had given more money and property to her than to any other woman. She had large revenues from Irish lands and an annual pension from the Post Office of almost £5,000. Whenever she had a quarrel with Charles he put things right by granting her plate from the Jewel House, and once she stunned everybody by appearing at a theatre matinée wearing £40,000's worth of jewels. Periodically the King made her gifts ranging from £10,000 to £30,000. No one knew how much capital she had accumulated, for she was very extravagant, but it was thought to be well over £100,000. She owned Berkeley House, a fine house between Whitehall and St James's Palace, and was soon to be the châtelaine of Queen Elizabeth's much-loved palace, Nonsuch, near Epsom. But Barbara liked ready cash better than property and eventually succumbed to the temptation of selling Berkeley House to a contractor for building plots at a very large profit.

At this point a welcome diversion presented itself in the form of her cousin, John Churchill – the boy who used to munch sweets in her apartment. Now he was a strikingly handsome officer of the Guards just back from the Mediterranean and the warm sun of Africa. He was welcomed enthusiastically by Barbara, who was always looking for adventure. Twenty-year-old John responded eagerly to the beautiful courtesan of twenty-nine and for the next three years 'this wanton and joyous couple shared pleasures and hazards'.[25]

John Churchill, of course, was attached to the Duke of York's household and the Duke and his family were now residing in St James's Palace, a stone's throw from Berkeley House. Although the King was involved in other romances, he still visited Barbara, and soon two stories were circulating about the Duchess of Cleveland and her glorious lover. The first was spread by Bishop Burnet, without mentioning names. He said that Charles had knocked on Barbara's bedroom door when Churchill was inside, and that the young ensign had leapt out of the window into the courtyard below in order to save

* She had parted from her husband and now was a duchess in her own right.

the lady's honour – or what was left of it. Barbara was so impressed by this quick-wittedness that she made him a gift of £5,000. The second story smacked of Court gossip as it was recounted by the French Ambassador, Barrillon, who was not even accredited to England at the time. Charles was supposed to have discovered the couple in bed together, but as he was familiar with such situations he let the officer off with the sarcastic observation: 'Go, you are a rascal but I forgive you because you do it to get your bread.'[26]

No one knows whether either of these tales is true but most historians prefer the first story, because there is a receipt from Lord Halifax showing that in 1674 John Churchill invested £4,500 in a life annuity yielding him £500 a year. No one but Barbara could have given him the money, which represented the first security he had ever known. The Duchess also gave birth to a daughter in 1672, named Barbara (her sixth child), for whom the King quite reasonably refused to acknowledge paternity as it was common knowledge that Churchill had been her lover for the past eighteen months. When the girl grew up she entered a French convent and became a nun – but not until she had run off with an Englishman, Lord Arran, and produced an illegitimate child!

The same year that Churchill returned from Tangiers, his sister Arabella gave birth to the Duke of York's son, who was named James FitzJames and eventually became the Duke of Berwick, one of Louis XIV's famous marshals. Before the child's arrival in 1670 James moved Arabella into a house in St James's Square where she lived for seven years, producing another son and two daughters, one of whom, Henrietta, married Sir Henry Waldegrave. The Duke of York was very fond of his two sons and at an early age sent them to France for their education. James joined the French army at the age of sixteen and had his first taste of combat when he was sent to fight the Turks on the plains of Hungary.

In 1671 Winston Churchill returned from Ireland and took up residence again at Mintern, his estate in the West Country. Did he feel that his eldest son, John Churchill, was on the road to success? 'All agreed', wrote Hamilton, 'that a man who was the favourite of the King's mistress and brother to the Duke's favourite was in a fair way of preference and could not fail to make his fortune.'[27] However, fame and fortune were not to be won merely by a lucky start.

Two

Arms and the Man

'A prince', wrote Louis XIV, 'gains *gloire* by conquering difficulties
... but he ought to be sure to achieve it with safety.'[1] Glory and safety
do not usually go hand in hand, but during the last thirty years of the
seventeenth century King Louis, thirty-two-years-old in 1670,
repeatedly launched wars of aggression and met with no serious
rebuffs. This was due to the fact that mighty France, with its
population of 20,000,000, exceeded the combined number of the
four largest states most frequently opposed to her. England had only
5,500,000 people, Holland 3,000,000, Austria 2,000,000 and Spain
(without her empire) 7,000,000.

Not only was France the strongest military power on the Continent
but the most civilized. Educated people learned her language and she
set the fashion in everything from food to sedan-chairs, from dainty
silver encased toothbrushes to smart clothes, pocket looking-glasses
and apricot paste. She led the world in architecture, philosophy,
literature and the art of war. Louis regarded warfare as a king's most
interesting occupation (as France was so strong he had nothing to
fear), and indulged in it with monotonous frequency.

In 1670, while John Churchill was serving in Tangiers and the ink
was scarcely dry on the Treaty of Aix la Chapelle, Louis was contemplating the destruction of Holland. He disliked many things about
the Dutch: their Republicanism, their Protestantism, and the fact
that they owned five times as many merchant ships as France and had
cornered the lion's share of Europe's trade. He referred to them
contemptuously as 'herring folk' and asked his ministers querulously
how men like this could stand in the way of a king who represented
the hereditary order that God had intended for the world?

Yet this was what they had done. When Louis had taken up arms to
vindicate 'the just pretensions' of his Queen, he wrote in his memoirs:

I found in my way . . . only the Dutch, who rather than being interested in my fortune . . . wished to impose their law upon me and oblige me to make peace, even dared to threaten me in case I should refuse to accept their mediation. . . .[2]

Although Louis knew perfectly well that the Dutch would not allow the French on their borders (if they could prevent it), he liked to dwell on the help that France had given them in the past and to accuse them of monstrous 'ingratitude, bad faith and insupportable vanity'. The vanity, however, seemed to be on his side for the truth of the matter was that the Dutch had committed the most heinous of crimes: a refusal to pay homage to Louis's *gloire*, for which the only fitting retribution would be annihilation. Holland would have to be stripped of her most important provinces and destroyed as a commercial and political entity.

The preparations took four years to complete. By a mixture of bribery and persuasion Louis neutralized most of the German principalities and even persuaded his potential enemy, the Emperor Leopold, to remain aloof. Only the Elector of Brandenburg (later the King of Prussia) resisted his spell. But his greatest triumph lay in winning England. Not only was England an ally of Holland but a Protestant country in possession of a formidable navy.

Charles II did not like the Dutch any more than Louis did. Basically he was a Francophile because of his French mother (a sister of Louis's father, Louis XIII) and the fact that he had spent his youth in France. Apart from this, he recognized France's strength as a land power and believed that it would be a good thing to join her in fighting England's chief naval and commercial rival. Furthermore, he was still smarting from the insult to his navy, when the Dutch had burned his men-of-war in the Medway and towed away his flagship. For this reason alone he was convinced that war against Holland would be popular.

Charles and Louis carried on clandestine negotiations for over two years until in 1670 the secret Treaty of Dover came into being. To secure Charles's signature to the final document the French King, always a great impresario, organized a dramatic scene. Charles's youngest and favourite sister, Henrietta Anne ('Minette' in family circles), was married to Louis's brother, the Duke of Orléans. This gentleman, always known as 'Monsieur', was a flamboyant homosexual who wore powder and paint and covered himself in diamonds, yet fulfilled his obligations by marrying twice and producing eleven legitimate children. He was very unkind to poor Minette. As a result she always longed to get away from him and jumped at the chance of travelling to England in the royal yacht to complete Louis's negotiations. Charles met her at Dover with his fleet while the French Court remained on the other side of the Channel in ignorance of what was happening. Louis left nothing to chance, and Minette's principal lady-in-waiting, Mlle Louise de Kéroualle, probably was selected as the enchantress most likely to captivate the English sovereign. Within eighteen months Louise had established herself as Charles's reigning mistress and before long had become an English fixture as Duchess of Portsmouth.

Minette was empowered to act as Louis's emissary, and brother and sister spent ten happy days picnicing and laughing in the Kent countryside while they argued over the final points. Minette had always dreamed of an *entente cordiale* between the two countries she loved so dearly and returned to France convinced that she had done a good piece of work for both. Two weeks later she was dead. Rumour spread that she had been poisoned by her husband who was jealous to see her playing such a large part in affairs of state. The French Court insisted angrily that 'Madame' had died of cholera and managed to convince Charles II that they were speaking the truth.

The document that Minette carried back to France called for a brutal act of aggression. The core of the agreement was a combined attack on Holland that would destroy the United Provinces as a factor in European politics. The integrity of the Spanish Netherlands (Belgium) would be respected because of England's insistence, but Louis would move his frontiers to the banks of the Rhine where it flowed through Holland. And as Holland would exist only in a truncated form, England would control most of the Dutch coastline including the Isle of Walcheren and its ports, Sluys and Cadsand, as well as the north of the Scheldt. England would send 6,000 soldiers to fight under French generals and the French would send a fleet to serve under an English admiral.

Yet it was not only the war clauses that prompted Charles to maintain the deepest secrecy. The dynamite was contained in Charles's admission that he was 'convinced of the truth of the Catholic religion' and his astonishing undertaking 'to declare it and reconcile himself with the Church of Rome as soon as the welfare of his kingdom will permit'. For this development Louis XIV guaranteed another £140,000 in subsidies, and graciously promised that, if necessary, French troops would cross the Channel to enforce the sovereign's will. Both Kings were aware that Charles's pledge to persuade – or force – his subjects to accept him as a Catholic King was tantamount to re-establishing the Church of Rome in England.

It is unlikely that Charles had any real intention of implementing this startling clause. He probably threw it in to loosen Louis's purse strings and perhaps even to please Minette. Nevertheless, the Duke of York was overjoyed as he himself had become a secret Catholic convert in 1668 and Jesuit priests had been holding clandestine masses for him in St James's Palace for nearly two years.

The subsidies that Louis agreed to pay Charles were dependent on the fighting and came to something in the region of £250,000 spread over four years. And as Parliament granted Charles £1,200,000 a year (including his life revenues from Customs and Excises) Louis's payments were not the 'vital subsidies' that Victorian writers sometimes suggest. The golden harvest that 1670 yielded was not due to France: when Parliament met that autumn it agreed to settle the sovereign's debts, which came to £1,300,000. Members not only discussed royal expenditure, but Sir John Coventry was particularly free in his criticism of Charles's ladies and their extravagant ways.

The Secret Treaty of Dover remained surprisingly secret. Charles II continued outwardly to support the Church of England and only two members of Charles's five-man cabal – Clifford (a Catholic) and Arlington (a man whose religious views were as uncertain as the King's own) – were allowed to read the original document in its entirety.* Later a second Treaty was trumped up as 'cover' confirming only the military provisions, and this was signed by the remaining three members of the group. The original and unabridged Treaty was not published until 1830 when no one who cared was alive.

When the preparations for war were complete in the spring of 1672, England had difficulty in finding a suitable *casus belli*. Although deeply jealous of the Dutch navy, she had no outward dispute with Holland which lent her determination to trump up a quarrel a slightly comic air. In the past century England had fought numerous battles with the Dutch for not lowering their flags when passing an English man-of-war in the Channel. So once again, the 'honour of the flag' was trumped up as an excuse. Charles sent Sir George Downing to The Hague to announce that the King was deeply disturbed because the Dutch fleet had not 'veiled bonnet' when the *Merlin*, a royal yacht, had gone to Holland to pick up the Ambassador's wife. The Dutch were so angry at this flimsy pretext for hostilities that Sir George feared for his life and fled from The Hague without waiting for an official reply. The French King, Louis XIV, was too grand to

---

* Lord Arundel and Sir Richard Bellings – both Catholics – also signed the document.

bother with detailed complaints. He simply declared war because 'he was displeased with the Dutch'.

Over 100,000 French soldiers, many of them equipped for the first time with the bayonet – a weapon introduced by General Martinet, famous for his strict discipline – took part in Louis's offensive. The Dutch could not withstand the strength of the assault and strongholds fell like ninepins. At the end of two months the French had taken 24,000 prisoners and captured four of the country's seven provinces. Cities such as Arnhem, Duisburg, Utrecht, Woerden and Naarden were in their hands, and the prize, the province of Holland with its rich and famous capital, Amsterdam, was on the verge of surrender.

But the surrender never came. Louis's army had crossed the Rhine by a bridge of boats; indeed, some of the troopers plunged their horses into the swirling water and actually swam the river, a feat immortalized in tapestries which still hang in Versailles. However, as soon as the French reached the other side, the Dutch cut the dykes and flooded the countryside between the Zuyder Zee and the Rhine delta. Amsterdam became an unapproachable island in an inland sea, the star in a galaxy of waterlogged, isolated towns. No one thought, however, that this drastic measure would give Holland more than a short respite. The States-General (the Dutch Parliament) offered to cede to France all the territory beyond the frontiers of the Seven Provinces that made up the republic. Although this included an important slice of Brabant and Flanders, and would have been judged a sweeping victory for France, Louis rejected the proposal out of hand. After all, the King argued, he had only to wait for winter to freeze the flooded fields to move his army and impose a settlement of his own.

A few weeks later the De Witt brothers, who ran the country, were murdered in the streets by citizens appalled by the disasters that had overtaken them. The people then turned to the twenty-two-year-old Prince of Orange, their Stadtholder and Captain-General, to save them. This great-grandson of William the Silent did not fail them. He imbued them with new courage and set about forming a coalition against the enemy. That winter, for the first time in years, the rivers and canals did not freeze. The bored and bewildered enemy remained in occupation, levying contributions, taking reprisals and kicking their heels.

Meanwhile the war was also being fought at sea. In May 1672 the English fleet, again under the command of the Duke of York, had passed through the Straits of Dover and lain off the Suffolk coast at Sole Bay (Southwold), where it took on food, ammunition and several thousand seamen and soldiers. Upon the deck of the Duke of York's flagship, *The Prince*, stood the 1st Regiment of the Foot Guards, acting as a naval battalion to fire the guns and beat off enemy attempts to board the vessel. It is not surprising that Ensign John Churchill was one of the officers, as this was the type of fighting that he had done at Tangiers.

Admiral de Ruyter's ninety ships lay off Walcheren and the Texel waiting for an opportunity to strike at the superior forces of the enemy. The best chance, the Admiral decided, was to attack before the English ships were at their stations. Consequently, when the Dutch fell upon them, the English were still loading their ships. They scrambled aboard their vessels and tried to form a line of battle, but only forty ships were in a position to fight. De Ruyter attacked *The Prince*, and a desperate struggle ensued at close quarters. The cannonade was heard for miles, drawing crowds of anxious sightseers to the Suffolk shores. The Duke of York's ship was not only pounded by batteries but assailed twice by fire-ships and swept by musketry. After two hours she was so wrecked in hull and rigging that she could no longer serve as a flagship and the Duke of York transferred to the *St Michael*; when this ship too was put out of commission, the Duke and his staff were rowed to the *London*. All this while the Foot Guards remained upon *The Prince*. The captain of the ship and over a third of the 600 men aboard were killed or wounded. The Dutch losses were just as great, but De Ruyter claimed a victory as he had prevented the enemy from approaching the Dutch coast. Later he said that the battle of Sole Bay was the 'hardest' of his thirty-two actions.

Unfortunately we have no details of the part played by John Churchill; we only know that he must have acquitted himself with great distinction for he was rewarded by a double promotion, jumping from Guards ensign to Marine captain. One of his comrades, Captain Picks, complained to Lord Arlington's* Under-Secretary that he had been overlooked:

> Mr Churchill, who was my ensign in the engagement, is made a Captain and I, without my Lord Alington's kindness and yours, I fear may still continue a lieutenant, though I am confident my greatest enemies cannot say I misbehaved myself in the engagement. . . . If you will oblige me with your kindness to get me a company I will present you with 400 guineas when I receive my commisssion. . . .[3]

* Lord Arlington was a Secretary of State; Lord Alington, to whom Picks refers in his letter, was a colonel of Foot Guards who took part in the fighting.

Captain Churchill could not complain of boredom. In June 1673 (a year after the Sole Bay engagement), he took part in one of the greatest sieges of the century. Louis was tired of waiting for the Dutch to submit to his demands and decided to capture the mighty fortress of Maestricht. This would give France control of the River Meuse (the Maas when it flowed through Holland) and assure her communications with the Rhine. Although the city belonged to the Elector of Cologne, the Dutch had fortified and garrisoned it to control the river. The French army had swept past it the year before because the fortifications were so strong that they feared its reduction might require a whole campaign. But now the King decided that its capture would add to his *gloire* and might even induce the Dutch to make the sort of peace he wanted.

The King led an army of 22,000 men into Flanders. He had driven from Paris to Tournai with the Queen and his current mistress, Madame de Montespan. The latter was expecting a baby, so the royal entourage established a Court at Tournai and waited until Madame had given birth to her child, a daughter. Louis then bid the ladies farewell and rode to Courtrai where he joined his army.

News that the King would be in charge of a siege operation had caused great excitement for weeks, although the fact that Maestricht was the objective was a closely guarded military secret until the very moment when the army appeared before it. The King always arrived surrounded by poets and painters to record the scene for posterity and always lived in magnificent style, appropriate to his *gloire*. His tent was made entirely of Chinese silk and contained three rooms apart from a bedroom and two offices. It was emblazoned with the insignia of power and was protected by a battery of secretaries, guards and officers.

The young bloods of England and France volunteered for the operation, not only to see the King but to make sure that the King saw them. The twenty-three-year-old Duke of Monmouth, King Charles's son by poor Lucy Walter, was serving in the French army as a lieutenant-colonel in command of 6,000 English soldiers. When he heard of the King's project he gathered a small group of friends, including John Churchill and thirty gentlemen troopers from the Life Guards, and they offered their services to Louis as an élite contingent, a gesture which was accepted with gracious thanks.

Maestricht was defended by 5,000 Dutchmen and was considered even more difficult than Lille. Once again the King made use of his protégé, M. Vauban. This time he was put in charge of the siege operations, the first time that an engineer had been given such an assignment. The tactics were as stylized as a ballet. First the fortress was invested; then came the opening of the trenches, usually formed in three parallels, after which the mines were laid; finally fighting ensued that led to the seizure of the counterscarps. After days of bombardment, the invasion of bastions or ravelins took place that opened the way into the fortress itself.

Under Vauban the siege was a masterpiece of military skill. He placed his trenches with such geometrical care that the fire from the fixed fortifications was at the wrong angle to damage the assault force as it moved closer and closer to the wall. The King went out every day to watch the progress. Sometimes he was on foot and stood by the parapet; sometimes on horseback saluting the besiegers and, according to the Gazette, 'appearing at places where lesser officers would hesitate to go'.

Two and a half weeks after the investment the siege-works appeared to justify an attempt to break in on the fortress. The attack, scheduled to take place at ten o'clock at night, was arranged to fall on Monmouth's tour of duty as a compliment to King Charles. Detachments from all the best regiments, including the King's Musketeers, were picked for the honour of taking part in an assault under the sublime gaze of the great Louis himself. The Duke of Monmouth, with Churchill at his side, led the French attack. The hand-to-hand fighting was fierce and the casualty list severe due to the explosion of two mines and 6,000 grenades; but at last the counterscarp galleries were occupied and Churchill was chosen to plant the lilies of France on the half-moon in front of the Brussels gate. It was now dawn and Monmouth and his officers retired to their tents.

However, it was not finished, for at noon the dull roar of a mine broke the quiet which told the camp that the Dutch were counter-attacking and by no means had thrown in their hand. Monmouth summoned a nearby group of French musketeers, amongst them M. D'Artagnan, one of the best swordsmen in France and later immortalized by Alexandre Dumas in The Three Musketeers. With these Frenchmen, twelve Life Guardsmen and John Churchill, Monmouth rushed back to the danger spot. There was no time to go through the zig-zags of the communicating trenches, so they scrambled over the top. The Life Guardsmen threw away their carbines and drew their swords to fight hand-to-hand. Later, one of Monmouth's officers, Lord Alington, wrote to Lord Arlington in London:

After the Duke had put on his arms, we went not out at the ordinary place, but leapt over the banks of the trenches, in the face of the Enemy. . . .

There was Mr Artagnan with his musketeers who did very bravely . . . but in passing that narrow place was killed with a shot through his head, upon which the Duke and we past where Mr O'Brien had a shot through his leages. The soldiers at this took heart the Duke twice leading them on with great Courage. . . . Then he sent Mr Villars to the king for 500 fresh men and to give him an account of what had past. When these men came, our Enemy left us without any further disturbance, masters of what we had gained the night before. . . . Some old Commanders say, this was the bravest and briskest action they had seen in their lives, and our Duke did the part of a much older and more experienced General, and the King was very kind to him last night.[4]

John Churchill was burning with ambition. He was determined to bring himself to the attention of the august assembly that had gathered to watch the fighting and volunteered for all the most dangerous tasks. He received a slight wound at Monmouth's side, while performing some service for his young colonel. We do not know what it was, but when the action was over Churchill was commended for the part he had played. He was publicly thanked by Louis XIV at a parade held to celebrate the victory and assured by the King that his good conduct would be brought to the attention of his own sovereign. There were others to commend him as well. Young Monmouth himself introduced Churchill to his sovereign-father with the words: 'Here is the brave man who saved my life.' There may have been a flicker of recognition in Charles's eyes as he registered that here also was the man who was sleeping with his ex-mistress, the Duchess of Cleveland. There was certainly no ill-feeling; Charles was now madly in love with the French seductress, Louise de Kéroualle, who proved to be so adroit that she maintained her influence with the King for the rest of her life.

At the end of 1673 Louis was alarmed by the strength of the coalition that the Prince of Orange was raising against him. Louis's cousin and rival claimant to the Spanish inheritance, the Habsburg ruler Leopold (Emperor of the Holy Roman Empire), had joined Holland; so had Spain, the powerful Duke of Lorraine, and several small German principalities. 'Most of the princes of Europe were leagued against me,' Louis wrote in his diary. 'So many powerful foes forced me to take guard . . . to sustain the reputation of my army, the advantages of the state, and my personal *gloire*. . . . My reactions had to be secret and prompt.'[5] He directed his generals to retreat from Holland and move closer to France.

Meanwhile there was trouble in England. Once again Charles II was short of money. Most of the French subsidies had been spent on refitting his navy and Charles was forced to repudiate interest on the loans he had received from bankers and goldsmiths and to recall the Houses of Lords and Commons.

The Parliament that met in February 1673 was extremely cantankerous as the King had not summoned it for nearly two years. Although many of the members were not opposed to fighting the Dutch, they were alarmed to see Catholic France extending her frontiers. Furthermore there were persistent rumours that the Duke of York had become a Catholic convert as he no longer attended the Anglican services. They therefore strongly objected when the King issued a Declaration of Indulgence giving Catholics (and dissenting Protestants) the same freedom as the Anglicans. Although the King's Act had been prompted by genuine tolerance, Parliament declared that Charles's Declaration infringed the prerogatives of the Church. It refused to vote him any money unless the Act was withdrawn and he gave his assent to a Test Act requiring every servant of the Crown to take the sacrament according to the Church of England. This, of course, meant the exclusion of Papists and Dissenters from all offices of state. Charles struggled hard against the demand, but in the end had no alternative but to give way because of his desperate need of money.

All eyes turned to the Duke of York and soon the country's worst fears were confirmed. James refused to acknowledge the Anglican Church or to declare himself against transubstantiation. So the Heir Apparent to the English throne really was a Papist! James had to resign his high offices including his military and naval positions. Although he was by far the most conspicuous casualty, there were other surprising revelations. The Duchess of Cleveland, for instance, had become a convert and now was obliged to relinquish her cherished role as the Queen's Lady of the Bedchamber, the position for which she had fought so fiercely twelve years earlier.

In 1674, in order to pacify his indignant Parliament, Charles made peace with Holland, in contravention of the solemn pledge he had given to Louis. Nevertheless, he allowed the 6,000 soldiers who were in French pay to continue to fight for France. This decision affected John Churchill who was serving in Westphalia under Marshal Turenne, the soldier who had taught Louis xiv the art of war and under whom the Duke of York had served. Although no important operations were taking place in this area, Churchill was well known for his outstanding courage and exceptional good looks. The French nicknamed him *Le Bel Anglais* and Turenne was said to have wagered, when a defile was captured too easily by the enemy, that *Le*

Bel Anglais would retake it with half the number of troops. Whether or not the Marshal collected his money is unknown; but the fact that he had formed such a high opinion of Churchill augured well for the young man's future.

As no English replacements were being sent to France many of the units were so far under strength that they had to be amalgamated. Even new commanders had to be found to replace the officers who had returned to England for good. Churchill benefited from these changes. On 19 March 1674, a newsletter from Paris announced that he had been chosen to command one of the composite regiments.

> Lord Peterborough's regiment, now in France, is to be broken up and some companies of it joined to the companies that went out of the Guards last summer, and be incorporated into one regiment, and to remain there for the present under the command of Captain Churchill, son of Sir Winston.

However, before Churchill could receive his colonelcy he had to receive the approval of King Louis. Although he would be in charge of a regiment of English infantry, he would be under French command. So, dressed in scarlet and gold, *Le Bel Anglais* was presented to the Great King at Versailles.* No doubt Louis remembered him from the Maestricht siege and gladly gave him his commission. Thus, at the age of twenty-four, Churchill was a full colonel in the French army. He had skipped the rank of lieutenant after Sole Bay; and now, in the French service, he had leaped over the grades of major and lieutenant-colonel.

Churchill fought two fierce engagements under Turenne when Louis ordered his Marshal to defend the French position in Alsace. One was at Sinzheim in June 1674, the other at Enzheim in October. The second encounter was the bloodiest. The Imperial general, de Bourneville, had an army of 40,000 men, twice as large as Turenne's, and was expecting the Elector of Brandenburg to arrive with further reinforcements of 20,000. De Bourneville crossed the Rhine at Strasbourg and dug himself in near the village of Enzheim about a mile from the River Breutsch. This virtually gave him command of upper Alsace, where provisions were plentiful and where he could invade France at will.

Turenne saw that he had no alternative but to attack, although he had half the number of men; if he waited for the Brandenburgers to arrive, he almost certainly would be driven back and, if he suffered

---

* Louis began holding Court at Versailles in 1674. Although the great château was not finally completed until 1682, the Grand Appartement, a splendid suite of seven rooms decorated by Le Brun, was ready for court functions much earlier.

heavy losses, the enemy would be able to lay waste the whole of Champagne. It was not an enviable task to launch an offensive as de Bourneville held an unusually strong position. On his right flank was Enzheim, now bristling with guns screened from view by hedges and vineyards; and on his left was a small forest known as 'the Little Wood'. This stronghold was about a mile long and half a mile deep. Who controlled the wood controlled the position, so this was where the battle would rage.

Turenne's first problem was to get his army over the River Breutsch. Oddly enough, the enemy had not destroyed the bridges and the French General moved his men across that night and was surprised to encounter no resistance. The enemy obviously welcomed a clash, believing that they were bound to inflict heavy losses on the attackers. In this they were not mistaken. Turenne threw his foreign troops into the forefront of the battle. Churchill's regiment, along with Hamilton's Irish battalion and Monmouth's Royal English battalion, fought in the Little Wood from nine in the morning until nightfall. The battle took place in pouring rain. Twice the English were driven out of the deadly wood and twice they retook it at horrible cost. They attacked for the third and last time over piles of dead and dying. When darkness fell, both sides were so exhausted that without knowing the other's movements, each retreated. Over 5,000 men had been killed and several thousand wounded. Churchill reported to the Duke of Monmouth :

> Your Grace's last battalion was on this attack, and both those of Hamilton and mine, so we have lost a great many officers, Hamilton, his brother and several others of the regiment. In your battalion Captain Cassels and Lee were killed and 2 wounded. I had Captain Dillon killed, Captain Piggott and Tutte wounded, and Lieutenants Watts, Howard, Tucker and Field killed. I had with me but 22 officers of which I have given Your Grace account of 11. Yet your regiment of horse was used much worse than we, for Lieutenant Colonel Littleton, Captain Gremes and Sheldon and 4 cornets with several lieutenants were killed. Their Major, Captain Kirke and most of the officers not killed are wounded, and above half the regiment lost with also several of their colours. I durst not brag much of our victory, but it is certain they left the field as soon as we did....[6]

Although Turenne could not claim to have won the battle, he had not lost it, and the following year he scored an undisputed triumph by throwing the imperialists out of Alsace for good.

Colonel John Churchill had fought with his customary brilliance and valour. Turenne mentioned him in despatches and Lord

Feversham,* Turenne's nephew, who was serving as his aide-de-camp, reported to London: 'No one in the world could possibly have done better than Mr Churchill has done and M. de Turenne is very well pleased with all our nation.'[7] Churchill's report to the Duke of Monmouth, however, was critical. 'Half our foot was so posted', he wrote, 'that they did not fight at all.'[8] Even at the age of twenty-four he realized that the greatest generals are not infallible. Nevertheless, he would become indebted to Turenne at a date far in the future if French claims are to be accepted. 'The French have well said', wrote Field-Marshal Wolseley in 1890, 'that Marlborough learned from a French General how to destroy French armies. It was Turenne's pupil who inflicted upon France those crushing defeats from which she never recovered . . . until Bonaparte.'[9]

No one knows whether Churchill was present at the battle of Sasbach in June 1675 when Turenne was killed by a cannon-ball. We know that he was sent to Paris on a mission for the Duke of York in August; and that in October he began to bring back his personal belongings, which seems to imply that his campaigning services in France had come to an end. In those days officers went to war with large supplies of silver plate to emphasize their status as gentlemen and to impress the guests who dined with them in the weeks before the battle. Now the plate was on its way to England and a warrant from the Customs House dated 8 October 1675 tells us that Churchill's equipage included one basin, two great dishes, three dozen plates, four candlesticks, two ewers, two pie dishes, chafing-dishes, one teapot, one chocolate-pot and cups and spoons.

Churchill again took his place in the Duke of York's household, but now he was one of the Gentlemen of the Bedchamber, a position that was bought for him by the Duchess of Cleveland. Many changes had taken place since Churchill's return from Tangiers five years earlier. In 1671 Anne Hyde, the Duchess of York, had died. As she was still in her twenties, her sudden demise came as a shock and puzzled her doctors who attributed it, rather fatuously, to 'overeating'; a century later the diagnosis was cancer of the uterus. On her death-bed and in the presence of her husband, the Duchess was received, very secretly, into the Church of Rome.

James was now free to make a suitable marriage, but his search for a bride and his negotiations with the various Courts of Europe provided

* Feversham was a French Huguenot of noble birth, born Count Louis Duras. He had become a naturalized Englishman in 1665 because of his friendship with the Duke of York. James put him in charge of his private Guard and a few years later secured him a peerage.

a hilarious comedy: he turned down one because she had 'a harridan as a mother', and another because she had red hair. In the end, forty-two-year-old James settled on the ravishing fourteen-year-old princess, Mary Beatrice of Modena, 'tall and admirably shaped' and with a complexion 'of the last degree of fairness'.[10] It was surprising that Charles agreed to this choice as Mary Beatrice was a Catholic and Charles had given a pledge to Parliament 'to provide for the ultimate succession of Protestants to the throne'. Indeed, he had forbidden James to influence the religious education of his two small children, Mary and Anne, who had been sent to live in Richmond Palace, away from their father's influence, with a governess from the Villiers family to bring them up as firm Protestants. However, as far as his marriage was concerned James was adamant and, in order to forestall any counter-moves, secretly married the Princess of Modeva by proxy in September 1672, although she did not take up residence in England until a year later. Naturally Parliament was angry; first they had been shocked by the news of James's conversion, now by his marriage to a Catholic. None of it boded well for the future.

When the fifteen-year-old Duchess moved into St James's Palace at the end of 1673, she was presented with a list of her Maids of Honour, among whom was thirteen-year-old Sarah Jennings, the daughter of Richard Jennings of Somersetshire, a land-owner and Member of Parliament, who had died when she was a child. She had grown up near St Albans – at Holywell House on the banks of the River Ver. She was a younger sister of the entrancing Frances, who had married Captain Sir George Hamilton six years earlier. Although people said that no one could hope to rival the beauty of Lady Hamilton, Sarah was soon being described as a worthy successor to her sister. She had a wonderful creamy skin, flashing blue eyes, honey-coloured hair and a slightly turned-up nose that gave her the audacious look that her character justified. She was amusing in a witty, provocative way, very self-confident for her years and had the 'temper of the devil'.

This temper had been inherited from her mother who, as a widow, was overburdened with debt. To escape the law, Frances Jennings had secured lodgings for her in St James's Palace where a summons could not be served on her. Although scurrilous pamphleteers frequently referred to Mrs Jennings as 'a witch' and a 'sorceress' – not because she did anything bad but because her appearance was dark and glowering – she was well-born and respectable, the daughter of Sir Gifford Thornhurst of Kent. But she often quarrelled fiercely with Sarah. 'Mrs Jennings and her daughter, Mayd of Honour to the Dutchesse,' Lady Chaworth wrote to her brother, have had so great a falling out that they fought; the young one complained to the Dutchesse that if her mother were not put out of St James's where she had lodgings to sanctuary her from debt, she would run away; so Sir Allen Apsley the controller of the Household was sent to bid the mother remove, who answered 'with all her heart' she should never dispute the Duke and Dutchesse's commands, but with the Grace of God she would take her daughter away with her, for two of the maids had had such great bellies at Court, and she would not leave her child there to have the third; so rather than part with her the mother must stay, and all breeches are made up again.[11]

But this was only the opening round. A month later Lady Chaworth reports that 'Mrs [Mistress] Sarah Jennings has got the better of her mother, who is commanded to leave the Court and her daughter in it, notwithstanding the mother's petition, that she might have her girle with her, the girle saying that she is a mad woman.'[12] The rupture was not permanent. As soon as mother and daughter were parted, they became deeply fond of each other again and perhaps even missed the excitement of their rows.

It is difficult to picture Sarah Jennings as a Maid of Honour at Charles II's boisterous Court, described by Bishop Burnet as 'a mad, roaring time full of extravagance'. Sarah was very different from the rather wild young maidens who rejoiced at being away from parental authority. These fifteen-year-old girls were allowed astonishing freedom. They came and went as they pleased and it was not in the least unusual for a Maid to receive her lover in her bedroom. The Queen's Maids were even less inhibited than those of the Duchess. They lived in a house near the river with a chaperone known as 'Mother Shipton', who only accepted the position of duenna on the understanding that her duties would not be arduous and that no one would object if she retired to bed early each night. This suited everyone, and her charges spent their evenings flirting outrageously or gambling at cards until the small hours of the morning with the Duke of Monmouth and his fellow officers. Sarah tells us that she once saw one of these girls, only thirteen years old, coming out of a room weeping, saying that her mother's advice had 'undone her' – not only her mother, but Thomas Thynne of Longleat who had put her in the family way. No doubt this drama made a deep impression on Sarah. 'I made it my business', she wrote, 'to observe things very exactly without being much observed myself.'[13]

Sarah was very much cleverer than her companions. Furthermore she was not a stranger to the Court, for at the ages of nine and ten she had frequently visited her sister Frances who, although she was married, still kept rooms at the palace. It was here that Sarah first became friends with little Princess Anne, a shy child five years younger than herself. However, it was one thing to be a visitor, another to be part of the establishment. Sarah found the Court routine boring, mainly because the endless chatter of the other Maids was so nonsensical. 'At fourteen,' she admitted, 'I wished myself out of the Court as much as I had desired to come into it before I knew what it was.'[14]

This was not entirely true, for Sarah refused to budge when her mother tried to take her away. Besides, there were plenty of amusements that she enjoyed. She loved playing cards for money and became an expert at the games then in fashion – ombre, basset and 'thirty and forty'. She also liked dancing and acting in plays. Before the Restoration, women never appeared on the stage, but now even the Princesses, Mary and Anne, begged to be given parts. Mrs Betterton, the best actress of the day, was employed to teach elocution to the Princesses and Sarah, and to produce the plays shown at Court. In the winter of 1674–5, *The Chaste Nymph* was performed, with females taking all the principal parts. The cast included the two Princesses, Margaret Blagge (the future Lady Godolphin), Lady Mary Mordaunt, Lady Henrietta Wentworth and Sarah Jennings. The only male intervention was that of the Duke of Monmouth and two of his colleagues who opened the performance by giving a spirited dance. Yet these light-hearted plays cast a long shadow. Apparently it was during rehearsals that the Duke and Henrietta Wentworth became enamoured of one another. Who could have foreseen that Monmouth would leave his wife for Henrietta; or that Henrietta would follow him into exile and die of a broken heart after he had fallen to the executioner's axe?

Sarah's life swung from boredom to rapture when eventually John Churchill began to court her and she fell in love with him. No doubt Churchill was aware of Sarah's existence in 1673 as they both served the Yorks, but at that time he was abroad half the year fighting and when he was at home he was preoccupied with Barbara. He did not return to England for good until the end of 1675. The Duke rewarded him with the Lieutenant-Colonelcy of the Regiment of Foot and luckily Barbara was still around to pay the fees. As a fearless young officer who had been praised by Louis XIV and Marshal Turenne, he was a hero and much admired at the English Court. Sarah had seen him about for several winters (war always stopped from November to April because of waterlogged roads) and no doubt followed his activities with close attention. 'He was', she wrote years later, 'naturally genteel without the least affectation and as handsome as an angel though ever so carlessly dress'd'.[15] Not only genteel and handsome but adven-

turesome and amorous, for his tempestuous affair with the Duchess of
Cleveland was notorious – not unlike the affair of his sister, Arabella,
who by this time had borne the Duke of York four children.

No doubt observant Sarah took note of the danger-signals flashing
when, in 1676, John began to be attentive to her, seeking her company
at dinner-parties and theatricals, and dancing with her at balls. That
same year the French Ambassador, M. Courtin, gave an amusing
account of London society in a letter to his Minister, M. Louvois.
After telling of a little party he is giving for four or five Court ladies,
including Sarah Jennings, the sister of *La Belle Jenyns*, he says that the
ladies' lovers are to be invited so that there will be plenty of dancing
while he is left at peace to play ombre; he then describes the fashions
of the day:

> There is nothing so dainty as the English woman's *chaussure*; their shoes
> fit them with great nicety; their skirts are short, and their stockings very
> clean and tidy. English ladies do not mind showing a great deal of their
> legs, which are perfect pictures. Green stockings are most in vogue, with
> black velvet garters, fashioned above the knees by diamond buckles.
> Where there is no silk stocking the skin is very white and satiny.[16]

Apparently Sarah's garters were irresistible, for Lord Bolingbroke*
declared that 'Colonel Churchill took special pleasure in tying and
untying the garters of Mistress Jennings.'[17]

No matter how audacious this pastime may seem to the reader,
fifteen-year-old Sarah was highly moral (like her sister Frances) and
took care to tread warily. The Churchills not only had a reputation
for being ruthless and ambitious but John was known as an expert
dissembler. Indeed, the Duchess of Cleveland confided to a relation
that she had given Colonel Churchill a great deal of money 'for very
little service done', a complaint that had become common gossip.
From this we deduce that his affair with Barbara was still drifting on,
despite his attentions to the young Maid of Honour.

John pursued Sarah for over two and a half years, and of the many
love letters that passed between them, only thirty-seven have been
preserved. All but eight are his. None have a beginning or an ending,
and none are dated, as though Churchill feared that they might fall
into the wrong hands and stimulate gossip, or even provide the Court
Wits with material for their outrageous verses. In her old age the
Duchess re-read the correspondence and on her own letters wrote:

---

* This Lord Bolingbroke, whose title lapsed with his death, was a distant relation of Mr
Henry St John, who later played a prominent part in the Marlborough story. The latter resurrec-
ted the family peerage in 1712 by becoming Viscount Bolingbroke.

'Some copys of my letters to Mr Churchill before I was married and not more than 15 years old.' When she re-read the letters in 1736, and again a few years later, she noted: 'Read over in 1743 desiring to burn them, but I could not doe it.'[18] Instead she instructed her woman-in-waiting, Grace Ridley, to take charge of the letters after her death and 'to burn without reading them'. Fortunately her orders were not carried out.

Some historians find the letters puzzling. John appears deeply in love. He swears his devotion over and over again, begging for a meeting anywhere, anytime, no matter how brief. Sarah's letters, on the other hand, are short and sharp, and often mocking. She must have written many more letters, but for reasons best known to herself only kept copies of her most combative missives.

The truth was that Sarah regarded John's advances as nothing short of a war which she intended to win. When the correspondence opened she was in such a strong position that the colonel could only make skirmishes:

> My Soul, I love you so truly well and hope you will be so kind as to let me see you somewhere today, since you will not be at Whitehall. I will not name any time for all hours are alike to me when you will bless me with your sight. You are, and ever shall be the dear object of my life, for by heavens I will never love anybody but yourself.*

What Sarah replied is not known. Perhaps she taunted him about Barbara. At any rate, he wrote repeatedly urging a meeting.

> I am just come and have no thought of any joy but that of seeing you. Wherefore I hope you will send me word that you will see me tonight.
>
> I fancy by this time that you are awake, which makes me now send to know how you do, and if your foot will permit you to give me the joy of seeing you in the drawing-room this night. Pray let me hear from you, for when I am not with you, the only joy I have is hearing from you.

Apparently joy was not a commodity that Miss Sarah Jennings was in a mood to give:

> My Soul, it is a cruel thing to be forced in a place when I have no hopes of seeing you, for on my word last night seemed very tedious to me, wherefore I beg you will be so kind to me as to come as often as you can this week, since I am forced to wait [to be in waiting]. I hope you will send me word that you are well and that I shall see you here tonight.

And again,

> I was last night at the ball, in the hopes to have seen what I love above my

---

* The love letters reprinted in this chapter are part of the Blenheim Papers, now in the British Library. The quotations are extracts and not complete letters. The spelling has been modernized. All of them have been published by Winston Churchill.

own soul, but I was not so happy for I could see you nowhere, so that I did not stay above an hour.

What was the trouble? Colonel Churchill must have found the Duchess of Cleveland difficult to handle to say the least. Not only was she thoroughly spoilt, having been the reigning beauty of the Court for a decade and a half, but she was the mother of Churchill's child and had lived happily with him for the past three years. Quite clearly she was not giving up her handsome colonel without a struggle. But Sarah had no pity and simply scoffed at him. Although she was only sixteen years old and deeply in love, she instinctively knew that any concessions would lessen her chance of victory. After all, she was dealing with the most handsome man of the day. Every flirtatious woman at Court (including Barbara) had her eye on him. 'Of all the men that I ever knew (and I knew him extremely well),' wrote Lord Chesterfield many years later, 'the late Duke of Marlborough possessed the graces in the highest degree, not to say engrossed them. ... His figure was beautiful but his manner was irresistible by either man or woman.'[19]

It was not irresistible to Miss Sarah Jennings, however, who continued to maintain her cold exterior. When Churchill tells her that he is ill, suffering from headaches, she appears quite unmoved. Did these attacks spring from the nervous strain of his courtship, just as in later years they plagued him during the tense hours on the eve of battle? Whatever the answer, nothing softened Sarah's heart. John to Sarah:

> I stayed last night in the drawing-room expecting your coming back, for I could have wished that we had not parted until you had given me hopes of seeing you, for my soul, there is no pain so great to me, as when I fear you do not love me; but I hope I shall never live to see you less kind than you are. I am sure I will never deserve it for I will by all that is good love you as long as I live. I beg you will let me see you as often as you can, which I am sure you ought to do if you care for my love, since every time I see you I still find new charms in you. ...

Clearly John was afraid that gossips were making trouble for him over Barbara, and adds rather desperately: 'Therefore do not be so ill-natured as to believe any lies that may be told you of me, for on my faith I do not only now love you but do desire to do it as long as I live.'

At the end of 1676 the Duke of Monmouth recommended that Churchill should be given the Colonelcy of the Royal English Regiment serving with the French army against the Dutch; but John was not a mercenary and, once England had made peace with Holland, he had no wish to continue fighting the hard-pressed and gallant Republic. But the French Ambassador in London, M. Courtin, had a different explanation. 'Mr Churchill', he wrote to Paris, 'prefers to serve the very pretty sister of Lady Hamilton than to be Lieutenant-Colonel in Monmouth's regiment.'[20]

However, John was not always successful in remaining close to Sarah. Early in 1677 the Duke of York sent him to France, probably to stress to the French King Charles II's urgent need for more subsidies to avoid the necessity of summoning Parliament again. Before Churchill left London he attended a Drawing-Room reception, but Sarah picked a quarrel with him, perhaps to ensure that she would remain uppermost in his mind.

> To show you how unreasonable you are in accusing me, I dare swear that you yourself will own that your going from me in the Duchess's drawing room did show as much contempt as is possible. . . . I suppose it is what pleases your humour.

John sounds genuinely puzzled by her actions:

> I cannot imagine what you meant by your saying I laughed at you at the Duke's side, for I was so far from that, that had it not been for shame I could have cried. And as for being in haste to go to the Park, after you went I stood for over a quarter of an hour, I believe, without knowing what I did. Although at Whitehall you told me I should not come, yet I walked twice to the Duke's back-stairs, but there was no Mrs Mowdie [Sarah's waiting woman]; and when I went to my Lord Duras's, I would not go the same way they did but came again down the back-stairs; and when I went away, I did not go in my chair but made it follow me, because I would see if there was any light in your chamber, but I saw none.

At this point the reader needs to be cautioned not to feel too much sympathy for the humble, earnest Colonel Churchill. Despite his protestations of undying love, he had not yet proposed marriage. Furthermore, it must be remembered that at the Court of Charles II, it was considered customary for the gayest sparks to try to seduce the Maids of Honour. Sarah's sister, Frances, had been courted by any number of amorous gentlemen including the Duke of York, but had turned a deaf ear to them all. Pert little Sarah, now sixteen years old, was carefully following Frances's lead; but, although she made every effort to give an impression of cheerful indifference, she did not come out of the combat unscathed. Throughout 1676 and half of 1677, she faced dangerous opposition which could have brought her romance to an end, causing her the deepest anxiety. Sir Winston and Lady Churchill got wind of their son's infatuation and moved into the arena. They were strongly opposed to his courtship and did everything they could to end it. With John's fine record, his charm and good looks, he could make a really advantageous marriage, not throw himself away on a slip of a girl without a penny to her name.

Money was an essential commodity for ambitious men, as promotions had to be bought – not only commissions in the army or posts at Court, but almost every position of distinction from judge to secretary of state. The money was not payable to those who gave the posts but to those who left them. Thus, even King Charles had to find money to buy from Lord Brandon the command of the King's troop of Life Guards which he wanted for his son, Lord Monmouth. Prince Rupert paid Lord Mordaunt £3,500 for the Governorship of Windsor Castle, but poor Sir William Temple had to decline the post of Secretary of State as he could not find the £6,000 demanded.

Up till now Barbara had paid for Churchill's promotions (they came to several thousand pounds), but what would happen when and if he married Sarah? If he fell out of favour with the royal family, he would be left with nothing. In favour he could provide a roof for wife and children and certainly keep them from starving. Apart from his annuity of £500 he had £300 a year as Gentleman of the Bedchamber and a few hundred pounds for his colonelcy. But he was an ambitious man, and how could he put his hands on the large sums required for the exalted positions he intended to fill? And what about Sarah? She had been introduced at Court in order to marry some rich peer like Lord Lindsay who, rumour had it, was paying her marked attention. To become the wife of a penniless soldier was as foolish for her as it was foolhardly for him.

Colonel John Churchill should marry an heiress. Sir Winston had it all planned. He had even discussed it with Sir Charles Sedley, one of the King's courtiers, whose only daughter, Catherine, would inherit a large fortune. Catherine was not pretty, but she had a good figure and fine eyes, was witty and amusing and greatly sought after as a sparkling conversationalist. Sir Charles gave his consent to the marriage and John's mother and father did everything in their power to make their son consider it. Sarah was well aware of the pressure being applied to her suitor who, despite his ardent letters, had not yet proposed marriage to her. She was right to be anxious, for no one understood the advantage of money better than Churchill himself. Contemporary gossip was firm in the belief that he was far too worldly to marry a woman without a sizeable dowry.

The French Ambassador saw Sarah at a party looking very unhappy and reported the incident to Versailles:

There was a small ball last Friday at the Duchess of York's where Lady Hamilton's sister who is uncommonly good-looking had far more wish to cry than dance. Churchill who is her suitor says that he is attacked by consumption and must take the air in France. I wish that I were as well as he. The truth is that he wishes to free himself from intrigues. His father urges him to marry one of his relations who is very rich and very ugly and will not consent to his marriage with Miss Jennings. He is also said to be not a little avaricious and I hear from the various Court ladies that he has pillaged the Duchess of Cleveland, and that she has given him more than the value of 100,000 *livres*. They make out that it is he who has quitted her and that she has taken herself off in chagrin to France to rearrange her affairs. If Churchill crosses the sea she will be able to patch things up with him. Meanwhile she writes agreeably to the Duchess of Sussex conjuring her to go with her husband to the country and to follow her advice but not her example.

7 December 1676[21]

We see from this that Barbara has flounced off to Paris, but we are in the dark as to Churchill's opinion of Catherine. All we know is that Sarah took a very unfriendly view and wrote an angry letter, to which John replied abjectly: 'I do love you with all the truth imaginable, but have patience but for one week, and you shall then see that I will never more do aught that shall look like a fault.' 'This letter', Sarah explains in an endorsement written many years later, 'was writ when I was angry at something his father and mother had made a disagreeable noise in the town about when they had a mind to have him marry a shocking creature for money.'[22]

Sarah decided that the time had come to force the issue. If John did not propose marriage, she would stop seeing him. She wrote to him in her brusque way, leaving no room for misunderstanding:

If it were true that you have that passion for me which you say you have, you would find out some way to make yourself happy – it is in your power. Therefore press me no more to see you, since it is what I cannot in honour approve of, and if I have done too much be so just as to consider who was the cause of it. . . .

John ignored the ultimatum and took refuge in his (by this time) monotonous declaration of love:

You say I pretend a passion for you when I have other things in my head. I cannot imagine what you mean by it, for I vow to God you do so entirely possess my thoughts that I think of nothing else in this world but your own dear self. . . .

And again,

> You complain of my unkindness, but would not be kind yourself in answering my letter, although I begged you to do it. The Duchess goes to a new play today, afterwards to the Duchess of Monmouth's there to dance. I desire that you will not go thither, but make an excuse and give me leave to come to you. . . .

Sarah was not taken in by soft words and refused to make an assignation. Sarah to John:

> As for seeing you I am resolved I never will in private nor in public if I can help it. . . . Surely you must confess that you have been the falsest creature upon earth to me. I must own that I believe I shall suffer a great deal of trouble, but I will bear it, and give God thanks, though too late I see my error. . . .

While John's courtship of Sarah was running into a rough sea, a royal marriage took place in a flood of tears, at least as far as the bride was concerned. Charles II married his pretty, fifteen-year-old niece, Mary (James's daughter), to William of Orange. William came to London in the autumn of 1677 to make the Princess's acquaintance and was pleased with what he saw. Mary, on the other hand, was appalled. Although the Prince was her first cousin (his mother was Charles's sister who had died in 1661), she found him gauche and ugly. He never smiled and had a nose that was much too long. Her father tried to reassure her, explaining that William had become one of the great men of Europe, a true hero who had saved his country from extinction and was now heading a coalition that was holding mighty France at bay.

But Mary was romantic and longed for love. The Prince, she pointed out, was a whole head shorter than herself and she did not care how many people admired him. Her father was sympathetic, but when she realized that the King was adamant and that there was no way to alter his decision, she wept for two days without stopping. She even went to Queen Catherine for sympathy, but the Queen talked about her own ordeal in being sent far away to marry a man she had never seen. Mary, with true English insularity, brushed her unhappy experience aside, saying: 'But Ma'am, you came *into* England, and I am going *out*!'

Poor Mary had no option but to do as she was told and married William with tears trickling down her face. The ceremony was conducted in the bedchamber at nine o'clock at night, and King Charles waited until the newly-weds climbed into their four-poster at eleven. He then pulled the curtains around the bed and cried: 'Now nephew to your work! Hey! St George for England!'

The melancholy marriage took place in a melancholy household, for Mary's younger sister, Anne, had contracted smallpox and was dangerously ill. Other members of the palace caught the infection including Lady Frances Villiers, the Princesses' governess, who had planned to accompany Mary to Holland. Instead, Lady Frances sickened and died. Even more tragic was the death of the Duchess of York's newly born and only son, Charles, Duke of Cambridge. Anne, believing herself entirely cured, had called on her stepmother on 3 December and unwittingly transmitted the disease. Nine days later the four-week-old infant was dead.

Anne was still in danger when Mary left for Holland. As the two sisters were very close, the Duke of York feared that Anne might suffer a fatal relapse if she knew Mary had gone; so every day fabricated notes were sent to the Princess to maintain the belief that she was still about. Indeed, Mary was so loath to leave her father, whom she idolized, that she refused to quit the stricken palace for a place of safety, and remained with James until the very moment of departure.

Her tears were an omen – her married life was deeply unhappy for many years. This was partly due to the fact that she took to Holland as one of her ladies-in-waiting Elizabeth Villiers (the daughter of her governess), who became William's mistress. Mary was not only indignant but deeply mortified as Elizabeth was very plain. She named her 'Squinting Betty', but the affair flourished. To make matters worse, Elizabeth's sister Anne married William's closest friend, Hans William Bentinck. Members of the Villiers family always seemed to dig themselves into entrenched positions.

Meanwhile John Churchill was struggling to get his relationship with Sarah back on an even keel. We can see from a letter which Harry Saville, the Duke of York's Vice-Chamberlain, wrote to a friend in the spring of 1677 that Churchill had brought to an end any idea of marrying Catherine Sedley:

> Mistress Sedley's marriage with Jack Churchill [he wrote] neither is nor ever will be any more talked of, both the knight and the colonel [Sir Charles and Sir Winston] being willing to break off fairly – which important matter is referred to me by both parties, and for both their goods I think it best it should cease.[23]

Luckily for Catherine, the Duke of York had become infatuated with her; so instead of marrying John she deposed John's sister, Arabella, as the reigning mistress and before long even took over Arabella's house in St James's Square.* Catherine was as modest as she was amusing. Referring to the Duke of York's mistresses, including herself and Arabella, she said: 'What he saw in any of us I cannot tell. We are all plain and if any of us had wit he would not have understood it.'[24]

John's thoughts were far removed from Catherine and once again he wrote professing his undying love. But Sarah did not think much of his declaration as she was still holding out for the final capitulation:

> I am as little satisfied with this letter as I have been with many others, but I find all you will say is only to amuse me and make me think you have a passion for me, when in reality there is no such thing. You have reason to think it strange that I write to you after my last, where I protested that I would never write nor speak to you more; but as you know how much kindness I had for you, you can't wonder or blame me if I try once more, to hear what you can say for your justification . . . pray consider if, with honour to me and satisfaction to yourself, I can see you; for it be only to repeat those things which you said so oft, I shall think you the worse of men, and the most ungrateful; and 'tis to no purpose to imagine that I will be made ridiculous in the world when it is in your power to make me otherwise.

Churchill seems to take refuge in telling her how ill he has been, as an excuse to ignore her demands:

> Yours last night found me so sick that I thought I should have died, and I have now so excessive a headache that I should not stir out all day but that the Duchess has sent me word that the Duke will see me this afternoon, so that at night I shall have the happiness of seeing you in the drawing-room. . . .

Sarah to John:

> At four o'clock I would see you but that would hinder you from seeing the play, which I fear would be a great affliction to you, and increase the pain in your head, which would be out of anybody's power to ease until the next new play. Therefore, pray consider, and without any compliment to me, send me word if you can come to me without any prejudice to your health.

These sarcasms stung the Colonel as no other letters had done and he wrote angrily to Sarah's waiting-woman, Mrs Mowdie:

> Your mistress's usage of me is so barbarous that surely she must be the worst woman in the world, or else she would not be thus ill-natured. I have

---

* Arabella sold her house for the huge sum of £8,000. It is not known whether the Duke of York or Sir Charles Sedley, Catherine's father, was the purchaser.

sent a letter which I desire you will give her. . . . I do love her with all my soul, but will not trouble her, for if I cannot have her love, I shall despise her pity. For the sake of what she has already done let her read my letter and answer it, and not use me thus like a footman.

Sarah to John:

I have done nothing to deserve such a kind of letter as you have writ to me, and therefore I don't know what answer to give; but I find you have a very ill opinion of me, and therefore I can't help being angry with myself for having too good a one of you; for if I had as little love as yourself, I have been told enough of you to make me hate you, and then I believe I should have been more happy than I am like to be now. . . .

John to Sarah, after an ominous silence:

It would have been much kinder in you, if you had been pleased to have been so good-natured to have found time to have written to me yesterday, especially since you are resolved not to appear when I might see you. But I am resolved to take nothing ill but to be your slave as long as I live, and so to think all things well that you do.

This letter is described by John Churchill's descendant, the great Winston Churchill of our day, as 'the only surrender to which the Duke of Marlborough was ever forced'. It was, he added with chagrin, 'to a chit of seventeen'.[25] Apprehensive that he might lose her if he did not come up to scratch, John Churchill finally spoke the words that Sarah longed to hear. They had very little money but plenty of confidence in the future. Because of the opposition of the Churchill family, the marriage took place in secret, under the auspices of the nineteen-year-old Duchess of York. Neither the place nor the date is known, but historians put it in the early winter of 1678, perhaps in Mary of Modena's apartments. It was not only a love-match, a rare occurrence in the seventeenth century, but it proved to be a great political partnership. Most rewarding of all, the magic that each had for the other lasted for the rest of their lives.

Three

Lady-in-Waiting

The young Churchills soon made their marriage known, but their mode of living changed very little apart from the fact that Sarah was obliged to relinquish her position as Maid of Honour. They resisted the impulse to use the little money they had to buy a house as John had hopes of a promotion and the required commission was bound to be substantial. They decided that when Sarah was in London they would live in John's bachelor lodgings in Jermyn Street; and when they were in the country they would divide their time between Mrs Jennings's house in St Albans and the Churchill house, Mintern, in Dorsetshire. Although John was very careful with money, eighteen-year-old Sarah was dissatisfied with the way he handled their meagre income and took over the task herself. 'Soon after our marriage,' she wrote,

> when our affairs were so narrow that a good deal of frugality was necessary, tho' Marlborough's inclination lay enough that way, yet by reason of an indulgent gentleness natural to him he could not manage matters so as was convenient to our Circumstances. This obliged me to enter into the management of my family.[1]

Like most girls of her age Sarah was uneducated; nevertheless, she had an exceptionally good mind. Her fresh, vigorous opinions were invariably diverting, and as she despised discretion she usually blurted out exactly what she thought. This meant that her acquaintances were divided into two groups: those who could not abide her and those who could not resist her. The letter she sent just before she was married to her only surviving sister, Frances Hamilton, gives one a better glimpse of her personality than her letters to John. Apparently Sarah's widowed brother-in-law, Edward Griffiths, had been dancing attendance upon her at Whitehall in the hope of securing a Court appointment. Sarah wrote to Frances that she was wearier of his company 'than anything in the world'.

> He has larnst French ever since my sister dyed, and thinks thar is nobody understands more nor pronounces it better than himself. I am in amazement every time I see him how my poor sister could have such a passion for him. Then he is soe ill-bred, and fancies himself such a wit, and makes such a noise from morning to night that, as my mother says, he turns my head, I beleeve I had not had his company but that he wants money. I cannot imagine how he will doe to live, being of a humor that makes him uncapable of anything but spending. I confess I have not much concern for him and all I desire is that he may not spend all at St Albans without paying the interest. . . . [2]

Sarah spent most of the first year of her marriage living with Sir Winston and Lady Churchill at Mintern. It is difficult to imagine this high-spirited girl, who read very little but who had decided views on everything from princes to housekeeping, adapting herself to the restricted outlook of her parents-in-law. No doubt the Churchills continued to regret that their son had not married Catherine Sedley, not only because she was rich but because she was even-tempered – something that could not be said for Sarah. Nevertheless, young Mrs Churchill did her best to get along with Lady Churchill, although the result was not always successful. Apparently her mother-in-law took exception to something she had written from St Albans and she asked John to read the letter she was sending in reply.

> If she takes anything ill that is in that letter [wrote John to Sarah] you must attribute it to the peevishness of old age, for really I think there is nothing in it that she ought to take ill. I take it very kindly that you have writ to her again for she is my mother, and I hope at last she will be sensible that she is to blame in being peevish.[3]

Sarah was always delighted when she could escape to her mother's roof, Holywell House in St Albans. Here she need not be on her best behaviour and could say what she liked. She had inherited her sharp tongue from Mrs Jennings, so it is not surprising that the two women continued to quarrel all their lives. These encounters were so stimulating that the combatants were inclined to patch up their differences as quickly as possible to get ready for the next round.

Their arguments often led to unexpected developments. Once Mrs Jennings was so annoyed with Sarah that she stopped the coach in which they were riding, got out and climbed up next to the driver, a seat unprotected from the rigours of the weather. 'I have thought very often since I left my deare mother', wrote Sarah, what was the reason for all the disorder and ill-humer the night and morning before I came away, and if I thought I had don anything that you had reason to take ill, I should be very angry with myself. . . . I beg you will consider how often I stop'd the coach as wee came home and beg'd you to come in which I could doe for noe other reason but for feare you should get your death and what reason had you when you came home to say soe many cruell things to me and bety Moody which I can't but take to myself, the post is going and I can't say noe more but that I hope I shall see you or heare from you very soone and that I will ever bee your most duty full Daughter whatever you are to me.

CHURCHILL[4]

John spent every free moment he had with Sarah, sometimes at Holywell House, sometimes at Mintern; but in 1678 trouble was brewing once more on the Continent and he was summoned frequently to Whitehall and twice sent abroad. This flurry of activity sprang from the fact that Charles II was playing a game of poker with France and more than once England seemed to be on the brink of war. Ever since parliamentary pressure had forced the King to withdraw from the alliance with France, he had been busily extracting payments from the two opposing interests. He persuaded Parliament to vote him large sums of money to arm the country against Louis's possible vengeance, and at the same time – February 1676 – he signed an agreement with Louis to prorogue Parliament (which he did for fifteen months) in return for three years of financial subsidies, payable each quarter.

Although Charles's Lord Treasurer, Lord Danby, knew that the King was receiving money from France, he did everything he could to promote an alliance with Holland. Indeed, it was Danby who finally persuaded Charles to appease Protestant England by marrying his niece Mary to William of Orange. When Louis XIV heard of the alliance he was so angry he behaved as though he had suffered a massive military defeat. The fact that the very opposite was true in 1677 did not improve his temper. 'You have given your daughter', he told the Duke of York, 'to my mortal enemy.' Louis's resentment was not entirely political. He still remembered the rebuff that William had given him years before when he had tried to draw him into his own family. He had offered the Prince his very young daughter by his mistress, Louise de la Vallière, but William had drawn himself up haughtily and said: 'In the House of Orange we marry the legitimate daughters of kings, not their bastards.'

King Louis showed his displeasure over the marriage of Mary and

William by cutting off his subsidies to Charles, then started a quarrel that went on for months. Charles reacted indignantly by recalling Parliament and informing his faithful Lords and Commons that he was ready to explore the possibilities of an alliance with Holland to resist Louis's invasion of Flanders. Parliament was delighted and voted Charles £1 million 'if the war actually broke out'.

Charles put the necessary preparations in hand and watched the mounting tension with a critical eye. He was still playing his game and had no intention of embroiling England in another conflict. Nevertheless he knew that if his threats were to prove effective, his actions would have to appear convincing. The Duke of York loyally supported his brother in his play-acting, and probably suggested making use of John Churchill, who was gazetted colonel in one of the new Foot regiments in February 1678. Churchill was becoming known for a cool head and an equable temperament; and the King was looking for someone to send to The Hague who had both military knowledge and diplomatic skill. James was convinced that Churchill was the right man and in March summoned him to London from Mintern. 'I got to town after three, very weary,' he wrote to Sarah from Whitehall. 'However I dressed and went to the Duke for to know what he had to command me. He told me that . . . he did believe that there would be occasion to send me to Holland and Flanders, and that he would have me here ready to go.'[5]

A few days later Churchill sailed for The Hague to arrange, on the King's authority, the military details for the intervention of English troops. He had met William of Orange when he had come to England the previous year, but this was the first opportunity he had had to talk to him. The two men took to each other at once. They were both twenty-eight years old and both experienced in the art of war, which they sat up half the night discussing. Churchill had been instructed to offer the Prince 20,000 men 'and guns proportionately' and had no difficulty in negotiating satisfactory terms.

Churchill was accompanied by Sidney Godolphin, a West Country man like himself, whom he had known at Court for many years, and who was destined to become his closest friend and Lord Treasurer of England during the great years of Churchill's military campaigns. Sidney had begun his career as a page at Charles's Court. The King liked his quiet efficiency and once praised him because he was 'never in the way and never out of the way'. 'He was the silentist and modestest man that was perhaps ever bred at court,' wrote Bishop Burnet,

... his notions were for the court; but his incorrupt and sincere way of managing the concerns of the treasury created in all people a very high esteem for him. He loved gaming the most of any man of business I ever knew; and gave one reason for it, because it delivered him from the obligation to talk much.[6]

The two Englishmen returned to London in May.* New regiments were in the process of being raised and recruits, who were paid much more than labourers, came pouring in on all sides. 'We are beating up drums every day for new levies,' wrote Lord Conway to his brother, 'and soldiers come in plentifully and cheerfully.'[7] The greater part of the new army was encamped on Hounslow Heath, where people came to stare at soldiers called grenadiers who were skilful at throwing a new weapon known as 'hand grenados'. They wore fox-tails at 3s6d apiece that hung from their caps and gave them a very fierce and barbarous look.

Meanwhile Louis had captured the great citadel of Ghent only thirty miles from the Dutch frontier, provoking an angry reaction from England. John Churchill was promoted again, this time to Brigadier of Foot. He was ordered abroad at twenty-four hours' notice to serve under the Duke of Monmouth. But he knew too much to believe in war. 'You may rest satisfied', he wrote to Sarah in September,

> that there will be certain peace in a few days ... therefore be not concerned when I tell you that tomorrow I go ... I believe it will be about the beginning of October before I get back which time will appear an age to me since all that time I will not be made happy with the sight of you. ... So dearest soul of my life, farewell. My duty to my Father and Mother.

Many years later Sarah endorsed the treasured letter: 'Lord Marlborough to ease me when I might be frightened at his going into danger.'[8]

Charles eventually won the game of poker, although at the last moment he was cheated of his financial reward. Louis could not be sure that England was bluffing and decided to open peace negotiations. He offered Charles £450,000 if he would disband his army, prorogue Parliament for four months and influence the Dutch to meet France's demands. Undoubtedly John Churchill was aware of the arrangement and probably saw the letter that the Duke of York wrote to William of Orange advising him to accept Louis's terms: 'I know such a peace as is offered is a very hard one for you and us to submit

---

* At the end of this year Godolphin's wife died giving birth to a son who, when he grew up, married Henrietta Churchill, John and Sarah's daughter. Godolphin never married again.

to: however I see no remedy, and [hope you] do not exasperate France [as she] may be of use to you. . . . '⁹

The negotiations were not difficult, as the capture of Ghent, so close to the Dutch frontier, had increased the desire of the Dutch for peace. Although Louis had failed in his original purpose – the destruction of Holland – he emerged from the conflict with the whole of Franche Comté, most of Lorraine, the city of Fribourg complete with a passage to Brisach, and a rationalized frontier between France and the Spanish Netherlands. (He gave up Oudenarde, Courtrai and other fortresses in the Low Countries and restored all the Dutch territory in his hands including Maestricht, the fortress that Churchill had besieged under Monmouth's command). However, at the last moment the French King suddenly demanded a concession that had nothing to do with Holland. Charles counter-manded the order to withdraw his troops from the Continent and declared angrily that Louis was playing him false – a move which cost him his £450,000. In the end, one of the Swedish Ambassadors suggested an acceptable compromise and the Peace of Nimwegen was signed in the summer of 1678. In France, Louis's prestige rose to new heights. He was called *Louis Le Grand*, and at the Palace of Versailles (which was still being built) his Court treated him almost like a god. Indeed, his courtiers adopted the habit of standing in the presence of any lady who seemed likely to become his mistress!

Nevertheless, Louis felt that he might have had an even greater success if he had not been thwarted by England. He was disgusted with Charles II for his endless swindles and still angry with Charles's Lord Treasurer, the self-assured Lord Danby, for pro-moting the marriage between William and Mary. Danby was particularly irritating because he always seemed to pick up the winning pieces from both sides of the table. The French King could not resist the chance of punishing him, particularly when his eye fell on Lord Montagu whom he recognized instantly as the necessary tool. Montagu had been dismissed from his post as British Ambas-sador to France by Charles, ostensibly for plotting against Danby, but in fact for seducing the convent-bred daughter of the Duchess of Cleveland. Still smarting with indignation at the loss of his post, Montagu agreed (for a sizeable fee) to appear at the Bar of the House of Commons with receipts, signed by Danby, for the various subsidies paid by France. The House was properly shocked. So Charles's anti-French, patriot minister had not hesitated to accept

French gold! Parliamentary indignation knew no bounds and instigated impeachment proceedings against Lord Danby.

This episode, distressing enough to the King and his Lord
Treasurer, was soon eclipsed by amazing revelations of a Catholic
conspiracy. Mr Titus Oates, a former naval chaplain who had been
dismissed from the service for homosexuality, declared that he had
uncovered an international Jesuit conspiracy to kill Charles and put
his brother James on the throne. This, he said, was a preliminary to an
invasion by French and Irish armies which would bring the whole
country under the Church of Rome. His accusations centred on a
meeting of Jesuits in the Strand. In the middle of the hearing the
magistrate to whom Oates had made sworn depositions was found
murdered on Primrose Hill. It was not the work of footpads as his
pockets had not been rifled. No one ever solved the mystery, but
people jumped to the conclusion that Catholics had killed him to
prevent his testimony from being heard.

This real life thriller plunged the whole country into a fever of
alarm. While the Catholic King of France was pillaging the Continent, the Catholic Church was conspiring to undermine the very
foundations of English freedom. These shocking revelations inspired
an anti-Catholic witch-hunt, the like of which had never been seen in
England before. Jesuit priests were hanged on the flimsiest of pretexts
and dozens of Roman Catholics flung into prison on trumped-up
charges. 'No kind of thing is thought here,' wrote Robert, Earl of
Sutherland, 'but Mr Oates and who he has accused and who he will
accuse.'[10]

Although Oates's allegations were eventually proved to be a tissue
of lies, there was no way to quell the rising storm.* Even Charles's
Cavalier Parliament, which had been sitting for eighteen years, refused to toe the line and, despite the King's protests, sent his faithful
servant, Lord Danby, to the Tower for five years. On the chance of
getting a more amenable assembly, Charles dissolved his Parliament
in January 1679. But the elections took place in such a floodlight of
Protestant indignation that the result was not all what he had hoped.
Nicknames such as 'Tory' and 'Whig' were used for the first time to
denote the factions for and against the Court; and everyone knew
that the main business of the new Parliament would be an attempt to
exclude James – or any other Popish prince – from the throne.

---

* Under James, Titus Oates was convicted of perjury and sentenced to life imprisonment, but
under William he was pardoned and given a pension. He never retrieved his reputation and
when he died in 1705 a contemporary wrote that he was 'a consumate chete, vicious, blasphemous . . . and not fitt to be remembered'.

This was exactly what happened. Parliament assembled in an atmosphere of crisis. The air was so thick with preposterous rumours that some people reacted wildly, clutching at any straw, no matter how unlikely; they insisted that the King had really married Lucy Walter and that her Protestant son, the Duke of Monmouth, was the rightful heir. Charles stood firm, refusing to bend in either direction. He publicly proclaimed the bastardy of Monmouth and, at the same time, exerted his influence against the Exclusion Bill that was being considered by his Parliament. He made no impression on the excitable Commons. In this Chamber the Whigs (sometimes described as crypto-Roundheads) had a large and implacable majority and argued, almost to a man, that parliamentary independence, even the safety of the realm, depended on a Protestant succession. The Tories controlled the Lords. Many – but not all – talked about the Divine Right of Kings and could be relied upon to reject the Bill. But Charles was not willing to take any chances. The oratory of the brilliant Whig leader, Lord Shaftesbury, might prove irresistible, so it was best to play safe. Charles therefore dissolved Parliament in July 1679. When he called an election a few weeks later, he no longer entertained the hope that the new Parliament would be less obstreperous than its predecessor but he had worked out a way of dealing with it. He prorogued the new assembly the moment it met; and, by repeating this process six times, did not give it a chance to function for a full year.

During this time the focal point of the increasingly bitter controversy, James himself, was far away. In an effort to reduce the velocity of the gale the King had sent the Duke of York abroad in March 1679 and instructed him to stay away until he gave him permission to return. Although many people believed that the frenzied atmosphere, whipped up by propaganda tales of Catholic plots, could at any moment explode into a second civil war, James was not at all pleased by the sacrifice he was called upon to make. Reluctantly, almost resentfully, he arrived in Brussels, capital of the Spanish Netherlands, in the spring of 1679. Accompanied by the Duchess of York, he moved into the same house that Charles had occupied before the Restoration. John Churchill and George Legge* (whom the snobbish diarist, Reresby, refers to as 'a scarce gentleman') served in their usual capacities. Sarah, who was expecting her first baby, came for a short spell as Lady-in-Waiting to the Duchess, while her sister, the beautiful Lady Hamilton, now a widow, appeared to keep her company.

---

* Legge, later Lord Dartmouth, was Groom of the Bedchamber to the Duke of York. He had served on the same ship as Churchill in the naval battle of 1672 against the Dutch.

James's daughter, fourteen-year-old Princess Anne, arrived for a brief visit with her Protestant chaplain.

Like other Stuarts, James was determined to extract some enjoyment from his exile. He instructed Legge to have his coaches sent over from England and ordered his Master of Foxhounds to see that horses and hounds reached Brussels by the autumn. 'I now begin to have very good sport stag-hunting,' he wrote to a friend, 'and the country looks as if the fox-hunting would be very good.'[11] As things transpired, James had no chance to try his hand at this. Charles II was struck down by an acute fever (probably malaria) and James hurried back to Windsor to be at his side. Not only was he deeply devoted to his brother, but friends in England warned him that if he were out of the country when Charles died the Duke of Monmouth would certainly try for the throne himself. Wherever Monmouth went crowds hailed him as 'our beloved Protestant duke' and he had begun to encourage his followers to toast him as the Prince of Wales.

Accompanied only by Lord Peterborough and Colonel John Churchill, not to mention the all-important barber, Mr Doyley, and two unliveried footmen, James rode post-haste to Calais where he embarked for Dover. He was in heavy disguise with 'a blacke peruque only and a plaine stuffe suit without his starre and Garter.'[12] The English officials had the good manners to pretend they did not recognize him, although his face was unmistakeable, and James and Churchill rode to London on horseback, far outstripping the rest of the party. The next morning they were at Windsor. By this time Charles had recovered and, although the two brothers clung to each other with tears of affection, he had no alternative but to send James away again. The King finally agreed, however, that the Duke could set up his household in Edinburgh – almost as distant as Brussels – so that he need not feel so cut off from home affairs. Charles also accepted James's complaints about the Duke of Monmouth. Although the young man was his best-loved son, Charles deprived him of his rank of Captain-General and sent him out of England.

No sovereign ever worked more doggedly to protect his brother than Charles, but it was an uphill task as James was fast becoming the most hated man in the kingdom. If it had not been for his change of religion none of this trouble would have come about. Why should the whole nation be thrown into turmoil because of the conscience of one man? Even James's friends were beginning to resent his obstinate nature which had begun to assume an aura of martyrdom. Charles's French mistress, the Duchess of Portsmouth, was so angry with James because of the anxiety he was causing the King that she came out openly in favour of exclusion. Other friends were less violent but less practical. They asked if it would not be possible for James, in the interests of the country, to renounce his faith, at least publicly? Even the Pope might bless him for it, as the cardinals were said to be joking that James ought to be excommunicated for destroying the last vestige of Catholic influence in England. James's brother-in-law, Laurence Hyde, was asked to point out to the Duke that he was not only jeopardizing his own succession but also rocking his brother's throne. Hyde put the matter squarely to him, but the reply was uncompromising:

> I will never try that way mentioned in yours to Churchill . . . even though I were sure that it would restore me into the good opinion and the esteem of the nation which I once had . . . what I did was never done hastily and I have expected many years and been prepared for what has happened to me, and for the worst that can yet befall me.[13]

As members of James's household, John and Sarah Churchill had no choice but to accompany their embattled and detested Prince into an exile that stretched over the first four years of their married life. When Parliament was not sitting, James and his staff came to London; otherwise Holyrood House in Edinburgh served as their main residence. Colonel Churchill, however, spent much of his time travelling. As there were no wars to fight, the Duke used him as a diplomatic envoy and found him extremely useful. Indeed, Churchill proved invaluable in keeping James in touch with the outside world. He was so shrewd and tactful that gradually the Duke empowered him to handle the most delicate matters. He was sent to The Hague to maintain James's façade of friendship with William of Orange; to Windsor to implore Charles to allow him to return to London; to Versailles to apologize for James having married his daughter to William and to beg for subsidies – which he did not get. The journeys were long and wearisome. Ships were at the mercy of winds and roads at the mercy of rain. Travel by post-chaise was always uncomfortable and, although horseback was preferable, journeys between London and Edinburgh exhausted the strongest of men.

The Yorks set out for Scotland in October 1679 and the trip took thirty-eight days as they made many stops along the way. John accompanied them, but Sarah remained at Jermyn Street with her sister, Frances Hamilton. At the end of the month she gave birth to a baby daughter whom she named Harriot, but who, sadly, died in infancy. From the following letter, probably written in December, we can see that John must have been sent south on another mission, for once again he is pounding his way back to Scotland.

Stilton, Monday night

You will see by this that I am got safe to this place and tomorrow night I intend to lie at Doncaster. I am a great deal wearier in riding this day than I ever was when I have ridden twice as far; if I continue so tomorrow I shall hardly get to Scotland on Saturday, but sooner I promise you I shall not, for all that I pretend to, is to be at Berwick on Friday night. You will be sure to hear from me as soon as I get to my journey's end, and pray believe that I love nobody in the world but yourself, and I do . . . with all my heart wish we were together. . . . Pray kiss the child once for me.[14]

Churchill's fatigue gave way to illness and at the end of January 1680 he wrote:

About an hour after I had written to you last night, I was taken ill of my old fits, and last night I had another of them so that for this two days I have had very violent headachings as ever I had in my life; I have this day taken physic so that I think I am better but . . . which makes me melancholy, for I love you so well that I cannot think with patience of dying, for then we must part for ever, which is a dreadful thing to me that loves you above all expression. The doctor is come in and will let me write no more, for he says it is the worst thing I can do. So my All, farewell.[15]

Churchill not only suffered physically from the gruelling hours of travel but felt that being employed as a courier – even a diplomatic courier – was no way to advance his career. Furthermore James's Catholicism had created an inevitable barrier between them. As a Protestant Churchill could not share his master's most precious concerns, yet as his servant he was forced to share much of the odium attached to him. Quite naturally this caused him considerable anxiety. What sort of life would he be able to make for Sarah? An important military post was what he hankered after but, as England was at peace and the army was being reduced, there was no prospect of this. He therefore did his best throughout 1680 to inveigle James into finding him some new employment which would hold out good prospects for the future. James appeared to be sympathetic and for a while Churchill tried to get the lucrative assignment of Master of Ordnance which eventually was given to his friend, George Legge. Other positions were discussed, such as the command of the Admiralty Regiment, the governorship of Sheerness, or perhaps even one of the foreign embassy appointments to The Hague or Paris. The French Ambassador in London wrote to King Louis that Churchill was favoured for The Hague because the Prince of Orange liked him. Even more important, 'Mr Churchill . . . has the entire confidence of his master, as your Majesty could see when he had the honour of presenting himself to you last year.'[16]

Despite the talk, none of the hopes came to anything. The truth was that the Duke of York was loath to part with such a competent servant as John. 'So long as I am away from the king', he told Laurence Hyde, 'I would not willingly have Churchill from me.'[17] In the summer of 1680, when Parliament was prorogued, the King allowed the Yorks to return to London. They went, accompanied by the Churchills, and took up residence in St James's Palace. Even without the House of Commons in session there was plenty of trouble. For one thing the Duke of Monmouth disobeyed his father and reappeared in England. Churchill had warmed to Monmouth many years earlier when they had served in the French army and together had stormed the Maestricht fortress, but since those days the Duke's head had been turned by Protestant leaders who were using him as a cat's paw. In August the high-spirited and foolish young man made a tour of the West Country where the public greeted him with acclamation and troops of horsemen met him at all the towns. The King was so angry that he stripped him of 'his places of profit' but, as Monmouth was married to the Buccleugh heiress, the loss of money did not worry him. He tried repeatedly to see his father, but Charles refused. Monmouth met this rebuff by removing from his coat of arms the *baton sinister** which proclaimed his illegitimate birth.

Before Parliament met – the King's third in eighteen months – the Yorks were packed off to Edinburgh with the Churchills again at their side. The new House of Commons was more truculent than ever and lost no time in drawing up its customary Exclusion Bill; but on this occasion there was the possibility that the resolution might get a majority in the House of Lords. Fortunately for the King, Lord Halifax came to his aid. This was the same man who, years before, had invested Churchill's £5,000 in a life annuity. Halifax had always been a friend and Churchill in turn admired him more than any other statesman. Indeed, if Turenne taught Churchill the art of war, Halifax certainly gave him ideas about the art of politics. Halifax was nicknamed 'the Trimmer' by his contemporaries because he refused to follow a party line. He hated extremes and always came down on the side of moderation, no matter which party advocated it. The Exclusion Bill was a case in point. Although Halifax was regarded as a Whig, he pronounced himself in favour of legitimate succession. Indeed, he made such a trenchant speech that Lord Shaftesbury's Bill

---

* A baton broken off at both ends, resembling a short truncheon.

was quashed. Three months later Charles dissolved his hostile assembly and held new elections for his fourth Parliament.

Up till now each Parliament had proved more intransigent than the one before and the gathering at Oxford, in March 1681, was no exception. Oxford had been chosen to avoid the pressures of the demonstrative London mass, but as it was a Tory stronghold the Whig members, wearing blue satin ribbons in their hats, arrived accompanied by troops. Nevertheless their leader, Lord Shaftesbury, was more confident and more demanding than ever. The Exclusion Bill was still uppermost in his mind. Indeed, after the Royal Speech he handed Charles what amounted to an ultimatum in favour of the succession of the Protestant Duke of Monmouth. 'My Lord,' said the King, 'As I grow older, I grow more steadfast.' Was this also a reproof to Shaftesbury who grew more treacherous with age? As Ashley Cooper, Shaftesbury had been a member of the King's Cabal; he had approved England's alliance with Catholic France in 1670 and two years later signed the Declaration of Indulgence that gave protection to Catholics. But now he was so violently opposed to all Catholics that he talked of civil war in the last instance as preferable to James. However, Charles had an ace up his sleeve. Once again he was on friendly terms with Louis XIV and had hopes of receiving badly needed subsidies from France; and once again he could afford to dismiss his no longer dearly beloved Lords and Commons. He enormously enjoyed what he knew was coming and spent a delightful day at the race meeting at Burford before meeting the newly elected Members.

The Lords and Commons sat only a week, during which time, as a prologue to the great business of 'Exclusion', they fell into a wrangle over a minor issue. This gave the King his chance. Quite secretly he donned his robes and put on his crown, the regalia necessary for dismissing Parliament. Then he took his place in the Lords, established in the hall of Christ Church, and sent for the Commons. The Members arrived bubbling over with excitement in anticipation of the victory for which they had fought so long. Instead, the King dissolved Parliament in one short sentence, observing that 'we are not like to have a good end when the divisions at the beginning are such.' The Chamber broke into an uproar of protests and indignation; yet there was nothing Members could do but pack their bags and go home. As Oxford was swarming with soldiers and the atmosphere was so taut that a single spark might start a conflagration, Charles departed by a secret stairway and travelled to Windsor under heavy guard.

Meanwhile a disgruntled James was ruling in Scotland as the King's representative, with special instructions from Charles to end the rebellion of the Convenanters which had been simmering ever since the Restoration. John Churchill had loved and admired the Duke of York when he first joined his household sixteen years earlier. At that time James was a lean and handsome man, open to new ideas. Although he had neither the charm nor the quickness of Charles, he was a brave and competent sailor who had won considerable acclaim. The Duke of Buckingham gave Dr Gilbert Burnet 'a short but severe' character of the two brothers: 'The King could see things if he would, and the Duke would see things if he could.'[18]

Since he had become a Catholic, however, James's nature had changed. Far less agreeable, far more didactic, he seemed to look upon compromise as a form of weakness. He believed passionately in the Divine Right of Kings and the absolute authority of the Crown. Indeed, he felt that anyone expressing even the mildest deviation from these precepts was guilty of treason. He certainly was the wrong man to deal with the Scottish Covenanters. Instead of approaching the problem with understanding, he tried to break the spirit of the rebels by unrelenting cruelty. As he was not a brutal man by nature, his actions dismayed members of his entourage, particularly the Churchills.

No doubt James saw no other way of achieving his objective, as the poor, misguided people with whom he came into conflict were members of a fanatical sect. He regarded them as blasphemous schismatics who in their heart denied the right of Charles Stuart to rule in Scotland and they must either be exterminated or made to recant. To many of the women he offered a reprieve if they would but utter the words 'God Save the King', but they preferred to die. The men, however, were subjected to dreadful tortures in full sight of the Council; and although most members begged to be excused, James sat in his chair quite impervious to the screams of his victims as they writhed in agony. Apparently Churchill 'preserved from ruin and destruction several poor people whose scruples of conscience rendered them obnoxious to the law. . . . '[19]

James summoned a Scottish Parliament, the first for many years, and managed to induce the assembly to pass an Anti-Exclusion Bill which at least ensured him the Crown in Scotland. He also persuaded the assembly to pass an Act demanding allegiance to the King 'and his lawful successors'. The most powerful noble in Scotland, the Earl of Argyll, took the oath with the rider 'as far as it is consistent with the Protestant religion'. As a result, James brought Argyll to trial and used his influence to have him condemned to death, but the Earl escaped to London on the eve of his execution. All her life Sarah looked back on the Duke's iron rule with repugnance:

> I saw it myself and was much grieved at the Trials of several People hang'd for no Reason in the World but because they would not disown what they had said, that King Charles had broke his Covenant. I have cried at some of these Trials to see the Cruelty that was done to these Men only for their choosing to dye rather than tell a Lye. . . . [20]

We can be sure that Colonel Churchill, who was to prove himself one of the most humane commanders ever to control an army, shared Sarah's sentiments. James, however, always seemed oblivious to the impression he was creating and continued to be as intransigent as ever. Even King Charles, who was worried about the growth in anti-Catholic feeling, found himself talking to a deaf man. He asked James if he would return to London and make one small but important concession: simply to appear at an Anglican service. After all, James had been present during the prayers of the Scottish Parliament. He need not do anything, only allow himself to be seen. Small as the gesture would be, it might turn the tide in his favour. Lord Halifax, who had destroyed the Exclusion Bill in the Lords, declared that unless the Duke agree, 'His friends would be obliged to leave him like a garrison one can no longer defend.'

Once again Laurence Hyde was entrusted with the task of persuasion. But nothing availed. James was told by his confessor that God would not forgive him for flirting with heresy. Churchill agreed with Halifax that James was being intolerably stubborn; but he, as a young man with no money and no other employment, felt that he had no choice but to remain on the sinking ship. 'My Lord Hyde,' he wrote disconsolately to his friend George Legge, 'who is the best man living, will give you an account of all that has passed. You will find that nothing is done in what was so much desired *so that sooner or later we must all be undone*. . . . My heart is very full so that if I should write to you of the sad prospect I fear we have I should tire your patience. . . . '[21]

At the very moment that Churchill was writing his letter – September 1681 – the storm that had been sweeping England for the past three years began to blow itself out. Charles's unexpected dissolution of Parliament at Oxford, when Lord Shaftesbury and his Whig followers were absolutely confident that the King would have to accept the Exclusion Bill in exchange for money supplies, had pulled the rug from under the feet of the opposition. Although no one admitted defeat at the time, many feared that the battle might be lost. Their presentiments were justified. Stripped of the rallying-point that a Chamber offers, they had no means of maintaining the solidarity proclaimed by their jaunty blue bows with the slogan: 'No Popery! No slavery!' By the autumn the tempest had subsided. At long last a new day was dawning.

Charles had been saved once again by that master of bribery who knew what was good for France and was always ready to pay cash for it. France required James's succession, otherwise the Crown might pass to France's hated enemy, William of Orange. So Louis offered Charles £300,000 spread over three years, plus an extra £40,000 for not making a fuss when France annexed Luxembourg. This was not a great sum of money, but just enough to guarantee Charles his independence. His hereditary income from Customs and Excises (not to be confused with his parliamentary grant) had risen to £1 million a year because of the increase in peacetime trade, which meant that he would not have to recall Parliament, and Louis's £100,000 a year allowed him the all-important frills that made life amusing.

Charles was not eager for James to return to England for fear that his presence might arouse emotions that had so mercifully abated. But in the end he gave way and James, who had come to London with Churchill to attend to financial matters, arranged to travel to Scotland by boat to collect his household. The trip resulted in a tragedy and contributed still further to the disillusionment that Churchill had begun to feel about his master.

Accompanied by a large number of nobles and servants, James embarked at Margate on the frigate *Gloucester*. Among the Duke's luggage was a large iron box containing the memoirs that he was writing and which were published eventually many years after his death. Why he carried this cumbersome box all the way to Scotland and back again, no one has ever fathomed; it is only mentioned because it played a part in this episode. Two days after the *Gloucester* had begun her journey, she was grounded in the early morning light on a dangerous sandbank three miles off the Norfolk coast. After about an hour she slipped off the bank and foundered in deep water. Although the sea was calm and several yachts were in the proximity of the royal vessel, only forty people out of the 400 aboard were saved.

Later various and conflicting accounts were given about what happened, but the majority blamed James for the loss of life. As Heir Apparent and a former Lord High Admiral, no one could move without James's orders and he could not make up his mind what to do. If he had acted swiftly and allowed himself to be taken away in the one and only long-boat, the captain would have been free to signal the yachts to come alongside and remove the remaining passengers and crew. Yet he was so irresolute that the precious minutes slipped by until the final disaster became unavoidable.

John Churchill and George Legge were among those accompanying the Duke, and Legge's son wrote that his father pressed James repeatedly to get into the boat, but that the Duke

> refused to do it, telling him that if he were gone nobody would take care of the ship which he had hoped might be saved if she were not abandoned. But my father, finding she was ready to sink, told him if he stayed any longer they would be obliged to force him out; upon which the Duke ordered a strong box to be lifted into the boat, which besides being extremely weighty took a great deal of time as well as room. My father asked him with some warmth if there was anything in it worth a man's life [and] the Duke answered . . . things of great consequence both to the King and himself.[22]

When Sarah Churchill wrote her memoirs many years later she echoed the same note. The Duke of Marlborough, she said, told her that all those who were drowned

> were lost by the Duke [of York's] obstinacy in not coming away sooner. And that was occasioned by a false courage . . . by which he was the [cause] of losing so many Lives. But when his own was in danger, and there was no hope of saving any but those that were with Him, he gave the Duke of Marlborough his Sword to hinder Numbers of People that to save their own Lives would have jumped into the Boats, notwithstanding his Royal Highness was there, that would have sunk it. This was done, and the Duke went off safe; and all the rest in the Ship were lost. . . . [23]

The calm that now settled on England was the calm of exhaustion – like a man, worn out by furious activity, who falls into a deep sleep. Although the Duke had failed to find his competent Gentleman of the Bedchamber a lucrative new position, Churchill had other rewards. In July 1681 Sarah had a second daughter whom she named Henrietta; and at the end of the year Churchill received a Scottish peerage and became Baron Churchill of Aymouth. He was also given the command of a troop of Life Guards, followed soon after by a second colonelcy in the King's Own Dragoons. The Dragoons were a new regiment in the British army. They were a corps of men, mounted, but equipped to fight on foot with musket and bayonet. The fact that Churchill, an infantry officer, had been made a colonel of what people persisted in calling a cavalry regiment, inspired innumerable lampoons:

> Let's cut our meat with spoons
> The sense is as good
> As that Churchill should
> Be put in command of the Dragoons.

1683 proved to be a watershed for Lord and Lady Churchill. After living from pillar to post for five years, they at last had a large enough income to run a house of their own. Sarah opted for the St Albans property that Mrs Jennings had made over to her three daughters. Since then Barbara Griffiths had died and the widowed Frances Hamilton had married again – this time the dashing Dick Talbot, an Irish–Catholic cavalier who had long been in love with her. As Frances had been carried off to live in Ireland, Sarah was able to buy her share of the estate. The young Churchills pulled down the family house and built a new one on a different site, a few hundred yards away, making use of a charming old fish-pond and marking off the space for a garden. They renamed it Holywell House.

Life suddenly became wonderfully relaxed; Churchill and Godolphin played tennis regularly with the King and Lord Feversham, all good players 'so that if one beats the other tis' alternatively'.[24] At other times they accompanied the King and the Duke of York to Newmarket for a day's racing. The highlight of the year, however, was the sudden growth of Sarah's friendship with Princess Anne. Sarah had known the Duke of York's two daughters since their mother's death in 1671, when they were nine and six years old. Charles II had sent them to live at Richmond Palace, away from James's Catholic influence, where they were put in the care of Lady Frances Villiers who brought them up with her six daughters as playmates. They were thoroughly grounded in religion, but in other respects their education was neglected. 'They studied or let it alone,' wrote an early anonymous biographer, 'just as it suited their inclination. It suited those of Lady Anne to let it alone, for she grew up in a state of utter ignorance.'

The Duke of York was very fond of his daughters and frequently visited them at Richmond Palace, while they in turn made an annual trip to Whitehall to take part in Court theatricals and other entertainments. It was here that Sarah, two years before she became a Maid of Honour, first met Anne. 'We used to play together when she was a child,' wrote Sarah in her memoirs,

> and even then she expressed a particular fondness for me. The inclination increased with our years. I was often at Court and the princess always distinguished me by the pleasure she took to honour me, preferably to others with her conversation and confidence.[25]

Sarah always wrote tersely, frequently telescoping the years into a single sentence which sometimes gave a misleading impression. In her adolescent years Anne saw little of Sarah. Instead her life revolved around Frances Apsley, the pretty daughter of Sir Allen Apsley, Comptroller of the Duke of York's Household. Anne wrote Frances romantic letters calling her 'faire Semandra' and posing as her husband Ziphares. When Anne was fourteen, she joined her father at Brussels, but almost as soon as she arrived James was summoned back to England because of the King's sudden illness. He was accompanied by Colonel Churchill and, as nineteen-year-old Sarah Churchill was expecting her first baby, she and her sister probably left for London at the same time.

Nevertheless, the trip was important to Anne's future development as it hardened her prejudices against Catholicism. She wrote to 'faire Semandra' that although she was not allowed to visit Catholic churches 'the more I hear of that Religion the more I dislike it.'[26] Some time later Anne made a long visit to her father in Scotland, but neither she nor Sarah make any mention of it. As Sarah's second child, Henrietta, was born in July 1681, Sarah may have been in London for most of the time.

When Anne was fifteen, Prince George of Hanover, the son of the Electress Sophia (and later George 1 of England), came to London, ostensibly as part of a Grand Tour but probably to take a look at Anne. Anne was not pretty but she had a round, open face, thick chestnut-brown hair and a good figure. Her best feature was her low, musical voice. As a child she had suffered from an eye disease which had slightly contracted her lids and gave a certain dullness to her countenance. She was too shy to talk and her silent presence often cast gloom on her surroundings. For over a year it had been widely rumoured that a marriage would take place between the twenty-year-old Protestant Prince of Hanover and James's daughter. According to the Modenese envoy, who had private access to the Duchess of York's household, Anne became infatuated with George at their very first meeting. Although the Prince remained in England for four months and the couple met regularly, he departed without committing himself. No one knows why, but apparently Anne felt that she had been rejected and for ever after nourished a strong prejudice against her eventual successor.

A year later Anne had a much less eligible suitor in the Earl of Mulgrave, a man eighteen years older than herself and a favourite of King Charles. The couple managed to take occasional rides in Windsor Park, and Mulgrave sent her poems and love letters. When

King Charles discovered the correspondence he banished Mulgrave to Tangiers – 'on a leaky frigate', the gossips said.* Mulgrave insisted that he had done nothing but 'ogle', but contemporary gossip believed that his letters 'intimated too near an address to her'.[27]

This is the point at which Sarah Churchill steps into the picture. In an unpublished memoir she mentions the Mulgrave affair and refers to herself as 'not having been in any degree of favour [with Anne] until after that.'[28] It is not surprising that the Princess came under the spell of the radiant, twenty-two-year-old Lady Churchill who 'was very young and very beautiful [but] had a capacity and Spirit great enough not to stand in need of those advantages as well as not to depend on them.'[29] This description of a young woman whose personality was as striking as her looks was written many years later by Sarah herself. It was fulsome self-praise but undoubtedly true as we know that Anne was thrilled to have this glorious creature near her.

Meanwhile Charles II was trying to find the Princess a husband. He was unwilling to run the risk of further flirtations and had made up his mind that she must be married with no more delay. Lord Churchill may have suggested the King of Denmark's brother, George, as a candidate, for his own brother, Charles Churchill, had been a page to King Christian ten years earlier and had accompanied George on a previous trip to England. The Danish Prince was a popular choice. He was a Lutheran Protestant and came from a small state, which meant that even Louis XIV had no cause for complaint. And, as he was tall and handsome and quite happy to fall in with any plan his brother the King made, Anne was content. The Prince adored eating and drinking but was not noted for his intelligence, and Charles II's famous remark is usually quoted to sum up his capacities: 'I have tried him drunk, and I have tried him sober and there is nothing in him.'

Nevertheless, as he met all the dynastic requirements, the marriage was arranged and took place in July 1683. The King gave Anne £20,000 a year which, added to the Prince's annual income of £10,000 from some small Danish islands, was thought to be enough. As a wedding present Charles also bestowed on the couple a four-storey residence newly built on the site of the old Cockpit lodgings where Lady Castlemaine had once lived, and from which the King had often been seen walking in the early hours of the morning. The new house was also known as the Cockpit and stood on ground which now forms the garden of No. 10, Downing Street.

---

* Surprisingly enough Mulgrave eventually married Princess Anne's half-sister, Catherine, the bastard daughter of James and Catherine Sedley.

Before her marriage took place, Anne persuaded her father to make Sarah one of her Ladies of the Bedchamber. 'The Duke', the Princess wrote happily to Lady Churchill,

> came just as you were gon and made no difficultys but has promised me that I shall have you which I assure you is a great joy to me. I should say a great deal for your kindness in offering it but I am not good at compliments. I will only say that I do take it extreemely kindly and shall be ready at any time to do you all ye service that lyes in my power.[30]

Once Sarah became a Lady of the Bedchamber, her time was no longer her own and she was often parted from John. Sometimes she was in waiting at the Cockpit, sometimes journeying with the Princess to Bath or Tunbridge Wells to take the waters. Early on, Sarah conveyed to Anne her intention always to tell her the truth and the whole truth. 'Young as I was,' she writes,

> when I first became this high favourite I laid it down for a maxim that flattery was falsehood to my trust and ingratitude to my dearest friend, and that I did not deserve so much favour if I could not venture the loss of it by speaking the truth and by preferring the real interest of my mistress before the pleasing her fancy. . . . [31]

Anne was clearly impressed by this declaration for when she accompanied her father to Portsmouth and Winchester she found time to write to Sarah:

> Let me beg of you not to call me 'your highness' at every word but be as free with me as one friend ought to be with another. And you can never give me any greater proof of your friendship than by telling me your mind freely in all things which I beg you to do; and if it were in my power to serve you nobody would be more ready than myself. I am all impatience for Wednesday – till then, farewell.[32]

'A friend', Sarah tells us, 'was what she most coveted and for the sake of friendship which she did not disdain to have with me, she was even fond of that equality which she thought belonged to it. . . . '[33] By the autumn of 1683 the two young women had another bond – both were pregnant. Sarah refused to curtail her duties and John, who was travelling with the Duke, wrote anxiously to St Albans:

> I hope to God you are out of all danger of miscarrying for I swear to you I love you better than all the rest of the world put together, wherefore you ought to be so just as to make me a kind return, which will make me much happier than ought else in the world can do.[34]

Sarah gave birth to a daughter in February 1684 whom she named Anne after her royal mistress. (The Princess also had a daughter, but the baby died a few weeks later.) Sarah was paid £200 a year as a Lady-in-Waiting and was proud of earning her own money, a rare experience for seventeenth-century females. She also liked the prestige attached to her service with the Princess and as soon as her confinement was over hurried back to the Cockpit. It is doubtful if any of the other ladies gave her much of a welcome as the Princess made it almost embarrassingly clear that Lady Churchill was her favourite. Anne particularly disliked her aunt, Lady Clarendon, who was first Lady of the Bedchamber and Groom of the Stole. According to Sarah, Lady Clarendon was a woman whose 'discourse and manner . . . could not possibly recommend her to so young a mistress, for she looked like a madwoman and talked like a scholar.' 'Indeed,' Sarah goes on to say,

> her Highness's Court was so oddly composed, that I think it would be making myself no great compliment if I should say her choosing to spend more of her time with me than with her other servants did no discredit to her taste.[35]

Sarah accompanied Anne to Tunbridge Wells for the whole of July and August 1684; and John often found himself alone at St Albans with four-year-old Henrietta and the baby Anne. 'You cannot imagine', he wrote to Sarah,

> how I am pleased with the children; for having nobody but their maid, they are so fond of me, that when I am home, they will be always with me, kissing me and hugging me. Their heats are quite gone; so that against you come home they will be in beauty. If there be room I will come on Monday, so that you need not write on Sunday. Miss is pulling me by the arm, that she may write to her dear Mama; so that I shall say no more, only beg that you will love me always as well as I love you, then we will be happy.

Then, to please the child, he added the postscript: 'I kiss your hands, my dear mamma. Harriet.'[36]

Lord Churchill was no longer chasing around London to keep pace with the Duke of York, but instead riding across England to snatch a glimpse of his wife. He wrote to Sarah that he was in London with the Duke who was going to Tunbridge Wells for one night. He would be 'forced to go back with him,' he explained, 'so that I hope you will take it kindly my coming a hundred miles for the happiness of one night.'[37]

King Charles was as popular in 1685 as he had been in the first year of his reign. Indeed, by the end of 1682 he had felt strong enough to open proceedings against Shaftesbury in the courts. The Duke of Monmouth cut his father to the quick by offering to stand bail for the accused, but nothing came of the gesture for Shaftesbury fled abroad and died in exile a short time later. Since that time the Rye House Plot, an alleged conspiracy to murder the King and his brother on their way from Newmarket, had swung public opinion back to the monarchy, and once again Charles was the darling of the crowds. Almost all the people unfortunate enough to have been in the tavern while the plotting was taking place, even though they had taken no part in the talk, were sent to the scaffold by perjured evidence and biased judges. Even the silver tongue of Lord Halifax could not save such fervent Whigs as Lord Russell and Algernon Sidney from the block, while Lord Essex, formerly one of the King's Lords of the Treasury, committed suicide in the Tower.

Charles was determined never to call another Parliament. His revenues from the Customs and Excises went on rising and Louis XIV was paying him subsidies – this time to turn a blind eye to his acquisitions along the Rhineland on the excuse of 'straightening his frontiers'. Louis had stumbled happily upon the idea of making acquisitions ('reunions'* he called them) on the spurious authority of *ad hoc* courts controlled by French directives, while the French army remained discreetly in the background! The novelty of the whole affair was that it was 'a cold war' carried out with the pretence of legality. Yet there was no limit to his high-handedness. He occupied the principality of Orange on the River Rhone which belonged to the Prince of Orange, and when William sent his agent, Heinsius, to Paris to protest, the French War Minister threatened to throw him into the Bastille. The fortifications of the city of Orange were dismantled and the fief transferred to the Duchess of Nemours.

Not all Louis's aggressions, however, were as bloodless as this. In 1683–4 he conducted a *blitzkrieg* in which he blockaded Luxembourg, bombarded the fortifications along the frontier of the Spanish Netherlands and took savage reprisals against Genoa. He was so powerful that the King of Spain and the Emperor Leopold eventually had no choice but to sign the twenty-year Truce of Ratisbon, leaving him temporarily with all his acquisitions, including Strasbourg and Luxembourg. Unfortunately for Europe, Louis had an insatiable appetite.

The English King, on the other hand, was at peace with the world and ready to enjoy what he had. He was making economies to spare

* From the doctrine of the reunion of ancient seigneurial domains.

him the necessity of convening Parliament ('they are devils who want my ruin'), but no one noticed the austerity. It was sad that Queen Catherine had never been able to give him a child, but he liked the company of his bastard children, who numbered a round dozen, and did what he could to ease their way through life. He followed the French example of marrying his daughters into the most illustrious families in the land and settled handsome benefits on his sons. His best-loved eldest boy, the Duke of Monmouth and Buccleuch, was still so intoxicated by the vision of the throne that he continued to behave disgracefully. The King finally had no alternative but to ban him once again from the kingdom, yet at the same time his fatherly love persuaded him to give the Duke £6,000 a year. This came as a godsend to Monmouth as he had left his rich wife and was living in Holland with Lady Wentworth. The King's other sons, also dukes, were well-behaved and represented an impressive addition to the aristocracy: Southampton, Northumberland, Grafton, St Albans, Richmond and Lennox. The Duke of Buckingham once remarked merrily that the King was supposed to be the father of his people and he certainly was the father of a great many of his people.

The Duke of York was now the King's closest adviser and in 1684 Sir John Reresby recorded that 'the Duke did now chiefly manage affairs, but with great haughtiness'. He was given the office of Lord Admiral (not the same as Lord High Admiral), but a year later this role was swept away by his accession to the throne.

In February 1685 fifty-four-year-old Charles II was struck down by a form of apoplexy that no one has ever been able to define satisfactorily. He lived for four days, during which the bewildered doctors applied agonizing and useless remedies. When no hope was left, James whispered in his ear asking if he would like to see a Catholic priest. 'Yes, with all my heart,' the King murmured. But how could a Catholic priest be brought into a room crowded with Protestant bishops and high dignitaries of state? And where could a priest be found quickly?

The Queen was not present because she was in such a distraught state that she was in her bedroom being bled; and quite by chance her confessor, Father Huddleston, happened to call on her. He was pounced upon, hustled into a disguise of wig and cassock and led to a closet which had a communicating-door to the King's chamber. James then announced to the assembly: 'Gentlemen, the King wishes everyone to retire except for the Earls of Bath and Feversham.' Lord Bath had known the King from boyhood and was his Groom of the Stole, while Lord Feversham (the Frenchman who had become a naturalized

Englishman) had served at Court for many years. As both Earls were Protestant, no one could protest. The priest gave His Majesty extreme unction, then sat by the bed reading in a low voice the Catholic prayers for the dying. The King survived the night but died at high noon.

Four

The Conspiracy

The succession passed peacefully to James, an occurrence which four years earlier people had said could never happen. '. . . It is impossible', Sir William Jones had told the House of Commons in the tumultuous days of 1681, 'that a Papist should come to the possession and quiet enjoyment of the Crown without wading through a sea of blood.'[1] But nations, like people, are emotional and fickle; grief at the death of Charles and the reassuring declarations of the new King combined to produce an unexpected mood of euphoria. Within fifteen minutes of Charles's death, James II met the Privy Council, whose duty it was to recognize a new sovereign, and declared his resolution to maintain in State and Church the system of government established by law. 'I know too', he added, 'that the laws of England are sufficient to make the King as great a monarch as I can wish and as I shall never depart from the just rights and prerogatives of the Crown, so I shall never invade any man's property.'[2]

The nation received the Royal Proclamation with relief and celebrated the accession with bonfires and loyal toasts at which Oxford University distinguished itself 'with the conduit at Carfax running claret'. Although James shocked some people by celebrating mass in public, he explained that 'dissimulation in religion was opposed to his way of life'. He then went on to demonstrate his impartiality by retaining in office Lord Sunderland and Lord Godolphin, both of whom had been Exclusionists, and by refusing to give important posts to many of his Catholic followers. Most impressive of all, during the first fortnight of his reign he issued writs for a general election.

However, if people had been able to read James's thoughts, they would not have been so happy. Everything he did was calculated to impress the new Parliament scheduled to meet in May, for he was determined to induce this august body to grant him the same Customs and Excise duties that had been given to Charles but which had lapsed with his death. These revenues had expanded with England's growing trade and now yielded twice as much as they had twenty years earlier. Indeed, they would be sufficient to make James virtually free of Parliament if – and this was the key – he could persuade the Commons to grant the revenues for life, as they had done with Charles. Although the Lords Lieutenants had instructions to make sure that all parliamentary candidates were loyal supporters of the Crown, M. Barrillon, the French Ambassador, suggested taking no chances and bribing the newly elected members. James had a different idea: if Parliament refused him, he would dissolve the assembly and take the money by force.

Before the confrontation took place, James decided to dispatch Lord Churchill to Versailles to make a formal announcement of James's accession. Overnight the Churchills had become people of importance. John Churchill not only was one of the nine Lords of the Bedchamber but he had the distinction of being the King of England's confidential envoy, while Sarah Churchill was the favourite of a Princess who now stood next but one to the throne. The new Queen, Mary Beatrice, had not given birth to a son since the death of the infant Duke of Cambridge in 1677; and the marriage of James's eldest daughter, the Princess of Orange, now in its ninth year, had proved barren. Anne of Denmark, therefore, was Heiress Presumptive after Mary of Orange.

When Lord Churchill reached Versailles he was lodged in the magnificent palace and accorded the honours due to an Envoy Extraordinary of His Majesty of Great Britain. He was attended by the most important English gentlemen residing in Paris, wearing deep mourning for the late King. He was officially received by the Dauphin and the Dukes of Burgundy, Anjou and Orléans. Of course he had an audience with the great French monarch who had first encountered the young officer eleven years earlier when, as a captain, he had fought with the French army. This was the last occasion on which these two historic personalities, and mortal enemies of the future, would meet face to face; and writers of succeeding generations often dwell lovingly on the hidden drama of the occasion. Apparently Louis took no particular notice of Churchill, receiving him in a perfunctory way; but a century later Charles James Fox delighted in describing how, in the years that lay ahead, Lord Churchill would journey abroad 'not to implore Louis for succour in enslaving England or to thank him for pensions to her monarchs but to combine all Europe against him in the cause of liberty.'[3]

Before taking his leave, Churchill talked to the Marquis of Ruvigny, a French Huguenot who was soon to seek refuge in England, about James's excessive Catholic zeal. 'If the King', he said, 'should attempt to change our religion, I will instantly quit his service.'[4] This remark is sometimes cited by historians as 'one of Churchill's rare indiscretions'. But Churchill did not make slips of this kind. What he said was what he wanted people to know.

Despite Churchill's apprehensions the Coronation which took place in April, a month before Parliament met, was celebrated in an atmosphere of enthusiasm. As a Lord of the Bedchamber, John took part in the procession, during which an unfortunate incident occurred. The Barons of the Cinque Ports, who walked on either side of the King carrying a canopy, let it fall on his head. And this was not all. The crown was so large that it slipped sideways and nearly dropped to the ground. Henry Sidney, an Englishman who lived in The Hague and had won the regard of the Prince of Orange, was standing next to His Majesty and put out a hand to steady it, remarking that it was not the first time a Sidney had supported the Crown. There were further mishaps, for after the ceremony the London *Gazette* advertised:

> Lost, at their Majesties' coronation, the button of His Majesty's Sceptre set about with twenty-four small diamonds, three rubies and three emeralds; [and] a pendant pearl from His Majesty's Crown. . . .

In the Coronation honours John received an English peerage which gave him the right to sit in the House of Lords. He chose the title Baron Churchill of Sandridge but did not hurry to take the seat.

James wasted no time in summoning his first Parliament, which met in June. When he asked Lord Halifax to comment on the draft of his speech, the statesman told the King in a shocked voice that the tone was far too domineering. He should caress the Lords and Commons, not bully them. But James refused to listen and delivered his address as he had written it. The gist of his message was: 'Give me the life revenues which are my due or beware of my displeasure!' To everyone's astonishment his tactless speech achieved the desired result. Parliament not only voted life revenues far larger than anything Charles II had been given but granted a supplement to pay for army and navy stores and to discharge the debts of the late King. Such royalists as Sir Winston Churchill, who once again sat in the House of Commons as Member for Lyme after an absence of six years, purred with pleasure at these satisfactory results.

James himself was both surprised and gratified. He could not know that at that very moment rebel subjects across the seas were planning a descent on his kingdom to snatch away his crown. Within a month, news arrived that the Earl of Argyll, who had been living in exile, had landed in the Western Isles with a small army. Next came an even more sensational report. A messenger galloped through the night and arrived at Sir Winston Churchill's house in London with an urgent communication from the Mayor of Lyme. The Duke of Monmouth, he said, had landed in Lyme and Winston's constituency was in revolt. Winston hurried to his son, John, and John led both father and messenger to the King. His descendant, Winston Churchill of this century, describes the scene as 'Sir Winston's apotheosis':

> The old cause was once more at stake in the old place; and here stood his son, Colonel of the Dragoons, the rising soldier of the day, high in the favour of the threatened monarch, long linked to his service – he it was who would march forward at the head of the Household troops, the *corps d'élite*, to lay the insolent usurper low.[5]

It was sad to think that the 'insolent usurper' had once been John Churchill's friend and fellow officer. The flamboyant, thirty-five-year-old bastard son of Charles II, who had delighted the young ladies at Charles's Court by his dancing and card-playing, had been living in exile in Holland since 1682 with his beautiful mistress, Lady Henrietta Wentworth. The Prince of Orange showed this agreeable, pleasure-loving man every hospitality and by his patronage encouraged Monmouth's dream of usurping the English Crown to further his own ends. The Prince, of course, himself had a claim to the throne through his mother (Charles II's sister) and his wife, Mary (James's daughter), but he kept his ambitions to himself and made it public policy to appear on terms of friendship with Monmouth. 'The Prince of Orange', wrote the French Ambassador, M. D'Avaux, 'knew how to caress Monmouth sufficiently; balls and parties were incessantly given for him. ... He likewise obliged the Princess and her Court to countenance Monmouth's mistress or secondary wife, Lady Harriet Wentworth.'*[6]

However, all this took place when Charles II was on the throne. When he died and James's succession did not create the expected strife, William's attitude changed and he asked Monmouth to leave Holland, explaining that he could not allow a rift to develop between himself and his father-in-law. This was an age of perfidy, but where

---

* Henrietta and Harriet (or Harriot) were interchangeable names – a fact that causes considerable confusion.

was it practised more skilfully: in London, Paris or The Hague? At a moment still in the future, the Prince of Orange would not hesitate to take up arms against his father-in-law, yet he now sent James a spate of sycophantic letters swearing that

> nothing can happen which will make me change the fixed attachment I have for your interests. I should be the most unhappy man in the world if you were not persuaded of it, and should not have the goodness to continue me a little in your good graces. . . .

At this period in history it was fashionable to carry deception to extremes. Thus the Prince of Orange ended his letter:

> I shall be to the last breath of my life, yours, with zeal and fidelity.[7]

The banished Duke lived in Brussels, but he frequently made secret visits to Rotterdam to meet the Duke of Argyll who fired him with the idea of landing in the west of England at the same time that he himself made his attempt in Scotland. Monmouth was carried away by a vision of enthusiastic crowds deposing his uncle and placing the Crown on his own Protestant head, and began making plans for an immediate invasion. Undoubtedly the Prince of Orange got wind of the affair – particularly as the ships were being fitted out in Dutch ports – but he turned a blind eye to the feverish preparations. Whatever the outcome, he would not lose – if Monmouth succeeded, the French threat against Holland would be diminished; if Monmouth failed, William would be rid of a troublesome claimant to the British throne.

Monmouth sailed from Amsterdam three weeks after Argyll had set out for Scotland. His squadron consisted of three small ships: a thirty-two-gun frigate which he hired for £5,500; a second vessel half the size of the first, and a one-masted boat, known as a 'dogger', no bigger than a fishing-craft. He had raised £6,000 in Holland for the purchase of arms but he needed £3,000 more. This Henrietta Wentworth provided by pawning her mother's jewels. With their £9,000 the Duke bought four field-guns, 1,500 cuirasses, 1,500 swords, pikes and muskets, a small number of carbines and pistols, and 200 barrels of powder. The men who accompanied him on the voyage, almost all British exiles, numbered about eighty and included Robert Ferguson, the fiery Scottish preacher, and Lord Grey of Werke, who later proved to be a coward. With this token force Monmouth hoped to attract thousands more to his banner. He landed at Lyme with no opposition.

Because of unfortunate winds and weather the journey from Amsterdam lasted twelve days. After taking possession of the town, the Duke issued a proclamation denouncing James as 'a usurper, a murderer, a traitor and a tyrant'. Loyalists sent the news to London post-haste and Parliament, which was still sitting, voted £400,000 to put down the rebellion and £5,000 for Monmouth's body, dead or alive.

John Churchill was delighted when James put him in charge of the royal forces. He had never had an independent command before and was grateful to be given a chance to show his prowess over the heads of older and more experienced men. He was promoted to the rank of Brigadier-General. As very few regiments of the regular army were available (six regiments were in Holland and one in Ireland) the Lords Lieutenants were ordered to call out the militia. Churchill left London for Chard, a town only a few miles from Ashe House, where he had grown up as a boy, and which he had selected for his headquarters. He had with him 300 mounted men drawn from the Dragoons and a few cavalry regiments.

Monmouth was encouraged to find that the militia, composed of agricultural labourers and weavers, mechanics and tradesmen, were overwhelmingly on the side of 'the Protestant Duke'. These simple rustics began to desert from the Lords Lieutenants' regiments in large numbers and Monmouth accepted as many as he could provide with arms. Others joined him brandishing scythes attached to long poles, and still others went to the village smiths who re-fashioned pitchforks into pikes.

Monmouth sent Lord Grey to attack Bridport, eight miles from Lyme, but unfortunately Grey was so neurotic that, when he stumbled upon an unarmed and unsuspecting group of militiamen, he panicked and bolted at the head of his mounted men. The incredulous militia could scarcely believe their eyes as Grey was running away from victory; and the victory would have given him the arms and supplies that his leader so badly needed.

Despite this fiasco Monmouth's forces had swollen to over 3,000 men. With these recruits he moved towards Axminster, each soldier wearing in his hat a green bough which had been adopted as the Protestant emblem. Not far from the town he came upon a junction where the militia from Somerset and Devon had joined forces under the command of Brigadier-General John Churchill. What happened next was a new experience for Churchill. His country yokels deserted to the enemy *en bloc*. When, he reported to the King, the militiamen learned that the Protestant Duke was in the neighbourhood, they 'threw down their arms and fled, leaving their officers and Colours behind; half, if not the greater part, are gone to the rebels.' Churchill went on to stress that 'unless speedy course be taken, we are likely to lose this country to the rebels; for we have those two regiments run away a second time . . . there is not any relying on these regiments that are left unless we had some of your Majesty's standing forces to lead them on and encourage them. . . .'[8]

Everything now depended on Monmouth's ability as a commander. His only chance of success was to launch a vigorous attack against the militia before the regular troops arrived from London. 'Had he boldly attacked them and pushed forward to Exeter,' wrote Field-Marshal Wolseley,

> there can be little doubt that a considerable number of them would have joined him – a proceeding which would have supplied him with money, arms and ammunition, all of which he sorely needed. He might then have marched rapidly upon Bristol with at least 10,000 fairly armed adherents, and the possession of that important seaport, with its supplies of arms, provisions and money, which would have given him a real chance of success. He failed to understand that loss of time was absolutely fatal to his cause, for every day brought the regular forces nearer to him.[9]

Instead, Monmouth marched in a leisurely fashion to Taunton, where young girls strewed flowers in his path and he was met with a tumultuous welcome. Then he made for Bridgwater, a centre of Protestant support, and finally set out for Bristol. When he reached the outskirts of the city he waited several days trying to decide whether or not to attack, during which time a small detachment of royal troops took possession of the great seaport with its wealth of supplies and its thousands of likely recruits. Monmouth's supporters still urged him to attack, assuring him that the inhabitants would open the gates and flock to his banner; but he had lost heart and gave the order to retreat.

Lord Churchill, who was waiting for reinforcements, used his cavalry to dog the footsteps of the rebels, so that he not only was familiar with their movements but aware of their problems. He was working out a plan of campaign when a piece of very unwelcome news overtook him. A letter from Lord Sunderland informed him that the King had given the French-born Lord Feversham the rank of Major-General and appointed him Commander-in-Chief over Churchill's head.

Churchill was not only angry at the change, but deeply chagrined as Feversham had never been given a military command of any importance and he did not regard him as a soldier of distinction. He knew, of course, that he was James's friend and protégé, and a nephew of the great Marshal Turenne. Feversham had been living in England for the past twenty years and, through James's influence, had been made Chamberlain to the Dowager Queen Catherine who loved her daily game of basset with him. Although Feversham belonged to a French Huguenot family, his two brothers had become Catholics to please Louis xiv and Feversham undoubtedly would have done the same for James if the latter had pressed him. However, James probably found it useful to have a neo-Catholic masquerading as a Protestant.

The King's unexpected alteration in the command may have sprung from a sudden, warm impulse to please an old friend, but Churchill felt it implied a lack of trust. Had James been mulling over the fact that Churchill was a West Countryman, and that the West Country was the heartbeat of Protestant England? Or did he recall Monmouth's admiration for Churchill when they had served together in France? Since that time Churchill had always taken a firm stand against Monmouth's aspirations. Indeed, during the last few days, Monmouth had written to John styling himself 'King of England' and claiming the latter's loyalty; Churchill told the trumpeter who brought the message that he knew no other king than James and had forwarded Monmouth's letter to Whitehall.

When Churchill wrote to Lord Clarendon, James's former brother-in-law and now one of his ministers, he did not try to hide his irritation:

> When you are at leisure ten lines from you will be a great pleasure to me who have not many things to please me here, for I see plainly that the trouble is mine and that the honor will be another's. . . .[10]

Churchill then put aside his disappointment and carried out his duties with patience and skill. The weather was appalling and at the end of twelve days of marches and counter-marches over waterlogged meadows and along hedge-lined lanes churned to mud, the two armies finally found themselves within three miles of each other in the neighbourhood of Bridgwater.

By this time Monmouth was in deep despair. Although thousands of peasants had flocked to his banner, none of the gentry had joined him. He was astonished by the change of mood in the three years since he had left England. Without powerful nobles at his side he would have neither the money nor the arms to continue his fight. Even now his rank-and-file were so hard-pressed for ammunition that when they passed through Wells they stole the lead from the cathedral roof to cast into bullets. Even more depressing was the news that the Earl of Argyll had been captured and executed. The Scottish chiefs who had answered his call had quarrelled among themselves and the rising had fizzled out before it got under way.

Although Monmouth's soldiers numbered over 5,000 (nearly twice as many as the royal force), he was not eager to provoke a confrontation as he did not believe that his undisciplined, untrained yokels would be any match for professional soldiers. Consequently he delayed too long in attacking Bristol, arriving twenty-four hours after Feversham had entered the city. He returned to Bridgwater more morose than ever and finally made up his mind to retreat to Cheshire. From here he secretly planned to make for a port where he could embark for the Continent. But as he was preparing his forces for the march, a farm labourer named Godfrey approached him with intelligence from his Protestant master. He not only gave Monmouth the exact position of the royal army, but told him that no watches had been posted as no one dreamed of the possibility of an attack, and that everyone in the camp had gone to bed roaring drunk. It was now early morning and Godfrey led Monmouth up the high tower of Bridgwater Church where he could see for himself, with the aid of a telescope, the enemy spread out loosely, even carelessly, before him.

The royal troops, all regular army units (one of which was commanded by Lord Churchill's thirty-year-old brother, Lieutenant-Colonel Charles Churchill), were encamped on Sedgemoor, a low-lying peat moor hemmed in between river and hills. The terrain was criss-crossed with wide ditches dug in ancient times as drainage systems to prevent the handful of villages, built on slight rises, from flooding. Feversham had billeted his cavalry and dragoons in the village of Weston Zoyland and placed his infantry a quarter of a mile away where they were protected by a wide ditch known as the Bussex Rhine. This had become a real obstacle as the recent rains had made it slippery and dangerous to traverse. There were only two crossing-places near the camp but they were adequate for waggons and guns. Monmouth's mood of despair gave way to exhilaration as he considered the advantages of a surprise night attack on a drunken enemy. He called a council, at which everyone enthusiastically supported his proposal, and scheduled the venture for that very night.

Lord Grey's cavalry led Monmouth's infantry on their four-mile march around and across the open spaces. They were relieved to find themselves shrouded by a dense mist rising from the moor; but that same mist proved to be their undoing. Their guide lost his way and could not find the crossing-place over one of the dykes. A royal trooper heard the confusion behind the blanket of fog, fired his pistol and made his way back to the Bussex Rhine where the main camp was sleeping. He rode up and down, crying: 'Beat your Drums, the enemy is come; for ye Lord's sake beat your Drums!'

Unfortunately for Monmouth the men had not gone to bed drunk, the troops were well posted and the General Officer of the Day was the redoubtable Lord Churchill. The drummers ran out barefoot and soon five battalions were drawn up parallel to the dyke. Lord Grey's 800 rebel horsemen made the mistake of riding along the other side, offering a splendid target for the royal infantry. At the first volley of musket-fire the untrained horses bolted and went crashing back through the lines of the approaching foot-soldiers.

Notwithstanding the cursing and shouting and general confusion, Monmouth managed to get three guns to the Bussex Rhine and began firing on the Royal Scots, causing heavy casualties. At the same moment Churchill learned that his own artillery could not be moved into position because the teams of civilian drivers who pulled the gun carriages had fled at the first alarm. Undaunted, he aroused Bishop Mew of Winchester, a visitor to the camp, and borrowed his coach, horses and servants to drag the guns into place. Once this was accomplished, he speedily brought the rebel fire to a close.

Feversham did not appear until four o'clock in the morning, an hour after the drums had sounded. Seven years earlier he had undergone the horrific operation of trepanning after sustaining terrible head injuries in trying to limit the fire in Temple Lane by explosives. These misfortunes had turned him into a very heavy sleeper, but there was nothing fundamentally wrong with his soldiering techniques. He had made his dispositions faultlessly and now ordered his men to wait until first light before pursuing the enemy.

Monmouth was doomed. When he missed the chance of breaking into the sleeping camp, and when Grey failed to set fire to Weston Zoyland, the gamble was lost. The Duke's simple, illiterate followers, who were fighting to set the Crown upon his head, continued to fire into the enemy camp until their ammunition ran out, while Monmouth and Grey, with fifty mounted men, rode off the battlefield leaving them to their fate. Monmouth's hope of escaping back to the Continent came to nothing, as both he and his lieutenant were captured later the same day. Although the Duke grovelled at his uncle's feet and even offered to turn Catholic if his life were spared, he was executed the following morning. A few months later Lady Henrietta Wentworth died of a broken heart.

What happened next was the worst part of the story. Feversham ordered the troops to scour the countryside for fugitives and to show no mercy. 'Our men', reported an eye-witness, 'are still killing them in ye corne and hedges and ditches whither they are crept.'[11] Feversham, however, favoured a more conspicuous form of punishment. He rode along with one of his lieutenants, an officer called Kirke, fresh from a Moroccan campaign, and hanged without trial whatever prisoners he captured on the way. He entered Bridgwater with a group of prisoners tied together like African slaves in tow. On that occasion he hanged twenty-two at once. The Bishop of Winchester, who accompanied him as 'his spiritual adviser', was so shocked by his refusal to hold trials that he warned him that if he did not stop this very un-English practice he might be charged with murder. This was not a likely contingency, however, for James 11 had already sent Feversham a letter deploring the fact that upon entering Frome he had not hanged 'any person found deserving, as he would have you do at other places if you shall see just cause.'[12] No one knows the exact number of those who died in this way, but the fact that their corpses dangled from trees for all to see made an unforgettable impression.*

Brigadier-General Churchill had no part in this sorry business; he hated vengeance and, although he hanged one of his prisoners (we do not know why), he recoiled from reprisals. Luckily he was able to take leave of the West Country as Feversham sent him to the King with a dispatch describing the victory. Before long Feversham was being toasted in the London cafés as a soldier whose talents lay in eating and sleeping. His delay in taking command during the night attack had become common knowledge. Indeed, the Duke of Buckingham was inspired to write a play about a general who won a battle while lying in bed. No doubt Churchill contributed to this uproarious picture as Englishmen loved stories proving that foreigners were as foolish as they were believed to be. As a result, contemporary opinion gave Churchill credit for the victory and left Feversham to come down through history as a nincompoop. Modern military historians, however, give him credit for the way he conducted his brief campaign.

No one, of course, dared to blacken Feversham's name to James, who was delighted with the swiftness of his victory. He bestowed the Garter on him and gave him the lucrative command of the First Troop of the Life Guards. Churchill received the colonelcy of the Third Troop of Horse Guards ten days after Sedgemoor and a year later received a financial award that greatly pleased him. In December 1686 the King gave him the lands and properties in Somerset of John Hucker, who had been executed for high treason. The goods and chattels were worth £500, the lands £250 a year.

Lord Feversham's brutality was followed by the notorious Judge Jeffreys's Bloody Assize. The Judge hated Dissenters and was pleased

---

* Estimates vary from 170 to 300.

to be able to demolish them on a charge of treason. He ordered over 1,000 men to be transported to the tropics and sold into slavery. Another 300 were hanged, causing Jeffreys to boast that he had hanged more men than all the judges put together since the Norman Conquest. James II was delighted by Jeffreys's 'severity', referring with grim humour to the latter's activities as 'Jeffreys's campaigns'.[13] He rewarded him by making him his Lord Chancellor. However, when James fled from England three years later Jeffreys was flung into the Tower; the cruel Judge begged for mercy,* writing to Lord Sunderland as 'dearest dearest Lord' and insisting that his Bloody Assize was by express orders and 'even that was not bloody enough for him who sent me there'.[14]

Churchill did his best to help the victims and on several occasions took petitions to the King on their behalf. When a young woman, Hannah Hewling, presented a petition on behalf of her twin brothers, Churchill waited with her in the ante-room for admittance. Churchill wished her success. 'But madam,' he said, 'I dare not flatter you with any such hopes, as that marble', and here he pointed to the mantlepiece, 'is as capable of feeling compassion as the King's heart.'[15] His fears were justified: both Hewling brothers were hanged.

Churchill was too experienced a courtier to allow the King to catch sight of the shadow that had fallen between them. Once again he was at his master's side, serving him with diligence and goodwill. No one could fail to notice, however, the change that had come over James since the Crown had been set on his head. He struck foreign envoys as 'very haughty', and even M. Barrillon, the French Ambassador, in whom he confided more freely than in his own ministers, reported to Paris that 'he suffers very impatiently the least contradiction'.[16]

The truth was that James's head had been turned by his unexpected success. Although he had been warned against taking a peremptory line with his Parliament, he had succeeded in securing the revenues he needed; and, although some of his advisers had expected Monmouth's landing to light a Protestant fire across England, he had extinguished the flame as easily as a candle. James now felt that he had nothing more to fear. Without further hesitation he would pursue his two secret aims: to rule without Parliament and to re-establish the Church of Rome in England.

First and foremost he needed a large standing army. When Parliament met in November 1685 he announced that he intended to replace

---

* Jeffreys died in prison a year later.

the national militia with professional soldiers, and planned to retain the Catholic officers he had enrolled in the Monmouth emergency. When the House of Lords began to bicker about the illegality of Catholics holding commissions in a public service, he simply prorogued the assembly and never summoned it again. He could afford to do this as his life revenues had swollen with the country's increased trade, and he had nearly £2 million per annum to spend. This meant that he could finance the army himself.

The King retained Lord Feversham as Commander-in-Chief and once again appointed Churchill second-in-command, giving him the rank of Major-General. The latter was not unhappy to be assigned the task of enlarging the army. Dozens of new companies were to be formed, and as each company of fifty men was controlled by an ensign (or cornet), a lieutenant and a captain, all of whom had to buy their commissions according to established practice, it was bound to prove a lucrative business.* Indeed, during 1687 Churchill made enough money to be able to invest £7,000 in government bonds at 6 per cent interest, and in February 1688 he put aside a further £3,000. 'He kept himself wholly out of the counsels of the King,' wrote Dr Gilbert Burnet, 'and so set himself to manage his post in the army, in which he made a great advantage, for money had as much power over him as he had over the King.'[17]

Whatever his counsels, nothing would have deflected the King from his adopted course. If he restrained himself from adding more Catholic officers, he made up for it by trying to convert his Protestant soldiers. Every summer a series of great reviews involving about 10,000 men took place at Hounslow which the King attended, dining afterwards with Lord Feversham or Lord Churchill in their tents. On the large field, 'between the Horse and the Foot', stood a wooden chapel on wheels which could be moved to make way for the parades. Here daily mass was said while priests moved among the soldiers looking for converts.

Across the Channel, Louis XIV was also seeking Protestant conversions, but in a less agreeable way. In October 1685 he had revoked the Edict of Nantes, which for nearly a century had given French Protestants – the Huguenots – freedom of religion. He had decided on the revocation, quite simply, to redeem himself for refusing to join the Christian princes in defending Vienna against the infidel Turk. The truth was that Louis wanted to see his Habsburg rival, Leopold I, defeated. This had not happened and now the French King was trying to regain the Pope's goodwill.

* Normally commissions were bought from retiring officers, but in this case the general who raised the new regiments could exact the payments.

At first James greeted the news of the revocation ecstatically, showering Louis with congratulations for his determination to stamp out heresy. By his act, Protestantism had become a crime in France; *dragonnades*, organized by military men, had been going about the countryside for some years tracking down Protestants and forcing conversions. Now they were given free rein and committed appalling cruelties, raping, whipping, torturing and killing. As a result, thousands of people fled the country and took refuge in England, Holland and Brandenburg. The burning hatred that Louis aroused throughout Protestant Europe against France, and against Catholicism, was incalculable. It not only contributed to the undoing of James, who would listen to no one but his confessor, but to the eventual undoing of Louis himself – with the help, of course, of General Churchill. But all this was far in the future.

Meanwhile, the Princess of Denmark's residence, the Cockpit, was becoming a place of increasing importance. Although the Duchess of York – now the Queen – had given birth to five children (two of them boys), none had survived. Of James's two daughters, Anne was the only one living in England, which made her a national focus for Protestant attention.

Anne was as fervent an Anglican as her father was a Catholic but, as he had made no attempt to tamper with her religion, she did not concern herself with politics. With James's approval she appointed her friends to key positions in her little Court, or 'family' as she called it, and set out to enjoy herself. She was delighted when the King sent Lord Clarendon to Ireland as Lieutenant-General, as Lady Clarendon was obliged to accompany him. This enabled the Princess to appoint Lady Churchill to her aunt's vacant post as First Lady of the Bedchamber, an office which Sarah retained for twenty-six years.

Other members of the Princess's Court included the eldest Villiers girl, Barbara (a sister of Squinting Betty, William of Orange's mistress), who was married to John Berkeley, Colonel of the Princess's Own Dragoons; 'Faire Semandra', now the wife of Sir Benjamin Bathurst, Controller of the Denmark Household; the Duke of Grafton, Charles II's son by Lady Castlemaine; and Churchill's two younger brothers, George, a captain in the navy, and Charles, a colonel in the army. The King gave further household positions as a reward for opposing the Exclusion Bills. One went to Lord Scarsdale, another to Lord Cornbury, Princess Anne's first cousin on her mother's side. Cornbury was second-in-command of the King's Own Dragoons under Churchill.

Although Anne was fond of her good-natured, unimaginative husband, who did his duty by keeping her almost continuously pregnant, Sarah was the true object of her love. Winston Churchill calls her obsession 'strange' and 'perfervid', for she loved Sarah as possessively as Sarah loved her own husband. Indeed, this odd quadrangle seems to have baffled biographers who gloss over it as though it were perfectly natural for royal princesses to be consumed with adoration for favourites of the same sex. Years later, when Sarah was an old lady, she wrote about her relationship with the Princess, referring to herself in the third person as 'the Dutchess'. 'The Dutchess', she says,

> . . . began to employ all her wit and all her vivacity and almost all Her time to divert and entertain and serve the Princess and to fix that favour which now one might easily observe to be increasing toward her every day. The favour quickly became a passion; and a passion which obsessed the Heart of the Princess too much to be hid.

Anne's feelings for Sarah were so intense that the emotion must have had its roots in physical attraction, although the Princess herself was probably unaware of it. Sarah was not only wonderfully diverting, but also a bold and dominating beauty – just the sort of woman to appeal to a shy and rather plain girl whose life had been reduced by Court restrictions to a tedious routine. In her narrative Sarah goes on to tell us that the Princess and the Duchess

> were shut up together for many hours daily. Every moment of absence was counted a sort of tedious lifeless state. To see the Dutchesse was a constant joy; and to part with her for never so short a time a constant uneasiness; as the Princess's own frequent expressions were. This worked even to the jealousy of a lover. She used to say she desired to possess her wholly; and could hardly bear that she should ever escape from this confinement, into other Company.[18]

But Sarah always did escape. Whenever John had leave from his duties they spent their time together at Holywell House. These days were balm to her spirit as the task of keeping her mistress permanently entertained could be exhausting. 'Her memory was exceedingly great, almost to a wonder,' explained Sarah,

> [but] she chose to retain in it very little besides ceremonies and customs of courts, and such like insignificant trifles; so that her conversation which otherwise might have been enlivened by a great memory, was only made the more empty and trivial by its chiefly turning upon *fashions* and rules of procedure, or observations upon the weather, or some such poor topics. . . .[19]

When Sarah was absent, the Princess divided her time between daily prayers, daily card-playing and daily letter-writing 'to my deare Lady Churchill'. Luckily for Sarah, both she and her mistress adored playing cards for high stakes, and every night when they were together the tables were set for ombre and basset. 'I am sorry you have soe ill success at dice,' the Princess wrote to Sarah, 'yesterday I won three hundred pounds but have lost almost half of it this morning.'[20]

Some people pitied the Prince and Princess of Denmark because they were so short of money. 'The Princess has but thirty thousand pounds a year,' wrote a contemporary, 'which is so exhausted by a great establishment that she is really extreme poor for one of her rank.'[21] However, it was not the establishment but the gambling that drove her into debt. She asked her uncle, Lord Rochester (the former Laurence Hyde), to use his influence with the King and ask for help, but he refused. Finally Sidney Godolphin, now Lord Godolphin and Chamberlain to Queen Mary Beatrice,* came to the rescue by persuading James to give her £16,000 as a Christmas present. This endeared Godolphin to the Princess, who drew him into her inner circle.

While Princess Anne was worrying about money, the Churchills were better off than ever before. John received £600 as a Gentleman-in-Waiting and another £600 for his various colonelcies, while Sarah's £200 would soon be increased to keep pace with her new responsibilities. Even so, they spent nothing on pleasure, saving every penny for the proverbial rainy day. Sarah won considerable sums at the card-table, giving rise to gossip that she made a point of enriching herself at the expense of her mistress.

No one could accuse Lord Churchill of gambling. He would not dream of risking his hard-earned funds on the turn of a card. According to Sarah, 'From his earliest days he never spent a penny beyond what his income was.' As the Churchills' only abode was St Albans and they had no house to keep up in London, they were able to save three-quarters of their salaries. The Princess gave them rooms in the Cockpit, and they still had John's lodgings in Jermyn Street. Soon stories were circulating about General Churchill's 'meanness'; how he preferred to walk home through muddy streets rather than pay a penny for a sedan-chair; how he never had a drink unless someone bought it for him ; how he only possessed three coats, one of which was reserved for state occasions. Perhaps all these accusations were true, but people conveniently overlooked the fact that Churchill was

* Under Charles II Godolphin had been First Lord of the Treasury, and regarded his present appointment as a setback.

one of the few men at Court who had married for love not money. He was determined to build up a fortune and was well aware that unless he could accumulate capital from his savings, he could not make it grow. This maxim was borne out in 1686 when he became governor of a Canadian fur company – the Hudson's Bay – which had received its charter from Charles II. The Duke of York had been the previous governor but had been obliged to relinquish the post upon his accession. Churchill was so impressed by the business that he put £1,000 of his savings into buying stock – an investment which doubled in the next five years.

Churchill had the responsibility of a growing family. During the first five months of 1686 both Lady Churchill and the Princess had babies. Sarah's fourth child (the first had died) was born on 12 January and was the son and heir for whom husband and wife longed. They named the baby John, and Sarah invited Lord Godolphin and her brother-in-law, Lord Tyrconnel (the former Dick Talbot), to stand as godfathers. As Lord Tyrconnel was a strong Catholic, Sarah's choice reveals how little concerned she was at that time with religion. Louis's revocation of the Edict of Nantes, which had taken place two and a half months earlier, was only beginning to make its full impact. Anne's baby was born in May, a girl whom she named Anne Sophia. She asked Sarah to be the godmother, but sadly the baby died a few months later. Poor Anne could not know that she was destined to have seventeen children, but that none would survive!

Anne spent the summer in Tunbridge Wells and found that people were becoming increasingly alarmed by the King's preoccupation with Catholics. He was infiltrating them into all sorts of positions ranging from Oxford Fellowships to Lords Lieutenancies. Indeed, there were rumours that James intended to convert the Princess of Denmark. This was pure gossip as the only step that James took was to send his daughter a religious paper, allegedly written by her mother, explaining her own conversion. Anne was unimpressed. 'I hope you don't doubt', she wrote to her sister in Holland, 'that I will ever be firm in my religion whatever happens. . . . The Church of Rome is wicked and dangerous and directly contrary to the Scriptures, and their ceremonies – most of them – plain, downright idolatory.'[22]

Despite the growing antagonism, the King continued on his way. In July 1686 the high courts ruled that James II possessed the power to dispense with the Test Act in appointing Roman Catholics to civil and military office under the Crown. This not only legitimized the action he had already taken but encouraged him to appoint four Roman Catholics to the Privy Council. James's Protestant advisers were deeply shocked, but the King had the bit between his teeth. He appointed Catholic governors at Hull and Dover, and gave the Catholic Duke of Berwick, his eighteen-year-old bastard son by Arabella Churchill, the governorship of Portsmouth. Some months earlier he had dismissed the highly respected Lord Halifax as Lord President of the Council because he would not work for the repeal of the Test Act of 1678, and now, in January 1687, he removed his two former brothers-in-law from office; in Ireland Lord Clarendon was replaced by Lord Tyrconnel, while Clarendon's brother, the able Lord Rochester, who was serving as the King's Lord Treasurer, was dismissed for declining to become a Catholic. Apparently he had listened to all the priest's arguments in favour of conversion and then announced that he was not impressed. This episode created such a furore that historians often cite it as the watershed of James's reign.

Churchill did not try to hide his anxiety from the King. His first biographer, an anonymous writer who claimed to be a close friend,* tells us that he spoke openly to James when they were strolling in the Deanery Garden in Winchester. He had accompanied his master on a royal progress in the west of England where James had touched people for the King's Evil. At Winchester James had been assisted by Catholic priests and asked Churchill what people thought of the ceremony. 'Why truly,' he replied, 'they show very little liking to it; and it is the general view of the people that Your Majesty is paving the way for the introduction of Popery.'

'How! Have I not given my royal word and will they not believe their King? I have given liberty of conscience to others; I was always of the opinion that toleration was necessary for all Christian people and most certainly I will not be abridged of that liberty myself. . . .'

But Churchill refused to be intimidated. He replied that nine out of ten Englishmen, including himself, had been born and bred Protestants and intended to remain Protestants. The natural aversion of English people for Roman Catholic worship made him fear 'some consequences which I dare not so much as name and which it creates in me a horror to think of.'

The King listened attentively, then replied that his aim was to ensure that all people were given the right to worship as they saw fit. 'As for the consequences, I shall leave them to Providence. . . .'[23] He then turned away and did not speak to Churchill again that night.

England was not the only battleground. By the beginning of 1687

* The book was published in 1713, while Churchill was still alive and well, and is therefore taken seriously by historians despite the fact that the author was never identified.

feeling in northern Europe against the persecution of Protestants in France was running high. A steady stream of refugees was crossing the Channel and in the English taverns songs were being sung mocking the periwigged tyrant at Versailles. 'I heare he stinckes alive,' declared Squire Edmund Verney, 'and his cankers will stincke worse when he is dead and soe will his memory to all eternity.'[24] Most of the gentry shared Verney's outlook. Nevertheless, King James still looked upon France as his closest ally, refusing to recognize the chasm that was opening between himself and his subjects. Every morning his confessor assured him that God would bless his inflexible will.

Lord Churchill was not an overly religious man, but he believed that Protestantism was synonymous with liberty; that it prevented England from being drawn into the French orbit, and thus guaranteed the country's political independence. Clearly James II was travelling on a collision course and equally clearly the Churchills were travelling with him, trapped in the same coach, heading for the same disaster. How could they extricate themselves? The best plan, Churchill decided, would be to accompany Princess Anne on a visit to her sister in Holland. That would enable him to find out whether Prince William had any plans to try and bring his father-in-law's runaway carriage to a halt. However, in January 1687, just as Sarah broached the idea of a journey to Holland, Anne had a miscarriage, which was attributed by her Court to 'a jolt in her coach' but which the Princess herself blamed on a new French dance, 'the Riggadoon . . . for there is a great deal of jumping in it'.[25] She had scarcely recovered from this mishap when tragedy overtook her. Her entire family – Prince George and her two babies – contracted smallpox. The infant girls died within a few days of each other and, although many people despaired of the Prince, he survived the dreaded disease. But the royal couple were devastated by the loss of their children. 'Sometimes they wept,' wrote Lady Russell, 'sometimes they mourned; in a word, they sat silent, hand in hand; he sick in bed, and she the carefullest nurse to him that can be imagined.'[26]

In March, when Prince George had recovered, the Princess asked permission of the King to visit the Princess of Orange. At first he gave his assent but a day later withdrew it without explanation. The French Ambassador, M. Barrillon, reported knowingly to Paris that 'the Princess had been worked up with the plan of going to Holland under the pretext of meeting her sister.'

> Once she was there [he continued] she would have been prevented from coming back and the Protestant party would have been fortified by the union of these two princesses, the lawful heirs to the Crown, who could

have made declarations and protestations against the whole Catholic movement. King James was not without suspicion that Churchill had his share in proposing such a journey and that his wife, the Princess Anne's favourite, had awakened her ambition.[27]

Anne was furious at the King's refusal. Not only was it an infringement of her rights as a Protestant, but of her privileges as a Princess. She blamed her step-mother for encouraging the King's Catholic zeal and before long was abusing her openly. 'The Queen', she wrote to her sister,

> is the most hated in the world by all sorts of people; for everybody believes that she pressed the King to be more violent than he would be of himself, which is not unlikely, for she is a very great bigot in her way, and one may see by her that she hates all Protestants. . . . She pretends to have a great deal of kindness to me but I doubt it is not real, for I never see proofs of it, but rather the contrary.[28]

Having failed to organize a visit to The Hague, Lord Churchill tried to get command of the six English and Scottish regiments stationed in Holland on Dutch pay; but he was told that James had earmarked these troops for the Duke of Berwick. However, when James ordered the regiments to be transferred to France, William of Orange flatly refused to let them go and for some weeks the relations between the two countries were at a very low ebb.

Because of her influence with Princess Anne, Sarah was attracting fire from two quarters. King James was told that Lady Churchill had received a bribe from Prince William to put the idea of the trip to Holland into the Princess's head, while the Princess of Orange was assured that Lady Churchill would become a Catholic if she was paid enough for it. Mary of Orange had known Sarah as a girl and had never liked her because she was 'irreligious'. Now she liked her even less because she was jealous of her. When she wrote to her sister, she took a sly dig at Lady Churchill's infrequent appearance at church, but Anne defended her stoutly. It was true, she said, that Sarah did not keep 'such a bustle with religion', but 'nobody in the world can have better notions of religion than she does.'[29] No doubt Mary's jealousy was increased by Dr Gilbert Burnet, who had moved from London to The Hague to serve as the Princess's spiritual adviser and who kept her abreast of the gossip. Lady Churchill, he wrote,

> is about the Princess Anne and has gained such an ascendant over her that there never was a more absolute favourite in a court. She is indeed

become the mistress of her thoughts and affections and does with her both in her court and in her affairs what she pleases.[30]

Meanwhile the Princess of Orange had sent a special envoy, Everard van Weede, Lord of Dijkvelt, to London, ostensibly to advise the King to modify his measures but secretly to sound out the opposition. One can sense the anxiety of the Churchills by the speed with which they nailed their colours – and those of the Princess Anne – to his mast. Churchill reported to the Prince of Orange that he had talked to M. Dijkvelt and that the Princess of Denmark wished 'Your Highness and the Princess her sister to know that she was resolved, by the assistance of God, to suffer all extremities, even to death itself, rather than be brought to change her religion.'

Churchill used less dramatic language to describe his own feelings. Nevertheless, on grounds of religious conviction, he made it clear that he was ready to serve the Prince:

I thought it my duty to Your Highness and the Princess Royal, by this opportunity to give you assurances under my own hand, that my places and the King's favour I set at naught, in comparison of being true to my religion. . . . I know the troubling you, sir, with this much of myself, I being of so little use to Your Highness, is very impertinent, but I think it may be a great ease to Your Highness and the Princess to be satisfied that the Princess of Denmark is safe in the trusting of me.[31]

Many other powerful nobles gave M. Dijkvelt similar assurances, and he left them in no doubt that they could count on William and Mary if matters came to a head.

We do not know exactly when the conspiracy against James began to form, or exactly when Churchill joined it. Churchill knew most of the great men of the realm – Lord Halifax, Lord Shrewsbury, Admiral Edward Russell – and no doubt had many private and secret conversations before the plans took shape. Because he had served in James's household for twenty years, he was singled out later and attacked for wicked ingratitude while other conspirators were praised for their Protestant 'zeal'. In Churchill's defence, it must be pointed out that he never concealed his views from James. The King's retention of his services was surprising, but the explanation probably lay in the fact that James's feelings were mixed. He not only found Churchill extremely useful but had known him so long that he looked upon him as part of his family. Yet when he gave him a high military command he took the precaution of placing his trusted friend, Feversham, over him.

Churchill's views, on the other hand, had hardened. He no longer wanted to leave the Court but was glad to be at his master's side, bland and watchful, as he believed with growing conviction that England's freedom was in jeopardy. In the years to come the Jacobites would refer to him as 'the great betrayer'. Even today some historians suggest that he should have left James's service and joined the English exiles in Holland; that, they say, would have been the honourable thing to do. But it also would have been the least effective thing to do. Churchill's role as second-in-command of the army was of crucial importance. The censure of him, therefore, depends on the importance one attaches to the issue involved. If Churchill was genuine in believing that the liberty and independence of England was at risk, it was his duty to use every weapon at his disposal to win the struggle. And that is what he did, laying his life on the line.

William of Orange was the soul of the conspiracy and Lord Danby (who had gone to the Tower because of Louis's subsidy payments to King Charles) was the self-appointed English leader. His chief helper was the twenty-eight-year-old Earl of Shrewsbury, a one-eyed man of irresistible charm, beloved by almost everybody, who became a close friend of the Churchills. Shrewsbury's father and brother had both been killed in duels, which was said to have affected his character: sometimes he was bold as a lion; at other times timid and uncertain. At the moment he was in a fearless mood and his house became the meeting-place for the conspirators. 'And there', wrote Dr Gilbert Burnet, 'they concerted matters and drew the declaration on which they advised the prince [of Orange] to engage.'[32] The 'declaration' was an audacious letter sent by Danby in the spring of 1688, inviting William to invade England. The latter replied that he must have a formal invitation from the country's leading statesmen and that he could not be ready until September.

These conditions took time to fulfil. Although most prominent Protestants were opposed to James's policy, many of them shrank from decisive action. Lord Halifax took refuge in being a 'moderate', while Lord Sunderland's loyalties remained as baffling as ever; Nottingham listened to the conspirators' plans and agreed to join them; then he had misgivings and retracted, upon which Shrewsbury calmly listened to the plan of one of his colleagues (he would not say who) to kill him. Eventually the others persuaded the anonymous lord to eschew violence and to trust Nottingham's oath of secrecy.[33]

The moment invasion developed into a likely possibility, Major-General Churchill became a key figure in the revolutionary plot. After all, everything would depend ultimately on the attitude of the army. Later Burnet described how some of the chief officers were approached:

> Churchill, Kirke and Trelawney [he wrote] went into it; and Trelawney got his brother that was Bishop of Bristol to join in it. Churchill did likewise undertake for Prince George and the Princess Anne; and those officers said they durst answer for the much greater part of the army, and promised to do their utmost endeavours to bring as many as possible they could into it.[34]

While Danby was coercing the statesmen and Churchill was quietly appraising the mood of the army, James II made the most disastrous move of his reign. He renewed his Declaration of Indulgence (giving latitude to Catholics), which he had introduced the previous year for a limited period, and ordered his announcement to be read in all the churches. On 18 May 1688 seven bishops, headed by the Primate of England, protested against this use of the sovereign's dispensing power, and the clergy throughout the country followed their superiors and refused to read the Declaration from their pulpits. James was furious and demanded that the bishops be tried for seditious libel. The bishops refused to provide bail and were put into the Tower to await trial.

For once, James's chief minister, the unfathomable Lord Sunderland, had reservations. Up till this moment he had encouraged the King in all his most extravagant designs, but he felt that the imprisonment of the bishops was a mistake. We do not know what else he thought, as Sunderland was one of the most mysterious personalities in English public life. He was a man of exquisite manners, a lover of the arts, a truly civilized milord. Even more important, he had such an insinuating personality that no one – particularly no king – could resist him. It did not seem to matter what blunders he made, what enormities he committed: he was always welcomed by each successive sovereign. He was, in fact, the English prototype of France's Talleyrand. Although he had voted for the Exclusion Bill, he managed to work his way back into Charles's counsels, and after Charles's death he won James's goodwill by taking instruction in the Catholic faith. Princess Anne hated Sunderland – perhaps because his wife was Sarah's friend – and in the spring of 1688 wrote to the Princess of Orange describing how this lord had 'turned backwards and forwards in the late King's reign' and now, 'he is working with all his might to bring in Popery. He is perpetually with the priests and I believe stirs up the King to do things faster than I believe he would himself.'[35]

About the time that Anne was writing this letter, an announcement was made that swept aside petty gossip and held the Court spell-bound. The Queen was pregnant. The news was greeted incredulously by Protestants as the Queen had not produced a child since 1682, when she had given birth to a daughter who lived only two months. In 1683 she had had a miscarriage and for many months had been in poor health, giving rise to talk that she was heading for an early grave. And now, as the Catholics put it, 'a miracle had occurred'.

Princess Anne was not only amazed by the news but jealous and angry. Ten months earlier poor Anne had lost her two baby daughters and in the intervening time had suffered two miscarriages. Not only was it cruelly unfair that her young stepmother should have what she was denied, but if the Queen gave birth to a son, he would displace both her sister Mary and herself in the line of succession; further-more, the boy would be brought up as a Catholic. The news was quite unbearable. 'No words can express', the Tuscan envoy in London reported to his master,

> the rage of the Princess of Denmark at the Queen's condition, she can dissimulate it to no one; and seeing that the Catholic religion has a prospect of advancement, she affects more than ever, both in public and in private to show herself hostile to it and to be the most zealous of Protes-tants with whom she is gaining the greatest power and credit. . . .[36]

Today, no one doubts Mary's pregnancy nor the birth of her son, James Francis Edward Stuart. But Princess Anne, encouraged by John and Sarah Churchill, refused for one minute to admit that the child sprang from the Queen's womb. Indeed, early in 1688 Anne began to hint at 'foul play'. In a letter to the Princess of Orange three months before the confinement she suggested that Roman Catholics were capable of any act. 'I can't help thinking Mansell's [the King's] wife's great belly is a little suspicious,' she wrote, 'it is true indeed that she is very big, but she looks better than ever she did which is not unusual. Her being so positive it will be a son, and the principles of that religion being such that they will stick at nothing, be it never so wicked, if it will promote their interest, give some cause to fear there may be foul play intended.'[37] A week later Anne wrote again, alleging that the Queen had refused to allow her to see her undressed and that 'these things give me so much just cause for suspicion that I believe when she is brought to bed nobody will be convinced it is her child, except it prove to be a daughter. For my part I declare I shall not, except I see the child and she parted.'[38]

But Anne had no intention of being present at the birth. Indeed, far from the confinement being a Catholic plot to foist a supposititious child upon the nation, it was a Protestant plot to ensure the succession of the Protestant Princesses. The plot was so well organized that undoubtedly the Churchills had a hand in it. The Princess, accompanied by her husband, departed for Bath to recover from what was later described as 'a false pregnancy' (perhaps this gave Anne the idea of fastening the same diagnosis on the Queen), and did not return until the confinement had ended.

The eminent Protestants who were invited to attend the royal bedchamber at St James's Palace made excuses to stay away so that they would not be compelled to testify to an event which might spell the end of Protestant England. 'The Lord Churchill among the rest', wrote Churchill's contemporary biographer, 'was summoned to attend and sent for in a particular Manner . . . but he had received some Intimations before and was purposely out of the way.'[39]

Luckily for the courtiers the birth took place on a Sunday morning, which allowed them to make the pious excuse of attending Divine Service. Lord Godolphin, Chamberlain to the Queen, had no option but to be present, but he took pains to stand where he could see nothing. As a result the great majority of witnesses were Roman Catholics who could not be trusted, leaving the Protestants to declare loudly that the baby had been smuggled into the Queen's bedroom in a warming-pan. It was amazing that anyone could truly believe this grotesque story. As Dean Swift, who was far from being a Catholic, pointed out, it was perfectly possible to squeeze a baby into a warming-pan if you did not mind breaking its back.

Among the affirmative witnesses was Sarah's sister, Frances, the wife of the Catholic Earl of Tyrconnel. Even Lady Isabella Wentworth, one of the few Protestants who attended the bedchamber, scoffed at the talk of fraudulence; years later, when Queen Anne was on the throne, she wrote, 'I am confident . . . Her Majesty . . . cannot disbelieve the Prince's birth'.[40] But Anne herself made no such admission. When she returned to London from Bath, five days after her stepbrother was said to have come into the world, she wrote to her sister, "tis possible it may be her child; but where one believes it, a thousand do not. For my part, except they do give very plain demonstrations, *which is almost impossible now*, I shall ever be of the number of unbelievers.'[41] And she maintained her very convenient disbelief for most of her life.

Two weeks after the announcement of the royal birth on the night of 30 June 1688, the trial of the bishops ended with the jury returning a verdict of 'Not Guilty'. The news was received throughout London with jubilation. On the same day a group of noblemen known in history as 'the immortal seven' – the Earls of Danby, Devonshire and Shrewsbury, Bishop Compton (a former tutor to Princess Anne), Henry Sidney (William of Orange's only English confidant), General Lumley and Admiral Russell (who had carried secret messages between the Princess and her sister at The Hague) – issued the formal invitation that the Prince of Orange had demanded before he would consider coming to England.

It was not until September that James began to fear that his son-in-law might really be planning to invade his realm. William of Orange had refused to denude Holland of ships and soldiers until he saw what Louis XIV was going to do. In September Louis took a calamitous decision. A month earlier he had offered James ships and soldiers with which to repel a possible Dutch invasion, but James had declined his help. Later people blamed Lord Sunderland who, they said, had persuaded the King that foreign intervention would be bitterly resented by his subjects. For once Louis was at a loss for what to do. If he tried to counter the invasion without James's co-operation, he would cut a ridiculous figure. At Versailles, Louis's ministers solved the problem by assuring him that a Dutch invasion would start a civil war in England which would serve French interests admirably. So, instead of sending an invasion fleet or even mounting an attack against Holland, Louis simply warned the States-General not to incur his displeasure by landing in England and gave orders for the capture of Philippsburg, a town at the northern corner of Alsace which controlled the traffic on the Rhine.

It would be difficult to say which King blundered the most, James or Louis. As September wore on and Whitehall received irrefutable proof that the ships and supplies gathering in Dutch ports were destined for England, James panicked and tried to reverse his policy. Roman Catholic schools would be closed; Protestant Fellows restored at Magdalen College, Oxford; Parliament recalled. But it was all too late. There was no way to stop the gathering storm.

A month earlier Churchill had sent William a letter written in his own hand which, if it had been intercepted, would have sent him to the scaffold.

4 August 1688

Mr Sidney will let you know how I intend to behave myself; I think it is what I owe to God and my country. My honour I take leave to put into your royal highness's hands, in which I think it safe. If you think there is anything else that I ought to do you have but to command me, and I shall pay an entire obedience to it, being resolved to die in that religion that it has pleased God to give you both the will and power to protect.[42]

Churchill was well aware of the risk he was running. The King's forces were three times as large as William's, which meant that anything could happen. Indeed, no one knew how the country would react to a 'foreign army' landing in England. The sympathy of the people might swing back to James overwhelmingly; in that case the conspirators would pay for their treason with their heads. Furthermore, there was always the possibility that the French might intercept William's fleet, or even land troops of their own. In an early draft of Sarah Churchill's memoirs, written in 1704 and only published recently, she recalls that 'the attempt of succeeding in the Revolution was subject to such a Train of Hazaards and Accidents that before the Duke of Marlborough entered into the Design he made settlements to secure his Family in case of Misfortune.'[43] The settlement was dated 27 July 1688.

William set out upon the seas on 19 October with 300 transport vessels escorted by fifty-two warships, which represented almost the whole of the Dutch fleet. His small army of 15,000 men was composed of volunteers and mercenaries from the leading Protestant countries of Europe and included Dutchmen, Swedes, Danes, Prussians, Englishmen and a band of French Huguenots. A violent storm scattered the Prince's ships and drove them back to their Dutch ports. Even when the gales subsided, the wind was so strong and wayward that it prevented the armada from landing in Yorkshire, where it was expected, and blew it south towards Devon. This was a genuine case of an ill wind blowing good, for the gale that sent the Prince off-course also prevented James's faithful servant, George Legge, now Lord Dartmouth* and Admiral of the Fleet, from intercepting the invasion. He could not come out of the Thames in a formation ready for battle; and, although he pursued the invaders and got as far as Portland, he was forced to take shelter at Spithead. Churchill's brother, George, on the other hand, was captain of the *Newcastle*, and did his best to persuade his brother officers to desert to William, but although they were sympathetic, they would not follow him.

The Prince of Orange landed at Torbay on the coast of Devon. The date was 5 November, the anniversary of the detection of the Gunpowder Plot; when Bishop Burnet, who accompanied William, explained the significance, the latter remarked provocatively: 'What

---

* Lord Dartmouth was Churchill's old friend who had fought with him on board James's flagship against the Dutch in 1667.

do you think of Predestination now?' The Prince set up his head-quarters at Exeter and waited for the powerful aristocrats who had pledged themselves to come to his aid.

James II immediately gave orders for units comprising 25,000 men of the royal army to move to Salisbury, not far from Exeter. Lord Feversham was still the King's Commander-in-Chief. His brother, the Count de Roye, a competent French general, had come from Paris to join him. It was odd to have two French-born commanders at the head of England's army, particularly as the third brother, the eldest, the Duke de Duras, was a Marshal of France in the active service of Louis XIV. But James reasoned that foreigners would not be infected by the emotional problems that plagued his own subjects. Still, it was neces-sary to have at least one experienced and outstanding English officer of high rank, so Churchill was promoted to the grade of Lieutenant-General and, as usual, made second-in-command.

What was this army to do? What were the conspirators after? Oddly enough, no one talked of deposing James, only of restraining him. Churchill probably hoped to play the role of a General Monck. If a large section of the army supported him, he would be in a position to negotiate between King and Prince. James would have to govern with Parliament; to promise to preserve the Protestant character of England; perhaps even to join a coalition against France. The immediate aim, of course, was to reach a satisfactory solution with-out William being forced to give battle.

James II and a small entourage, including the Prince of Denmark and General Churchill, set out for Windsor on 18 November. Lord Godolphin and the enigmatic Lord Sunderland, who now appeared to be on the side of the conspirators, accompanied them as far as Windsor. When they arrived at the castle, they received news that Lord Clarendon's son, Lord Cornbury, had deserted to William. Cornbury, who was Prince George's Master of the Horse and a first cousin of Princess Anne, had been appointed acting commander in Salisbury until his superiors arrived. Churchill was seen in the com-pany of Sunderland and Godolphin 'going hand in hand along the gallery in the greatest transports of joy imaginable'.[44] Later, people declared that Churchill himself had given Cornbury his temporary command in order to lend weight to his defection.

Lord Feversham begged the King to arrest Churchill, even going down on his knees to implore him to act before it was too late. James nodded and talked of imprisoning Churchill at Portsmouth. Then he changed his mind, saying that the shock to the army might start a chain-reaction which would result in large-scale desertion to the enemy. So he put the matter out of his head until he arrived at Salisbury; there, on 23 November, a council of war was held. Churchill, supported by the Duke of Grafton (another conspirator), recommended an attack, while Feversham and his brother proposed a retreat. The second plan was adopted.

By this time Churchill had probably heard rumours of his impending arrest; on that very night, accompanied by Grafton, Colonel Berkeley and several hundred officers and troopers, he rode fifty miles to Axminster and joined the Prince of Orange. Twenty-four hours later Prince George of Denmark and the Duke of Ormonde followed suit. They were accompanied by Brigadier Trelawney and some of his junior officers, including Lord Churchill's brother, Captain Charles Churchill.

The letter that Churchill left for James declared that he would 'always with the hazard of my life and fortune (so much your Majesty's due) endeavour to preserve your royal person and lawful rights'. He explained that the desertion

> of one who lies under the greatest personal obligation to your Majesty . . .
> proceeds from nothing but the inviolable dictates of my conscience, and a
> necessary concern for my religion (which no good man can oppose) and
> with which I am instructed nothing can come in competition.[45]

This letter was the only explanation that Churchill ever gave for leaving James. By making his conscience the decisive factor he avoided the necessity of telling James the brutal truth. Everything that Churchill did now, and for the rest of his life, points to the fact that he was convinced that James had become a danger to England. If the King continued to favour and promote Catholicism, as he had done for the past three years, he would undermine England's Protestant zeal – the zeal that was prepared to challenge the rapaciousness of Catholic France. That spirit, and that spirit alone, carried with it both the salvation and the future glory of his country. Months earlier he had thrown in his lot with the 'immortal seven'; and, once the die was cast, he never looked back.

The spate of desertions broke the King's spirit. Despite Feversham's warnings he had never believed that Churchill, who had served him since boyhood, would abandon him. And the more he thought about it, the angrier he became, saying that he would never, never forgive him. He called his defection the blackest of crimes and put him at the head of the enemies who would feel his vengeance when he came into his own again. Nevertheless, Churchill's flight had the effect of opening James's eyes to the chasm between himself and his subjects. From this moment he had no will to fight, for how could he rely on his army? His only thought was to remove his wife and child to the safety of France and to follow them as soon as possible.

Yet the military revolt had not worked out as the conspirators had hoped. Lord Cornbury, for instance, had attempted to lead three regiments of Horse into William's camp but had been foiled by his officers. He told them that he had received instructions to proceed towards Axminster to engage the enemy; but after a long and ill-prepared march his officers grew suspicious and demanded to see his orders. Cornbury beat a hasty retreat and rode off to William's head-quarters with 200 men, while the rest of the brigade angrily extri-cated itself from the trap and returned to base.

This fiasco should have comforted James; and so should the fact that Churchill, despite his efforts to achieve a wholesale defection, had only been able to persuade 400 officers and men to desert the King. The truth was that Englishmen were nettled by the foreign army on their soil and had a strong aversion to treason. When Sarah wrote her memoirs many years later, she tells us that she never for a moment envisaged James II leaving his throne.

> When he [Churchill] left King James which was with the greatest regret imaginable, but he saw it was plain that King James could not be preven-ted any other way from establishing Popery and Arbitrary Power to the Ruin of England. And I really believe that he thought the Army would force the Prince of Orange to go back to Holland, when they had found some way to secure the Prince of Orange's interests and to have the laws of England continued. . . .[46]

If James had understood the deeply rooted feelings of his subjects and been willing to call a Parliament, he might still have retained his crown, even at this late hour. But the only decision he seemed capable of taking was to send orders that Lady Churchill and Mrs Berkeley were to be placed under house arrest until His Majesty's return. Both Lord Churchill and the Prince of Denmark had expected their wives to leave the metropolis before they deserted the army, but the two ladies were still in the Cockpit. News of the King's imminent arrival preceded his detention orders and gave Sarah time to arrange for the Princess's escape. Anne was in 'a great fright', wrote Sarah. 'She sent for me, told me her distress and declared that rather than see her father, she would jump out of a window.'[47] That night the Princess went to bed leaving instructions that she was not to be disturbed; then she dressed again, and went down the back-stairs, a secret stair-case especially built for this purpose. Accompanied by Lady

Churchill, Mrs Berkeley, Bishop Compton and the Earl of Dorset, the Princess began a journey that took them as far north as Nottingham. When the King returned to London the following day and learned that his daughter had fled, he was shaken to the core. 'God help me!' he moaned. 'Even my children have forsaken me.'

In her memoirs Sarah described her flight with the Princess as 'a thing sudden and unconcerted'. This was deliberately misleading as everything had been planned weeks in advance. The staircase had been built, Bishop Compton had been put on the alert, the route had been mapped, and the houses at which the Princess would pass the nights on her journey had been chosen.

When the Princess and her party reached Nottingham they learned that revolts had broken out in many parts of the country. Danby was up in arms in Yorkshire, Devonshire in Derby, Delamere in Cheshire. The Princess was received enthusiastically and a huge dinner was given by Lord Devonshire in her honour. As there was a shortage of attendants, the poet, Colley Cibber, was asked to stand near Lady Churchill's chair and to supply her with whatever she called for. Mr Cibber was overcome by Sarah's appearance. 'At the sound of her voice asking for some wine and water', he wrote,

> all my senses were collected into my eyes, which during the whole enter-tainment wanted no better amusement than stealing now and then the delight of gazing at the fair object so near me. . . . An emanation of beauty, such a commanding aspect of grace, struck me into a regard that had something softer than the most profound respects in it. . . .[48]

Early in December 1688 James declared his willingness to enter into negotiations with William of Orange, who had been keeping very quiet, waiting unobtrusively with his static army to see how things developed. But James was only playing for time so that he could arrange for the Queen and her son to leave for France. Two days after her departure he fled to the coast in the middle of the night. As he crossed the Thames he threw the Great Seal into the river, believing that no business could be done without it, and hoping to plunge his kingdom into some chaos. At the same time he ordered Lord Feversham to disband the army. The Frenchman did as he was told but, as an act of revenge, did not disarm his soldiers, allowing them to roam over the countryside at will, robbing the local citizens at gunpoint.

James did not get far, for he was pulled off his ship and mauled by a group of fishermen who mistook him for a Jesuit. His faithful Gentleman of the Bedchamber, Lord Ailesbury (who had been in his service for many years and was a friend of Lord Churchill), set forth in a coach to bring him back to London. Ailesbury found James unshaven, unfed and under arrest. He secured his release and set about collecting food. When he asked His Majesty if he would like to dine in state, James replied in the affirmative; so a handful of astonished local dignitaries were admitted while his Gentleman of the Bedchamber somehow managed, despite his jack-boots, to serve his King on bended knee. Throughout the day servants arrived: a barber, a cook, a valet carrying fresh clothes, and finally saddle-horses and an escort of Life Guards.

The Prince of Orange was appalled to hear that James had returned to London. The last thing he wanted was to deal with his father-in-law. So he sent a message advising the King to take up residence in Rochester. This was a clever move, as Rochester was the back-door to the Continent. Lord Ailesbury, who was still attending the distraught monarch, begged him repeatedly not to leave England, but James was convinced that he would be sent to the Tower 'which no king has ever quitted except for the grave'. Insisting that it was his duty to preserve his royal presence from such a fate, he made a second attempt to leave his kingdom and this time succeeded. He sailed for France on 23 December 1688, never again to return to his native land.

Five

William and Mary

No perilous undertaking has ever unfolded more methodically, even prosaically, than the Prince of Orange's invasion of England. With scarcely a shot fired, James had fled across the Channel, enabling William to fulfil the main purpose of his intervention – he gave the French Ambassador twenty-four hours to pack his things, making it clear that England was committed to the alliance against France.

But there were other things to settle. William summoned a Convention, explaining to one of his generals, Prince Waldeck, 'that according to law there can be no Parliament if there is no king; but the Convention will do pretty much the same as Parliament. . . .' William's sagacity lay in his ability to keep his mouth firmly shut; he watched over the scene in silence, never proferring an opinion unless asked. 'I must remain passive in the whole affair,' he continued to Waldeck, 'without having spoken of it to anyone, although I have been extremely tormented to do so. Indeed, if I had wished to give the least encouragement I am persuaded that they would have proclaimed me King, a thing I do not covet, not having come here for that end. . . .'[1]

Without realizing it, Lady Churchill confirmed William's reluctance to grasp power when she tells us again that she discounted him as a possible ruler. 'I do solemnly protest', she wrote,

that . . . I was so very simple a creature that I never once dreamed of his being King. Having never read, nor employed my time in anything but playing cards, and having no ambition myself, I imagined that the Prince of Orange's sole design was to provide for the safety of his own country by obliging King James to keep the laws of ours, and that he would go back as soon as he had made us all happy. . . .[2]

One must accept Sarah's testimony with reservation, for even if we look upon her as the giddiest of card-players, she must have understood that when her husband threw in his lot with William of Orange the Churchills' future would not be altogether promising if the *ancien régime* was re-established. However, Sarah was not alone in discounting the Prince as a contender for the throne. Most Tories talked of a Regency, but this idea was rejected by William and defeated in the Convention Parliament by fifty-one votes to forty-nine – with Lord Churchill and several of his friends taking care to abstain.

The next most popular suggestion was that Mary of Orange (the natural successor if James and his son were ruled out) should reign as Queen. Once again, William objected, saying that he would not be 'his wife's gentleman usher'. He then decided to speak out and proposed himself as King. English people, even William's friend and adviser, Dr Gilbert Burnet (soon to become Bishop of Salisbury), were shocked by his callous disregard of Mary's prior rights – although in truth Mary was so subservient that she would agree to anything her husband wanted.

Nevertheless, the aristocratic cabal that had brought William to England dug in its toes and said that William and Mary must rule jointly, although the administrative power could reside in the Prince's hands. William shrewdly insisted, however, that it must be clearly established that if Mary died first he would reign alone. This was more complicated than it sounded, for it rested on Anne's willingness to renounce her right to succeed her sister. When Lord Halifax suggested to William that Churchill 'might perhaps prevail with the Princess of Denmark to give her consent', William bristled with resentment. 'Lord Churchill', he said, 'could not govern him nor his wife as they did the Princess of Denmark.'[3] Nevertheless, Sarah was convinced that it was in Anne's interest to surrender her rights until William's death. 'I quickly found', she explained, '. . . that the settlement would be carried in Parliament, whether the Princess consented or not. So that in reality there was nothing advisable but to yield with good grace.'[4] Later Anne referred to this settlement as her 'abdication' and remarked that it seemed a little strange that less ceremony should be required in passing away the interest of three kingdoms than in the conveyance of a cottage. Sarah was surprised by William's sudden indifference towards Anne and noted cynically 'that the Prince and Princess [of Denmark] had been of more use than they were likely to be again.'[5]

The new King, William III, appointed Churchill a Gentleman of the Bedchamber and in the coronation honours gave him an earldom.

John took the title 'Marlborough' from his great-aunt's husband who had been killed in a sea battle with the Dutch in 1665. Even more important, William confirmed Churchill as Lieutenant-General and assigned him the task of reconstructing the English army with particular regard to the five regiments of Horse and three of Foot that had been raised by James and officered by Roman Catholics. Although the eighty-year-old Marshal Schomberg (a Protestant who had left Louis XIV's service when the Edict of Nantes was revoked) was nominally William's Commander-in-Chief, and William Bentinck, who had served the Prince since boyhood, was the King's right-hand man, neither interfered with Marlborough's decisions. Indeed, Schomberg remarked drily to Lord Ailesbury: 'My Lord Churchill proposes all, I am sent for to say the general consents, and Monsieur Bentinck is the secretary for to write all.'[6]

Churchill's task of weeding out and replacing James's Catholic officers proved to be even more remunerative than the expansion of the army under James. The unfortunate Catholics, by their very dismissal, forfeited reimbursement from the sale of the commissions; instead the payments went to Churchill. 'The harvest my Lord Churchill made by this was vast,' wrote Lord Ailesbury in his memoirs,

> for all is sold. Colonel Selwin of the Foot Guards, of little merit and service, obtained a regiment and Governor of Tilbury etc.; and his footman told one of mine that his master gave him twice a purse of a thousand guineas to hold for him until his master entered into that lord's lodgings at the Cockpit.[7]

Lord Marlborough continued to reap his golden harvest for some time as the King decided to expand the army and added eighteen new regiments of Foot and four of Horse.

When people congratulated the Marlboroughs on their good fortune, Sarah had a tendency to toss her head and say that the reports were exaggerated. Lord Ailesbury visited them in St Albans and walked in the garden with the talkative thirty-year-old Sarah, who exclaimed: 'Lord [a word common with her] they do keep such a noise at our wealth. I do assure you that it doth not exceed £70,000 and what will that come to when half is laid out in land?'[8] She then went on to talk about the cost of providing for her son and daughters, intimating that £70,000 was barely enough to keep the wolf from the door. In these days of inflation it is not possible to estimate the purchasing power of this sum, but we no longer need to think of the Churchills as an impoverished couple!

Their newly found riches, however, did not result in the slightest alteration in their way of life. They continued to live in the pretty manor-house they had built at St Albans and in London still had no house of their own. They lived in the few rooms at the Cockpit and used John's bachelor lodgings on Jermyn Street for their children when they came to London. They did not even keep carriages and horses, preferring to hire what they needed. The truth was that neither John nor Sarah could bear to 'waste' money; and luxuries of every kind came into this category. Their aims were perfectly clear: to leave their son an inheritance and to provide their numerous daughters with handsome enough dowries to make good matches. Sarah now had one son and four daughters, the last two girls, Elizabeth and Mary, having been born in 1687 and 1689.

King William was fully aware of the vital contribution that Marlborough had made to the success of the invasion, and had a high opinion of his ability; yet he made no attempt to draw closer to him. The truth was that William had none of the affability of his Stuart predecessors. He suffered from ill-health and, as Bishop Burnet pointed out, 'he was apt to be peevish', and to conceal his fretfulness 'put him under a necessity of being very much in his closet'.[9] He was thought to have a tubercular lung, was afflicted with asthma and was partially crippled.

Although Prince William's mother and wife were English, he disliked England; and although his Dutch boyhood had been regimented and unhappy, he perversely adored Holland. His father had died before he was born and his anguished and pregnant mother had draped the empty nursery in black. Even the cradle was black down to the rockers. This sombre introduction to life foreshadowed the pattern of William's youth. During his early years he lived in the Palace of the Woods at The Hague, but when he was nine his mother died of smallpox and he was brought up by his austere and aged grandmother, Amalia of Solms. He made several visits to the sophisticated Court of his English uncle, Charles II, but the courtiers found the puny Prince something of a trial for he refused the French wine that was offered to him and asked for Holland gin. Even worse, he went to bed each night at ten.

Despite the care he took of his constitution, he nearly died of smallpox (as both his parents had done) during the period when the French were in partial occupation of his country. The 'pox' did not erupt and the poison spread through his body until there seemed no hope for him. 'His physician declared', wrote a biographer, 'that if some healthy young person who had not had the disease would enter the bed and hold the Prince in his arms for some time, the animal warmth might cause the postules to appear. . . .'[10] This announcement caused consternation, for nobody cared to be a guinea pig. Suddenly, one of the Prince's pages, the handsome, aristocratic William Bentinck, stepped forward. He did as he was asked, but caught the disease and nearly died himself. In the end both he and his master survived and Bentinck became the Prince's favourite, which he had remained ever since.

When William married Charles II's niece, Princess Mary, he treated her ruthlessly. Upon reaching Holland he dismissed her English servants and kept her under strict confinement until he was satisfied that he had broken her will and that she saw everything through his eyes. She became so servile that she ignored her filial obligations and helped her husband in the conspiracy against her father. The Princess's compliance was surprising as she deeply resented the fact that her Lady-in-Waiting, Elizabeth Villiers, had become the Prince's *maîtresse en titre*. What made the relationship very odd was that William disliked the company of women and paid scant attention to Elizabeth. In sophisticated Paris, gossips pointed to Bentinck, who had moved even closer to the Prince by marrying Elizabeth's sister, and whispered that the female connections of both men were simply a cover for homosexuality.

King William's rough manners and unconcealed contempt for the English did not endear him to Whitehall. The slights he administered bordered on insults yet he showed no concern. He upset people by banishing from London the 1st Guards and Coldstream battalions, resplendent in their scarlet uniforms and bearskins, and installing his own drab Dutch soldiers to pace the beats of Whitehall and St James's. He was just as tactless inside the palace. A young page, Dillon, who later rose to be a general, wrote in 1689 that,

> he never saw English noblemen dine with the Prince of Orange, but only the Duke of Schomberg who was always placed at his right hand and his Dutch general officers. The English noblemen that were there stood behind the Prince of Orange's chair but never were admitted to eat or sit.[11]

Lord Marlborough and the other English lords-in-waiting were 'dismissed when the dinner was half over'. Dillon goes on to say that he was present for several days and never heard the King utter a word at table. When he asked the King's newest page, the handsome young Arnold van Keppel (who would one day supersede Bentinck as the favourite), if William never spoke, Keppel replied 'that he talked enough at night over his bottle when he has got with his friends.'[12]

William's greed at table prompted the ladies to refer to him as 'a low Dutch bear'. However, the Prince's Dutch friends had no reason to complain: he not only gave them titles, but large estates from the Crown lands. Bentinck became Earl of Portland; Zulestein, Earl of Rochford; Ruvigny, Earl of Galway; old Schomberg, Duke of Schomberg; young Schomberg, Duke of Leinster. Only one Englishman was the recipient of his largesse: the good-looking, thoroughly undistinguished Henry Sidney, known as 'Beau' Sidney, became the Earl of Romney.

No matter how gauche and disappointing the King was in private, his public activities commanded deep admiration. Still only thirty-nine years old, he had spent most of his life fighting against the repeated attempts of Louis XIV to extend his frontiers to the Rhine. Indeed the heart of the weak and misshapen Prince of Orange burned with a fire that forged him into one of Europe's greatest leaders. Perhaps no one has ever surpassed William in statecraft or, for that matter, in the duplicity that made the statecraft so successful. The behaviour of Princess Anne and her simple-minded husband pale in comparison to that of William and Mary, whose protestations of loyalty to James, even when the invasion fleet was assembling in Dutch ports, persisted until the eleventh hour. Later innumerable Jacobite ballads were written about

> Mary and William, George and
> Anne
> Four such children never had man.

However, there was no deceit when it came to William's fierce animosity toward Louis XIV. 'It almost seemed that a being had been created', wrote the twentieth-century Winston Churchill,

> for the sole purpose of resisting the domination of France and the Great King. His public hatred of France and his personal quarrel with Louis XIV constituted the main theme of his life. All his exertions were diverted against the tyrant who not only had encompassed the ruin of the Dutch Republic but had actually seized and dragooned the small principality of Orange from which he had sprung. . . .[13]

Even during the months that William was making himself King of England he was busy assembling a coalition to resist Louis's capture of Philippsburg. He found no difficulty in collecting allies because that very winter – 1688–9 – Louis embarked on a 'scorched earth' policy, destroying and burning dozens of beautiful and innocent German towns and villages – Heidelberg, Mannheim, Heilbron, Spier, Worms, Tübingen, Eslingen and many others.

These 'atrocities' were new for the times, and aroused such hatred against Louis that William's coalition expanded rapidly.

What was the French King aiming at? The answer was both simple and mistaken: he wanted to compel the German states to accept *permanently* the gains made by France's 'reunions' which the Truce of Ratisbon had confirmed for only twenty years. Louis explained to his ministers that his war was a blitz – something 'short and sharp'. In fact the war lasted nine years and is sometimes referred to quixotically as the 'War of the English Succession'.

Very little worked out as Louis planned. He promised England's deposed King, James II, 6,000 seasoned French soldiers (in exchange for 6,000 Irish soldiers) to make a landing in Ireland as the first step towards regaining his throne; from there the way would be open for an invasion of England. Furthermore, Louis was confident that James's presence in Ireland would prevent the English from joining his enemies on the Continent. But the opposite happened. As soon as James made a reconnaissance – landing in March 1689 with a few French military advisers – England declared war on France and dispatched an army across the Channel. King William gave Marlborough command of 8,000 British troops and instructed him to join Prince Waldeck's army of Dutch and Swedish soldiers on the Rhine.

At long last Lord Marlborough, now thirty-nine years old, was able to follow his chosen profession. Apart from Sedgemoor, he had not done any fighting for over ten years, and then it had been on the side of France. He knew that opportunities in life were few and far between and, when he left England, made up his mind to seize any chance, no matter how hazardous, to distinguish himself. Although at first the situation did not look promising, the god of Luck did not desert him. While the Imperialists under the Duke of Lorraine were manœuvring on the upper Rhine, while the Spanish were advancing on Courtrai and the Elector of Brandenburg was preparing to attack Bonn, Prince Waldeck's army (of which Marlborough was part) was motionless, awaiting developments. The very fact, however, that Waldeck was operating in Flanders meant that Louis was obliged to keep the French divisions opposite him at full strength to prevent an incursion into France. These troops were commanded by the haughty Duc d'Humières who was determined to have a fight. In August, Waldeck crossed the River Sambre and settled in rolling and wooded country near the village of Walcourt, nine miles from Charleroi and thirty miles south of Brussels. Next morning, he ordered Marlborough to send out a number of foraging parties so that he could test French combatitiveness.

Marlborough protected his raiders with a battalion of English infantry, composed of 600 men, and Dutch cavalry numbering another 300. The officer-in-charge, Colonel Hodges, saw a French detachment advancing over a hill and as it came nearer realized that it was no isolated unit but the vanguard of the whole French army. Cannons were fired to recall the foragers and to alert Waldeck's camp, two miles away. Marlborough appeared on the scene within a few minutes and ordered his troops to delay the enemy advance until Waldeck had time to occupy the town of Walcourt and post his army in advantageous positions. Hodges's men, firing cannon and mortars, managed to hold up the French troops for nearly two hours; then they made an orderly retreat to higher ground.

Marshal d'Humières was exasperated by the inconvenience he had suffered, and perhaps excited by the sharp fighting that had taken place. At any rate, he decided to teach the enemy a lesson. Although Walcourt was surrounded by a heavy wall and stood on top of a hill favourable to the defenders, d'Humières ordered eight battalions of the French Guards to carry the town by assault. His troops were wonderfully brave, but Marlborough's batteries were well placed and the attacking force was raked by fire. Soon the ramparts were strewn with over 500 dead and wounded.

By now d'Humières was so furious at being baulked that he lost control of himself. Like a gambler refusing to accept defeat, he threw all his remaining resources into the combat: in this case his whole army. This was the moment for which Marlborough – and Prince Waldeck – had been waiting. General Slangenberg led the Dutch infantry from the western side while Marlborough attacked from the east. Placing himself at the head of his cavalry, composed of Life Guards and Blues, and supported by two English infantry regiments, Marlborough charged the French right flank, inflicting enormous injury. As night fell d'Humières withdrew with a loss of six guns and 2,000 of his best soldiers. His ill-starred attack not only cost him his command – in the next campaign he was replaced by Marshal Luxembourg – but found him special mention in military text-books. 'This combat', wrote a French critic, 'should never be cited save as an example to avoid.'[14]

Marlborough led a charmed life. Although he never spared himself and always appeared in the forefront of every battle, he was not wounded. Indeed his audacious conduct was singled out repeatedly for praise. '. . . the Earl of Marlborough', Waldeck wrote to King William, 'is assuredly one of the most gallant men I know.' He went on to add that Marlborough had displayed in this one battle 'greater military capacity than do most generals after a long series of wars'.[15] William wrote to Marlborough in unusually flattering terms, giving him full credit for the successful action, and telling him to 'rest assured that your conduct will induce me to confer on you still further marks of my esteem and friendship.'[16] This praise was not excessive as Walcourt was the only sizeable gain won by the Dutch or English that year.

When Marlborough returned from the Continent in the autumn of 1689 he found that his wife had become a bone of contention between Queen Mary and Princess Anne. The Queen had never liked the Churchills. She felt that they were ambitious and untrustworthy, and resented the ascendancy which Sarah had over her sister. At one time Anne had been devoted to Mary, but now she yearned for Lady Marlborough and, when the latter was away, sat moping or writing her letters. Sarah gives different reasons for the division between the Princesses. In her memoirs she tells us that, when Mary arrived from Holland, the royal sisters met at Greenwich 'with transports of affection which soon fell off and coldness ensued'. This was because their 'characters and humours' were very different.

> It was indeed impossible [continued Sarah] that they should be very agreeable companions to each other because Queen Mary grew weary of anybody who would not talk a great deal and the Princess was so silent that she rarely spoke more than was necessary to answer a question.[17]

Even their marriages had played a trick on them by casting them into roles contrary to what might have been expected. Whereas Mary's strong-willed husband demanded submissiveness, Anne's consort was so preoccupied with the pleasures of eating and drinking that he gladly left all responsibility to his wife.

Nevertheless, the royal sisters were still on friendly terms when Anne gave birth to a son in July 1689 – her sixth pregnancy in seven years and the first of her children to reach boyhood. Everyone was determined to avoid Mary of Modena's mistake and all the right people were summoned to the delivery-room. 'Queen Mary was present the whole time, about three hours,' reported the London *Gazette*, 'and the King, with most of the persons of quality about the Court, came into Her Royal Highness's bedchamber before she was delivered.'[18]

The birth of an heir to the throne greatly enhanced Anne's importance, and when she asked for new quarters in Whitehall she expected them to be given to her. She already had been assigned the luxurious

Whitehall apartment that once had belonged to Charles II's mistress, the Duchess of Portsmouth; she now wanted the adjoining apartment for her servants. But the Queen told her that these rooms had been promised to the Earl of Devonshire and no decision could be taken until he had made up his mind. Sarah caused trouble by suggesting that the Earl was deliberately hanging onto his option in the hope that he could secure the Portsmouth lodgings himself. So Anne replied coldly that she had no wish 'for my Lord Devonshire's leavings'. At the same time she asked for the palace at Richmond, where she had been brought up as a child and where she wanted the newly born Duke of Gloucester to live, away from the noise and dirt of central London. But this request also was refused as Catherine, yet another one of the Villiers sisters, held the lease and was unwilling to give it up.

The Princess was particularly upset by this last refusal as little Gloucester had been seized by convulsion fits a month after his birth and the doctors hourly expected his demise. When he surprised everyone and recovered, Anne was determined to take him to the good air of the country. Eventually, she rented Camden House – near Kensington Palace, the residence that William and Mary were remodelling for their own occupancy.

These changes imposed a severe financial burden on Anne. William had not been in the least generous as far as his sister-in-law was concerned. He had confiscated the whole of James II's huge private income (mainly from his lands in Ireland) and not assigned her any part of it. Sarah Marlborough and other members of the Cockpit circle felt that Anne should be given a parliamentary grant that would free her from William's control. It was unprecedented for an heir to the throne to be independent of the reigning monarch, but it was also unprecedented for an heir to sacrifice hereditary rights as Anne had done.

The motion was introduced in the House of Commons in March 1689 but not debated until December. At first the Queen refrained from alluding to it, but when she saw that Anne was not going to bring up the matter herself she confronted her at a Court gathering. 'She asked her', wrote Sarah,

> what was the meaning of these proceedings? To which the Princess answered, she heard her friends had a mind to make her some settlement. The Queen hastily replied, with a very imperious air, 'Pray what friends have you but the King and me?'

Anne was infuriated by this remark. When she returned to the Cockpit that night, Sarah tells us: 'I never saw her express so much resentment as she did at this usage.'[19]

That autumn the hostility between the Court and the Cockpit became common knowledge as both sides solicited support from the House of Commons. The Queen's jealousy of Sarah's influence over her once-docile sister turned to bitter animosity. Quite rightly, no doubt, she blamed Sarah for Anne's intransigence, while others suggested that Lord Marlborough was behind the whole affair and had his own sinister reasons for wishing to see the Princess establish an independent position. Lord Wharton, a leading Whig minister, 'warned the King that the design was plain to give the Princess a great revenue and make her independent upon your Majesty that she might be the head of a great party against you.'[20]

Sarah's closest friend in the Cockpit circle, Lady Fitzharding (formerly Mrs Berkeley), told her that if she did not 'put an end to measures so disagreeable to the King and Queen' it would spell the 'ruin' of her family; and, as Lady Fitzharding was a great gossip and a sister of Elizabeth Villiers, the warning should not have been ignored. Nevertheless, Sarah refused to heed it, insisting that she was only doing her duty by her mistress. The King did not intervene until the eleventh hour. The motion came before the House on 16 December 1689, and the following day William sent Lord Wharton and Lord Shrewsbury to persuade Princess Anne to drop the matter. Queen Mary wrote in her memoirs that when Shrewsbury first approached his long-standing friend, Marlborough, the latter 'begged he would not own he found him as his wife . . . was like a madwoman and said the Princess would retire if her friends did not support her'.[21]

Furthermore the affair was already before Parliament. Indeed the very next day the House voted Anne an annual grant of £50,000, a sum so generous that it represented a humiliating defeat for the Court. By now the argument had become something more than a family quarrel over money; the extent of the Princess's victory revealed a large following in the country. Perhaps Lord Wharton's warning of a 'design' with the Marlboroughs behind it had some truth in it. In a private memorandum of 3 March 1690, the Queen wrote that the 'Revolution government' was threatened by a republican party, a Jacobite party, 'and I have reason to fear that my sister is forming a third'.[22]

The King was too busy with the war to worry about his sister-in-law. Louis's diversion in Ireland, where his 6,000 soldiers had landed, was meeting with success. Although William had sent two of his best generals across the Irish Channel to deal with James II, their campaign had been disastrous. By the end of the year James reigned over most of the island except for the Protestant settlements in the north and even Charlemont, in Ulster, was under Jacobite control. It was not surprising that Parliament was fearful that Louis might launch a two-pronged attack on England from Ireland and France. Members begged the King to abandon the idea of taking command of the army in Flanders and to deal first with James. William bowed to the pressure and personally led 15,000 men across the Irish Sea to reinforce Schomberg. Thus Louis, at a cost of only 6,000 French soldiers, succeeded in preventing the King from taking part in the main European battle.

William appointed Marlborough Commander-in-Chief in England and gave him a seat on the Council of Nine, which ran the country under the Queen's direction. Mary's animosity towards Sarah had become so great that it now included Sarah's husband: 'I can never either trust or esteem him,' she told her husband.[23] Nevertheless, she always did as William instructed and took care to get on well with him. Thus Marlborough, who had scored the only success the previous year, was left kicking his heels in London while William's army on the Continent and his navy off the English coast suffered two resounding reverses within a few weeks of one another. Prince Waldeck, who commanded the troops in Flanders, was routed by General Luxembourg while the combined fleets of England and Holland met with a crushing defeat in a sea battle off Beachy Head. 'The Dutch got the honour, the French the advantage, and the English the shame,' reported a London newsletter.[24] There was no time, however, to brood on the shame. Although the Admiralty ordered new ships to be built as speedily as possible, England's coasts were now open to the French, and the population could think of nothing but the likelihood of an invasion.

Indeed, if it had not been for King William's splendid victory in Ireland, it is probable that the 'two-pronged invasion' everyone had talked about for so long actually would have taken place. This was one of William's only triumphs in his nine years of waging war. Taking command of his soldiers in person, he took the field against James II's army which was covering Dublin near the River Boyne. The Irish troops were outnumbered and fought badly; after an hour and a half they broke and fled, and James followed suit. Escorted by 200 cavalry soldiers he made full speed for Dublin and the following day continued to Kinsale where he embarked for France.

At this point Marlborough proposed taking an invasion force to Ireland to seize the ports of Cork and Kinsale, and thus prevent the French from reinforcing their Irish allies. Most members of Queen

Mary's Council vetoed the project because they feared a French assault across the English Channel, but King William overruled them and authorized the expedition. The day before Marlborough departed, Sarah bore her last child, whom she named Charles. Her husband wrote to her from Portsmouth before embarking:

> The regiments are all here, but as yet no more of the Fleet, but I believe tomorrow morning we shall have them, and then I shall lose no time in shipping off the men, so that I may get the sooner back again to you whom I love beyond my own life; and if you are just to me you will believe that I have no pleasure in this world equal to that of thinking you love me. As ambitious as you sometimes think me, I do assure you I would not live in this place to be emperor of it. I shall have no true satisfaction till I see you again; therefore if you have kindness for me you will have care of your dear self.[25]

This was Marlborough's first command and it resulted in a swift and imposing victory. However, the Dutch commander, General Ginkel, was not very co-operative. According to a prearranged plan, Marlborough expected 5,000 English troops from him; instead he received only a handful of English soldiers and 5,000 Danes, Dutch and Huguenots under the command of the Duke of Würtemburg. Although Würtemburg was inferior to Marlborough in rank, he was superior in birth and claimed the right to direct operations. Fortunately Marlborough managed to cope with this seemingly 'insuperable' problem. As there was no time to appeal to King William, he proposed that they divide the command, taking alternative days. They drew lots and when the first day fell to Marlborough he chose 'Würtemburg' for the password. The Duke was so flattered that he not only returned the compliment next day but from then on quietly followed Marlborough's lead. Among the English troops was the latter's brother, Colonel Charles Churchill, who distinguished himself by leading the infantry across the tidal estuary at Cork without mishap.

Within twenty-three days Marlborough had captured both Cork and Kinsale, achieving more, Field-Marshal Wolseley wrote two centuries later,

> than all William's Dutch commanders had done both in Ireland and abroad during the whole of the previous year. . . . All things considered, this campaign of Marlborough's was the best planned and the neatest, as well as the most successful military operation in William's reign.[26]

Marlborough's young friend, the Duke of Grafton (the son of Lady

Castlemaine and Charles II), was killed aboard one of the troop ships; but the Duke of Berwick, the son of Arabella Churchill and James II, who served with the Jacobite army, lived to fight another day.

Marlborough left his brother Charles as Governor of Kinsale, but all the Churchills seem to have had an eye on the main chance. George, the naval captain, had been sent to the Tower by the House of Commons the previous year for disreputable conduct concerning convoy money, and before long Charles was under grave suspicion for the embezzlement of stores and supplies taken at Kinsale. When an official enquiry took place he insisted that what was missing had been given to him by the Jacobite governor, but no one believed such a bizarre story.

Marlborough returned to London with a greatly enhanced reputation. The skill and originality of his tactics, hallmarks of his genius, not only delighted his contemporaries, but went into the military text-books for special attention. The King, who longed for glory on the battlefield but lacked the Englishman's ingenuity, paid him a double-edged compliment. 'No officer living,' he said, 'who has seen so little service as my Lord Marlborough, is so fit for great commands.'[27] Unfortunately the great commands were not forthcoming as it was part and parcel of William's policy to keep all important military posts in the hands of his Dutch officers. He was unwilling to allow any Englishman, particularly an ambitious Englishman like Marlborough, to become a hero on the battlefield and a powerful figure at home.

Perhaps the King was jealous of Marlborough, the 'inexperienced' Englishman who seemed to know instinctively how to win a battle, for he refused to bestow any honours on him. When the Prince and Princess of Denmark requested the Garter for Marlborough, William did not even answer; and when he was asked to appoint him Master of Ordnance – a post that Marlborough had always coveted because of the financial return – he pointedly gave it to the handsome and inconsequential 'Beau Sidney', his one and only English favourite.

King William's high-handed attitude, underlined by his indifference to his English subjects, was making him increasingly unpopular. He was not only remote in spirit but also in body, as he had moved away from Whitehall because the dampness from the Thames was bad for his asthma. He settled down in the great Tudor palace near Richmond, Hampton Court, where he employed Sir Christopher Wren to build a magnificent series of State Rooms around the Fountain Court. Lord Halifax grumbled about the long

journey from Whitehall and complained that it was 'very incon-
venient for the Council to meet the King there', whereupon William
snapped back, 'Do you wish to see me dead?'[28] Eventually, however,
the sovereign bowed to mounting pressure and purchased Nottingham House, a mansion in Kensington which he directed Christopher Wren to extend and adapt as a royal residence. Thus Kensington Palace was created and became William's chief abode.

Although the King made a practice of spending one or two nights
a week at Whitehall, Stuart gaiety was a thing of the past. A grim,
new atmosphere prevailed at Court. William sat through meals
uncommunicative and scowling. He still refused to admit
Englishmen into his circle and still made it clear that the only
company he enjoyed was that of his own hard-drinking countrymen.
His ungracious manners offended Princess Anne and her well-
meaning husband. Prince George had taken part at his own expense
in William's Irish campaign, fighting side by side with him in the
battle of the Boyne. But William apparently found Prince George so
boring that he never once invited him to ride in the royal coach,
taking 'no more notice of him', wrote Sarah, 'than if he had been a
page of the backstairs.'[29] Even worse, a few months later, when the
Prince volunteered for service with the navy and had put his
equipage and baggage aboard the ship to which he was assigned, he
received a peremptory order from the King refusing him permission
to sail.

It is not difficult to imagine the discord that this created. Princess
Anne, the Churchills, and even Prince George, had all taken dangerous risks to put the Crown on William's head and had every reason
to feel affronted by his apparent ingratitude. In letters to Sarah, the
Princess began to refer to William as 'a monster', 'an abortion'; and
Sarah, who was piqued that John had not been given the Garter for
his victories at Cork and Kinsale (although Anne herself had requested the King to bestow it), replied in equally scathing terms. The two
ladies now used pseudonyms in writing to each other as the Princess
wanted Sarah to feel a sense of true 'equality'. Although not intentional it was also a precaution in case the letters were intercepted.
The Princess became 'Mrs Morley', Sarah 'Mrs Freeman' and the
King 'Mr Caliban'. Anne's very dull and devoted husband, Prince
George, refused to involve himself in controversy, and overcame his
irritation by an excessive and happy indulgence in good English
spirits. Anne on the other hand turned her attention back to gambling at basset and the pleasures of the table. About this time a ditty
was being sung:

> King William thinks all,
> Queen Mary talks all,
> Prince George drinks all,
> And Princess Anne eats all.

While witty jingles at the expense of the royal family were being recited in taverns and coffee-houses, rumours were growing that James II would soon be back on his throne. Many Tories had come to regret his departure. They were exasperated by William's boorish manners and his blatant preference for everything Dutch. Indeed, his own particular shortcomings seemed just as distasteful as James's religious bias, and of the two evils they might as well have the 'true King'. Talk of a Stuart restoration, however, did not spring merely from the wishful thinking of a disgruntled minority but from the ever present possibility of a French assault. Since the French naval victory at Beachy Head the previous year English shores had been wide open to invasion. When James departed from England 50,000 people (a large number of whom were Irish) followed him to France. Jacobite agents were recruited from these expatriates and many of them now swarmed back to the island kingdom to gather intelligence for their master. James had set up his Court at St Germain, near Versailles, and was treated by Louis XIV as grandly as though he were still on the throne.

The presence of the Jacobites in England (even Jacobite agents) was not proscribed and spies found themselves in the agreeable position of being able to contact whomever they pleased. Indeed the dividing-line between the two sides recognized no boundaries and cut through hundreds of families. For instance, even though Lord Shrewsbury had been one of the 'immortal seven' who had invited William to England, his mother was one of James's most vociferous supporters; Sarah Marlborough's sister, Frances, was the wife of the Catholic Duke of Tyrconnel, James's Governor-General of Ireland; and Lord Feversham, who had been Commander-in-Chief of James's army when William invaded, was now allowed back in Whitehall because Charles's widow, Queen Catherine, wanted him as her chamberlain. Last, but certainly not least, Marlborough's nephew James Fitzjames, now Duke of Berwick, was a general in the French army.

Many people talked to Jacobite agents out of straight curiosity. They were eager for news about the possibility of an invasion and liked to judge for themselves James's chances of retrieving his throne. The agents reported to St Germain that they were in touch with most of the leading men of the day, including Lord Shrewsbury, Admiral

Russell, Lord Godolphin and Lord Marlborough. We do not know how accurate these claims were, but some of them may have deemed it expedient to have a pardon up their sleeves in case of a restoration. They expressed regret for the part they had played and promised to make amends at some later, unspecified date. Others felt it worthwhile to keep tabs on what James (and his French allies) were planning for the future. An agent named Harry Buckeley, who had served as James's courier and who, of course, had known Marlborough and Godolphin for many years, informed St Germain that he was in contact with them. Indeed, he sent pleasing reports describing how much these gentlemen missed their former master and repeated other niceties suggesting that James still had a large following in England.

However piqued Marlborough might have been from time to time, he could not complain that he had not been rewarded for his part in the revolution. William had given him an earldom, promoted him to Lieutenant-General and appointed him one of the Lord Justices who assisted the Queen in running the country when William was abroad. Far more important, the King recognized Marlborough's ability as a soldier; in 1689 he had put him in charge of the British troops on the Continent and in 1690 had allowed him to mount an offensive in Ireland. But in 1691 Marlborough's star suddenly seemed to lose its ascendancy, and he began to feel that his career was moving backwards not forwards.

Privately Marlborough was critical of the unimaginative way in which the war was being fought. What he was striving for was a high military command that would enable him to determine – or at least influence – the strategy of the army as a whole. He was perfectly willing to earn his promotions step by step, but the campaign of 1691 was so lackadaisical (except for a burst of fighting at the beginning and end) that there was no chance for him to employ his splendid troops, even in the smallest undertaking. The French general, Marshal Luxembourg, appeared before the fortress of Mons with 100,000 men a month before King William expected him and took the citadel with almost no opposition. After that, the two armies spent their time manoeuvring and reconnoitring within sight of each other, happy to think that if nothing was being gained, at least nothing was being lost. In the middle of September, when the King expected Marshal Luxembourg to retire to winter quarters (and retired himself to the palace of Het Loo near The Hague), the Frenchman suddenly mounted a cavalry charge, routing the Dutch cavalry and cutting them down as they fled. Before the Allies could gather themselves for a counter-attack, Luxembourg had disengaged and withdrawn for the season. The verdict was that King William had 'entered the field too late and quitted it too soon.'[30] In Paris a cartoon appeared showing the rising sun over a dead lion.

Marlborough had been forced to stand on the side-lines watching the missed opportunities, convinced that if he had been in command he would not have let the enemy off so easily. One of William's generals, the Prince of Vaudemont, seemed convinced of it too, for when the King asked him his opinion of English generals he replied:

> Kirk has fire, Lanier thought, Mackay skill and Colchester bravery; but there is something inexpressible in the Earl of Marlborough. All their virtues seem to be united in his single person. I have lost my wonted skill in physiognomy if any subject of your Majesty can ever attain such a height of military glory as that to which this combination of sublime perfections must raise him.

'Cousin,' the King replied politely, no doubt controlling a surge of jealousy, 'You have done your part in answering my question, and I believe the Earl of Marlborough will do his best to verify your prediction.'[31]

King William brought Portland and Marlborough back to England in his own coach. On the road from Margate to London, at Shooter's Hill, the carriage overturned and Marlborough announced in a funereal voice that his neck was broken. William snapped back that this could not be so 'since he could still speak'.[32] This was a convincing rejoinder and, when the vehicle was righted, Marlborough climbed back dazed but unhurt.

Unfortunately the long hours of travel did not bring Marlborough any closer to his sovereign. Indeed, the conversation on this particular journey may have led to the rift that sprang up between the two men with grave consequences for the future. There is little doubt that William discussed his plans for the military campaign of the coming spring. Was it at this time that he voiced the idea that he would give the command of the British troops to General Ginkel? And talked about taking Marlborough to Flanders with him as a Lieutenant-General attached to his own person? This proposal, whenever it was made, fell on stony ground. Marlborough had no intention of travelling about with the King as a mere adviser, particularly as he knew that he would have no real authority yet would be blamed for any failure. This was not at all what he hoped for; perhaps he never would be given a real chance to display his military skills, and to win the *gloire* that he learned to value when he was serving in the French army!

Marlborough's apprehension gradually turned into suspicion and he became convinced that the King was deliberately barring his way. We do not know what brought him to this conclusion (perhaps Sarah had a hand in it), only that he reached it. He was so resentful that he behaved in an entirely uncharacteristic way. He threw caution to the winds and began to hit out in every direction. He referred to the Earl of Portland as 'a wooden fellow' and told the King to his face that it was a mistake to reward Dutch favourites by bestowing English Crown property on them. On this occasion William turned his back on Marlborough. Our hero was undeterred. He talked openly in army messes against the policy of employing Dutch officers to command English troops; and once even suggested that the officers band together and make a joint protest. All these criticisms got back to William, sometimes through Lord Portland, sometimes through Lady Fitzharding, whose sister, Elizabeth Villiers, told the King.

William III was used to plain words from his notable subjects and remained on reasonable terms with Marlborough. Queen Mary, however, flew into a rage when she learned, early in January 1692, that Princess Anne was making Lady Marlborough an annual payment of £1,000 out of her parliamentary grant. She summoned Anne and asked her angrily if she thought that was what parliamentary grants were for? As we know, Mary always believed the worst of Sarah. For some time she had suspected the favourite of deliberately fleecing Anne of thousands of pounds a year at cards; and news of the large yearly salary seemed to be the last straw.* After berating her sister for some time, she threatened to use her influence to see that her parliamentary grant of £50,000 was cut in half. But Anne knew that Mary had no power to do this and refused to be rattled.

The next morning a far more serious event took place. Two hours after the King's levee, when Marlborough as Gentleman of the Bedchamber had the duty of handing His Majesty his shirt, Lord Nottingham was sent to find him. Without a word of explanation he told Marlborough that the King no longer required his services and that he must sell his offices and consider himself banned from Court. Admiral Russell, England's most illustrious sailor, was so angry that he expostulated 'with great rudeness to King William on Marlborough's disgrace, demanding to see the proofs of his fault, and reminding the King in a tone "not very agreeable" that it was he who

---

* The Princess's debts amounted to £50,000, of which £16,000 was said to be owing to Lady Marlborough.

carried the letters between His Majesty and Marlborough before the Revolution.'[33]

This stormy interview had no effect, and the Court continued to buzz with excitement, particularly as the King and Queen refused to make any comment. Indeed, even today we are still not certain what sparked off the King's action as Marlborough himself never offered an explanation nor, for that matter, ever referred to the incident. Later Bishop Burnet wrote that the King told him that

> he had very good reasons to believe that Marlborough had made his peace with King James and was engaged in a correspondence with France; it is certain he was doing all he could to set on a faction in the army and nation against the Dutch and to lessen the King [and that he] as well as his wife, who was so absolute a favourite with the Princess that she seemed to be the mistress of her whole heart and thoughts, were alienating her both from the King and Queen. . . .[34]

Lord Nottingham echoed the same theme, saying that the King had told him that 'he had disgraced Marlborough for sowing dissension and breeding factions in the army and for holding correspondence with the Court of St Germain', but added that Marlborough had 'rendered such valuable service' that he had no wish 'to push him too far.'[35] The Prussian Minister, Bonet, followed suit, but blamed Marlborough's misfortunes on 'an excessive confidence in his own talent and from his belief that he could not be done without.'[36]

Although these explanations, inspired by the King, were accepted by historians for over two centuries, it is difficult to believe that an astute politician like William could have been seriously alarmed by Marlborough's contacts with St Germain. Even the Jacobites themselves, who were inclined to clutch at every straw, were sceptical of Marlborough's sincerity. Would he really have wanted to bring back James, the King he had betrayed, to the detriment of 'La Cadette' – the Princess Anne – who offered him his best hope for the future?

It seems clear that it was not James, but Anne, with the Marlboroughs behind her, whom the King regarded as his real threat. Anne had the respect of Church and State and, with Churchill's backing, undoubtedly could command a large following in the army – even the Jacobites might rally to her. This was probably the reason that Marlborough had induced Anne to try to make amends to her father. 'I have been very desirous of some safe opportunity to make you a sincere and humble offer of duty,' she had written to James in December 1691. She then went on to stress her 'repentant thoughts' and to assure her father that 'if wishes could recall what is past I had long since redeemed my fault.'[37]

Although this surprising letter has been cited by many historians, we cannot be sure that it was not a fabrication as the original has never come to light. Whatever the truth, the Queen had always been distrustful of the Marlboroughs and had thought for some time that Anne was capable of taking a political stand against her. After her furious altercation with Anne over Sarah, she probably persuaded William that Marlborough might be toying with the idea of forming an opposition movement around her sister. There was no evidence against Marlborough, and William could only act on suspicion. However, he had not braved the perilous voyage to England to be worsted by an ambitious English general, so he acted swiftly and decisively, accusing Marlborough of communicating with St Germain.

The offices that Marlborough was compelled to sell had yielded him an annual income estimated at £12,000 a year and ended all hope of his taking part in the war. Nevertheless, he presented to the world a bland and imperturbable appearance. Sarah was much angrier, thrashing about and blaming Lord Portland and Elizabeth Villiers for bringing about the débâcle. She knew that she was regarded as her husband's link with Anne and, when she wrote her memoirs, she stated bluntly: 'The disgrace of my Lord Marlborough was designed as a step toward removing me from the Princess Anne.'[38] As far as the King and Queen were concerned, they had succeeded in killing two birds with one stone, for after the disgrace of Sarah's husband it was unthinkable that Sarah could remain with the Princess.

But the unthinkable became a fact. Two weeks later, on 4 February, Anne attended a formal Drawing-Room at Kensington Palace accompanied by Sarah. This was such a violation of prescribed etiquette that the following day the Queen wrote a furious letter to Anne declaring 'that never anybody was suffered to live at Court in Lord Marlborough's circumstances' and that it therefore 'is very unfit that Lady Marlborough should stay with you since that gives her husband so just a pretense for being where he should not.' 'I have all the reason imaginable', the letter continued,

> to look upon your bringing her as the strangest thing that was ever done
> . . . it was very unkind in a sister, would have been very uncivil in an equal
> and . . . I must tell you I know what is due to me, and expect to have it from
> you. 'Tis upon that account I tell you plainly Lady Marlborough must not
> continue with you in the circumstances her lord is. . . .[39]

Anne, with all the stubbornness of her Stuart ancestors, answered this angry letter affectionately but firmly: '. . . there is no misery that I cannot readily resolve to suffer rather than the thought of parting with her [Lady Marlborough].'[40]

The Queen countered by ordering the Marlboroughs to vacate the Cockpit, and Anne moved her household to Syon House, situated on the banks of the Thames about five miles from Whitehall. This lovely house was owned by the Duke of Somerset, so rich and powerful that royalty held no fears for him. The Queen countered again, taking the initiative, this time by removing the guards who protected the Prince and Princess, and instructing the soldiers on duty in St James's Park not to stand to arms when either the Prince or Princess of Denmark passed. 'These things', Anne wrote merrily to Sarah, 'are so far from vexing either ye P. or me that they please us extremely.'[41]

Notwithstanding the Princess's good humour, Sarah feared that her continued presence might lead the Princess to even more serious trouble, and on several occasions suggested that Anne let her go. Anne was horrified. '. . . How would all reasonable people despise me,' she wrote to Sarah.

> How would that Dutch abortive [William] laugh at me. . . . No my dear Mrs Freeman, never believe your faithfull Mrs Morley will never submit. She can waite with patience for a Sunshine day and if She does not live to see it She hopes England will Flourish againe. Once more give me leave to beg you would be so kind never to Speake of parting more for lett what ill happen that is ye only thing that can make me miserable.[42]

Nevertheless, Sarah was fearful that further humiliations might be inflicted on Anne and urged her to make a conciliatory gesture to the Queen. On 17 April 1692 the Princess gave birth at Syon House to her seventh child, a son who was christened at once but who died an hour after the ceremony. In deference to Sarah's pleas the Princess sent the sad news to the Queen, who decided impulsively to visit Syon House that very afternoon – but she did not come with any sympathy. 'I could not believe it', Sarah wrote in her memoirs,

> that the Queen upon such Misfortune would come to an only Sister, and never ask her how she did or express the least Concern for her Condition nor so much as take her by the hand. The little word she said was, that she had made the first step in coming to see her, and that she now expected that she would make the next in removing me.[43]

The poor Princess, suffering from the aftermath of a prolonged and difficult labour, and grieving for the loss of yet another child, lay back weakly against the pillow, but she still refused to dismiss Lady Marlborough. When Prince George handed the Queen into her coach, she was so angry that she scarcely said goodbye.

Far more urgent problems, however, awaited Mary's attention and temporarily distracted her mind from her sister. And these same happenings dragged the Churchills into a dangerous whirlpool. The trouble began as soon as the Queen returned to London from visiting Anne; she was given the chilling news that the French were planning to invade England during the next few weeks. William had departed for the war and Mary was left in sole charge of the realm. She countermanded the embarkation of six regiments intended for Flanders and ordered six more to be recalled from Ireland. All these troops were hastily sent to the south coast. Marshal Schomberg's son, now the Duke of Leinster, was appointed to the command of the English troops at home; the militia was called out; and all horses and cattle were driven fifteen miles inland. By this time the whole country was in a state of consternation. Mary was so apprehensive that she burned her private journals.

Across the Channel every port in Normandy was alive with French *poilus* and noisy Irish musketeers – most of them soldiers of fortune – who looked forward to the joy of looting London. But although the military preparations were completed by the middle of April, and King James and the Duke of Berwick were waiting in Caen, severe storms upset the schedule. Several ships were damaged and the sea was so rough it was impossible to embark the troops. Even worse for the would-be invaders, Admiral Tourville's fleet, which had inflicted such damage on the Anglo–Dutch ships at Beachy Head, was weather-bound in harbour for over six weeks.

England was tense with excitement when Lord Portland arrived from William's headquarters on 3 May 1692. The Queen called a Council but some of the business that came under review was quite unexpected. A disreputable character named Young, who had already served a gaol sentence for fraud, informed the Government that there was a plot afoot to capture the Prince of Orange, dead or alive, and to restore James to the throne. He alleged that the incriminating document was a bond of association signed by a dozen prominent men, including Lord Marlborough, Lord Cornbury and the Bishop of Rochester. The paper, he said, could be found in one of the Bishop of Rochester's flower-pots. It was all so bizarre that three members of the Council led by Devonshire refused to sign the warrants of arrest; the most that could be said for the reprehensible Young, they claimed, was that 'he had not yet had his ears cropped'. However, the times were so threatening that the Queen insisted on taking every precaution. As a result of the accusation, Marlborough and several other nobles were arrested on a charge of high treason and sent to the Tower.

Sarah was frantic. She left Syon House and moved to London to be close to her husband. She did not find it easy to get permits to visit him as they were issued for 'one day only' and had to be signed by the Secretary of State. She was particularly annoyed when an official charged her £2 2s od to visit her husband on a 'closed day' and she arrived to find it was an open day after all. But the pin-pricks paled into insignificance when news arrived from St Albans that her second son, two-year-old Charles, had died. We do not know the cause; indeed, the only allusion to this sad event is a letter from the Princess who, 'knowing very well what it is to lose a child', sent Sarah love and sympathy, stressing that 'time is the only cure for all misfortunes'.[44]

While the Bishop of Rochester's flower-pots were being searched for the compromising documents, Admiral de Tourville finally sailed out of his harbour. The long delay had cost him his advantage. Admiral Russell, the splendid sailor who had berated King William over Marlborough's dismissal, used the respite to amalgamate the ships of England and Holland, and now had a fleet of ninety ships equipped with over 7,000 guns and manned by 41,000 men of whom Captain George Churchill was one. The battle that took place is known as La Hogue. De Tourville fought gallantly, but was outnumbered and easily defeated; and when Admiral Russell pursued him the following day he put out of action half the French fleet.

That was the end of all talk of invasion, at least for the time being, but England had learned her lesson and never again allowed her naval superiority to be whittled away. Meanwhile, Anne wrote to Sarah nearly every day to console her for John's imprisonment. 'I hope when the Parliament sitts care will be taken that people may not be clapt up for nothing or els there will be no liveing in quiet for anybody but insolent Dutch and sneaking mercenary English men.'[45] When Sarah again suggested leaving the Princess's service to spare her further mortifications, Anne 'fell into the greatest passion of tenderness and weeping that it is possible to imagine.' 'I beg it for Jesus's name,' Anne cried out,

> that you would never name it any more to me. For be assured, if you should ever do so cruel a thing as to leave me, from that moment I shall never enjoy one quiet hour. And should you do it without asking my consent (which if I ever give you may I never see the face of heaven) I will shut myself up and never see the world more, but live where I may be forgotten by human kind.[46]

The paper incriminating Marlborough was at last found in the Bishop's flower-pot, but when Young was closely examined he broke down and admitted that he had forged the signatures. He had hoped to gain notoriety by the case; how he hoped to make money is not apparent. Indeed, it was so far from clear that Sarah declared that Lord Sidney, a Secretary of State, had paid Young to embarrass Marlborough. Marlborough was eventually released from the Tower on bail of £6,000, which was paid by Lord Halifax and Lord Shrewsbury. The Queen was so angry that she personally struck the names of these guarantors off the list of Privy Councillors. Sarah was grateful that John had such good friends: 'But', she wrote, 'one of his best friends was a paper that lay upon the table and which I have often kissed, the Act of Habeas Corpus.'[47]

Marlborough had accepted his dismissal with astonishing coolness and continued to present a façade of supreme self-assurance, allowing no one to glean the slightest trace of anxiety in his bearing. His remarkable self-control and perfect good humour would be regarded eventually as his most famous characteristics. Yet his heart must have been heavy. Here he was, standing on the side-lines while a great war was being fought, forty-two years of age with his youth slipping away, unable to put to the test the military talent which he was sure he possessed. His friends were indignant at the King's harsh treatment: Russell berated William to his face, Shrewsbury spoke in his favour and Godolphin threatened to resign from the Government. George Churchill actually did resign, surrendering his commission in the navy and remaining out of active service for three years.

Marlborough, however, maintained an unswerving faith that the tide would turn in his favour as suddenly as it had run against him. Sarah, of course, acted as a perpetual tonic by entertaining everyone with her sharp, amusing talk. She was inordinately proud of her husband and liked to boast of the fact that he had received none of his promotions through privilege, but had worked his way up the ladder by victories in the field. 'I think it more Honour', she wrote many years later,

> to rise from the lowest Step to the greatest than, as is the Fashion now, to be Admirals without ever having seen water but in a Bason or to make Generals that never saw any Action of War and only felt from the Generosity of their Temper that they were not to pursue a flying enemy.[48]

When Sarah was not on duty with the Princess, she spent her time with John at Holywell House near St Albans. Brusque, quiet little Sidney Godolphin, who had been a widower for many years, had become a close friend of both the Marlboroughs and frequently jour-

neyed to St Albans to spend weeks at a time with them. He was
now the outstanding man at the Treasury, with a firm grip of the
country's economic problems, and was often spoken of as a future
first minister. He loved gambling at cards, and recently had
acquired a second hobby which became the ruling passion of his
leisure-time – horse-breeding. He became a regular attendant at the
Newmarket races, studying pedigree and performance with rapt
attention, and before long introduced his own line of bloodstock.

> He is the unchallenged father of English horse-breeding [wrote Winston
> Churchill, himself a lover of horses]. If all his life time of Ministerial
> work was blotted out his fame would be secure. . . . He it was who
> imported the Godolphin Arabian, 'who was allowed to have refreshed
> the English blood more than any foreign horse yet imported' and
> brought into being a race of horses never previously known to man,
> more cherished and admired than all other quadrupeds in human
> history.[49]

Godolphin was as proficient at the Treasury as he was in
developing his hobbies, and John Marlborough never went into a
commercial transaction without consulting him. When the latter
was dismissed by King William, he was forced to relinquish the
governorship of the Hudson's Bay Company, but in 1694, on Godolphin's advice, he seized the chance to buy shares in the newly
founded Bank of England. Both Marlborough and Lord
Shrewsbury invested £10,000 each while Godolphin, who was not
a rich man, managed to raise £7,000 for his own equity. Godolphin understood the function of money better than most people
and for years had been pressing for a proper credit system. He
prophesied that the Bank of England would not only finance
England's overseas trade but would carry the burden of her wars.
As far as trade was concerned, the company he favoured most was
the East India Company and he advised John Marlborough to
invest in this too. The latter took his advice, and in 1697 asked Sir
Benjamin Bathurst, a former governor of the company, to purchase
stock for him. Although the Marlboroughs were now well off,
John still counted every penny. He stipulated that Bathurst should
buy the stocks 'before Wednesday that I may not lose the ten shil-
lings [premium]'.

The Marlboroughs were wonderfully happy together although it
would be difficult to find two people more different in personality
and temperament. Whereas Marlborough had complete control of
his emotions and rarely revealed his innermost thoughts, Sarah

'tumbled out' everything that crossed her mind, regardless of the effect on her listeners. Furthermore, when her temper burst its confines it was as dramatic as a river flooding an entire countryside. She stormed and railed and sometimes even threw things. Once, when she was in a passionate rage with John, and every reprisal seemed inadequate, she picked up the scissors and cut off her wonderful blonde hair – simply because her husband admired it so much! But she received no satisfaction as John appeared to be oblivious to what she had done. He never alluded to it, even much later, although her cropped head was far from attractive. It was not until after her husband's death, when Sarah was going through his belongings, that she suddenly came upon her shorn locks in his strong-box where they had lain for over thirty years.

In London the Marlboroughs were always surrounded by people, so when they arrived at St Albans they did their best to keep time for themselves. They refused to adopt the pattern of life that earls and countesses were expected to follow. For instance, most aristocrats kept an open table to which neighbours and friends and relations could come whenever they chose. 'Having Children whom both L Marl and I loved very tenderly', Sarah explained in her memoirs,

> it was natural for us to desire to be easy in our house with our Children and a few friends and both L Marl and I agreed perfectly in that to abhorre a promiscuous mixture of all sorts of people and the E of Godolphin who was so united to us both in friendship and alliance that he was much with us hated the dining with such a rout about us as much as we did. . . .[50]

Despite Sarah's professions of love for her children, she was not a good mother. Not only was she strict and censorious but she seemed to be utterly humourless when dealing with her young. In 1693 her family consisted of an eleven-year-old boy, John (little Charles had just died), and four girls, later known as 'Marlborough's beautiful daughters'. Henrietta was twelve years old and longed for attention from her beautiful 'Angel Mama'. Sarah was at St Albans nursing her own mother who had had a stroke and was dying, and the children had been sent to London to get them out of the house. 'If my dear Mama', wrote Henrietta, 'would stay any time at St Albans, if she would but write to me I should be extream proud of it and the over-joydest creature in the whole world.' Anne, too, clamoured for notice, saying (probably in response to some reproof) that she would 'rather go through fire and water' than displease her mother.[51] Mary Churchill was the most beautiful and the most spirited of all the daughters. Although at this date she was only four years old, by the time she was ten, she refused to take the responsibility for losing her clogs and was writing to her mother with an aggressiveness that hinted at trouble to come:

> I can't help thinking my case very hard [she complained] that you will give me over for so small a thing & which is not my fault, for if I should buy a pair every day I should never have any for the moment I take them off they are lost. . . . I will say no more but that since you have been so angery with me I have been so miserable that I have wish'd and pray'd for nothing so much as to dy that I might be no trouble to my dear mama & I hope much happier myself.[52]

Although Sarah was uneducated herself, she liked the role of school-teacher. When her children were young she taught them reading and writing (we hope not spelling) and later set them to writing essays. Their studies whetted her own appetite and before long she had embarked on a programme of self-education which consisted mainly of reading the classics. Though her mind was untutored, it was an exceptionally good machine; it is not surprising, therefore, that she craved stimulating talk. 'If I were a great man', she said, 'I should prefer keeping the best Company I could get with Independancy before any pleasure this world could give.'[53] John was very proud (and a little awed) by her intellectual interests and, when she felt strongly on a subject, invariably accepted her view. Sarah's dominance, however, was due far less to her powers of reasoning than to the boldness and originality of her views. She was adored, not only by her husband and Princess Anne, but by Sidney Godolphin and other men who came into her life later.

Sarah's great fault lay in her intransigence as an enemy. Her in-laws – the Churchills – qualified for her disapproval because they had urged John to marry Catherine Sedley. Nevertheless, John went regularly to Mintern to see his mother (his father had died in 1688) and kept in close touch with his brothers Charles and George. As for John's only sister, Arabella (the one-time mistress of James II), she is seldom mentioned by Sarah. Soon after leaving James, Arabella had married one of John's fellow officers, Colonel Charles Godfrey,* and became a respectable housewife. In 1681 she stood as godmother to Sarah's daughter, Henrietta, but after that faded out of sight. The two women must have quarrelled, for we never hear of them meeting again. Marlborough was very fond of Arabella and left her a handsome legacy when he died in 1722. Sarah, on the other hand, criticized one of her husband's biographers for deigning to mention Arabella

---

* Very little is known about Godfrey, but he may have been Arabella's cousin.

and her 'Train of Bastards'. 'Because they had titles he seems to think that was an Honour. . . . I think it quite the contrary,' she added waspishly.[54]

While Sarah bustled about, nursing her mother and encumbering the lives of her children with rules (for their own good, of course), John Marlborough complained of the depressing and indecisive way the war was being conducted. William of Orange had no outstanding talent as a military commander and, when the magnificent and self-assured French army forced him to fight, he was usually defeated. However, in those days most generals made a point of avoiding confrontation with the enemy, preferring to pass the campaigning months in futile manœuvres or by entrenching themselves in positions that could not be attacked. Occasionally a commander decided to risk a battle. This happened in the summer of 1692 when Louis XIV captured the fortress of Namur and King William felt that he must strike back, if only for reasons of prestige.

He decided to throw his whole army against the Duke of Luxembourg at a moment when the latter's forces were divided. He gave command of the splendid English troops trained by Marlborough to his cousin, the arrogant Count Solms, whose high military rank was due to birth, not talent. Consequently, eight English regiments led by General Mackay surprised the French in the early morning near Steinkerk. After fierce fighting, they broke the enemy lines, but General Luxembourg did not enjoy his reputation as France's best general for nothing. He threw his crack Household Troops into the battle and fierce hand-to-hand fighting with sword and bayonet took place. The English stood their ground, but when Luxembourg began to pour in reinforcements, Mackay called for help. Solms, however, refused to comply. 'Now we shall see', he said sneeringly, 'how the bulldogs will come off.' The poor bulldogs not only lost their two best generals – Mackay and Lanier – but half their strength, with over 3,000 killed and wounded.

Marlborough was so indignant when he heard what had happened that he spoke in the House of Lords in favour of a bill prohibiting foreigners from commanding English troops. Resolutions were passed in both Houses, but the Whigs in the Commons praised the merits of the Dutch command, and voted William all the supplies he needed for the coming campaign. The result was not encouraging as it brought the Allies an even worse disaster. In July the battle of Landen, in Flanders (part of the Spanish Netherlands), cost William nearly 20,000 men, an unparalleled slaughter for the time.

Marlborough's brother, Colonel Charles Churchill, took part in the battle and by a bizarre stroke of fate emerged a richer man! The main fighting revolved around the village of Neerwinden which changed hands several times during the course of the day. One of Churchill's main adversaries was his nephew, the twenty-three-year-old Duke of Berwick, now a general in the French army. Berwick was an inspired fighter and at one point drove his enemies out of the village and took possession of it. However, before long, a counter-attack reversed his good fortune and he suddenly found himself caught in a trap. He removed the white cockade from his hat and tried to pass through the general *melée* as an Englishman. This might have worked if Churchill had not spotted Berwick's aide-de-camp and immediately looked around for his nephew. He took Berwick prisoner and conducted him to King William, who, wrote Berwick in his memoirs, 'made me a very polite compliment, to which I only replied by a low bow: after looking steadfastly at me for an instant, he put on his hat and I mine; then he ordered me to be carried to Lewe.'

Perhaps William did not think Berwick's response to his salutations had been polite enough. At any rate, Berwick had the impression that his release might not be easy to manage. 'The Prince of Orange', he continued,

> certainly had a design of sending me prisoner to England where I should have been closely confined in the Tower of London, though that would have been contrary to all the rules of war; for though he pretended that I was his subject, and consequently a rebel, yet he had no right to treat me as such, since I was not taken prisoner in a territory that belonged to him. We were in a country of the King of Spain and I had the honour to serve as Lieutenant-General in the army of the Most Christian King. . . .[55]

In the end the Duke of Berwick was exchanged for the Duke of Ormonde and each gentleman returned to his own lines. According to the custom of the day William allowed Charles Churchill £1,200 in ransom money which he invested in government bonds. Although Charles was promoted to the rank of Major-General the following year, he never for one moment imagined that he possessed the same gifts as John. He was a competent professional soldier, truly devoted to his disgraced brother, whom he recognized as the genius of the family.

The Marlboroughs took heart in April 1694 when King William dismissed the Tory, Lord Nottingham, as Secretary of State and appointed the Whig, Lord Shrewsbury, Marlborough's close friend, in his place. Shrewsbury was a perfect bridge between the two quarrelling sisters (not to mention the Marlboroughs and William and Mary) because he was esteemed by the King who made him a duke, and by the Queen who was in love with him. Bishop Burnet declares that if Mary had been a widow she would certainly have married Shrewsbury. Lord Dartmouth tells us that when Mary's Vice-Chamberlain led her into the chapel and 'the Duke of Shrewsbury stepped forward to speak to her she trembled all over.'[56] William III obviously had a sense of humour, for he nicknamed the one-eyed Shrewsbury 'King of Hearts', a soubriquet which clung to him for the rest of his life.

Shrewsbury was not able to effect a reconciliation between the King and Marlborough. He wrote to William begging him to make use of the latter's services:

> Since I very well remember when your Majesty discoursed with me upon it in the spring, you were fully convinced of his usefulness; but some points remained of a nature too tender for me to pretend to advise upon and of which your Majesty is the only and best judge; who, if those could be committed to your Majesty's satisfaction, I can but think he is capable of being very serviceable. It is so unquestionably his interest to be faithful that single arguments make me not doubt it.[57]

But William replied coldly, 'concerning Lord Marlborough I can only say no more than that I do not think it for the good of my service to entrust him with the command of my troops.'[58]

This interchange suggests that Marlborough's offence was of a fairly trivial, perhaps even personal nature. Was it criticism of William's Dutch officers? Or his favourites? Or perhaps the letters he induced Anne to write to her father? Whatever the answer, Marlborough's enemies were delighted by his continuing disgrace. Most of them were Tories who were still loyal to James because he was their rightful King and who accused Marlborough of the blackest treachery. (George Legge's son, Lord Dartmouth, once described him as 'a bad grate man'.) Even those who had been glad to see James deposed censured him for unforgiveable disloyalty to a master of twenty years. The fact that Marlborough was being punished for establishing links with St Germain (or so people thought) was regarded as rough justice, but not considered much of a sin. The truth was that everybody knew that Jacobite agents, connected to the other side by blood and marriage and friendship, were swarming about trying to get in touch with England's leading men. Although their reports were secret no one would have been surprised to learn that they had made contact with the Dukes of Newcastle and Leeds, the Marquis of Normandy, the Earls of Shrewsbury, Marlborough and Godolphin, Admiral Russell and many others.

But a century later, when a life of James was published, claiming to have been compiled from the ex-King's memoirs, the 'immortal seven' who had arranged for William's arrival in England were portrayed in a shameful light. And none more so than Marlborough. He is seen as a penitent, eager to make up for his deception by re-establishing James on the throne and, even worse, of betraying an assault on Brest in 1696 which resulted in a serious loss of British life. According to Lord Macaulay, the purpose of this was to make himself so important that he would be reinstated by William and given a high command.

These charges of perfidy, which were accepted by many Victorian biographers without challenge, and which for a century and a half badly damaged Marlborough's reputation and dimmed his posthumous glory, must be examined. Today, it seems incredible that any sensible person could suppose that Marlborough would wish to restore James – the man he had taken such risks to depose – at the expense of his staunch admirer, Princess Anne, next in line to the throne. Yet nineteenth-century historians believed just that. Lord Macaulay painted an odious (and ridiculous) picture of Marlborough, and even the fair-minded and greatly esteemed twentieth-century historian, G.M.Trevelyan, in his study of Queen Anne's reign (the first volume of which was published in 1930) unquestioningly accepted Marlborough's betrayal of the Brest expedition, castigating it as 'a base thing for an English soldier to do'.*

Fortunately Marlborough's famous descendant, Winston Churchill, came to the great soldier's rescue. In 1933 he published the first volume of his four-volume biography of Marlborough. With the help of a team of researchers he had carried out an intensive study of all relevant documents and had left no stone unturned to discover the truth. He paid special attention to the two books on which historians had based their charges: *The Original Memoirs of James II . . . Writ in His Own Hand* and *The Life of James II Collected out of Memoirs Writ in His Own Hand*, edited by James Clarke, 1816.

James's memoirs were scribbled on scraps of paper of various sizes. When the latter fled to France in 1688 he managed to take the manuscript with him (the same manuscript that he had clutched when the *Gloucester* sank) and eventually entrusted it to Louis Innes, Principal of the Scots College in Paris, for safe-keeping. Soon after James's

---

* The only source that Trevelyan gives is one of Marlborough's Victorian biographers, General the Viscount Wolseley.

death (probably some time around 1707) the exiled 'Prince of Wales', later known as 'the Old Pretender', commissioned a biography of his father to be compiled from James's memoirs and other documents. This work was written anonymously by a Roman Catholic exile, William Dicconson, who was employed at St Germain as a treasury official. Dicconson spent five years, from 1710 to 1715, at the Scots College in Paris completing his undertaking and the biography ran to four volumes. Throughout most of the eighteenth century these manuscripts – James's original memoirs and Dicconson's anonymous life, both of which were written in the third person – lay side by side in the College under lock and key. A handful of scholars such as Hume, Dalrymple and Carte, and a Tory Member of Parliament, Mr James Macpherson, visited the College at various times to study James's memoirs 'writ with his own hand'. However, there is evidence that none of them ever saw the original work but were shown instead Dicconson's biography.

These scholarly excursions to Paris came to an end in 1793, when the French Revolution was raging, and the College arranged to send James's original memoirs to England. The gentleman who acted as messenger was arrested in St Omer and his wife, fearing that the royal arms of England which decorated the binding might compromise her, first buried the memoirs and then later dug them up and burned them. Meanwhile, Dicconson's biography fared better. The manuscript was dispatched by the owner (the Young Pretender's illegitimate daughter) to the English Benedictines in Rome during the Revolution and was purchased eventually by the Prince Regent of England. After six years of being shunted from pillar to post, the manuscript arrived in London just after Napoleon's defeat in 1815. The Prince realized his good fortune in retrieving Dicconson's manuscript (which, of course, was still anonymous) and commissioned his historiographer, the Reverend J.S. Clarke, to edit and publish it. The work appeared in 1816 as a life 'collected out of memoirs written by His Majesty's own hand'.

The book shocked England – especially Victorian England. According to James II, most of the men who had taken a leading part in putting William on the throne had feet of clay. What was surprising was the fact that nineteenth-century historians accepted the odious light in which these heroes were cast. Churchill was hated by the Jacobites more than any other individual as his defection from the army was believed to have been the chief cause of James's undoing. Therefore no stone was left unturned to portray the 'deserter of Salisbury' in the blackest colours. He was not only a villain but a despicable villain, who was soon grovelling before the master he had betrayed and begging for pardon.

However, when Winston Churchill was working on Marlborough's life in the 1930s, he came across a letter which had lain buried in the Royal Archives at Windsor for over a century. It had been written in 1740 by Thomas Innes, brother of Louis, who had succeeded him as Principal of the Scots College in Paris, and stated categorically that James's memoirs 'writ with his own hand' had ended at the time of the Stuart Restoration in 1660.[59] Churchill pounced triumphantly on this letter, pointing out that the calumnies about Marlborough in Dicconson's books, purporting to come from James, had sprung instead from Dicconson's own malicious pen. But this argument was not wholly conclusive. As James's manuscript was believed to have consisted of nine folios, and the finished memoirs only occupied three of them, it was possible that the remaining six folios, lost for ever, had consisted of a hodge-podge of cuttings, comment and random jottings that spread over many more years of James's life.

Nevertheless, Innes's statement was a timely warning to historians to be on their guard. Undoubtedly much of Dicconson's work had been based on the hearsay of the Jacobite Court, which thrived on the exaggerated reports of secret agents.* The forlorn little group of exiles at St Germain lived on the bounty of Louis XIV and, as that bounty depended on the value Versailles placed on them, they always felt the need to present their case as forcefully as possible. Jacobite agents had no difficulty in making contact with England's leading men, including the members of William's Council. But when these agents revealed the disenchantment of the revolutionary leaders with their Dutch King (despite his Protestant faith), and gave a picture of them bewailing the wrong they had done to James, the reports verged on absurdity. The aim, of course, was to convince the French King of Jacobite support in England so that he would mount an invasion to restore James to his rightful throne. Yet for two centuries historians accepted Clarke's life based on Dicconson based on James as the unvarnished truth.

In his research Winston Churchill also discovered that there was not a single letter autographed by Marlborough in Jacobite possession, and that the shameful letter revealing the attack on Brest was also non-existent. A French translation of the purported missive was

---

* One of James's biographers, Maurice Ashley, points out that Dicconson makes no reference to volumes 4, 5 and 6 of James's memoirs and that when he (Dicconson) refers in Part II to volumes 7, 8 and 9, his work is untrustworthy.

filed among the official papers of Sir David Nairne, an Englishman who served as Under-Secretary of State to the exiled James. However, as Nairne was a passionate Jacobite whose papers were drawn from flamboyant secret service accounts with the aim of inducing Louis XIV to invade England, they are regarded today as 'untrustworthy and mendacious documents'.[60] Indeed, it is quite possible that the treacherous 'betrayal', the translation of which was in Nairne's own handwriting, had been concocted by himself (or one of his entourage) to impress James. Otherwise, where is the autographed letter from which the translation was made?* If it had ever existed, can anyone seriously imagine that the French would not have used it to destroy the great Duke of Marlborough, if not at that moment, at least a few years later when he was pulverizing the armies of France?

Finally, Marlborough's correspondence with St Germain was not, as some historians had suggested, simply 're-insurance' against James's return. Contact with the enemy was part and parcel of a system which he followed through the years of his greatest triumphs. He always talked to Jacobite agents for the simple reason that he learned more from them than they learned from him. The King knew of his contacts with St Germain and was not worried by them, for William was not foolish enough to imagine that Marlborough would put James back on the throne and ruin the chances for Princess Anne. On the contrary, Lord Ailesbury, the faithful courtier who served both Charles and James, wrote in his memoirs that William was glad of Marlborough's Jacobite connections. 'It is very certain', he declared,

> that the King William gave leave to the Earl of Marlborough, my Lord God-olphin, the Duke of Shrewsbury and Admiral Russell to correspond with my Lord Middleton at St Germain. They infused into the King the great advantage that might arise to him by it, and on my conscience I believe it. The plausible pretext was that my Lord Middleton should be deluded, that he should know nothing of what passed in England of high secret moment, but that they four would wire-pull all out of my Lord Middleton. . . .[61]

Marlborough lived in an era of such intense partisanship it is not surprising that he was furiously maligned. But as he would not have known what charges the embittered Jacobites in St Germain were trumping up against him, his silence is understandable. Nevertheless, as modern scholarship is coming to the conclusion that the 'perfidious acts' of which he was accused are not only tendentious, but perhaps fabricated, new appraisals are being made of his character.

* In the translation, Marlborough is made to address James as 'you' rather than 'Your Majesty', something that a former courtier would be unlikely to do.

As well as living in Syon House, Anne had rented Berkeley House, a large residence on Piccadilly on the site where Derby House stands today. She led a circumscribed existence, dependent almost entirely on her own household for company, as the Queen had forbidden those who wished to be received at Court from paying their respects to her. However, in February 1693, when Anne reviewed the events of the past year, she assured Sarah that she had no regrets. 'You cannot expect any news from Berkeley House', she wrote, 'but as dull and as despicable as some people may think it, I am so far from being weary of my way of living or repenting . . . that weare ye years to run over again I would tread ye same steps.'[62]

Anne would have been blissfully happy if only she could have produced healthy children. But in her ten and a half years of marriage she had had eleven pregnancies of which only five had resulted in living babies. Of these, two had died immediately after birth, and another two as very young children. The only survivor was the five-year-old Duke of Gloucester whom Anne referred to as 'my poor boy' – he was suffering from water on the brain, but it was not known at the time. During the spring of 1694, he ran a high fever and suffered from paroxysms which occurred at regular intervals. Anne was deeply worried, as she not only adored the child but feared that if he should die the King and Queen might adopt James's son, the Prince of Wales, and bring him up as their Protestant heir.*

To make matters worse, Anne herself was not in good health. She had begun to suffer from gout (at that time all rheumatic ailments were attributed to gout) and at times had such bad attacks she had to be carried into her garden in a chair. As she was only twenty-nine years old, many people prophesied that Queen Mary would outlive both her younger sister and her asthmatic husband; but during the Christmas holidays of 1694, Mary contracted the dread disease of smallpox. For many months Sarah had urged the Princess to try and make it up with her sister. On this occasion Anne sent one of her ladies to Kensington Palace with a letter of sympathy, adding that if Her Majesty would allow her the happiness of waiting on her, she would be only too glad to come despite her condition. The Queen's Groom of the Stole, Lady Derby, replied in a letter to Lady Marlborough that the Queen could not be disturbed and that the Princess should defer

---

* This rumour was in almost constant circulation until William's death. Indeed, some historians claim that the reason Marlborough first got in touch with St Germain and prompted Anne to make amends to her father was to forestall any idea of allowing the Prince of Wales to become William's heir. However, as James never for a moment considered the proposal, the consternation was unjustified.

her proposed visit. She then added a postscript: 'Pray madam, present my humble duty to the Princess.' 'This civil answer', Sarah recorded, 'and my Lady Derby's postscript made me conclude more than if the college of physicians had told me the disease was mortal.'[63]

The Queen died on 28 December 1694, having declared that she had nothing in her heart against her sister. King William was so distraught that his attendants feared for his sanity, a surprising epilogue for the cold-hearted little man who disliked women and for so many years had treated his wife with scant consideration.

Six

The Grand Alliance

The death of Queen Mary gave a sharp upward turn to the fortunes of the Marlboroughs. Although King William detested the Princess of Denmark, he could not afford to be at loggerheads with the Heiress Apparent to the throne. So when Anne sent William a letter of sympathy, William invited Anne to Kensington Palace. The Princess was pregnant and suffering from what she called gout, and when she arrived was carried upstairs in her sedan-chair. An eye-witness described how the King came forward to greet her, and how 'she told His Majesty in faltering accents that she was truly sorry for his loss'. William then led her into his private room where 'she staid three quarters of an hour'. Soon after 'His Majesty presented the Princess with most of her sister's jewels.'[1] Not only that, but William restored the Royal Guards outside Anne's house and urged her to move into St James's Palace where she could keep Court 'as if she were a crowned head'. She took up residence there at the end of 1695.

Word of the reconciliation swept the Court; Anne's first Drawing-Room was crowded with people whom she had not seen for three years. In a letter to Sarah she commented cynically on 'the great appearance at Mrs Morley's', and later described a courtier who announced loudly: 'I hope your Highness will remember that I came to visit you when none of this company did.'[2] The Duke of Shrewsbury informed Admiral Russell that things were going well between the King and his sister-in-law, and that the Princess was missing no opportunity 'to show her zeal for His Majesty and his government; and our friend [Marlborough] who has no small credit with her seems very resolved to contribute to the continuance of this union. . . .'[3]

The King, however, was not in a hurry to receive Marlborough and kept him waiting for two months before he was allowed to kiss hands.

We can be sure that Sarah poured scorn on her husband for putting up with this discourtesy, for nothing would induce her to heal the breach. She flatly refused to go near the Court for over a year. 'Having taken great Pains till then', she wrote, 'to avoid all Places where the King was and I believe I should have continued it, but that my Lord Sunderland disswaded me from it.'[4] After spending three years giving King James disastrous advice (and pretending to become a Roman Catholic to boot), Lord Sunderland had fled to Holland. Now he was back at Court, once again a Protestant and once again confidential adviser to the reigning monarch. We do not know the explanation of his irresistible charm. Some people say he knew all the secrets of the great families of England and kept his royal masters amused by his animated gossip. Queen Anne could not abide him and once described him as 'the subtilest workingeste [she meant 'most subtle working'] villain in the whole world'.[5] As Sunderland had been a friend of the Churchills for many years, he tried to persuade the King to re-employ Marlborough but met with no success.

At first Marlborough maintained his air of unconcern, but before long his aplomb was shattered by an unexpected development: early in 1696 he was accused of high treason. Not surprisingly, the trouble stemmed from St Germain. This gloomy Court, overladen with priests, was staffed by exiles with barely a penny to their names. They spent half their day in prayer and the other half intriguing with each other for sinecures of posts that would keep them in food and shoe-leather. Their only chance for the future was an uprising that would put James back on the throne, but this likelihood seemed to recede with the passing months. Queen Mary's death, however, produced a sudden gleam of hope. From London the courtiers at St Germain learned that clandestine Jacobite meetings were being held all over the country, as it was believed that William was too unpopular to rule without his English Queen. James II agreed to send the Duke of Berwick to England (in disguise) to spy out the land and concert the measures for an armed uprising. King Louis promised to support a revolt (when and if it took place), but would only guarantee an invasion force of 2,000 men.

But this was not all. Other invasion attempts had been planned in the past and had never come to anything. This time James's political advisers decided to give the Jacobite rebellion a proper impetus. They would begin by assassinating King William. We do not know whether James was familiar with the details of the plot, but he agreed to send Sir George Barclay to London to mastermind the plans; he also agreed to allow twenty members of his bodyguard to make their way surreptitiously to the English capital and, by pre-arranged signals, to put themselves in touch with Barclay. Every Saturday King William went hunting and returned by way of Turnham Green, where he crossed the river by boat and was met on the other side by a new guard and a new coach. This was the spot where the murder would take place. However, Barclay estimated that, as William's guard would have to be overpowered, he needed at least forty men to do the job, and he set about recruiting another twenty volunteers.

Meanwhile, the Duke of Berwick was appraising the Jacobite uprising to decide whether or not it was determined enough to warrant a French invasion. He travelled about England in heavy disguise, conferring with the men pledged to his cause. The reader should take note that Berwick did not get in touch with his uncle John – a challenge to the veracity of the Jacobite reports on Marlborough's partisanship! Berwick sent news back to France that 'two thousand Horse well-appointed and even regimented were ready to take the field'. In his memoirs he goes on to say that it was not until he returned to London from his fact-finding trip that he learned of the murder plot. It is difficult to believe that James would allow Berwick to go to England in ignorance of an undertaking as dangerous as an assassination attempt. 'I thought', Berwick continues airily, 'my principal commission being at an end, I ought to lose no time to return to France that I might not be confounded with the conspirators, whose design appeared to me difficult to execute.'[6] Apparently Lord Ailesbury warned Berwick to flee for his life – advice which the young man accepted, escaping only a few hours before his lodgings were searched.

The assassination of King William was scheduled for February 1696. When Berwick crossed the Channel he found the ports crowded with soldiers waiting to embark. He met James II on the road to Paris, turned around and accompanied his father back to Calais. There they waited for the bonfire on the cliffs of Dover that would tell them that the fatal deed had been done. But the fire was never lit. At the eleventh hour two of the men recruited by Barclay lost their nerve and informed the Earl of Portland (William Bentinck) of the plot, and he in turn persuaded William not to go hunting on the following day, the 15th.

England was furious when news of the plot was made public. The whole country rallied around the King. The conspirators were tried and some of them executed, and William enjoyed a popularity that he had not had since the first days of his rule. In the general round-up, other men, who had nothing to do with the murder plan, were arrested and sent to the Tower. One of these was Lord Ailesbury;

another, a respectable citizen, Sir John Fenwick, who was married to the daughter of the Earl of Carlisle. Fenwick had been active in stirring up the Jacobite revolt but that was all. When he was questioned he tried to protect his accomplices by writing out a confession in which he repeated the names of those men so often bandied about by Jacobite agents – Shrewsbury, Godolphin, Russell and Marlborough. He accused them all of treasonable correspondence with St Germain. William III saw through him at a glance and sent the report back to his Council with assurances to those incriminated that he placed no value on such absurd charges. When Fenwick was brought to the Bar of the House of Commons, Colonel Charles Godfrey, Marlborough's brother-in-law, invited him to state fully the allegations against Marlborough, but he had nothing to say. Each of the persons named reacted in their own particular way. Marlborough had recovered his composure and appeared to be completely unabashed. In a speech in the House of Lords he not only denied Fenwick's charges but went on to say that since he had left King James in 1688 no one 'was able to accuse him of the least thing'.[7] Lord Shrewsbury responded very differently. Despite the fact that he was accused of nothing more than seeking James II's pardon, he was deeply mortified and begged the King to relieve him of his duties. Although William assured him his trust in him was as great as ever, Shrewsbury simply retired to the country and sat brooding for several months. In the end Fenwick was executed, probably unjustly, while Lord Ailesbury, equally unjustly, was exiled for life.

Meanwhile, Louis XIV was showing ever-growing eagerness to bring the war on the Continent to a close. Although King William had won only two major battles in all the years of fighting – the battle of the Boyne in 1690 and the recapture of Namur in 1695 – he certainly had not lost the war. The truth was that the maritime powers, with their large merchant fleets, were in a much stronger position than Louis XIV to wage long drawn-out conflicts. Whereas the French were suffering from poor harvests, the English and the Dutch could bring in grain from the Baltic. Even more important, the newly founded Bank of England seemed to have stumbled on a magical system that enabled the English government not only to finance the war quite painlessly but to subsidize its allies. Louis could not persuade William to negotiate peace until he finally managed to reach a secret agreement with the Duke of Savoy. William saw the danger of his allies negotiating separate treaties and sent the Earl of Portland to France to secure satisfactory terms. William Bentinck was almost as much a Frenchman as he was a Dutchman. He spoke the language perfectly and was a skilled diplomatist. Apparently he thrashed out the peace terms with Marshal Boufflers while pacing up and down an orchard.

The French King surrendered most of the gains that France had made since the Treaty of Nimwegen in 1678, but refused to return Strasbourg to Emperor Leopold. Although he recognized William as the *de facto* King of England, he would not hear of James II being driven from France as this would detract from his *gloire*. He also promised that neither he nor his subjects would assist the Stuart pretenders – 'any of them' – to retrieve their lost throne. Lastly he returned the province of Orange to its distinguished owner with the proviso that French Huguenots would not be allowed to live there.

General Vauban considered the Treaty of Ryswick, which was signed in 1697, a humiliating defeat for the King, but Louis put a happy face on it, ordering a *Te Deum* to be sung in Notre Dame, and a great celebration to be organized on the theme: 'Louis XIV Gives Peace to Europe'. The King went on to talk of 'the happy success with which it has pleased God to favour my enterprises', although later he explained: 'I sacrificed the advantages that I gained in the war . . . to [the needs] of public tranquillity.'[8]

Portland had wrung such good terms from Louis that he should have been greeted as a hero when he returned to London. Surprisingly, William's only desire was to send him abroad again as soon as possible. He achieved this by naming him Ambassador to France and encouraged him to establish an embassy so magnificent that even the French were impressed. Portland took the house of the Prince d'Auvergne and, as the dining-room was too small for his needs, built one into the garden which was completed in three weeks. Portland kept open house for any English gentleman either living in or passing through Paris. He had wonderful food and wine, stables containing ninety horses (the Prince d'Auvergne only had ten horses) and seven coaches. On his staff were six of England's grandest lords.

Portland wrote the King heartbroken letters, for he knew that he had been replaced as the 'favourite'. His successor was a handsome youth of twenty-seven, Arnold Joost van Keppel, recently made Earl of Albemarle. Everyone in Paris gossiped about this love affair, as sodomy was a fashionable pastime, particularly in the set of Louis's brother 'Monsieur', who once had been married to Charles II's sister, Minette. People said that William was in love with Albemarle, like a woman, and sometimes kissed his hands in front of the whole Court.

Lord Marlborough had taken note of Keppel's rise in the world and had gone out of his way to make friends with the young man. They found common ground in their detestation of Portland; and, perhaps because Portland had been one of the chief obstacles in preventing the King from patching up his differences with Marlborough, Albemarle decided to show his power by healing the breach. Suddenly it was announced that Lord Marlborough had accepted the post of 'governor' to Princess Anne's son and heir, the nine-year-old Duke of Gloucester. This was a far cry from Churchill's dream of glory on the battlefield, yet it was the first step back into favour. He was restored to his rank in the army and readmitted to the Privy Council. The *Gazette* of 16 June 1698 announced with an almost embarrassing flourish:

> His Majesty has been pleased to appoint the Right Honourable the Earl of Marlborough to be Governor of His Highness the Duke of Gloucester, as a mark of the good opinion His Majesty has of His Lordship's zeal for his service and his qualifications for the employment of so great a trust. . . .

The position certainly was of great importance as the little Duke of Gloucester was Anne's only living child. As a baby, his health was so poor none of his doctors thought he could live, but he had confounded their predictions and grown into a boy whom everyone loved, but who still suffered from distressing bouts of fever. 'My poor boy had his ague again yesterday,' Anne once wrote to Sarah, 'and though Dr Ratcliffe said it was nothing I thought it a very long fit for it lasted seven hours and made him very sick but an hour after it was gone he was mighty merry and seemed to be as ever he was in his life.'[9]

Marlborough's post as 'governor' was purely supervisory: to see that the child had the right tutors; that his time was divided sensibly between work and recreation; and, above all, to make sure that he was surrounded by children of his own age who would keep him amused and contented. Princess Anne, of course, was delighted by the appointment. She not only was a friend and admirer of Marlborough but was gratified by her son's enthusiasm. Little Gloucester liked nothing better than playing soldiers and was thrilled to think that a *bona fide* general would direct his daily routine. He was devoted to King William and made all his playmates, including the Marlboroughs' twelve-year-old son, Jack Churchill, sign a letter swearing to serve His Majesty until they were down to their 'last drop of blood'.

Anne hoped that Marlborough's appointment would mean that she would see even more of Sarah than she already did. Anne had moved into St James's Palace early in 1696 and spent her time producing babies that died at birth. Her dependence on Lady Marlborough was not surprising, as she had almost no distractions apart from card-playing. She seldom read, and when strangers were present sat (in her own words) 'silent and moros'. Although she loved the idea of large receptions and hundreds of people laughing and talking, when they actually appeared she refused to go near them as she could not think of anything to say – only that 'it was hot or cold' or 'to enquire of them how long they had been in town or such like weighty matters'.[10]

The Marlboroughs still had no house of their own in London and when they were required at Court lived in St James's Palace. Sarah was meticulous in carrying out her duties, but Anne was less inter-ested in looking over the Privy Purse accounts than in listening to her friend's amusing and often outrageous talk. Sarah, on the other hand, complained that it was 'extremely tedious to be so much where there could be no manner of conversation. I knew she loved me & I suffer'd by fearing I did wrong when I was not with her. For which reason I have gone a thousand times when I would rather have been shut up in a dungeon.'[11]

We cannot give a fair judgement of the relationship of the two women as Sarah insisted that the Princess destroy her letters. Indeed, she made such a fuss about it that we frequently come across Anne's plaintive cries:

> In obedience, after having read & kissed your dear kind letter over & over I burnt it much against my will & I do assure you you need never be in pain about your letters for I take such care of them 'tis not possible that any accident will happen that they should be seen by anybody.[12]

When Sarah was not at Court Anne pursued her relentlessly. Once when she went to Tunbridge Wells to take the waters with John, Anne wrote:

> Your faithfull Mrs Morley has a mind some time next week to come & inquire how they the spa waters agree with you a maunday if it be a convenient day or els a fryday sevennight or if ye had rather ye later end of this week or ye beginning of ye week after the next whatever time is easiest to you & your deare Mr Freeman do but name it & I shall fly with joy to my dear Mrs Freeman.[13]

Anne sometimes wrote to Sarah twice a day. The communications abounded in the extravagant expressions of an ardent lover writing to his mistress. It is frustrating that we will never know what Sarah said in reply. One of the Duchess's biographers, David Green, gives us extracts from Anne's undated letters written before she became Queen. 'Oh beleeve me you will never find in all ye search of love a hart like your poor unfortunate faithful Morley.' 'A hart soe truly soe sincerly soe intirely without reserve nor soe passionately yours'. 'I am', she insists, 'as unchangeable as fate', and 'To ye last moment of her life your fatifhull Morley will ever be ye same.' No letter from Sarah means desolation; and then, when it arrives 'Just as I had writ thus far I received your deare kind letter which I have kissed a hundred times. . . . If I writt whole volumes I could never express how well I love you nor how I long to see you. . . .'[14]

Marlborough's appointment was the first move in a decision to establish a separate household for the little Duke. The time had come, Parliament decided, for the boy to be taken out of women's hands and placed under male governors, and for this purpose they voted an annual sum of £50,000. The King, however, decided that this was too generous and allotted the Princess only £15,000 a year, pocketing the rest himself. Needless to say, this caused a great deal of bad blood. More was engendered when, without any consultation, William appointed Gilbert Burnet (the Bishop of Salisbury, renamed by Anne the 'Blabbing Bishop') as Gloucester's chief preceptor. Anne was furious as she had her own choice for the post and looked on Burnet as one of William's spies. The Bishop was well aware of the Princess's antipathy towards him, which made him all the more grateful to the Marlboroughs for their friendship. Indeed, Burnet fell under Marlborough's spell so completely that he rewrote the passages in his history which dealt with the latter's desertion of James. Unfortunately, he forgot to destroy the original version which was unearthed 'to his posthumous mockery'.[15]

However, the Bishop was not the only cause of Anne's quarrel with the King. Under pressure from Lord Sunderland, William sent word that Anne could select the lower servants in Gloucester's household and she set about choosing the sons of her friends as grooms and pages. But the King forgot what he had promised and, when he heard what she was doing, declared angrily that 'she shall not be Queen before her time' – he, alone, would nominate the household servants. The Princess referred to 'this brutal usage', but in the end everything was smoothed out by the useful Keppel who persuaded William to let the matter drop.

Among the names in the list of the Duke of Gloucester's household staff was the woman in charge of the laundry, put down merely as 'Hill'. This ominous surname – destined to alter the course of history – belonged to Alice Hill, whose mother had appeared out of the blue and made herself known to Sarah as her aunt. 'I can't be positive', Sarah wrote in her memoirs, whether it was before, or just after the revolution that Mrs Chudleigh, a cousin of the Duke of Marlborough, came to me and told me that I had a relation, Mrs Hill, with a husband and four children that she believed I did not know which were reduced to want of bread by projects [i.e. speculations] & losses at sea & that Mr Hill had kept his misfortunes as long as he could from his wife, but now he could struggle no longer and they were in so miserable a condition that she was sure I would do what I could to relieve them, upon which I presently gave her what I had about me which was ten Guineas & after that I did what I could to support them till opportunitys happened that I could provide better for them.[16]

Sarah had never heard of her aunt, Mrs Hill, as her Jennings grandfather had sired twenty-two children and her mother had lost track of her husband's twenty-one brothers and sisters. Nevertheless, Sarah took the Hills's four children in hand and with Lord Godolphin's help found the eldest boy a place in the 'publick revenue', which he kept till he died of smallpox a few years later. 'His brother . . . was a tall boy whom I clothed (for he was all in rags) and put to school at St Albans. . . . After he had learned what he could there, a vacancy happening of Page of Honour to the Prince of Denmark, his Highness was pleased at my request to take him.'[17] By 1698 the boy had outgrown his post and the Duke of Gloucester's household proved to be a merciful refuge. Not only was Alice Hill put in charge of the Prince's laundry (with Princess Anne's approval), but Jack Hill was slipped into the household, unbeknownst to the King, as a third Groom of the Bedchamber. 'It being reasonable', Sarah wrote, 'to have more than two Grooms of the Bedchamber who were to run after a child from morning till night.'[18]

This left only Abigail Hill to be looked after. Abigail was the eldest daughter and the one closest in age to Sarah. Her long nose prevented her from being pretty, but she had an even gaze and a quiet way about her that appealed to her benefactress. Although she contracted smallpox while she was staying with the Marlboroughs, Sarah nursed her through the dread disease; and in 1697, when Sarah heard that Princess Anne's old nurse, Ellen Bust, who served as a bedchamber-woman (not to be confused with Lady of the Bedchamber), was seriously ill, she asked the Princess if, in the event of a vacancy, her cousin Abigail might be considered. 'As to what you say about Mrs [Miss] Hill,' wrote the Princess to Sarah,

you may assure yourself she shall have ye place you desire for her whenever Bust dyes. I . . . never will engage myself in nothing without knowing first whether anything that lyes in my power can be ye least serviceable to deare Mrs Freeman. . . .[19]

Thus, sometime in 1698, Sarah secured the position that was to enable her cousin Abigail to insinuate her way into Anne's favour – and from there to conspire against the Marlboroughs and eventually bring about their downfall. But this was still a long way in the future and the present cast no shadows.

Marlborough was not only a member of the King's Privy Council but in July 1698, when William made his annual journey to Holland and a Council of Regency was established, he was also one of the nine Lord Justices appointed to exercise the sovereign power. In the autumn, when Parliament reassembled, he played an important part in trying to prevent that august body from slashing to pieces the British army of 87,000 men. William himself addressed Parliament and begged the members not to risk the good terms they had obtained from France by disarming too quickly. After all, the question of the Spanish succession had not been settled and might once again plunge Europe into war. But his words had no effect against the Tory majority in the Commons and a motion was passed which cut the army to 7,000 men. The King's heart bled to see the troops who had fought for him so gallantly thrown on the rubbish heap. In the seventeenth century soldiers were simply turned adrift with no means of support. Many who had shed their blood for King and Country roamed the countryside as footpads and outlaws and ended their days on the gallows.

William was disgusted by the behaviour of Parliament. The House of Commons, led by Robert Harley, a Whig lawyer about whom more will be heard later, even passed a resolution (once desired by Marlborough) 'that the troops that remained in England should consist, both officers and men, of natural born subjects.' This was a wounding decision, as it meant that the King's faithful and well-loved Dutch guards would have to leave the country. In his own hand William wrote to the House asking Members to make an exception in this case, but they took no notice of his request and the guards started their march to the coast. Indignantly, William talked of abdication. Having rescued England from impending ruin, he said, he intended to leave her to herself. 'He has spoken of it to my Lord Marlborough,' wrote Lord Somers, '(which one would wonder at almost as much as at ye thing itself) to Lord Montague, and to my Lord Oxford, and, I believe, to divers others.'[20] The King got as far as composing his abdication speech, but the Lords Sunderland, Somers and Marlborough dissuaded him from such a drastic course.

While all this was going on, Sarah Marlborough was busy arranging the marriages of her two very pretty daughters. Everyone was delighted to hear of seventeen-year-old Henrietta's engagement to Lord Godolphin's only son, Francis. Henrietta was not in love with her fiancé, but she was eager to escape from her mother's dominance. Sarah seemed to find fault with everything her daughter did and Henrietta once cried out that her 'dear Mama would be much better satisfied if only she did but remember she was once my age herself.'

This was impossible. Nevertheless, Henrietta (or 'Lady Harriot' as she was sometimes called) was Princess Anne's favourite among the Marlborough girls, and she now wrote to Sarah, asking to give her a humble gift, 'my poor mite . . . being offer'd from a heart that is without any reserve, with more passion and sincerely, my deare deare Mrs Freeman, than any other can be capable off.'[21]

The following day the Princess explained that her 'poor mite' was £10,000 – a truly colossal sum by the standards of the time. Indeed, it was so large that the Marlboroughs decided to accept only half of what the Princess offered, but Sarah took care to thank her in a letter of warmth and affection. The Princess replied with a spate of letters expressing her devotion. 'As long as I live I must be endeavouring to show', she wrote, 'that never anybody had a Sincerer passion for another than I have for my deare deare Mrs Freeman.'[22]

Anne's wedding took place a year after Henrietta's, but this time Princess Anne could scarcely have been enraptured. The bridegroom was the son of a man she had always hated – the devious Lord Sunderland. However, his son and heir, Lord Spencer, was very different from his father. Instead of trying to please people he did everything to shock and annoy them. He claimed to be an ardent republican who looked forward to the day when not only the monarchy but the whole aristocracy would be abolished and he could be plain Mr Spencer. Marlborough was not at all pleased at the thought of having this hot-headed, rebellious young man, who was still mourning the death of his first wife, as a son-in-law; but Sarah was enchanted by Spencer's intellectual gifts and fascinated by the fact that he was in the process of collecting one of the most important libraries in England. Although many Whigs would have been shocked by his attack on the monarchy, Sarah liked what she called his robust outlook, and in the end she persuaded her husband to consent to the marriage.

On 24 July, the Marlboroughs were staying at Althorp with the Sunderlands while Princess Anne was celebrating her son's eleventh birthday at Windsor. That night the little boy complained of chills and a sore throat. Two days later he developed a fever and, although the doctors let blood, 'he went into a delirium with broken sleep and Incoherent Talke'.[23] The Princess spent day and night at her son's bed, but there was no way to escape the terrible diagnosis of smallpox. The Marlboroughs arrived from Althorp on the afternoon of the 29th and in the early hours of the 30th the child died.

Gloucester's body was taken by barge from Windsor to Westminster and, after lying in state in the Painted Chamber, was interred in the Stuart tomb at Westminster Abbey. The Princess was so distraught she would not come to London but remained in seclusion in Windsor, seeing no one but Lady Marlborough. From this time forward she invariably signed her letters to Sarah 'from your poor unfortunate faithful Morley' – a transposition of the Churchill family motto, 'Faithful but Unfortunate'.

The King was in The Hague when he received the news of Gloucester's death. He wrote to Anne with a simplicity that revealed the depth of his feelings: 'It is so great a loss to me and for all England that my heart is pierced with affliction.'[24] Grief, however, was not allowed to obscure duty and when the King returned to London he was plunged into the question of the succession. Gloucester's death had torn a large gap in the accepted order. Now there were no young heirs and once again people were murmuring that the King might adopt the twelve-year-old Prince of Wales. Whatever the truth of this story, Anne was appeased when King William and his Tory ministry drew up an Act of Settlement which was passed by Parliament in June 1701. After the reigns of William and Anne and their issue, the succession would pass to the Electress Sophia of Hanover (a grand-daughter of James I) and her Protestant heirs.

During the last half of 1700, while Princess Anne was in seclusion mourning the loss of her son, Europe was embroiled once again in the problem of the Spanish inheritance. As Marlborough felt certain that he would be caught up in the approaching storm, he followed developments with rapt attention. In 1698 the childless King of Spain, Carlos II, who had defied the doctors' predictions of imminent death for over thirty years, seemed at last to be nearing his end. This poor Prince was a product of in-breeding between the Habsburgs of Vienna and the Habsburgs of Madrid. He was not only a physical wreck but mentally deranged and, as his life flame began to flicker, he became obsessed with the idea that he was possessed of the Devil. For hours each day he submitted to the mumbo-jumbo of priests who pretended to be exorcizing his evil spirits.

Yet he had an important decision to make. Two families claimed the Spanish inheritance: the Bourbons represented by Louis XIV and the Habsburgs represented by Leopold I. Both these dynastic heads were intimately connected with Spain and intimately connected with each other. Louis and Leopold were the sons of the two sisters of Philip II, and had married the two daughters of Philip II. Louis claimed to have the prior right, as both his mother and his wife were elder daughters; however, his wife had renounced the Spanish throne on condition of a dowry payment which had never been made. So which family had the better claim, the Habsburgs or the Bourbons?

Louis felt sure that King Carlos would leave the inheritance to Leopold, as he was married to Leopold's sister-in-law who was said to have great influence over him. Nevertheless, Louis was determined to see that his wife's 'rights', as he called them, were acknowledged by the cession of some piece of Spanish territory; indeed, it was necessary for his *gloire* to achieve this. At the same time he did not wish to become embroiled in another war so soon after the last – no doubt he wanted time to reorganize and to put his country on a better economic footing – so he decided to negotiate a Partition Treaty with King William. William controlled the Maritime Powers and whatever he decided would have to be endorsed by Leopold, who could not fight France alone.

Louis's proposals were surprisingly modest. As the Earl of Portland, then Ambassador to France, had impressed on him that England and Holland were determined to keep the Spanish Netherlands (Belgium and Luxembourg) from his grasp, he agreed that the Spanish Crown, complete with most of its overseas and European possessions (Mediterranean islands and huge tracts of territory in North and South America), should go to Leopold's grandson, the seven-year-old Electoral Prince of Bavaria. There would be only two exceptions: Leopold's younger son, the Archduke Charles, would be given the Milanese (the province in the north of Italy) and Louis's son, the Grand Dauphin, would be ceded Sicily and Naples, a large province consisting of most of southern Italy. Leopold I, however, flatly refused to acknowledge the treaty. He wanted the whole of the Spanish inheritance and was not willing to part with even a fraction of it. While he was protesting indigantly, the question dissolved into thin air as the Electoral Prince died (very mysteriously, no one ever knew what of) and everyone had to start negotiations all over again.

In 1700 King William and King Louis set about drawing up a Second Partition Treaty. They agreed that no immediate heirs to the French throne or the Habsburg possessions should rule Spain. So the

Spanish Crown would go either to Leopold's second son, the Arch-duke Charles, or to Louis's grandson, Philip, Duke of Anjou. After much bargaining it was agreed once more that Austria could have the Spanish Crown and France Spain's possessions in Italy. The Archduke Charles would be given Spain, the Spanish Netherlands and the Spanish Empire overseas; and the Dauphin would take Naples and Sicily as in the previous agreement, but this time he would also take the Duchy of Milan on the promise of exchanging it with the Duke of Lorraine for the duchies of Lorraine and Bar. This would greatly improve France's eastern border and sever the land connection between Austria and Spain.

Once again the Viennese Habsburgs refused to sign the Treaty, insisting that the entire inheritance should come to them. The Castilian nobles in Madrid were equally insistent on the preserva-tion of the Empire as a whole and began to apply pressure to poor, demented Carlos II to sign another will. Meanwhile, the only stories from Madrid were macabre accounts of the dying King staggering down the stairs to the family mausoleum. There he would open the coffin of his dead first wife and gaze at her remains. At other times he would lie in his own coffin, draped in the shroud that awaited his death.

Carlos II died on 1 November 1700, shortly after putting his signature to a new will. Like the priests and nobles who attended his bedchamber, he was convinced of the necessity of preserving the Spanish Empire in its entirety. But what decision had he made? Into whose hands had he delivered his magnificent gift: Habsburg or Bourbon?

When the Spanish envoy arrived at Fontainebleau he presented the King with a copy of the will, which confounded everything Louis had been led to believe. Carlos II's last testimony stipulated that the Spanish Crown should be offered first to Louis's youngest grandson, Philip, Duke of Anjou; and if Louis rejected it, it would then be offered to Leopold's second son, the Archduke Charles. The Spanish had made their decision in the belief that mighty Louis would be able to enforce the terms of the will more effectively than the disorganized Emperor.

Louis's Partition Treaty with England and Holland presented a problem, but the King's advisers pointed out that there was no way to avoid a war with Leopold whatever France did. And if there was going to be a war it was better to fight for something great than something small. These arguments were conclusive, but when the Court went to Versailles only a few members of Louis's entourage knew what had been decided. When the Spanish Ambassador entered the King's *cabinet* Louis made a gesture towards the eighteen-year-old Duke of Anjou and said: 'You may salute your King.' The Ambassador fell to his knees and made his salutations in a flood of Spanish. 'He does not yet understand Spanish. It is I who will answer for him.' The double doors leading to the Grand Gallery were then opened and Louis announced to the assembled courtiers: 'Gentleman, there is the King of Spain. His birth called him to the Crown. The Spanish nation has wished it and demanded it of me. I have granted their wish with joy. It is the command of heaven.' When the Ambassador took his leave he kissed Philip's hand with emotion. 'What joy,' he said, 'the Pyrenees no longer exist; they have been levelled and we are one.' This remark has sometimes been attributed falsely to Louis, who knew perfectly well that the Pyrenees still existed.[25]

Surprisingly, Louis's acceptance of the Spanish throne for his grandson found a good deal of popular support in England. Fundamentally, no one in the island kingdom wanted another war, particularly as the peace of 1697 had resulted in an explosion of trade and prosperity. The Tories had a further argument: it was better, they said, for a French prince to become King of the Spanish Empire than for parts of the Spanish Empire to be hived off and given to France, thus further strengthening Louis's already powerful kingdom. The Second Partition Treaty was a case in point. If it had been implemented, it would have transferred Sicily and Naples, which the English navy regarded as key positions in the Mediterranean, to France. Indeed, the Tories were so angry that the Treaty had been drawn up without reference to Parliament that they tried to impeach the four Whig architects: Halifax (not 'the Trimmer' who was Churchill's friend, but Montague, the founder of the Bank of England), Russell, Somers and Portland. Although, some months later, the Impeachment Bill was defeated in the House of Lords, it created bitter animosity between the two parties that continued throughout Anne's reign.

King William watched these irrelevant quarrels with a heavy heart. He knew Louis's insatiable appetite and he believed reports that the eighteen-year-old King of Spain, Philip v, was an indolent, weak-willed young man entirely under his grandfather's control. He was convinced that Louis would unite the two crowns in a common purpose, and was deeply disturbed by England's inability to sense the growing danger. Marlborough shared the King's views on France's insatiable appetite and was not surprised when Louis suddenly abandoned the unnatural restraint he had been practising for the arrogant pose to which Europe was accustomed. He embarked on a series of foolish and dangerous acts – encouraged, no doubt, by the sorry plight of his enemy across the Channel. No longer was William the leader of a powerful coalition, no longer the inspiration of a powerful fighting force. He was the servant of an English Parliament that mocked and thwarted him; that disbanded his army and sent his faithful Dutch guards marching back to Holland. What did Louis have to fear from England? The English accepted Philip as King of Spain and were making it clear that they wanted peace at any price.

So first, in contravention of his 'gentleman's agreement', he drew up a paper officially recognizing that his grandson, Philip v of Spain, was still eligible for the succession to the French throne if Fate so decreed. The document flatly rejected the English view that sovereigns were subject to the will of man, and triumphantly proclaimed the Divine Right of Kings. Despite a groundswell of resentment in England and Holland, the claim was registered by the French Parliament in February 1701.

Louis's next move was more serious. The great fortifications along the frontier with the Spanish Netherland had been regarded by Holland for over half a century as a 'barrier' against French aggression; so much so that when the Ryswick peace treaty was signed in 1697 and the Spanish complained about the cost of maintaining the fortresses, the Dutch had sent twenty-two battalions of their own troops to assume the duties and the expense. Now, within a week of the compliant Philip v mounting the Spanish throne, French troops suddenly appeared before the barrier fortifications. The Spanish commanders were still lighting bonfires and drinking loyal toasts in celebration of Philip's succession and happily swung open their gates to admit their new French allies. The Dutch were too surprised and too bewildered to break the peace and offered no resistance; the French disarmed and imprisoned them and eventually sent them back to Holland. Thus the great forts that whole armies had fought over for months at a time collapsed like ninepins: Antwerp, Mons and even Namur, captured by William in 1697, Léau, Ath, Venlo, Ostend, Nieuport and Oudenarde. Without a shot being fired, they now belonged to the Sun King who glibly explained that as Holland had not recognized Philip v, Dutch soldiers could scarcely be allowed to remain in the Spanish Netherlands. Furthermore, Louis's move was a contribution to peace as it prevented the Dutch from the temptation of using the bases to attack France.

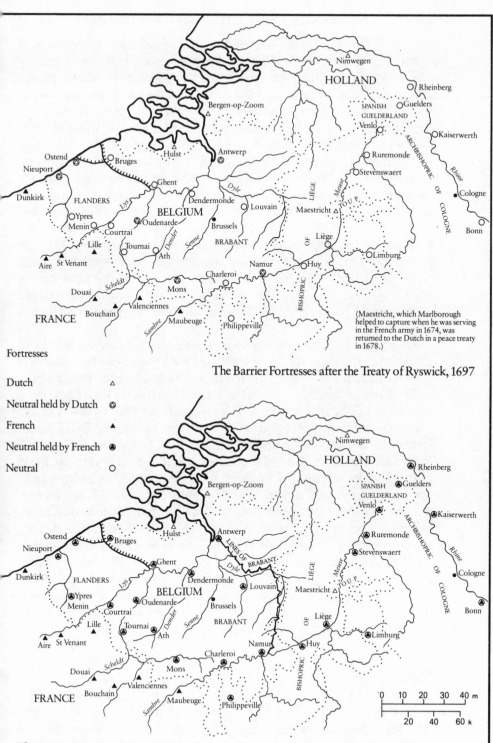

Fortresses

Dutch	△
Neutral held by Dutch	◎
French	▲
Neutral held by French	◉
Neutral	○

(Maestricht, which Marlborough helped to capture when he was serving in the French army in 1674, was returned to the Dutch in a peace treaty in 1678.)

The Barrier Fortresses after the Treaty of Ryswick, 1697

The Barrier Fortresses in April 1702, when Marlborough assumed command of the Grand Alliance

The War of the Spanish Succession

At long last, England, even the England of unbelieving Tories, was aroused and furiously indignant. People not only accepted the inevitability of war but some even tried to hasten it. In May a deputation from Kent begged the House of Commons to grant supplies to enable the King to help their allies 'before it is too late'. At the same time the burghers of Amsterdam, staunch pacifists a few months earlier, were begging William to look to his defences. The King had foreseen every move on the chessboard, but he was in poor health and sensed that he, himself, would not be able to carry on the fight for long. He needed someone to head the Grand Alliance, to negotiate the treaties, to lead the armies into battle. In other words, he needed someone to take his own exalted place. The choice could only be an Englishman, as England would not follow a foreign general. Only one man seemed to fulfil the necessary and multiple requirements – a man who was a brilliant negotiator, a man who knew the demands of war. And that man had the added advantage of being the trusted servant of the sovereign who would mount the throne upon William's death.

Thus Lord Marlborough, who had been punished and scorned and ignored by the King, was now entrusted with the most important and sacred duties that William had the power to bestow: the preservation of the life and liberties of England and Holland. On 31 May 1701 Marlborough was appointed Commander-in-Chief of the English forces assembling in Holland; and on 28 June he became Ambassador Extraordinary to the United Provinces. To Marlborough himself it must have seemed as though someone had rubbed a magic lamp, for in his wildest dreams he could never have foreseen such a sudden leap to power. He knew, of course, that William's choice had fallen on him not only because of his training and ability but because of Sarah's influence over Princess Anne. William's whole life had been dedicated to the containment of Louis xiv and he was determined that France would not find Europe an easy prey after his death. With Lord Marlborough heading the Grand Alliance and Lady Marlborough directing Anne, William's struggle would continue in the next reign. And that mattered to the passionate, frail, asthmatic, valiant Prince of Orange more than anything else.

On 1 July 1701, the royal yacht carried King William and the Earl of Marlborough to Holland. Marlborough's responsibilities were prodigious but he was accompanied by two able personal assistants who would prove themselves indispensable in the ten years of campaigning that stretched ahead. The first was Brigadier William

Cadogan, a big, burly Irish Protestant soldier, twenty-five years his junior, who had first come to his notice during the attack on Kinsale and Cork in 1690. Cadogan had been only fifteen years old then, and was serving with the Inniskillen Dragoons as a boy cornet. Ten years later, when Cadogan's regiment (renamed the 1st Irish Dragoons) was sent to Holland to serve under William III, Marlborough encountered him for the second time. Twenty-six-year-old Cadogan was now Quartermaster-General, with the rank of Major. Marlborough promptly seconded him, gave him the rank of Brigadier and made him Quartermaster-General of the whole army. One can understand Marlborough's choice of an energetic, high-spirited young officer as his right-hand man; young men have a zest and enthusiasm that often deserts the middle-aged. Cadogan proved to be worth his weight in gold. His outstanding ability became so obvious that the roles of Chief-of-Staff and Director of Intelligence – functions that had not existed before – were added to his duties.

Marlborough's other helper was Adam Cardonnel, the son of a French Protestant who had entered the War Office at the early age of fourteen and risen to the position of Chief Clerk. He was immensely capable and possessed the added advantage of speaking French and English equally well. The fact that he was bilingual explains why Marlborough employed him as a secretary as early as 1692. Cardonnel had proved himself not only an astute and reliable assistant but a trusted confidante. He knew his master's mind so well that in a pinch he could draft Marlborough's official letters himself – whether to English political leaders or to the princes and generals of the Grand Alliance.

Marlborough's new duties fell into two main categories. He was to make one last attempt to try and end the war, but if that failed he was to work out an offensive and defensive alliance against France with England's two main partners, Holland and the Empire. When this was accomplished he was to try and draw into his net such powerful states as Prussia and Denmark and as many of the independent German principalities as could be persuaded to throw in their lot with the Grand Alliance. This was the diplomatic part of his task. The other side was concerned with his fighting men. He had to decide the number of troops and seamen which each signatory would provide and to train and command the British army now assembling behind the Dutch frontier.

Marlborough's official residence in The Hague was Prince Maurice of Nassau's beautiful house near the palace. (This house was burned down in 1707 and re-built on its present site.) Marlborough cut a memorable figure as he stood at the top of the stairs receiving his distinguished guests. A 'finer work of art' had never been shown there – 'a glorious living portrait of a Milord, every inch a soldier and a courtier; said indeed to be fifty years of age but in the prime of manly beauty, with a complexion like a girl's; talked charmingly in bad French; seeming to understand all and to sympathize with everyone.'[26]

Here in the Mauritshuis Marlborough did all his business, beginning with one last attempt to retrieve the fast-fading peace. On behalf of the Maritime Powers – England and Holland – he once more demanded the withdrawal of French troops from the barrier fortresses, and the guarantee of a reasonable settlement for the Emperor Leopold. But Louis XIV, swollen with self-confidence, refused to attend a conference or to make any concessions. As an excuse he pointed out that his soldiers were already fighting the Emperor's troops in Italy.

This was perfectly true, but the outcome was not at all what Louis expected. The Emperor's army was led by the brilliant thirty-seven-year-old Prince Eugene of Savoy, who had been fighting wars for the past nineteen years. Marlborough had often heard Eugene praised as one of the foremost generals in Europe and he now had a chance to judge his skill and audacity for himself. Louis XIV's famous commander, Marshal Catinat, proclaimed mockingly that if Eugene wished to get past his line in Italy, he and his army would have to learn to fly – and Eugene seemed to do just that. He debouched into the country by little-known passes, marched through Vicenza and finally confronted Catinat on the plains to the south. Catinat declined to take the initiative and tried, instead, to defend the line of the River Adige. Eugene turned his front and drove Catinat back first to Lake Garda, then to the River Oglio behind Chiari.

The whole operation was one of supreme bravado – almost like a present-day commando operation – and Marlborough was both amused and impressed. The French were so annoyed they sent Marshal de Villeroy to replace him. 'It is important that I shall be seen in the city', Villeroy wrote to King Louis, 'to persuade people that your Majesty disapproves of the past conduct of the campaign.' A few days later he assured the King that 'the dispositions are favourable for our enterprise . . . your Majesty can wait with calm and tranquillity.'[27] But unfortunately, from the French point of view, the engagement was a disaster. Eugene drove Villeroy's army back with withering fire that cost the French 250 officers and 3,000 men. Worse was to come. A few months later the pugnacious Eugene, in a battle for Cremona, kidnapped Villeroy and with that final *coup* retired to winter quarters.

Marlborough longed to meet the gallant Prince. He could not know that he was destined to forge a glorious brotherhood of arms with Eugene – so much so that one day in war they would be referred to as 'twin captains'. Yet Eugene had nearly missed his vocation. He was a grandson of Duke Charles Emmanuel of Savoy and a son of Cardinal Mazarin's beautiful niece, Olympe Mancini. Eugene was brought up in France, but in his youth was frail and unprepossessing. Although he had a burning desire to enter the army, his slender physique and slightly vacant stare did not commend him to the military. The King went so far as to forbid him to enter the army, and forced him into the Church, referring to him patronizingly as '*le petit abbé*'. This disappointment, coupled with his father's exile, prompted Eugene to leave France. He moved to Vienna and offered his services to Leopold, who enlisted him in the fight against the Turks. He had risen in the army, rank by rank, and now was recognized as 'the most renowned commander in Europe'.

Sarah had journeyed to The Hague to be present for the signing of the Grand Alliance between England, Holland and the Empire, which took place on 7 September 1701. Marlborough signed for England, and Sarah was thrilled to be among the brilliant throng of spectators. She was even summoned to the palace at Loo where, wrote Cardonnel, she 'had the honour of a visit from the King in her apartment.' Sarah's vivacity lifted John's spirits and when she started back to England he felt as though someone had suddenly rung down the curtain and blown out the candles. 'I must own to you', he wrote to Godolphin when she was on her way home, 'that I have a great many melancholy thoughts, and am very much of the opinion that nobody can be very happy that is in business. . . .'[28]

Marlborough had too much to do to remain dejected for long. In the Grand Alliance Treaty William had taken care to pitch the demands of the Allies in a low key. They had acquiesced in Philip's Spanish sovereignty but stipulated that the Crowns of Spain and France must never be united. The Habsburgs would receive 'satisfactory' compensation in the form of most of Spain's European possessions, including the much fought-over Spanish Netherlands; and the Maritime Powers would receive 'satisfactory' commercial rights in the West Indies. Finally, the contracting powers agreed to negotiate jointly with France rather than separately.

In spite of dotting the i's and crossing the t's the Allies were not yet at war with France. But a few days after the treaty was signed an event took place that catapulted Europe to the brink of the abyss. James II died at St Germain and Louis XIV, despite all his promises at Ryswick – his recognition of William as King of England and his Solemn pledge not to assist the Stuarts to retrieve the throne – gave way to his emotion at the bedside and hailed the Prince of Wales as James III of England. It was not an accidental blunder; the Sun King had made up his mind that war was inevitable and felt so supremely confident of France's power that he decided to throw down the gauntlet.

England took Louis's words as a mortal insult. Not only had he repudiated his pledges but he was treating England as though she was a vassal of France. Indeed, the country was engulfed by such a storm of anger that William asked Marlborough to make sure that Anne did not mourn her father as a monarch (that meant putting the whole of her house in mourning) but simply as a close relation. Marlborough sent William's message via Godolphin, but Anne seemed to miss the point, referring to it as 'the ill-natured, cruel proceeding of Mr Caliban which vexes me more than you can imagine, and I am out of all patience when I think I must do so monstrous a thing as not to put my lodgings in mourning for my father.'[29]

William decided to exploit the popular outcry against Louis by holding a general election. He hoped, of course, to rid himself of the hated Tory opposition in the Commons that had slashed his army to bits. His Commander-in-Chief, however, did his best to dissuade him. Although Marlborough was a Tory by birth and breeding, and had only established friendly relations with the Whigs after abandoning James for William, he felt that a new election would be a serious political mistake. Not only were the Tories much stronger than the King imagined, but they were now doing their best to make up for their former lapse. They had fulfilled all William's demands from strengthening the army to providing munitions. Indeed, Marlborough believed that 'only the party of peace could draw the sword of war', and that it would be much better to enter a conflict backed by the Tories than to leave them to form a hostile opposition. Godolphin agreed with Marlborough. The Tories, wrote Godolphin, 'provided ... the greatest supplies that ever were given when the Kingdom was not in actual war.'[30] Marlborough read this letter to William but the King persisted in holding his election. The result was not very different from the previous Parliament, with the Commons fairly evenly balanced between Tories and Whigs. As Marlborough had feared, however, the Tories felt deeply affronted. Their respect for William turned to bitter hatred and they said openly that they longed for his death.

Europe now stood on the brink of a long and terrible war in which Louis XIV would be a clear favourite. France's allies were numerous enough to give an impression of invincibility: Portugal, Savoy, Bavaria, Cologne and, of course, Spain, with her world-wide empire and her European possessions – Belgium, Luxembourg and most of Italy. Even more serious, the whole Dutch barrier was in French hands, and Louis, by his occupation of the archbishoprics of Cologne and Trier, was master of the Moselle and the lower Rhine.

William did not live to fight this new war. In February, while hunting in Richmond Park, his horse stumbled over a molehill and fell. The King was thrown off and broke his collar bone. At first the injury seemed comparatively unimportant, but William, weakened by tuberculosis and in poor health, deteriorated rapidly. (In the years to come Jacobites would lift their glasses to toast the killer-mole as 'the little gentleman in black velvet'.) The man who loved the King more than anyone or anything in the world was at his bedside when he died – William Bentinck, the Earl of Portland; the newest favourite, the Earl of Albemarle, was kept away. However, it was Queen Mary who triumphed at the end. When William breathed his last, at eight o'clock on the evening of 8 March 1702, he was wearing a locket containing a piece of Mary's hair.

Queen Anne's great moment had come. It was, as she had written to Sarah ten years earlier, 'a Sunshine day'. But would the rest of her prediction come true? Would England, faced by a hostile Europe dominated by the formidable Louis, really 'flourish againe'?

Seven

The Sunshine Day

Although Queen Anne was barely thirty-seven years old, she was in a state of physical decline. Apart from the debilitating effect of eighteen pregnancies in seventeen years, she suffered from rheumatism and gout (probably arthritis) and had recently contracted dropsy, a malady that caused her body to swell in alarming proportions. She could only walk a few steps at a time and was usually carried about, even inside the palace, in a sedan-chair.

Her first public engagement called for an address to Parliament but she feared that her poor health would prevent her from carrying it out. She discussed the problem with her long-standing friend, Lord Godolphin, who, as Sarah pointed out, 'had conducted the Queen with the care and tenderness of a father or a guardian through a state of helpless ignorance and had faithfully served her in all her difficulties before she was queen.'[1] 'She is very unwieldy and lame,' Godolphin wrote to Robert Harley, Speaker of the Commons. 'Must she come in person to the House of Lords, or may she send for the two Houses to come to her?'[2] Harley replied that if possible the Queen should attend in person.

Consequently, on 11 March, accompanied only by the Marlboroughs, Anne arrived at the Palace of Westminster. Her infirmities were effectively disguised and her costume was carefully chosen for its historical significance. Her dress was red velvet lined with ermine and edged in gold galloon. She wore the crown and heavy gold chain of St George, and bore the Garter ribbon on her left arm. Her clothes were modelled on a portrait of Queen Elizabeth.

Queen Anne was not a clever woman but she had a priceless asset in her low, sweet, musical voice which always charmed and often thrilled. Her speech was never to be forgotten because of a single sentence – words suggested by her uncle, Lord Rochester: 'I know my own heart to be entirely English.' This not only was a stab at the late King William but at the French-educated Prince of Wales, and it delighted her parochial listeners. 'Her Majesty charmed both Houses on Wednesday last,' declared one observer,

> for never any woman spoke more audibly or with better grace. And her pressing to support our allyance abroad will commute for what the Dutch may take amiss in that emphasis which her Majesty layd on her English heart. But it did very well at home and raised a hum with all that heard her.[3]

The Queen loaded John and Sarah with honours. Within five days of her accession she bestowed the Garter upon Marlborough; and before he set off on a brief trip to The Hague to stress Anne's determination to prosecute the war (still undeclared) she gave him three important offices: Captain-General of her army both at home and abroad; Master-General of the Ordnance (a lucrative post that he had always coveted); and Ambassador Extraordinary to the Dutch Republic. Apart from this he was, of course, a member of her Cabinet Council.

Marlborough's family was the recipient of many more honours. His daughters, Henrietta and Anne, were made Ladies of the Bedchamber, while Sarah – beloved Sarah – became Groom of the Stole (the officer closest to the sovereign), Mistress of the Robes and Keeper of the Privy Purse. This was not all. A few months later, when the Queen relieved Lord Portland of his perquisites, she passed on to Sarah his position as Ranger of the Great Park at Windsor. This was a life appointment and brought with it the Lodge at Windsor, a charming place that became the Marlboroughs' favourite house. Altogether, Sarah received £5,600 a year, a huge salary for the time. This was dwarfed by John's income, which eventually totalled nearly £60,000 per annum.* Not everyone rejoiced at the Churchills' good fortune. Lord Dartmouth, the Tory son of John's old friend George Legge, wrote maliciously that Churchill 'was undoubtedly the most fortunate man that ever lived, having always received the reward before the merit, and the appearance of having deserved it came afterwards, for which he expected and constantly received a second gratification. . . .'[4]

On this occasion Marlborough needed all the encouragement he could get, for the task facing him was prodigious. No Englishman, and certainly no Dutchman, could gaze on a world map in 1702

---

* In these days of inflation this figure would have to be multiplied by fifty.

without acute anxiety. With far-flung Spain as an ally, rapacious Louis XIV not only controlled many of the ports of North and South America, but dominated the strategically important Mediterranean and three-quarters of the European Continent. The Archbishop of Cologne and the Bishop of Liège had become French allies, and the Elector Max Emmanuel of Bavaria was in the process of following suit. The Dutch barrier had passed into French hands, while the territories owned by Spain – Belgium, Luxembourg and most of Italy – were France's willing partners. Louis's fortresses bristled with cannon all the way from Bonn and Kaiserwerth to the sea, and the Dutch were certain that his baleful eye would fall once again on Holland as a desirable military objective.

Louis looked so impregnable that in England the High Tories argued that it was folly to send an army across the Channel. England should subsidize her Continental allies and limit herself to a naval war, striking at her enemies' overseas possessions. Although this view was defeated in the Cabinet Council, Marlborough organized a combined naval and military expedition in the Mediterranean. Queen Anne appointed her husband, Prince George, to the position of nominal High Admiral and Marlborough's brother, Admiral George Churchill, became his right-hand man. Marlborough, therefore, had no difficulty in controlling naval strategy. He decided to follow William III's plan and capture Cadiz, and from this base perhaps take Minorca which would give them control of the Mediterranean. This would keep the Tory opposition quiet, but there would be no question of not playing a leading part in the Continental war.

The die was cast on 4 May 1702, when the King-at-Arms rode out from St James's Palace surrounded by heralds and, to the blare of trumpets and the crash of cymbals, read out the Queen's declaration of war against France. When Louis XIV was informed, he remarked laconically: 'I must be growing old if ladies are now declaring war on me.' Like all the wars of the period, this one – the War of the Spanish Succession – was fought with close relations on opposing sides. Queen Anne was ranged against her first cousin, Louis XIV, as well as her two half-brothers, one legitimate, one not – James, the Pretender, and James, Duke of Berwick. Berwick was in arms against his uncle, the Duke of Marlborough; Louis XIV against his first cousin and brother-in-law, the Emperor Leopold; and the Emperor's celebrated general, Prince Eugene, against his first cousin, the Duke of Vendôme. The Duke of Savoy (after changing sides) became the opponent of his own daughters who were married to Louis's grandsons – the Duke of Burgundy and Philip of Anjou, who became King of Spain.

A few days before Marlborough sailed for Holland, the Queen acceded to his urgent request that his close friend, Lord Godolphin, be granted the office of Lord Treasurer. This was vital to the Captain-General's peace of mind, as wars could not be fought without subsidies and arms. Everything, a contemporary quipped, was being arranged for his benefit: while he ran the war, his friend ran the country, and his wife ran the Queen. 'He sailes with a full Gale of Favour,' a local paper observed. Yet the thought of being separated from Sarah for long periods made Marlborough inexpressibly sad and, as the Margate skyline faded into the distance, he withdrew to his cabin to write her his thoughts. 'It is impossible', he began,

> to express with what a heavy heart I parted with you when I was by the water's side. I could have given my life to have come back, though I know my own weakness so much that I durst not, for I know I should have exposed myself to the company. I did for a great while, with the perspective glass, look upon the cliffs in hopes I might have had one sight of you. If you will be sensible of what I now feel you will endeavour ever to be easy to me, and then I shall be most happy.[5]

This is a remarkable letter from a man of fifty-two who had been married for twenty-five years. As Sarah made John burn her letters, there is, sadly enough, only a one-sided picture of the deep devotion that bound these two together. But judging from the way Sarah fought for her lord, both wisely and unwisely, John's affection was amply returned.

In The Hague, Marlborough found everything at sixes and sevens, because no one could decide on a Commander-in-Chief for the joint Anglo–Dutch forces. The Dutch General Ginkel (whom William had made Earl of Athlone) had been given the task temporarily and, needless to say, was agitating for permanent command. Marlborough, however, had a close friend and supporter in the Grand Pensionary, Anthonie Heinsius, who was Holland's *de facto* head of government. The two men liked and trusted each other and talked with complete openness. Heinsius believed that his hero, King William, had intended Marlborough for the overall command and gave the Englishman his backing; but some of the Dutch generals were indignant to think they might be by-passed. They argued that, although Marlborough was a gallant soldier, he lacked experience – except for the attack on Cork and Kinsale, he had never been in command of a major undertaking. Ginkel, Overkirk, Opdam and Slangenberg, who had been fighting wars for over twenty years, were all rivals for the top post, and even stressed that they should be given priority as the Dutch had pledged 100,000 troops to the Alliance compared with England's 42,000 men. However, Heinsius had the final word when he pointed out that although England and Holland were jointly pledged to subsidize the war effort of the smaller states, England was carrying the lion's share of the financial burden. And this was more important than the length of a soldier's service.

The Dutch were not Marlborough's only rivals. Surprisingly enough, Queen Anne intervened and urged the States-General to install her husband as Commander-in-Chief. Although she sent a letter in her own hand, everyone knew that poor, foolish, kind-hearted Prince George (now nominal High Admiral) was quite incapable of fulfilling a colonelcy, much less of coping with the marshals of France, and left her letter unanswered. The final contender was the Elector of Brandenburg,* who had joined the Alliance when the Emperor Leopold promised to recognize him as King of Prussia, but he, too, was ignored. Fortunately the lesser royalties made no attempt to project themselves. In their ranks were the Electors of Mainz and Trier, the Landgraves of Hesse-Cassell and Hesse-Darmstadt, and the Elector Palatine. They joined the Alliance supported by English subsidies, and were quite content to serve under the orders of Marlborough or whatever Anglo–Dutch leader was chosen. The Margrave of Baden may have coveted the position, but as a ruling prince his first obligation was to defend his own large estates between the upper Rhine and the Neckar, and to lead his own army into battle. As the Emperor's senior general, he could not possibly be spared from home duties.

Not until the war had been in progress for nearly two months was the matter brought to a conclusion. By this time the operation theatres had been decided by the French. They had sent two marshals to the Italian front with an army of 60,000 men to confront the Emperor's troops; another 20,000 men under the command of Marshal Catinat to defend Alsace against the Margrave of Baden; and 60,000 men into the Low Countries under Marshal Boufflers – a former colleague of Marlborough when they both had served under Turenne in the attack on Sinzheim in 1674. Another army was commanded by Louis's grandson, the Duke of Burgundy.

Boufffler's force had moved into a strongly entrenched position between the Rhine and the Meuse, in the territory of Cleves, close to Nimwegen, the gateway into Holland. When Marlborough left for

* The title 'Elector' was given to the German princes empowered to elect the Holy Roman Emperor.

this theatre on 30 June Heinsius informed him that the States-General had held a secret meeting that morning and awarded him the top command. That was as close to acknowledging him as Commander-in-Chief as the Dutch would go. He was not, in fact, in command of all Dutch troops, only those serving in the Grand Alliance at the side of English and German soldiers. Indeed, as far as Holland was concerned, his status was deliberately undefined and remained so throughout the war. Marlborough's secretary, Adam Cardonnel, looked on the bright side. 'The States have given directions to all their generals and other officers', he wrote to England, 'to obey my Lord Marlborough as their General.'[6] Three days later, Marlborough wrote from Nimwegen thanking the Dutch for giving him command of all the British, Dutch and hired German forces of the Grand Alliance, a post that he held until 1711. He continued to play his hand quietly to overcome the jealousy that his appointment had aroused. When Godolphin sent his congratulations, he replied that 'the station I am now in . . . would have been a great deal more agreeable to me if it could have been had without dispute and with a little less trouble; but patience overcomes all things.[7]'

Unfortunately, patience does not always triumph. Although Marlborough was tactful and charming, he met with nothing but rebuffs and disappointments. The truth was that his idea as to how a battle should be fought was very different from the standard practice of the day. Eighteenth-century warfare was surprisingly leisurely. Because of waterlogged roads, the army only fought in the spring and summer. In the autumn it went into winter quarters for six months; and, because of the difficulties of feeding men and beasts when they were on the move, objectives became severely limited. An average fighting force of 60,000 men, equipped with an appropriate number of guns and supply-carts, and carrying an average amount of baggage, often stretched along the road for twenty miles. The problem of supplying each soldier with a daily ration of a kilo of bread – not to mention the thousands of tons of fodder needed to feed the horses – discouraged generals from moving too far afield and inclined them towards the relative security of a fixed target. Gradually, campaigns were designed to carry out a series of sieges during which the bulk of the army was employed to cover or break up investments and then to retire to winter quarters for recruitment and drill.

Marlborough had not been at headquarters a week before his Dutch colleagues began to realize that his idea of fighting was very different from theirs. He was not interested in a cautious campaign – in the capture of a town here, a fortress there – indeed, he would go to any lengths to provoke a confrontation. He sought a great battle on an open plain: a test of skill that would enable him to drive the French army out of Flanders. That was what he wanted – a decisive win! However, he soon discovered that far from being a free agent he was in trammels. The constitution of the Dutch Republic stated that two members of the Government – civilians – should accompany the Captain-General throughout his operations, and that no important action could be fought or, for that matter, no town besieged, without their consent. Their consent depended on the mood of the Government, and at this moment the mood was very cautious. The United Provinces had been invaded once and the Deputies flatly refused to allow the Dutch army that was barring the enemy's path at Nimwegen to move from its entrenched positions.

Marlborough understood their feelings but was determined to coerce them into a decisive undertaking. One of the two Dutch Deputies was a former Ambassador to England, Herr Geldermalsen. He was deeply impressed by Marlborough's reasoning and was soon arguing vigorously with his own countrymen. Poor Lord Marlborough, he wrote to Heinsius, was in lively distress to find himself 'at the head of a stronger army tied to the gates of a town .... In the name of God,' he implored, 'work unceasingly for a resolve to do something effective.' Meanwhile, Marlborough himself was hammering at the Dutch, trying to convince them that as long as Marshal Boufflers remained in the Nimwegen-Clèves area, the Allies would be relegated to the defensive; and as long as the French retained control of occupied territory they would emerge from the war victorious.

For a brief moment it looked as though Marlborough's arguments were prevailing, but what happened next proved to be a cruel disappointment. The Earl had a very simple plan that was bound, he said, to draw the enemy away from Nimwegen. If he crossed the Maas and marched south, Boufflers would be compelled to come running after him to protect the line on which the French army depended for its food, and to save the Spanish Netherlands. It took Marlborough ten precious days to win the necessary consent; at last, on 26 July, he was allowed to start his southward move. Exactly what he had predicted happened; in the words of Captain Parker, one of his infantry officers, the enemy was obliged 'to quit their camp and dance after him'. Boufflers saw the full danger of his position on the Maas with hostile Maestricht behind him. He had no choice but to march across Marlborough's front to reach his lines in Spanish Brabant. This was a perilous operation, as Marlborough was almost bound to attack him when he was at his greatest disadvantage.

The decision was reached on the night of 1 August. Marlborough told the Dutch Deputies that his intention was to attack Boufflers and his whole army the next day as they streamed past his front. It took several hours to gain their agreement, but at last all was settled. Baggage was sent to the rear and the army assigned to its battle positions. Dawn broke and Marlborough was on horseback, about to give the order for the general attack; in the distance he could see the heads of the enemy's columns as they approached from the south-west, ready to cross his front.

At this point a shattering scene took place. The Dutch Deputies suddenly appeared and withdrew their consent. They knew that if he chose to ignore them they would not have a leg to stand upon, so now they were forced to change their tactics and humbly begged him not to risk the army of the Republic on the terrible gamble of a battle. There was always the possibility of defeat, they said, and defeat could mean the end of Holland's very existence. Marlborough argued with all the force at his command, but he could not overcome their fears. Convinced that he was losing the chance of victory – perhaps even the chance of driving the French out of Flanders – he nevertheless bowed to their distraught feelings. 'It may be doubted', comments G.M.Trevelyan,

> if a man ever underwent a more bitter disappointment. But without any sign of annoyance, he [Marlborough] invited the Deputies to ride forward with him to see the enemy pass over the heath, which they and most of the General Officers did, and saw them hurrying over it in the greatest confusion and disorder imaginable. Upon this they all acknowledged that they had lost a fair opportunity of giving the enemy a fatal blow.[8]

This is a puzzling and not altogether commendable example of Marlborough's famous compliance. Others might have gambled on victory and flatly refused to withhold the order to attack; indeed, a sense of outrage would have made most men temperamentally incapable of accepting such a reversal. Was Marlborough's 'self-control' a virtue or a failing? As a courtier he had been trained to gain consent by placating and cajoling, knowing that if, in the end, he failed he would have to submit gracefully; as a military man dealing with his allies he adopted the same tactics. Not only was it against his nature to ride roughshod over his fellow beings, but he believed that in the long run he would fare better by winning their goodwill than by thwarting them. Indeed, the sharp contrast between the audacious, lion-hearted soldier with the sword, who refused to entertain defeat, and the even-tempered, unruffled courtier who frequently hoisted the flag of surrender, makes Marlborough one of the most enigmatic characters in history.

Although on the morning of 2 August the Deputies ruefully admitted that a great opportunity had been lost, a second chance made itself felt that very same night. The French were forced to pitch camp at a town called Zonhoven, a position almost as dangerous for them as crossing the enemy's front. Marlborough hoped that the experience of the morning would have altered the outlook of the Deputies and once again urged an attack at dawn. But the Deputies still could not bring themselves to run a risk – any risk – no matter how small. The Duke of Berwick, who was serving under Boufflers, gauged the true difficulty of his uncle's position. 'The Earl of Marlborough', he wrote,

> proposed to march up to us by passing the defile of Peer, by which a battle on the heaths would have been unavoidable; but the Deputies of the States-General would never consent to this, any more than to attack us in our camp at Sonoven. This was very fortunate for us; for we were posted in such a manner that we should have been beaten without being able to stir, our left being very high, and our right sunk in a cul de sac between two rivulets.[9]

Although Marlborough was seething inwardly with rage and frustration, he continued to present his usual bland appearance to the world. He preserved his balance by writing daily letters to Sarah, sending loving messages to his children, and enquiring about his garden. Occasionally the strain showed through his placid observations. 'These last three or four days', he wrote, 'have been very uneasy, I have been obliged to take more *pains than I am well able to endure.*'[10]

Lord Marlborough did not expect life to run on a trouble-free path, but although he was familiar with the role of Dutch civilian Deputies responsible to a Dutch civilian Parliament, he had not expected to be constantly baulked and humiliated by them. No one but a man with heroic self-control could have continued to serve the Alliance so wholeheartedly, even managing to remain on friendly terms with the exasperating 'overlords' who followed him about vetoing his plans. Lord Ailesbury, Marlborough's friend of long standing, who had been exiled from England for his Jacobite activities in 1696, and was living now in Flanders, gives us a vivid glimpse of Marlborough at the front. He first sent his secretary, Mr West, to ask the Commander-in-Chief for a pass allowing him to go to England for a few days. Mr West, with an assistant trailing behind him, found Lord Marlborough at the front under cannon-fire, standing in a circle of generals. Apparently the

Portrait of John Churchill, 1st Duke of Marlborough, by John Closterman

Miniature of Charles II in 1665 by Samuel Cooper

Barbara Villiers, Lady Castlemaine and later Duchess of Cleveland, who was the mistress of both Charles II and John Churchill (painting by Sir Peter Lely)

Louis XIV, the Sun King

James II by an unknown artist, *c*.1690

Arabella Churchill, John's sister and the
mistress of James II (portrait by Mary Beale)

The Duke of Berwick, son of Arabella
Churchill and James II, who rose to be a
marshal in the French army and was witness to
many of his uncle's triumphs (portrait by
Niccolo Cassana)

Sarah, Duchess of Marlborough, *c.*1700
(portrait after Sir Godfrey Kneller)

e burning of the *Royal James*, 1672, during the battle of Sole Bay where John Churchill
rned a captaincy in the Admiralty Regiment

Companion portraits of William and Mary, Prince and Princess of Orange,
by William Wissing, 1685

The Marlborough family painted by John Closterman, c.1696

nce George of Denmark painted
Michael Dahl in 1704

Portrait of Anne as a young woman
by William Wissing

igail Hill, Lady Masham, who beguiled
een Anne and saved Louis xiv from
ominious defeat

Prince Eugene of Savoy painted
by Sir Godfrey Kneller

Engraving of the battle of Blenheim, 13 August 1704

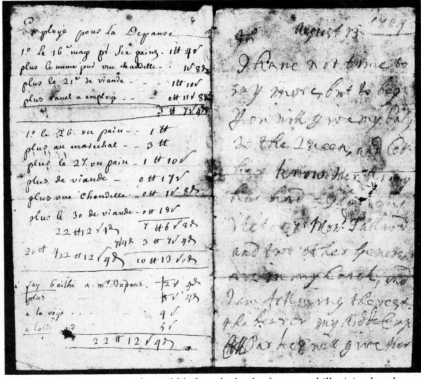

Marlborough's note to Sarah, scribbled on the back of a tavern bill, giving her the news of the victory at Blenheim

(*Above*) Portrait of Sydney, 1st Earl of
Godolphin, holding his white wand of office as
Lord Treasurer, by Sir Godfrey Kneller, *c.*1705

(*Left*) Robert Harley, 1st Earl of Oxford, the
man Marlborough hated more than any other
(portrait by Sir Godfrey Kneller, 1714)

Henry St John, Viscount Bolingbroke
(portrait attributed to J.Richardson)

Mareschal de Tallard.

Marlborough's French adversaries: (top left)
Marshal Villars, (top right) Marshal
Villeroy, (left) Marshal Tallard and (above)
the Duke of Vendôme

Contemporary engraving of the battle of
Ramillies, May 1706

The Battlel of Ramillies where ÿ D: of Marlbo
roug.ᵗ &c: took 26. Standards & 63. Enʃigns the
French loʃing 20000, men all their Baggage
Amunition &c.

The Ramillies playing card showing the
cannonball shearing off the head of
the Duke's equerry

Portrait of the 1st Duke of Marlborough
by Sir Godfrey Kneller

Sarah, Duchess of Marlborough, when she was
in mourning for her son Charles
(portrait by Sir Godfrey Kneller)

Detail from the tapestry showing the battle of Oudenarde, 1708

sketch of the Duke of Marlborough at the battle of Malplaquet, 1709

Detail from the tapestry
showing the siege of
Bouchain

The rich and powerful Duke of Somerset, who courted the
widowed sixty-two-year-old Duchess of Marlborough with
ardour and persistence (portrait by Sir Godfrey Kneller,
c. 1703)

An engraving of the north face of Blenheim Palace c.1745

cannonade had been begun by Marshal Boufflers in celebration of St Louis's Day. The serenade was particularly appropriate as all French guns were marked *Ultima Ratio Regis* – 'The King's Last Argument'.

Marlborough recognized his visitor and, turning away from his officers, said: 'Mr West, my humble service to my Lord. You see I cannot write now, but I will send an express to Aix.' He added that the spot where the two visitors were standing was dangerous but, just as the men began to move back, there was an ominous whistle and a cannon-ball carried off the head of Mr West's companion. Mr West hastily took his leave. 'Not being used to such hot work,' Lord Ailesbury tells us merrily, 'no doubt he was severely affrighted.'[11]

During the first months of Marlborough's appointment all eyes were fastened on him to see what sort of man he was. His courage and his clever tactics had already won him widespread recognition, but now for the first time his army had a chance to appraise his personality. What impressed his soldiers most was his unfailing courtesy – very unusual in a general; and what surprised them most was that his courtesy was not limited to officers but embraced the rank and file – absolutely unknown for a general! Indeed, he showed the roughest soldier the same courtesy that he would give to the finest gentleman. 'For his natural good humour', wrote Lord Ailesbury, 'he never had his equal, he could not chide a servant and was the worst served possible, and in command he could not give a harsh word, no, not to the meanest sergeant, corporal or soldier.'[12] This point was emphasized some years later when a story went the rounds about the Duke of Marlborough's 'soldier-servant'. Marlborough was inspecting some line positions with a colleague, Commissary Marriott, when it began to rain. He called for his cloak but his attendant did not bring it. Apparently the man was puzzling about straps and buckles.

> At last the rain increased very much, and the Duke repeated his call, adding, what was he about that he did not bring the cloak? 'You must stay,' grumbled the man, 'if it rains cats and dogs, till I can get at it.' The Duke only turned to Marriot and said, very coolly: 'Now I would not be of that man's temper for all the world.'[13]

Marlborough believed that harmony was the mother of efficiency, and insisted that the nationalities under his command establish good relations with one another. On one occasion his English soldiers were so incensed with the Dutch that he had a hard time healing the breach. Lord Athlone, the former General Ginkel, Holland's most distinguished soldier, had quite wrongly allowed his soldiers to steal the forage that belonged to Marlborough's men. Harsh words passed that might have ended in bloodshed, but Marlborough settled the matter with a terse warning: 'Advertise my Lord Athlone's men', he said, 'to beware of doing that twice.' Ailesbury goes on to say that 'if we had had a general of another disposition, the two nations might have come to hostilities, for the English hated the Dutch mortally and the footguards and soldiers of all other regiments and troopers had a great deal of Jacobite spirit among them.'[14]

This was not the only example of Marlborough's cool-headed judgement. Whenever Monsieur Geldermalsen, who was responsible for organizing food and transport for the Dutch army, reported to Lord Marlborough the clash of wills between the Dutch and the English, the Commander would reply: 'Mr Geldermalsen, that may be as you say, but it is our business to look forward to the common cause, and', putting his hand before his face, 'let us wink at all this and when we have a peace it will be then time to come to a discussion.' 'This same gentleman told me', Ailesbury continued, 'that when there appeared difficulties as to this or that enterprise, that one would be of this opinion and another of that, and that my lord would always say, "Done it must be, one way or the other, and let us resolve on what may be of less difficulty".'[15]

Lord Marlborough did not live in the style expected of a Commander-in-Chief. Although in 1702 the superb French military machine was admired from one end of Europe to the other, and not only laid down a pattern for waging war but for enjoying it as well, the Englishman was disconcertingly austere. The Duke of St Simon tells us that when he himself was an ordinary trooper in the Mousquetaires de Roi he had three valets, a private field-kitchen and a wonderful service of silver plate 'at least as good as that of a general officer'. French generals occupied luxuriously equipped tents and competed with each other over food and wine. Marshal Tallard, of whom we shall hear more later, made a point of entertaining 100 officers on the first rest day of every march 'keeping two mule trains laden with good things to eat – and wines too – at the head of the army for this very purpose'.[16] Marlborough, on the other hand, almost never entertained (unless one of the princes of the Alliance arrived at his headquarters). Eventually he curtailed the amount of baggage that an officer could take with him. Not that anyone was unduly stinted: infantry generals on campaign were allowed three wagons of furniture and personal effects for their tents – which must have been veritable homes-from-home. Brigadiers, however, felt badly used as they were limited to one wagon each.

Lord Marlborough, on the other hand, seemed able to do without trappings of any kind. When Lord Ailesbury visited his headquarters in 1702, he found him established in an old abbey from which he was just about to move. Even so, Lord Ailesbury was dismayed by the bleakness of his surroundings as the room where he received his visitors was almost empty. Apparently he had sent the furniture ahead or perhaps into storage for use another time. 'His moving furniture', wrote Lord Ailesbury, 'was suitable to his natural temper of keeping what he laid up . . . so he had but one great chair that was to be portable, and a chair with a back.'[17]

Marlborough's headquarters were usually better furnished than this. After ten or twelve hours in the saddle on reconnaissances or countless hours given to inspecting troops and garrisons, he spent his evenings in his rooms working with Cadogan and Cardonnel. A Commander-in-Chief was responsible for almost everything from food and forage to horses and wagons, guns and ammunition and, of course, victory or defeat. After his sessions with Cadogan came hours with Cardonnel writing to Godolphin in London, Heinsius in Holland, Leopold in Austria. More letters to the German principalities about the number of troops committed to the campaign, arrangements for the payment of English subsidies, letters to the leading men in Parliament, to the generals in Spain and to the Queen about foreign policy. No Commander-in-Chief in history appears to have had so many responsibilities or so many tribulations.

In the summer of 1702, Marlborough's worst trial was frustration. In July he made one more attempt to overcome Dutch intransigence. When a friendly convoy of 800 wagons, guarded by 6,000 Dutch soldiers, approached his lines, he had the clever idea of using the vehicles as a decoy by which he could lure the enemy into battle. He therefore ordered his army to retire southwards, keeping the convoy just close enough to attract the French vanguard. He was a great believer in this type of feint as a retreating army always has the advantage of turning and fighting when it reaches the right terrain.

Everything worked according to plan and, after three days with Marshal Boufflers close behind him, Marlborough emerged from the difficult country on the Heath of Helchterem, a wide expanse that seemed to be especially made for a cavalry charge. As Marlborough had superiority in this arm, he drew up his army in battle array, to the surprise and dismay of the enemy. For once, the Dutch Deputies could see the advantage of attacking and gave their consent. But this time the Dutch generals were so slow in organizing their troops that the battle was postponed until morning. When dawn came, Marlborough still wanted to attack, although the chances were not quite as favourable as the preceding day; but by this time the Deputies intervened with their usual change of mind and said he must wait yet another day. 'Tomorrow', Marlborough insisted, 'Marshal Boufflers will be gone.'[18] And gone he was, his army remaining unsullied by the hand of war.

Eighteenth-century warfare was full of surprising gestures, one of which was made by Marlborough. He took considerable pride in his military reputation and could not bear to think of Marshal Boufflers and the Duke of Berwick scoffing at him for missing yet another splendid opportunity for victory. So he sent a trumpeter through the lines apologizing for not attacking and making it clear that the decision had not been his. With so many relations and friends fighting against one another the two sides sometimes assumed the pose of friendly opponents. Thus Marlborough found time to send young Berwick a permit permitting him to purchase eight coach-horses in Holland and have them sent to France!

It was clear that the Dutch would not allow their troops to take part in a battle. Yet Marlborough was determined not to let the campaign end with no visible success and, with only a few weeks of summer left, turned his attention to the siege warfare so dear to the military heart of the eighteenth century. He encountered no difficulty in winning Dutch approval to reduce the fortress towns of the Meuse valley. Within six weeks he had scored a staggering success, becoming the master of territory five times greater than anything King William had gained in eight years of war.

He began with Fort St Michael on the west bank which contained such heavy guns that it could protect the fortress of Venlo on the east side. By an artful manœuvre, he threw the French off-balance and drew a net around his targets on the lower Rhineland. From intelligence reports reaching Versailles, Louis XIV could see that his grandson, the Duke of Burgundy, and Marshal Boufflers were in difficulty. 'If they take Venlo,' he wrote to Boufflers, 'then Guelders will be lost, and in the end you will be driven from the whole territory of Cologne. . . .'[19] Marlborough might be inexperienced, but it did not take the French long to know that they were up against a master of war. Louis XIV sent his famous engineer, General Vauban, to help Marshal Boufflers, but the latter seemed to be suffering from a loss of nerve. Not only did he recognize the brilliance of Marlborough's movements, but he knew that on three previous occasions the Englishman had manœuvred him into positions where, if the Dutch had not interfered, his army would have been routed.

Letters from the Duke of Burgundy began to reflect the gloom that pervaded Boufflers's headquarters. He complained to his grandfather that the Anglo–Dutch horses had more to eat than the French horses, which were in such wretched condition that they could no longer be used in important operations. The young Duke felt that the near future held nothing agreeable, and decided to return to Paris before he became tarred with the brush of failure. It was an unhappy surprise for the Sun King. 'I had not expected the Duke of Burgundy to leave the army so soon,' he wrote to Boufflers. 'I fear that his departure will have a bad effect on my troops and give confidence to the enemies. . . .'[20]

Events turned out exactly as Burgundy had foreseen. Marlborough pinned down the French defenders and prevented reinforcements coming to their aid. He then besieged and captured one fort after another without giving the defenders the customary opportunity to surrender and march out with the honours of war. The sieges of Venlo, Ruremonde, Stevenswaert and Liège were carried through with speed and panache. Louis watched the fighting with a fascination bordering on horror. 'I knew when you said that all the general officers felt that it would be impossible to aid Venlo that the whole province was lost,' he wrote Boufflers, 'but I was convinced myself that you could save Liège.' And a little later, when it was clearly not going to be saved,' you know the pain the siege of Liège causes me and the importance of the fortification for the war . . . it is a long time since anyone has seen conquests as rapid as these. . . .'[21] Liège was indeed an important fortification for it was the only remaining passage by which the French garrisons on the Rhine could be speedily supplied.

At the end of the campaign, the situation was completely transformed. Despite Marlborough's deep despondency, and despite the fact that he had been forced to miss chances that might have made a profound impression on the course of the war, he had emerged from his first year of command as a hero. When the Dutch had reluctantly given him effective command, they had been cowering under the guns of Nimwegen, afraid to move for fear the French would push their way through the Nimwegen gateway into Holland. Now, less than five months later, the French had been expelled from the Meuse and the lower Rhine; and the navigation of the two great rivers was open to the Allies and the Allies alone. During Marlborough's blackest days, Sarah's daily letters, as sprightly and provocative as ever, had helped to bolster his morale, and he now sent her his thanks in what must rank as the most flattering letter a man ever wrote to his wife: 'I do assure you that your letters are so welcome to me that if they should come in the time I was expecting the enemy to charge me, I could not forbear reading them.'22

However, of all the officers in the army, Marlborough was the least satisfied, as 'he had not been allowed to make war – only to play military chess.'23 Nevertheless, he had succeeded in impressing his skill on his prickly rival, General Ginkel, Earl of Athlone. 'The success of this campaign', wrote Athlone, 'is solely due to this incomparable chief, since I confess that I, serving as second-in-command, opposed in all circumstances his opinions and proposals.'24 Marlborough's greatest triumph was the conquest of Athlone.

However, the campaign nearly ended in disaster as, on the way to The Hague, Marlborough had the traumatic experience of being captured by the French. In those days the quickest way to travel from the lower Rhine to The Hague was by river. Marlborough therefore embarked on a yacht at Maestricht, accompanied by a Dutch soldier, General Opdam, the two Dutch Field Deputies and an escort of twenty soldiers. The vessel was towed, and arrangements were made for a posse of cavalry to keep pace with it along the river bank and stand guard over it at night. Meanwhile, an enemy raiding-party at Guelders, a town in alliance with the French, anticipating the yacht's journey, had laid a trap in the hope of capturing high-ranking officers. After Venlo there was a bend in the river and a stretch where the escort no longer could hug the bank. The raiders chose this spot to pounce on the yacht, pulling it to the side by the tow-rope.

The officer in charge of the operation was an Irish deserter from the Dutch service named Farewell. He had been chosen by the French to lead the raid as he was familiar with the terrain. He immediately set about scrutinizing the papers of his captives in the lantern light of his cabin. The two Field Deputies and General Opdam all had passes signed by the Duke of Burgundy to free them from annoyance on their way home – the granting of passes was a common courtesy extended by high officers to their opposite numbers. Marlborough, however, had airily brushed aside this precaution, insisting that he wanted no favours from the enemy.

Fortunately, while he was waiting his turn to be questioned by Lieutenant Farewell, his servant, Stephen Gell, slipped into his hand a pass made out to his brother, General Charles Churchill, which had never been used. The fact that it was out of date and did not cover transit by water was a stumbling-block, but Marlborough was equal to the occasion. Unfortunately no one knows what was said; only that the attempt to secure a favourable decision from the Lieutenant was prolonged. 'I have desired Mr Cardonnel to send you a particular account of my having been in the power of a French party near five hours,' Marlborough wrote in November to one of the Secretaries in England, Sir Charles Hedges. 'But I thank God they did not know me but took me for Lieutenant-General Churchill.'[25] Lieutenant Farewell stripped the yacht of cash and silver (which he turned over to his colleagues) and removed as prisoners the cook, the crew and the military escort. He then allowed the three gentlemen passengers and their servants to continue to float down the stream. The yacht soon overtook Cohorn and his armed guards and once again the passengers proceeded to The Hague.

The Imperial Ambassador, Count Goes, reported to Vienna that the Irish Lieutenant 'did not sin through ignorance' but was well aware of whom he had in his hands. Apparently he decided that he had more to gain from the Dutch than from the French, and so did not accompany his fellow raiders back to Guelders but vanished into thin air. Two months later he turned up in The Hague where he received a free pardon and a captaincy in the Dutch service. Marlborough, however, remained convinced that his escape was due to his servant's presence of mind and rewarded the estimable Gell with a pension of £50 a year for life.

Before Marlborough's arrival at The Hague, the rumour, emanating from Venlo, spread through Holland and France that the Commander-in-Chief had been captured. 'Till they saw me,' he wrote to Godolphin,

> they thought me a prisoner in France so that I was not ashore one minute before I had great crowds of the common people, some endeavouring to take me by the hands, all crying out welcome. But that which moved me most was to see a great many of both sexes cry for joy.[26]

While Lord Marlborough had been struggling to impose his views on the Dutch, Lady Marlborough had been struggling to impose hers on the Queen. The new House of Commons which assembled in October 1702 had a comfortable Tory majority, due to the fact that the Queen had all but nailed her colours to the party mast. 'My own principles must always keep me entirely firm to the interests and religion of the Church of England,' she had told Parliament in the spring, 'and will incline me to countenance those who have the truest zeal to support it.' And, as she always referred to the Tories as 'the Church Party', no one was in any doubt where her sympathies lay.

Unfortunately, Sarah did not see eye to eye with the Queen. Although she had taken very little interest in politics before Anne's

accession, she now found herself the centre of attention. 'The eleva-
tion of my mistress to the throne', she wrote,

> brought me into a new scene of life and into a new sort of consideration
> with all those whose attention either by courtesy or ambition, was turned
> to policies and the Court. . . . From this time I began to be looked upon as a
> person of consequence, without whose approbation at least neither places
> nor pensions nor honours were bestowed by the Crown.[27]

Assiduous in winning Lady Marlborough's support was her son-in-
law, the brilliant, awkward Charles Spencer, who inherited his
father's title, Earl of Sunderland, a few weeks before Parliament met
in the autumn of 1702. Charles was one of the five magnificoes who
ran the powerful Whig Junto and he found Sarah an eager pupil.
Although she knew very little about politics she was 'a natural Whig'.
She did not care whether Protestants worshipped in church or in
chapel and she certainly did not think that kings were divine. She
hated despots, believed passionately in freedom, and the more she
talked to Lord Sunderland the more convinced she became that the
Whigs – and only the Whigs – had the right message for the country.
Neither her husband nor her close friend, Sidney Godolphin, shared
her strong convictions. Although they both came from Tory back-
grounds, they disdained party politics and made a point of keeping
themselves independent of both factions.

Nevertheless, Sarah was determined to change the Queen's opinion
of the Whigs. She wrote in her memoirs that she knew it would not be
an easy task as, from early childhood, Anne 'had been taught to look
upon all Whigs not only as republicans who hated the very shadow of
regal authority but as implacable enemies of the Church of England.
This aversion to the whole party had been confirmed by the ill-usage
she had met with from her sister and King William.'[28]

Sarah was confident of influencing Anne, whom she regarded as a
well-meaning, rather simple woman who eventually came round to
her dearest friend's point of view. (After all, it was ridiculous to be so
anti-Whig when Anne only sat on the throne because the Whigs had
brought William from Holland.) Although Sarah flung herself into
the controversy, she was shocked to find that her arguments made no
headway. All she could draw from the Queen was a stubborn defence
of the Tories and a humble apology for disagreeing with her. 'I would
not have you and your poor, unfortunate faithful Morley differ in
opinion in the least thing. . . .' Nevertheless, poor unfortunate
Morley stuck to her guns. 'My dear Mrs Freeman,' she wrote with a

touch of asperity. 'You are mightily mistaken in your notion of a true Whig for the character you give of them does not in the least belong to them but to the Church. . . .'[29]

While Anne and Sarah argued about the two parties, the two parties fought for the Queen's favour, using every trick, exploiting every issue, to further their cause. What Sarah did not understand was that no matter how partisan the Queen might appear on the surface, she was determined not to allow either party to get the upper hand with her. She was unflagging in asserting her right to choose her ministers from one or other of the factions, or both, or none at all, as it suited her. '. . . If I should be so unfortunate as to fall into the hands of either party,' she wrote to Lord Godolphin, 'I shall not imagine myself though I have the name of Queen to be anything but their slave.'[30]

The truth was that the Queen's convictions cut across both factions: she was a moderate Tory who actively disliked the High Tory policy of 'appeasement', and was whole-heartedly committed to the Whigs' Continental war to keep the Catholic King of France from dominating Europe. When Marlborough arrived back in England in December 1702 and was greeted as a hero, Anne seized the opportunity to show her esteem. Although the High Tories praised the Captain-General because he had 'retrieved the ancient honour and glory of the English nation', their words were chosen as a deliberate slight on the memory of King William. And although the expedition sent to Spain, led by Admiral Sir George Rooke and the Duke of Ormonde, had been a near fiasco (Cadiz had not been captured and the seizure of the Spanish treasure fleet in Vigo Bay had been a happy accident), the Tories maliciously coupled the names of Ormonde and Marlborough in giving their thanks. Indeed, the leader of the High Tories, the Queen's uncle, Lord Rochester, did not attempt to conceal his opposition to the war on the Continent, favouring instead a series of naval attacks on the enemy's ports. Partly as a reproof for this hostility, Anne decided to offer her Captain-General a dukedom. 'I hope you will give me leave,' she wrote to Sarah. 'I know my dear Mrs Freeman does not care for anything of that kind, nor am I satisfied with it because it does not enough express the value I have for Mr Freeman, nor nothing ever can how passionately I am yours my dear Mrs Freeman.'[31]

Sarah was against the idea. John had a huge income as Commander-in-Chief, but what if he was removed from his post? Or killed? Who would support a dukedom then? And what could be more ridiculous than a poor duke? John was abroad and Sarah wrote begging him to refuse. But John fancied the idea of being a duke; he replied saying that Anthonie Heinsius, the Grand Pensionary, felt that his new rank would increase his standing among the princes of the Alliance. The Queen came to the rescue promising a grant from the Post Office of £5,000 a year during her lifetime; the next step would be to transform the payment into a permanent parliamentary pension. Sarah agreed, and John became the first Duke of Marlborough. Unfortunately, however, the Queen's request for a parliamentary grant in perpetuity was refused. The Commons politely pointed out that King William had been censured for the same sort of thing, and much to Marlborough's chagrin there was no alternative but to let the matter drop. In order to soften the Commons' rebuff, Anne offered the Marlboroughs £2,000 a year from the Privy Purse which would have been a private and secret transaction. Sarah was deeply grateful, but this time she refused.

That winter Sarah completed the arrangements for the marriages of her two remaining daughters. Her youngest child, fourteen-year-old Mary, became engaged to the fifteen-year-old Viscount Monthermer, the son of the former Ambassador to France, the Earl of Montagu, who had created such a furore by seducing the Duchess of Cleveland's daughter. At the same time the Marlboroughs' third girl, Elizabeth Churchill, married 'Scroops' Egerton, the Earl of Bridgwater. Although the bridegroom was notoriously stupid, the Queen pleased Sarah by making him a Gentleman of the Horse to Prince George. And if a vacancy should occur for a better position, Her Majesty wrote to the Duchess, 'I shall be glad to let him have it, for although he is no Solomon, he is a man of great quality and young enough to improve.'[32]

In February 1703, two weeks after Elizabeth's wedding, a tragedy took place – almost the worst tragedy that either John or Sarah could have imagined. Their only son and heir, seventeen-year-old John, Marquis of Blandford, died of smallpox. The boy was studying at King's College, Cambridge, and in the autumn of 1702 spent several weeks with his godfather, Lord Godolphin, at the latter's house at Newmarket. As a public servant, Godolphin was a hard-working, silent, incorruptible man with an almost uncanny understanding of finance; therefore it was amusing to see him in his moments of leisure at the racing capital. Young Blandford poured out his innermost feelings to him. He wanted to enlist in the army and join his father in Flanders, but his mother would not hear of it. Godolphin probably advised him to play his hand carefully, telling him that when the right time came he would help him. In the meantime he wrote to Sarah regularly:

My Lord Churchill is now at Cambridge but today he comes hither for 5 or 6 days. What you write about him, I think extremely just, and reasonable, and the smallpox has been in the town, yett as he is going into no house but mine will I hope bee more defended from it by ayr and riding, without any sweating exercise, than possible he could bee anywhere else.[33]

On the following Tuesday, 13 October, Godolphin returned to his house in London and once again wrote to the Duchess 'of your pretty son' whom he had just left. 'I assure you without flattery or partiality', he wrote, 'that he is not only the best natured and most agreeable, but the most forethinking and reasonable creature that one can imagine of his age; he had twenty pretty questions and requests. . . .'[34]

Sarah was still anxious about the smallpox epidemic, but by February the danger seemed to have passed. Now a different kind of trouble arose. Blandford suddenly got into a scrape – it is not known what – that infuriated his mother. He wrote two letters to his parents begging their forgiveness. His brother-in-law, Francis Godolphin (Henrietta's husband), intervened on his behalf. 'Dear Mama,' Blandford wrote,

I received a letter from Mr Godolphin last post and the joy I had when I found I had some hope of being friends with my dear Mama is not to be expressed, but I can't think myself so happy till my dear Mama can find some time to let me have a letter from her, & I am sure there can be no greater pleasure than would be to my dear Mama, your most Dutyful Son, Blandford.[35]

The ink was scarcely dry on his letter before news came from Cambridge that Blandford had smallpox. Sarah rushed to his bedside and the Queen dispatched her own doctors to Cambridge to attend him. By 19 February, however, the boy's condition was declared hopeless. Anne sent a letter to the Duchess praying that 'Christ Jesus comfort and support you under this terrible affliction, & it is his mercy alone that can do it.'[36] With both parents at his bedside, Blandford died on 20 February, and the Marlboroughs left Cambridge for St Albans.

The Queen, remembering the death of her own little boy, the Duke of Gloucester, could think of nothing but Sarah's grief, and suffered with her almost hour by hour. In a moving letter, she offered to join the Duchess at St Albans 'for I must have one look at my dear Mrs Freeman & I would com ye way that will be least uneasy to you.'[37] But Sarah was so distraught that she rejected Anne's suggestion that 'the unfortunate ought to come to the unfortunate', and when Lord Godolphin returned to London he found the Queen deeply hurt that the woman she loved so profoundly did not need her consolation, or for that matter even want her around during this terrible period. This realization undoubtedly affected Anne's feelings towards Sarah in the days to come. 'We hear', wrote a contemporary, 'the Duchess of Marlborough bears not her affliction like her mistress, if reports be true that it hath near touched her head.'[38]

Poor Sarah was not in her right mind. A few months later she thought for a brief moment that she might be pregnant again, but instead she discovered that she was undergoing the menopause period that marks the end of a woman's child-bearing years. The fact that this coincided with her terrible loss undoubtedly contributed to her inability to gain control of herself. Added to this, her personality seemed to undergo the subtle change that is a fairly common occurrence at this time in a woman's life.

Marlborough was almost as depressed as his wife. He spent a week trying to recover his spirits at St Albans and, when he returned to Holland in March 1703, had to struggle to keep his mind from his misfortune. 'I have this day', he wrote from Cologne to Lord Godolphin, 'seen a very great procession, and the thought how pleased poor Lord Churchill would have been with such a sight has added very much to my uneasiness. Since it has pleased God to take him I do wish from my soul I would think less of him.'[39]

He not only mourned for the person of his delightful son, but lamented the loss of his only heir. He had convinced himself that the purpose of his life was to found a dynasty; and although, before going on campaign, he made out a new will leaving his estate to his elder daughter, Henrietta, the wife of Francis Godolphin, it was not at all the same as the vision of a male Churchill following in his footsteps. When he encountered Lord Ailesbury in The Hague he said dejectedly: 'I have lost what is so dear to me it is fit for me to retire and not toil and labour for I know not who. . . .'[40]

However, he was careful not to express his sadness to his wife. He wrote to her tenderly, telling her how often he thought of their 'living quietly together, till such happy time comes I shall not be contented.' He even tried to comfort her by an expression of religious faith. 'You and I have great reason to bless God for all we have,' he wrote,

> so that we must not repine at his taking our poor child from us, but bless and praise him for what his goodness leaves us. The use I think we should make of this his correction is that our chiefest time should be spent in reconciling ourselves to him, and having in our minds always that we may

not have long to live in this world: for I am persuaded that by living in the world we may do more good than by being out of it, but at the same time to live so that one could cheerfully die when it shall be his pleasure to call us.[41]

Historians who portray Marlborough as a villain have not known what to make of this gentle, philosophic letter. Even G.M. Trevelyan seems hard pressed for an explanation. 'It cannot be conscious hypocrisy', he wrote, 'for the woman to whom alone it was addressed insisted on no such sentiments; nor can it be mere custom, for such was not the conventional language of the Whitehall where he and his wife were brought up. It must represent', he concludes, 'one of the genuine moods of this most secret man.'[42] However, this was not a 'mood'. Marlborough, like most soldiers, believed in God and in God's protection and never went into battle without saying his prayers. Sarah was the agnostic and one wonders what she thought of her husband's sentiments. She grieved for her son for many months, no doubt tormented by the quarrel she had had with him just before his fatal illness.

Strangely enough, the tragedy of Blandford's death led to another family misfortune of a very different kind – the gradual alienation of Sarah and her eldest daughter, Henrietta. Much to her mother's disapproval Henrietta became enamoured with the celebrated playwright, William Congreve. This gentleman had been so moved by the death of Lord Blandford that he had written a pastoral lament, *The Tears of Amaryllis for Amyntas*, which he had dedicated to the boy's godfather, Lord Godolphin. He sent it to members of the bereaved family; Henrietta asked Congreve to call on her and a close friendship developed. Sarah, for all her 'free-thinking', did not regard poets and actors as respectable company for members of the aristocracy and did everything she could to sever the relationship. When she learned that Henrietta had contributed to a new playhouse in the Haymarket, backed by Congreve and Vanbrugh, she wrote indignantly that her daughter had given '100 guineas to a very low poet [John Gay] that will tell her that she is what she knows she is not.'[43] Needless to say, these acrimonious remarks did not bring her any closer to Henrietta, and Sarah then tried to enlist her husband's help. 'I wrote to her myself', Marlborough replied in August 1703, 'that she could never find any lasting happiness in this world but from the kindness of Mr Godolphin. . . . I should be glad to know if it had any effect, for I love her, and think her very good so that I should hope . . . it is for want of thinking. . . .'[44]

Marlborough was wrong. Henrietta's greatest happiness came

from the love that blossomed between herself and Congreve and lasted until the playwright's death.

Every year the Queen's physical condition seemed to deteriorate, yet she stubbornly refused to look upon herself as an invalid. 'I am I thank God very well in my health,' she wrote to Sarah in June 1703, 'but I fear it will be a great while before I can walk alone.'[45] Her fears were more than justified, for a year later she could not walk at all. The only out-of-doors pastime of which she was physically capable was driving about in a *chaise-roulante* with two men walking beside the horses' heads, holding the reins. In this way she watched herds of deer being driven past her in Windsor Park or 'hunted the hare', which was not nearly as dashing as it sounded, but merely consisted of meeting the huntsmen at certain fixed times.

Despite her disabilities the Queen attended a Cabinet Council almost every week, read State papers and made up her mind about appointments put forward by Lord Godolphin (usually at the Duke of Marlborough's suggestion). She was a generous woman with simple benefits and prejudices, and the famous Stuart stubbornness. She never contributed ideas at her Councils, but her presence was mandatory as Cabinets could not be held without her. Her greatest worry was her inability to communicate with her subjects. She longed to be the centre of great social gatherings, but when they took place she was overcome with shyness. The receptions at St James's or Kensington Palace were embarrassingly uncongenial 'with Foreign Ministers and ladies sitting for a quarter of an hour about the Queen in dead silence'.[46]

What the Queen had always liked best was listening to Sarah's sparkling conversation, but throughout most of 1703 the Duchess of Marlborough lived at Windsor Lodge, seeing very few people apart from her family and grieving for her son. Although she had important duties, she rarely attended Court. Instead, encouraged by young Lord Sunderland, the most fervent of the Whig leaders, she showered the Queen with letters on political matters which would have been better left unwritten. Very foolishly she returned to the controversy over the merits of the two parties, asserting that all Tories were secret Jacobites. Could she seriously have hoped to turn the Queen into a Whig by this type of argument? It was true that some of the High Tories, who still clung to Divine Hereditary Right, regretted that they had passed an Act of Settlement in favour of the House of Hanover, and in the congenial atmosphere of the coffee-house aired the possibility of 'James III' succeeding Anne. But these sentiments reflected a minority view and the Queen put up a stout defence. 'I own I cannot have the good opinion of some people that you have, nor that ill one of others,' she wrote to Sarah in June,

> and lett the Whiggs brag ever soe much of their great Services to their country & of their numbers, I believe the revolution had never bin, nor the Succession setel'd as it is now, if the Church party had not Joyned with them. . . .[47]

Sarah was like a dog with a bone and refused to allow the controversy to end. But after a week in which her letters were delivered to the Palace every day, the Queen tried to break off the correspondence: 'Finding you are so fixed in ye good opinion you have of some & ye ill opinion you have of other people that it is to no manner of purpose to argue anything with you. . . .'[48] Sarah was always annoyed by the Queen's independence. Formerly, her royal mistress had concurred eagerly with everything she said; she could not accustom herself to the change and wondered who had put the words into her mouth. Anne took pains to soften her rebuke by using the kindly language of earlier days. 'I must Confess', she wrote,

> it is no small mortification to me that differences of opinion should make you cold to your poor unfortunate Morley and hinder you from Coming to me, for whatever you say I cannot take it ill knowing as I have said already, that you mean it kindly. . . .[49]

The truth was that clever Sarah was contemptuous of poor, muddled Anne who disclaimed Divine Right yet touched for the Queen's Evil; who disliked the Jacobites yet refused to admit that her High Tory churchmen had Jacobite leanings. Sarah's assault, of course, was delivered because these same High Tories were increasingly opposed to her beloved 'Lord Marl' and his European 'land war', and still talked of fighting a naval war against the enemy's overseas possessions – as if that would be an adequate substitute. Nothing nettled Sarah more than failure to make an impression on her once-receptive mistress, and she found it impossible to hide her irritation. 'Your poor, unfortunate faithfull Morley . . . expects nothing but uneasiness this winter,' the Queen complained in October. 'And your Coldness added to it will make it unbearable.'[50] But Sarah refused to respond.

While the Duchess was bickering with the Queen, Marlborough's troubles were on such a heroic scale that they embraced the possibility of total defeat. Indeed, 1703 was destined to stand out as one of the most disagreeable years of his whole life. His difficulties began when he returned to Flanders hoping to find the Dutch generals more co-operative than they had been during the previous campaign. Unfortunately, Lord Athlone had died, and the other generals were as determined as ever to restrain Marlborough from an unorthodox move. When he produced a masterly plan to capture Antwerp and Ostend they refused their consent, and he expostulated to Lord Godolphin: 'I shall not be very fond of staying with an army that is to do no more than eat forage.'[51] A few months later, when the French were working feverishly to construct 'lines' from Antwerp to Namur (a distance of ninety miles) to protect the Spanish Netherlands, Marlborough spotted a point near Ramillies where the earthwork barrier was still incomplete. He proposed forcing the lines and managed to secure the approval of the German and Danish generals, and for once even won the approval of the Dutch Field Deputies. But as usual the Dutch generals said no. Marlborough was close to despair. 'Even if I were given millions,' he wrote to the Grand Pensionary Heinsius, 'I would not again serve in the field with such obstacles and forced to depend upon the unanimous consent of the generals. I would rather die than put up with it again. . . .'[52]

Indeed, Marlborough was so sick with anxiety and frustration that he began to suffer again from blinding headaches. His concern was not centred on Flanders – although he felt it was reprehensible not to attack the enemy, at least the enemy was not preparing an attack on him. In Flanders the position was reasonably safe (for the moment) whereas in South Germany it was not only alarming but desperate. There the enemy seemed poised for a victory that might end the war. Prince Max Emmanuel, the rich and powerful Elector of Bavaria, with an army of 40,000 men, had defected from the Allies and joined the French in 1702. Needless to say, Louis XIV had offered him irresistible incentives – namely that, if France was victorious, he would make Max Emmanuel Holy Roman Emperor in place of Leopold; and what Wittelsbach could resist a chance to replace a Habsburg? As Louis XIV favoured an all-out attack on Vienna, his best general, Marshal Villars, led 30,000 men across the Rhine and through the passes of the Black Forest to join forces with the Elector on the Danube. The Franco–Bavarian army, far stronger than anything the Emperor Leopold could put against it, now stood in the centre of Germany, and Villars reckoned that the capture of Vienna was 'an affair of eight days'. To Marlborough, at the other end of Europe, it looked as though nothing could save the city; and with the fall of the capital, the Grand Alliance was bound to splinter as each country would try to wrest its own peace terms from the Sun King.

Marlborough could only pray that some unexpected happening would halt the awful sequence of events, and this is exactly what transpired. First of all, the blunt, professional Marshal Villars could not get on with the devious Max Emmanuel. 'I cannot recommend strongly enough', Louis XIV wrote to Villars, '. . . not to be haughty with a man of his birth and rank.'[53] The Marshal did his best to keep the peace, but when the Elector suddenly abandoned his undertaking to mount a joint drive towards Vienna and instead led an impromptu attack in the Tyrol, Villars's wrath knew no bounds. The explanation was not difficult to find: Max Emmanuel had a secret treaty with Louis allowing him to keep whatever enemy territory he could seize, so he decided to appropriate what he coveted in the Tyrol before peace broke out. But things did not happen as he hoped. Fierce Tyrolean resistance developed, with the result that the joint attack on Vienna had to be postponed until the following year. So Marlborough was given the reprieve for which he had been praying and Villars was so disgusted that he asked Louis to relieve him of his command. He was sent to the south of France to deal with the Huguenot uprising while Marshal Marsin, a man of far less ability, took his place in Bavaria.

For weeks Marlborough had been threatening to resign unless he could come to a better arrangement with the Dutch; and now Godolphin was also talking of leaving, complaining of being caught in an intolerable crossfire between the two parties. Sarah informed the Queen of the disillusionment of her two most trusted servants (they referred to themselves as 'galley-slaves') and at the end of October, two weeks before Marlborough returned to England, Anne composed one of the most remarkable letters ever penned by a sovereign. 'The thoughts that both my dear Mrs Freeman and Mr Freeman seem to have of retyering', she wrote to Sarah,

> gives me no small uneasiness and therefore I must say something on that Subject, it is no wonder at all people in your posts should be weary of ye world who are so continually troubled with all ye hurry & impertinencys of it, but give me leave to say, you should a little consider your faithful friends & poor Country, which must be ruined if ever you should putt your melancholy thoughts in execution, as for your poor unfortunate faithful Morley she could not beare it, for if ever you should ever forsake me, I would have nothing more to do with the world, but make another abdycation, for what is a Crown when ye support of it is gon, I never will forsake your dear self, Mr Freeman nor Mr Montgomery, but always be your constant faithfull servant & we four must never part till death mows us down with his impartial hand.[54]

Marlborough was so moved by this simple call for help that he resolved to stop complaining, to solve his impasse with the Dutch by his own efforts, and to serve the Queen to his dying breath.

In November, the Duke of Marlborough left the fractious Dutch to return to the fractious English. Parliament only sat during the five months that the army was in winter quarters as William III had organized English political life to suit his military requirements. Marlborough was present, therefore, to hear the Queen's Speech – a futile plea for 'perfect Peace and Union'. 'The parties are such bugbears,' Anne had written to Marlborough shortly before his return, '. . . I pray God keep me out of the hands of both of them.'[55]

The Queen's major concern throughout her reign was to maintain her right to appoint whichever ministers she wanted, regardless of parliamentary pressure. As both factions were equally determined to force the sovereign to select her ministers from the predominant group, party warfare was continually on the boil. The general election of July 1702 had given the Tories a majority in the House of Commons, and the Whigs had a permanent majority in the Lords, which made the battle fairly even.

The Queen liked to think that she was conducting a non-party Government by selecting her ministers from the Tory 'moderates'. This was a rather indeterminate group which sometimes referred to itself as 'the Queen's Servants'. (Godolphin calculated in 1702 that the House of Commons consisted of 190 Tories, 160 Whigs and 100 Queen's Servants.) Although Marlborough and Godolphin were Tories by upbringing, they had moved on to the central ground between the High Tories and the Whigs and encouraged the Queen to follow their example – to disdain party warfare and to play both ends against the middle. Someone, however, had to control the strong currents running through the Commons and Mr Robert Harley, leader of the Tories and Speaker of the House, was Godolphin's natural choice.

As Harley was destined to play the role of a villain in the Marlborough story, we must take a closer look at him. He had begun life as a Whig and a Non-conformist but had worked his way to the middle ground and now called himself a 'Tory moderate'. He was, in fact, a twentieth-century manipulator operating in an eighteenth-century setting. He made himself indispensable to Marlborough and Godolphin by organizing and producing majority votes for them in the House of Commons. His prestige was based on his knowledge of constitutional history and parliamentary procedure, but his brilliant management was due to a superb network of political intelligence which he had built up by hard work. In some ways Harley was a baffling character as everything about him was contradictory. He was a Puritan and a humbug; an unscrupulous man who concealed his driving ambition under a cloak of flowery sentiment and lavish flattery; a false man who gloried in his duplicity and once boasted that 'he was ready to howl with the wolves and, if his friends wished it, to call black white or white black.'[56]

Harley never had any difficulty in knowing on which side his bread was buttered and for some years served Marlborough and Godolphin with loyalty and skill. They had been quick to recognize the usefulness of 'the Sorcerer' – as some people called him – and even before King William's death had drawn him into their orbit. In 1701 Harley had proved indispensable in rallying Tory support for the signing of the Grand Alliance Treaty and the enactment of the Act of Settlement giving the succession to the House of Hanover after Anne's death. And now, when the initial euphoria over the war was beginning to fade, Harley was more indispensable than ever. The money and supplies for Marlborough's campaign depended on the vote in the Commons. 'It is necessary above all the rest', Godolphin wrote to Harley in November 1703, 'that the Duke of Marlborough and you and I should meet regularly at least twice a week, if not oftener, to advise upon everything that should occur.'[57]

Godolphin sensed that the new session of Parliament would be sticky, particularly where the war was concerned. In seven months of costly belligerence Marlborough had been able to do no more than capture Bonn, Huy and Limburg. But whereas Godolphin expected trouble to come from the Tories, it was the Whigs who dropped the bomb-shell. They opened the session by demanding Marlborough's resignation as Commander-in-Chief. They had nothing personal against the Duke; on the contrary, his son-in-law, Sunderland, was one of the leaders of the party. But they were eager to replace him by George, Elector of Hanover, son and heir of the Electress Sophia and a future King of England. This could have great advantages for the Whig Party. If the Queen suddenly died, the Prince would be in a position to enforce the Act of Settlement against a possible Jacobite challenge; then, of course, he could reward his Whig supporters by allowing them to form a government.

To everyone's surprise Marlborough welcomed the suggestion of making the Elector supreme commander. A royal prince, he agreed, would have far more influence on the Dutch than he had had; and he was quite willing to serve as second-in-command. Far from illuminating Marlborough's character, this incident renders him more baffling than ever. How could a man as ambitious as the Duke agree so equally to the relinquishing of his post? Did he have a premonition of disaster? Or did he truly believe that the Elector could overcome Dutch stubbornness? Whatever the answer, the Dutch themselves quickly killed the new proposal. Although they took pleasure in thwarting Marlborough, they disliked the Germans almost as much as the French and flatly refused to allow the Prince to take over their army. So there the matter rested.

1703 was such an ill-starred year for the Marlboroughs that even good news carried a hidden sting in its tail. The agreement bringing Portugal into the Grand Alliance was the one event of the season that won the unqualified approval of Parliament. No one was more delighted than Marlborough although, as fate would have it, it carried the seeds of his own destruction. The Treaty was the result of many years of negotiation on the part of two British Ambassadors – father and son – John and Paul Methuen. Portugal was uncertain which side to support, but was persuaded at last that English sea power would offer more advantages (and more protection) than the armies of France. As a result Portugal opened Lisbon to Allied shipping, enabling England to seize Gibraltar and eventually Port Mahon in Minorca. Thus Britain established herself as mistress of the Mediterranean – a position which she retained for nearly 250 years.

In return for the Portuguese alliance, however, Lisbon demanded that England agree to expel Philip v from the Spanish throne and to put in his place the Emperor Leopold's youngest son, the Archduke Charles. Not only this, but she should support Charles's claim for the whole of the Spanish inheritance with nothing for Philip. This was a complete reversal of the Allies' war aims. With one fell swoop it swept away William III's carefully thought-out demands based on the partition of the Spanish Empire. At the time no one, including the Duke of Marlborough, raised a voice in protest. The war was in such a critical state that Portugal's support, under any terms, could only be regarded as a miraculous intervention. Furthermore, the likelihood of Louis XIV being reduced to utter ruin (the only condition that could possibly induce him to accept the new *dictat*) was so remote that no one gave it much thought. Nevertheless, it committed the Allies to a Peninsular war and, although no one seemed aware of it, ended any hope of a negotiated peace with France.

When the Whigs finished attacking Marlborough's war effort, the Tories leapt into the fray and attacked the Whigs. They tried to ensure the passage of an 'Occasional Conformity' bill that would prohibit

Whig Dissenters from holding public office, but the Queen stood on her newly discovered 'middle ground' and dismissed seven High Tory ministers (she had rid herself of her uncle, Lord Rochester, a year earlier). Robert Harley became Secretary of State, retaining at the same time the Speakership of the Commons; and one of his brilliant young followers (also a protégé of Marlborough), Henry St John, became Secretary of State for War. The Queen would have liked to have given Lord Shrewsbury a place in her Government; he was the sort of cryptic Whig that she liked – a man almost indistinguishable from her middle-of-the-road Tories. But Shrewsbury had taken himself off to Italy just before King William's death and refused to return. He remained in Rome for six years, pleading ill-health and accumulating a splendid collection of pictures.

The Queen now made her position crystal clear and nailed the word 'moderation' to her banner. It remained there for the duration of her reign. She placed her entire faith in her three trusted advisers: in the military skill of the Duke of Marlborough; in the financial skill of Lord Godolphin; and in the managerial skill of the new arrival, Robert Harley. It was difficult to know exactly where quarrelsome Sarah, the once-adored favourite, fitted into the picture, but it was impossible to leave her out. The Queen was not as dependent on her as once she had been, but she still sent her plaintive letters, begging that Sarah, 'would never lett difference of opinion hinder us from living together as we used to do.'[58]

Meanwhile, Marlborough had taken the most momentous decision of his life. His assertion that he would 'rather die' than submit again to Dutch interference had not changed and he adhered to the decision he had taken the summer before. 'I will for the future command the troops that are in the pay of England,' he had written to Heinsius in September 1703, 'and the States can supplement them by as many battalions as they think advantageous to their own interest.'[59] Marlborough had made up his mind to leave the Dutch to stew in their own juice and to move far enough afield to throw in his lot – and the lot of the Grand Alliance – with the Austrians. Three plans ran through his head, any one of which might be put into operation to carry the war to the Moselle (the half-way mark between Holland and Austria); or to the upper Rhine; or, most ambitious of all, to the Danube itself. Although he made a hurried trip to The Hague in January 1704, the despondency and pessimism did not encourage open discussions. After emphasizing that he would not be fighting again in Brabant or the Spanish Netherlands, he ordered two German units to take up positions on the Moselle. But he offered no explanation, waiting and hoping that the Dutch (whose troops he needed) would come forward with suggestions of their own.

Before he left the shores of England for the Continent, Sarah delivered a thunderbolt, accusing him of carrying on a clandestine love affair. The woman was unnamed and all that is known of this surprising charge are Marlborough's fervent and unhappy denials. 'I never sent to her in my life,' he declared over and over again to the furious Sarah, 'and may my happiness . . . depend on the truth of this.' John's humble, defeated letters recall the declaration he had made in his courtship, twenty-five years earlier, when he had sworn to be Sarah's 'devoted slave' for the rest of his life. 'May I and all that is dear to me be curs'd if ever I sent to her'; and again, 'Your suspicion . . . will vanish but . . . the thought has made me take no rest this night and will for ever make me unhappy.'[60]

None of his protests succeeded in melting Sarah's heart. She came to Margate to bid him goodbye, but she remained cold and aloof and handed him a paper listing her complaints. For once he was not sorry to tear up her letter. He embarked on 8 April 1704 with a retinue that included his brilliant staff officer, Brigadier-General Cadogan; his brother, General Charles Churchill; his old friend and military colleague, Lord Orkney; his faithful secretary, Adam Cardonnel; and the Imperial Ambassador, Wratislaw. His ship was accompanied by a fleet of transports carrying four infantry regiments and several thousand drafts, and protected by a convoy of warships.

The future was fraught with peril. Marlborough knew that unless he took a gamble, unless he won a spectacular victory that would alter the outlook of the war, now so favourable to France, the Grand Alliance would collapse, giving Louis xiv the mastery of Europe. Deeply distressed by his breach with Sarah, but excited by the audacious plan that had taken shape in his head, he bade farewell to England.

Eight

The Blenheim Gamble

Never had Louis xıv been so confident of bringing the war to a successful conclusion as in the spring of 1704. His splendid armies and famous marshals were assembled at key points across Europe. In the Low Countries Marshal Villeroy stood on the defensive; in Italy Marshal Vendôme was preparing an attack on the renegade Duke of Savoy; and in Germany Marshal Tallard was contemplating an offensive down the upper Rhine. The main thrust, however, would take place along the Danube valley to Vienna. Marshal Marsin's troops had united with the flamboyant Elector Max Emmanuel of Bavaria, whose army had been badly mauled by the Tyrolese and was now in need of replacements. The two Generals had moved into a strongly entrenched camp below Ulm and, as soon as their armies were at full strength again, would launch an offensive to capture the Habsburg capital and knock the Empire out of the war.

All winter Marlborough had been considering ways and means to prevent the enemy from delivering a final blow. His determination to give himself latitude by leaving Flanders – and the Dutch – was inflexible. For this reason he had obtained a letter from the Queen commanding him 'to send speedy succour to His Imperial Majesty and the Empire'. This purposely vague order allowed him a number of possibilities and for a while he toyed with the plan of taking his English soldiers and his English-paid mercenaries to Coblenz, then turning south and driving through the Moselle valley into France itself. In February he made a hurried trip to The Hague to discuss the matter with Cadogan and Cardonnel, giving them instructions to set up food magazines at Coblenz.

He did not reveal any of his plans to the Dutch and put them off the scent by talking in general terms about the necessity of reducing the Moselle fortresses at Trarbach and Trèves. Meanwhile Count Wratislaw, the Imperial Ambassador to London, was imploring him to take direct action against the Elector of Bavaria and bombarding him with arguments. It was an accepted maxim that, if Vienna fell, the Grand Alliance would fall to pieces and bring the war to an end. So why not extinguish the blaze at the centre rather than on the perimeter? It is not known what finally changed Marlborough's mind; only that, by the time he returned to England, he had come round to Wratislaw's view.

All this continued to be carefully hidden from the Dutch. When Marlborough arrived in The Hague on 22 April to start his spring campaign he found his allies in a bad mood, as determined as ever to keep all their forces in Holland. He could see that they were prepared to veto any unorthodox idea, so he decided to try and bamboozle them into helping him without knowing what they were doing. Indeed, at the time the Duke's plans were still so secret that he had not even confided them to his great friend, Sidney Godolphin. 'My intentions', he disclosed on 29 April,

> are to march all the English to Coblenz and to declare here that I intend to command on the Moselle. But when I come there to write to the States [the Dutch] that I think it absolutely necessary, for the saving of the Empire, to march with the troops under my command and to join those in Germany that are in Her Majesty's and in the Dutch pay . . . for the speedy reduction of the Elector of Bavaria.[1]

However, when Marlborough asked leave of the Dutch to command the Moselle campaign himself, they protested strongly at his leaving Flanders. So much so that he suddenly changed his tactics and announced that he would march to Coblenz with all the troops in English pay, with or without the consent of his allies. He then showed them the Queen's command 'to send speedy succour of His Imperial Majesty and the Empire'. He closed the meeting very grandly by saying that, as it was an order from the Queen, he could not allow any further discussion. He wrote to Godolphin on 1 May:

> I am very sensible that I take a great deal on me. But should I act otherwise the Empire would be undone and consequently the confederacy. . . . If the French shall have joined any more troops to the Elector of Bavaria I shall make no difficulty of marching to the Danube.[2]

The following day, 2 May, he wrote to his still-estranged wife:

> I shall not continue in this country long for I intend to go higher up into Germany which I am forced as yet to keep here a secret, for fear these people would be apprehensive of letting their troops go so far.

Nothing would make me take so much upon myself in this matter but that I see the French must overrun the Empire if we do not help them at this time. I am very sensible that if we have not success I shall be found fault with . . . but I shall have the quiet of mind to know that I have done what I think is the best. . . . Whatever happens to me I beg you will believe that my heart is entirely yours, and that I have no thoughts, but what is for the love of my country. Remember me kindly to my dear Children.[3]

The day after Marlborough had confronted his stubborn allies, the Dutch yielded. They not only wished him well on the Moselle but promised to send troops from their own command to join him. On 5 May, the day of his departure for his headquarters at Maestricht, he received the best news of all: a warm and loving letter from Sarah who had at last overcome her furious suspicions and now asked penitently for permission to join him. He was overjoyed and wrote back ecstatically: 'I do this minute love you better than ever I did before.' However, it would be impossible for her to come as he was 'going into Germany'. 'But love me as you do now', he continued, 'and no hurt can come to me. You have by this kindness preserved my quiet and I believe my life; for till I had this letter I had been very indifferent of what would become of myself. . . .'[4]

The British-born troops numbered about 16,000 and consisted of fourteen infantry battalions and nineteen cavalry squadrons. They were not short of generals. Marlborough's chief officer was his brother, General Charles Churchill, who had fought with him at Sedgemoor and at Cork and Kinsale, and whom he put in charge of the whole body of English infantry. After this came four lieutenant-generals, three major-generals, eight brigadiers, an adjutant-general, a quartermaster-general, a wagon-master-general, a provost master-general, a judge advocate-general, seven brigade majors, twenty-one aides-de-camp, and the Duke's own chaplain. The lieutenant-generals were George, Earl of Orkney, a well-respected soldier who had married 'Squinting Betty' Villiers, for many years King William's mistress; the Hon. Henry Lumley, a brother of the Earl of Scarborough, and Richard Ingoldsby, both of whom had fought at Namur; and the incredibly brave Lord Cutts, known as 'the Salamander' because he always emerged from the hottest fire unscathed. Dr Francis Hare, who had been tutor to the poor Marquis of Blandford at Cambridge (and later became Bishop of Chichester), was Chaplain General.

The British troops marched from Brabant to Bedburg, a town about twenty-five miles from Bonn which had been chosen as an assembly point. Here they were joined by twenty foreign squadrons in English pay, bringing their numbers to 19,000.* Contingents from other members of the Alliance – Hessian, Hanoverian, Prussian, Danish – were scheduled to join them as the march progressed, more than doubling Marlborough's army. The Duke's secretary and confidant, Adam Cardonnel, must have anticipated these additions when, writing from Maestricht, he put Marlborough's force at 'upwards of 40,000 very good men' which the enemy 'would not be able to match for goodness'.

'The annals of the British Army', declared Winston Churchill, 'contain no more heroic episode than the march from the North Sea to the Danube.' Although only a handful of people were aware of the Duke of Marlborough's intentions, this fifty-four-year-old English general, who had never commanded a major battle, was about to take one of the greatest military gambles in history; and unless every factor worked in his favour, the plan would come to grief. The great march across Europe would have to be a masterpiece of deception. If he did not deceive the Dutch, they would not lend him the troops necessary to bring his army up to strength; and if he did not deceive the enemy, they would overwhelm him at his final destination. These conditions were not easy to fulfil as an army of 40,000 men, marching 300 miles across Europe, was scarcely a private matter. Yet the ultimate objective had to be kept secret until the eleventh hour and the final battle had to be a resounding victory! Punters would have been considered generous if they had put the odds against the Duke at ten to one.

As Marlborough understood the vital importance of discretion, he did not even inform his brother Charles of his plans. In those days there was no 'Q' department to organize the logistics, nor even a general staff to complete the military arrangements. A Commander-in-Chief was expected to direct and supervise most of the details himself, and this is exactly what Marlborough did with the help of three trusted colleagues. Closest to him was the bulky Irishman, twenty-nine-year-old Brigadier William Cadogan, sometimes described as the Duke's Quartermaster-General, sometimes as his

---

* Battalions were usually reckoned at 700 and ~quadrons at 150, but these were considerably over strength. However, none of the recognized authorities agree on the size of Marlborough's army at the start of the march. G. M. Trevelyan accepts Cardonnel's estimate of 40,000 and gives his figure of forty battalions and eighty squadrons; the military historian David Chandler quotes thirty-one battalions and sixty-six squadrons (21,000 men); and Winston Churchill estimates fourteen battalions and thirty-nine squadrons – nineteen British and twenty foreign – and puts the total at 19,000 of which 16,000 were British. Churchill's figures are followed.

Chief of Staff or personal assistant or special adjutant.* In some ways he was the Duke's alter ego for he seemed to know his chief's mind as well as his own and carried out his duties – planning, reconnoitring and organizing – with superb efficiency. He arranged for the siege-trains, bargained with the bread contractors and sent out scouts to survey the roads.

Marlborough, of course, took all the decisions. Instead of the supply-wagons generally employed by the army he would use the new, two-wheeled and sprung carts pulled by two horses. Although he placed the highest importance on the use of artillery, he came to the conclusion that the large field-guns – the three-ton brass and iron monsters which required ten horses to pull each one – would have to be left behind. Even the standard twenty-four-pounders created a problem. Although they could be shipped along the Rhine as far as Philippsburg, after that they would have to be dragged along the roads for perhaps as much as 100 miles. As most of the draught horses and drivers were provided by civilian contractors on two-day service agreements, this called for a complicated rota system of re-placements.

These were only a few of the difficulties facing Marlborough. With the help of Adam Cardonnel he had been in touch with the various princes of the Alliance all winter, but now he had to settle the number of soldiers each would contribute, and when and where they would join the main army. The most important aspect of the whole under-taking – the money and credits to pay for it – was causing the least trouble. This was due to the persuasiveness of the Duke's financial agent in Frankfurt, Henry Davenant. By his skilful arrangements the British Exchequer guaranteed a steady flow of credits to Continental bankers that enabled Marlborough to meet the immense charges of the war and keep his soldiers in comfort and plenty.

The first lap of the journey was a seventy-mile stretch from Bedburg to Coblenz. The road followed the Rhine and Marl-borough's artillery expert, the well-named Colonel Blood, had the pleasure of travelling on the barge that carried his train of guns, while his colleagues sweated it out on the dusty highways. The cavalry led the procession, always several days in advance, followed by the serried ranks of red-coated infantrymen, spread out for many miles. The rear was brought up by several thousand carts carrying all the necessities of war from saddlery to horse shoes, lamps, nails, rope,

* Present-day historians have found papers to prove that Cadogan was in the Duke's confi-dence, contrary to Winston Churchill's assertion. See David Chandler, *Marlborough as Military Commander.*

bricks, shovels and medical supplies. Then came hundreds of carts packed with ammunition; and last, but not least, the officers' personal baggage including everything from tents and furniture to silver for their tables.

As Marlborough's army approached Coblenz, a charming old town on the strip of land at the confluence of the Rhine and the Moselle, Marshal Villeroy, the French Commander in the Spanish Netherlands, became certain that this was the Englishman's objective. He had always felt that Marlborough would attack here, and without more ado struck out for Coblenz himself on a parallel road with a force of 21,000 men. The Duke had predicted this move, and was pleased as it drew pressure away from the Dutch. Furthermore, it showed that his carefully planned deceptions were effective. As well as employing agents to spread false rumours, he had set up supply-bases as 'blinds'. For instance, in Coblenz he established such a large magazine store that even his own men were convinced that he intended to fight in this area. 'And now when we expected to march up the Moselle,' wrote Captain Robert Parker, an infantry officer,

> to our surprise we passed over that river by a stone bridge and then the Rhine over two bridges of boats, and proceeded on our march to the country of Hesse-Cassell where we were joined by the Hereditary Prince (now King of Sweden) with the Troops of that country; which makes our army 40,000 fighting men compleat.[5]

The bridge of boats mentioned by Parker was composed of hundreds of small boats which worried Marshal Villeroy as they were capable of fulfilling a dual purpose. Because of the strength of the Rhine currents, they could carry Marlborough's army downstream very swiftly, covering eighty miles in a single day. Some French soldiers, including Villeroy, were tormented by the fear that the wily Englishman might not attack there at all, but suddenly double back on his tracks and attack in Flanders before the rest of them could retrace their steps. But this anxiety passed as the great army continued its march.

The soldiers were in high spirits as they made their way over the hill roads to Mainz, and from Mainz through the romantic wooded country to Heidelberg. No doubt the Rhine wine added a sparkle of its own, not to mention the inhabitants who greeted them as deliverers and the pretty girls who lined the roads to wave them on '. . . some of them much handsomer', wrote Lieutenant Pope, 'than we expected to find in this country.'[6] Only the Scottish Bible-reading Colonel Blackader complained: he objected to the oaths and profane language of his comrades, and found the army 'a bad place to be on the Sabbath'.

During the ten days of this second lap of the journey the enemy readjusted his original assessment and came to the conclusion that Alsace was the objective and that Marlborough's attack would begin with the siege of Landau. This idea took root because the governor of Philippsburg was busy constructing bridges over the Rhine and storing grain in one of the huge magazines. The prospect pleased the two French Marshals, Tallard and Villeroy, as they were within easy reach of one another and could quickly form a joint army with which to repel the incursion.

Meanwhile Tallard was leaving nothing to chance. He had just made his way through the Black Forest with 10,000 recruits, badly needed by the Elector of Bavaria, for his summer assault on Vienna. Tallard had met Max Emmanuel and Marshal Marsin in Villingen, turned over the drafts and returned to Strasbourg without mishap. This incident caused both Marlborough and the Emperor Leopold much concern, for Prince Louis of Baden, the Emperor's Commander-in-Chief, was only a few miles from Strasbourg with an army of 30,000 men. Surely he could have intercepted Tallard before he reached Villingen? Or attacked the Elector on his way back to Ulm? While Tallard resumed his station on the upper Rhine, some blamed the Margrave for stupidity, others hinted at duplicity.

Marlborough's mastery of detail and his brilliant organizing ability gave most of his officers their first glimpse of their chief's superb quality of leadership. All along the way detachments of troops had been joining his army according to pre-arranged plans. In early June he learned to his satisfaction that the Dutch not only had forgiven him for not launching a campaign along the Moselle (they now thought it would be in Alsace), but as a mark of friendship were sending him 8,500 Danish soldiers in the pay of the Dutch. The provisioning of this army was no easy task, yet everything ran easily and smoothly due to Marlborough's careful preparations. First of all, quite unlike most army commanders of the day, he carried gold – supplied by Henry Davenant – and paid on the nail for everything his army consumed or required. According to Marlborough's spirited chaplain, Dr Hare, this idea was so novel it created a sensation. 'Regular payments', he wrote,

> for everything that was brought into Camp was a thing hitherto unknown in Germany, where in all former Wars, both the Imperial and French Generals have subsisted their armies at the Expense of those Princes whose countries they marched thro; and to prevent any failure herein he [the

Duke] ordered the Treasurer of the Army to be always in Cash to answer Bills, and duly to have a month's subsistence beforehand. . . .[7]

As a result, wherever the troops encamped, 'grand' and 'petty' sutlers and *vivandières*, supplying meat and brandy and other luxuries, were awaiting them. Marlborough always moved his army in the dark hours of early morning so that Villeroy's troops – across the distant valleys – could not pinpoint their position by the tell-tale dust arising from the roads. Every fourth day the army came to a halt for twenty-four hours while field-ovens were set up and bread baked for a few days. 'We generally began our march', wrote Captain Robert Parker,

> about three in the morning proceeding about four leagues or four and a half by day, and reached our ground about nine. As we marched through the countries of our allies commissaries were appointed to furnish us with all manner of necessaries for men and horse; these were brought to the ground before we arrived, and the soldiers had nothing to do, but to pitch their tents, boil their kettles and lie down to rest. Surely never was such a march carried on with more order and regularity, and with less fatigue to man and beast.[8]

The truth was that the men loved marching through glorious country in fine summer weather – particularly when they were moving through friendly states and receiving an ecstatic welcome as 'deliverers'. Not only were the troops superbly fit but also superbly well-clothed. General Churchill's infantry soldiers wore 'a tricorned hat, leather shoes, white or grey breeches with gaiters, and a red coat embellished with linings and facings of varying hue according to regiment'.[9] The men were so proud of their appearance they were always glad to be inspected. Thus when Count Schönbrunn, the brother of the Elector of Mainz, invited General Churchill and his officers to a ball, the latter accepted with pleasure but insisted that the Count and the Elector must first inspect the Brigade of Guards at Cassell. According to Dr Hare, the Elector was so impressed by 'their cleanliness and their arms, accoutrements, clothes, shoes and linen' that he exclaimed to General Churchill: 'Certainly all these gentlemen are dressed for the Ball!'[10]

Unlike most commanders of the day Marlborough took an intense personal interest in the welfare of his men. 'His camps', wrote a contemporary biographer, Thomas Lediard,

> were like a quiet and well-governed city and perhaps, much more mannerly. . . . His Army was the best Academy in the world to teach a young gentleman Wit and Breeding, a Sot and a Drunkard being what they scorn'd. The poor soldiers who were (too many of them) the Refuse and

Dregs of the Nation became, after one or two Campaigns . . . tractable, civil, orderly, sensible and clean. . . .[11]

Marlborough's preoccupation with the physical well-being of his soldiers was not only altruistic but practical as it was essential that they should arrive at their destination 'fighting fit'. But his private letters show that his concern about their welfare ran deeper than military expedience. He frequently mentions them to Sarah and Godolphin and, on the march, kept in daily touch with his brother Charles to make sure that the infantry was in good heart. Marlborough was several days ahead with the cavalry and on 3 June sent Charles a message advising him to direct his troop along the route to Heidelberg as the road he had taken to Ladenburg 'will be too difficult for you'. He asked Charles to keep him informed as to where he was camping each night; and when he passed through hilly country sent instructions: 'You must take care beforehand to ease your artillery horses all you can, and if in the rest of your route . . . you find any difficulty in reaching to the place appointed, in case it can be done and the forage brought to you, you may camp a little short, provided you do not come more than a day later to Gieslingen. . . .'[12] And again, 'I hope this warm weather you take care to march early so as to be in your camp before the heat of the day.' Later, the Duke scribbled a hurried postscript that gives a rare glimpse into his inner feelings. 'I long to have you with me being your loving brother Marlborough.'[13]

The Duke's most spectacular move, however, was his 'pre-order' of footwear on a large scale, all paid for by Frankfurt credits. When the infantry reached Heidelburg, every soldier found a new pair of boots awaiting him. The 'poor Foot' had never received such attention before and were delighted to discover their own importance!

Meanwhile, Marlborough continued to apply pressure on Godolphin to make sure that the flow of money credits was maintained. 'Notwithstanding the continuous marching,' he wrote from Mainz in early June, 'the men are extremely pleased with this expedition so that I am sure you will take all possible care that they will not want.'[14] Although Marlborough never spent a penny on himself, he did not stint when it came to his army. 'The troops I carry with me are very good,' he wrote to Sarah, 'and will do whatever I will have them.'[15] This was no exaggeration. Because of the care he lavished on them, they nicknamed him 'the old Corporal'; and when it came to the clash of cold steel they showed that their respect was worth having.

Marlborough was not only a big spender on boots and blankets. During the two years that he had been in command of the Allied army he had built up a superb intelligence service. It was expensive because he enrolled highly placed informants in almost every important city in Europe. One of them, the confidential secretary of the Elector of Brunswick, got hold of the French plan of battle for the summer of 1704 and sent it to Cardonnel at Coblenz. It did not tell Marlborough anything he did not know, but it was reassuring to have his views confirmed. 'Nothing is beyond the power of the march of gold,' commented Napoleon's historian a hundred years later, 'and it looks as though Marlborough, although blamed for avarice, knew how to spend money to some point.'[16]

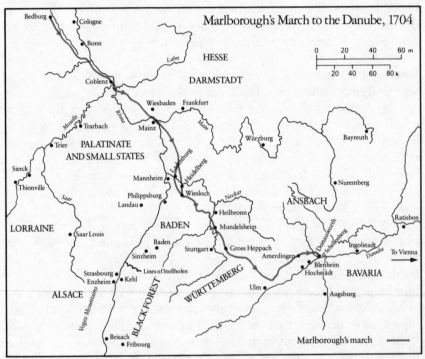

On 3 June Marlborough led his cavalry, now swollen in number to 12,000 troopers in eighty squadrons, across the River Neckar, a few miles from Heidelberg. He took the floating bridge at Ladenburg and encamped on the far side for three days. This was to allow his brother, who was following with infantry and cannon, time to catch up with him. It was there that Marlborough wrote to the States-General and revealed his true destination. He reminded them that the Queen of England had commanded him to go to the aid of the Empire and he appealed to them to allow the Danish contingents and certain Dutch

detachments which he had collected in the course of his march 'to share in the honours of this memorable expedition.'

On 6 June he proceeded to Wiesloch and on 7 June turned sharply away from the Rhine and headed eastwards to Sinzheim where he had fought as a young man with Turenne. At long last the French knew his destination. For over three weeks he had kept them wondering and guessing, rooted to their camps for fear of making the wrong moves. When Marlborough began his march to Coblenz, Marshal Marsin had abandoned his plan to attack Nuremberg and hung on at Ulm to see what the Duke would do. Marshal Bedmar and Marshal Tallard followed suit – one remaining on the Maas, the other at Strasbourg. But when it became clear that the Duke would not fight at the Moselle, all eyes moved higher up into Germany. Although news that the Governor of Philippsburg was building bridges across the Rhine seemed to give them their answer, some French officers still had lingering fears that the Duke might suddenly send his army down the Rhine at eighty miles a day in a masterly attempt to overwhelm the French positions in Flanders!

Not until Marlborough suddenly veered off to Sinzheim did everything become horribly clear. The Allied army, which had now grown to 50,000 men, would be joined by the Margrave of Baden, who could command almost as large a force again. Together, the two commanders would fall on the Elector of Bavaria and Marshal Marsin and destroy them. Marlborough had been so successful in deceiving the enemy that he had managed to place himself in a perfect strategic position. He was midway between the Rhine and the Danube, and within easy reach of the Margrave. Tallard and Villeroy, on the other hand, were on the west side of the Rhine, while Marsin and the Elector were many miles east on the banks of the Danube. The Duke's army was in a splendid position between the two.

At this point the French panicked. 'In view of the superiority of the enemy forces between the Rhine and the Danube,' wrote Tallard to Louis xiv, 'assistance in Bavaria is so difficult as to appear almost an impossibility.' What could they do? The King would have to decide. 'Your Majesty', wrote Villeroy despairingly, 'understands war better than those who have the honour to serve him.'[17]

Word soon reached England that the Duke of Marlborough had led his army 300 miles across Europe – under the very noses of the enemy – and was now close to the Danube. Although the journey had taken thirty-five days (twenty-five marching days, little over the average speed), the long-sustained effort was hailed as a remarkable feat. Not only had the Duke managed to fool the French, but by his superb organization had kept his troops in such fine fettle that they were, literally, fighting fit – an almost unheard of accomplishment for the time. Indeed, some Members of Parliament were so impressed by the great march that they even declared themselves reconciled to the Land Tax. But others, like High Tory Sir Edward Seymour, who had recently been dismissed by the Queen, declared sourly that if Marlborough should fail, 'we will break him up as hounds upon a hare.'[18]

Marlborough met the famous Prince Eugene for the first time when the latter called on him in the little town of Mundelsheim, forty miles from the Danube. The Duke received his illustrious guest – the greatest general in the Emperor Leopold's service – with full honours, which included a magnificent banquet. Afterwards the two men talked for several hours; although they were not at all alike in temperament or appearance, they thought of war in the same aggressive way and were immediately attracted to one another. Eugene was small and ugly and charming; so much so (John told Sarah) that he reminded him of Lord Shrewsbury, the irresistible 'King of Hearts'. Eugene offered a sharp contrast to his English host. With a mixture of French, Austrian and Italian blood in his veins, he was impulsive and talkative, while the handsome, polished Marlborough, full of compliments and *politesse*, never revealed his true thoughts unless he judged the time propitious. 'Certainly they were very different characters,' wrote Winston Churchill, 'yet when their eyes met each recognized a kindred spirit in all that governs war. They were in action, as has been well said, "two bodies with one soul".'[19]

Next day, when Marlborough took his cavalry to Gross Heppach, twenty miles away, Prince Eugene rode with him. As they started off, all nineteen squadrons were lined up for Eugene to inspect. The Prince was genuinely amazed that men and horses could be in such fine condition after a march of 250 miles. Indeed, it was common knowledge that Marshal Tallard's march to Ulm a few weeks earlier had resulted in so many desertions that his effectiveness had been cut by a third. 'My lord,' exclaimed Eugene in unfeigned delight, 'I never saw better horses, better clothes, finer belts and accoutrements; but money which you don't want [lack] in England will buy clothes and fine horses, but it can't buy that lively air I see in every one of those trooper's faces.' 'Sir,' replied Marlborough, who was never to be outdone when it came to compliments, 'that must be attributed to their heartiness for the public cause and the particular pleasure and satisfaction they have in seeing your Highness.'[20]

In Gross Heppach the two Generals awaited the arrival of the Emperor's Commander-in-Chief, Prince Louis, the Margrave of

Baden. Prince Eugene revealed to Marlborough that he not only disliked Prince Louis but distrusted him. Louis had been in communication with the Elector Max Emmanuel (his friend of many years standing but now supposedly his greatest enemy) and Eugene suspected that the two men had come to an understanding, based on the likelihood of a French victory. If so, it would explain why Louis had not prevented Max from forming his recent juncture with Tallard near Strasbourg.

The fifty-year-old Margrave of Baden was not what Marlborough had expected. Although he had distinguished himself against the Turks and had a reputation as a fine soldier, he was ponderous and slow and talked a great deal about the importance of fortified lines, revealing an excessively conservative approach to war. However, as he was a prince with a large army, he had to be treated with consideration. The three Generals came to the conclusion that the best way to ensure the safety of Vienna – and the position of the Emperor Leopold – was to force the Elector Max Emmanuel of Bavaria to change sides. And the best way to achieve this was to carry the war into the heart of Bavaria. But first they must organize large supply-depots and establish a bridgehead across the Danube.

Marlborough's eye had already fallen on the fortified town of Donauworth, which not only would provide the necessary bridgehead but be an ideal place to set up magazine-stores. However, it would not be an easy prize as it was dominated and protected by a cone-shaped hill, known as the Schellenberg, bristling with enemy guns. It had been established as a fort by the famous Gustavus Adolphus of Sweden.

This was the position that must be taken first, and Marlborough declared that it must be taken at any price as it was the gateway to Bavaria. It was decided that Eugene should lead an army to the upper Rhine to try and delay Marshal Tallard and Marshal Villeroy from bringing reinforcements to the Elector, while Louis of Baden and Marlborough would join forces to storm the Schellenberg. Although the command between these two was supposedly 'shared', Marlborough took control and Louis reluctantly followed his lead.

The attack could not take place until Marlborough's infantry and siege-guns had caught up with him. The heavy artillery had travelled along the Rhine for 150 miles but when the road turned away from the river, poor Colonel Blood had to struggle along muddy, waterlogged roads with horses, guns and wagons, and was frequently held up for hours at a time. The Duke waited for him at Giengen, about thirty miles from Donauworth. 'As I am writing', he reported to Sarah, 'I am forced to have fire in the stove in my chamber. But the poor men, that

have not such conveniences, I am afraid will suffer from these con-
tinual rains. As they do us hurt here, they do good to Prince Eugene
on the Rhine, so that we must take the good with the bad.'[21]

On 1 July the army camped at Amerdingen, fifteen miles from
Donauworth. Although Marlborough and Prince Louis had hived
off 30,000 men for Prince Eugene, they still had a fairly impressive
total between them, numbering about 60,000. That afternoon Marlborough drew 130 men from each of the English infantry battalions
under his command, amounting to 6,000 picked men who, in
modern parlance, would be known as 'storm-troopers'. Meanwhile,
the Count d'Arco, who had been despatched only two days earlier
from the Elector's camp with 14,000 men, with instructions to hold
the Schellenberg at all costs, was feverishly trying to repair his defences. The Elector had been warned by Villars a year earlier not to
neglect the fortifications of this strategic hill, but Max Emmanuel
had done nothing about it until now. Two weeks earlier he had sent
engineers, pioneers and ordinary labourers to the Schellenberg to
strengthen the two miles of entrenchments that had been overlooked
so long. The work was proceeding rapidly and the Count was confident of finishing the defences by 3 July, the day that additional
troops were expected to arrive from the Elector's camp. The Count
d'Arco was therefore not worried. After all, Schellenberg was
famous as an impregnable fortress; a gap of only 1,200 feet was all
that was left in the defences, and preparations were being made to
receive reinforcements on the day of completion.

What neither he nor any of his officers foresaw was that Marlborough might attack *before* the 3rd. Such a possibility was out of
the question – the date was already 1 July and the Duke's infantry
was a day's march away; the earliest the Allies could arrive was late
afternoon of 2 July, and no one would attack at sundown after a
long march. Yet this is exactly what the Duke did. His soldiers
broke camp at 3 a.m. on 2 July and by late afternoon the slopes
leading to the foot of the Schellenberg were crowded with men in
brilliant uniforms. Some were on foot, some mounted, others were
dragging cannon or bringing up ammunition; and all were converg-
ing on the space between the wood and the hill, the most likely
place to start an assault. Marlborough had decided that despite the
lateness in the day, the fortifications were proceeding so rapidly that
every hour he delayed in launching his attack would cost him a
thousand more lives. And if reinforcements arrived from the Elector,
as rumoured, the position might prove impossible to take whatever
the cost.

If the timing of Marlborough's attack was unexpected, the deploy-ment of his troops was just as surprising. He thrust a large number of English infantrymen, conspicuous in their scarlet coats, on to the enemy's most heavily guarded point, then pressed home his attack ruthlessly. Some generals, accustomed to the stately warfare of the day, regarded the Duke's disregard of human life as most ungentle-manly. Nevertheless, these were the tactics he introduced at the Schellenberg and used again at Blenheim and Ramillies. His purpose was simple and severe. If his first violent onslaught on the enemy's strongest position succeeded, victory was his; if it did not succeed the reinforcements brought forward from other parts of the line would create vulnerable spots which he could exploit.

This, then, was the formula. At 6.15 the drums beat and the Dutch-man, General Goor, led the first assault force up the hill between the old fort and the woods. Most of the 6,000 leading storm-troopers were British; they walked at a slow step, shoulder to shoulder, in long columns, many lines deep. Behind them came another 6,000 men – Hessians, Hanoverians, Dutch – as a support column. And bringing up the rear, 5,000 cavalry – all the English, and 2,500 Danes and Prussians. Colonel Blood's batteries were on a hill a short dis-tance away and one of the French officers defending the fort, M. de la Colonie, tells us that cannon-balls killed eighty of his grenadiers before the fighting began, while he himself was splashed with the blood and brains of a company commander.

The soldiers moved up the steep slope in perfect formation, each carrying a fascine in his left hand to use in crossing the ditch outside the parapet. When half the distance was covered, the Bavarian guns fired point-blank into their midst and the breastworks blazed with musketry. General Goor fell dead and gaping holes were torn in the oncoming formations, but the ranks closed and the lines kept moving. Unhappily, the leading column mistook a gully for the main obstacle and used their fascines before they reached the wide ditch. Here, they once again met such withering fire that the columns following had to make their way over the bodies of their comrades to reach the ram-parts. By this time they were furious for revenge. 'The enemy broke into the charge', wrote de la Colonie,

> and rushed at full speed, shouting at the top of their voices to throw themselves into our entrenchments. The rapidity of their movements, together with their loud yells, were truly alarming and as soon as I heard them I ordered our drums to beat the 'charge'. ... By this means I animated my grenadiers, and prevented them hearing the shouts of the enemy, which before now have produced a heedless panic.

The English infantry led this attack with the greatest intrepidity, right up to our parapet, but there they were opposed with a courage at least equal to their own. Rage, fury and desperation were manifested by both sides, with the more obstinacy as the assailants and assailed were perhaps the bravest soldiers in the world. . . .

During this first attack, which lasted a good hour or more [in fact less than half an hour] we were all fighting hand-to-hand, hurling them back as they clutched at the parapet; men were slaying or tearing at the muzzles of guns and the bayonets which pierced their entrails; crushing under their feet their own wounded comrades, and even gouging out their opponents' eyes with their nails, when the grip was so close that neither could make use of their weapons. I verily believe that it would have been quite impossible to find a more terrible representation of Hell itself than was shown in the savagery of both sides on this occasion.

At last the enemy after losing more than 8,000 [in truth about 3,000] in this first onslaught were obliged to relax their hold, and they fell back for shelter to the dip of the slope, where we could not harm them. . . . The ground from our parapet was covered with dead and dying in heaps almost as high as our fascines; but our whole attention was fixed on the enemy and his movements. We noticed that the tops of his standards still showed at about the same place as that from which they had made their charge in the first instance, leaving little doubt but that they were re-forming before returning to the assault.[22]

Marlborough ordered two more attacks in the same sector – by this time almost all the top officers were killed or wounded. Then he probed to the right, found little resistance and directed his eight reserve battalions to attack here; the Margrave and his troops were already heading for the same spot. Meanwhile the third attack on the central position was proving successful and suddenly the battle was over. Marlborough signalled the Imperial cavalry, which poured through the gap and, as the enemy broke and ran through the cornfields to the river, thousands were ridden down and killed. Of Count d'Arco's 14,000 men, scarcely 5,000 rejoined the Elector's army. As for the English, nearly half of the 4,000 men who had been in action were killed or wounded. The list of casualties included eleven lieutenant-generals, four major-generals, twenty-eight brigadiers, colonels and lieutenant-colonels. Although Prince Louis of Baden had had a horse shot from under him, he had escaped with a bruised toe.

The capture of Schellenberg brought with it the surrender of Donauworth which could not be held under enemy gunfire from the hill. Donauworth was the gateway to Bavaria. It had to be taken at any cost; and the cost had been paid in full.

At first Marlborough tried to bribe the Elector of Bavaria to abandon the French. This was not an easy proposition as Louis XIV had promised to help Max Emmanuel to become Emperor of the Holy Roman Empire in place of Leopold, and the Allies had nothing so important to offer. However, Max loved intrigue, and on this occasion complained loudly of his disillusion with the French and declared his willingness to join the Allies if the terms were enticing enough. However, when he learned that Marshal Tallard was actually on his way with the promised relief of 35,000 men he, not unexpectedly, broke off relations.

Marlborough refused to accept defeat and decided to take drastic measures. 'We are advancing into the heart of Bavaria', he wrote to the Pensionary Hensius the following day, 16 July, 'to destroy the country and oblige the Elector one way or the other to a compliance.'[23] Twelve years earlier, when Louis XIV had ordered his troops to adopt a scorched earth policy in the Palatine, Europe had been outraged. Now the civilized, kindly, equable Marlborough was prepared to use the same barbarous methods. 'We sent this morning 3,000 horses to . . . Munich, with orders to burn and destroy all the country around it,' he wrote to Sarah.

> So uneasy to my nature that nothing but an absolute necessity would have obliged me to consent to it. For these poor people suffer only for their master's ambitions. There having been no war in this country above 60 years and their towns and villages are so clean and neat you would be pleased with them.[24]

Although Marlborough convinced himself of the necessity of this action, he seems to have been ashamed of it. Captain Robert Parker, who was present, tells us that 372 villages were set on fire, but adds that the Duke 'would not suffer any of the Troops that were immediately under him to go out on that burning command.' Perhaps he knew that this alien practice would not be acceptable to English soldiers; or even more likely he may have wished to spare his countrymen (and his country) the odium that was bound to attach to them.

Marlborough assigned the major part of the undertaking to his colleague, the Margrave of Baden, who disapproved deeply of the affair. At first the latter flatly refused to carry out the Duke's instructions, saying angrily that 'he would not make war like a hussar' but only 'like an experienced general'. Count Wratislaw, the Emperor's diplomatic agent, who was accompanying the army, finally convinced Prince Louis that he must obey Marlborough's orders. 'As a result of the ravaging, the fires and the forced contributions,' he wrote scathingly to the Emperor, 'in a short time there may be little of Bavaria left. I hope that I have taken the right course for your Majesty's service in accepting other people's opinions.'[25]

However, there seem to be conflicting opinions as to the amount of damage done. Although several hundred *sorties* were made, M. de la Colonie, another eye-witness, tells us that the destruction was far less severe than generally believed. 'I followed a route through several villages said to have been reduced to cinders,' he wrote, 'and though I certainly found a few burnt houses, still the damage was as nothing compared with the reports current through the country.'[26] This seems to suggest that many officers simply refused to carry out their instructions.

Meanwhile Prince Eugene was champing at the bit, dissatisfied with what he termed Marlborough's 'indecisiveness'. The month of July was drawing to a close. Tallard would soon be joining the Elector with his large army, and the Allies had done nothing for the past two weeks but ravage Bavaria – quite pointlessly as they now realized, for Max Emmanuel had not changed sides after all. 'They have amused themselves with . . . burning a few villages', Eugene wrote to the Duke of Savoy, 'instead of . . . marching straight upon the enemy. . . . I don't like this slowness on our side, the enemy will have time to form magazines of food and forage, and all our operations will become the harder.'[27]

What Marlborough was waiting for, of course, was an opportunity to strike at the enemy with a chance – even an outside chance – of success. But as the days passed he saw that his foes were not going to make the sort of blunder he needed. After all, they had everything to gain from inactivity. The Allies could not spend the winter in Bavaria; and if the Elector Max Emmanuel and Marshal Marsin remained entrenched, Marlborough would be forced eventually to relinquish the Schellenberg and return to the Rhine empty-handed. Prince Eugene understood his predicament and felt that his reluctance to make a bold decision was due to his lack of experience. Although he was a man of the highest quality, he wrote to the Emperor, 'He understands throughout that one cannot become a general in a day, and is diffident about himself.'[28]

Eugene's appraisal was not entirely correct. During the first ten days in August the enemy moved into new positions which gave Marlborough his first glimmer of hope. On 6 August, 60,000 men, representing the full concentration of the Franco–Bavarian army and including Marshal Tallard's 35,000 men, effected a junction at Biberback. A few days later they moved to Hochstädt, a small town on the Danube close to the village of Blindheim (Blenheim) and set up a

camp on the large plain spread out before them. At once Marlborough made up his mind to act. No one guessed his intention as he
encouraged Prince Louis of Baden to march away with 15,000 men to
besiege Ingolstädt, the last enemy stronghold between Donauworth
and Vienna. Although there were advantages in capturing this fort,
people later claimed that he had deliberately rid himself of Prince
Louis's presence (and interference) even though the price in man-
power was high. Later Louis himself came to this conclusion, which
did nothing to improve relations between the two men.

On 11 August, while the Franco–Bavarian army was filing across
the Danube *en route* to its new camp, Marlborough was on his way to
join forces with Prince Eugene and his 18,000 men at Munster. He no
longer had any doubts about what he must do: even if the odds
against him were unfavourable, he must confront the enemy, for
without a battle all would be lost. 'The French make their boast of
having a great superiority,' he wrote to Godolphin, in a letter
weighted with unspoken words,

> but I am very confident they will not venture a battle. But if we find a fair
> occasion we will be very glad to venture it, being persuaded that the ill
> condition of our affairs in most parts requires it.[29]

The marshals of France would have been amazed to read this letter.
The last thing they contemplated was an enemy attack, particularly
when they had encamped in such an impregnable position. Settled on
a plain made up of huge, harvested fields, nearly four miles square,
they were protected on every side by natural obstacles: river,
marshes, woods and just past the village of Blenheim, a stream
known rather grandly as the River Nebel. Apart from being well-
entrenched, the French felt that there was not the slightest danger of
an assault. Armies of equal strength did not fall on one another in a
death grapple designed to win all – or lose all – in a day. Such furious
paroxysms were not worth considering as men were too valuable and
materials too costly to be risked in made gambles.

But the Duke of Marlborough and Prince Eugene had different
ideas. If the obstacles did not appear utterly insurmountable, they
would put the war to the test. On 12 August they rode out together to
study the dispositions as the Franco–Bavarians moved into their new
camp. The two Generals surveyed the scene through telescopes from
the tower of Tappheim Church, five miles away. What they saw
satisfied them that the situation was not hopeless, and they resolved
then and there to fight a battle at dawn. Agreement was not unanimous. 'Almost all the generals were against my Lord's attacking the

enemy, they thought it so difficult,' wrote Dr Hare, Marlborough's chaplain, the day after the battle. Lord Orkney, one of the Duke's most respected subordinates, reflected the same misgivings: 'I confess it is entirely owing to my Lord Duke, for I declare, had I been to give my opinion, I had been against it, considering the ground where they were camped and the strength of the army. But his Grace knew the necessity there was of a battle.'[30]

'That night', wrote Count Mérode-Westerloo, a Belgian officer in the French army, 'spirits were at their highest in the Franco–Bavarian camp, for no one doubted that Marlborough and Eugene would be forced to retire.'[31] This conviction was rooted in the belief that no commander would flout military conventions to the extent of delivering a frontal attack on a numerically superior army in a strong position. If no battle was fought, and Marlborough was made to retire, the war was as good as won. This made the evening unusually congenial.

Marlborough and some of his high-ranking officers were acquainted with Marshal Tallard, who had spent several years in London as French Ambassador. Louis XIV considered him as good a soldier as he was a diplomat which was no small compliment, but his colleagues thought him over-cautious and frequently referred to him in private as an old woman. As Tallard commanded the largest army, the sector under his control extended for two miles along the Nebel stream. In a corner, bounded on one side by the stream and on the other by the fast-flowing Danube, lay Blenheim village to which Tallard's strong right flank was securely pinned. It contained 300 houses with pretty, south-German gardens, a picturesque church and a stone-walled churchyard. As soon as the army moved in, Tallard gave orders that the approaches to the village should be strongly fortified; and there he set up his headquarters.

Count Mérode-Westerloo also established himself in Blenheim, sleeping in a barn which his soldier-servant made comfortable by scrounging a bed and putting a carpet on the floor. 'Never I believe', wrote the Count in his memoirs, 'have I slept a sleep more sound and tranquil. . . .' However, at seven o'clock in the morning (after a very late night), the terrified servant burst into the room. 'Milord,' he cried, 'the enemy are there.' 'There?' laughed the Count. 'Where?' 'There. There,' replied the man, flinging open the barn door to reveal the large plain on the other side of the Nebel flooded with sunshine and covered with hostile squadrons and battalions. It was the surprise of his life. All around him the camp was springing to life as alarm-bells, jangling incessantly, rent the air, and signal-guns boomed to call back the foragers.[32]

Unfortunately for Marshal Tallard, he had sat up half the night writing an optimistic summary for the King. When one of his officers returned from an outpost in the early hours of the morning and reported that Marlborough and Eugene were getting ready to leave their camp six miles away, Tallard added a postscript to his letter:

> This morning before daybreak the enemy beat the *generale* at 2 o'clock and at 3 the *assemblée*. They are now drawn up at the head of their camp and it looks as if they will march this day. Rumour in the countryside expects them at Nordingen. If that be true, they will leave us between the Danube and themselves and in consequence they will have difficulty in sustaining the posts and depots which they have taken in Bavaria.[33]

There was a heavy mist on the morning of 13 August; and when the two French Marshals and the Elector Max Emmanuel finally discerned the large forces gathering along their front at six o'clock all three of them clung to the belief that the advance was only a covering operation for the main body. Cheerfully, Tallard dispatched a messenger with his report to the King. But soon after seven, when the enemy columns began to deploy into long lines of scarlet, blue and buff, there was no mistaking their intentions.

Marlborough derived grim satisfaction from the shock he had given to the enemy. Through his glasses he could see aides-de-camp galloping about in a frenzy of motion; tents being dismantled; horses saddled, guns wheeled into position. By half-past eight the formation of his own army had so developed that it was within cannon-shot and the French guns opened fire. As the French columns came within range the English field-batteries began to reply and the cannonade became general.

Although contemporary authorities differ widely, the two armies were not far apart in size – probably 53,000 and 59,000, with the French in the lead.[34] The harvested fields of golden stubble on which the troops were massing were four miles in length, bordered on one side by the Danube, on the other by the woods of Lutzingen. The front extended the whole way and, for most of it, the dividing-line between the sides was the Nebel stream running between marshy banks.

At nine o'clock the French Marshals and the Elector had a conference and decided that General Marsin and Max Emmanuel would defend the line from the far hills to the village of Oberglau, while Marshal Tallard, reinforced with extra squadrons of cavalry, would be responsible for the two-mile sector between Oberglau and Blenheim, and the 200-yard stretch from Blenheim to the Danube. There was some disagreement about the best method of dealing with the enemy's advance across the Nebel. Marsin and the Elector wanted to take up positions close to the marshy bank to prevent the Allies from crossing the stream. But Tallard was more ambitious. He would hold his fire until at least ten battalions were on his terrain, then he would attack them from all sides and push them into the marshy water. 'Beware of these troops,' warned the Elector, who knew only too well the story of Schellenberg. 'They are dangerous; you cannot afford to concede anything.' 'Well then,' replied Tallard testily, 'I can see that today the victory will be my own.'[35]

The Allied commanders had perfected their own plans the previous day. Prince Eugene, with his Austrian cavalry and his Prussian and Danish infantry, would attack and hold the enemy's left wing (the front between Oberglau and the far hills which, as things turned out, placed him opposite Marsin and the Elector), while Marlborough would overwhelm the French right wing. The Duke's army would be larger than Eugene's, consisting of all the English cavalry and a mixture of Dutch, Danish, Hessian and Hanoverian soldiers of both Horse and Foot. His front would extend from Blenheim to Oberglau opposite Marshal Tallard; and, although the Franco–Bavarian army was believed to outnumber the Allies by 6,000 men, Marlborough had complete confidence in the excellence of his soldiers. He was particularly proud of his English contingent and, just as at the Schellenberg, designated his fellow countrymen to undertake the most crucial operations. Englishmen, he often asserted, are 'better than what can be had anywhere else.' At other times he expanded his point and included the Scots among his 'best troops'.[36]

The battle could not begin until Prince Eugene had taken up his position near the Lutzingen Hills. Although he had reckoned to be ready at eleven o'clock, the terrain over which he had to drag heavy artillery was broken and at times swampy, causing him unexpected delays. He was also slowed down by the enemy's artillery for, although the French waited politely for the Allies to reach their selected positions, etiquette did not prevent them from mounting a bombardment. As the Franco–Bavarian army had many more guns than the Allies (ninety as opposed to sixty-six) the barrage not only hindered Eugene's progress but took a heavy toll of Marlborough's army, causing 2,000 casualties before the battle even began.

The Duke's men were formed in columns in the order of battle, with the troopers sitting by their horses and the infantry lying back on the stubble. As it was Sunday morning, the Duke tried to distract his men when the cannonade began by ordering Divine Service to be held at the head of every regiment. The crash of cannon-balls mixed with the cries of the wounded and the frightened neighing of the horses must have provided a macabre background for the prayers and hymns. The presence of the Duke of Marlborough moving along the lines on his splendid white horse was a comforting sight. A magnificent figure in scarlet coat and Garter sash, all eyes were fixed upon him when a round shot hit the ground, covering him in a shower of mud. A gasp of anxiety broke from the ranks, but not a muscle moved in the Duke's face as he continued his stately progress.

During these anxious hours, Marlborough's engineers, known as 'pioneers', repaired a stone bridge and, using pontoons and faggots, constructed five causeways across the marshes between Blenheim and Oberglau. At the same time, five splendid English battalions from Lord Cutts's command, led by Brigadier Rowe, dispelled the enemy from two watermills on the Nebel. The mission accomplished, Rowe posted his column on the river-bed, 150 yards from Blenheim, to await the signal to advance. Here, wrote Sergeant John Millner, 'with wonderful resolution . . . they withstood the Fire of six Pieces of Cannon, planted on a Height near that village.'[37]

This awful period of waiting seemed intolerably long to Marlborough who was well aware of all that the approaching battle could mean. His most perilous task would be moving 15,000 foot soldiers and nearly 9,000 troopers with their horses across the causeways and coping with an enemy attack at the same time. Because of this hazardous prospect he had formed his lines in a most unorthodox way. His first line, several columns deep, consisted of 9,000 infantry soldiers; his second and third lines, also several columns deep, of 8,500 cavalry troopers; and his rear of 6,000 foot soldiers. The enemy stared through their field-glasses at this strange formation, but before the day was over they understood its significance. Marlborough was a great believer in the fire-power of his infantry and often drilled his platoons himself to achieve both rapidity and accuracy. The infantry had instructions to leave lanes running through their ranks so that if their cavalry was driven back the troopers could retreat into their midst and the infantry could rout the pursuing enemy horsemen with their withering volleys.

Although the Duke seemed quite unruffled by the ordeal of waiting, his tension revealed itself when he sent two aides-de-camp, and finally his Quartermaster, Cadogan, to find out what was keeping Eugene. However, shortly after twelve o'clock word arrived that the Prince was ready. Marlborough mounted his horse and turned to his circle of officers: 'Gentlemen, to your posts.' General Charles

Churchill's infantry began to move towards the Nebel and Lord Cutts gave Rowe the signal to attack Blenheim.

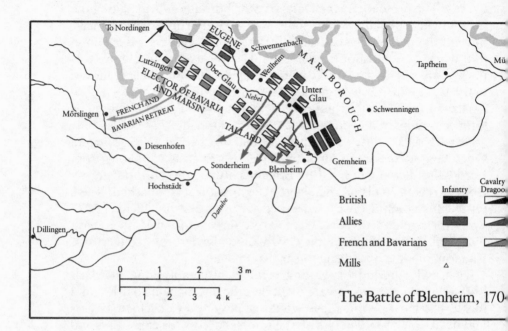

The Battle of Blenheim, 170∘

Blenheim was Marlborough's initial target: first, because it would be the least expected move; second, because, as the reader knows, he believed that if the assault were violent enough (as shown at the Schellenberg) the enemy could be relied upon to bring up reinforcements, weakening other portions of his line which could then be exploited. Blenheim was heavily fortified and defended by a garrison of nine battalions and another eighteen battalions in reserve at the rear of the village – a total of 13,500 men.* Furthermore, the 200 yards between the village and the Danube were defended by a barricade of farm-carts, behind which were 1,200 dismounted dragoons whose horses had died of disease.

Marlborough had chosen his most fearless commander for the Blenheim attack – the dashing, witty, black-eyed Lord Cutts, who fought 'like a madman' and prided himself on the bravado of his men. Cutts, 'the Salamander', commanded four brigades – two British, one

---

* Allowing for wear and tear at this date battalions are calculated roughly at 500 (instead of 700) and squadrons at 120 (instead of 150).

Hessian and one Hanoverian. For this crucial operation he had picked Brigadier Rowe's British brigade, made up of five battalions, to seize the village. For two hours these men had been under fire in the river-bed. Now they shouldered arms* and began to move in orderly columns towards the village. Rowe was in the vanguard and instructed his men not to fire until he struck the pallisades with his sword. As the men moved forwards, an ominous calm descended which lasted until they were within thirty yards of their objective, when the French poured a withering volley into their ranks. Rowe gave his signal and fell back, mortally wounded. The British fought furiously, some of them firing through the openings in the barrier, others trying to tear the pallisades apart with their bare hands, or using their bayonets to stab the enemy through the pales. As the French continued to pour lead into their ranks the attackers fell in swathes, until over 1,000 of them lay in front of the defences. It was the Schellenberg all over again.

When Rowe's two senior officers tried to carry their General to safety they were shot dead. The assault had not succeeded and now it was beginning to recoil. At this point three squadrons of the famous French *gens d'armerie*, in scarlet uniforms and riding magnificent horses, swept around the corner of the village and fell upon the attackers. They sent many of them running back across the stream and even captured the colours of Rowe's regiment. However, at the edge of the marsh, Lord Cutts's Hessian infantry brigade had formed up and assailed the horsemen with such accurate and devastating fire that they not only routed them but recovered the Brigadier's flag.

Cutts now ordered another attack, adding the Hessians and the second British brigade to the survivors of Rowe's battalions. Although, once again, the attackers could not get into the village, they pressed the defenders 'against the walls of the houses'. The casualties were now over 2,000 and the engagement so fierce that the French commander, M. de Clérambault, panicked. During the first assault he had drawn into the village seven supporting battalions and now he called in the eleven reserve battalions. This meant that over 15,000 men were inside Blenheim (including the 1,200 dismounted Dragoons), so closely packed that most of them could not use their arms.

Marlborough saw what had happened and sent a signal to Cutts to abandon further attacks as his object had been realized. Although Cutts's two assaults had failed to capture the stronghold, the flower

* The British had adopted the relatively new 'ring bayonet' which meant that every musket had a dual role as sword or rifle.

of the French infantry was penned up inside the village and could neither fight nor break away, as the three Allied brigades, only half the number of those inside, blocked every outlet. 'It was not possible for them to rush out upon us', wrote Captain Parker, 'without running upon the very points of our bayonets. The great body of troops therefore was of no further use to Tallard, being obliged to keep on the defensive, in expectation that he might come to relieve them.'[38]

Meanwhile, Marlborough had moved the first line of his infantry across the Nebel and now columns of troopers were leading their horses over the causeways. On the long front which stretched from Blenheim to Oberglau, he had a slight numerical superiority over Marshal Tallard, but this advantage was far from outweighed by the danger involved in crossing the marshland and the delay imposed in forming up for battle.*

In the beginning, however, there was no challenge from the enemy, as Tallard adhered to his decision to allow his foes to cross the stream unimpeded. Marlborough's soldiers could scarcely believe their luck; Sergeant Millner was amazed to be given 'all the time we wanted' while the enemy 'kept very quiet on the hill', and General Kane relates how the squadrons and battalions 'passed over as well as they could and formed as fast as they got over, Tallard all this while as a man infatuated, looking on.'[39]

Tallard's hope, of course, was to win a spectacular victory that would set the whole of Europe talking. As soon as enough of Marlborough's men had crossed the Nebel he would direct one flank attack from Blenheim, another from Oberglau, and a third cavalry assault against the centre, completely demolishing the Duke's army. This was the Marshal's design, but when he heard the news that twenty-seven of his infantry divisions were at that very moment bottled up in Blenheim, and that fierce fighting was taking place at Oberglau, he began to sense that his plans might go awry. As this unhappy thought occurred to him, he witnessed a distressing incident. Five of Lord Lumley's cavalry squadrons, under the command of Colonel Palmes, had scrambled across the rivulet ahead of the others and were in the process of forming up. Tallard's cavalry commander saw a chance of catching them off balance and ordered his eight squadrons of *gens d'armerie* (some of whom had already been in action) to attack. Colonel Palmes's troopers met the assault full on and, in a brilliant display of horsemanship, not only managed to break the enemy's wings but, wheeling inwardly, smashed the centre

---

* Prince Eugene's army faced Marshal Marsin and the Elector of Bavaria on the front from Oberglau to the far hills.

and completely routed the famous French unit. The Elector of Bavaria, who had been dashing about madly, far from his own sphere of command, happened to witness the action and could scarcely believe his eyes. 'What!' he cried. 'There is the *gens d'armerie* running away! Is it possible? Go gentlemen, tell them that I am here in person. Rally them and lead them back to the charge.'[40]

This irritating commentary did nothing to lift the spirits of Marshal Tallard. The sight of his eight celebrated squadrons being put to flight by little more than half their number seemed to be a portent of disaster, and he later cited the incident in explaining the French defeat. However, when he again directed a cavalry charge against the Duke's newly formed left he fared better. This time the French horsemen managed to roll up four or five English squadrons, but as they drove their beaten foe back to the Nebel, Marlborough's infantry, under the command of the redoubtable Lord Orkney, was waiting for them at the stream. The men turned their rapid fire on to the pursuers with satisfactory results. 'I really believe,' wrote Orkney, 'had not ye Foot been here, that the Enemy would have driven our Horse from the field.'[41] Now the puzzled French Marshals understood the meaning of Marlborough's interlocking formations of Horse and Foot.

The Duke did not launch his central attack until he had seen the outcome of Blenheim. When he finally gave the signal, the whole, long front burst into conflict – cavalry charges, bayonet attacks, musket-fire, artillery barrages, all had their moments. 'From one end of the armies to the other', wrote Count Mérode-Westerloo, 'everyone was at grips and all fighting at once – a feature very rare in battles.'[42] 'My Lord Marlborough', wrote Dr Hare, 'was everywhere in the action to encourage our men, exposed to infinite dangers.' The Duke had posted each battery himself and, when the fighting was under way, paid close attention to the range and accuracy of his fire. Surrounded by a handful of aides-de-camp, who were constantly galloping this way and that with messages to his front-line subordinates, he kept a sharp eye on the shifting battle. Like a chess-player who can see the game many moves ahead, he had an almost uncanny understanding of what the enemy would do in any given circumstance.

When a situation appeared threatening – as it suddenly did at Oberglau – he took charge himself. One of General Churchill's infantry commanders, Prince Holstein-Beck, had just crossed the Nebel with two battalions, when M. de Blainville, the French Commander of Oberglau, threw nine battalions against him. The Irish Brigade, known as the 'Wild Geese', led the attack with chilling whoops and screams; Prince Holstein was mortally wounded and his battalions soon overwhelmed. From afar the Duke saw that there was nothing to stop Marsin's cavalry from moving through the gap to attack the allied formations behind the Nebel. In a flash he crossed the stream and took command: he ordered Colonel Blood to bring up his guns, flung three of the Prince's reserve battalions against the Irish and sent an urgent message to Prince Eugene asking for the use of one of his cavalry brigades, the 'Imperial Cuirassiers'. Although Eugene was in the middle of a highly critical battle, he complied without a moment's hesitation, immediately ordering the brigade to advance towards Oberglau. At the same moment that Marsin instructed his cavalry to charge, Marlborough's line, the Cuirassiers, mounted a counter-charge, striking the French horsemen at an angle on the bridle-hand and throwing them back in total disorder.

The battle wavered back and forth for half an hour with the cavalry scoring successes first on one side, then on the other. When Marlborough saw one of his officers retiring with a posse of troopers in disarray he rode up to him and said with his famous *politesse*: 'Mr ———, you are under a mistake; the enemy lies that way; you have nothing to do but to face him and the day is your own.'[43] This proved to be only too true, for by three o'clock in the afternoon Blainville's two battalions had been driven back to Oberglau, and the Dutch battalions which had formed the centre of Marlborough's attack were able finally to pen them into the village. On a smaller scale it was a repeat performance of what had happened in Blenheim.

Meanwhile, a mile away, Prince Eugene was fighting an enemy twice as strong as himself. The Elector and Marsin had more squadrons, nearly double the battalions and more than double the cannon of Eugene, yet they had been hard put to defend themselves. Although there was no prospect of Eugene overrunning their positions, he was certainly giving them a run for their money. On the other hand, if he failed to prevent the enemy from breaking through his lines the whole day could be lost. But there was little chance of this; the Prince's indomitable spirit always communicated itself to his troops for he led them wherever the battle was hottest. Indeed, he put himself in dire peril so often that his survival was a miracle. Once his coat was clutched by an enemy horseman and he only escaped through the devotion of his troopers. He demanded from his soldiers a courage equal to his own, and when he saw two of his horsemen fleeing from the battle, he shot them with his own hand. Like all Latins he was prone to furious bursts of emotion and, when he led his Austrian squadrons in a charge that failed for a third time, he left his cavalry with bitter words, saying that from now on he would fight and die with the gallant infantry and not with cowards. The Danish and Prussian soldiers pushed the enemy two miles back over the rocky foothills.

Dr Hare, who had been accompanying Marlborough around the battlefield, admitted later: 'Before three I thought we had lost the day.' The two villages had not been taken and Eugene was having a struggle holding his own. Yet, even then, Marlborough knew that victory was within his grasp, and he sent Eugene a message of encouragement. Twenty-seven enemy battalions were penned up in Blenheim while the whole of Marlborough's force was safely across the Nebel marsh banks. The Duke now had a large, unused army at his disposal. Eighty squadrons of cavalry (only half of which had been in action) to the enemy's fifty or sixty squadrons; and twenty-three battalions of infantry* against Tallard's nine battalions of young cadets.

Marlborough's final charge did not take place until half-past five in the afternoon. For over an hour his horsemen had battled with the French cavalry, the tide of war ebbing and flowing enigmatically. Suddenly the Duke began to sense 'a lack of stomach on the part of the French Horse' and decided that the moment had come for the decisive attack. He rode along the ranks of his squadrons, then drew his sword and ordered the trumpets to sound the charge. Now, for the first time, the whole body of the cavalry broke into a trot, the swords of the troopers gleaming in the evening sun. 'With trumpets blaring, the kettle-drums crashing and standards tossing proudly above the plumage and the steel, the two long lines, perfectly timed from end to end, broke into a trot that quickened ever as they closed upon the French.'[44]

The French did not wait to receive the shock. They fired their pistols half-heartedly, then turned their horses and galloped away, leaving the four or five thousand young infantry recruits to their fate. These nine devoted battalions held their ground with inspiring bravery and were cut down to a man. 'I rode through them next morning', wrote Captain Parker, 'as they lay dead in Rank and File.'[45]

Some of the cavalry, including the famous Maison du Roi, the King's most exalted regiment, made for Hochstädt, four miles away; others made for the Danube. The horsemen were riding so close together that when they came to Sondenheim, where the river bank falls

* The remaining battalions were engaged at Oberglau and Blenheim.

twenty feet, 2,000 of them were driven headlong over the drop into the swiftly moving river, where most of them were drowned. Our old friend, Count Mérode-Westerloo, was imprisoned in the mob and says that 'his horse never put its feet to the ground' until he was thrown into 'a marshy meadow and buried beneath several falling cavaliers'.[46]

Meanwhile, Marshal Tallard, only a short distance away, was trying to make his way into Blenheim to tell his infantry to lay down their arms. He was recognized by a Hessian regiment because of the Order of the Saint Esprit which he was wearing, and taken prisoner along with several of his officers. He was conducted to Marlborough who graciously placed his coach at the Marshal's disposal.

This was the moment when Marlborough borrowed a piece of paper – a bill of tavern expenses – from an officer and wrote on the back his famous message to Sarah:

13 August 1704

I have not time to say more but to beg you will give my duty to the Queen and let her know her army has had a glorious victory. Monsieur Tallard and two other generals are in my coach and I am following the rest. The bearer, my aide-de-camp Colonel Parke, will give Her an account of what has passed. I shall do it in a day or two by another more at large.

Marlborough

When Marshal Marsin saw Tallard's line broken and Marlborough's infantry advancing in solid formations over the wide plain between Blenheim and Oberglau, he knew that the moment had come to retreat. The Elector and the other generals concurred. By seven o'clock the whole of Marsin's army was heading for the gap above Morselingen, followed by all the troops that Prince Eugene could muster. General Charles Churchill had encircled Blenheim with his twenty-three battalions so that none of the French infantry locked inside could escape.* It was Churchill who asked Lord Cutts to stage a final attack. What was left of Rowe's British Brigade led the assault and when Marshal Tallard saw this fierce outburst from afar, he sent a message to the Duke declaring that 'if he would let these poor fellows retire' he, Tallard, would prevent further firing by the French. 'Inform Monsieur de Tallard', Marlborough replied tartly, 'that in the position in which he now is he has no command.'[47]

Inside Blenheim the Marquis de Clerambault was distraught, reproaching himself for having drawn so many battalions into the village. He suddenly broke out of his confines (exactly how is not

* Apparently some hundreds had already managed to get away.

explained) and galloped like a madman to the Danube. No one knows whether he was trying to cross the swirling waters or seeking death to shield him from disgrace; only that he threw himself into the river and drowned.

Meanwhile General Churchill, Lord Orkney and Lord Cutts continued their assault until they finally managed to induce their proud foe to surrender. The fury of these unbeaten troops, the flower of the French infantry, was at fever-pitch. The Regiment of Navarre burned its standard with tears of rage and many officers refused to sign the convention placed before them. As the village contained over 12,000 men, Marlborough and Eugene decided that they had quite enough prisoners to look after without pursuing Marsin's army.

About nine o'clock at night the prisoners were ordered to file out of the village and bivouack in a field while the officers were billeted in the nearby village of Unterglau. Dr Hare visited a group of sixty or seventy prisoners and found them in a state of deep depression.

> Some were blaming the conduct of their own Generals,* others walking with their arms folded, others were laid down lamenting their hard fortune and complaining for want of refreshment until at last, abandoning all reflections of this nature, their chief concern was for their King, abundance of these mutterings and plaintly saying, *Oh que dira le Roy!*[48]

British soldiers with fixed bayonets were ordered to guard the thousands of prisoners in the open until relief squads took over from them at dawn. As they had been actively engaged since two o'clock in the morning, only high spirits kept them awake. 'I am hardly able to give you an account of the great victory we gained yesterday, I am so weary,' wrote Lord Orkney to his wife. 'I bless God I have no wounds tho' my horse was shot under me . . . it is the greatest [battle] that has been fought these 50 years. . . .'[49]

Marlborough spent the night in a watermill near Hochstädt filled with kegs of enemy powder. No doubt he was too weary to reflect on the shifting fortunes of the day, or even to take pride in the success of his tactics. Most things had worked out as he had hoped: neutralizing the flanks at Blenheim and Oberglau; trusting Eugene to hold the enemy's superior force on his front; and finally the victory by smashing through the centre.

The next morning, accompanied by Eugene, the Duke went to visit Tallard. He felt particularly solicitous towards the Marshal who not

---

* In a letter which Hare wrote to his cousin the day after the battle, he says that the French command was generally blamed 'for not bringing their troops down to the rivulet to hinder our passing it . . .' HMC, 14th Report Appendix 9, p. 200.

only had suffered the bitterness of defeat but whose son had been slain at his side. He sent a trumpet with a small escort to fetch the Marshal's coach from the enemy lines and allowed Tallard to dispatch his own account of the battle to King Louis.

The officers were fascinated by the 'Great Twin Captains' as they called Marlborough and Eugene:

> There were a great many of the French generals with the Marshal [wrote Dr Hare] all of whom came crowding around his Grace and admired his person, as well as his tender and gracious behaviour towards them. They had all something to say for themselves, which His Grace and Prince Eugene received with the greatest modesty and compassion. Prince Eugene ... frankly told how often and how bravely they had repulsed him. ... After staying with the Marshal above an hour, the Duke and all his company returned to our army which he ordered to march beyond Hochstädt ... whilst he rode over the field of battle, from the right to the left, the dead of both armies lying stripped, upon the ground.[50]

The Allies had lost over 13,000 men killed and wounded – about a quarter of their whole – while the enemy's casualties amounted to 23,000 killed, drowned and wounded, plus another 14,000 taken prisoner. This made a total of 38,000 out of 59,000. Louis XIV was astonished by the number of prisoners and remarked plaintively that he 'had never heard of an army being taken before'. But the result of the battle could not be computed by casualty figures alone. Blenheim marked Louis's first great defeat and, by shattering the myth of French invincibility, it changed the balance of Europe. That night, when Marlborough sat down to write Sarah, a sense of wonderment still enveloped him – the gamble had been so great, the victory so complete.

14 August

> Before the battle was quite done yesterday I wrote to my dearest soul to let her know that I was well, and that God had blessed Her Majesty's army with as great a victory as has ever been known; for prisoners I have Marshal de Tallard and the greater part of his general officers, about 8,000 men and near 1,500 officers. In short the army of M. de Tallard which was that which I fought with is quite ruined; that of the Elector of Bavaria, and the Marshal de Marsin, which Prince Eugene fought against, I am afraid has not had much loss, for I can't find that he has many prisoners. As soon as the Elector knew that Monsieur de Tallard was beaten, he marched off so that I came only time enough to see him retire. ... I am so very much out of order with having been 16 hours on horseback yesterday, and not having been able to sleep above three hours last night, so that I cannot write to any of my friends. However I am so pleased with this action that I can't end my letter without being so vain as to tell

my dearest soul that within the memory of man there has been no victory as great as this; and as I am sure you love me entirely well, you will be infinitely pleased with what has been done, upon my account as well as the great benefit the public will have. For, had the success of Prince Eugene been equal to his merit, we should in that day's action have made an end of the war.*[51]

Neither Paris nor London knew about the outcome of the battle for over a week. On 21 August Louis XIV wrote to Tallard: 'The large number of letters from officers of my troops who are now prisoners-of-war, leave me no doubt that there has been an action at Hochstädt in which the enemies have had a considerable advantage. . . .' But Louis still continued to hope: 'I do not know how it is that I still have no news from you, Tallard, nor from M. de Marsin . . . in waiting I still hope that the situation is not as bad as the enemies have asserted.'[52]

The situation could scarcely have been much worse for the Sun King. The one thing he had not envisaged was Tallard as a prisoner-of-war. Although the Marshal was treated with every courtesy, the sensibilities of his captors, dulled by exuberance, were not acute. The first Sunday after the battle they held a Thanksgiving service, followed by a victory review of the troops. They invited Tallard and some of the other high-ranking officers whom they held prisoner to come out with them 'to see the army fire'. Tallard did his best to escape this experience but his excuses were not accepted. 'As they rode along the lines', wrote Captain Parker,

> our Generals paid Tallard the Compliment of riding next to the army, and ordered all the Officers to salute him. When the firing was over, the Duke asked Tallard how he liked the army. He answered with a shrug, Very well but they have had the honour of beating the best Troops in the World. The Duke replied readily, What will the world think of the Troops that beat them?[53]

The same day that Louis wrote his anxious letter to Tallard, Colonel Parke arrived in London with Marlborough's scribbled message to Sarah telling her of his stupendous victory. Parker had ridden across Europe at breakneck speed, spreading his joyful news through the German and Dutch cities as he passed. Eight days after the battle of Blenheim, on 21 August, he delivered his note to Sarah at St James's Palace. She sent him on to Windsor with the original scrap of paper.

---

* Marlborough was praising Eugene but he expressed himself in such a clumsy way that historians later accused him of a surprising lack of generosity.

There is a story dear to the heart of historians, but almost certainly untrue, which tells us that when Parke was admitted to the Queen he found her seated by a window overlooking the terrace and playing chequers with the Prince. Parke fell on his knees and told Her Majesty that he personally had witnessed the rout of the French. It was customary for the Queen to give the messenger of good tidings £500, but Anne told Parke that 'he had given her more joy than ever she had received in her life'[54] and rewarded the gallant Colonel with 1,000 guineas.

Soon, the whole of London was celebrating. Godolphin arranged for copies of the Duke's note to be struck off the presses and circulated in thousands. At the Tower cannon were fired, church bells rang and people poured into the streets. That night everyone talked of the wonderful note 'writ on horseback with a black leaden pencil', while in the taverns each bumper was downed to the health of the Queen and the Duke.

Marlborough was not able to return to England for another four months. After Blenheim he felt so ill he had to be bled. At fifty-four, he had been the oldest soldier on the battlefield and the strain, both physical and mental, had taken its toll. 'Ever since the battle', he wrote to Godolphin on 17 August, 'I have been so employed about our own wounded men and the prisoners, that I have not had one hour's quiet, which has so disordered me, that if I were in London I should be in my bed in a high fever.' And a week later, 'Nothing but my zeal for Her Majesty's service could have enabled me to have gone through the fatigues I have had for the last three months; and I am but too sure when I shall have the happiness of seeing you, you will find me ten years older than when I left England. . . .'[55] Nevertheless the trouble he took over his prisoners made a deep impression at Versailles. 'Whereas Prince Eugene was harsh,' wrote Saint-Simon, 'the Duke of Marlborough treated them all, even the humblest, with the utmost attention, consideration and politeness, and with a modesty perhaps even more distinguished than his victory.'[56]

Sarah was distressed by his letters and urged him to wind up his business and return home; but a further three months of the campaigning season stretched before him and he was already deep in plans with Eugene for the coming year. The 'twin captains' were closer than ever. Neither disagreement nor jealousy disturbed their relationship and together they shared the gratitude of the countries they served. The Emperor Leopold, of course, was not only overjoyed but relieved, as he had been in immediate danger. He heaped congratulations upon his adored Eugene and told him how much he had feared for his safety; 'the Imperial House and the whole Alliance', he said, 'was dependent on him.' He issued a decree making Eugene's Vienna *städtpalais* free from taxes for ever. His reward for Marlborough was more complicated; he talked of making him a Prince of the Holy Roman Empire but, as the gift involved the transfer of a principality, the arrangements would take months to complete.

Behind the tattered remnants of the French army, Marlborough and Eugene led their victorious troops back to the Rhine, receiving a hero's welcome all along the route. The Margrave (still furious at being deprived of the glory of Blenheim) conducted a siege against Landau on the Main, while Marlborough reduced the two fortresses on the Moselle – Trarbach and Trèves. This was in preparation for a campaign on the Moselle which the Prince and the Duke were eager to fight the following year.

There were further demands. Berlin was clamouring to meet the famous Marlborough and, as the latter needed a large contingent of Prussian and German troops for the new undertaking, he lumbered 800 miles over bad roads to visit the capital. At Berlin he got the support he needed and received 'a hat with a diamond button and loop and a diamond hairband valued at between twenty and thirty thousand crowns and two fine saddle horses with rich furniture.'[57] On the way home he stopped at Hanover and made the acquaintance of the Heiress Presumptive to the British throne, the seventy-four-year-old Electress Sophia. She was so charmed by his manners that she deemed him as 'skilled as a courtier as he is brave as a general'.

The Dutch gave him an equally enthusiastic welcome. The Grand Pensionary and seven Deputies received him on behalf of the Republic and presented him with a basin and ewer of solid gold. In the middle of December he sailed from Rotterdam for home.

Nine

The Duke Triumphant

'She cannot set her foot to the ground,' Lady Russell wrote of the Queen to Lady Granby in November 1704. 'She has a chair made so well that it is lifted with her in it into the coach, and then she moves herself to the seat, and the chair is taken away.'[1] All autumn the Queen had been suffering from gout, at one time not even being able to write as her right hand was 'bound up'. Despite her infirmities she rode in state to St Paul's in September (while the Duke was still abroad) to give thanks for the battle of Blenheim. The route along the Strand, Fleet Street and Ludgate Hill was draped with blue cloth and lined by city militia. The diarist, John Evelyn, saw Her Majesty drive past 'in a rich coach with eight horses, none with her but the Duchess of Marlborough, the Queen full of Jewels.'[2] Inside Wren's great cathedral, which was not quite completed, two battalions of foot-guards made a lane from the west door to the choir. The invalid Queen was carried to her seat in a chair and Sarah sat at her side, 'the proudest subject in England that day'.

Across the Channel Louis XIV was plunged in gloom. While the Queen of England was thanking God for His blessings, the King of France was begging God for His forgiveness. He had suffered many disappointments in his life, but never a military defeat on the scale of Blenheim. It was the first time that his army had been so badly mauled that it could no longer fight. It was also the first time that the enemy had captured one of his marshals. The sixty-six-year-old monarch felt old and tired. Not only had he lost most of his teeth but his *esprit* had departed as well. It was clear that God was punishing him for his sins, his pride and his arrogance. This conviction was shared by his morganatic wife, Madame de Maintenon, who always knew what the Almighty was thinking. In the privacy of Madame's boudoir they shed many tears, but the gloom was only temporary as Louis never allowed himself to remain downcast for long. 'We must hope', he wrote to his War Minister in September, 'for more happy opportunities, and that the enemy will not gain other advantages from this battle beyond that of forcing me to recross the Rhine and to abandon Bavaria.'[3]

In England people were too busy celebrating the summer's successes to think of next year's campaign. Even the moderate Tories had joined the Whigs in their enthusiasm for Marlborough and the war. Tory rhymesters, however, managed to stir up discord by comparing Marlborough's 'triumphs' to William's 'fourteen empty years'. The High Tories went a step further. In July a landing-party from Admiral Sir George Rooke's Mediterranean fleet had seized Gibraltar and in August Rooke's guns had defeated the French in a battle off Malaga. So now the Tories championed Rooke and the navy as the equal of Marlborough and the army. 'The High Church Party look on Sir George Rooke as their own,' wrote Daniel Defoe to his patron, Robert Harley. 'I am obliged with patience to hear . . . the sea victory set up against the land victory; Sir George exalted above the Duke of Marlborough and what can be the reason of this but that they conceive . . . their High Church Party will revive under his patronage?' 'By the visible dissatisfaction of some people,' Sarah observed caustically, 'one would have imagined that instead of beating the French he [Marlborough] had beaten the Church.'[4]

Marlborough landed at Greenwich on 14 December with a ship full of distinguished prisoners headed by Marshal Tallard. They included sixteen generals and sixteen lesser officers, none lower in rank than lieutenant-colonel. The following day Parliament gave the conqueror its thanks and on 3 January London spilled on to the streets to cheer a victory parade that wound its way through the capital to show the trophies captured from the enemy. Although the Dutch had asked the English to share the spoils with them, pointing out that British soldiers had only composed a quarter of the whole, the request was rejected with the polite observation that Dutch soldiers represented an even smaller proportion of the total. The largest part of the army was drawn from the German principalities subsidized by England. So London saw the troopers of the Blues and the pikemen of the Guards carrying the thirty-four standards and 128 colours that their comrades, still serving abroad, had captured at Blenheim. Starting at the Tower, they marched through the City, down the Strand along Pall Mall to St James's Palace and into the park, where two salvos of forty cannon were fired. They then proceeded to Westminster Hall where the banners were received and set up for all to see.

Three days later the Lord Mayor and Aldermen entertained Marlborough and his officers, together with Lord Godolphin and the Queen's ministers, at a banquet in the Goldsmith's Hall. Marlborough rode in one of the royal coaches, leading a fleet of carriages carrying foreign ambassadors and the most illustrious members of the English aristocracy. However this dinner, like most City galas, had a special purpose: in the hope of raising money for the spring campaign, annuities were to be sold costing £250 each and yielding £10 a year. The dinner was so successful that when the lists were opened a few days later the entire sum of nearly £1,000,000 was raised within two hours.

Across the centuries it is easy to see that the battle of Blenheim marked the beginning of a new era for Britain, but even at the time people were conscious that an epoch-making event had taken place. England and Holland, with a total population of less than nine million people, had vanquished the armies of mighty France and altered the balance of power in Europe. Although the full implications may not have been grasped at once, the fact that England had won a victory over her most dangerous foe was understood by the meanest of the Queen's subjects.

It is not surprising, therefore, that Anne set about heaping honours on her General. On 17 February 1705, she informed the Commons that she proposed to convey to the Duke of Marlborough the royal Manor of Woodstock and 15,000 acres. She also proposed that the grant of £5,000 a year, which she had settled upon him for her lifetime, should become by Act of Parliament (previously rejected) a permanent charge on the Civil List. Finally, the Queen would plan and build at her own expense a splendid residence for the Marlboroughs which would be called the Palace of Blenheim. She had selected as architect her Controller of the Board of Works, Sir John Vanbrugh, who had already submitted a model of the proposed building which would be on display at Kensington Palace.

Marlborough was delighted by the magnificence of Vanbrugh's conception and warmed to the idea of spending his last years in such a vast palace. But the project struck Sarah as much too grandiose. 'I opposed it all that was possible for me to doe,' she wrote many years later, claiming that from the very first she was convinced of 'the maddnesse of the whole Design.'[5] Marlborough's ideas of splendour had been formed as a young man on his visits to Versailles and secretly he was thrilled at the prospect of living in a palace built on a comparable scale to that of the Great King. However, he knew better than admit his weakness to Sarah and avoided a quarrel by telling her that he was not prepared to find fault with the Queen's decisions. The Duchess was not easy to please. She even tried to prevent her husband from becoming a Prince of the Holy Roman Empire, arguing that it was quite enough to be an English duke. However, as the Queen had given John her warm consent, he was able to silence Sarah by insisting once again that the rise in his status would help him in dealing with the princes of the Grand Alliance.

In London John had no chance to lead a private life. He was always present at the Queen's Councils, which sometimes took place twice a week, and he was assiduous in attending the House of Lords. Apart from official functions, he was besieged by people clamouring to meet him. Even John Evelyn, who a year earlier had complained that the Duke had been given 'an excess of honours', was delighted to be spoken to by the great man. 'I went to wait on my Lord Treasurer,' he wrote, 'where the victorious Duke of Marlborough came to me and took me by the hand with extraordinary familiarity and civility, as formerly he used to do, without any alteration of his good nature. He had a most rich George in a sardonyx set with diamonds of very great value; for the rest very plain. I had not seen him for some years and believed he might have forgotten me.'[6]

Whenever he could snatch a few days Marlborough went with Sarah to Windsor Lodge which had become her favourite home. Most of his time here was spent in a whirl of preparations for the marriage of his youngest and prettiest daughter, Mary. On 20 March, two weeks before Marlborough returned to The Hague, she married Lord Montagu's son and heir, Viscount Monthermer. Once again the Queen offered the bride a dowry of £10,000 and once again only £5,000 was accepted. Mary was not in need of money as her father-in-law was one of the richest men in the kingdom. His vast London house stood on the site now occupied by the British Museum and his country house, Boughton (now owned by the Duke of Buccleuch), was even then regarded as a show-place. Shortly after the wedding, the Queen, still in a beatific mood, created him Duke of Montagu, so that little Mary could have something to look forward to. This was inspired planning, as within four years old Montagu died and Mary became a duchess.

Marlborough was in high spirits when he returned to The Hague. During his three and a half months in England he had thought of little else but his forthcoming campaign. With Prince Eugene's encouragement, he had fastened again on the Moselle plan which he had abandoned to march to the Danube. Unfortunately Eugene could not join him as he was in command of the force in Italy. The Moselle pointed the route into France and if Marlborough's attack succeeded it might even foreshadow the beginning of the end of the war. With 90,000 men he would sweep through Lorraine and take the road to Paris. His army would be divided into two sections, each part operating in close proximity with the other to guarantee the maximum protection. Prince Louis of Baden would lead 30,000 men and approach the French frontier by Saar-Louis while Marlborough, with 60,000 men, would make his way through the Moselle valley from Coblenz and Thionville, and from there into France.

All the details had been worked out with great care. In England, Marlborough had spent hours each day with Cadogan and Cardonnel exacting promises from the German princes of troops and supplies, studying secret service reports, consulting engineers on roads and river-crossings, arranging for draught-horses and, most important of all, organizing the building and stocking of grain-magazines. Feeding an army was a horrific problem for an eighteenth-century commander. A modern professor gives us a glimpse of the requirements of 60,000 soldiers. Assuming that each man consumed a half a kilo of bread a day,

> at least 60 ovens operated by a staff of 240 bakers would be needed to undertake the baking of four days' rations. Armies habitually marched for three days and halted the fourth, which was needed for rest and re-supply. To build a single oven called for 500 2-kilogram bricks, so to supply the basic requirements for 60 ovens called for 60 carts of bricks, and it required several days' work to establish an efficient bakery and the necessary stores around it. The fuel problem was even more dramatic. To fire the 60 ovens seven times a month required all of 1,400 wagonloads of fuel (a single baking called for 200 loads). The milling of flour also presented daunting logistical problems; local mills were often targets for enemy interdictive action so armies had to carry grinding equipment with them, still further enlarging the train.[7]

The force of 90,000 men that Marlborough had earmarked for the Moselle campaign represented less than half the Allied army. The Alliance had 60,000 men in Flanders, 30,000 in Italy and 15,000 in Portugal, while the Emperor had another 25,000 dealing with the Hungarian insurrection – a total of 220,000. The French amazed everyone by fielding a new army 'more numerous and more brilliant than ever', estimated at 200,000. Louis XIV used his troops to defend the long semi-circular front from Breisach near Switzerland to the Spanish Netherlands, dividing them into three sections headed by

three marshals: Marshal Villeroy and the Elector of Bavaria commanded in Flanders; Marshal Marsin on the upper Rhine and Marshal
Villars on the Moselle.

The Great King bombarded his generals with precautionary advice,
making it clear that he expected them to rush detachments to the
support of any sector that might be threatened. Louis recognized the
Duke of Marlborough, the glamorous 'bel anglais' of yesteryear, as a
dangerous opponent, 'a bold predatory soldier who threatened the
kingdom of France itself.'[8] He also recognized that the Duke's
English soldiers were always sent to the hot spots, and gave his secret
service instructions to report every movement of these troops.

Louis XIV had a marked advantage over his opponent. Whereas he
was an absolute Commander-in-Chief with indisputable authority,
Marlborough 'was only an informal chairman of a discordant
committee'.[9] The Duke had not been at his headquarters more than a
few weeks before he discovered that all his plans were going awry.
The 12,000 Prussians and the 7,000 Palatine troops that were due to
arrive early in May would be three or four weeks late; and when the
Duke set up his headquarters at Trèves on the Moselle (the fortress he
had captured the previous October) he discovered that the grain-
depot was half empty. He had instructed his agent to fill the magazine
to overflowing but the Dutch had intervened, saying that a lower
tender had been received. Unfortunately the new contractor had
failed to obtain the necessary supply and, fearful of showing his face,
had deserted to the enemy.

Last but not least, Louis of Baden, who had agreed to join Marlborough with 30,000 men, showed no sign of appearing. On 5 May
1705 the Emperor Leopold died, and Baden seized upon this as a
reason for delay. However, the succession of Leopold's son, Joseph,
caused no dislocation as the new Emperor was as fervent a supporter
of the war as his father had been. After this excuse had worn off, the
Prince of Baden fell back on 'ill-health'. The toe that he had injured at
the Schellenberg had become infected, he said, and the inflamation
was spreading up his leg. Marlborough was conscious of the fact that
the Margrave had been bitterly angry with Eugene and himself for
excluding him from the battle at Blenheim, so he made a supremely
uncomfortable journey across country to find out whether the
Prince's incapacity was real or feigned. It was not easy to tell. The
Margrave seemed in reasonably good spirits and was well enough to
conduct Marlborough around his palace, which was in the process of
being constructed, with hundreds of workmen and gardeners engaged
in the task. However, he did not seem in the least ashamed to tell the

Duke that he was unable to provide either the soldiers or the supplies that he had guaranteed him. Indeed, he could scarcely rustle up half the number he had promised which, of course, ruled out the possibility of forming a separate army. Nevertheless he would join up with Marlborough's main army and take part in the offensive. He solemnly pledged himself to arrive at Trèves not later than 10 June.

Prince Louis's tardy revelations spelled the ruin of Marlborough's campaign plans for the greater part of 1705. If he could have undertaken the siege of Saar-Louis by himself he would have done, but – as he wrote to General Overkirk from Trèves – 'another difficulty which gives me much pain, is the 3,000 horses that the local princes should have furnished me with for bringing up the artillery and munitions for the siege, but of which I have no news. . . .'[10] Without guns no siege was possible. By this time, Marlborough's frustration was so great that he decided to try on his own to lure Marshal Villars into battle. Who knows, perhaps this desperate venture might even act as a spur to the leisurely Margrave? The shortage of food and forage would be his greatest problem, but if he could force the issue quickly he might overcome it.

Villars was in a strong, entrenched position twenty-five miles from Trèves, near the town of Sierk. Marlborough started his march at two in the morning of 2 June and after twenty-one miles, much of it over hills and broken country, reached his objective before dark. He established his headquarters in the castle of Elst, on top of a hill overlooking Villars's position, while his soldiers encamped on the plain of Sierk where Villars could see their rows of tents. It soon became plain that the Marshal, despite all his bravado, was not going to fight. The decision, however, was not his. The moment he saw that Marlborough was heading his way, he bombarded Versailles with requests to engage in battle, but Louis XIV gave him a flat refusal. Instead he ordered Marsin to send detachments to strengthen Villars – such was the impression that Blenheim had made on the Great King!

Although Villars, reinforced by Marsin, had a much stronger army than his adversary, Marlborough would have given battle if he had come out from behind his entrenchments. Indeed, if only the Margrave would arrive, Marlborough might launch an attack against his fortified positions. He sent General Cadogan galloping off to find Prince Louis and beg him to hurry. Then, to take his mind off the anxiety of a dwindling food supply, he opened a correspondence with Marshal Villars. He began by asking for a return of stragglers who had been cut off from General Charles Churchill's battalions on the march through Luxembourg. Villars was happy to oblige, and sent

Marlborough some intercepted letters, apologizing for having opened them. Marlborough replied with gifts. 'M. de Marlborough', Villars wrote to his War Minister, 'had sent me a quantity of liquors of England, Palm wine and cider; one could not have received greater civilities. I have paid him back as much as possible. We shall see how our serious business will settle itself.'[11]

How it 'settled itself' pleased no one. Cadogan caught up with Prince Louis's army but found that the Margrave was not in command, having taken himself and his injured toe to a nearby spa for a rest cure. The new commander, Comte de Frise, was following instructions by taking a long and unnecessary detour, adding many extra days to his passage. Despite Prince Louis's solemn promise, it was clear that he had no intention of allowing his army to join the main force.

Marlborough had no alternative but to retire. Luckily Marshal Villeroy offered him a good excuse by threatening Liège. The Duke pulled out during the night of 17 June and, when he was past the danger-points of the river-crossings, sent a trumpeter to the Marshal's lines explaining why he had not attacked. 'Tell Marshal Villars that . . . the Margrave has broken his word, and that I can hold only him responsible for breaking up our plans'. Another source claims that he added: 'Be assured that my contempt of him does not equal my respect for you.'[12] To Godolphin he wrote: 'I may assure you that no one thing – neither for the troops nor the subsistence of the Army – that was promised me has ever been performed.' And a few days later: 'I have for these last ten days been so troubled by the many disappointments I have had that I think if it were possible to vex me for a fortnight longer it would make an end of me.'[13]

Despite his air of imperturbability, Marlborough was a man of strong and changing moods which only those close to him – Sarah and Godolphin – were allowed to see. Sarah was his sheet anchor. He wrote to her every day, and by the reaffirmation of his love managed to derive the strength and purpose that enabled him to maintain his outward calm. Here are a few extracts from his campaign letters, 1703 to 1706.

> If you had not positively desired that I should always burn your letters, I should have been very glad to have kept your dear letter of the 9th, it was all so very kind, and particularly so upon the subject of our living quietly together, till which happy time comes I am sure I cannot be contented.
>
> The greatest ease I now have is sometimes sitting for an hour in my chair alone, and thinking of the happiness I may yet have, of living quietly with you, which is the greatest I propose to myself in the world.

I can refuse you nothing.

I am sure I can never be happy until I am with my dearest Soull.

You may be assured that you are dearer to me than all the world.

Pity me and love me.

My dearest soul I love you so well, and have set my heart so entirely on ending my days in quiet with you, that you may be so far at ease as to be assured that I never venture myself but when I think the service of my queen and country requires it.[14]

Marlborough never remained depressed for long. He had not been at Maestricht more than a few days before he had become absorbed in an exciting new idea. The only way to save his 1705 campaign from utter failure, he decided, was to force a passage across the Lines of Brabant and face Villeroy's superior army in battle. The 'lines' were a defensive position that had been built up by the enemy over the years. They stretched seventy miles from Namur to Antwerp and were made up of a series of natural and imposed obstacles: felled trees, dammed-up streams, palisades with forts, ditches and ramparts and redoubts. All the side roads leading from the entrenchments were kept in good condition so that the army could move quickly, and large magazines of grain, forage and ammunition were in guarded forts behind the entrenchments. The purpose of the lines was not to prevent but to delay an enemy incursion, giving the defenders time to concentrate behind the threatened sector, thus ensuring heavy losses for any aggressor.

Marlborough had hoped that his Blenheim victory would make his Dutch colleagues less intractable but, to his surprise, found the reverse true. One of Holland's most respected commanders, General Slangenberg, was so eaten up with jealousy that he could not conceal his hatred of Marlborough. He called him a 'court favourite' and prophesied that his lack of military expertise would end in complete disaster. Meanwhile he said no to every proposal the Englishman made. And as Slangenberg's word carried weight with the Dutch Deputies, Marlborough found himself once again up against a brick wall. He played his hand brilliantly; before he had spoken a word, he sensed the opposition and kept his plans to himself. He pretended that he would simply 'tease' the enemy by a series of feints and manoeuvres. The Dutch could scarcely object to this but forbade him to take the offensive without 'permission'.

When one tries to compare Marlborough' s genius with that of the great generals who followed him – Frederick the Great and Napoleon – one must always bear in mind the severe limitations under which he operated. If he had enjoyed their freedom and authority he might have brought Louis XIV to his knees in two years. As it was, once again he had to employ all his cunning to deceive his own side before he could turn his thoughts to the enemy. The Lines of Brabant offered (for the second time) a splendid example of the Duke's brilliance at confounding friends and foes alike. Many experts would have deemed it impossible to fool Villeroy, sitting behind his defence system with his massive army, determined to teach the hero of Blenheim a lesson. The Marshal was anxious and alert. His scouts were reporting regularly on enemy movements and his troops stood at readiness, prepared to move at a moment's notice.

How did Marlborough pull off his coup? He divided his army into two sections and sent one part north and the other south. Marshal Villeroy had always believed that Marlborough would attack in the south, in the Namur area and when his scouts reported that the Duke's pioneers were throwing pontoon bridges across the Mehaigne until 'it was all one, as if there was no river', he became increasingly sure of his opinion. This deduction was fortified by deserters from Marlborough's army who convinced their interrogators that the march to the north was a feint. Villeroy hesitated no longer and gave the order for 40,000 men to take up positions along the threatened Namur front.

In the middle of the night General Overkirk, who was moving south, suddenly received orders to do an about-turn – to retrace his steps to the River Mehaigne, recross it and proceed north as fast as possible. There was no time for the Dutch Deputies to hold a council or even, for that matter, to protest. Furthermore, as Marlborough was merely carrying out the bewildering marches that the Deputies had endorsed, there was no room for objection. The other half of Marlborough's army – the English troops and cavalry – moving in the opposite direction, also received an order to change their angle of march. Instead of continuing due north they were to veer north-west to Landen, and from Landen to the Little Geete River which bordered the Lines of Brabant. At four in the morning they reached their destination, and at three separate places – Elixem, Wangé and Orsmael – began to cross the bridges into almost empty entrenchments. Three regiments of French dragoons at Orsmael fled without fighting, heading for Léau, and further disgraced themselves by not even sounding an alarm. At Elixem, Dr Hare, who was at Marlborough's side, reported that the red-coated cavalry 'stormed the bridge and made for the earthworks, and were over before one thought they were at them'. By 5 o'clock in the morning, 60,000 men had occupied the French positions; 'without the loss of half a dozen men', Hare commented, 'they passed those lines which was thought would have cost at least as many thousands.'[15] Beyond the Geete a fine piece of flat country stretched to Tirlemont. The English cavalry had formed into two lines, reinforced by the infantry whose numbers were growing all the time.

The French communications system was so deficient that it gave the Allies a great advantage. The negligence of the fleeing dragoons meant that the French cavalry leader, the Marquis d'Alègre, who was only three miles south of Elixem, did not receive news of the Allies's assault until 5 a.m. He immediately assembled his French, Spanish and Bavarian troopers and sent word to Caraman, commander of the French infantry, four miles further away, to join him as quickly as possible. Marshal Villeroy and the Elector Max Emmanuel, seven miles away at Merdorp, seem to have been totally ignored. Although the Marshal had ordered his 40,000 men to 'sleep on their arms', and was almost unbearably keyed up, no one bothered to tell him the news until eight o'clock. By this time the battle was over. When Marlborough appeared at Elixem at 7 o'clock, twenty-five enemy squadrons had formed into battle-lines. The enemy horsemen consisted of many of the Bavarian units that had survived Blenheim. They wore armour and were a magnificent sight with their black cuirasses and helmets glinting menacingly in the early morning light. A mile behind them the first infantry battalions were in the process of deploying their troops.

Marlborough rode up to the front line of his English cavalry and took his place among them as an ordinary trooper. A buzz of excitement ran along the line. The men drew their swords and the Duke gave the order to charge. This was done knee to knee at a fast trot. Although the Bavarians had new 'triple-barrelled' guns with rapid firing, nothing could stop the massive red wave of oncoming horsemen; nor could the glinting armour overcome the shock of the charge or protect the enemy from the swords of their assailants. The Scots Greys routed four squadrons without losing a single man. The enemy, reinforced by five new squadrons, attempted a counter-charge, but Marlborough attacked a second time, again riding with his troopers. This charge was decisive and the enemy galloped off the field in disorder.

Marlborough was lucky to escape with his life. One of the Bavarian officers recognized him and tried to cut him down. 'My Lord Marlborough in person was everywhere', wrote Lord Orkney,

and escaped very narrowly; for a squadron, which he was at the head of, gave ground a little, though [it] soon came up again; and a fellow came up to him and thought to have sabred him to the ground, and struck at him with that force, and, missing his stroke, he fell off his horse. I asked my Lord if it was so; he said it was absolutely so. So what a happy man he is.[16]

The whole action had lasted well over an hour. Caraman's infantry got away by forming a hollow square, while the cavalry was dispersed far and wide. The trophies left behind included kettle-drums, standards, guns, and over 3,000 prisoners. Lord John Hay, head of the Scots Greys, had himself captured the senior enemy general, the Marquis d'Alègre. But the hero of the day was Marlborough. The victory had been a *tour de force*, achieved by superb subterfuge, and at so little cost of life that it was nothing short of magic. The English troopers were so impressed by the brilliance of the whole affair that when Marlborough rode down the lines they all began to cheer him. He was their commander, their Lord Duke; but he was also 'Corporal John' who had ridden beside them to charge the enemy.

Marlborough was in such high humour that for once we catch a glimpse of him as a man – not as a courtier, not as a diplomat, nor even as a Commander-in-Chief – just as a trooper boyishly elated by the good fortune of the day. He laughed with his officers over the double necessity of having to fool the Dutch as well as the enemy: 'I was forced to cheat them into it,' he wrote to Godolphin. 'He dared not offer to persuade the Deputies of the States,' explained Dr Hare, 'but perfectly bubbled them into it.'[17] That night John wrote to Sarah, '. . . it is impossible to say too much good of the troops that were with me, for never men fought better. . . .' And two days later, 'I was so pleased when I wrote my last, that had I writ on I should have used expressions which afterwards I should have been ashamed of. The Kindness of the troops to me had transported me. . . .'[18]

It is possible to imagine Sarah sitting at home receiving news of the fighting first from John, then from Godolphin and gradually from close friends whose husbands were serving with Marlborough. They would not be slow to tell her of John's two cavalry charges and his narrow escape from the sword of an enemy horseman. Knowing as she did that the campaign season was only half over, her apprehension at the thought of the danger lying ahead must have been great. Could this moment have prompted her to send her husband the following letter, tender and sad and loving? The lines bear no address, no date, no signature, but Sarah's writing is unmistakable. It is the only one of her war messages that has survived:

Wherever you are whilst I have life my soul shall follow you, my ever dear Lord Marl, and wherever I am I shall only kill the time, wish for night that I may sleep and hope the next day to hear from you.[19]

Marlborough's triumph was not a big affair but it spelled the end of the famous Lines of Brabant which for many years had protected the

Spanish Netherlands from attack. Within the next few months the Allies demolished fifty miles of fortifications, bringing to a close the stalemate in the northern theatre. Furthermore, the episode had its own personal importance, because it sealed the Duke's position as an incomparable leader and inspired in his men the admiration and trust that he never lost.

Nevertheless, Marlborough was severely criticized by some of the Dutch officers under his command for not exploiting his victory more vigorously. If he had continued his pursuit towards Louvain, instead of pulling up at Tirlemont, he might have surrounded the whole retreating army and scored a victory as spectacular as Blenheim. However, this only became apparent with the benefit of hindsight; at the time it was believed that the way was blocked by Marshal Villeroy with a force of 40,000 men. Perhaps Marlborough felt that he had had his share of good fortune and decided not to push his luck too far. Whatever the reasons, when the Elector of Bavaria, looking across the valley, saw the Dutch pitching their tents, 'he cried out three or four times in a rapture "*Grace à Dieu*"'.

Marlborough made up for his lapse by a flood of new ideas and energy, but the Dutch general, Slangenberg, stepped forward to prejudice the Dutch Deputies against everything the Duke suggested. The most serious obstruction came when Marlborough, after a series of brilliant feints and manoeuvres, created a second opportunity to inflict a massive defeat on the enemy. Villeroy's army was trapped near the town of Oversocche, fifteen miles south of Brussels; and Marlborough, after winning the consent of the Dutch commander, General Overkirk, began to deploy his forces which were now within gunshot of the French. Suddenly he was told that the artillery train was still on the road. As he had sent orders several hours earlier to hurry the guns forward – the attack could not take place without them – he was amazed. Soon he learned that the delay was not accidental. 'We were drawing near the enemy', wrote Captain Robert Parker, 'and his Grace had sent orders that the English train of artillery should make all possible haste to him; but as they were just upon entering a narrow defile Slangenberg came up to the head of them, and stopped them for some hours, until his baggage had passed on before them, a thing never known before. . . .'[20]

For sheer insolence nothing like this had been seen before, yet the jealous Slangenberg ('that beast Slangenberg', as Dr Hare called him) had only begun his obstructionist tactics. He now used all the authority and prestige at his command to persuade the Dutch Deputies to withdraw from Marlborough the permission to attack.

General Overkirk should have overruled him, but he was old and timorous and left it to Marlborough to do the arguing. Nothing availed; although the Duke had a superiority in men and materials, although the opportunity was golden and the result close to a fore-gone conclusion, they refused. 'Should we neglect this opportunity,' pleaded Marlborough in desperation, 'we must be responsible before God and Man.'[21] Nevertheless, neglect it they did, and in the end Marlborough had no alternative but to withdraw his army. 'We have been obliged to retire from the enemy, notwithstanding we were at least one third stronger than they,' he wrote to Godolphin,

> which I take to be very prejudicial to the common cause and scandalous for the army . . . the enemy will see very plainly that they have nothing to fear on this side, nor can I ever serve with them [the Dutch] without losing the little reputation that I have; for in most countries they think I have power in this army to do what I please.[22]

Marlborough correctly gauged the enemy's reactions, but the French made a mistake in holding the Duke responsible for the fiasco. 'I am overjoyed to learn that the great bragging that they made', Louis XIV wrote to Villeroy, '. . . ended in shameful retreat.'[23] The French Minister of War, M. Chamillart, also wrote to Villeroy that he had 'only a mediocre opinion' of the Duke's capacity and considered that the victory of Blenheim 'ought to be attributed to luck alone'. Villeroy was delighted with these observations and in his reply referred to Marlborough as 'an adventurer mortified with the scanty success of his campaign'.[24] A dire punishment awaited the author of these words.

Meanwhile Marlborough fought the Dutch obstructionists with all the power at his command. Some of his tactics were decidely comical. He wrote to the Grand Pensionary Heinsius begging him to invite his Dutch generals to draw up an Allied plan of campaign, promising that he would cheerfully co-operate! A week later he sent a happy note from Tirlemont saying the decision he had taken 'of being governed by your generals . . . gives me a great deal of quiet so that I am now drinking the Spa waters.'[25]

The irony was not lost either on the Dutch people or the Dutch Government, particularly as Queen Anne made representations to the States-General saying that they seemed to place 'less confidence in the Duke of Marlborough this year than last'. Indeed, when the story about the withdrawal from battle became public knowledge, the Dutch people were as angry as the English. 'They are so enraged against Slangenberg', wrote the Duke of Shrewsbury who was passing through Holland on his way back to England from Italy, 'for his being his [Marlborough's] enemy, as well as a Jesuitical Papist, that had he come to Amsterdam this summer, after he had hindered the battle, he would have been de Witted.'[26] The outcome of all this was that Slangenberg was dismissed the service, and it was agreed that in future Dutch Deputies would not be allowed to harass and thwart the Commander-in-Chief.

At the height of Marlborough's troubles in the middle of September, he ran into his old friend the Jacobite Earl of Ailesbury at a dinner-party in Tirlemont. Despondent and angry as the Duke was, he presented to the world his usual unruffled appearance. There are so few intimate pictures of Marlborough that Ailesbury's description is compelling:

> That night my Lord Orkney gave me a vast supper . . . and who should come in but my Lord Marlborough. . . . He was perfectly merry and for him ate much and drank heartily, and we all found the effects of the excellent wine, and I never saw more mirth. The next day he asked me where I dined. I told him where he was to dine – at Count Oxenstiern's. 'I shall not be so happy,' said he, 'for I am condemned to dine with base company, and shall have as base a dinner.' The three States Deputies of the Army [Dutch] had invited him, and that year they were three sad fellows and great pedants, and continually thwarting him.* The next day . . . Marechal Overkirk posted his troops and auxiliaries the left line of the army in review, and my Lord Marlborough promised to come, but we going to see him in the morning he entertained us and the company so long that I put him in mind of going. He whispered me in the ear that it was very indifferent to him. At last he went in his chaise for one person and one horse, and in getting up he set foot on ground again, and told me he had forgot to show me the plan of his house and gardens at Woodstock. . . . I asked him who was his architect (although I knew the man who was) he answered 'Sir Jo. Van Brugg'. On which I smiled and said, 'I suppose my Lord you made choice of him because he is a professed Whig.' . . . It was at my tongue's end to say that he ought as well to have made Sir Christopher Wren the Architect Poet Laureate. In fine, I understand but little or nothing of this matter, but enough to affirm (by the plan I saw) that the house is like one mass of stone without taste or relish.[27]

These frivolous episodes give us an insight into Marlborough's powers of concealment, for what a multitude of anxieties were hidden beneath his bland exterior! Not only did he have to deal with the shortcomings of his Allies but – surprisingly enough – he was confronted suddenly with peace proposals from the Great King himself.

---

* Marlborough's lack of enthusiasm is not surprising as these were the very same Deputies who had refused to allow him to attack the enemy.

Louis XIV was thankful to have escaped defeat in Flanders but his campaign had not brought him any victories. In Italy Eugene had prevented Marshal Vendôme from overrunning Turin; and in Spain an Anglo–Dutch–Imperial landing at Barcelona had allowed the Archduke Charles (brother of the new Emperor) to appear as 'Charles III'. These results were disappointing to Louis, but far more serious was the fact that the war was being fought in so many theatres that France could not find the money to pay for it. If only Paris could produce a miraculous invention like London's Bank of England which seemed to pour out gold quite effortlessly! Lacking this miraculous fountain Louis had no alternative but to try to initiate peace talks.

When the Marquis d'Alègre (captured at the Brabant battle) was given two months' leave by Marlborough to return to France, Louis XIV made the maximum use of it. Marlborough had asked the Marquis to convey a message of ceremony to the King and Louis lost no time in appointing d'Alègre his special emissary and sending him back to the enemy with peace proposals to be shown first to Marlborough, then to Heinsius. The terms were too favourable to France to be acceptable to England: Philip would not only remain on the Spanish throne but retain the Milanese, and the Spanish Netherlands would become independent. (In William's treaty, the Spanish Netherlands had been assigned to Charles and the Milanese to the Dauphin on the understanding that he would exchange it for Lorraine with the Duke of Lorraine.) If the Elector of Bavaria – Louis's ally – would agree to give up his southern German homeland in exchange for Naples and Sicily, the Emperor Joseph could compensate himself by taking Bavaria. The Dutch would be given a satisfactory barrier and France, of course, would remain as strong as ever. Attached to these proposals was a rider saying that if the Duke of Marlborough could assist in bringing about peace terms along these lines, Louis XIV would be happy to offer him a reward 'worthy of a man of his standing'. The reward was not only worthy, but quite startling – two million French livres, reckoned in those days at £300,000 (to day, anything from three to thirty million!).

Obviously the French King had been told that Marlborough liked money and had decided to find out if he was venal as well. The Duke was much too worldly to take umbrage at this massive bribe. He thanked the King warmly and got in touch with Heinsius urging him to reject the proposals out of hand as France was still too strong a power. '. . . England can like no peace but such as puts King Charles in possession of the monarchy of Spain,' he wrote to Heinsius.[28] At the time he sent this letter, August 1705, King Charles and his allies did not have a single foot of land in Spain and the Indies, apart from Gibraltar;* nor did they occupy Milan, Naples, Sicily or the Netherlands. Marlborough's self-confidence was admirable, but his insistence on the subjugation of Spain before even France had been humbled was plain bravado.

Marlborough was a man with big ideas. That winter he decided to open his spring campaign by leading his army across the Alps to Turin to help Eugene. Affairs there were in a critical state as the Prince had not been able to join forces with the Duke of Savoy, and if the enemy proved successful in besieging Turin (which Eugene had prevented the previous summer) their victory would spell the end of Austrian supremacy in the north of Italy. Although Marlborough confided his plan only to his closest confidants the fact that he ordered six hand-mills for grinding corn to be distributed to British regiments provided his officers with a clue. 'This occasioned the report', wrote Captain Robert Parker, 'that he designed a march into Italy to the relief of the Duke of Savoy, which had been a fine jaunt indeed.'[29]

The length of this staggering march did not seem to cause Marlborough undue anxiety. However, in April 1706, soon after he had won the reluctant approval of the Dutch, Marshal Villars upset his plans. The French Commander launched a surprise attack on Prince Louis of Baden and hurled his army back across the Rhine. Once again the Alliance was gripped by fear. Not only the Dutch but the Prussians, Hessians and Hanoverians said that all talk of Italy must be abandoned as they could not allow their troops to move so far from home. Marlborough was left with no alternative but to remain where he was. The only gesture he could make was to send 10,000 troops to Eugene to make up for the latter's losses. 'In Flanders,' he wrote mournfully to Sarah in May, 'where I shall be forced to be, I am afraid the whole summer, there will be very little action, for the French will not venture in this country. . . .'[30]

Marlborough was wrong. The Great King had been brooding about the stalemate in Flanders and the ruinous cost of the war. Encouraged by Villeroy's disparaging remarks about Marlborough, and heartened by Villars' success on the Rhine, he decided to change his tactics. Instead of urging his generals to play safe, he would strike out boldly, for only by frightening his enemies could he coerce them round a peace-table. 'I can think of no better way to force my enemies to negotiate peace', he wrote to Villeroy, 'than to make them realize

---

* Barcelona was not taken until October 1705.

that I am strong enough to attack them everywhere.'[31] He therefore ordered Villeroy to cross the Dyle, to lay siege to Léau and, if confronted by Marlborough, to accept the challenge.

Marlborough could not believe his ears when he was told that the French were coming out from behind their entrenchments; but when he learned that Villeroy was actually marching towards Tirlemont, his heart leaped with joy. This could mean only one thing: that the French were ready for battle. Well, come on then! He would see that they had it! He began moving his own army at three in the morning of 23 May. He hoped to attack the enemy somewhere near the great plain of Ramillies, a watershed ringed by the marshland from three rivers – the Mehaigne, and the Little and Great Geete. Although the two hosts were not more than a few miles apart, the French had encamped for the night and the Allies were uncertain of their position. Marlborough had sent General Cadogan ahead to find the enemy and to mark out a camp. On that particular night the darkness was more impenetrable than usual as there was a thick fog – indeed, it was impossible to see more than a few yards ahead even at eight in the morning – and when General Cadogan passed the village of Merdorp he suddenly came up against a small posse of French Hussars. There were shots and scamperings and both sides quickly retired. Half an hour later the mist rose a little and the General could see that the French were moving on to the Ramillies plain, near the Mont St André plateau, the exact spot where he had intended to pitch his own camp. He sent a trooper galloping back to Marlborough with the news.

The Duke joined Cadogan at ten o'clock. At the very moment of his arrival the fog lifted, like a theatre-curtain, and there before his eyes was the picture that he had longed to see for so many months. Spread out before him over a space of several miles were the enemy's 60,000 men, some of them in battle formation, some of them still deploying. It was a truly magnificent sight, for the plain was covered with the light green of spring corn and the soldiers in their multi-coloured uniforms looked like a field of Dutch tulips; the French infantry was in white, the Bavarians in light blue with red trimmings, the Swiss Guards in red with blue trimmings, the *gens d'armerie* in scarlet, the Household Troops (the *Maison du Roi*) in white, and the troops of the Spanish and Waloon Horse in greens, blues and greys.

The French and their Bavarian allies were itching for battle. They had completely recovered their lost morale and talked with mounting excitement of avenging themselves for the Blenheim disaster.

The 'Old Campaigner', the French officer who had fought at the Schellenberg, tells us in his memoirs that the French Marquis who accompanied him to Ramillies remarked

> that France had surpassed herself in the quality of these troops; he believed that the enemy had no chance whatever of breaking them in the coming conflict; if defeated now we would never again hope to withstand them. . . . So vast was the plain of Ramillies that we were able to march our army on as broad a front as we desired, and the result was a truly magnificent spectacle. . . . The army had but just entered on the campaign; weather and fatigue had hardly yet had time to dim its brilliancy, and it was inspired with a courage born of confidence.[32]

There was no doubt about the army's splendid appearance; even the Duke of Marlborough remarked that it 'looked the best of any he had ever seen'. But something else was required to settle the contest, and the Duke had implicit faith in the 'goodness' of his own men. He did not doubt for a moment who would carry off the honours of the day.

With both sides convinced of their superiority it was clear from the start that Ramillies would be no ordinary battle. Marlborough rode along the broad front at eleven o'clock accompanied by a handful of officers (all of them with the shoulder-length periwigs and the three-cornered hats that were *de rigueur* at the time) while his army, a mile distant from that of the enemy, began deploying and forming into battle-lines.

Marlborough was familiar with this particular piece of ground as he had camped there two years earlier. Added to this, he had an amazing eye for country and could memorize it the way other people could memorize poetry. Oddly enough the battleground was similar in many ways to that of Blenheim. The enemy's right was attached to the villages of Taviers and Franquenée close to the River Mehaigne (like Blenheim village and the Danube) while his left stretched out to the village of Autre Eglise. This small community lay at the far side of the plain which – like the Blenheim plain – was four miles in width and looked as though Providence had designed it expressly for a cavalry charge. In the foreground, about half a mile in front of the French formations, was the village of Ramillies. As Marlborough rode along he sited the position for every one of his thirty big guns. Unlike other commanders, he attached great importance to his artillery and on this occasion was happy to have a superiority in field-guns.

Marlborough's two wings on opposite sides of the plain began to move at 2 o'clock in the afternoon. On the left were the famous Dutch Guards supported by nine squadrons of Dutch and Danish cavalry –

nearly 10,000 men in all. The attack began when General Wertmuller, under the command of General Overkirk, led four battalions of Guards against Taviers village. The men in the vanguard dragged two twenty-four-pound cannon with them. Apparently, this was a surprise as the use of artillery by front-line troops was quite unheard of in those days. The cannon smashed garden walls and houses, and the Dutch storm-troopers took the two villages – Taviers and Franquenée – in the space of half an hour. The French command countered by ordering two battalions of Swiss infantry and fourteen squadrons of dragoons to retake the villages. The dragoons made the mistake of leading their horses rather than riding them across the strip of marshland formed by the River Mehaigne. In the middle of this operation the Danish cavalry broke upon them and routed them completely. Their horses bolted and the 'Old Campaigner', who was about to bring a Franco–Bavarian battalion into the attack, reported that when the enemy forces 'came tumbling down upon my battalion . . . they brought such alarm and confusion in their train that my own fellows turned around and fled [as well] . . . .'[33]

While this was going on, Marlborough's spirited General Orkney, in command of the right wing, four miles distant, was leading twelve battalions of English troops – about 9,000 men – towards the villages of Autre Eglise and Offus. These two hamlets, about three-quarters of a mile apart, were protected by a large area of marshland formed by the Little Geete River and its tributary streams, which most military men deemed 'quite impassable'. Nevertheless, Orkney's men fought their way forward supported some of the way by General Lumley's cavalry. They waded through the bog, cursing and panting and swearing, and to their surprise got to the other side. Even more surprising was the fact that several of Lumley's supporting squadrons managed to get there as well. Marshal Villeroy and the Elector of Bavaria were watching the 'redcoats' with rapt attention through their telescopes, recalling the words of their King. 'It would be very important', Louis xiv had written only a fortnight earlier, 'to have particular attention to that part of the line which will endure the first shock of the English troops.'[34] As the dreaded attack of the English was about to fall on the sector near Autre Eglise, it was understandable that Villeroy should give an order to transfer troops from the French centre to the threatened zone on his left. This was just what Marlborough intended him to do; neither Orkney nor the enemy suspected that Orkney's attack was being mounted as a feint.

Meanwhile the Duke, mounted on his white horse, was directing the battle from a small rise about a mile short of Ramillies. The mind boggles when one thinks of the responsibility resting on the shoulders of one man who, without any of the modern means of communication, was expected to control a front four miles long, where literally thousands of men were locked in hand-to-hand combat. Marlborough's sharp eyes could see more through a telescope than most men, but when the guns began to fire, heavy smoke often blotted out the landscape. He kept in touch with developments through his aides-de-camp, a steady stream of whom came galloping up to him with front-line intelligence. These aides were not just messengers but highly trained observers whose eye-witness accounts provided the Duke with the information on which he based his crucial decisions. He knew, of course, that Taviers village had been taken by his soldiers and that Lord Orkney was making spectacular progress through the 'impassable' marshland on his extreme right. He also knew that Villeroy was still withdrawing troops from the centre to reinforce his stand against Orkney's dreaded 'redcoats'.

Now it was time to test the strength of the enemy's weakened centre. Marlborough's attention focused on the plain between Taviers and Ramillies. Here, trotting in two dense lines, Overkirk's blue-grey Dutch squadrons rode hard into France's most famous cavalry regiments, the aristocratic and celebrated Maison du Roi, the equivalent of England's Household Cavalry. The severe, head-on clash provoked ferocious fighting and for a while it looked as though the French might break through the Dutch lines. But when the enemy came up against the infantry which Marlborough always used to support his 'Horse', they met a hail of bullets – the 'platoon firing' which the Duke's foot soldiers were obliged to practise all winter. This finally turned them back. Nevertheless, Marlborough had taken note of the fact that General Overkirk's line had bent dangerously and immediately sent word to Lord Orkney to break off his flank assault, explaining that the main attack would come in the centre, and that he needed Lumley's cavalry and Orkney's infantry to support him. In order to make sure that the hot-blooded Irishman understood and obeyed, Marlborough sent ten aides-de-camp to deliver his orders, and finally even dispatched General Cadogan himself. As Orkney was on the point of seizing the village of Autre Eglise he could scarcely believe his ears; we do not know what words were exchanged, but he did as he was told. 'I confess', he wrote in his memoirs in a famous piece of understatement, 'it vexed me to retire.'[35]

Marlborough's plan for the transference of Orkney's cavalry to the centre (first eighteen then twenty-one squadrons) was ingenious.

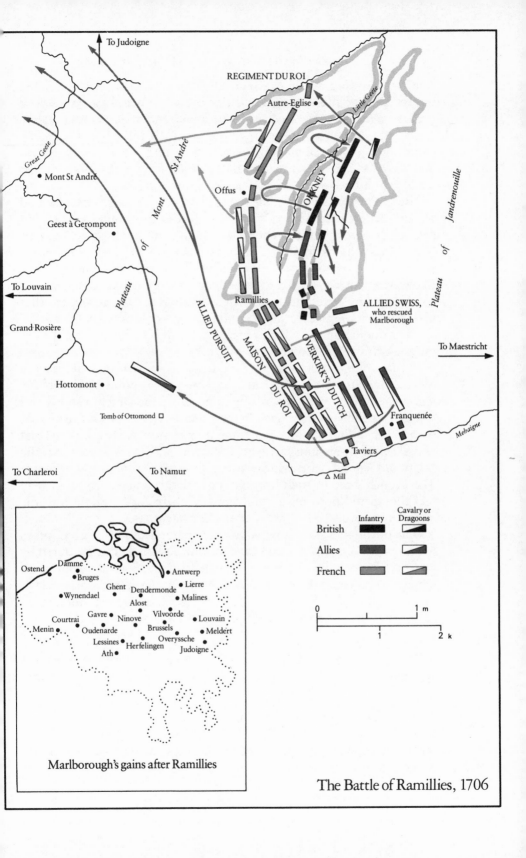

To Judoigne

REGIMENT DU ROI

Autre-Eglise

Great Geete

Mont St André

St André

Offus

Mont

OKNEY

Plateau of Jandrenouille

Geest à Gerompont

To Louvain

Plateau

ALLIED PURSUIT

Ramillies

ALLIED SWISS,
who rescued
Marlborough

Grand Rosière

MAISON

OVERKIRK'S DUTCH

To Maestricht

Hottomont

DU ROI

Tomb of Ottomond □

Franquenée

Mehaigne

Taviers

△ Mill

To Charleroi

To Namur

	Infantry	Cavalry or Dragoons
British		
Allies		
French		

0   1 m

1   2 k

Ostend

Damme

Bruges

Antwerp

Ghent

Dendermonde

Lierre

Wynendael

Alost

Malines

Courtrai

Gavre

Vilvoorde

Menin

Ninove

Louvain

Oudenarde

Brussels

Meldert

Lessines

Overyssche

Herfelingen

Judoigne

Ath

Marlborough's gains after Ramillies

The Battle of Ramillies, 1706

They were to traverse the 'dead ground' between a series of rises in the terrain so that the enemy could not see what was happening. The French were also to be deceived by Orkney's infantry. The second line was to halt just short of the crest of a long, low hill where the enemy could spot their regimental colours and imagine them to be re-grouping. Meanwhile the rest of the infantry would move across 'dead ground' to join Marlborough's centre as reserves.

The Duke now appeared at the spot where the Dutch cavalry had put up its fierce resistance. It was vital to Marlborough's whole plan of battle to prevent the French horsemen from breaking through his lines. Altogether a total of 25,000 horsemen were preparing them-selves for the second encounter. Suddenly, to everyone's amazement Marlborough trotted up and joined the Dutch line. No doubt he was encouraged by the enthusiasm he had aroused at Elixem, and felt that his participation might strengthen the resolve of his troops. However, it was a foolish move which nearly cost him his life and might have put the war itself in jeopardy.

Marlborough's scarlet coat stood out like a sore thumb among the blue-coated Dutch horsemen and became a focal-point for the enemy who were not slow in recognizing him. Twice the Dutch recoiled and Marlborough was swept back in the general retreat. His horse pecked in jumping a ditch and he was flung to the ground. He got to his feet and, despite the encumbrance of jack-boots and heavy wig, ran for the safety of General Murray's Swiss troops – two Protestant battalions. The French were in such hot pursuit that they rode over Milord; in fact they could not pull up and some of them rode straight into the Swiss infantry and were impaled on their bayonets.

Marlborough's staff immediately surrounded him and Captain Molesworth dismounted and gave his horse to the Duke. Sheltered by Murray's troops, he directed the battle from this vantage-point until his equerry, Major Bingfield, rode up with another charger. Marl-borough changed horses, but as the devoted Bingfield was holding his stirrup a cannon-ball knocked off the latter's head.

> Milord Marlborough was rid over [Orkney reported the next day] but got other squadrons which he led up. Major Bingfield holding his stirrup to give him another horse was shot by a cannon-ball which went through Marlborough's legs; in truth there was no scarcity of 'em.[36]

This incident gripped the imagination of the British public to such an extent that playing-cards were made showing Marlborough, his leg half over the horse's back, and the headless Major standing at the horse's side.

Soon Marlborough had a superiority of Horse – 'five to two' he reckoned – counting Orkney's eighteen squadrons which were on their way, and another twenty-one squadrons called in from his immediate right. Even the Maison du Roi with their wonderful golden banners embroidered with the lilies of France could not stand against such numerical superiority and were finally routed. At five o'clock Marlborough ordered his victorious horsemen to wheel right and form a line facing north so that they could roll up the enemy's exposed flank. It took almost an hour to complete this complicated manoeuvre, involving 100 squadrons and over 10,000 men. Their lines were spread out over the mile between Ramillies and the Tomb of Ottomond. Meanwhile the Allied infantry with twenty cannon were moving forward between Ramillies and Offus.

At six o'clock the signal for the final cavalry charge was given. The remaining fifty French squadrons, representing the last reserves, refused to take the shock and simply turned their horses and rode off the field. The French infantry held its ground, but when the Allied Foot began coming at them from two directions, supported by more cavalry, the morale broke. 'We had not got forty yards on our retreat', wrote Peter Drake, the Irish renegade fighting for the French, 'when the words *sauve qui peut* went through the great part, if not the whole army, and put all to confusion. Then might be seen entire brigades running in disorder.'[37]

Soon the whole countryside was a scene of fleeing troops hoping for safety in the darkness of the night. The panic was understandable, as the Allies, drunk with excitement, were taking no prisoners. For four hours they pursued the shattered remnants of what had been a magnificent army. All the enemy's guns and trophies, even their baggage, fell into the victors' hands. The 5,000 unwounded prisoners who surrendered were fortunate, as jubilant horsemen with flashing swords were so excited by the chase that they showed no mercy. Thousands of escaping men who had missed the bullets of the battlefield were given no quarter and cut down.

Louis xiv did not hear of the disaster for three days. 'I was at Versailles,' writes Saint-Simon. 'Never has one seen such anxiety and consternation. . . . In ignorance at what had happened and of the consequences of such an unfortunate battle and amid everyone's fears for kith and kin, the days seemed years.'[38] As no official dispatch arrived, the French King finally was forced to send his Minister of War to Villeroy's headquarters to learn the details.

With news of Villeroy's defeat, the towns and fortresses of the Spanish Netherlands began to fall like ninepins. Brussels led the way, recognizing the Emperor Joseph's brother as Charles III of Spain – an example followed by many others. '. . . we have done in four days', Marlborough wrote to Sarah on 16 May, 'what we should have thought ourselves happy if we could have been sure of it in four years.' This was a truly epic encounter, for the battle had brought every aspect of Marlborough's genius into play: his eye for the contours of the land, his understanding of infantry fire-power, his superb communications, his use of artillery, his personal courage, and his never-faltering ability to deceive and surprise. Even so, one of the secrets of his success lay undoubtedly in a simple human emotion: the admiration and affection of his soldiers, rough men who showed their gratitude for his kindness and courtesy by laying victory at his feet. Unfortunately Marlborough's success was blighted by the fact that he was again suffering from blinding headaches. 'So that', he admitted in the same letter to Sarah, 'I have not as yet all the pleasures I shall enjoy of the blessing God has been pleased to give us in this great victory.'[39] But four days later he had recovered enough to rejoice in his superb triumph.

> We are now masters of Ghent [he wrote to Sarah] and tomorrow I shall send some more troops to Bruges. So many towns have submitted since the battle that it really looks more like a dream than truth. My thoughts are now turning to the getting everything ready for the siege of Antwerp. . . .[40]

However, the siege never took place because Antwerp surrendered without a blow; and on 3 June John was sending Sarah more good news:

> Every day gives us fresh marks of the great victory, for since my last we have taken possession of Bruges and Damme, as also of Oudenarde which was besieged the last war by the King, with 60,000 men, and he was at last forced to raise the siege. In short there is so great a panic in the French army as is not to be expressed. Every place we take declares for King Charles* . . . . I am so persuaded that this campaign will bring us a good peace, that I beg of you to do all you can so that the house at Woodstock may be carried up as much as possible, that I may have a prospect of living in it. . . .[41]

Meanwhile England and Holland were astonished and overjoyed by the wonderful news of their victories (the Dutch were particularly proud because of the role their soldiers had played), while poor Marshal Villeroy was in the depths of despair. 'The only happy day which I foresee in my life', he said in a letter to the King, 'is the day of

---

* The Allies' candidate for the Spanish throne.

my death.'[42] Although Villeroy was a great favourite at Court, his defeat was on such a scale that the King had no alternative but to dismiss him. As Louis XIV was famous for his good manners, he did his best to ease the blow. 'At our age', he told his Marshal comfortingly, 'we must no longer expect good fortune.'[43] Nevertheless, Villeroy's critics complained that it was sad that he was not as irresistible to the enemy as he was to the ladies! The Duke of Vendôme took Villeroy's place and was soon writing to Louis how grieved he was at the 'sadness and dejection that appears in the French army'. 'I will do my best', he declared, 'to restore their spirit. But it will be no light matter for me to do so, for everyone here is ready to take off his hat at the mere name of Marlborough.'[44] Indeed, the French army was beginning to look upon Marlborough as a universal hero. Not only was he a brilliant commander and a brave, pugnacious warrior, but he was a man of infinite kindness and courtesy – something quite rare among military men. Saint-Simon was deeply impressed by the fact that he looked after the enemy wounded with the same care that he gave to his own men, and also praised his willingness to set many of his 'prisoners of mark' at liberty for three months upon their parole.[45]

When Brussels capitulated and the Estates of Brabant transferred their allegiance from the Bourbons to the Habsburgs, Marlborough entered the capital in state. As Commander-in-Chief he handled the many decisions forced upon him with wisdom and forbearance. He guaranteed the country's civil and religious rights and laid down stringent regulations to protect the inhabitants from military excesses. He even took care to heed Catholic sensibilities. As a result, word spread that a firm and fair hand had taken control. Food and forage poured into the city; the country came into the war alongside the Allies; and everyone began to clamour for the Duke's permanent authority.

At this point the Emperor Joseph invited Marlborough, on behalf of his brother Charles III, to become Governor-General of the Spanish Netherlands. It was the most important and richest civilian post in Europe, carrying a salary of £60,000 a year. The Duke was delighted by the offer and wrote to the Queen asking Her Majesty's permission to accept it. While he was awaiting her reply he made a point of calling on the celebrated M. de Vos, the most renowned artist in tapestry in the whole of Europe. No doubt de Vos had been recommended to Marlborough by Prince Eugene, a great lover of the arts, who was familiar with his work because the Emperor Leopold had hung several of his tapestries in the Imperial Palace in Vienna. De Vos had only been in Brussels a year. He had set up his looms in 1705 and was being accorded many honours in recognition of his skill. That summer Marlborough commissioned him to depict a scene (to do 'a hanging' as the Duke called it) from the battle of Blenheim. This wonderful tapestry was given eventually the place of honour at Blenheim Palace. Sarah put it in the Duke's bow-windowed room where he most often sat, and it still hangs there today.

The Queen had replied to Marlborough that both she and her Government were wholly in favour of the Duke's acceptance of the Governorship of the Spanish Netherlands. Unfortunately, the Dutch were so violently opposed to the plan they were furious that Marlborough dared to consider it. The truth was that they wanted to govern the Netherlands themselves, at least as long as the war lasted. Conveniently, they overlooked the fact that the Southern Netherlands – the Belgians – would rather be governed by anyone but the Northern Netherlands – the Dutch. But Heinsius argued that the great sacrifices that Holland had made – not to mention the fact that Ramillies had been won mainly by Dutch soldiers – entitled them to the position. After all, the chief reason why Holland was fighting the war was to erect a 'barrier' against France. The only way the Dutch could be sure of a satisfactory Barrier Treaty, they said, was to control the Southern Netherlands. Marlborough did not argue. The strength of the Dutch reaction convinced him that the Grand Alliance itself was threatened and, without any further hesitation, he refused the Emperor's offer; adding up the pros and cons, the salary of £60,000 a year would not compensate for the disunity of the coalition. Eventually an Anglo–Dutch condominium was set up to take over the government until the war ended, when the province could be transferred to Charles III.

The remainder of the fighting season – from June to the first week in October – was devoted to four successful sieges: Ostend, Dendermonde, Menin and Ath. The familiar red-coated figure of the Duke, with his black tricorn hat and his shoulder-length periwig curls, mounted on his white horse, always caused a ripple of excitement that frequently broke into cheers. His agreeable personality had become a byword in the army; as a result even the most cantankerous men made a point of paying their respects to him. Marlborough knew hundreds of them by sight as he always rode out with Cadogan and a group of officers and aides to examine the siege-lines and site the guns. At Menin he was galloping across open ground when he dropped his glove. Instead of turning to one of his equerries, he asked Cadogan to pick it up. The latter instantly dismounted and fulfilled the Duke's request. That night in camp Marlborough told Cadogan that he wanted a battery posted at the spot where he had dropped his glove and Cadogan replied that he had already given the order. Marlborough, in surprise, asked how he had known his intention. Because, Cadogan explained, the Duke was much too considerate to ask him to dismount and pick up his glove without an ulterior motive, and he had guessed what it was.

That summer, July 1706, Prince Eugene began his wonderful march from the foot of the Alps, around Garda, and up the valley of the Po to relieve the siege of Turin and to bring aid to his kinsman, the Duke of Savoy. Crossing countless rivers, outmanœuvring hostile armies, his force of 20,000 men (half of whom had been supplied by Marlborough at great risk to his own campaign) moved towards the valley of Turin. Eugene was well aware of his friend's sacrifice and for this reason was particularly delighted by the news of Marlborough's magnificent victory at Ramillies. The Prince was also aided by the recall of Marshal Vendôme from Italy to take over Villeroy's command in Flanders. The Duke of Savoy was in desperate straits, but in September Eugene finally succeeded in joining forces with him. Together they attempted to raise the siege of Turin. Although their joint army numbered only 35,000 men and the French besiegers were 60,000, the two Savoyards saw a gap in the enemy's defences. After a short and fierce battle, the enemy's lines of circumvallation were carried. The French army fled across the Alps and Turin declared for Austria. Within the next few months the French garrisons in Milan, Naples and Sicily followed suit. Italy had now passed into the hands of the Allies and no longer belonged to France.

Marlborough was never jealous. Although people always tried to make trouble between the two commanders by praising one at the expense of the other, neither deigned to listen to gossip. When Marlborough heard the news of Eugene's triumph, he wrote to Sarah: 'It is impossible for me to express the joy it has given me; for I do not only esteem but I really love that Prince.'[46]

Occasionally, the war must have struck the Duke as a happy, even a peaceful escape from the bickerings at home – particularly the bickerings between his beloved Sarah and his own beautiful daughters. For some time Sarah had been complaining of the girls' behaviour and in May John had begged her to pass over 'little faults' and to remember that they were 'very young'. As tactful as ever, he added that 'they must be barbarians if they do not make a kind return to so good a mother.'[47] But daughter Mary – the chief culprit – was not easy to handle; she had the imperious ways of her mother and did not welcome criticism. However, in this particular case, the fault was Sarah's. Although Mary was a married lady of high rank, Sarah insisted that when they met in company Mary must drop her a curtsey and call her 'Madam'. This deference was not part of the etiquette of the day and Mary refused to comply. 'One of Lady Mary's fancies', Sarah wrote later, 'was when she was first married, that if I met her in any public place she would not make me a curtsey . . . [so] I desired her to give me the ease of not coming to my house – and in this way we lived a great while, and when I have met her in the street in her chair she would not let down her glass and bow. . . .'[48] In July (while Prince Eugene was marching across Italy), John wrote to Sarah that he was pleased to hear that she was on good terms with three of her children, and hoped to God that Lady Mary 'will in time be truly sensible of the great obligations she has to you.' But unfortunately Lady Mary was destined to be a permanent thorn in her mother's flesh.

Ten

Abigail

Although Marlborough's sword was raising England to new heights, Queen Anne's appearance suggested anything but glory. When she received a visitor from Scotland, Sir John Clerk, at Kensington Palace in the summer of her triumph – *annus mirabilis* 1706 – he could scarcely believe that he was in the presence of his sovereign lady. 'Her Majesty', he wrote in his journal,

> was labouring under a fit of Gout, and in extream pain and agony, and on this occasion everything about her was in much the same disorder as about the meanest of her subjects. Her face, which was red and spotted, was rendered something frightful by her negligent dress, and the foot affected was tied up with a pultis and some nasty bandages. . . . Nature seems inverted when a poor, infirm Woman becomes one of the Rulers of the World.[1]

The 'poor, infirm Woman' showered praise and gratitude on Marlborough for Ramillies, and as town after town in the Southern Netherlands continued to fall, she described as astonishing 'ye great progress ye hav made since ye battle', adding the fervent hope that God would make her Captain General 'the happy instrument of giving a lasting peace to Europe'. 'Now', she told Godolphin, 'we have God be thanked soe hopefull a prospect of a peace.'[2]

The Queen's instinct for peace was sound. By the end of the year the war aims of William III, as set out in the Treaty of Grand Alliance of 1701 – the withdrawal of French troops from Italy and the Netherlands – had been realized. And, as the Treaty accepted the 'partition' of the Spanish Empire between Bourbon and Habsburg candidates, even this knotty problem presented no difficulties. Louis XIV had been stunned by the news of Ramillies, and in the privacy of Madame de Maintenon's apartment, he again wept bitter tears. How long would the Almighty continue to punish him for his pride and arrogance? Apparently, the Almighty encouraged him to take a practical step. In August, while the Queen of England was still talking about the blessings of peace, the French King made new and secret proposals to Marlborough which he forwarded to Heinsius. The terms were very different from those suggested by Louis six months earlier. Spain and the Indies would go to Habsburg Charles, while Bourbon Philip would be compensated in Italy – he would have the Duchy of Milan, the ports of Tuscany and the two kingdoms of Naples and Sicily. The future of the Spanish Netherlands would be decided by the Dutch themselves.

When Marlborough received these communications, he was directing the siege of Menin. On 17 August his Chief-of-Staff, General Cadogan, was taken prisoner by a French raiding-party, and for several days the Duke did not know whether he was dead or alive. Fortunately he was hale and hearty and was returned within a fortnight in exchange for a French general. This brief picture gives a glimpse of Marlborough's hectic life. Here he is, Commander-in-Chief of two campaigns in two separate theatres waiting for news from Italy (a third theatre) which might affect his plans; directing his own siege operations in Flanders; twelve hours a day in the saddle, but no rest for the weary until he had wrestled with a vast correspondence demanding decisions on everything from troop movements to peace initiative. 'As a good Englishman', he wrote to Heinsius on 21 August, referring to the French peace proposals, 'I must be of the opinion that both by treaty* and interest, we are obliged to preserve the Monarque of Spain intier. At the same time, as a friend I must own that I believe France can hardly be brought to a peace unless something be given to the Duke of Angou [Philip v].'[3]

In this case, Marlborough adopted the official line, yet at the same time he reveals that, in his own personal opinion, a refusal to adopt William III's scheme of partitioning Spain would prevent France from making peace. Everything for Charles, nothing for Philip ('Spain intier') was tantamount to a demand from France of unconditional surrender. Nevertheless, the Queen's ministers, led by the Lord Treasurer and supported by Whig bankers and merchants, were so dazzled by the year of victory that they wanted just this. They saw themselves benefiting hugely by picking up the pieces – particularly in trade – of a ruined France. Furthermore, if they could remove Louis's

---

* Marlborough is referring to the Anglo–Portuguese Treaty of 1703 in which England agreed to support Charles's claim to the whole Spanish Empire. This clause could easily have been renegotiated in view of the reduction of French power.

grandson from the Spanish throne (and substitute an ineffectual Habsburg), they might reap all sorts of trade concessions in the New World, now monopolized by Spain. Indeed, the Bourbons must not be allowed a foothold anywhere outside France; they were too clever, too predatory. 'No Peace Without Spain' became a rallying cry for all patriotic Englishmen. 'No good Englishman or servant of the Queen', wrote Lord Godolphin to the Pensionary of Amsterdam in September 1706, 'can advise the dismembering.[the partitioning] of the Spanish Monarchy.'[4]

The prevailing wind of bellicosity carried all before it. Not only the Dutch but even the Queen herself was swept along by the gale. However, she went out of her way to assure Marlborough that she had 'no ambition after the King of Spain [Charles III] is settled on his throne but to see an honourable peace, that whenever it pleases God I shall dye, I may have the satisfaction of leaving my poor country and all my friends in Peace and quiet.'[5]

At that very moment, July 1706, even the difficult war in Spain seemed to be going Marlborough's way. Barcelona, the Allies' only stronghold, under siege by Marshal Tessé and on the verge of capitulation, had been saved at the eleventh hour by the arrival of Admiral Leake and 5,000 troops. The French had been driven back into their own country (with Philip v in their midst); and Lord Galway, the French Huguenot, who had become a naturalized Englishman, had marched from Portugal to Madrid. There he was awaiting the arrival of the English commander, Lord Peterborough, from Valencia and, even more important, the Archduke Charles from Catalonia. As soon as the twenty-one-year-old Habsburg Prince entered the capital, the Allies would crown him Charles III of Spain.

Then, suddenly, everything began to go wrong. Quarrels and vicissitudes of one kind and another intervened and Charles got no further than Guadalajara, a town thirty-five miles from Madrid, where he joined Galway and Peterborough. By this time the Duke of Berwick was marching on Madrid with such a strong force that the English had no alternative but to evacuate the capital. As things turned out, the Allies' brief interlude in Madrid proved to be their high-water mark in Spain. Indeed, when peace finally came in 1713, the events of 1706 could be seen as prophetic. France would be forced to return to her own frontiers, but Charles would never be crowned King of Spain.

With the advantage of hindsight, 1706 stands out as the year that Marlborough should have asserted himself in the interests of peace. As the most celebrated man in Europe, he was perhaps the only individual who might have drawn the two warring sides into an agreement. Even Marshal Vendôme was obliged to pay tribute to him. 'Everybody', he wrote to the French Minister of War in August, 'is ready to doff his hat to Marlborough.'[6] 'He had the qualities William lacked,' wrote the eminent Professor G.M. Tevelyan, 'for he could not only plan but win a war; but he was to fail where William succeeded for he could not make a world peace. Indeed, he can scarcely be said to have tried.'[7] One might add that, whereas William had time to consider and to plan a world peace, Marlborough had none.

Furthermore, in 1706 Marlborough was not at all convinced that Louis's peace offers were genuine. He wrote to Heinsius that France might be bartering for the time to put her affairs in order before beginning 'a new warr'. 'You must give me leave to tell you', he wrote in October to General Slingelandt, Overkirk's future successor as commander of the Dutch forces, 'that I am one of those who believe that France is not yet reduced to her just bounds, and that nothing can be more harmful to us on this occasion than seeming over-forward to clap up a hasty peace.'[8]

While the Duke of Marlborough was conducting the war abroad, the Duchess of Marlborough was fighting her own battles at home. Once again she was back in regular attendance at Court, the dominant figure among the Queen's ladies. At forty-six she was still beautiful. Her sparkling blue eyes and English rose complexion turned many heads when she entered a room, but it was the exuberance of her personality that captured (or alienated) most people. Whatever their reaction, no one ever called her boring. 'Did you know her but half as well as I have the happiness to do,' Lord Hervey wrote to a friend,

> she would make you think of her as one said of the sea, that it infinitely surprised him the first time he saw it, but that the last sight of it made as wonderful an impression as if he had never observed it before. She had a most acute and elevated understanding . . . she ought to have been born in the golden age.[9]

Sarah had spent most of 1703 away from London grieving for her dead son, and during the next two years had allowed her political differences with the Queen to spoil the pleasures of her Court life – no more cards, no more gossip. But now her resentment had given way to a more affable mood which was combined with her usual brisk efficiency. As the Queen's closest friend she occupied a commanding position. Dozens of people clamoured to see her, presenting petitions, asking for royal appointments, even requesting pardons for relations sentenced to the pillory.

Sarah performed her duties with authority and good sense. First she laid down new rules for the Privy Purse (no more bribes, no more bought places); then she tackled the Queen's clothes. It was ridiculous, she decided, to spend large sums of money on clothes for a woman in Anne's sorry physical condition. For state occasions the Queen would wear velvet and ermine, but on ordinary days her clothes would be good but simple. As a result, irate tradespeople criticized the Duchess, saying that 'her Majesty was not fine enough for a Queen'. 'But it would have been rediculous with her person and [one] of her age', wrote Sarah, 'to have been otherwise drest. Besides her limbs were so weakened with the Gout for many years that she could not indure heavy clothes & she really had everything that was handsome and proper for her.' Occasionally, Anne longed for more magnificent attire and talked about 'two diamond buttons and loops upon each sleeve', but Sarah invariably broke off the discussion by returning to the original decision and saying lightly: 'Lord, Madam, it must be so !'[10]

In April, Sarah became the Princess of Mindelheim. At long last the Emperor Joseph had carved out a small principality in Swabia (territory confiscated from Max Emmanuel of Bavaria) and bestowed it upon the Duke. This meant that he could take his seat as a *bona fide* Prince of the Holy Roman Empire. Sarah refused to use the title, but John was pleased because it gave him £1,500 a year and Prince Eugene addressed him as 'cousin'. Sarah preferred to be an English duchess.

Even so, English duchesses were not people that Sarah cared to see often. English politicians were much more up her street. Ever since the election of 1705 the Whigs had commanded a majority in the House of Commons.* They had done everything they could to ingratiate themselves with the Queen. They had wholeheartedly supported the union between Scotland and England enabling Anne, in the early spring of 1706, to appoint Scottish and English commissions to draw up a treaty. But by the summer the Whigs were tired of being kept out of the Government and decided to bludgeon their way into the Queen's favour. They informed Lord Godolphin that unless Anne selected one of the members of the Whig Junto as Secretary of State, they would no longer co-operate with the Government. They put forward Marlborough's son-in-law, Lord Sunderland, as the most

---

* Although neither Whigs nor Tories had emerged from the election of 1705 with a clear majority, the Whigs always persuaded enough 'non-party' members to support them to give them control.

likely candidate to breach the Cabinet walls, or, as they put it, 'in driving the nail that would go'. Here they miscalculated, as the Queen had an almost pathological hatred of all Sunderlands. She had loathed the young man's father because of the shocking way in which he had changed his religion from Protestant to Catholic and back again, to suit the requirements of James II and William III, and she disliked the present Lord Sunderland because she suspected him of republican leanings. Even more important, the Queen was fighting to retain the royal prerogative of selecting Cabinet ministers regardless of party pressures (she was the last sovereign to enjoy this privilege as an uncontested right) and replied vigorously to pressure from Lord Godolphin. 'All I desire', she told her Lord Treasurer, 'is my Liberty in encouraging and employing all those that concur faithfully in my service whether they are call'd Whigs or Torrys. . . .'[11]

At this point Sarah picked up the cudgels. She had avoided arguments with the Queen for over eighteen months, but now – no doubt prodded by Godolphin and Sunderland himself – she could no longer be silent. ''Tis certain', she told Her Majesty, 'that your Government can't be carried on with a part of the Torrys, and the Whigs disobliged. . . .' Sarah tried to be tactful but the last lines of her letter caused the Queen great offence. 'Your security and the nation is my chief wish,' wrote Sarah, 'and I beg of God Almighty as earnestly as I shall do for his last pardon at my last hour, and Mr and Mrs Morley may see the errors as to this *notion* before it is too late. . . .'[12]

What impertinence for the Groom of the Stole to lecture the Queen of England in such a way! It was not until a week had passed that Sarah discovered that, through Sidney Godolphin's mediation, the Queen had read Sarah's word 'notion' as 'nation'. However, this revelation only increased Sarah's annoyance. The fact that the Queen, once so gentle and loving, should take umbrage over a single word was becoming quite ridiculous. Furthermore, Lord Godolphin and the Duke of Marlborough were only urging the Queen to take Sunderland into her Government because Whig support was essential in providing the necessary war credits. The Queen's behaviour was so out of character that Sarah began to be suspicious. 'The only fear I have', she wrote to Anne,

> is that there is someone artfull that takes pains to mislead Mrs Morley for otherwise how is it possible that one whom I have formerly heard say, she was not fond of her own judgement, could persist in such a thing soe very contrary to the advice of two men that has certainly done more

service both to the Crown and the Country than be found in any history.[13]

Sarah could not put her finger on anyone or anything except Mr Robert Harley who, as Secretary of State, worked closely with Godolphin. With great skill, he had always managed to keep the moderate Tories (of whom he was one) toeing the line. Although it was obvious that he could not welcome an overflow of Whigs into the Government who might threaten his position, Sarah had no evidence that he was acting contrary to her husband's wishes; and her husband refused to think ill of him. So Sarah went slogging on, trying to make the Queen see reason about Sunderland. In the end she lost her restraint; she wrote to Anne enumerating the risks her husband was taking on Her Majesty's behalf, then proceeded to a sweeping indictment of the Stuarts, which was particularly galling because it was true.

> I desire you would reflect whether you have never heard that the greatest misfortunes that ever happen'd to any of your family has not been occasion'd by having ill advises & an obstinacy in their tempers that is very unaccountable.[14]

Early in December the Queen capitulated and appointed Lord Sunderland one of her two Secretaries of State; but she deeply resented the pressure applied to her, and was determined to seize the first opportunity to stop this dangerous trend.

Once again the Duke of Marlborough returned to England a hero; once again Parliament voted its thanks and gave him a handsome reward. This time it was the pension of £5,000 a year, refused in 1702 and settled for life in 1704, which now was granted in perpetuity. The statute stated that it should go for ever to his heirs, male or female, 'in order that the memory of those deeds should never lack one of his name to bear it.'[15]

Although Marlborough was the most celebrated figure in Europe, and one of the richest men in the world (he saved three-quarters of his annual income of £60,000), he did not change his way of life. Sarah and he were still without a London house, living in the free lodgings in St James's Palace provided by the sovereign. Indeed, the Duke's parsimony was rapidly becoming legendary as the public loved to fasten on the foibles of the great. As a result, all the stories of meanness ever invented began to be attributed to Marlborough. People repeated patently ridiculous tales: how when Marlborough's private carriage was not available he borrowed sixpence from a friend, then pocketed it and walked home through the rain; how when a messenger arrived at the Duke's tent in the middle of the night and His Grace learned that the communication was not to be read but to be delivered by word of mouth, he said, 'Then put out the lantern'; how when the Commander-in-Chief's gaiters were so drenched they had to be cut off, he insisted on having them ripped down the seams so they could be sewn up again. Finally, there is the story of a general trying to read one of Marlborough's letters aloud to Prince Eugene; when he stumbled over the words and explained that the Duke had not dotted his i's or crossed his t's, Eugene remarked drily: 'That saved ink.'

The Duke's niggardliness about money did not extend to the wonderful palace being built for him at Woodstock. He had already started collecting fabrics and treasures for it from all over Europe. He was so delighted with de Vos's tapestry that he commissioned the artist to depict all the great battle scenes of his many campaigns. At Antwerp he bought a set of hangings that William III had greatly fancied for £1,800; and when the Duke's army besieged and captured Tournai the following year, Marlborough made off with the immense bust of Louis XIV which stood over the gateway. Eventually it was placed on the roof of Blenheim, where it stands to this day.

In these circumstances it is not surprising that Marlborough was always badgering Sarah to speed up the work on Blenheim. Yet his distinguished, forty-one-year-old architect, John Vanbrugh, was exasperatingly slow – no doubt because he had more than one string to his bow. A famous playwright as well as an architect, Vanbrugh was the author of such brilliant Restoration comedies as *The Relapse* and *The Provok'd Wife*,* plays so witty and timeless that they are still being performed today. Vanbrugh hero-worshipped Marlborough and was enchanted by what he called 'the more than common delight the Duke had from the beginning being taken in this work at Woodstock.' He knew the joy it would give Marlborough to be told that the gardens had actually been started and in 1705 reported: 'The Garden wall was set ago-ing the same day with the House: and I hope it will be done against Your Grace's return, all but the coping which 'twill not be right to Set till next Spring.'16

For the next ten years, thousands of trees and shrubs and flowers poured into the estate, proving that the charm of a garden is the fact that it is never finished. Although the edifice seemed to grow very slowly, Godolphin wrote in September 1706 that 'the building is so far advanc'd that one may see perfectly how it will be when it is don.'

---

* A critic wrote that *The Provok'd Wife* was 'a piece of the indecencies of which ought to explode it out of all reputable society'.

Sarah, on the other hand, found fault with everything, and the Duke retorted, '. . . the great fault I find is that I shall never live to see it finished. . . .' Marlborough had a point, for in 1707 Vanbrugh suddenly changed the order from Doric to Corinthian, which meant that there was more pulling down than building up. But when Sarah complained that it was all too big and unwieldy, Marlborough replied that as it would be 'a monument of the Queen's favour and the approbation of my services to posterity, I can't disapprove of the model.'[17]

The very mention of the word 'approbation' seemed to tempt Fate, which immediately sent everything spinning in the wrong direction. 1707 proved to be a cruel disappointment. First of all, Louis XIV, annoyed that his peace efforts had failed, managed to field a formidable fighting force and to breathe new fire into it. Marshal Vendôme and the Elector of Bavaria again worked as co-commanders; with 100,000 troops under their command, they were instructed by the Great King to recover Huy and Liège but not to risk a battle with Marlborough; Marshal Tessé, with 8,000 men in the south of France, was told to stand on the defensive; Marshal Villars, with 40,000 men, to take the offensive against the Margrave of Bayreuth (the military successor of Louis of Baden, who had died of blood-poisoning). The Duke of Orléans and Marshal Berwick, with a large Franco–Spanish army, were ordered to clear the Allies out of Valencia and Aragon.

The Duke of Marlborough's offensive – which he called the 'Great Design' – was organized to deal with all Louis's schemes at once. He planned it with the precision of an artist. The centrepiece would be a combined operation of army and navy against the great Mediterranean naval base of Toulon. The Duke calculated that, as soon as the threat became apparent, the French would rush troops from Spain, Germany and Flanders to defend the port. The British navy liked the idea and gave the Duke full backing. This support was more or less a foregone conclusion as Admiral George Churchill, Marlborough's younger brother, was director of naval operations, a position equivalent to the First Sea Lord of modern times.

Admiral George did everything he could to further his brother's naval schemes. He threw himself into the Toulon plan, echoing Marlborough's contention that if the port could be captured, the Allies would be able to drive deep into the heart of France and bring Louis XIV to the peace-table as a supplicant. England and Holland were delighted to co-operate in a joint naval venture and the Emperor

Joseph agreed to allow Eugene – the key figure in the plan – to lead the land attack. However, in the next breath, he threw a spoke in the wheel. Before he could release Eugene, the Prince must occupy Naples. Marlborough did everything in his power to dissuade Joseph, even promising him the help of the Maritime naval fleet if he would postpone his Italian venture until Toulon had been taken, but the Emperor refused to listen. What was disappointing was that Prince Eugene himself showed very little enthusiasm for the Toulon operation, probably because he was a land animal who knew next to nothing about sea power. So Marlborough, who had hoped to see the Toulon assault started in May, was forced to sit back twiddling his thumbs until Prince Eugene was free to begin his march from Italy.

Meanwhile, one blow after another fell on him. In Spain, Lord Galway made an appalling blunder. On 24 April 1707, with only 13,000 troops, he attacked Marshal Berwick's army of 25,000 men at Almanza. The result was not only a disaster for Galway but for the Allies' hopes of settling Charles III on the Spanish throne. The massive defeat opened the way for the Duke of Orléans to sweep northwards into Aragon and Berwick to sweep south to Valencia, capturing town after town. The Allies were left finally with only a toe-hold in Catalonia and were back where they had started three years earlier. At the time no one could have known that Berwick's victory would prove to be a watershed. Marlborough sent reinforcements from Flanders, but the army in Spain never re-established its ascendancy for any length of time. Indeed, Marlborough's nephew was destined to go into the history books as 'the Marshal Duke of Berwick who saved the Bourbon Succession'. Winston Churchill of the Board of the Green Cloth had bred a formidable strain!

A week after Almanza came news of a second disaster, this time on the Rhine. Marshal Villars launched a masterly surprise attack, captured the famous Lines of Stollhofen and advanced as far as Stuttgart. This meant that once again even the Danube was threatened. Only in Marlborough's theatre was the French army quiet, as Louis had forbidden his marshals to chance their arm against the brilliant English general. At home Sarah could not know that John was both idle and safe. She worried constantly. Was his army on the move? Was he taking part in another cavalry charge? In June she forwarded one of Godolphin's letters to John on which she scribbled a postscript. It was only a single sentence and, because it was at the end of an official paper, it survived destruction, giving us a glimpse of the tenderness that Sarah refused to let the world see: 'God send good news of you my dearest life.'

Now, more than ever, the Toulon plan was of vital importance. Yet it was not until July 1707 that Eugene's army of 35,000 men began their search. But although the distance was only ninety miles, he did not reach the outskirts of the city for twenty-six days. Seventy warships under two British admirals lay off the coast, eager to give every assistance, but Eugene's heart was not in the project. Furthermore he resented the entreaties of the admirals to make haste to besiege the fortress before the defences were complete. Instead, he insisted on opening formal trenches, an operation that took days of preparation.

Marlborough, who could do nothing but watch and wait from his headquarters in Flanders, began to suffer from headaches. 'I have been uneasy in my head,' he wrote on 4 August, 'but if the siege of Toulon goes properly, I shall be cured of all diseases except old age.'[18] Alas, the siege did not go well; in fact it did not go at all. After sitting around for three weeks staring at the obstacles in front of them, Prince Eugene and the Duke of Savoy decided to march home again. The admirals, Eugene reported to Vienna on 14 August, 'insist on staking everything on the siege of Toulon, although the impossibility of success is as clear as daylight. . . .'[19]

On 21 August, Eugene's army struck its tents and in five columns began its march back to Italy. The fleet evacuated the guns, the sick and the wounded. The Toulon adventure had collapsed. Although it was a crucial blow, it did not affect Marlborough's friendship with the Prince. He felt that the Emperor had delayed the project so long by his selfishness over Naples that he had ruined Eugene's chances. It is not surprising that when Marlborough returned to England four months later Colonel Cranstoun found him 'much out of humour and peevish'. However, he could look back on one unequivocal success. That was when he had travelled to Altranstädt to charm the young warrior-king of Sweden. He delighted Charles XII with praise of his military prowess and urged the spirited young monarch to suspend his quarrel with the Emperor Joseph over Saxony – very troublesome for the Grand Alliance – and to turn his attention to Russia. Charles accepted his advice to the great benefit of the Allies but, unfortunately for Charles and Sweden, the King suffered a calamitous defeat at the hands of Peter the Great.

When the Duke returned to England in December 1707 he found trouble on the home front to make him even more 'peevish' than he was abroad. This was because Sarah's war was proving even more disastrous than his own campaign. Gone were the days when Mrs

Morley clamoured for Mrs Freeman's company and told her she really believed that 'one kind word from Mrs Freeman would save me if I was Gasping'.[20] When Sarah was alone with Anne she could not mistake the air of aloofness or the faint trace of embarrassment. At first Sarah ascribed their strained relations to political quarrels and was confident that she could get things back to the old footing. But when the Duumvirs (as the Whigs called Marlborough and Godolphin) began to complain that Anne seemed reluctant to gratify requests essential to the war effort, Sarah's wits sharpened. The Sunderland issue was followed by fierce inter-party wrangles over the distribution of bishoprics, and it was worrying to see that on more than one occasion the Queen ignored Godolphin's requests and bowed ostentatiously to Tory demands.

Suddenly, in the middle of 1707, Sarah stumbled on the answer. At first she could scarcely believe her senses. Although she had been suspicious of Robert Harley for some time, the last person to cross her mind as a possible adversary was her humble, twenty-eight-year-old cousin, Abigail Hill, whom she had persuaded the Queen to take as a bedchamber-woman. Yet now she discovered that Abigail had become Anne's 'favourite', and that Harley was using her to further his own ambitions. The reader will recall that ten years earlier Sarah had befriended the four children of Mrs Hill, who was one of her father's many sisters. Mrs Hill had married an Englishman who traded in the Levant and had gone bankrupt. She had appealed for help and Sarah had found places for the cousins she had never seen.

As Abigail played a crucial part in the lives of the Marlboroughs, the lowly duties that she performed for the Queen assume unusual importance. A sharp line was drawn between 'ladies of the bedchamber' – aristocrats who stood around and supervised the work done by menials – and 'bedchamber-women'. Some years later Abigail Hill wrote a description of the post which gave her a place in history:

The bedchamber-woman came in to waiting before the Queen's prayers which was before Her Majesty was dressed. The Queen often shifted in a morning: if Her Majesty shifted at noon the bedchamber-*lady* being by the bedchamber-*woman* gave the shift to the *lady* without any ceremony, and the *lady* put it on. Sometimes, likewise the bedchamber-*woman* gave the fan to the *lady* in the same manner; and this was all that the bedchamber-*lady* did about the Queen at her dressing.

When the Queen washed her hands, the page of the back-stairs brought and set down upon a side table the basin and ewer; then the bedchamber-*woman* set it before the Queen, and knelt on the other side of the table over against the Queen, the bedchamber-*lady* only looking on. The bedchamber-*woman* poured the water out of the ewer upon the Queen's hands.

The bedchamber-*woman* pulled on the Queen's gloves, when she could not do it herself.

The page of the back-stairs was called in to put on the Queen's shoes.[21]

None of the bedchamber-women were of gentle birth except for Mrs Danvers, who was the daughter of Lord Chandos 'but who had lost the advantage of her birth by marrying a tradesman'.[22] Nevertheless, Mrs Danvers's presence made the position respectable and Abigail was pleased to accept it when it was offered. According to Swift, Mistress Hill was 'a person of plain sound understanding, of great truth and sincerity . . . full of love, duty and veneration for the Queen her mistress.'[23] The Earl of Dartmouth saw her in a far less rosy light, describing her as 'exceedingly mean and vulgar in her manners, of very unequal temper, childishly exceptious and passionate.'[24] Despite the difference in these two opinions, no one doubts that Abigail knew how to make herself agreeable to her royal benefactress.

Sarah discovered Abigail's close relationship with the Queen by accident. Someone told her that her cousin had married Mr Masham, who had been a courtier for twenty years and, according to Sarah, was 'a soft, good-natured, insignificant man, always making low bows to everyone and ready to skip to open a door.'[25] Sarah asked her cousin if it was true she had married and Abigail 'owned it was and begged my pardon for having concealed it from me.' Sarah then offered to help her break the news to the Queen and Abigail looked up at the ceiling in confusion and said she believed the bedchamber-woman had already told her. By this time Sarah was annoyed and asked the Queen why she had not been informed of her cousin's marriage. 'All the answer I could obtain from her Majesty', wrote Sarah, 'was this, I have a hundred times bid Masham tell you but she would not.'[26]

Sarah was quite shocked by these revelations and pursued her enquiries still further. Very soon all the pieces had fallen into position, and Sarah was able to date the first display of the Queen's favour to Abigail from the royal visit to Bath in 1703. Mrs Danvers, the aristocratic bedchamber-woman, told Sarah that Mrs Hill (Abigail) disliked the lodging she was assigned and told the Queen that she would 'sett-up' all night.

Upon which [wrote Sarah] there was the most rediculous scene as Mrs Danvers acted it and that ever I saw, of Mrs Hills sorley ill-bred manner & the Queen going about the room after her & begging her to goe to bed, calling her Dear Hill twenty times over.[27]

Sarah soon had a chance to appraise the situation herself. On one occasion she went to the Queen's bedchamber by a secret passage and was having a private talk with her Majesty when Abigail burst in 'with the gayest air possible, but upon seeing sight of me stopped; and immediately, changing her manner, and making the most solemn courtesy, *did your Majesty ring*? And then went out again.'[28]

When one considers the Queen's wretched health, it is not difficult to understand her dependence on Abigail. The latter was cheerful and adaptable and a first-rate nurse. She had no education and no pretentions, but she did her best to make the poor Queen comfortable and above all offered her the companionship that Sarah had not given her for many months. Furthermore, she had a gift for mimicry and a talent for the harpsichord, both of which were said to assuage Her Majesty's pain! In less than a week's time, the Duchess of Marlborough tells us,

> I discovered that my cousin had become an absolute favourite; that the Queen herself was present at her marriage in Dr Arbuthnot's lodgings . . .; that Mrs Masham came often to the Queen when the Prince was asleep, and was two hours every day in private with her.[29]

A bizarre part of this story was the fact that Robert Harley suddenly discovered that through Abigail's father, the impecunious Mr Hill, he too was a cousin of Abigail. He did not become aware of the relationship until she entered the Queen's service and showed her potential usefulness. Sarah tells us angrily that she discovered 'beyond all dispute Mr Harley's correspondence and interest at Court by means of this woman.'[30] Sarah was not someone who understood reticence and immediately confronted Abigail, accusing her of trying to alienate the Queen's affections. 'To this she very gravely answered', wrote Sarah,

> that she was sure the Queen, who had loved me extreamly, would always be very kind to me. It was some minutes before I could recover from the surprise with which so extraordinary an answer struck me. To see a woman, whom I had raised out of the dust, put on such a superior air, and to hear her reassure me, by way of consolation, that the Queen would always be very kind to me![31]

Sarah's fury at being superseded by her drab, unprepossessing cousin unbalanced her. Some writers ascribe her lack of control to the menopause; others to the death of her son. It is simpler, however, and probably just as convincing to put it down to humiliation. That one

of the most unselfish acts in her life (helping the penniless Hills) had
proved to be her undoing, was insupportable. Even worse was the fact
that it had been accomplished by a cousin whom she considered
beneath her notice! Chagrin and resentment took possession of her
and she deluged the Queen with furious criticisms of the
'bedchamber-woman'. Finally, even Sarah decided she might have
gone too far. 'You seem'd soe much offended when I nam'd my cousin
Hill's speaking to you of business', she wrote to the Queen, 'that I
have a mind to explain that . . . I doe believe she does not directly
medle in anything of that nature but without knowing it, or intending
it, she is one occasion of feeding Mrs Morley's passion for Torrys.
. . .'[32]

The Queen replied in what Winston Churchill describes as 'a
masterpiece of sarcasm and polished hostility.'

> Your Cousin Hill, who is very far from being an occasion of feeding Mrs
> Morley in her passion (as you are pleased to call it) she never medeled in
> anything. I believe others that have bin in her Station in former Reigns
> have been tateling and very impertinent but she is not at all that temper.
> . . .[33]

None of this improved Sarah's temper and when she next ran into
the hated Abigail she gave her a thunderous look which the latter
described to Robert Harley: 'As she passed by me I had a very low
curtsey which I returned in the same manner, but not one word passed
between us and, as for her looks, indeed they are not to be described
by any mortal but her own self.'[34]

Nothing could stop Sarah's pen from scribbling its way across sheet
after sheet of paper for the Queen's attention. Finally, Anne begged
her not to mention

> that person Abigail any more who are pleased to call ye object of my
> favour for whatever caracter ye Malittious world may give her, I do assure
> you it will never have any weight with me, knowing She does not deserve
> it, nor I can never change ye good impressions you once gave me of her,
> unless She should give me Cause, which I am very sure She never will.[35]

Sarah probably knew that she was attempting the impossible in
trying to influence her mistress against Abigail. Anne's feelings for
her favourites were intense and emotional. To defend them became
almost a point of honour with her, as Sarah herself had seen years
earlier. 'There is nothing she will not disown, dissemble or deny',
the Duchess had written, 'if she bee but prepared for it by those that

she has a passion for.'[36] Sarah knew what she was talking about, for in her day she had not only persuaded Anne to give up her rights to succeed her sister on the throne in favour of William, but influenced her to oppose her father and put the idea into her head that her stepmother's son had been smuggled into her bed in a warming-pan. She therefore was fully aware of what she was up against when she discovered that Abigail had become 'an absolute favourite'.

By this time Abigail and Harley had merged in her mind as 'the enemy' – a formidable enemy bent on ruining her husband and her friend Godolphin. She still had no real evidence against Harley, but the fact that he was hand-in-glove with Abigail was enough to make her hate him. 'The mischievous darkness of his soul', she declared, 'was written in his countenance.' Lord Cowper described him in the same vein, as Harley was a singularly unattractive man who made his way in the world by fawning, flattering and deceiving. His best points were that he was a hard worker, a good judge of people and clever at persuading uncongenial men to co-operate with one another. This was why he had proved so useful to Marlborough and Godolphin. His worst quality was his falseness – he refused to deal openly with people and, as Lord Cowper pointed out, employed tricks 'even when not necessary but . . . from an inner satisfaction at applauding his own cunning.'[37] Sarah summed him up with a sweep of the hand: 'He was a cunning and a dark man of too small qualities to do much good but of all the qualities required to do mischief.'[38]

As early as June 1707 Sarah was writing to John that Harley was 'doing hurt' to England by encouraging the Queen in her dislike of the Whigs; by August Godolphin was echoing the same theme. Marlborough suddenly had a vision of himself being thrust into another period of humiliating inactivity by discord at home and abroad. He wrote fiercely to Godolphin in November, threatening to hand over his command in Flanders to George of Hanover rather than be made to look a fool by remaining idle. If things, he stressed in his letter 'should go as I think they will both in England and Holland nothing shall prevail with me to lose the reputation I have hazarded in this war.'[39]

But this was only a mood and by the time Marlborough returned to England in December he was determined to impose his will. He had plenty of weight when he chose to exert it. Despite his frustrating campaign, his prestige had been mounting steadily – 'the greatest man in Europe', his admirers said. So many people clamoured to see him that when he was in London he held regular levees (a practice he had begun in Brussels), which were as crowded as those of a sovereign. He even followed the example of Louis XIV by receiving in his bedroom. 'Every morning when he is in London,' the Genoese envoy reported to his government, 'he has in his antechamber gentlemen of the first quality including ambassadors and ministers of foreign princes; he dresses, even shaves, and puts on his shirt in public.' This routine excited a great deal of criticism but Marlborough managed to allay some of it by his unexpected modesty.' He behaves', the Genoese envoy concluded, 'in a manner calculated to offend no one at least by words, and affects a gentle and gracious air with all.'[40]

Whatever is said of Robert Harley, it cannot be denied that he was a man of exceptional courage. To take on a titan like Marlborough, backed by the tigerish Sarah and the tenacious Godolphin, was no minor resolve. Harley's weapons were not plentiful but they were formidable. For months he had been sympathizing with Anne over attempts by Whigs to try and wrest political power from her hands. Anne was a timorous woman who genuinely feared the Whigs. To her they were a rough lot who basically cared nothing for the monarchy. They had shown that they were perfectly willing to throw out one sovereign and substitute another when their policies demanded it. The Tories, on the other hand, not only believed in the monarchy but had a sentimental leaning towards 'the Divine Right of Kings' and every- thing that implied. Furthermore, they were the protectors of her blessed Anglican Church. The war was the stumbling-block. Anne had to admit that the Whigs were more bellicose than the Tories, but ever since the great victory of Ramillies Anne had felt safe; and the warm glow of security had persuaded her (secretly) that the time had come for peace. Her advisers told her that the fighting must continue and she paid lip service to this unhappy fact; but in her heart peace was what she wanted and peace was what she intended to have. Even on this issue Harley was sympathetic, suggesting that perhaps the Duke had a vested interest in the war because of the vast financial returns it brought him.

The struggle between Marlborough and Harley did not come to a head until the Duke had been home for nearly six weeks. As the union between England and Scotland had been signed and sealed in May, Marlborough arrived back in London in December 1707 to take part in the first session of the first Parliament of the United Kingdom of Great Britain. After a debate on the progress of the war, both Houses passed a resolution endorsing 'No Peace Without Spain', the slogan that gave the whole of the Spanish Empire to Charles, and Charles alone. Thus the nation departed officially from William III's 'partition' solution. The irony was that the impossibility of the new war aim was already becoming evident. For years the Spanish people had been indifferent as to which monarch – Bourbon or Habsburg – was foisted upon them. But after the battle of Almanza they had rallied fiercely to the side of Philip and taken him to their hearts – he was now the idol of the nation. Although three years earlier Marlborough had confided his personal misgivings to Heinsius about abandoning partition, he seems to have bowed to the pressure of the Whigs (mesmerized by the prospect of huge trade advantages) for he made no protest in the Lords. On the contrary, he gave his full support to the foolish war aim that was destined to bring about his downfall.

Meanwhile, Harley was scurrying around secretly trying to form a new government composed of moderates from both parties – Queen Anne's dream of an ideal ministry. Naturally, Harley saw himself as the first minister of the new combination which meant the expulsion of Lord Godolphin. Therefore, when the House of Commons was probing the cause of the Allied defeat at Almanza, Harley's right-hand man, Henry St John, Secretary of State for War, committed what the Duumvirs thought was a calculated 'indiscretion'. He blurted out that, of the 29,000 men voted by Parliament for service in Spain, only 9,000 had been present at the battle of Almanza. Behind the scenes, the blame was put squarely on an administrative blunder on the part of Lord Godolphin.

The crisis had arrived. On Sunday evening Marlborough and Godolphin and Sarah visited the Queen and told her that unless she dismissed Mr Harley they would have to offer their own resignations. Each one saw her separately and, although she appeared to accept the departure of Godolphin with composure, and of Sarah with relief, she begged the Duke to change his mind. 'If you doe, my Lord, resign your sword, let me tell you you will run it through my head.'[41] She implored and wept, and for a moment even appeared to be suffocating, but she refused to alter her course, obdurately clinging to Harley. This gives us a clear picture of Anne's stubbornness in defending her 'rights'. Harley had promised her a government of moderate Tories, while all that Godolphin could do was to enslave her with hated Whigs. All thoughts of the war, all thoughts of the years of loyal service were put aside as she battled for what she considered her sovereign rights.

Small wonder that Harley was in a buoyant mood when he attended the Cabinet Council following these interviews. The Queen seated herself in her State chair at the head of the table and Harley opened the business of the meeting. While he talked, the other members turned to each other with uneasy looks and, after a few

minutes, the Duke of Somerset, a moderate Whig, interposed, declaring that he could not imagine what business could be done as
'neither the General nor the Treasurer were there'. This was one
report. According to Swift he was much more blunt, simply pointing
at Harley and saying: 'If your Majesty suffers that fellow to treat of
affairs of the war without the General, I cannot serve you.'[42] The
others murmured their approval and the meeting broke up in confusion. Apparently, that night Prince George pointed out to his wife
the dangers of the step she had taken and within twenty-four hours
Harley was dismissed and both Marlborough and Godolphin were
reinstated.

A number of ministers followed Harley into the wilderness, leaving
a vacuum for the hungry Whigs to fill. The most conspicuous departure was that of Henry St John. He idolized Marlborough and had
been thrilled to serve him during the years of Blenheim and Ramillies.
But now that the choice seemed to be between serving Marlborough
or taking a step that might lead to the Tory leadership, he followed
Harley, the 'dear master' who had brought him into the Government.
Henry Boyle, a Whig moderate, replaced Harley; and Robert
Walpole, another Whig, replaced St John. Even the position of Chancellor of the Exchequer went to a Whig, John Smith. From now on, no
one in the Government, including Lord Godolphin, would oppose the
policies of the Junto.

The Queen was humiliated at losing her power struggle and did not
recover her spirits for many months. Letters to and from Harley show
that he did not see the Queen for nearly eight months, despite Sarah's
claim to the contrary. Abigail wrote to him in the summer of 1708
telling him that the Queen was still so mortified by her defeat that she
was afraid to take an independent line.

> Oh my poor Aunt Stephens [the Queen] is to be pitied very much, they
> press her harder than ever; since what happened lately she is altered more
> than is to be imagined, no ready money [courage] at all to supply her with
> common necessaries.[43]

There were other things that frightened Anne as much as political
defeat. In March, Louis XIV lauched the twenty-year-old Pretender
(Anne's brother) on an invasion attempt. With an army of 6,000
soldiers he was to land in Scotland as 'James III' and try to start a civil
war over the union with England. For two days there was a real scare.
'The Duke of Marlborough, the Lord Treasurer and Lord Sunderland
went to Kensington at 5 in the morning and there was a counsel
summon'd immediately which met between 7 and 8.'[44] Later that day

the Queen informed the Lords that Admiral Byng was pursuing the French with a superior fleet; but that night she moved from Kensington Palace to St James's to be able to dispatch orders more easily. 'The Queen herself', declared Sarah, 'had terrible impressions about his coming in a forcible manner & showed the greatest signs of fear and concern about the matter. . . .'[45] The Queen quickly recovered her composure when news came that Byng had captured one of the Pretender's ships and driven the rest back to France.

The fright the Queen had suffered drew her closer to Marlborough and before he went abroad in April 1708 she asked him to help her with Sarah, who was causing a good deal of gossip by absenting herself from Court. 'She has taken a resolution not to come to me', she wrote to Marlborough,

> when I am alone and fancies that no one will notice the change. She may impose on some poor simple people, but how can she imagine she can on any that have a grain of sense? Can she think that the Duchess of Somerset and my Lady Fitzharding, who are two of the most observing, prying ladies in England, won't find out that she never comes near me nor looks on me as she used to do, that the tatling voice will not in a little time make us the jest of the town?[46]

But when John showed this letter to Sarah she pushed it aside saying that Mrs Morley was 'always the greatest decembler [dissembler] in the world', ready to 'act a part and say anything that was not true.' And on 10 April, when the Queen wrote to 'Mrs Freeman' regretting their quarrels, she shrugged it away and refused to reply.

> I am very sorry all I can say will not prevail with you to live with your faithfull Morley as we did seven years agoe, that being ye Manner I am & shall allways be desirous to live with you, & whenever you will be easy with me I will be soe too. . . . It has not bin my fault, that we have lived in ye Manner we have don ever since I came to the Crown. . . .[47]

Sarah was not wrong in doubting the Queen's goodwill. She knew that Anne could not afford to lose the services of her Captain-General and rightly suspected that she was merely trying to put the relationship with 'Mrs Freeman' on an easier footing until she felt strong enough to dispense with both Marlboroughs.

That same April a general election was held which for the first time gave the Whigs a large majority. The result was a direct challenge to the Queen's cherished prerogative of choosing her own ministers regardless of party pressure – how much longer could she refuse office to the hated Whig leaders? Inwardly seething that the independence for which she had struggled throughout her reign was in the process of being destroyed by the 'mercyless men', she stubbornly resolved to go on fighting – in the spirit if not in the flesh. She would bide her time and wait for her revenge.

Once again Marlborough was looking for a knock-out battle that would bring the war to an end. He proposed that the Elector of Hanover, the future George I of England, should take command of the army of the Rhine; that Prince Eugene should operate on the Moselle; and that he, Marlborough, would command in Flanders. At a given moment, Eugene would march through the night, link up with the Duke and together, with an army of 120,000 men, they would fall on the French and try to put an end to the war.

Meanwhile Louis XIV had resolved on equally drastic action. Encouraged by the gains of 1707, and annoyed that his peace terms had been rejected, he decided to make an attempt to retrieve all that he had lost in the Spanish Netherlands. For this great enterprise he chose his bastard cousin, the Duke of Vendôme (a grandson of Henri IV) and his own twenty-five-year-old grandson, the Duke of Burgundy, son of the Dauphin.

At fifty-four, Vendôme was old, fat and bestial. He was bisexual – anyone or anything could assuage his needs – but, as he was also a superb warrior, the King refused to hear a word against him. However, any man less likely to appeal to the fastidious Duke of Burgundy would have been hard to find. Vendôme always wore a shirt bespattered with tobacco which he refused to change more than once a week and often received his visitors seated on his *chaise percée*. Although Burgundy was the nominal commander, being a Prince of the Blood, Vendôme was the acknowledged leader. He was infuriated therefore when the royal whippersnapper argued with him and occasionally even had the audacity to countermand his orders. Indeed, one can say that Marlborough's great victory at Oudenarde – still in the future – was due not only to the skill of Eugene and himself but to the incessant quarrelling between the French commanders.

At first, things went badly for Marlborough. First, the Emperor found so many things for Eugene to do that the latter was not able to leave Coblenz to join him until the end of June; second, Marlborough was again suffering from severe headaches which developed into a fever so that he could barely sit on his horse; third, the French mounted a surprise attack which caught him off-balance.

Belgium, which the Duke had wrested from the French, was seething with discontent over the Dutch rule to which they were now subjected. The French army was fully briefed on this and suddenly sent a small detachment of troops to Ghent; without a shot being fired the gates were opened by conspiracy within, and the town went back to France. On the same day a similar scene took place at Bruges, and a few days later the French army took up protected positions behind the Bruges canal. 'The States', wrote the Duke to Godolphin, 'have used this country so ill that I no way doubt that all the towns will play us up the same trick as Ghent has done whenever they have it in their power.'[48]

This sudden, unexpected French coup, combined with Marlborough's poor health, plunged the Duke into deep gloom. No doubt the underlying cause of his depression was the Queen's alienation – perhaps, for a while, it all seemed too much to bear. When Prince Eugene finally joined his comrade-in-arms he was astonished at the plight in which he found him. Marlborough talked about the loss of Ghent and Bruges as being utterly 'ruinous' to their campaign. He stressed the fact that Ghent was the key to all the waters and riverways of Flanders and that Bruges was only a trifle less important. Eugene was full of gaiety and did his best to cheer him up. Brigadier Grumbkow, the Prussian commissary at the British headquarters, wrote to Frederick I that the Prince

> drew me aside and asked me what exactly all this meant. The Duke was incomprehensively exhausted and talked as though everything was lost, which the Prince did not consider appropriate, for unless he [Marlborough] lost his life we should with God's help obtain satisfaction. This morning My lord Duke had a severe fever and was so ill that he had to be bled. . . .[49]

Natzmer, the Prussian cavalry general, also remarked on Marlborough's distress over the Flanders losses but added that Prince Eugene's 'timely arrival raised the spirits of the army again and consoled us.' The 'two Princes', as they were now known, closeted themselves and after a few hours emerged with their plans co-ordinated. It was clear that the enemy's next move would be to occupy the town of Lessines, on the River Dender, then to besiege and capture Oudenarde, a town twenty miles from Ghent. The Duke and the Prince therefore decided to try and reach Lessines before the enemy so that they could cross the Scheldt and sever Vendôme's communications with his main bases at Lille and Tournai.

However, on the evening of 7 July, Marlborough collapsed and was carried to bed. The orders for the 8th went forward as agreed, issued by General Overkirk. 'His Grace', wrote Hare on the night of the 8th, 'has been confined to his bed today by a hot fever fit, but something he took in the afternoon carried it off with a gentle sweat and he was much mended.' On the 9th, Marlborough was riding his horse in front of his men. 'In all appearance', stated Hare with relief, 'he was very well.'[50]

The timetable rolled forward according to plan. Marlborough and Eugene formed a junction at Herfelingen and marched swiftly to Lessines, bivouacking there on the 10th. At one o'clock the following morning Marlborough sent his Chief-of-Staff, the burly, jovial Brigadier Cadogan, along the Oudenarde road with sixteen battalions of British infantry, and eight squadrons of Hanoverian dragoons commanded by the future George II of England. He also had the whole of the pontoon-train and a strong detachment of pioneers. His instructions were to construct five pontoon-bridges across the River Scheldt just below Oudenarde. After a march of fifteen miles they saw below them the valley with the river winding through marshes, and the little fortress-town of Oudenarde in the distance. Far more interesting, however, was the sight of the French army, six miles away, encamped above the heights of Gavre. Cadogan had won the race with time to spare and speedily set about constructing his bridges. Each pontoon was about seventeen feet long, and was carried upside-down on special wagons. Made of wood, most of them were sheathed with copper plates, and referred to as 'tin boats'. They had to be launched into the water and anchored at set intervals. When they were linked by beams, a plank roadway was built on top of them.

If Burgundy and Vendôme had been on more amicable terms, they might have spotted what was going on and mounted an attack to push Cadogan's men into the water; but the French commanders were too far apart in spirit to concert the simplest plans. Burgundy was a sensitive young man who preferred the mirrored ballroom of Versailles to the battlefield. He saw nothing amusing in fighting a war, and did it simply because his grandfather insisted on it. Vendôme, on the other hand, gloried in everything to do with the army and liked descending into the maelstrom and fighting hand-to-hand. As a result his soldiers would follow him anywhere. According to one writer:

> At the front Vendôme paraded gluttony, sloth, sodomy and practically all the deadly sins – and amused the soldiers who adored him . . . the holy set at Versailles said that God would never bestow victory on one so wicked. Vendôme got to hear of this and observed that he did not imagine that Marlborough went to church much more than he did.[51]

As soon as Cadogan began to lay his bridges, he sent a messenger back to Marlborough at a gallop to tell him the way was clear. The

Allied army, which numbered about 80,000 men (almost the same as that of the enemy) and consisted of English, German, Dutch, Scandinavian and Huguenot troops, came forward at a tremendous pace to make sure of crossing the Scheldt before the enemy. Marlborough had trained his infantry to march briskly, despite their heavy packs, and now, although they felt they had been moving at breakneck pace, the Duke politely requested them 'to please step out'. 'It was no longer a march,' wrote one observer, 'but a run.' Strict orders were issued that wagons carrying the baggage of generals and other high persons were not to be allowed on the roads until the army had passed; whenever a breach occurred, the soldiers simply hurled the wagon from the track and confiscated whatever spoils they could carry.

When they reached Cadogan's pontoons and in the far distance saw the white coats of Louis's splendid army crossing the river in a leisurely fashion, their enthusiasm knew no bounds. The red-coated Foot ran across the bridges despite the heavy weight they were carrying, while the blue-coated Prussian Horse went over at full gallop. When the French scouts reported back to the Duke of Vendôme at half-past one that Marlborough's main army was crossing the Scheldt, the Frenchman could scarcely believe it. 'If they are there, the Devil must have carried them; such marching is impossible.'[52] In the past sixty hours they had covered fifty miles.

The battle of Oudenarde was about to begin, and from the first, the dissensions in the French camp played into the Allies' hands. Vendôme gave orders for seven Swiss battalions to occupy the village of Heurne in preparation for an attack, but Burgundy interposed (perhaps quite rightly) and gave orders for a line to be formed at a different place. Unfortunately for the Swiss, nobody bothered to inform them of the counter-order and they occupied the village of Eyne, waiting for further instructions. An hour later the British infantry moved forward until they were within twenty yards of the Swiss. Then there was a roar of musketry and the battle was joined. The Swiss, angry at having been forgotten and left on their own, surrendered with no more ado.

The battle that now ensued was later described by experts as an 'encounter action'. It was unplanned and unco-ordinated. It did not take place in broad fields with troops drawn up in formal lines, but was a fierce, hand-to-hand affair, fought through villages, over ditches, across hedges and gardens and clumps of woods. 'The fight was very desperate on both sides,' wrote private Deane of the Foot Guards,

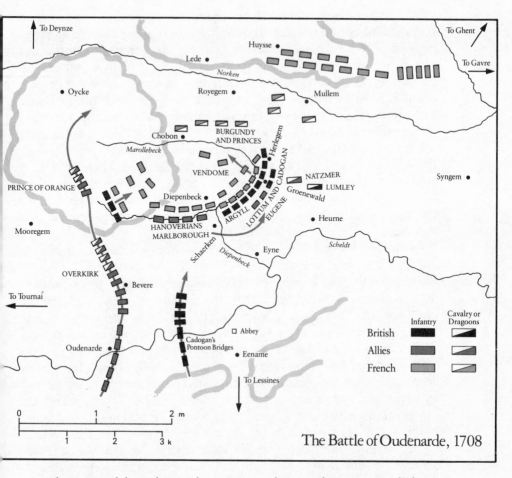

The Battle of Oudenarde, 1708

and continued from five in the evening as long as there was any light; in
which time the enemy was beat from hedge to hedge and breastwork to
breastwork . . . one would have thought it impossible for them to have lost
the battle, they having had time to secure themselves of strong ground as
they always do, getting into villages, possessing themselves of houses and
making every quickset hedge a slight wall that we cannot come at them.[53]

But Marlborough, with his usual intuition and brilliance, was reinforcing units here, withdrawing others there, and at the same time
slowly enveloping the enemy's forces. On the other side, Vendôme
had thrown himself into the maelstrom and was doing what he liked
best – hand-to-hand fighting – or, as one writer put it, 'crashing
around like an enraged animal'. The Duke of Burgundy, his brother,
the Duke of Berri, and the pathetic English 'Pretender' had set up

headquarters near the mill of Royegem. Here they were surrounded by the nobility and the military courtiers who gloried in accompanying Princes of the Blood to battle. There were hundreds of orderlies and valets and grooms holding the horses of the royal circle. The battle was raging along a wide crescent, a mile away, and the Princes could see the infantry locked in a fierce struggle with the innocent little puffs of smoke above them that meant musket-fire. At one point General Rantzau, with the Electoral Prince (later George II) in tow, and eight squadrons of Hanoverian horsemen, suddenly charged into the whole of the French cavalry flank on his right. There was wild confusion. The Prince's horse was shot from beneath him and one of his squadron commanders killed. Nevertheless, Rantzau got out of the maelstrom without serious loss; how much good he did no one was sure.

By this time Vendôme was in a fighting frenzy, determined to take Groenewald whatever the cost. At five o'clock he sent an order to Burgundy to bring the whole of the French left wing – 30,000 men – into action by attacking across the Ghent road to the east of Groenewald. This was a crucial order. The Allies had only twenty-eight squadrons of cavalry – Natzmer's 2,000 Prussian horsemen and Rantzau's 1,000 Hanoverian troopers, who were still re-forming. That was all. Morale was high but the defence would not have been able to withstand Burgundy's 30,000 men, horse and foot, supported by artillery. And defeat would have left General Cadogan and his 8,000 infantrymen an easy prey for a continued onslaught. The Duke of Burgundy, however, did not execute Vendôme's order. He was told by his Chief-of-Staff that the ground was so swampy it was impassable. So he sent an aide-de-camp to Vendôme, but the messenger was killed before he reached him, leaving the French Marshal in total ignorance of the fact that his left wing was not going to support him in his renewed attack on Cadogan.

Most military experts regard this mistake – and mistake it was, as there was no morasse that could have obstructed them – as the stroke of luck that won the battle for Marlborough. No one knows what could have happened if Cadogan had been driven back upon Eyne. If Vendôme had not been busy fighting, pike in hand 'like a private soldier rather than a Marshal of France charged with the supreme control of 90,800 men', he might well have ordered his troops to fall upon Cadogan in irresistible numbers.

Up to this point, the battle had been touch and go; now Marlborough turned his right wing over to Eugene and took charge of the left himself. The fighting was fierce and uncertain, and no one would have been happy to predict the outcome. 'We drove the enemy', wrote our old friend Millner, 'from ditch to ditch, from hedge to hedge, and out of one scrub to another in a great hurry and disorder.' Suddenly, Marlborough's encircling movement was seen to be gaining ground. Dusk had begun to fall when the Princes at the windmill saw, in the distance, the enemy driving all before them. The French cavalry in the fields wheeled to meet the shock. The troops of the French right, only a mile away, 'gave ground so fast', wrote Saint-Simon, 'that the valets of the suites of all who accompanied the Princes fell back upon them with an alarm, a rapidity and a confusion which swept them along . . . towards the main battle on the left.'[54] There, too, all was panic and disorder.

It was ten o'clock and pitch-black when the French commanders met in the village of Huysse on the high ground behind the River Norken. Although two-thirds of the army was ringed by a horseshoe of enemy troops, Marshal Vendôme appeared at last, dishevelled with the sweat of battle and furious with Burgundy, saying that they must continue the fight at first light. His staff officers tried to point out to him that two-thirds of the French army was caught in a horseshoe surrounded by enemy troops, but this did not appear to suffice. When Burgundy tried to speak, Vendôme told him to hold his tongue: 'Your Royal Highness must remember that you only came to this army upon condition that you obeyed me.'[55] Then he went on to remark scathingly, in reference to the idle left wing, 'I cannot comprehend how 50 battalions and 180 squadrons could be satisfied with observing us engaged for six hours and merely look at us as though watching the opera from a third-tier box.'[56] It would be difficult for a commander-in-chief to damn himself more thoroughly than this. Whose responsibility was it to see that the left wing played a part in the battle?

All Vendôme's officers declared that the army was in total disorder and their only recourse was to retreat to Ghent. 'Very well gentlemen,' said the Marshal, 'I see you all think it best to retire. And you, Monseigneur,' fixing the Duke of Burgundy with his bloodshot eyes, 'have long had that wish.'[57] With this insult he gave the order to retire, and made straight for Ghent where he slept for thirty hours. Large numbers of French troops made their way through the gaps in the enemy cordon and struck across the Scheldt towards France. Others surrendered to the Allies. Eugene hit upon a device by which Huguenot officers went into the darkness calling out the names of famous regiments: 'A moi, Picardie', 'A moi, Rousillon', thus taking hundreds more prisoners. Although Marlborough had at least 20,000 troops which had not been engaged and planned to continue the attack at dawn, the early morning light showed a battlefield on which there were only dead and wounded, or prisoners waiting to be rounded up.

Marshal Vendôme had not suffered the same casualties that Villeroy had sustained at Ramillies, but his army had been badly mauled. He had lost 6,000 men, killed or wounded, another 9,000 were taken prisoner, and a further 15,000 scattered around the countryside completely out of touch with their units. But the psychological effect of the defeat was far greater than the numbers suggested. 'I hope I have given such a blow to their Foot', Marlborough wrote to Godolphin the day after the battle, 'that they will not be able to fight any more. My head aches so terribly that I must say no more.'[58]

Needless to say, Marlborough had re-established the ascendancy which the French had challenged the year before; and, from the speed with which Vendôme and Burgundy had hurried their forces into the strong defensive position behind the Ghent–Bruges canal, it was not difficult to gauge the fear that the English commander again inspired. Indeed, Marlborough's invincibility was fast becoming a legend from one end of France to the other. Naughty children were told that if they did not behave, 'Malbrouk' would get them; and French women sang songs about *Malbrouk se va t'en guerre* – as though he was some sort of terrifying monster about to devour them. The awe his name aroused did not escape Marlborough's notice and he was delighted by it. 'That which is our greatest advantage', he wrote proudly to Godolphin, 'is the terror that is in their army. . . . The Duke of Vendôme's army is so frightened I am very confident if we could get them out of their entrenchments and from behind the canal . . . we should beat them with half their number. . . .'[59]

Once again Marlborough was in a buoyant mood. Headaches and depression vanished and he spent his evenings dining and wining with his officers. Apparently General Biron, a French officer who had been taken prisoner and lived at Allied headquarters for several days, was struck by 'an almost royal magnificence at Prince Eugene's quarters and a shameful parsimony at those of the Duke of Marlborough who ate the more often at the tables of others.'[60] Although Marlborough's baggage-train included all the wonderful table-silver and ornaments suitable to his position – including fabulous silver 'pilgrim bottles' for carrying wine on pack animals, engraved with his arms and the imperial eagle of a German princedom (a gift from the Emperor after Blenheim) – these spectacular pieces only saw the light of day when some visiting royalty appeared.

The Allied casualties at Oudenarde were comparatively light – only about 3,000 men – and Marlborough wrote happily to Sarah as soon as the battle was over:

> ... I thank God the English have suffered less than any of the other troops; none of the English horse having been engaged. I do, and you must, give thanks to God for his goodness in protecting and making me the instrument of so much happiness to the Queen and nation if she will please to make use of it.[61]

When the Queen heard the news, however, she did not respond joyfully, as she had after Blenheim and Ramillies. As long as the war continued she was a helpless victim of the Whigs. Although in numbers Oudenarde was the largest battle so far waged, and although it had been fought under unprecedented circumstances, Anne's first reaction was: 'Oh Lord, when will all this bloodshed cease?' Marlborough, of course, knew nothing of this as the Queen soon recovered herself and sent him one of her usual letters filled with thanks and gratitude. The Whigs, however, were determined to force the Queen to acknowledge their contribution to the war effort and to reward them accordingly. In an attempt to show their strength they put the story about that the Electoral Prince was planning a short visit to London. Anne became furiously agitated. The Elector George, who had commanded Marlborough's troops on the Rhine, and his son the Electoral Prince, who had fought so gallantly at Oudenarde, were both eager to come to England, if only for a few days to show themselves to their future subjects. But Anne was adamant: three weeks after the battle she wrote to Marlborough begging him to put such an idea out of the Prince's head, so that she would not be faced with the 'difficulty of refusing him leave to come if he should ask it, or forbidding him to come, if he should attempt it. . . . I cannot bear to have any successor here, though but for a week.'[62] No one could understand the Queen's reaction to such a harmless proposal. Did she still resent the Elector's unsatisfactory courtship of so many years ago? Or did she secretly harbour the notion that when she died her Stuart brother might succeed her? Whatever the answer, she managed to scotch the idea of a Hanoverian visit.

In the interim Sarah had forwarded to Kensington Palace a copy of the private letter that she had received from her husband, thanking God for the victory he had won for the Queen 'if she be pleased to make use of it'. Her Majesty at once wrote to the Duke asking him to explain his meaning. 'What I meant', he replied,

> is that you can make no good use of this victory, nor of any other blessing than by following the advice of my Lord Treasurer who has been so long faithful to you; for any other advisers do but lead you into a labyrinth, to play their own game at your expense. . . .[63]

The Queen in her reply denied that she was influenced 'by Mr Harley through a relation of his' and asked Marlborough why it was 'something very extraordinary' that she did not always adopt his opinions?

> And why then should it be wonderful that you and I should differ in some things, as well as other people, especially since my thoughts are the same of Whigs that ever they were from the time that ever I have been capable of having notions of things and people, and I must own I can see no reason to alter mine.[64]

Marlborough no longer had any doubt where they all stood. There was not a hint of reconciliation in the Queen's letter. 'The Tories', he wrote to Sarah, 'have got the heart and entire possession of the Queen, which they will be able to maintain as long as Mrs Masham has credit.'

If Marlborough had known how his beloved Sarah was passing her time, he would not have been in the least surprised that the Queen had turned to Mrs Masham for comfort. Sarah had made a disastrous new friend, Mr Arthur Maynwaring, who prodded her into being even more outrageous than she already was. Maynwaring was an ardent Whig and a barrister of the Inner Temple; he edited the Whig journal, the *Medley*, and was a close friend of all the members of the Whig Junto. He was a stimulating conversationalist with a fund of mocking banter, and idolized the Duchess. He referred to himself as 'Her Grace's unpaid secretary' and threw himself into her quarrels with alarming enthusiasm. He praised everything that Sarah said or did, even encouraging her indiscretions – which were plentiful enough without added stimulus. Sarah's daughter, Lady Sunderland, refused to meet Maynwaring because he was 'mallitious' but this, of course, was what endeared him to the Duchess.

Together, throughout the spring of 1708, they composed long, outrageous letters to the Queen, only a few of which were sent; and equally long and outrageous letters to Abigail, which probably were never sent. Maynwaring wrote draft after draft for Sarah's approval. 'Choose anything you like,' he tells her,

and though I sometimes press your Grace . . . to do things that you seem
adverse to. . . . I do not think that you were ever in the wrong in your life
. . . the letter for Mrs Mor [the Queen] as I have put it together . . . shows
that I have not imitated your stile so long quite in vain.[65]

Maynwaring's adulation seems to have drawn many confidences
from Sarah. She described her life at Court with Princess Anne and
apparently talked of the latter's deep attachment for her which
Maynwaring defined as latent lesbianism. Sarah probably had never
thought of this before, but once the idea took root in her mind she
could not rid herself of it. Perhaps she now began to recall occasions
when Anne's passionate devotion had worried her, but this is only
conjecture. All that remains from Sarah is a cryptic sentence referring
to Anne's girlhood friendship: 'There are yet many things untold',
she wrote, 'for want of a name.'[66]

Whatever Sarah's true thought, in July 1708, the same month that
Oudenarde was fought, she made one of her rare appearances at
Court to show the Queen a scandalous ballad about Abigail (undoubtedly written by Maynwaring) which, she said, was being sung
about the town to the tune of *Fair Rosamund*.

> When as Queene Anne of Great Re-
> nown
> Great Britain's scepter sway'd
> Besides the Church she dearly lov'd
> A dirty Chambermaid
>
> O! Abigail that was her Name
> She stich'd and starch'd full well
> But how she pierc'd this Royal Heart
> No Mortal Man can tell
>
> However, for sweet Service done
> And Causes of great Weight
> Her Royal Mistress made her, Oh!
> A Minister of State
>
> Her Secretary she was not
> Because she could not write
> But she had the Conduct and the Care
> Of some Dark Deeds at Night.[67]

As the Queen was a semi-invalid, often swathed in bandages, the
idea of an unnatural relationship between herself and Abigail seems
fairly grotesque; but Sarah was out of control and refused to drop the

subject. Had she really come to believe it? Or was her fury at being set aside for her cousin so great that she could not resist the pleasure of cruelly embarrassing the Queen? This last supposition seems the most likely; and with Maynwaring to egg her on, she went to astonishing lengths. On 26 July, a few days after delivering the outrageous ballad (and on the heels of the Oudenarde victory), she wrote to her royal mistress accusing her in unmistakable language of lesbian tendencies:

> ... and tho your Majesty was pleased to desire me not to speake any more of her [Abigail] which I know to bee but her own request & what would bee of great advantage to all her designs if she could obtain it, yet I must humbly beg pardon if I cannot obey that command, the rather because I remember you said att the same time of all things in this world you valued most your reputation, which I confess surpris'd me very much, that your Majesty should so soon mention that word after having discover'd so great a passion for such a woman, for sure there can bee noe great reputation in a thing so strange & unaccountable, to say noe more of it, nor can I think the having noe inclination for any but of one's own sex is enough to maintain such a character as I wish may still bee yours.[68]

This was not all, for Sarah's anger mounted as she wrote. Abigail was 'a wretch', 'a woman I took out of a garret'; Harley, 'a very ill man'. No history, she said, had ever been written of a Queen brought to misfortune 'because she would believe nobody but a chambermaid'. She then went further: she reminded Anne of that day in January when 'the base woman and the creature who governs her' had forced Marlborough and Godolphin to tender their resignations. 'I earnestly desire of Your Majesty', she threatened, 'not to make a second tryall of removing them, which will certainly cost you much dearer than the last.'[69]

The Queen left these unforgiveable, almost lunatic diatribes unanswered and Marlborough (unaware of what Sarah was writing) sent a warning to his wife: 'You say Mrs Morley has taken no notice of your letter. I think this is a trew sign that she is angry.'[70] Nevertheless, the very fact that Sarah was able to upset the Queen encouraged her to continue her line of attack. A few weeks later a pamphlet was circulated (again undoubtedly written by Maynwaring), entitled *The Rival Duchess*, in which Abigail tells Madame de Maintenon: 'Especially at Court I was taken for a more modish lady, was rather addicted to another Sort of Passion, of having too great a Regard for my own Sex, insomuch that few People thought I would ever have Married.'[71]

The Queen suspected Sarah of instigating these slanderous jibes and never forgave her. The last lingering trace of affection for her friend turned to bitter dislike. Even so, Anne could not afford to lose the services of her great Captain-General, and therefore had no alternative but to retain Sarah in her duties as Groom of the Stole, First Lady of the Bedchamber and Keeper of the Privy Purse.

Eleven

The Lost Peace

When the Queen went to St Paul's in August 1708 to give thanks for the victory at Oudenarde, the Duchess of Marlborough had to be invited to ride in her carriage. Although Anne loathed the very sight of her former friend, Sarah was a state figure and it was necessary to keep up appearances. But even on this thanksgiving occasion, Sarah managed to create a scene. She had taken pains in laying out Anne's jewels for the ceremony, but at the last minute the Queen decided not to wear any. Sarah interpreted the omission as a personal affront instigated by Abigail, and on the journey to St Paul's accused Anne of trying deliberately to humiliate her. When they arrived at the Cathedral and stepped out of the carriage the Queen opened her mouth to answer but Sarah, fearful that they would be overheard, bade her 'Be quiet'. The Queen was deeply offended. Two days later Sarah forwarded to Anne one of Marlborough's letters with a covering note in which she complained that 'Your Majesty chose a very wrong day to mortify me, when you were just going to return thanks for a victory won by Lord Marlborough.'[1] The Queen replied icily:

> After the commands you gave me on the thanksgiving day of not answering you, I shoul'd not have troubled you with these lines, but to return the D of Marlborough's letter safe into your hands, & for the same reason do not say anything to that nor to yours which enclosed it.[2]

Sarah was like a runaway horse that no one could rein in. Her outrageous affronts were always on the same subject – the wickedness of Harley and the vileness of Abigail. Mr Bertie, the Queen's Vice-Chamberlain, reported in September 'two terrible Battles' between the two women, 'and when the Queen was seen afterwards her Eyes were red and it was plain she had been crying very much.'[3] It is not surprising that the palace seethed with gossip, and undoubtedly much of it was exaggerated. Lord Dartmouth, who hated the Marl-boroughs, added many disobliging footnotes to Burnet's History, and in one of them he tells us that at Windsor the Duchess spent an hour with the Queen. He claims that Sarah enumerated

> her own and her family's services, in so loud and shrill a voice, that the footmen at the bottom of the back-stairs could hear her; and all this storm was raised for the Queen's having ordered a bottle of wine a day to be allowed her laundress without having acquainted her grace with it. [This was an infringement of Sarah's prerogatives as Groom of the Stole.] The Queen, seeing her so outraged got up, to have gone out of the room; the Duchess clapped her back against the door, and told her she should hear her out, for that was the least favour she could do her for having set and kept the Crown upon her head. As soon as she had done raging, she flounced out of the room, and said she did not care if she never saw her more: to which the Queen replied very calmly that she thought the sooner the better. . . .[4]

In October the Queen's gentle, unpretentious husband, Prince George, who had been in poor health for some time, sickened and died. Despite the fearful rows that Sarah had provoked with her royal mistress, she pushed herself forward and insisted on being at the Queen's side. She was present in the death-chamber (another pre-rogative) and tells us that the Queen was 'in a paroxysm of grief and continued kissing her husband even after the breath had left his body.'[5] Sarah's harsh, unfeeling description of the Queen's emotions and the persistence with which she took part in the sad and intimate scenes, ignored and unwanted, shows a repellant side to her character. She was there not to ease the Queen's pain, but to prevent Abigail from doing so.

She went even further, and set herself up as the arbiter of 'grief-stricken behaviour'. Without being asked, she ordered the removal of the Prince's portrait from the Queen's bedchamber. After the funeral Anne begged her 'once more for God's sake to lett the Dear picture you have of mine, be put into my Bedchamber, for I cannot be without it any longer.'[6] Sarah remarks in her memoirs that she had only taken the portrait away 'because I thought she loved him and if she had been like other people its terrible to see a picture while the affliction is still upon one.'[7]

While the tension between Sarah and the Queen was nearing breaking-point, Marlborough was busy working on a new 'strategic design' that would bring France to her knees. Louis XIV had been bitterly disappointed by Oudenarde, but bad news no longer shocked him as it formerly had done. Defeat had become the expected lot of his once-proud and magnificent army. Although his generals were forced to admit that 'forty of our regiments are reduced to a wretched condition' the outcome at least had not been as calamitous as Ramillies. Indeed, Marshal Vendôme wrote furious letters insisting that the defeat had been entirely due to the fact that his command to send the left wing into action had not been obeyed. The unnamed culprit, of course, was the King's own grandson, Burgundy. We do not know how Louis viewed this criticism, but he seemed to ignore it, simply begging his generals and marshals not to lose heart, and predicting better times ahead.

The Allies were jubilant. Marlborough, despite his blinding headaches, had seized the initiative and was confident that his next stroke would end the war. Once again he was planning an amphibious operation. The entire Allied army would ignore the great French fortresses at Ghent and Bruges and Lille and invade France, using Abbeville (which could be supplied by a combined Anglo–Dutch fleet) as a base. This town, now in French possession, would be seized by General Erle and 6,000 men coming from the Isle of Wight; and British and Dutch ships would ferry the mass of stores, cannon and equipment required for the operation from Holland. From Abbeville, Marlborough and Eugene would march on Paris at the head of 100,000 men and bring the war to a triumphant close.

Marlborough was convinced that his action would draw in its wake all the French forces in the fortress areas. Although he knew that the Dutch, invariably opposed to new ideas, would be reluctant to give their approval, he won the enthusiastic backing of the British Cabinet. There was only one snag – Prince Eugene was a land animal and Prince Eugene did not like the scheme. He could not visualize setting up a supply-base dependant on the hazards of the sea, while heavily defended fortresses bristling with guns were ready to repel an advance – or even a retreat – by land. After much thought he pronounced it too great a gamble, and for the second time put an end to the possibility of an amphibious operation.

Poor Marlborough; someone always managed to scotch his wonderfully ingenious plans. Without Eugene's enthusiastic co-operation there was no hope of putting the proposal into operation, because the Dutch supported the Prince. 'I have acquainted Prince Eugene with the earnest desire we have for marching into France,' the Duke wrote to Godolphin, '[but] he thinks it unpractical till we have Lille for a *place d'armes* and magazine. . . .'[8] Marlborough had so much respect for Eugene's experience that this honest disagreement did not create one iota of animosity. Even so, the Duke could not forbear writing to Lord Halifax, 'Were our army all English, it would be feasible, but we have a great many among us who are more afraid of wanting provisions than of the enemy.'[9] If only he had been his own master! 'In Marlborough's whole military career', wrote the historian C. T. Atkinson, 'this proposal [the seizure of Abbeville and the invasion of France] is the most daring, the most original and the most interesting of his unfulfilled projects.'[10]

The fact that the Duke's brother, Admiral George Churchill, had been *de facto* head of the Admiralty for so many years had helped to give Marlborough a grasp of amphibian warfare which was far in advance of his time. His proposal in the preceding year – 1707 – to attack Toulon, relying on naval guns and naval rations (and even on a naval promise to evacuate his infantry if necessary) was bold and imaginative. But his plan to seize Abbeville as a naval base so that he could thrust deep into France, ignoring the triple line of frontier fortresses, and supplying his whole army from the sea, was nothing short of genius. Judging from the instructions sent by the French Minister of War to Marshal Berwick, Marlborough's design would have drawn the French from their fortresses and sent them hurrying after him (just as he had prophesied), leaving their strongholds an easy prey for the troops left to defend the Netherlands. 'You must be very attentive', the French Minister wrote anxiously,

> to any movement which the enemy may make . . . toward the Somme or the Authie. That would be a sure way of completing the ruin of Picardy and of spreading terror throughout Normandy to the very gates of Paris.[11]

Alas, these anxieties never moved beyond the realm of conjecture.

Marlborough's disappointment, on the other hand, was heightened by two severe personal blows: the shattering of the close links between himself and his two brothers, one by illness, the other by politics. In the spring of 1708, General Charles Churchill, who had served John devotedly in all his major campaigns, suffered a stroke. Luckily, he had a rich wife which made it possible for him to live comfortably at the Churchill family home at Mintern which he had inherited. He had no legitimate children, but was very proud of a bastard son whom he named Charles Churchill. His retirement was a great loss to John who liked his quiet, serious manner and trusted him implicitly.* When

---

* Although Charles retired and went to England, Marlborough kept his name on the active army list so that he continued to draw his full pay; this went on until Marlborough was superseded.

Marlborough was called away he often left Charles in command in the Netherlands. Even more regrettable, however, was the severance of his ties with George because of bitter political altercations. Like his father, Sir Winston Churchill, Admiral George was a dyed-in-the-wool Tory. A large, moon-faced man with a huge curly wig and an unsmiling mouth, he was more emotional and more assertive than Charles. Although he had always been fiercely loyal to Marlborough, sometimes to his own detriment, he could not abide the Whigs. The trouble probably arose because the Whigs made a point of disparaging the navy, talking as though the army was the sole defence of the kingdom.

The Whigs, on the other hand, found Admiral George rude and cantankerous. Behind his back they accused him of being a Jacobite and complained to Marlborough that he spent his time encouraging the Queen (through her husband) to refuse their just demands. The most ardent Whig of all, Lord Sunderland, prevailed upon his mother-in-law, Sarah, to urge the Duke to muzzle his dangerous brother. Sarah nagged at John for several months until he finally sat down and wrote George a curt letter demanding that he hand in his resignation or prepare himself for an ignominious dismissal. As George had always been the soul of loyalty to John, it is not surprising that this letter resulted in a permanent breach between the two. George was not a man to be pushed about, so he simply ignored John's threats and continued to urge the Queen and the Prince to stand firm against the Whig Junto.

At this inopportune moment Prince George died. Inevitably, the Admiral was thrown out of a job. Although he was a member of Parliament for St Albans, he made it known that he would spend the winter in the country. 'He continues in town', wrote one of Harley's correspondents, 'till the funeral is over and then retires to Windsor with the intention not to appear this winter in Parliament.'[12] In fact, Admiral Churchill never appeared in Parliament again for he died eighteen months later. Meanwhile, he lived in a villa in Windsor, tending the wonderful aviary that he had built up over the years. Like Charles, he was married but had no legitimate children. He refused to patch up his quarrel with John and Sarah and, although the Marlboroughs spent much of their time at Windsor Lodge, a stone's throw away, he also refused to meet them. When he died he left part of his aviary to his brother's chief military rival, the Duke of Ormonde, and the remainder to his sister Arabella's son, Brigadier Godfrey.

Apart from Marlborough himself, Arabella Godfrey was the only hale and hearty member of the family left. She outlived everyone except Sarah, holding onto life until 1730.

Marlborough never lingered over disappointments. As soon as
Eugene argued against the amphibious Abbeville operation, he
turned his attention to Lille. Next to Paris this was France's most
important town – 'a large and well-fortified place with a very strong
citadel, the capital of French Flanders, the staple of all trade between
the Netherlands and France. . . .'[13] The capture of Lille would be no
humdrum affair as it was so cleverly fortified it was known as
'Vauban's masterpiece'. The town was surrounded by double-moats
protected by stone-built covered ways, and defended by a pentagon-
shaped fortress, capable of standing a second siege. It was not surprising that most people considered Lille impregnable, but Marlborough and Prince Eugene were not among these. The 'twin
captains' liked nothing better than a challenge, particularly a challenge which, if it ended in success, would reverberate throughout
Europe. Furthermore, there was every reason to believe that a satisfactory result would force Louis to sue for peace.

Marlborough's first problem was to transport siege-guns and
ammunition from Holland to Lille. As Vendôme's army controlled
Ghent, the artillery was sent by ship to Antwerp, and by canal to
Brussels. For the remaining seventy-five miles it had to travel by road.
The 'Great Convoy', as it came to be known, was divided into two
sections and stretched over thirty miles. Fourteen thousand horses
(commandeered from the unlucky peasants of Belgium and France)
were used to pull the eighty heavy siege-guns, the twenty mortars and
3,000 wagons (with four horses each) containing supplies and
ammunition. General Cadogan, assisted by the Prince of Hesse-
Cassel, was in charge of the convoy which had to pass between two
French armies, neither of which was more than twenty miles distant.
Vendôme and Burgundy were behind the Ghent–Bruges canal and
Berwick was in the Mons area. 'For God's sake, be sure you do not
risk the cannon,'[14] Marlborough wrote in his own hand to Cadogan.
What Cadogan was supposed to do to eliminate the risk is not known,
but the convoy was accompanied by an Allied force of 50,000 men
commanded by Prince Eugene. Later, the French military critic, M.
Feuquières, wrote that posterity would not be able to believe that this
'prodigious convoy', travelling at a snail's pace, had been allowed to
pass unmolested. The truth was that the French commanders were
still at odds with each other: Berwick had no use for Vendôme and
Vendôme none for Burgundy. Furthermore, Vendôme was still suffering from the humiliation and shock of Oudenarde. Although
Berwick suggested that they join forces and intercept the convoy on
the River Dender, Vendôme refused; nor would he agree to a joint

attack on Brussels. No doubt he was afraid to leave his entrenched position in case the terrifying Marlborough should fall on him and cut him to pieces. Thus, while all Europe watched with baited breath, the slow-moving procession successfully completed its journey on 13 August. 'The Prince of Savoy', wrote Marlborough that same night, 'has invested the town of Lille on all sides and the cannon has arrived at Menin a few miles from Lille within reach of the siege, which will be pressed with all possible vigour, and this may at last convince the enemy that they have lost the battle of Oudenarde.'[15]

Marshal Boufflers, a fellow officer of Marlborough's when they both served Turenne, was the defender of Lille. He knew perfectly well that no fortifications, whatever their strength, could withstand weeks of pounding by heavy guns; and that, as long as the besiegers had plenty of ammunition, they were bound to win in the end. There were only two ways that the French could save Lille: by preventing food and gunpowder from reaching the assault force which was commanded by Prince Eugene, or by attacking and defeating the covering army which was commanded by Marlborough. Tension was high in Versailles, as Lille was the lynchpin of the line of fortresses protecting the French frontier. Lous XIV was in constant touch with his quarrelling generals at the front, advising them, soothing them, encouraging them. As Vendôme and Berwick commanded a joint army of 110,000 compared to Marlborough's 60,000, the King instructed them to attack, whatever the cost. And when his order was not obeyed, he sent his War Minister, Chamillart, to find out why.

Marlborough had taken up a strong defensive position to the south of the city, and although Vendôme and Berwick effected a junction near Tournai at the end of August, they could not agree on what the next move should be. Indeed, their only point of accord was their mutual dislike of Louis's grandson, the Duke of Burgundy. Where Vendôme wanted to attack, Berwick refused; and when Berwick wanted to attack, Vendôme would have none of it. Marlborough's men were amused by the cannonades that came to nothing and boasted that Oudenarde had taken the heart out of them. 'We might wait until Doomsday', wrote Private Deane, 'for the enemy to advance. We are continually fatigued and bug-beared out of our lives by those who had as much will to fight as to be hanged.'[16] In the end, however, even Chamillart came to the conclusion that Marlborough's position was too strong to attack, and the French struck their tents and retreated.

The siege itself was anything but easy. 'The outworks are so large and numerous', wrote a subaltern in the Scots Fusiliers, 'that whatever way we make our approaches we are always flanked and our men very often kill'd both with small cannon and shot at the very bottom of the trench.'[17] Not only was shot used, but mines and mortars and occasionally such fiendish devices as boiling oil. On this particular sortie, Prince Eugene was struck by a musketball which grazed his forehead above his left eye. The force of the blow was broken by his tricorn hat which, Lediard tells us, 'was beat off his head'. Although the Prince dismissed his injury, he suffered severe concussion which kept him out of action for over a week. That same night the Allies suffered 1,000 casualties.

By this time Marlborough's supplies were running dangerously low. Although the French generals refused to risk the battle that Louis demanded (and which Marlborough himself ardently desired), they fought a war of attrition with all their energy. During the last fortnight in September, Vendôme and Burgundy occupied the whole line of the Scheldt from the Lille approaches to Ghent. They cut all communications between the Allies and Brussels and beyond Brussels with Holland. The Allies were surprised to find themselves in urgent need of ammunition because of the miscalculation of their engineers. 'We have already fired very near as much ammunition as was demanded for taking of town and citadel,' Marlborough wrote to Godolphin on 20 September, 'and as yet we are not entire masters of the counterscarp.'[18] To Sarah he voiced grave anxieties: 'The siege goes on so very slowly that I am in perpetual fears that it may continue so long and consequently consume so much stores that we may at last not have the wherewithall to finish, which would be very cruel. . . .'[19]

Fortunately, Marlborough had a brilliant alternative. Six weeks earlier, when he was planning his great march to Paris, General Erle had been assigned the task of seizing Abbeville. Erle was still cruising around the North Sea with his detachment of 6,000 men awaiting further instructions. Marlborough now gave him new orders: Erle was to disembark at Ostend, which was in Allied hands, and take the necessary steps to organize a convoy for Lille.

Erle lost no time in establishing a post and bridges over the Nieuport Bruges canal at Leffinghe, and gave orders for 700 wagons to be assembled at Ostend. The convoy started its march on 27 September escorted by twelve battalions (probably about 8,000 men). The French were determined to prevent the arrival of these vitally important supplies and Berwick despatched 12,000 men, under the command of General de La Motte, to interrupt the journey. Marlborough always had a reliable secret service, and knew of the plan in plenty of time to send General Webb with 6,000 men to Thourout, and Cadogan with another 6,000 men and twenty-six squadrons of cavalry to Roulers.

La Motte's first attempt to disrupt the convoy was foiled by General Erle's posts at Leffinghe, and after that he came up against Webb's spirited resistance at Wynendael. Webb had no cavalry and no artillery, only 6,000 infantrymen, while La Motte's force of 12,000 men comprised all three arms. When Webb saw the French commander meant business, he sent the convoy on its way and took up a defensive position in the Wynendael woods. His cleverness lay in planting an ambush on either side of the enemy's approach. But first the Allies had the ordeal of a French bombardment which went on all afternoon. In the evening, the French horse and foot delivered their attack and were caught unawares by the formidable crossfire of the ambush. This was a perfect example of the deadly fire-power of Marlborough's infantry; his men had been trained for years in rapid and accurate shooting as 'infantry fire-power' was an article of faith with the Duke. In the space of half an hour the enemy had lost 3,000 men. Count de La Motte ordered a second attack but his troops were suffering such a loss of morale that they refused to carry it out, and he had no option but to retire. 'If our convoy had been lost,' Marlborough wrote to Godolphin, 'the consequences must have been the raising of the siege next day.'[20]

With the convoy's safe arrival the attack was renewed, and by the end of September the besiegers were in possession of 'most of the outworks that were of consequence'. They had the counterscarp and a bastion covering a gateway known in Flemish as the *katte* but referred to by the British soldiers as 'the Cat'. Soon the Allies were able to drain off the water in the moat and to cannonade the base of the main wall until it was breached. It was clear that Boufflers's days were numbered.

Vendôme was now so desperate he was ready to go to any lengths to stop supply convoys from reaching the Allies. He marched around Ghent to Oudenberg and cut the dykes between Bruges and Nieuport, flooding the land for miles around; a new Allied convoy which had just set out from Ostend was forced to return to dry land. However, Cadogan solved the problem by providing flat-bottomed boats in which the supplies, after being taken by road from Ostend to Leffinghe, were carried across the floods and picked up by a new convoy of wagons. Vendôme countered by organizing a huge flotilla of rowboats carrying soldiers who attacked and captured Leffinghe. By this time the Allies had succeeded in getting several convoys through to Lille with large consignments of ammunition, and on 22 October Boufflers surrendered the city of Lille. As he still had the citadel, the fighting continued night and day, claiming enormous casualties.

Although only 3,000 British soldiers were engaged, they lost half their number before the struggle ended.

While the final struggle for the citadel was taking place, Marlborough wrote an astonishing letter to his French nephew, Marshal Berwick, suggesting that the time had come for peace talks. If King Louis was interested he might like to authorize the Duke of Burgundy to appoint himself and Prince Eugene as intermediaries. The letter then said: 'You may be assured that I shall be wholeheartedly for peace not doubting that I shall find the goodwill which was promised me two years ago by the Marquis d'Alègre. . . .'[21] This, of course, was a direct reference to the bribe of two million *livres* that Louis had offered him the year before. Marlborough's audacity in putting such a compromising suggestion in writing is staggering. He seemed perfectly aware of the risk he was running for he ended with the admonition: 'As I trust you without reserve I conjure you never to part with this letter except to return it to me.'

Marlborough's trust in his nephew was not misplaced and his letter produced no ill effects. Did he really want the money? Or did he mention it to make his French adversaries believe in his sincerity? It certainly impressed Berwick, who wrote to Torcy that he was inclined to believe in his uncle's 'good faith' because 'he speaks in it of a certain matter by which you know he sets great store.'[22] The French Court was accustomed to pay for services rendered and Chamillart took the whole thing in his stride, writing to Torcy that Marlborough's goodwill 'would not be bought too dearly at Monsieur d'Alègre's figure.'[23]

Despite a flurry of interest at Versailles, the King, encouraged by Chamillart, began to suspect that Marlborough was writing from weakness, not strength, and that the fortunes of war might be reversed in the next campaign. Berwick, therefore, was instructed to reply to Marlborough that the situation of the Allies,

> although most brilliant in appearance cannot prevent those who have experience of war from perceiving that it is strained in all sorts of ways, and may at any moment be so transformed that even if you took the citadel of Lille you might be thrown into extremities which would destroy your armies and put it out of your power to supply with munitions and food the strong places you occupy beyond the Scheldt, to recruit and re-establish your forces, and to put your armies in a state to resume the war in the next campaign. . . .[24]

Marlborough not only was affronted but outraged that his assessment of the military situation was suspect. The Duke of Berwick sympathized with his uncle: 'Monsieur de Chamillart prescribed the answer for me to make,' he wrote in his memoirs, 'and I thought it so extraordinary that I sent it in French in order that the Duke of Marlborough might see that it did not come from me.'[25] Berwick returned his uncle's letter and there the matter ended.

Marlborough turned his attention back to the siege, still smouldering with anger. Five weeks later, on 9 December, Marshal Boufflers was forced to capitulate. He marched out of his citadel with all the honours of war, but he had only 7,000 men left out of 16,000. The cost to the Allies, however, was much greater – 15,000 men, five times as many as at Oudenarde. 'This murdering siege', wrote Private Deane, who took part in the action,

> has destroyed more than Namur did last war and those that were the flower of the Army for what was not killed or wounded were spoiled by their hellish inventions of throwing of bombs, boiling pitch, tar, oil and brimstone with scalding water . . . likewise many other inventions enough to puzzle the Devil to contrive.[26]

Although it was well past the time customary for the army to go into winter quarters, Marlborough refused to lay down arms until Ghent and Bruges had been recovered. These two towns were of great strategic importance, as they controlled the whole waterways system in Flanders, rivers and canals alike. Although Vendôme pleaded with the King to be allowed to give battle in their defence, Louis called him home (because of Burgundy's jealousy) and appointed the luckless Count de La Motte in his place. Marlborough began the siege of Ghent in the middle of December. 'To be in some quiet this Winter,' he wrote to Sarah on the 17th, 'and to enable the making of a good Campagne the next Yeare, we must be masters of this town.'[27] Marlborough had no need to worry as La Motte's resistance proved to be so feeble that the whole operation was finished in a fortnight. The fickle population surrendered gladly and cheered the latest conquerors as heartily as they had welcomed the French six months earlier.

Marlborough arrived back in England in January 1709 to find that Sarah was engaged in a new battle – this time with their celebrated architect, John Vanbrugh. The Duke had made the mistake of urging Sarah to keep a close watch on what was happening at Blenheim and from that moment tranquillity became a rare thing. Although the Duke was accused of avariciousness, the Duchess was one of the most money-conscious women who ever lived. This characteristic, allied with an overbearing arrogance, made her a horrendous person for any architect to deal with. She refused the stone-carters their extra penny a foot, beat down the wages of the carpenters, and neglected to transfer £350 to Mr Vanbrugh's account when he undertook the work of one of his assistants who had died. Sarah never saw two sides to a question and told everyone that her quarrels with Mr Vanbrugh arose simply because she persisted in curtailing unnecessary expenditure. Vanbrugh had a different view of the situation and bewailed his ill luck in finding himself under the direction of so arbitrary a mistress:

> Tis this that makes me avoid all Company and haunt the Building like a Ghost from the Time the Workmen leave off at Six a Clock till tis quite Dark. . . . Studying how to make this the Cheapest, as well as (if possible) the best Haus in Europe, which I think my Ld Duke's Services highly deserve.[28]

Sarah refused to be taken in by Vanbrugh's remonstrances and lectured him repeatedly on priorities. The main body of the house must come first; all luxuries such as courts, grottoes, bridges and the like could be considered later. As for the imposing ruin known as 'Woodstock Manor', once a royal hunting-lodge where Henry II made love to fair Rosamund, and where Princess Elizabeth was imprisoned for a year at Bloody Mary's command, she did not wish to hear his endless pleas to preserve it.

When the Duke returned home after the long drawn-out siege of Lille, Sarah could talk of nothing but Woodstock Manor. Apparently Vanbrugh, enchanted by the romantic relic, had spent £1,000 to prevent the ceilings from collapsing and another £1,000 to beautify it. Sarah was outraged; it was 'not very agreeable', and she wanted it pulled down as it spoiled the view from the palace. Vanbrugh, on the other hand, argued that visitors were fascinated by its history, and that far from spoiling the view, it endowed the estate with glamour and the nostalgia of antiquity.

In January 1709 Sarah insisted that her husband and Sidney Godolphin accompany her to Blenheim to pronounce on it. Godolphin said exactly what she wanted to hear – 'there could be no more a dispute than whether a man that had a great wen upon his cheek would not have it cut off if he could.'[29] Apparently Marlborough was not so sure. He gave directions that nothing more was to be done to embellish the Manor but did not completely order it to be pulled down. What interested him much more than these rather tiresome details was the furnishing of the palace. For years, Marlborough had been collecting ornaments and works of art for his splendid abode:

silks from Genoa, marble from Alicante, pictures and hangings from all the capitals of Europe. The Spanish Ambassador in Rome had presented him with a full-scale model of the Bernini fountain in the Piazza Navona and he had collected many superb tapestries and statues. In 1706 he had written to Sarah that he was 'so fond of some pictures I shall bring [home] with me that I could wish you had a place for them till the Gallery at Woodstock be finished.'[30] Among them was Van Dyck's famous equestrian portrait of Charles I, which had been given to the Emperor by the Elector of Bavaria and passed on to the Duke. 'I have been to see the hangings for your apartment and mine; as much as are done I think very fine,' he wrote in 1706. '. . . I should be glad, at your leisure, you would be providing everything that may be necessary for furnishing these two apartments . . . for I am resolved to finish the room with the finest pictures I can get.'[31]

The creation of Woodstock, however, was not Sarah's only housing project. In 1708, she decided to build herself a London residence. She had been toying with the idea for some time and, in 1706, with Lord Godolphin's help, had leased a strip of Crown land adjacent to St James's Palace and secured the Queen's permission to build on it. The former tenant, sixty-three-year-old Catherine of Braganza, widow of Charles II, had died in 1705, and the land was known as Friary Grounds because Catherine had used the now tumbledown buildings that stood on it to house the dozens of priests who had accompanied her when she had first come from Portugal over forty years earlier. Lord Godolphin acted as Sarah's intermediary with the Crown estate for, although Queen Catherine died in 1705, the lease could not be transferred until the latter's estate was settled – something that took many months. What induced Sarah, already burdened with the responsibility of Blenheim, to push ahead with her town house in 1708? Was it because she anticipated losing her position at Court and her apartment at St James's Palace? Or was it because she wished to annoy the Queen who, by now, must have deeply regretted having granted her the lease? Or was it to spite Mr Vanbrugh by choosing seventy-seven-year-old Sir Christopher Wren as her architect?

Whatever the reason, when Sarah unfolded her plan to her husband, soon after his victory at Oudenarde, Marlborough was taken aback and much against the idea. 'As for myself', he replied,

I am so desirous of living at Woodstock that I should not much Care to do anything but what is necessary anywhere else. . . . And you may depend on it, 'twill cost you double the Mony they have estimated. 'Tis not a proper place for a great House . . . so that if you have not set your Heart upon it I

should advise you to think well of it. For 'tis more advisable to buy a
House than to build any.[32]

But Sarah *had* set her heart upon it and thus began the building of
Marlborough House which, before it was finished, cost her £50,000.
'Almost incredible,' she admitted, 'but not really as extravagant as it
appears, because it was the strongest and best house that ever was
built.' Of course she quarrelled with Wren over money and sacked
him before he finished the job. 'The poor old man', she writes,

> undertook this business very readily. . . . Then I began to find that this
> man from his age was imposed upon by the workmen and that the prices
> for all things were much too high for ready money and sure pay, upon
> which I took the finishing part upon myself, and I had the good fortune
> with much pains to do it as I was told toe everybodys satisfaction.[33]

The Marlboroughs' concern with houses and homes was significant
as the Duke was confident that the war was drawing to a close. In this
he was wrong, as 1709, far from being a year of peace, was a year of
violence and unparalleled bloodshed. Even worse, that winter the
weather was so severe that it was 'almost glacial'. The Great Frost, as
it was known, wrought havoc from one end of the Continent to the
other. Ice-floes appeared in the Channel and the North Sea. The
Thames froze solid; so did the Seine and all the canals in Venice.
Cattle and sheep perished all over the Continent.

France was hit hardest of all. There the tragedy turned into disaster. The harvest the year before had failed, and now it was
discovered that the seed corn was dead in the ground. The French
Treasury was nearly bankrupt but Louis XIV set an example by
melting down the silver furniture in the *Galléries des Glaces* and
contributing it to the Exchequer; the purpose was to buy corn from
the Beys of Africa, but this hope was shattered by squadrons of British
and Dutch warships. Soon, an economic boycott of France was
organized by the Allies, which caused widespread misery and terrible
hunger. The churches were crowded and, on 15 February, the relics of
St Genevieve were paraded through the streets of Paris. Not everyone
was content to pray. Some sang songs mocking the King and his heirs,
or chanted parodies of the Lord's Prayer which began with the words:

> Our Father who art in Versailles, whose name is no longer hallowed,
> whose kingdom is no longer large, give us our daily bread which is lacking
> everywhere. . . .

With the fall of Lille, Louis saw that he could never win the war;

and·now, with the threat of famine, peace became a desperate necessity. No doubt the King regretted the patronizing letter he had allowed Chamillart to write to the Duke of Marlborough only four months earlier. He sent his Foreign Minister, the Marquis de Torcy, to The Hague to make secret arrangements for the opening of a peace conference. However, when Philip v heard that the Allies were determined to throw him out of Spain, he wrote to his grandfather that he would never leave Spain alive or relinquish the 'throne that God had given him'. 'I praise the sentiments of your Majesty,' Louis replied, '. . . but knowing that my kingdom cannot hope to sustain much longer the weight of this war . . . it is necessary to end it at any price. . . .' And, a few days later: '. . . my subjects are now reduced by famine to the point where it is no longer possible to negotiate. . . .'[34]

The Allies, however, were cock-a-hoop, confident that they could dictate whatever terms they liked. Marlborough was England's chief plenipotentiary, while the Pensionary Heinsius and Prince Eugene acted for Holland and the Empire. A fourth delegate, Lord Townshend, arrived from England at Marlborough's special request as a nominee of the Whig Junto. His task was to negotiate with the Dutch the complicated Barrier Treaty – the ring of cities and fortresses which the States-General regarded as essential for their future security and which was their main reason for entering the war. As the Dutch were bound to antagonize the Emperor Joseph and his brother, Charles, with their demands for cities in the Spanish Netherlands, Marlborough had evolved this plan to escape from the inevitable crossfire of bad feeling.

Louis xiv's negotiator, the Marquis de Torcy, was a sophisticated man who knew the ways of the world and consoled his despondent King by insisting that things might not turn out as badly as he anticipated. He would proceed gingerly and follow a carefully contrived plan. First, he would seduce the Dutch by offering them a better 'barrier' than they had dared hope for; then he would turn around and seduce the Duke of Marlborough by giving him a colossal bribe. 'Marlborough holds the key,' he explained, 'and there are means of making him choose peace.'[35]

As Torcy was a meticulous man he set up a precise tariff and got the King's approval before he departed for The Hague. If Marlborough could persuade the Queen and her Cabinet to override the absurd policy of keeping the huge Spanish Empire intact, and offer Philip the kingdoms of Naples and Sicily in exchange for leaving Spain, the French would pay him two million *livres*. If the fortifications or harbours of Dunkirk were left to France, or Strasbourg was spared, he would receive another two millions – this made a possible total of 4,000,000 *livres*.* 'Such was the view which the French took of their conqueror,' wrote Winston Churchill acidly, 'they can hardly be blamed for doing so after his letter to Berwick.'[36]

However, much to Torcy's surprise, he met with a courteous rebuff. 'When', he wrote, 'I spoke about his private interests, he reddened and appeared to wish to turn the conversation.'[37] Biographers are baffled by this incident, as indeed was poor Torcy. Only a few months earlier Marlborough had proposed himself to the French as an intermediary and hinted at a monetary reward; now, when he was a fully-fledged plenipotentiary and the monetary reward was proferred on a hand-some scale, he scorned it. Some writers suggest that the good and bad sides of his character often struggled with each other for suprem-acy, but this applies to mankind in general and is not a satisfactory explanation. However, it must be emphasized that Marlborough was not corrupt. He loved money and was delighted by the large sums he earned but no one ever proved him guilty of dishonourable dealings. As he turned down offers of French gold in 1707 and 1709 we are driven to the conclusion that his letter to Berwick was part of a design to impress the enemy with his good faith. Thus Torcy's whole plan of defence crashed to the ground, leaving him exposed to a series of unbridled demands. 'Every sovereign prince', wrote Torcy to the King, 'assumes that he has the right to formulate his claims against France, and would even think himself dishonoured if he had extorted nothing to the injury of the French crown.'[38] The clamour was heard from voices as far apart as Portugal and the Diet of Ratisbon. The Emperor Joseph asked for Strasbourg and Alsace; the English for Newfoundland; the Dutch for Lille. Some of these claims were accepted, others not, but Torcy's careful reflections on Naples and Sicily never became a topic of discussion as the English remained ada-mant on the subject of the Spanish Empire. Just as their Parliament had decreed, everything should go to 'Charles III' and nothing to Philip. And, as though this was not enough, the Allies decided that the French King must deliver Spain in person. They were not prepared to incur the trouble or expense of conquering that country themselves. Indeed, they were doing so badly in Spain it was much better to force Louis to secure his grandson's abdication by peremptory 'command'.

Although he protested vehemently, Torcy had no alternative but to accept these stringent conditions; but when the Pensionary Heinsius,

* £300,000.

on behalf of his colleagues, asked for guarantees of good faith in the form of three French and three Spanish fortresses, now occupied by French troops, the Marquis dug in his toes. Even more outrageous was a further stipulation by the Allies that if Philip v did not obey Louis's order to withdraw from his adopted country, the French King would join the Allies in taking military action to force his compliance. Torcy was outraged by a 'condition so unnatural'. Lord Townshend tried to jolly him along and make him see that the paragraph – known as Article XXXVII – was not as bad as it sounded. It might, he argued brightly, 'have the good effect of making the Spaniards actually declare for King Charles when they saw the French king was under an obligation to joyn with the Allies. . . .'[39] But Torcy indignantly refused to sign, saying that he would advise the King to reject the preliminaries. Marlborough then suggested rephrasing the offensive clause so that Louis would not be obliged to take up arms against his grandson, but Townshend argued him out of it; as Philip v was bound to do as the King demanded, the paragraph was of no particular importance. Marlborough acquiesced and the document was left as it stood and sent on to Louis.

The part played by the great victor is puzzling. A resplendent figure in scarlet and ceremonial gold, handsome, brave and the hero of Europe, the Duke was the cynosure of all eyes. Yet his contribution to the negotiations was negligible. He spent his time being immensely agreeable to everyone, never arguing, never challenging, only occupying himself with minor issues, solving no problems and contributing no new ideas. What was he thinking? One can only conclude that he deliberately stayed in the background as he felt that the peace was won, and was determined to remain on the best of terms with all members of the Grand Alliance.

This happy state of affairs, however, did not last long. When Madame de Maintenon was given details of the terms, she could scarcely believe her ears. 'The news brought by Torcy', she wrote on 3 June, 'fills everyone with a drop of French blood in his veins with indignation.'[40] Louis's son and heir, the Dauphin (the father of Philip v), was as outraged as Torcy; and so was Philip's brother, the Duke of Burgundy. Louis agreed that the terms were quite unacceptable. Famine, bankruptcy, desertion, mutiny – none of it mattered any more; 'If I must needs fight,' said the King, 'I would rather fight my enemies and not my own children.'[41]

For a while the plenipotentiaries continued to live in a fool's paradise at The Hague. Marlborough was so sure of peace that he asked Sarah to send him a chair of state and a canopy so that he could sign the treaty in surroundings compatible with the dignity of an Ambassador Extraordinary to the Dutch Republic. 'I beg you will take care', he wrote to his wife, with his usual display of economy, 'to have it made so that it may serve for part of a bed when I have done with it here, which I hope will be at the end of the summer.'[42]

Like the rest of his countrymen, Marlborough overestimated France's impotence. When Louis made public his refusal to sign the treaty Marlborough was stunned. 'Is there, then, no counter-proposal?' he asked. Yet in his heart he knew perfectly well that Article XXXVII was an impossible demand for the simple reason that Louis was no longer in control of his grandson's kingdom. '. . . I call God to witness', he wrote to Heinsius on 4 July, 'that I think it is not in the power of the King of France so that if you persist in having three Spanish towns in Spain, it is in my opinion declaring the continuance of the war.'[43] And on 10 July, again to Heinsius, 'If I were in the place of the King of France I should venture the loss of my country much sooner than be obliged to join my troops for the forcing of my grandson.'[44]

It is a pity that these forthright observations were not made before, rather than after, Louis's rejection of the preliminaries. But the truth was that Marlborough was too confident. Stories that the French army was unable to supply its soldiers with either pay or rations, and that large-scale desertions were taking place, had made a deep impression on him. He had forgotten that there was always a point at which a man would rather fight and die than tamely submit. In London the public was utterly dismayed by the breakdown, as peace had been regarded as a certainty. Lord Godolphin was so shocked that at first he refused to accept the King's pronouncement as final. 'I can hardly bring myself to believe the French will persist in not signing the preliminaries.' he wrote to Lord Coningsby,

> nothing but the hope of peace has kept the people within any bounds for this last month, and if they find themselves like to bee disappointed, I believe we shall hear of no small disorder in that kingdom. . . .[45]

But this was wishful thinking. Instead of disorder, stricken, hungry France took on a new spirit. Louis appointed Marshal de Villars to command his troops – the last army that could be raised – and issued a stirring proclamation to his people, calling on them to defend the sacred soil of France with their last breath.

Despite Marlborough's disappointment over the lost peace, both he and Eugene believed that France was on the verge of collapse and that the war would soon grind to a halt. To make sure of destroying Villars, England and Holland increased the size of their armies to

120,000 men, nearly twice the number that had taken part at Ramillies. Villars, on the other hand, had difficulty in scraping up enough
recruits to bring his numbers to 80,000 and many of his men were half
starving. When he arrived at the Franco–Belgian frontier he found the
privates selling their arms and jackets for bread, and even the
subalterns bartering their shirts. Villars was a boastful, competent
Gascon, a man of the people who despised incompetent princes, and
was both shrewd and sensible when it came to war. He had a common
touch that endeared him to his men and within three months had
infused a new spirit into his army.

Once again Marlborough would have liked to use the navy to seize
Abbeville, and with this base drive deep into France; and once again
Eugene voted in favour of besieging a fortress – this time Tournai.
Marlborough submitted; the reduction took two months and cost
5,000 men. The Allied statesmen were disappointed, as they longed
for a sensational victory which would set the ceremonial cannon
booming and the populace dancing in the streets. Villars used the
precious weeks to advantage by constructing the Lines of La Bassé
which extended from Aire to Douai and were forty miles long. The
marshy reaches of the Rivers Lys and Scarpe added to their strength
while the heavy rains of June increased the difficulty of the
approaches.

Marlborough and Eugene were now so impatient to attack Villars
that they were not looking for favourable conditions. However, the
Marshal's lines were so heavily fortified that an attempt was out of
the question. Perhaps if they drew siege lines around Mons he would
be tempted to emerge from his lair? This plan met with success, for
Villars suddenly moved forward and occupied the Gap of Malplaquet, an opening between two forests.

What the Allies could not know was that up till this moment the
Marshal had been under strict orders from Louis XIV not to allow
Marlborough and Eugene to draw him into battle. Indeed, when
Villars suggested a surprise attack on Brussels, Louis reminded him
that his primary duty was 'to prevent the enemy from entering my
kingdom . . . and always to be situated so that you will not be forced
to fight unless you enjoy a great advantage.'[46] Nevertheless Villars
continued to tell the King that there was no wheat for bread and to
insist that only a successful battle could end the dire threat that the
Allies were posing. 'God help us,' the Marshal finally exclaimed, 'but
the more I think of the problem of food, the more I find that we must
have peace or a battle . . . it is a miracle to maintain the army without
food . . . and it is dangerous to the state.'[47]

Villars was so persistent that Louis finally gave him permission to fight. 'The King leaves it entirely in your hands to do what you believe yourself forced to do, . . .' the new French Minister of War, M. Voisin, wrote to the Marshal.[48] The French commander breathed a sigh of relief, but bided his time and did not stir from his fortified lines until Marlborough and Eugene moved towards Mons. The King had sent Marshal Boufflers to join Villars and together the two French Generals decided that the time had come for a battle. 'I have the honour to inform your Majesty', Villars wrote to the King on 8 September,

> of the resolution to assemble the army and seek a battle. . . . M. de Boufflers is here to testify that, if we attack, it will be with good reason; if we do nothing it will also be true that a brave man will be witness that we have done our best.[49]

This was the moment when Villars moved forward and occupied the Gap of Malplaquet. He fastened his wings on to the forests on either side of the open space – the great Wood of Sars on his left and the Wood of Lanières on his right. And this was the place where the famous battle was fought. He ordered his men to entrench themselves in the open ground by building earthworks behind which they could establish their batteries. In the wood they constructed a series of redoubts, fortified by felled trees. The soldiers worked feverishly, within forty-eight hours creating a strong defensive position. They were proud to be fighting for hearth and home; proud to be serving under the competent Villars; proud that the gallant Marshal Boufflers had come to join them. Whenever Villars approached they assured him that the defences they were building would be held at all costs.

Marlborough's plan of attack was based on his Blenheim strategy. He would strike hard at the two flanks pinned to the forests on either side of the Malplaquet Gap. When Villars's centre was weakened it would be assaulted by the infantry reserve (mainly British) and finally overrun by the huge cavalry arm, numbering over 30,000 men. They would move through the Gap and attack the French cavalry in the plain beyond. If they succeeded in routing the French horsemen all the troops drawn into the two flanks would be cut off as had happened at Blenheim.

Marlborough began to deploy his troops shortly after half-past five on the morning of 11 September. Luckily for him, a thick fog enveloped fields and woods so that he was not subjected to artillery fire. When it lifted it revealed the Allied army, 100,000 strong, moving to the attack. The infantry was three deep, and the cavalry followed. 'While over their heads flapped like sails a forest of huge flags, unfolding the blazonry of a score of the greatest States and Princes in Europe.'[50]

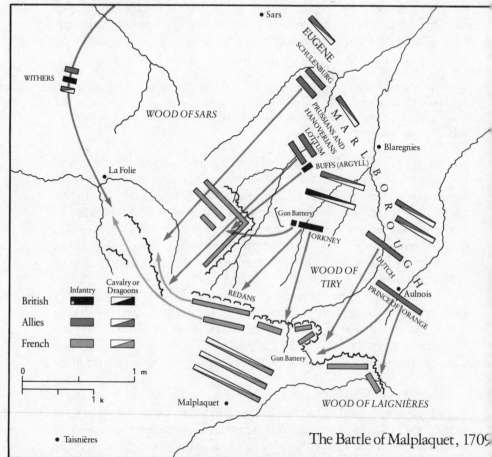

The Battle of Malplaquet, 1709

The battle that followed was horrific. Not only was each side equipped with heavy artillery that tore into the ranks of the other, but each side was in a fever of bellicosity, having been told that the very outcome of the war could depend on this day alone. Count Schulenburg and Count Lottum, under Eugene's orders, led the assault on the Wood of Sars which spread out for nearly a mile and supported the French left. Schulenburg's 20,000 Germans were formed in three lines but, in the 800 paces which they had to cross before reaching the forest, French musket-fire blazed into their first line, slaughtering hundreds of men, among them two major-generals and six colonels. The assailants were carried forward by the second and third lines and before long were strengthened by Count Lottum's battalions. Within the hour, over 50,000 Allied soldiers were fed into the salient. Although they outnumbered the enemy four to one, the latter was so well-entrenched that every inch of ground was contested, and an almost unimaginable death-grapple developed in which 60,000 men were engaged in a furious mêlée of hand-to-hand fighting. Hour after hour the glades re-echoed to the thunder of the volleys and the crash of companies bursting through the underbush. 'Before the end of the day', wrote Marlborough, 'we had 80 battalions in that wood and I believe there were more.'[51]

The attack on the French right in the Wood of Lanières began half an hour after Schulenburg's advance, and was even more severe. The young, devil-may-care Prince of Orange led thirty Dutch battalions and a Scottish brigade in Dutch service into the attack. His troops were met by the finest regiments of France – Picardy, Navarre, Piedmont and the French Royal Marines. This time the French not only outnumbered their assailants but had a nest of concealed batteries, consisting of twenty cannon. The Dutch advanced in perfect order but the cannon ripped through their ranks and they fell in swathes. They re-formed and continued to advance. The Prince's horse was shot from under him and a staff officer killed at his side. He lost 5,000 men before he was driven back. Luckily, the Prince of Hesse-Cassel with twenty-one squadrons of cavalry stopped the pursuit. Unsupported infantry had no chance against the murderous crossfire of the cannon, yet the Prince of Orange ordered a second assault and would have tried a third time if Marlborough had not appeared and commanded him to break off.

During this time Schulenburg and Lottum were moving slowly forward through the lethal woods on their right. The French soldiers were behind redoubts and at one moment 30,000 Allied infantrymen were trying to press forward within a triangle no more than 600 yards on each side. They had to make their way over ground on which 7,000 men lay dead and dying. Fighting forward foot by foot, they steadily gained ground; and at noon, after four hours of fierce combat, bloodstained and exhausted, the Allied line reached the plain on the other side of the wood.

Marlborough now ordered an attack on the centre. Lord Orkney with his British corps and several Prussian battalions were given the signal to advance, and to their great surprise took the position with no opposition. This, of course, was exactly how Marlborough had planned it: attack the wings and force the enemy to weaken his centre. The Duke now considered the battle as good as won. The cavalry would be left to rout the enemy. However, Marshal Villars had not finished fighting. He gathered together 3,000 soldiers and was determined to launch a counter-attack against the disorganized forces of Schulenburg and Lottum, just emerging from the woods. But as he rode forward with his staff he was caught by a burst of fire. The Marshal's horse fell dead and he tumbled onto the ground unconscious, his left leg smashed below the knee. He knew nothing more until he awoke in the hospital at Quesnoy. There he learned that General Chemerault had been killed and that General Albergotti had a broken thigh.

Marshal Boufflers was now in command and placed himself at the head of the Maison du Roi. All morning the French cavalry had been subjected to heavy cannon-fire and were so angry and discomforted they could scarcely wait to get to grips with the enemy. The Allied horsemen began to pour through the gaps in the woods on to the wide plain beyond. The Prince of Auvergne with thirty Dutch squadrons led the way, followed first by General Wood with the British cavalry, then by General Bulow and the Duke of Wurtemburg with the Prussian and Hessian horse.

As many as 30,000 horsemen took part in the cavalry battle, yet very little is known about it, apart from Lord Orkney's disjointed sentences. Orkney's infantry battalions now manned the whole line of redans and watched the fighting at close quarters. The French attacked the Allies piecemeal as they emerged from the wood and before they had a chance to form up; but wave after wave kept coming. All the fighting was done with the sword and Marshal Boufflers led the Maison du Roi in person. Six times the Allies charged these redoubtable French troopers, but each time they were repulsed. 'Sometimes they gained a little ground and were as fast beat back again.' However, Orkney's infantry poured such a volume of fire into the ranks of the pursuers that it made them 'retreat prodigiously'. 'I really believe', continued Orkney, 'had not ye foot been there they would have drove our horse out of the field.'[52]

However, it was the French, and not the Allies, who finally were forced to give way. Although Marlborough appeared when things were going badly and led the British and Prussian squadrons himself, it was Eugene's arrival with several thousand Imperial horsemen that turned the tables. Marshal Boufflers had no option but to withdraw; his centre was pierced, both his wings were in retreat and his cavalry was outnumbered. By three o'clock the French had left the field and were marching in orderly ranks towards the towns of Mauberge and Buvaï. Unfortunately, the Allied troops were too exhausted to pursue them. Marlborough went to his tent and wrote to Sarah:

> 11 September 1709
> I am so tired that I have but strength enough to tell you that we have had this day a very bloody battle; the first part of the day we beat their foot, and afterwards their horse. God almighty be praised, it is now in our powers to have what peace we please, and I may be pretty well assured of never being in another battle; but that nothing in this world can make me happy if you are not kind.[53]

The Allies lost 25,000 men killed and wounded, and the French another 11,000. For days the woods were crawling with mutilated beings. Marlborough had at least 15,000 wounded men of all nationalities on his hands. He invited the French to send wagons to collect their men and eliminated all red tape to avoid delay; he took every penny out of his military chest and spent it on the relief of the wounded, regardless of whether they were friends or enemies. 'I have hardly time to sleep,' he wrote to Godolphin, 'being tormented by the several nations for care to be taken of their wounded.'[54] To Sarah he wrote that his heart grieved at the numbers who had perished, 'for in this battle the French were more obstinate than in any other war.'[55]

Even the ebullient Lord Orkney could not forget the horrors of this particular battlefield. He wrote to his brother, describing how in many places, the dead

> lie as thick as ever did a flock of sheep. I really think I never saw the like; particularly where the Dutch Guards attacked it is a miracle. I hope in God it may be the last battle I may ever see. A very few of such would make both parties end the war very soon.[56]

The campaign was not yet finished as both Marlborough and Eugene insisted on capturing Mons – if only to prove that Villars's battle, fought to save the city, had been abortive. The siege was successful and in the course of it his jolly, young Quartermaster-General, Cadogan, got a bullet in the neck which, amazingly, was not fatal. 'I was with him this morning when they dressed his wound,' the Duke wrote anxiously to Sarah. 'As he is very fatt their greatest apprehension is growing feaverish. We must have patience for two or three dressings before the Surjeans can give judgement. I hope in God he will do well, for I can intierly depend upon him.'[57] Much to Marlborough's relief Cadogan recovered and lived to fight another day.

After the battle Marlborough suffered once again from blinding headaches. He wrote to Godolphin explaining why he had not answered his letters, and Godolphin passed the news on to Sarah who was beside herself with anxiety. 'Lady Marlborough has been so much alarmed at these letters, that it was with difficulty that she was prevailed with not to go over in the next packet boat to you,' Godolphin wrote to the Duke.[58] But Marlborough replied that he did not believe that his illness was due to physical reasons, but to his distress at the great number of men who had died in the battle. 'I believe it the chief cause of my illness, to see so many brave men killed with whom I have lived these eight years when we thought ourselves sure of a peace.'[59]

Twelve

Sarah's Dismissal

The Duke of Marlborough's failure to make peace at The Hague conference seemed to set in motion a cycle of misfortune which caught him in its grip. Nothing he did went right. In September 1709, after Malplaquet, he brushed aside the assurance he had given to Lord Cowper and made another request for a life appointment as Captain-General. This time the Queen refused him outright. Marlborough's reaction was uncharacteristic: he lost his urbane manner and replied in a snide, almost disrespectful way, as though Sarah's spirit was guiding him (which may well have been the case). He had made his request, he said, because he had been told that Mrs Masham had assured Mr Harley 'and some of his wretches that let my services or success's be what they would I should receive no encouragement from your Majesty which . . . must oblige me to retire.'

If it was foolish to make a request that was more than likely to be refused, it was amazingly tactless to mention Mrs Masham. And now the Duke made an even worse blunder by complaining of 'your Majesty's Change from Lady Marlborough to Mrs Masham & the several indignitys Mrs Masham has made her suffer,' and ended his letter,

> hoping that in time you will be sensible of the long and faithfull services of Lady Marlborough and that God will bless you with the opening of your eyes, soe that you may avoid the danger these people are running you into.[1]

The Queen was so annoyed by Marlborough's letter that she took nearly a month to answer it. Indeed, her sprightly reply suggests that a helping hand stirred the broth. 'It is not to be wondered that you should be so insensed against poor Masham since the Dutchess of Marlborough is soe . . . but she never said to Mr Harley or anybody what you are informed she did. . . .' The Queen then switched to the provocative Sarah:

> You seem to be disatisfyed with my behaviour to the Dutchess of Marlborough. I do not love Complaineing, but it is impossible to help saying on this occasion I beleeve no body was ever soe used by a friend as I have bin by her ever since my coming to ye Crown. I desire nothinge but that she should leave off teasing and tormenting me & behave herself with the desensy she ought both to her friend and Queen, and this I hope you will make her doe, & is what I am sure no reasonable body can wonder I should desire of you, whatever her behaviour to me, mine to her shall always be as becomes me.
>
> I shall end this letter as you did yourse to me, wishing both your eyes and the Dutchesse of Marlboroughs may be opened and that you may ever be happy.[2]

And to Sarah the next day:

> It is impossible for you to recover my former kindness but I shall behave myself to you as the Duke of Marlborough's wife and as my Groom of the Stole.[3]

It was unfortunate that Marlborough's altercations with the Queen should have come at the same time that Sarah was behaving in a particularly offensive way. Encouraged by Maynwaring the Duchess picked a series of quarrels with the Queen over trivial details stemming from Anne's failure – no doubt intentional – to honour the prerogatives of Sarah's offices. For instance, the Queen appointed Mrs Danvers's daughter, Belle, as a bedchamber-woman and raised the salary of Elizabeth Abraham, the royal laundress, without consulting Sarah, who saw these acts as a display of Abigail's power. When, on top of this, Sarah learned that Abigail had been given rooms in St James's Palace near her own, she went to the Queen requesting these same rooms for her husband. The Queen, of course, refused and Sarah asked if she might repeat in public how, after the great services Lord Marlborough had done her Majesty, he was not allowed 'a miserable hole to make a clean way to his lodgings'.[4]

Sarah's anger with the Queen, of course, still sprang from jealousy. She could not accept the fact that the devotion she had inspired in Anne for so many years had been transferred to her dull and rather ugly cousin, and that none was left for her. When she discussed it with Maynwaring he only laughed and said that what she had lost was the Queen's passion and, as she had not cared for that, he would not offer his condolences. Nevertheless, Sarah refused to allow the subject of

Abigail to drop and when she saw the Queen privately (which was not often) she invariably made a point of referring to the latter's 'passion for Masham'. Apparently, Maynwaring had convinced Sarah that by disparaging her cousin she could turn her into such a figure of fun that the Queen would lose interest in her. 'A good ridicule', he said, 'has often gone a long way in doing a business; and this I am sure is such a thing that it needs only to be mentioned to make it ridiculous.'[5] But Sarah had no gift for light-hearted ridicule, and, far from impairing Abigail's influence, only made her own presence increasingly unwelcome.

However, nothing deterred her and she now composed a tedious sermon, described as a 'Narrative', which she sent to the Queen on 29 October. (The Queen's letter to Marlborough complaining of the Duchess's behaviour had just been written and sent abroad.) The sermon began by recounting Sarah's great services to Anne during the reign of James II, then went on to exhort her to follow the precepts of *The Whole Duty of Man* by intense self-examination before receiving the Holy Sacrament. Such 'self-examination' would force the Queen to admit Mrs Masham's 'dominance' and perhaps even to recognize that 'such things can proceed from nothing but extravagant passion'. 'Ask your heart seriously', she wrote, 'whether you have ever told me of any fault but that of believing as all the world does that you have an intimacy with Mrs M. and whether those shocking things you complain I have said was any more than desiring you to love me better than her & not to take away your confidence in me.' The letter finishes with the usual attack on Mrs Masham – this time because the favourite has dared to accuse Sarah of 'inveteracy and malice': 'I do not comprehend how one can properly bee said to have malice and inveteracy for a viper because one endeavours to hinder it from doing mischief.'[6]

Later the Duchess explained to Maynwaring that she had written her 'Narrative' 'for tho it will never cure her passion . . . the truths I tell her tho it makes her hate me, makes it more easy for her ministers to govern her.'[7] No matter how vindictive her actions, Sarah always managed to dress them in an altruistic guise which Maynwaring accepted with genuine admiration. Marlborough had no idea of the sort of letters his wife had been composing. Nevertheless, when he returned to England on 10 November 1709, he managed to persuade her to break off her correspondence, at least for the time being.

Mr Robert Harley was a much more dangerous adversary than cousin Abigail. Nevertheless, the favourite played an important role in destroying Marlborough's influence with the Queen, as her hatred of Sarah, fanned by the latter's slanders, extended to all members of the Churchill family. Abigail was delighted to act as Harley's intermediary and in 1709 frequently led the little man up the back-stairs of Kensington Palace for secret talks with the Queen. He could not hope to get rid of Marlborough until the fighting stopped, so he kept this plan to himself and merely stressed the blessings of peace. Nevertheless, he launched a campaign against the Captain-General by repeating the vicious lies circulating in Tory political circles. All of them were based on Marlborough's well-known partiality for money. He was deliberately prolonging the war, they said, because of the huge emoluments he was receiving; and he always supported the Imperialists because the Emperor's offer of the governorship of the Spanish Netherlands at a salary of £60,000 a year was still in the offing. The most monstrous slander, however, concerned Malplaquet. He had heedlessly sacrificed the lives of many of his officers in order to sell their commissions! This vile accusation was particularly outrageous as Marlborough himself had discontinued the practice of selling commissions when Anne appointed him Captain-General. He probably did this because he felt it might prevent him from picking the best man for the job. Further grist to Harley's mill was the Duke's request for a life-appointment as Captain-General. Was he planning a new Cromwellian dictatorship and aiming at the Crown itself? Abigail seized this point and went about referring to Marlborough as 'King John II'.

In January 1710, when Lord Essex died, the Lieutenancy of the Tower of London, together with that of the Oxford Regiment, fell vacant. Harley had another chance to strike a blow at Marlborough. On his instructions Abigail probably put the idea into the Queen's head that it would be amusing to demonstrate to the Captain-General that the sovereign, and the sovereign alone, was head of the British army for life. The Queen fell in with the suggestion and appointed Lord Rivers (a follower of Harley) to the Tower post. Marlborough was flabbergasted. It was customary for the commander to propose a name and he had already promised the post to the Duke of Northumberland. Far worse, on the same day Anne wrote a peremptory letter to Marlborough instructing him to appoint to Lord Rivers's vacant regiment no other person than Abigail Masham's brother, Colonel Hill. This was the individual who had come into Sarah's life twenty years earlier, and is described in her memoirs as 'Jack Hill, a tall boy whom I clothed (for he was all in rags) and put to school.' She had done everything to help him, getting him a job first as a page in Prince George's household, then as groom to the Duke of Gloucester.

If it had not been for Sarah, he would not be in the army at all, for she had insisted that her husband take him as an aide-de-camp although 'he always said he was good for nothing'. In the past ten years 'he had never distinguished himself unless it were over a bottle',[8] and now the Queen was demanding a regiment for him to please her favourite.

Marlborough realized that the Queen's request was a studied insult planned by Harley. To promote Mrs Masham's brother over the heads of far more competent officers, who had risked their lives in battle, would be an injustice of the most flagrant kind. Furthermore, it would destroy Marlborough's authority in the army, for his officers could scarcely fail to see where the real control lay. When the Duke had an audience with the Queen and protested, she was like a stranger. The Majesty who once had been so warm and gracious, so overflowing with gratitude, so solicitous of the Duke's well-being, was now cold and aloof. Although he used every argument he could muster to show her what damage the promotion would do to army morale she never once smiled, and ended the discussion with the words: 'You will do well to advise with your friends.'

Both Lord Somers and Lord Cowper urged the Queen to reconsider her decision, but she was adamant. At the same time she went out of her way to emphasize her high regard for Marlborough and to insist that she was asking for very little, much less than 'most princes'. 'It is the Queen's change to me', Marlborough replied to Cowper, 'that has brook my sperit . . . for I can't but think the Nation wou'd be of opinion that I have deserv'd better than to be made a sacrifice to the unreasonable passion of a bedchamber-woman.'[9]

Mr Maynwaring had several close friends in the Whig Junto, and he now stepped forward to try and help. 'It is Children's play', he told Sarah, 'for any men to hold the first Posts in a government and not have it in their power to remove such a slut as that Abigail.'[10] Maynwaring attended meetings with Marlborough and his Cabinet colleagues, and on 19 January made the novel suggestion to Lord Somers (a member of the Whig Junto) and Lord Sunderland of introducing a petition in the House of Commons asking the Queen to remove Abigail from her household. Although the two ministers accepted the plan, other members of the party protested that 'it was impossible for any man of sense, honour or honesty to come into an Address to remove a dresser from the Queen . . . only to gratifie my Lady Marlborough's passions.'[11] Nevertheless, Sunderland made arrangements to introduce the petition in four days' time, on 23 January. When the Queen heard of their intention, she flew into a furious rage. One of her ladies-in-waiting said that the anger was such that in the thirty years she had served, 'she had never seen the like'.[12] However, the threat was effective, for the next day, 20 January, she told Lord Godolphin that Hill would not be appointed.

Meanwhile, Marlborough drafted a letter telling the Queen that he could not continue to execute his duties while Abigail was advising her Majesty, and asking her to choose between them. Godolphin, however, was a timid man who hated taking issue with the Queen and begged Marlborough not to send the ultimatum. After much argument the Duke deferred to him, but some of his colleagues felt that he had missed a splendid opportunity to quash the Abigail–Harley faction. However, considering Anne's obstinacy and the fact that twenty years earlier she had remained impervious to far more serious threats involving Sarah, Marlborough may have done the wise thing. Despite his withdrawal, the Queen never forgave him for the threat, and if a date can be put to the time when her resentment against Marlborough began to outweigh her gratitude, this was undoubtedly the moment. In February 1710, when he left for the peace conference at Gertruydenberg in Holland, his son-in-law travelled to the coast to say goodbye to him: 'None of our heads are safe', Lord Sunderland remarked gloomily, 'if we don't get the better of what I am convinced Mrs Morley designs.'[13]

The new peace conference offered Marlborough one more chance of ending the war. The most bellicose people in Europe were the Whig leaders who were now at the zenith of their power in England. 'No Peace Without Spain' (a phrase which Marlborough himself had coined many years earlier) had become ingrained in their thinking; and, although the conception eventually proved to be as absurd as it sounded, they were still obsessed with it. Nine days after the battle of Malplaquet, Lord Godolphin had a talk with Sir Gilbert Heathcote, Governor of the Bank of England, which he described in a letter to Marlborough:

'Pray, My Lord,' he said to Godolphin, 'don't let's have a rotten peace.' 'Pray tell me,' I answered, 'What do you call a rotten peace?' 'I call a rotten peace,' he said, 'unless we have Spain.' 'But Sir Gilbert,' I said, 'I want you a little to consider the circumstances of the Duke of Marlborough and me; we are railed at every day for having a mind, as they call it, to perpetuate the war.' He replied very quick, 'They are a company of rotten rogues; I'll warrant you we'll stand by you.'[14]

The five lords of the Whig Junto, all of whom had managed to push their way to the Queen's council-table by the end of 1709, reflected the same opinions as Sir Gilbert, but by this time Marlborough knew that if the Allies wanted the sort of peace they were talking about, they could only get it by signing a separate treaty with France and fighting another full-scale war with Spain. Although the Alliance had done badly in the peninsula (once again they had been pushed back to Catalonia), the Duke was confident they could depose Philip 'in less than six months if just and vigorous [military] measures are taken by England and Holland.'[15] But there was no enthusiasm for a second major war. The Dutch flatly refused to consider it, and the English recoiled from fighting it alone. 'A Spanish war may prove very troublesom as well as expensive,' Marlborough's chaplain, Francis Hare, wrote in August 1709, 'and the load will lie entirely upon England when the other Allies have got what they want.'[16] So Spain remained the stumbling-block, with the Allies clinging fatuously to the notion that the King of France must be forced to deliver the Spanish prize at no cost or trouble to themselves.

Unfortunately, the French were not so complacent in the immediate aftermath of Malplaquet. 'The last battle', claimed Torcy, 'had rather raised the courage of our nation than weakened it.'[17] To the surprise of military observers, Marlborough and Eugene had failed to crush the enemy's resistance; the frontiers of France remained inviolate and Villars still had an army with which he could continue the war. Indeed, Boufflers wrote ecstatically to Louis suggesting that Villars's wound had forced the French withdrawal. 'But I can assure your Majesty that never has a misfortune been accompanied by so much *gloire*.'[18] Villars's letters were equally buoyant and soon the following parody was circulating throughout England:

> This is to let Your Majesty understand that to your immortal Honour, and the destruction of the Confederates, your troops have lost another battle. Artagnan did wonders, Rohan performed miracles, Guiche did wonders, Gattion performed miracles; the whole army performed miracles and everyone did wonders. And to conclude the wonders of the day I can assure your Majesty, that tho you have lost the field of battle, you have not lost an inch of ground. The Enemy marched behind us with respect, and we ran away from them as bold as lions.[19]

Despite the English mockery of the French, Malplaquet at the very least was a moral victory for Louis. The Allies had not believed that the King could even field an army, much less an army that could hold at bay two such brilliant commanders as 'the twin princes'. France not only had protected her soil from invasion but had demonstrated that she could continue the war. Indeed, she was already recruiting soldiers for the next year's campaign.

Although France was not as abject in 1710 as she had been the year before, she still was desperately eager for peace. She made it clear that she was willing to sign the preliminary articles if the negotiators could find a way around Article XXXVII. Apparently this was beyond the capability of the Allies, who refused to abandon the idea of winning Spain effortlessly. The French did their best to reach an agreement. They pledged strict neutrality if the Allies attacked Spain; and if the Allies did not wish to attack Spain, Louis would try to persuade his grandson to abdicate in exchange for some inducement such as Naples and Sicily, or Sardinia and another of the Mediterranean islands. However, as extracts from Marlborough's letters show, Holland and Austria found it impossible to reach an accord.

> 12 March
>
> The Court of Vienna had much rather not have a separate peace than allow any part of the Monarque of Spain to the Duke of Anjou [Philip v].

> 19 March
>
> The States-General are as positive in putting an end to the war at once by giving the Duke of Anjou a partage [of the Spanish Empire].

> 13 April
>
> The Imperialists Continue Very obstinat in never consenting to any Partage.[20]

It is sad that the great Duke of Marlborough lacked the will to pull the dissident factions together and to fight for peace with the same energy with which he waged war. Considering that in 1708 he had written secretly to France suggesting that the time had come to discuss peace, historians have been baffled by the minor part he chose to play in 1709 and 1710. Although his failure at The Hague is understandable – a straight case of miscalculation – his performance at the second conference is more difficult to fathom. At home things were not going well for him – he had every incentive to knock his Allies' heads together and force them to reach an agreement. Despite all that has been written about the strident demands of the Whigs and their dominant position in Parliament, he, and he alone, had the stature to impose a settlement. The Queen and the Tories were eager for peace, and the Whigs would have been obliged to acquiesce, particularly if they felt that the Duke's resignation was on the line.

It was worth a pitched battle to reach a solution, but Marlborough seemed to have no clear idea as to what sort of a Europe he would like to see. He deplored the rapaciousness of his Allies and had been shocked by the demand that Louis fight his grandson. The aim of the Grand Alliance seemed to have swerved from the preservation of liberty to the destruction of France. Now was the time to revert to the conviction that Marlborough had expressed several years before: that peace would never be negotiated unless the Spanish Empire was divided as William III had suggested. Why did he not grasp this solution and push it forward with all his authority? Certainly it would call for a change of front on his part, and stir up a hornet's nest of Whig resistance at home. Sarah would have been the most indignant of all – was he afraid of her waspish antagonism?

His failure to make any acceptable proposal to the French prompted his critics to say that he had gained so much from patience that he had lost the quality of revolt. The truth was that Marlborough was a great soldier and a great public servant, but not a great statesman. He always shrank from verbal confrontation. He was a secret man who preferred the by-ways to the open road. His weapons were charm and dissimulation but these were not the guns that could forge a peace. By allowing the talks to drift on inconclusively, he automatically staked his future on a *dictated* peace, which meant marching to Paris.

> If his countrymen and his colleagues [wrote an anonymous critic], if the States-General, if the Empire, chose to frustrate the French desire for peace and conjure him to lead the strongest armies yet known to the invasion of France and march to Paris he would willingly, too willingly, be their servant and commander.[21]

This probably comes as close as anything to summing up Marlborough's attitude. War, not peace, was his *métier*. What would he do when he reached Paris? In one of his letters, he talks of deposing Louis XIV and setting up a constitutional monarchy, although judging from the violent birth-pains of parliamentary government under Queen Anne, the experiment probably would have proved dramatically unworkable. But all this is only conjecture. Marlborough's refusal – or inability – to grasp the nettle and make peace was the greatest failure of his life. It not only gave his enemies the handle they needed to damage his credibility but detracted from his posthumous fame.

No one, of course, was more delighted than Mr Harley to learn that the talks in Gertruydenberg were leading nowhere. The Queen –

indeed the whole country – was chafing with impatience; but as Harley's chance of regaining office depended on Marlborough's diminishing prestige, he rejoiced at the Duke's second failure to reach an agreement. No one could see far ahead politically, but Harley was never idle and had begun to gather the support of ambitious and powerful aristocrats who were acceptable to the Queen. His first three recruits were impressive: although nominal Whigs they were independent of the Junto and prepared (secretly) to back the moderate Tories.

His most important convert was the one-eyed Duke of Shrewsbury – the King of Hearts – once a close friend of Marlborough. He had conspired with Churchill against James, and had sprung to Churchill's defence when William had dismissed him. Towards the end of William's reign Shrewsbury had left England and gone to live in Rome; there he had married a well-born Italian lady with deplorable manners and strong social ambitions. In 1706 she finally induced him to return to London so that she could become a great hostess. Although on the surface the Shrewsburys and the Marlboroughs were still friends, some people detected a certain coolness on the part of the Italian Duchess which they attributed to Sarah's tales about the lady's pretensions and her peculiar manner of expressing herself. The fact that Shrewsbury shifted his support from the Duumvirs to Harley was said to be due to his wife's ambition. As long as Sarah Marlborough held the Gold Key of her high office, there was no opening at Court for the Duchess of Shrewsbury.

Another independent Whig, recruited by Harley, was the Duke of Somerset, one of England's greatest 'milords'. He had loaned Syon House to Princess Anne when she was quarrelling with her sister, Queen Mary, over Sarah, and had forced Harley's resignation in 1708 by refusing to sit at the Cabinet without Marlborough. Somerset's wife was the Percy heiress who had been married three times before reaching the age of sixteen and was a companion of the Queen. Harley was anxious to recruit her husband because, apart from great wealth and influence, he had direct access to the sovereign. Harley seduced Somerset quite easily by hinting that he might be the right man to succeed Lord Godolphin at the Treasury – a grotesque suggestion which people laughed at behind his back, but which Somerset took seriously. The Duke of Argyll completed Harley's triumvirate. He was a general who had served under Marlborough but was bitterly jealous of his chief and shockingly disloyal. His father had been beheaded by James II, so he had no love for the Stuarts; nevertheless, he was prepared to follow Harley if he could pull down Marlborough and increase his own influence in the army.

Although Harley's activities created rumours that ministerial changes were in the offing, it was difficult at the beginning of 1710 to see how they could be brought about. The hated Whig Junto dominated the Queen's Council Board and the Whig party commanded large majorities in Parliament. The Queen still smouldered with anger at the way they had managed to impose themselves on the royal will, but what could she do? Then, on 27 February, nine days after Marlborough's departure for his headquarters in Flanders, a trial opened in London that unleashed a blaze of resentment against the Government which, until this moment, had seemed impregnable. Thus Harley's faith in the unexpected was justified.

The spark that caused the conflagration was a sermon preached in St Paul's at the invitation of the Lord Mayor by a crypto-Jacobite parson, Dr Henry Sacheverell. His subject, 'The Perils of False Brethren both in Church and State', was a muddled diatribe which might be construed as an attack on the Government, the Revolution settlement and the Hanoverian succession. Normally, Sacheverell's bombasts went unnoticed as he was a fanatic who ranted and raved each Sunday. Sarah described him as 'a lewd, drunken, pampered man' and 'an ignorant, impudent incendiary'.[22] 'Incendiary' was an apt description, for he suddenly caught the popular imagination and the Lord Mayor printed and distributed 40,000 copies of his sermon.

Lord Godolphin was particularly incensed as he recognized himself as one of the 'false brethren'; in this case he was depicted as 'a wily Volpone' who had deserted the Tory party for political gain.[23] For once his common sense deserted him and, with the support of Sunderland and Wharton, he rashly set in motion an impeachment for 'high crimes'. Sir Christopher Wren was ordered to construct scaffolding in Westminster Hall that would provide seating for the world of rank and fashion, and a special area was roped off for the Queen and her ladies.

The trial was a great spectacle but not a great occasion. Indeed, one observer deplored 'so solemn a prosecution for such a scribble'. Although Sacheverell had not uttered a word against the Queen, he had talked about the duty of people to accept the Divine Right of Kings with mental 'non-resistance'. This enabled the Whig prosecution to hinge the trial on the question: was the monarchy based on hereditary or parliamentary right? The Whigs, of course, championed the parliamentary case, arguing that James II had broken his contract with the people, therefore resistance had been right and proper. Indeed, William and Mary and Anne herself owed their titles to the decision of Parliament. In order to give further weight to their case, they went on to admit that the famous warming-pan story, which they had put into circulation in 1688 to prove James's son was an imposter, was pure invention. This meant, of course, that the Pretender was the hereditary heir. However, they took pains to stress that Anne had an even stronger claim as she was Queen by will of Parliament and the nation.

The London mob cared nothing about Divine Right or the fine points of the Anglican belief; the only thing they knew was that a Tory clergyman had attacked the Whig Government, and that the Whig Government was responsible for their poverty and unemployment. So they decided to demonstrate in favour of the parson. Riots broke out, the pews of dissenting chapels were ripped out and made into bonfires, and there was even talk that gangs were planning to assault that sacred Whig institution, the Bank of England. Mr Hoffmann, the Imperial resident who had resided in London for twenty-five years, reported home that the kingdom had not experienced such convulsions since Cromwell's time.

The rioters believed their miserable living conditions were due to the Whigs' never-ending war. In London, grain prices had soared to new heights and the cost of bread had doubled. During the Queen's reign the National Debt had risen from £10,000,000 to £50,000,000. Inflationary prices, increased taxation, compulsory military recruitment, all were direct results of the war, and Dr Sacheverell was a humble Tory parson championing the downtrodden against the Whig persecutors. So the crowds gave enthusiastic support to the 'doctor', surrounding the coach in which he rode to and from Westminster Hall each day and cheering him loudly. Beggars even pressed forward to touch his garments.

On 22 March Sacheverell was found guilty by such a narrow vote (sixty to fifty-two) that it was tantamount to a defeat for the Government. 'So all this bustle and fatigue', exclaimed Godolphin, 'ends in no more than a suspension of three years from the pulpit and burning his sermon in the Old Exchange.'[24] Sacheverell was given a living by a Tory supporter and enjoyed a popularity quite new to him.

The Duchess of Marlborough, who attended the trial each day, was far less interested in the defendant than in the etiquette observed by the Queen's ladies. She took umbrage at the fact that the Duchess of Somerset (the Percy heiress) insisted on standing all day in deference to Her Majesty. Sarah had asked the Queen for permission to sit, which had been readily granted, but when she imparted this information to the rival Duchess the latter stared at her as though she had done something impertinent and refused to avail herself of the royal graciousness. 'It was easy to see the meaning of all this,' wrote Sarah, 'and that my gold key was the thing aim'd att. . . .'[25]

A few weeks later Sarah heard that 'false and malicious stories' had been told to the Queen and asked to see Her Majesty 'to vindicate' herself. The Queen, however, had no wish to see the Duchess of Marlborough and on 3 April commanded her to put her thoughts in writing. Sarah refused to be fobbed off and replied that nothing would thwart her determination to talk privately to the Queen.

> If this afternoon be not convenient I will come this very day and wait till You please to allow me to speak to you.

Sarah then gave a fatal promise of which the Queen made the maximum use:

> *And one thing more I assure Your Majesty which is, that what I have to say will have no Consequence either to oblige you to answer or to see me oftener hereafter than will be easy to you.*[26]

The Queen saw Sarah that same afternoon in her small dark closet at Kensington Palace. Years later Sarah wrote many drafts of this famous interview which proved to be the last meeting between the two women. One of the versions was in dialogue form. When she began to speak the Queen interrupted her coldly, saying several times: 'There is nothing you can have to say but you may write it.' But Sarah quickly came to the point.

> LADY MARLBOROUGH: There is a thousand lyes made of me, which are so rediculous that I should never have thought it necessary to goe about to clear myself of what never entered into my head . . . and I do assure your Majesty that there is severall things which I have heard has been told to your Majesty that I have said of you, that I am no more capable of than I am of killing my children.

(Sarah does not reveal what she was alleged to have said, but undoubtedly it referred to lesbianism, for she tells us that when she repeated it to the Queen 'she turned her face from me as if she fear'd blushing upon something I might say to her.')

> QUEEN: There is without doubt many lyes told.

> LADY MARLBOROUGH: Pray Madam, tell me what you have

> heard of me that I may not trouble you to repeat more disagreeable things than is necessary.
>
> QUEEN: You said you desired no answer & I shall give you none.

Sarah begged again to 'know what you have heard that I might be able to clear myself.'

> QUEEN: You said you desired noe answer and I shall give you none.

After an attack on the Duke and Duchess of Somerset, Sarah returned to the charge.

> QUEEN: I shall make you noe answer to anything you say.
>
> LADY MARLBOROUGH: Will your Majesty make me some answer att some other time, since you won't now?
>
> QUEEN: I shall make you no answer.

Then my tears dropt again, which was strange, but I could not help it & suppose it must be at such inhuman usage.

> LADY MARLBOROUGH: You know, Madam, how much I have dispised interest in comparison of serving you & of doing what was right & you are sure I would not disown anything that were true, & I assure your Majesty I have never don any thing that you have reason to be displeased att, then I cryd again.
>
> QUEEN: I shall make you noe answer to anything you say
> at which I made my chursey, saying I was confident she would suffer in this world, or the next for so much inhumanity, & to that she answered, that would bee to herself.[27]

When Sarah reached the Long Gallery she sat down and dried her tears and tried to compose herself. Apparently she could not bear to think that the long friendship had ended on such a dismal note and went back to the Queen's closet and knocked on the door. Anne herself opened it. It would be difficult to imagine more of an anti-climax. There stood the Duchess of Marlborough with nothing in particular to say, only that when her Majesty went to Windsor Sarah would avoid being at the Lodge. 'To this she readily answered that I might come to her to the Castle and she would not be uneasy at it.'[28] But Anne had no intention of seeing Sarah again if she could avoid it.

The riots and street demonstrations provoked by the Sacheverell trial heralded the end of the Whig Government and marked the in-evitability of the Marlboroughs' fall from power. At last Harley saw the way ahead. The Queen's breach with Sarah was permanent; how long would Her Majesty deem it necessary to put up with her Captain-General? The general election would not be held until Octo-ber as bargains had to be struck with the Lords-Lieutenant that might be called 'rigging'. However, the Tories were so joyful that many of them who had not been in London for months visited Kensington Palace to pay their respects. 'Your Majesty', said the Jacobite Duke of Beaufort, bowing deeply, 'is Queen indeed.'[29]

Harley was so confident of victory at the polls that his first move was to encourage the Queen to start making ministerial changes. His advice was faultless. Her first move was to dismiss the Earl of Kent as Lord Chamberlain and to appoint the Duke of Shrewsbury in his stead. Anne did not make the change until Godolphin had gone to Newmarket, so that she had an excuse for not informing him of her decision. Nevertheless the Lord Treasurer was under no misap-prehension as to what was happening and protested strongly at not being consulted.

Two months later, in May 1710, rumours were rife that the next victim would be Lord Sunderland. This was a much more serious proposal as Sunderland was the ablest member of the Junto and a son-in-law of Marlborough, which was bound to cause a stir abroad. However, the Whigs were so demoralized by the result of the Sacheverell trial that ministers were more concerned in saving their own skins than in combining to defend one another. As a result none of them lifted a finger to save Sunderland except Godolphin, who did everything in his power to try to alter the Queen's decision. Marl-borough wrote a strong letter of protest which Godolphin showed to Anne, but it had no effect. 'It is true indeed', she replied to her Lord Treasurer,

> that ye turning a son-in-law out of office may be a mortification to the D. of Marl but must the fate of Europe depend on that & must he be grate-fyed in all his desires and I not in soe reasonable a thing as parting with a

man who I took into my Service with all ye uneasyness emaginable & whose behaviour to me has bin soe ever since & who I must add is I believe obnoxious to all people except a few. . . .[30]

The Queen ordered Henry Boyle, a joint Secretary of State, to procure the seals from Sunderland. When Boyle protested that he was Sunderland's friend, Anne replied briskly, 'Best done by a friend'. As the Queen had no reason for dimissing Sunderland except personal dislike, she offered him a pension of £3,000 a year, but he declined the money, saying: 'If I can't have the honour of serving my country I will not plunder it.'[31] Then he retired to Althorp where he immersed himself in his wonderful library and waited for a change in the political scene.

The men jostling for power knew that this was only a beginning, as Harley would not be satisfied until he had driven Lord Godolphin from the Treasury and taken his place as the Queen's first minister. Anne, however, was nervous about dismissing Godolphin – not because he had served her for thirty years and was competent and incorruptible but because she feared that his departure would cause a furore in the City and might damage the nation's new credit system. However, Abigail Masham did useful work for Harley by reminding the Queen of Godolphin's close friendship with Sarah Marlborough. This line of attack was so successful that in May 1710, a month after the Queen's final meeting with Sarah, Anne complained to one of her doctors, Sir David Hamilton, 'that the Duchess made my lord Marlborough and my lord Godolphin do anything, and that when my lord Godolphin was ever so finally resolv'd when with Her Majesty, yet when he went to her [Sarah] she impress'd him to the contrary.'[32]

According to Hamilton the Queen often lamented: 'O, that my lord Godolphin would be parted with the Duchess of Marlborough I should be very happy.' Hamilton was a man of exceptional charm and tact and the Queen decided to use him as an intermediary. On 15 May she asked him 'to see, if it was possible, to bring my lord Godolphin off from the Duchess; for that would be one of the happiest things imaginable. That she did believe the City would be in an Uproar if he was turn'd out, and she was perswaded that he greatly study'd her Ease.'[33]

The following day Hamilton reported back to the Queen that Godolphin would not consider severing his ties with Sarah. 'It was impossible', he said, 'their Relation being so near, and their Circumstances so united, for him to break off with the Duchess.'[34] The Queen accepted this answer as final and for the time being allowed the matter to drop.

Meanwhile the eyes of Europe were fastened on the Continent where the two great commanders, Marlborough and Eugene, were assembling their armies. The Allies were so anxious to see Marlborough bring the war to an end that they had given him the largest army ever – 120,000 men compared to Villars's force of 85,000. Would the twin captains try to force a decisive battle? Or would they revert to the untried plan of seizing a coastal town as a supply-base and drive into France? With the new climate in England, and the threat of a Tory victory at the polls, the Whigs felt that a sensational victory in the field was the only thing that could save them.

Yet of all Marlborough's campaigns, the campaign of 1711 proved to be the least sensational, the most conventional. The reason was not discernible by the public but Marlborough's close colleagues were aware of it. The great Duke was suffering from an acute loss of nerve (not physical: he did not know the meaning of fear on the battlefield), arising from mental stress. With the loss of the Queen's favour and the increasing animosity of the Tories, he feared that his enemies might fabricate charges that would strip him of his *gloire*. Indeed, they might pounce on a single military mistake to remove him from his command, even to subject him to an impeachment. He wrote to Godolphin that the Tories would like to see his army beaten – even though it was their army too! 'But if I live I will be ever so watchful', he continued, 'that it will not be in their power to do much hurt.' He referred bitterly to Harley's recruit, the Duke of Argyll, and claimed that the latter was telling people

> that when I please there will then be a peace. I suppose his friends speak the same language in England, so that I must every summer venture my life in a battle, and be found fault with in the winter for not bringing home peace, though I wish it with all my heart.[35]

In order to avoid an error of judgement, Marlborough adopted the uncharacteristic attitude of extreme caution. As a result, when Marshal Villars arrived to take command of the French army, the Allies were playing safe and concentrating on reducing the heavily fortified citadel of Douai. Eugene was conducting the siege operations under the protection of the Duke's military umbrella. Although Villars should have been convalescing, he appeared with his knee clamped in a special iron device that caused him excruciating pain but enabled him to review his troops on horseback. On 4 May the Marshal moved his troops forward to within two miles of the chain of redoubts that they had built and 'seemed determined to give the Duke battle', wrote Captain Robert Parker. 'He began to cannonade us with great fury and this brought Prince Eugene from the siege with as many guns as could be spared.'[36] Villars spent twenty-four hours of indecision, but after consultation with the Duke of Berwick decided that Marlborough's position was too strong, and withdrew. Although Douai capitulated on 27 June, Marlborough was criticized in England for not having launched his own attack, particularly when the Marshal was manœuvring in front of him.

Many people attributed Marlborough's refusal to take the offensive to the ghastly slaughter at Malplaquet which they claimed had made a deep impression on him. This may have played some part, but the news from England was more to blame. A few weeks before the surrender of Douai, Marlborough learned that Sunderland had been dismissed and Lord Dartmouth appointed in his place. 'What I hear from England', he wrote to Heinsius in Holland, 'gives me so much spleen that I long extremely to be out of all publick business.'[37] Stories of Tory vindictiveness edged his distress with alarm, and he began to fear that false accusations might be trumped up against Sarah to get her out of the way. If only she would stop sending letters to the Queen! 'For God's sake,' he wrote to her in cypher, 'let me begg of 240 [Sarah] to be careful of her behaviour for shee is in a country of Tygers and Wolves.'[38] But Sarah was in a reckless mood and refused to end her unsolicited correspondence. 'I will vex her [the Queen] so much', she wrote to Maynwaring, 'as to convince even her own stupid understanding that she has used me ill and then let her shutt herself up with Mrs Masham.'[39] As we know, one man's poison is another man's meat, so while the Marlboroughs were lamenting Sunderland's dismissal the Marquis of Torcy was rejoicing. He saw it as the first step in a Tory revival that might save France; and without more ado broke off the peace negotiations at Gertruydenberg and sat back waiting for the tide to turn.

Marlborough remained anxious and depressed. The impression he gave of imperturbability was misleading, for he had the volatile temperament of the artist. He flourished on admiration and encouragement and was profoundly affected by the Queen's indifference. Gone were the panache and audacity that prompted him to take incredible risks and score incredible successes. Marlborough himself was the first to admit his loss of confidence. 'I long for an end to the war,' he wrote to Lord Godolphin on 12 June, '. . . but I can't say that I have the same sanguine prophetic spirit I did use to have; for in all former action I never did doubt of success, we having had constantly the great blessing of being in one mind. I cannot say it is so now. . . .'[40]

Marlborough pondered over his old idea of an amphibious operation, and looked at Calais and Boulogne as possible supply-bases of a march to Paris. But once again he rejected the idea, this time for a very different reason. He would be dependent on supplies from England and he did not believe that he could rely on English support! 'The little consideration that the Queen has for you and me', Marlborough wrote to Godolphin on 2 August, 'makes it not safe for me to make any proposal for the employing those regiments now in the Isle of Wight; though if things were as formerly I could attempt a project on the sea coast that might prove advantageous.' Marlborough ended his letter gloomily: '. . . as everything is now, I dare attempt nothing, but what I am almost sure must succeed; nor am I sure those now in power would keep my secret.'[41] The fact that the Queen's Commander-in-Chief was afraid of being betrayed by the Queen's ministers indicates the peril of walking in the corridors of power at that time! Marlborough and Eugene were accustomed to sudden changes of fortune and simply shrugged their shoulders and turned their attention to capturing Bethune, Saint-Venant and Aire. The Bethune attack was prolonged and bloody, costing the Allies 4,000 men.

In August, in the middle of this offensive, Marlborough learned of Godolphin's dismissal. Sarah wrote to him with the details. On 7 August the Lord Treasurer had had a long talk with the Queen who received him with marked cordiality. When he took his leave he asked: 'Is it the will of your Majesty that I should go on?' Without a moment's hesitation she said 'Yes', but the next morning one of her servants (Sarah claimed later that it was the Duke of Somerset's groom) brought him a letter complaining of his 'unkind returns' which made it 'impossible for me to continue you any longer in my service. But I will give you a pension of £4,000 a year, and I desire that, instead of bringing your staff to me, you will break it which, I believe, will be easier to us both.'[42]

Harley was not given the coveted job of Lord Treasurer as it was thought wiser to put the Treasury into commission until things quietened down. Instead, he was made Chancellor of the Exchequer. However, the Queen did not honour her promise to give Godolphin a pension, and he would have been very badly off if it had not been for the unexpected death of his elder brother a week after his dismissal. He inherited a sum of money which gave him an income of £4,000 a year.

Prince Eugene reported the news to his Emperor. 'I am afraid', confided the well-known misogynist, 'that we must expect things to go from bad to worse in England as long as a woman is in charge. She lets herself be led by many wrong-headed people. . . . I have spoken about it to the Duke of Marlborough and implored him not to despair but to wait and see what the next campaign brings forth.'[43] Marlborough had already made up his mind to remain as Commander-in-Chief until the bitter end, in the hope of reaching Paris. The campaign was completed in October with the capture of the fourth fortress, Aire. Although the Allied gains were not impressive to the layman, Marlborough now controlled the River Lys and a wide front invaluable for the drive into France.

In September, the Queen dissolved Parliament and a month later a general election took place in which the Tories swept the board. The Whigs lost over 200 seats and the Tories emerged with a House of Commons majority of 151, the greatest party triumph since the Queen's accession. Most ministers had resigned upon the dissolution of Parliament and the Queen began to fill their places. Henry St John (later Lord Bolingbroke) became one of the Secretaries of State and Simon Harcourt the Lord Keeper. By the end of 1710 no prominent Whig enjoyed high ministerial office. On 8 November, when a general thanksgiving was held for Marlborough's military success, Harley's propaganda hack, Jonathan Swift, noted: 'I was at Court when the Queen past us by with all Tories about her; not one Whig.'[44]

One of Harley's first acts as Chancellor of the Exchequer was to suspend payment on the building of Blenheim. The Queen herself had chosen John Vanbrugh as the architect and had displayed a model of the house in Kensington Palace. Like other architects before and after him, Vanbrugh had underestimated the construction cost, putting the figure at £100,000. Already £134,000 had been spent and the palace was only half-built. Parliament was becoming irritated by the incessant demands for money and referred to the project as 'the golden mine of Blenheim'. When Harley stopped payment, Vanbrugh wrote to the Duchess asking for a letter assuring him that the workmen would not suffer. At the same time the workmen wrote to the Duke asking for wages that had fallen in arrears. The Duchess was too shrewd to stumble into this trap, knowing that if she responded sympathetically Harley would be only too glad to shift the entire burden onto herself and her husband. Without more ado she 'stopped the works . . . until the Crown should direct money for it.'[45] Even John, who for years had dreamed of spending his last days at Blenheim, lost his enthusiam. 'I am grown very indifferent,' he wrote to Sarah, 'for as things are now, I do not see how I can have any pleasure in living in a country where I have so few friends.' 'Let them keep their heap of stones,' Lord Godolphin commented drily.[46]

In November 1710, when the Whigs complained that Marlborough was being treated with ingratitude, Jonathan Swift attacked him in the Government-backed *Examiner* (No. 17) in a piece that is still read today as a model of invective laced with wit. He suggested that Marlborough was trying to set himself up as a second Cromwell. Then he drew up a balance-sheet. On one side was 'Roman Gratitude', listing items that included frankincense and earthen-pots (£4 10s 0d); a sacrificial bull (£8 0s 0d); a crown of laurel (2d); a triumphal arch (£500 0s 0d). The grand total came to £994 11s 10d. On the other side of the balance-sheet was 'British Ingratitude', with such items as Woodstock, Marlborough House, Mindelsheim, jewels, pictures, etc., etc., amounting to £54,000.[47] Before ending his attack, Swift accused the Marlboroughs (under fictitious names) of avarice, suggesting that the Duchess had been fraudulent in handling the Privy Purse. Sarah had many failings, but she was not dishonest. 'To be printed and cried about the country as a common cheat and pickpocket', Sarah wrote indignantly to Dr Hamilton, 'is too much for human nature to bear.' Hamilton showed her letter to the Queen and Sarah later recorded: 'All the Queen said to this letter was "Nobody thinks cheating is the Duchess of Marlborough's fault".'[48]

Meanwhile Sarah had resumed her battle with the Queen, using Dr Hamilton as an intermediary. Before long she was writing the same sort of letters that she used to write to Anne and, as he showed the letters to Anne, it amounted to the same thing. The Queen did not dare to dismiss Sarah as Marlborough was still indispensable to her; furthermore she feared her friend's acid tongue. The Duchess, on her part, was determined to hang on until John relinquished his command of his own accord. Then they could both retire together and her 'disgrace' would be minimal.

Consequently, Sarah seized every means of defence to circumvent the Queen's action. At the end of June she threatened to publish Anne's letters, written to her over the years and filled with passionate phrases, to show the world the fickleness of her royal mistress. Hamilton advised Anne that when she turned Sarah out it should 'be done in a way the least provoking, for a woman of Sense and Passion provok'd dos often turn Malicious, and that may force her to print what has happened for her own justification.'[49] The Queen defended herself to Hamilton by saying that 'when people are fond of one another they say many things, however indifferent, that they would not desire the world to know.' But Sarah refused to give way and told

Hamilton that she intended to print letters that 'contayn'd what would reflect upon her Majesty's piety such as breaches of Promise and Asservation.' She also said, Hamilton reported, 'that she took more pleasure in justifying herself than your Majesty did in wearing your Crown and that she wondered that when your Majesty was so much in her Power, you should treat her so.'[50]

The Queen ignored Sarah's threat, but the Duchess refused to let the matter drop. In July she talked to Hamiton about the Queen's 'solemn promis' to distribute her offices among her daughters when and if she retired. She had taken pains to extract this promise from the Queen in 1708 in order to frustrate Abigail, but the Queen now dismissed the matter lightly saying 'that persons may promise and yet Occurance change'. Later Anne told Hamilton that she regarded the promise as 'null' and would not have the Churchill girls under any circumstances. Henrietta, the wife of Lord Godolphin's son, was 'willy and Imprudent and had lost her reputation'; Lady Sunderland (Anne) was 'cunning and dangerous'; and even worse, Mary Montague was 'just like her mother'.[51]

Sarah never ran out of topics with which to rile the Queen and cited the following extracts from Anne's letters as examples of 'breaches of promise':

I wish I may never see the face of Heaven if I ever consent to part from you.

I wish I may never enjoy happiness in this world or the next, for Christ Jesus' sake do not leave me.[52]

Sarah's claim that these declarations were 'oaths' upset Dr Hamilton, who spent some time with divines discussing the strength of the Duchess's accusation.

The bickering simmered down and it looked as though Sarah had won the day, for there was no more talk of 'putting her out'. However, on 27 December, the day that Marlborough arrived back in England from the Continent, the Queen again raised the subject with Hamilton. She told him why her friendship with Sarah was dead, explaining that 'the Duchess had said shocking things even to herself, Yea, as much to herself and afterwards in Company, and that she lied.'[53]

Undoubtedly the Queen was referring to Sarah's charges of 'intimacy' with Abigail. This subject seems to have been so irresistible to the Duchess that on 6 December, when her employment was hanging by a thread, she had again referred to lesbianism in a letter to

Hamilton. The excuse was the publication of scurrilous pamphlets that 'I knew to be a lye . . . but that which I hated was the disrespect to the Queen & the disagreeable expression of the dark deeds in the night.'[54] Any reference more calculated to inflame the Queen would be difficult to imagine. The blinding impulse to wound seems to have been stronger with Sarah than self-preservation. Three days later the Queen told Hamilton that she was 'positive she would never see her more, and it would look odd to keep her in, and she never come to her.'[55]

The Duke returned to England at the end of December accompanied by Hans von Bothmar, the new Hanoverian envoy to Great Britain. Marlborough dreaded what lay in store for him, as he was sure that his royal mistress was only awaiting his arrival before turning Sarah out of her employments. 'As soon as winter comes', he had written to Sarah in September, 'they will put into execution what they have so unjustly designed.'[56] Rumours of Sarah's dismissal were so widespread on the Continent that before Marlborough left his headquarters, the Elector of Hanover (the future George I of England) made the Duke promise that whatever provocations he received he would not resign his command; and he sent Bothmar to London with him.

As a result Marlborough was determined to do everything in his power to smooth matters over, both for his wife and himself. In the military field he had been forced to swallow intolerable humiliations; so much so that Count Gallas, the Imperial Ambassador, was struck by the change in his appearance. 'The Duke has suffered so much', he reported to Vienna, 'that he no longer looks like himself.'[57] The most recent rebuff had been administered to him on the eve of his departure for England. He had received orders addressed to his three best young generals. When the letters were opened, it was found that all three were being cashiered on the Queen's authority for drinking a toast to Marlborough and 'confusion to his enemies'. The enemy was astonished because toasts like these were commonly drunk and no one had ever taken notice of them before. Hoffmann, the Emperor's minister in London, felt that it boded ill for the future. 'All officers speak on behalf of these three,' he wrote to Vienna. 'If generals are cashiered on information supplied by an informer, even the most guiltless are no longer secure. . . .'[58]

When Marlborough was received by the Queen on 28 December he tried to persuade her to rescind her order, telling her that the three generals had distinguished themselves on the field of battle, but she refused to listen. Otherwise he was humble and submissive and did his best to calm down the explosive atmosphere that Sarah always created. When he talked to Dr Hamilton the next evening and learned some of the details of his wife's correspondence, he adopted a long-suffering attitude and told the doctor that 'he long's to have his wife quiet'. Hamilton reported this to the Queen who was 'quite melted'. 'Her Majesty said that she was sorry to see him [the Duke] so broken. That there was no thought of putting him out.'[59]

This goodwill did not extend to the Duchess. On 10 January 1711, Hamilton was directed by the Queen to tell the Marlboroughs that Sarah must relinquish her offices. Once again the Duchess lashed out wildly, threatening that 'such Things are in my Power that, if known by a Man that would apprehend and was a right Politician, might lose a Crown.'[60] Although Sarah had known for months that her dismissal was hanging fire, now that it had come she was in the furious rage that her husband both had anticiapted and dreaded. She refused flatly to send any reply to the Queen. Four days later, Hans von Bothmar, accompanied by Lord Sunderland as an interpreter, called on Sarah and told her that the Elector of Hanover did not want anything to jeopardize Marlborough's position as Commander-in-Chief. Sarah took the hint and agreed to relinquish her offices.

At this point Dr Hamilton intervened and told the Duchess that in his opinion it might not be too late for a reconciliation. Sarah would have to write an abject letter of apology and the Duke would have to use all his powers of persuasion with the Queen. They both followed his advice but what happened at the interview is uncertain. The Archdeacon Coxe, in his biography of Marlborough published in 1820, claims that the Queen read Sarah's letter unwillingly, and then said: 'I cannot change my resolution.' Whereupon Marlborough dropped to his knees and begged for his wife's employments. The Queen declared that her honour was involved in the dismissal and gave him three days to bring her Sarah's Gold Key. He asked for ten days and she cut the time to two. When he got home Sarah flung her Gold Key on the floor and told him to take it to the Queen then and there.

Dr Hamilton gives us a less dramatic but more convincing account, particularly as he played a central part in the drama. On 18 January he wrote in his diary:

> Visiting the Queen she told me that the Duke had been there, and was not so tender as one might have expected; and [the Queen] said it would be more for his and her quiet, to prevail with her [Sarah] to Lay down; he said he would endeavour it; and if in a fortnight he could not accomplish it, she might do what she thought best.[61]

19 January

The Queen told me the Duke brought the Key last night.

The fact that the Queen said Marlborough 'had not been so tender as had been expected'[62] would seem to dispense with the tale of the Captain-General having pleaded for his wife 'on his knees'. Sarah felt that Dr Hamilton had tricked her into writing her contrite letter to the Queen by holding out false hopes of a reconciliation, and bitterly regretted having listened to him. Hamilton's assertion that Sarah's Gold Key was returned on the night of the 18 January (not the same night that the Queen told him that Sarah must go) was correct. Apparently Marlborough went to see the Queen for a second time on army business, but she refused to discuss anything until she had the Key. When he went home Sarah may or may not have flung it at him. At any rate, he returned the Key that night. The Duchess of Somerset became Groom of the Stole and Mrs Masham became Keeper of the Privy Purse.

It took Sarah some time to recover her composure. She convinced herself that no servant had ever served her mistress more devotedly, more honestly and more efficiently. She then demanded, and received, the £2,000 per annum that the Queen had offered her in 1702 and which she had refused. The total came to £16,000. Sarah's greed, or perhaps one should say anger, was so comprehensive it extended to trivialities. When she was asked to leave her lodgings at St James's Palace in the spring of 1711, she became convinced that Abigail was planning to move in. According to current gossip she stripped the rooms of their chimney-pieces and even took the brass plates and locks off the doors. Although Harley had authorized a further £10,000 for the building of Blenheim the Queen threatened to stop the work. In a letter from Maynwaring written in cypher, Sarah was told:

> 42 [the Queen] is so angry that she says she will build no house for 39 [Marlborough] when 242 [Sarah] has pull'd hers to pieces.[63]

Sarah, however, was maligned. She had not in fact taken the chimney-pieces and the Queen finally admitted that the brass locks were of Sarah's 'own buying'.

Thirteen

Marlborough's Last Campaign

'Abigail', the Duke of Shrewsbury remarked cheerfully, 'could make the Queen stand on her head if she wanted to.' And that appeared to be exactly what Abigail was doing. Gracious, kindly Anne was suddenly behaving with uncharacteristic ruthlessness that seemed to be gaining momentum as the days passed. Her dismissal of Sarah was understandable, but her treatment of the Duke of Marlborough was surprising. After all, by preventing Louis XIV from establishing a hegemony in Europe, he had kept the crown upon Anne's head. As Sarah pointed out, the Queen now appeared to love 'only those whom she once hated and hated those whom she once loved', and gloried 'in breaking the contracts and unravelling the schemes'[1] which she had taken so much trouble to develop.

The Queen made no effort to spare the Duke the humiliations which Mr Harley and Mr St John delighted in heaping upon him. To demonstrate that Marlborough was no longer a power, St John took the whole business of army promotions out of his hands; as this was the only way that a Commander-in-Chief could reward enterprise and gallantry, the move was well calculated to lessen Marlborough's control. St John went even further. He set up a board in London under the Duke of Ormonde, Marlborough's chief military rival, and empowered it to scrutinize the claims of officers. Whenever possible, advancement was to be given to those who opposed the Duke, and particularly to those who had attacked him in Parliament.

Marlborough did not find these affronts easy to endure. 'I can so little bear mortyficiations', he had written to Godolphin in the summer of 1710, 'that it is all I can do to keep myself from being sick.'[2] Yet he had made up his mind to stay at his post, whatever the cost. He loved the polyglot army that he had welded together and led to victory in nine campaigns, and clung to the hope that he might retain his command just long enough to lead his men to Paris. Count Gallas, the Emperor's Ambassador in London, was doubtful that he really had a command. The Duke's authority, he said, was so severely undermined that soon he would be left with 'hardly anything more than the mere name'. Yet the reverse was true. Officers and men rallied fiercely to the Duke's side, outraged that their great General should be the target of such mean abuse. 'No man but the Duke of Marlborough', wrote Captain Robert Parker, 'could have borne with the treatment he received.' However, the strain took its toll and the Duke had several prolonged bouts of illness. On 18 May he wrote to Sarah that he was suffering from severe headaches and ear-aches and troubled by 'giddiness and swimmings in my stomach.'[3] At this time he may have been close to the stroke that affected him five years later.

Marlborough needed the smile of fortune in the spring of 1711, but all he got was a frown. While he was anxiously awaiting Eugene's arrival, the Emperor Joseph died of smallpox. Joseph's brother, the Archduke Charles, who was fighting in Spain as 'Charles III', inherited all the Habsburg lands in Austria, Hungary, Bohemia and Silesia; undoubtedly, he would be elected Holy Roman Emperor when the Electoral Princes met in October. This, of course, raised problems for the Allies. Would it be sensible to insist that the 'whole of Spain' should go to a Habsburg prince who had such vast possessions in Central Europe? Apart from this, Spain itself was a problem. At first the Allied army, led by Charles III, Count Starhemberg (an Austrian general) and James Stanhope, a brilliant young protégé of Marlborough, made impressive gains which led to the occupation of Madrid. For the second time Philip V was forced to flee from his capital.

At this point Marshal Vendôme, the French General who liked to fight alongside his soldiers with a pike and who had been severely chastised by Marlborough at Oudenarde, arrived to take command of Philip's army. In January, a few weeks after his arrival, he regained his lost reputation by capturing General Stanhope and 5,000 men at Brihuega. Once again, the Spanish people flocked to Philip's colours and Vendôme managed to turn Charles's retreat into a rout. He drove him back to Barcelona and restored the Peninsula to its Bourbon King. 'If you can drive them from Spain', crowed the seventy-three-year-old Louis XIV in a letter to his grandson, 'I trust that the advantages will not be less useful to my kingdom than they will for your Majesty. . . .'[4]

In the eyes of the world this spectacular defeat, coupled with Charles's inheritance of the Habsburg Crown and property, again threw the Spanish problem into the melting-pot. Only the Duke of

Marlborough seemed to hold fast to the idea that Charles must have Spain; and that Spain could be won by reaching Paris. However, this was not the Duke's only problem in the spring of 1711. When Eugene finally joined him at the end of May the two Generals had an army of 140,000 men, which gave them a superiority of 20,000 over Villars. Marlborough and Eugene were determined to try to force a battle but, as the Marshal had dug himself into a very strong position, they decided that they must feel their way, waiting for the right opportunity to strike. Meanwhile, they would try to circumvent Villars's strongly defended lines. While the two Generals were studying the area, Marshal Villars suddenly dispatched fifteen squadrons and fifteen battalions to the Rhine. Eugene's government panicked (as Louis XIV had foreseen) and ordered the Prince to pursue the French and fend off a possible attack. This left Marlborough with only 90,000 men – 10,000 fewer than Villars's force. 'I send you the enclosed copy of Prince Eugene's letter,' he wrote gloomily to Heinsius, '. . . as the conjection is now I fear we must not venture any siege.'5

In London a number of dramatic episodes had taken place that affected both the war and the peace. In March, the Marquis de Guiscard tried to assassinate Mr Harley. Guiscard was a French refugee who had been employed by the British Government to plan an invasion of Normandy which never took place. He became the profligate friend of the profligate Mr Henry St John. Both men shared the same mistress and argued about the paternity of her child. Guiscard had no money apart from a pension of £500 a year from the British Government which, he complained, was not enough to live on. He had an interview with the Queen and begged her to ask the Treasury to increase it. Instead, the new Chancellor of the Exchequer, Mr Harley, cut the pension by £100 a year to register his disapproval of Guiscard's disreputable mode of life. Financially desperate, the Frenchman entered into treasonable correspondence with Versailles. By chance his letters were intercepted and he was arrested. He was interrogated at a Cabinet Council and, when he was being led away, suddenly lunged at Harley and stabbed him in the breast with a penknife. Pandemonium broke out and in the excitement St John and the Duke of Ormonde attacked the assailant, running him through the body with their swords; Guiscard died in prison. When the scene was reported to Queen Anne she became hysterical and four doctors were required to calm her.

Although Harley's wound was not serious, there was always the danger of blood-poisoning which could prove fatal. He was obliged therefore to remain at home for six weeks under the care of a doctor. His plight commanded widespread sympathy and the Queen consoled him by raising him to the peerage as the Earl of Oxford and Mortimer. A few weeks later she made him Lord Treasurer.

While Harley was convalescing, St John grabbed the reins of government. He revived a proposal to launch an expedition that would sail up the St Lawrence and capture Quebec. Formerly Harley had rejected the idea, arguing that it was more sensible to settle the affairs of Europe before moving so far afield. Now Harley was not present to interfere, and St John wasted no time in organizing the largest fleet of ships that had ever crossed the Atlantic. He took 6,000 men from Marlborough's army and appointed as commander Abigail Masham's brother, Brigadier Jack Hill – Sarah's 'once ragged boy', who was known as 'four-bottle Jack'. Abigail was thrilled and made sure that the Queen gave the Minister everything he wanted.

The expedition consisted of nine warships and forty troop transports. St John chose Rear Admiral Hovenden Walker to lead the enterprise. The Admiral was a charming man and a staunch Tory, but unfortunately he did not understand the navigation of the St Lawrence. When he reached the mouth of the river he was beset by dense fogs and torrential gales; eight transports went on the rocks and 800 of Marlborough's soldiers were drowned. Admiral Walker and Brigadier Hill lost heart and after a council of war decided it was best to return home as speedily as possible. No congratulations awaited them when they reached England on 17 October, and when the Whigs eventually returned to power Admiral Walker was struck off the list of admirals and deprived of his half-pay. Abigail was not only chagrined at her brother's failure but furious because Harley had disassociated himself from the affair – although he had every right to do so as he had always opposed it. Only St John seems to have emerged happily from the disaster. He netted thousands of pounds from military and naval clothes contracts, and made trouble between Abigail and Harley which was to his own advantage. Only part of this story had unfolded by mid-summer when Marlborough began the moves that were to be the highlights of his tenth campaign.

By July the Duke had recovered both his health and his spirits and, although he was making a very late start, moved his troops near the town of Arleux which controlled the main approach to the fortress at Bouchain. Villars was certain that Marlborough would not dare to attack him across the formidable barrier he had erected. For the past six months the French Marshal had employed hundreds of peasants to work alongside soldiers and engineers in constructing a formidable barrier based on river-lines and marshes, both natural and man-made. These 'lines' were strengthened by earthworks, felled trees, palisades and redoubts, and stretched for ninety miles from Namur to the Channel. They incorporated the rivers of Gy, Scarpe, Sensée and the upper Scheldt, and were supported by a number of fortresses including Arras, Bouchain and Cambrai.

Villars was so certain that his barrier was impregnable that he named his lines after an expression used by Marlborough's scholarly army tailor – or so it was said. Apparently, when the tailor saw a splendid red coat that Marlborough had brought from London he exclaimed, '*Ne Plus Ultra!*' – 'Nothing further is possible!'[6] The flamboyant Villars now wrote boastingly to Louis that the Duke of Marlborough had been brought at last to '*Ne Plus Ultra*'.

Marlborough had other ideas. He was not prepared to risk a frontal attack but he was determined to cross the famous lines. That meant he would have to outmanœuvre the enemy, outmarch him and completely hoodwink him. And that was exactly what he did. The piercing of Villars's famous *Ne Plus Ultra* lines has come down in history books as a superb example of military deception; so sly and adroit that it bordered on the comical; so successful that not a single soldier's life was lost; so satisfying that it put the whole Allied army in high good humour for weeks to come.

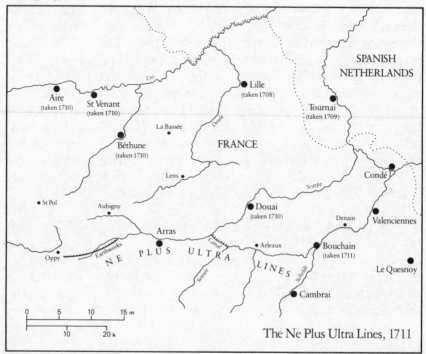

The Ne Plus Ultra Lines, 1711

Marlborough began by capturing Arleux, a small French fort that dominated the causeway across the River Scarpe and opened the way to the larger fort of Bouchain. He wanted to demolish Arleux, but if he did, the enemy would know that he intended moving his troops across the causeway. So he would have to trick the French into doing it for him. How he managed this shows his profound understanding of the enemy's reactions, and gives us a glimpse of the cunning that made him the greatest commander in Europe. He strongly fortified Arleux, then deliberately left it with a very light guard of only 600 men. Villars made up his mind quickly. If Marlborough felt that the fort was important enough to strengthen, it must be demolished. The task was easier than Villars had imagined; he attacked it on 22 July, and although Marlborough sent Cadogan with thirty squadrons of grenadiers to forestall him, they travelled in a very leisurely way. 'Not much haste,' commented General Kane, 'as the occasion seemed to require.' Subsequently Arleux was captured by the French, the garrison taken prisoners-of-war and the fort razed to the ground. Marlborough feigned acute annoyance. He gave a rare demonstration of bad temper, declaring that he would get even with Villars for the 'affront'. 'This gave Villars another occasion of bouncing,' declared Captain Parker, and once again Villars assured Versailles 'that these lines were the *Ne Plus Ultra* of the Duke of Marlborough.'[7]

As if to show his determination to punish Villars for snatching Arleux from him, the Duke moved his army near Vimy Ridge, facing the Arras sector of the lines. 'We may probably attempt to force his lines before two days are at an end,' wrote Cardonnel, tongue-in-cheek, to a Hanoverian friend who was famous for his indiscretions. 'All possible preparation being made for that end. The weather is not the most favourable; it having rained continually to Day, from noon to this hour. . . .'[8]

Meanwhile Villars was sending every available man to the threatened area. He was confident that he could repel the attack but was taking no chances. On 4 August, Marlborough reconnoitred the enemy lines at close quarters, protected by a large body of cavalry and accompanied by a good many staff officers. Captain Parker asked his Brigadier if he could ride out with the Duke.

This was readily granted, and thereupon I kept as near His Grace as I possibly could. He rode upwards of a league along their lines, as near as their cannon would permit. From thence I could discern plainly by the help of a perspective, that the lines were very strong and high and crowded with men and cannon, and that the ground before them was levelled and cleared of everything that might be any kind of shelter to those that approached them.

Notwithstanding all this, the Duke's countenance was now cleared up, and with an air of assurance, and as if he was confident of success, he pointed out to the General Officers the manner in which the army was to be drawn up, the places that were to be attacked and how to be sustained. In short, he talked more than his friends thought was discreet, considering that Villars had spies at his very elbow. And indeed, some began to suspect that the ill-treatment he met with at home, or the affront he had lately received from Villars, might have turned his brain and made him desperate.[9]

While all eyes were fastened on the spectacle of Marlborough and his escort inspecting the lines, the Duke's field artillery was secretly being withdrawn, piece by piece, and sent in an easterly direction. Apparently the undulations between Vimy Ridge and Arras (where two centuries later a terrible battle would be fought) concealed these moves from the enemy. Other mysterious exertions were taking place. When Parker returned to his unit he saw General Cadogan 'attended by one servant' steal out of the crowd. A short while later the General rode out of the camp with forty Hussars and galloped off to Douai where he joined General Hompesch's garrison and units from Lille, Tournai and Saint-Armand.

Meanwhile, in the Arras sector Marlborough was circulating the order of battle for a dawn attack. As the sun went down faces were sombre. No one relished a frontal attack on a position that appeared impregnable, and some men began to wonder if the Captain-General, so harassed by his political opponents in England, was in his right mind. Then, suddenly, came the surprising command to strike tents and to march eastwards 'without beat of drum', leaving the camp-fires burning behind them. Marlborough's army was on its way to Arleux to breach the *Ne Plus Ultra* lines; and everything depended on reaching the causeway before the French could intercept them.

The Duke had five hours start on Villars who did not catch on to what was happening until eleven o'clock at night and who took another three hours to reassure himself that he was not being fooled twice over. He finally put himself at the head of the Maison du Roi and ordered his whole army to march eastwards. The Allied infantry was moving through the moonlit night at a brisk pace. As dawn broke they could see the enemy on parallel lines for, although Villars had started much later, he was using his own specially built lateral roads that cut miles from his route. 'It was', wrote Captain Parker, 'a perfect race between our two armies but we, having the start of them by some hours, constantly kept ahead.'[10] At this moment Marlborough received word that General Cadogan and General Hompesch had found the Arleux causeway undefended and had crossed it at three in the morning with twenty-two battalions and twenty squadrons. They were now in possession of the enemy's much-vaunted lines but could only maintain their position if Marlborough's soldiers beat Villars's men to the causeway.

The Duke sent a dozen aides-de-camp the length of the marching columns explaining what was happening and what was required. Once again (just as at Brabant) the order was 'My Lord Duke wishes the infantry to step out!' The men believed that they had been marching as fast as humanly possible, considering the weight they were carrying, but soon the pace was so hot that literally hundreds of soldiers fell by the roadside. However, the Duke knew what his punishing order would do and had assigned General Albemarle's cavalry to pick up the stragglers 'behind their saddles'.

By eight o'clock the Duke and the cavalry were pouring through the lines near Arleux! Two hours later the leading (and surviving) infantry battalions made their appearance; despite their fifty-pound packs and the rough country over which they had walked, some of them had covered thirty-nine miles in eighteen hours. The distraught Villars arrived on the scene at eleven o'clock accompanied by 200 troopers. He could scarcely believe that Marlborough was behind his lines with an army of men – had they come on a magic carpet? He was so rattled he threw caution to the winds and galloped ahead so far that 100 of his men were captured and he only escaped himself by a hair's breadth.

By mid-afternoon, Marlborough's army was formed up and ready to fight if Villars chose to attack. But the Marshal decided that the Allies' position was too strong and drew off to shelter beneath the walls of Cambrai. Marlborough did not take the offensive either (which later aroused some criticism) as his generals pronounced the ground unfavourable. Instead, he adhered to his original plan of capturing the fortress of Bouchain which would lay open to him the best way into France.

The siege of Bouchain rivalled the forcing of the *Ne Plus Ultra* lines as a model of military skill. General Cadogan wrote to a friend that its success was in keeping with

> My Lord Duke's Glory and Reputation. His Grace undertook it in sight of the enemy's army, tho' superior to his by above 30 battalions, and commanded by a general that France looked on as its last hope and who, piqued even to rage by being duped in the Passage of the Lines was determined to leave nothing unattempted to repair his faults and to relieve Bouchain.[11]

Despite Villars's angry determination, Marlborough made his dispositions so cleverly, and placed his guns so advantageously, that the Marshal's efforts were unavailing and Bouchain was forced to surrender fifteen days after the Allied guns began to fire. Nevertheless, there were several tense moments and Captain Parker tells us that, while he was awaiting an order to attack an entrenchment 'crowded with men and cannon', the Duke himself intervened:

> The Duke of Marlborough (ever watchful ever right) rode up quite unattended and alone, and posted himself a little on the right of my company of grenadiers, from whence he had a fair view of the greater part of the enemy's works. It is quite impossible for me to express the joy which the sight of this man gave me at this very critical moment. I was now well satisfied that he would not push the thing, unless he saw a strong probability of success; nor was this my notion alone; it was the sense of the whole army both officer and soldier, British and foreigner. And indeed we had all the reason in the world for it; for he never led us to any one action that we did not succeed in. He stayed only three or four minutes and then rode back . . . [soon] orders came to us to retire.[12]

This glimpse of the great Duke gives us an unforgettable picture of his attention to detail and an illustration of the faith that his men placed in his judgement.

The surrender of Bouchain brought the season's fighting to an end. No one could know that it would prove to be Marlborough's last command. Technically his superiority over Villars was so indisputable that General Kane described the campaign as 'among the greatest he ever made' and General Natzmer (one of his Prussian commanders) as 'the most glorious for my Lord Duke'.[13] Marlborough himself was pleased, as Bouchain was the passage 'through which our whole army is to creep into the heart of France & so force Spain from them.'[14] Except for two minor fortresses, the way was clear down the whole of the Oise to Paris.

Two months earlier Marlborough had written to Oxford asking for extra money so that the Allied troops could spend the winter on the French frontier instead of going into their usual army quarters. This would entail the building of shelters for the troops and stabling for the horses; however, it would enable the campaign of 1712 to begin early, with great advantage to the Allies. Oxford assented in what Lord Stair described as 'a bamboozling' letter. He had no intention of allowing Marlborough to take his army to Paris.

Rumours of peace moves had reached Marlborough more than once on the battlefield. 'It is look'd upon here as certain', James Brydges wrote to him in June 1711, 'that there are Propositions in agitation for a General Peace.'[15] And again in August: 'We have a strong report in town of a secret negotiation of peace being carried out . . . whether the treaty has been desired by the French and what promises have been offered or asked I am wholly a stranger to. . . .'[16]

In April a paper had been submitted to the British Cabinet, purporting to come from France, formally requesting peace negotiations. In reality, the talks had been instigated by Mr Harley, now Lord Oxford. As intermediaries he had used Lord Jersey (who had a Roman Catholic wife) and the Abbé Gaultier, a Roman Catholic priest known to the Jersey family. Gaultier officiated in the Austrian chapel in London and was Torcy's confidential agent in England. He visited Paris twice in the early months of 1711, laying down Harley's conditions. First, the initiative must appear to come from France; second, the early talks must take place between England and France alone, and be held in strict secrecy as they breached Britain's pledge to the Grand Alliance not to negotiate a separate peace; third, the massive Allied defeat at Brihuega a few months earlier had convinced England that 'No Peace Without Spain' must be abandoned – Philip v would be recognized as King of Spain in return for important concessions in the Mediterranean and South America. Lastly, England's new ministers were prepared to support the claims of the Pretender against the Hanoverians 'if he thinks like us' – in other words, if he embraced the Protestant faith.[17]

Torcy could scarcely believe his eyes as he read what was being offered to him. Here was France, floundering in a rough sea, being thrown a lifebelt by the Queen's Chief Minister. It was quite plain that the English had decided to abandon their Allies and strike out on their own. 'Who could have foreseen', exulted Torcy, 'that the prosperity of an Alliance so formidable for France and Spain was at an end; that the Supreme Being who fixes the boundaries of oceans and calms the impetuosity of the waves . . . should stem the torrents of so many victories.'[18] Torcy lost no time in making a formal request to London for new peace talks. He sent a vague outline of what would come under discussion, which the British Government forwarded to Heinsius in Holland. That was the last the Dutch heard about the matter until October 1711, when the draft preliminaries were signed.

Never had the affairs of Britain been in the hands of two such unprincipled and unscrupulous men as Lord Oxford and Mr St John. They were not in the least dismayed at the prospect of peace with dishonour, and peace with dishonour is what they finally got. They coerced the simple-minded Queen into filling a deplorable role which she did without a tinge of dismay. She betrayed her Allies and disgraced the man whose sword had raised her to her present exalted position; before she was done, she even humiliated the army that had vanquished her enemies.

The preliminaries were negotiated by St John behind tightly closed doors, and were based on a startling new concept: instead of England and her Allies confronting France, England and France joined hands in confronting the Allies. Of course the dealings could not be presented in this light; the preliminaries therefore were divided into two parts: the 'official' section which was published in October 1711, and the 'secret' section designed to serve as a basis for Anglo–French negotiations when the formal peace conference opened in Utrecht in 1712. The secret pages outlined the advantages that the very able St John managed to wring from the French at the expense of everyone else: a thirty-year concession to import African slaves into the West Indies and South America, known as the 'Asiento'; trade rights in Spain and sovereignty over Gibraltar and Minorca; St Kitts Island and Arcadia; Newfoundland and Hudson's Bay.

While the finishing touches were being put on the draft, Lord Oxford informed the Duke of Marlborough of what was happening in a letter that stands out as a masterpiece of misrepresentation. 'The French made an offer to the Queen of a general peace . . .' he wrote to the Duke in September 1711.

> The Queen's answer was that she would enter no separate treaty neither should it be transacted here; she had several things to demand for the good and quiet of her dominions, but she was resolved nott to act without her allies, and particularly the States. They sent a paper in general promising satisfaction to all the Allies, in barriers, in trade, and all other articles. . . .[19]

Oxford made every effort to dress up the 'official' preliminaries to appeal to the Allies, but when the *Daily Courant* published the terms on 13 October they were such a far cry from the concessions that France had offered in 1709 that they aroused a storm of protest. Count Gallas referred to 'the new scandalous preliminaries' and declared that they rendered Tories and Whigs 'terrified and dumb'.[20] Certainly Louis XIV had escaped with the minimum sacrifice considering that Marlborough was poised to strike the final blow that would take him to Paris.

Oxford and St John had no intention, of course, of allowing the war to progress to this stage for, if Louis was utterly vanquished, England would not be allowed to enjoy her exclusive advantages but be obliged to share the spoils with her allies. As things stood, the Queen had reaped immense secret benefits and it was hoped that the official document which was now being published would keep the Allies quiet. In this, Louis promised to recognize the Queen of England and the established Protestant succession; to satisfy all and each of the Allies in their reasonable demands; to restore international trade; to dismantle the fortifications of Dunkirk; to negotiate a barrier for the Dutch; and to prevent the amalgamation of the Crowns of France and Spain. This last sentence was revealing. It showed that England had agreed that Philip v should remain King of Spain; otherwise there would be no need to specify the separation of the Crowns.

The Whigs and their candidate for the Spanish throne – Charles, now Holy Roman Emperor – protested vehemently; and the heir to the British throne, the Elector of Hanover, was even louder in his opposition. '. . . Ye fruits of this war will be lost', he wrote to Lord Oxford, 'if Spain and the Indies remain in the hands of the Duke of Anjou for this will soon render France once more in a state to give the law to Europe.'[21]

Marlborough was in close touch with Hanover and gave the Elector his full support. Oxford recognized the Duke as his most formidable enemy and turned his attention to completing his downfall. He was wonderfully ingenious. When he told the Queen about Marlborough's request to keep his army on the frontier during the winter, he twisted the information in such a way as to arouse deep suspicion. 'Ye Duke of Marlborough', she replied, 'shows plainer than ever by this new project his unwillingness for a peace, but I hope our Negotiations will succeed and then it will not be in his power to prevent it.'[22]

Oxford had other plans. When Marlborough arrived in The Hague in November, on his way to England, he learned that the British Government – directed by Oxford – was sponsoring a parliamentary investigation of his accounts, suggesting that he had misappropriated a percentage of the payments made by foreign princes for the maintenance of their troops. Marlborough immediately wrote to the Commissioners, explaining what he had done with the money. His conscience was so clear that he regarded the matter as closed, but before long he realized that his enemies had prejudiced a good many people against him. When he had his first audience with the Queen on 17 November, she reported to Oxford that 'he seemed dejected and very uneasy about this matter of the publick accounts.'[23] According to Sarah, 'she put on ye guise of great kindness and said "she was sure her Servants would not encourage such proceedings" or to that effect. Yet it appear'd afterwards that not only Her Servants but She herself encouraged this very proceeding against him. . . .'[24] Apparently the Queen entreated Marlborough (at Oxford's instigation) to resume his place in the Cabinet and to support the peace proposals, but he refused, warning her that Oxford's ultimate goal was restoration of the Pretender.

Meanwhile Lord Oxford and St John were encouraging their tame writers to produce a sea of propaganda against the Whigs, the Allies and the Duke of Marlborough. Jonathan Swift performed brilliantly with an outrageous 'history' entitled *The Conduct of the Allies*. This travesty depicted the partners of the Grand Alliance as selfish, grasping ne'er-do-wells who sponged on Britain and bled her white. The Elector of Hanover hit back at once through his English representative, the Baron von Bothmar. The Baron's protest was published in the *Daily Courant* and created a sensation. It accused the British Government of violating the Treaty of Grand Alliance by negotiating separately with France, and prophesied that, as soon as Philip v had been accepted by Europe as King of Spain, France would support the Pretender as King of England.

The war that was being fought between the Queen's ministers and the angry Whigs was moving towards a flash-point. Anne recognized Marlborough's hand in the Hanoverian attack and when she opened Parliament on 7 December 1712, she inspected the deferential rows of nobles drawn up outside the House of Lords with the purposeful look of a commander reviewing his troops. Bolingbroke had written the Queen's speech and even her announcement that a peace conference would gather at Utrecht was couched in spiteful language: 'notwith-standing the arts of those who delight in war,' she said referring to the famous General who had saved her throne, 'both place and time are appointed for the opening of a Treaty of a general peace.' Marl-borough's reply to this jibe was a model of self-control. He bowed to the Queen, then pointed out that he had always informed 'Her Majesty and her Council of all the proposals of peace that have been made' and had asked her repeatedly 'for instructions for my conduct.'[25]

The Queen's address did not go down well with the Lords, the majority of whom were Whigs. Even the Tory Lord Nottingham was ready to oppose her and at once put down the motion: 'No peace could be safe or honourable to Great Britain or Europe if Spain or the Indies were allowed to any branch of the House of Bourbon.' When the motion was put to the test, the Queen was dismayed to find that it had been carried by eight votes.

The Queen was now ready to heed Oxford's advice: Marlborough would be dismissed, and twelve new peers created to carry the peace

plans through the House of Lords. Everything was done with precision. First of all, an excuse must be found for relieving the Duke of
his command. The Commissioner of Accounts was instructed therefore to lay before the House of Commons a *prima facie* case of peculation against him, although both the Queen and Oxford knew that
the charges had no foundation. The House was adjourned on 22
December before the report could be debated. On 29 December the
Queen's letter of dismissal was delivered to Marlborough. It is not
known what it said, as for once the Duke lost control of his temper
and threw the paper into the fire. However, he replied with his usual
dignity:

> I am very sensible of the honour your Majesty does me in dismissing me
> from your service by a letter of your own hand, though I find by it that my
> enemies have been able to prevail with Your Majesty to do it in the manner
> that is most injurious to me. . . . I wish your Majesty may never find the
> want of so faithful a servant as I have always endeavoured to approve
> myself to you. . . .[26]

The repercussions of Marlborough's fall reverberated far and wide.
Louis XIV could scarcely believe his good fortune. The affair of
displacing 'the Duke of Marlborough', he said brusquely, 'will do all
for us we desire.'[27] The Allied army, on the other hand, was swept by
anger and amazement. 'You know the bottom of my heart,' wrote
General Cadogan to a friend, 'therefore can better imagine than I can
describe the affliction and weight of Grief I am under.' Corporal
Matthew Bishop describes his dismay in his diary: 'Oh! said I, must
we part from such a Man, whose Fame has spread throughout the
World? It terrified my soul to such a degree', he added, 'that I could
not rest night or day.'[28] Lieutenant Haswell refers to the event as 'a
moral reflection on the unsteddiness of human affairs – a great man
and one of the Greatest Generals and subjects of the world, stript of
his glory in a moment when neither his friends nor foes expected it.'[29]
General Kane blamed 'a set of vile profligate Men who had insinuated
themselves into the favour of the weak Queen.'[30] Even the partisan
Swift felt that the Government had taken a huge risk: 'We have had
constant success in arms while he commanded,' he wrote. 'Opinion is
a mighty matter in war, and I doubt the French think it impossible to
conquer an army that he leads, and our soldiers think the same: and
how far even this step may encourage the French to play tricks with
us, no man knows.'[31]

On 31 December 1711, the same day that the London *Gazette*
announced Marlborough's dismissal, it also informed the world that

the Queen had created twelve new peers. One of them was Abigail Masham's husband. According to Lord Dartmouth, the Queen had been reluctant to elevate Mr Masham to the peerage for fear of losing his wife as a good body-servant. 'I was desired to propose her [Abigail's] husband being made a Lord, which I found was not very acceptable,' wrote Dartmouth. 'The Queen told me, she had never had any design to make a great lady of her, and should lose a useful servant about her person, for it would give offence to have a peeress lie upon the floor, and do several other inferior offices, but at last consented upon condition she remained a dresser and did as she used to do.'[32]

The newly created Lady Masham continued to perform menial tasks; the Tories had enough support in the Lords to pass the Queen's peace plan; and the Duke of Ormonde took Marlborough's place as Commander-in-Chief of the Allied armies.

Within five days of Marlborough's dismissal Prince Eugene appeared in England. The Imperialists invariably arrived too late – for six months Herr von Hoffmann had been begging the Emperor Charles to send someone to London to try to alter the Queen's policy, but Vienna made its plans in a leisurely way and the Prince did not learn that Marlborough had been relieved of his command until he reached Harwich. There hundreds of people gathered to welcome Eugene, but in view of his colleague's fall from favour he decided to avoid public demonstrations. He sailed up the Thames and disembarked at the Whitehall Stairs where no one expected him. He drove to Leicester House, formerly occupied by Count Gallas, but now empty, where he met Marlborough and talked for several hours. The Government hoped to separate him from his fellow General but the Prince did not mince words with members of the Court. 'I had to tell him', Eugene reported to his Emperor after a meeting with Oxford's agent, John Drummond, 'that since it was known all over the world what a firm and intimate friendship I had fostered with the Duke of Marlborough I could not do otherwise. . . .'[33]

Eugene spent two months in England. He saw the Duke of Ormonde several times to discuss the coming campaign, but when he had an audience with the Queen she refused to discuss business of any kind, and none of her ministers paid him a formal call. Nevertheless, his ante-rooms at Leicester House were filled with distinguished visitors and on the streets people who recognized his carriage cheered and clapped him. He created a stir by attending the opera with Marlborough, and when the Duke of Portland, son of William III's favourite, gave a ball for him, crowds gathered to see the two comrades-in-arms. Apparently neither Marlborough nor Eugene could be persuaded to dance. 'I don't think', wrote an anonymous correspondent, 'they could kick their heels like Nero or Louis XIV . . . tho' both have very handsomely kicked the grand monarch at the Great Balls of Blenheim, Ramillies and Oudenarde. . . .'[34]

Throughout February London resounded to rumours floated by Oxford's agents that Marlborough and Eugene were plotting to depose the Queen. Eugene, people said, would set fire to London while Marlborough seized the Queen. These tales, however, were too wild to disturb Anne and on her birthday she held a reception for the Prince. Swift was furious that the Whig ladies were 'too spiteful' to attend and hoped the Queen would be 'against them forever'. 'I saw Lady Wharton,' he continued, 'as ugly as the Devil coming out in the crowd in an undress; she had been with the Marlborough daughters and Lady Bridgwater in St James's looking out of the window, all undressed to see the sight. I do not hear that one Whig lady was there, except those of the bedchamber.'[35] However, the Tory ladies apparently made up for the Whig embargo by looking 'monstrous fine'.

At the reception Anne, who was carried about in her sedan-chair, summoned Eugene and presented him with a diamond-hilted sword valued at £4,000, but quite understandably she still refused to discuss her peace negotiations. Before the Prince left England he had an inconsequential talk with Lord Dartmouth, one of the Secretaries of State, and a secret rendezvous with Lord Oxford, but learned nothing of interest. Throughout his stay, Eugene refused to let anyone demean his great friend and colleague, the Duke. When Bishop Burnet told the Prince that one of the Tory ministers had admitted that Marlborough perhaps 'had been once fortunate', Eugene replied that 'no greater tribute could be given him since he was *always successful.*'[36]

Eugene's visit had no effect on the Queen as it was apparent that her ministers were determined to destroy the Grand Alliance. Not only Marlborough but Marlborough's secretary, Adam de Cardonnel, and Marlborough's friend and former colleague, Robert Walpole, were indicted by the House of Commons on trumped-up peculation charges. The House then moved gladly to the task of renegotiating the Barrier Treaty with Holland. These inflammatory acts provoked rumours that the Whigs were planning riots to overthrow the Government. The appearance on the street of a group of young bloods, known as 'Mowhawks', added fuel to the fire. These young men, it was claimed, roamed about molesting pedestrians. One tale led to another and soon stories were circulating that a Whig conspiracy was under way to kidnap the Queen and to assassinate her ministers. The report was taken so seriously that the Queen's guard was reformed and Oxford and Shrewsbury were moved to the security of St James's Palace. Why Bolingbroke was not protected nobody knows, except that Oxford probably would have been glad to see the last of him. As things transpired, no violence took place and men went about their business, nefarious and otherwise, in perfect safety.

Marlborough House had been finished just in time to provide a sanctuary for the embittered Duchess and her philosophical husband. She had sacked poor old Christopher Wren, now in his eighty-first year, because 'his workmen were taking advantage of him' (another way of saying it was costing too much money) and took charge of the building herself. She was a good manager and furnished the house in record time, but John begged her to be careful of moving in too soon. 'My only design in building that house was to please you,' he wrote from his headquarters in May 1711, 'and I am afraid your going into it so soon may prejudice your health, so that you must be careful to have it well examined at the end of September: for should it not be thoroughly dry, you ought to stay one year longer.'[37]

The Duchess complained that the Tories spied on her from their windows in St James's Palace to see who was going in and out. Lord Cowper was one of John and Sarah's most steadfast friends and gave Lord Dartmouth a graphic description of the Marlboroughs at home. Cowper found the Duke in bed with 'a great deal of company in the chamber, and the Duchess sitting at the bedside, railing in a most extravagant manner against the Queen, [saying] that she had always hated and despised her; but that fool, her daughter Henrietta (who stood by) had always loved her [the Queen] and did so still, which she should never forgive her.' Apparently Lord Cowper was embarrassed by Sarah's wild remarks, but the Duke told him, 'he must not mind what she said, for she was used to talk at that rate when she was in a passion, which was a thing she was very apt to fall into, and there was no way to help it.'[38]

The Duchess was not always in such a passion about Queen Anne. For the past year she had been encouraged by the admiring Maynwaring to write what he called 'the great history' but which was, in fact, Sarah's memoirs, beginning with the revolution of 1688 and continuing until the present time. 'You always write so clearly and properly,' he told her, 'and with such natural expressions in which you excel everybody.'[39] Sarah was utterly engrossed in her project; although she did not publish her work for thirty years, she polished and revised and added to it for the rest of her days.

John, on the other hand, seemed imperturbable and surprisingly content to do nothing. Yet peace and quiet were not his for long. First came the peculation charge. The Commissioners of Accounts, instigated by Lord Oxford, had laid the matter before the Commons in December, and at the end of January 1712, the House debated it in an atmosphere charged with furious party faction. The Duke faced two charges. One was the 2½ per cent that he had deducted from the pay of foreign troops in Her Majesty's service. This practice had been begun by William III to avoid asking Parliament for money for the secret service, and had been followed by Marlborough. Indeed, the Duke held the Queen's warrant for the transaction dated 6 July 1702. Although his defence was irrefutable, Tory Members of Parliament followed instructions and brushed it aside, declaring that the money paid to him – about £200,000 over ten years – was 'public money and should be accounted for'. The second charge was more difficult to counter. The chief army contractor, Sir Solomon de Medina, had paid the Duke an annual commission of £6,000 for the contract to supply the army with bread; this money, too, had gone to the secret service. No one could deny that Marlborough's troops were well fed, or that Marlborough's secret service was the best in Europe, but as the Duke could not reveal names or show receipts, there was no way that he could prove what sums had been expended. The Commons therefore seized its opportunity and by a vote of 276 to 165 declared the commissions 'unwarrantable and illegal'. Yet when the Duke of Ormonde was appointed to succeed Marlborough he was empowered to draw the same on the bread contracts from Medina, and to deduct the same 2½ per cent from the pay of foreign troops!

Many of the foreign princes in the Grand Alliance wrote indignant letters in defence of Marlborough. The heir to the British throne, George of Hanover, was particularly emphatic about the legality of the 2½ per cent deduction:

> We declare that we are fully convinced and satisfied that the Prince Duke of Marlborough has annually applied these sums to the Secret Service . . . and we are persuaded that his wise applications of these amounts has forcibly contributed to the gaining of so many battles.[40]

Although the vote against Marlborough was large, the case against him was so obviously trumped up that the Government did not ask for an impeachment. Oxford was bitterly disappointed that despite searching the records tirelessly for two years he had found nothing about the Duke that smacked of corruption or malversation, not even the commonplace practice of selling commissions. Sarah stresses this point in a letter written many years later. 'I have heard him [Marlborough] solemnly swear,' she wrote, 'when it was of no Significance to do it to me, that he never in the whole Reign of Queen Anne sold one Commission, title, or anything to anybody when he had so much favour. . . .' Sarah went on to elaborate proudly:

> The Duke of Marlborough had never any vanity, and therefore living so many years with great Employments, he left a great Estate, which was no wonder he should do, since he lived long and never threw Mony away. And Mony was for many years at six per cent. . . . He had a great deal of Compassion in his Nature and to those that he had long been acquainted with he gave Mony out of his Pocket to those who were poor, tho' they were not of his Opinion. I am a living Witness of this: for I was directed by him to pay some persons Pensions when he was abroad and have letters that prove the truth of it from the Persons.[41]

Nothing would have pleased Oxford more than to cast a permanent slur on Marlborough, but the mud he threw refused to stick.

Meanwhile trouble had erupted in Utrecht where representatives of England, France, Holland and the Empire had gathered to negotiate peace terms. The significance of Marlborough's dismissal had not been lost on Louis XIV. He deduced that Oxford and St John were not thinking of another military campaign, but gambling on a quick peace. He therefore instructed Torcy to brush aside the secret agreements he had made with England in the preliminaries and to adopt a more aggressive attitude. Torcy complied by confronting the conference with a series of proposals 'so monstrous that even the English were aghast.'[42] The French not only demanded the return of a long list of frontier fortresses, the prizes of hard-fought sieges, but talked as though they had won the battle of Ramillies and had the whole of Belgium at their disposal. Indeed, Torcy airily suggested that Belgium should go to France's most important ally, the Elector of Bavaria.

This was enough to provoke an angry reaction, but when the idea began to gain credence that England had been carrying on secret negotiations to gain commercial advantages at Holland's expense, the atmosphere became even more embittered. The fact that Philip V would be allowed to retain Spain and the Indies unconditionally was regarded as the price England had paid for her special advantages. Needless to say, this aroused furious resentment among the Dutch. Gallant Holland had poured out her blood and treasure unstintingly, only to be double-crossed by her ally on the home stretch. Harley was so embarrassed by the hurricane of bad feeling he had aroused that he persuaded the Queen to let 'negotiations sleep in Holland'. Instead, he authorized St John to re-open his secret negotiations with Versailles – this time to hammer out the terms to be accorded to the Allies. The Allies would be told quite bluntly to take them or leave them; and as they could not do better alone, they certainly would 'take them'.

At this point a series of deaths took place in the French royal family which startled the world and once again thrust the Spanish question to the forefront. Louis's son and heir, the Dauphin, had died in 1711. Now, in February 1712, the Dauphin's son, the Duke of Burgundy (who had become the new Dauphin), contracted smallpox and died, and in March his heir, a child of five, also succumbed. This left only Burgundy's second son, a child of two,* so sickly he was not expected to live for long, between the throne and Philip v of Spain. Thus, by the accident of death, the very contingency that the Allies had fought so long and so hard to prevent – that Philip should wear two crowns – seemed likely to come about.

The English dug in their toes. Such an eventuality was unthinkable. But when St John suggested that Philip renounce the throne of France, French lawyers pronounced the idea 'contrary to the principles of the French monarchy'. St John then proposed that Philip renounce the throne of Spain, when and if he was called to the French throne, and that Victor Amadeus, Duke of Savoy, be named as his successor. At this point Philip interceded and announced flatly that he was King of Spain and intended to remain King of Spain. Once again the quest for peace had reached a deadlock. Philip could not renounce the French Crown and Philip would not renounce the Spanish Crown.

The Allies had no alternative but to call for a renewal of the war. Although the Duke of Ormonde had supplanted Marlborough as Commander-in-Chief of the British paid troops – about 40,000 men, amounting to nearly a third of the total – he had not succeeded him as Generalissimo. That position had been given to Prince Eugene. Ormonde was instructed to act in conjunction with the Allies 'in pushing the war with all possible vigour' and Eugene regarded him as 'the finest cavalier and the most complete gentleman that England bred, the glory of that nation.'[43]

Unfortunately, neither Ormonde nor the nation contributed much glory to what happened next. While messengers hurried between

---

* The child survived and reigned as Louis xv.

London and Versailles and Madrid, carrying suggestions as to how Philip's complicated future could be ironed out, the Allied armies were assembling near Tournai. Eugene planned to follow Marlborough's blueprint by laying siege to Quesnoy – the last remaining northern fortress, small but important – and then to push on to Paris. Ormonde took the field as part of an army of 122,000 men against Villars's badly equipped force of 100,000. After Quesnoy there was nothing to stop the march to Paris. Yet Oxford and St John were determined to prevent it, as the utter defeat of the French would rob England of the particular and separate advantages that she had won in the preliminaries and force her to share her gains.

On 9 May St John received the long-awaited news from France that Louis XIV had sent an ultimatum to Madrid demanding that Philip choose between the Savoy plan and renouncing his throne. Acting on the belief (which was proved correct) that a decision was in the offing, he dispatched a letter to Ormonde, known in history as the 'Restraining Orders'. It not only led to one of the most shameful episodes in British public life, but later provided the fuel for St John's impeachment.

> Her Majesty, my Lord, has reason to believe that we shall come to an agreement upon the great article of the union of the two monarchies, as soon as a courier, sent from Versailles to Madrid, can return; it is therefore the Queen's positive command to your Grace that you avoid engaging in any siege, or hazarding a battle, till you have further orders from her Majesty. I am, at the same time, directed to let your Grace know that the Queen would have you disguise the receipt of this order. . . . Her Majesty thinks that you cannot want pretenses for conducting yourself so as to answer her ends, without owning that which might, at present, have an ill effect if it was publickly known.

This astonishing letter carried a postscript:

> P.S. I had almost forgot to tell your Grace that communication is given of this order to the Court of France; so that if the Mareschal de Villars takes, in any private way, notice of it to you, your Grace will answer accordingly. . . .[44]

Winston Churchill, who led Britain in a later and even more fateful war, declares that this was 'an indelible stain' on England's honour:

> For an English Minister acting in the name of the Queen to conceal from the Allies his intentions, while disclosing it secretly to the enemy, was in fact to encompass the defeat of Eugene and the slaughter of the Allies and comrades with whom British troops had so long stood shoulder to

shoulder. Nothing in the history of civilized peoples has surpassed this black treachery.... Ormonde, so popular and magnificent, so gallant in his youth, now showed himself the weak, base creature he was at heart. With his eyes open he lent himself to this shame....[45]

Fortunately the Allied generals were not deceived by Ormonde's flimsy pretexts for refusing to attack the enemy, particularly as Villars did not bother to entrench the French troops facing the British. When Ormonde floundered about saying that he was 'waiting for letters from England', Prince Eugene and the Dutch Deputies replied sharply that his answer supported 'the suspicions they had for some time entertained'. Other commanders were less polite and began to refer to 'the English traitors'. In The Hague there even was talk of disarming and arresting all 12,000 native-born British soldiers. Who could have imagined that the famous red coats, heroes of so many of Marlborough's battles, would become the subject of such recrimination!

Word soon reached London of the bitter animosity at the front caused by Ormonde's 'delaying tactics' and on 28 May Lord Halifax moved in the House of Lords that their new Captain-General should be ordered 'to prosecute the war with the utmost vigour'. Nottingham hinted that the General had been told not to fight because the Government was aiming at a Stuart restoration and did not want to weaken France. Oxford lied his way out of the impasse with breathtaking composure. After admitting that if the Duke of Ormonde declined to act offensively he probably was 'following instructions', he went on to assure the House that the basic Anglo–French peace agreement was nearing completion and would be laid before their lordships within a few days. 'The Allies', he said, 'are acquainted with our proceedings and satisfied with our terms.' This was followed by an even more reckless lie. 'The idea of a separate peace', he said,

> had never been entertained for one moment. Nothing of that nature was ever intended, and that such a peace would be so base, so knavish and so villainous a thing, that everyone who served the Queen knew that they must answer it with their heads to the nation.[46]

This lie was so effective that the Lords supported him by sixty-eight votes to forty. Yet at that very moment St John was secretly informing Torcy that if the French agreed to surrender Dunkirk to the British, 'her Majesty would not hesitate to conclude a separate peace leaving the other powers a period in which to submit.'[47]

Meanwhile, the Duke of Ormonde was left in the dark. Although he had written to London three or four times, he had received no replies and his position was becoming unbearably awkward. On 8 June Prince Eugene began his investment of Quesnoy and Ormonde could think of no further reasons for not taking part. 'I have done all that I could to keep secret and to disguise the orders that I received from Her Majesty by Mr Secretary St John,' he wrote to Oxford on 13 June, '. . . and now I can't make any more excuses. . . .'[48] He therefore allowed 6,000 troops in the joint pay of Britain and Holland to take part in the siege and positioned the best of his army between the French and the besiegers. This drew an indignant query from Marshal Villars as to what he thought he was doing? He replied that he had been obliged to furnish troops in order to allay suspicion, but that he had not provided 'one single man solely in the Queen's pay'.

Although the Queen's ministers did not keep the Duke of Ormonde in touch with political developments, matters in London were coming to a head. On 6 June the Queen told the House that progress was being made at Utrecht: Philip v had agreed to renounce publicly the throne of France. She then went on to reveal the splendid conditions that Britain had wrung from the French in the secret negotiations of the previous year. She began with the acquisition of naval bases in Gibraltar and Minorca, went on to the cession of Nova Scotia and Newfoundland, and ended with the thirty-year monopoly of the Spanish slave trade. Their lordships were so delighted with these splendid trade concessions – Whigs and Tories alike – that they gladly accepted Oxford's untrue contention that the Allies supported the agreements that were being made. After all, things had changed so drastically since Marlborough's peace conferences two and three years earlier, that the old cry 'No Peace Without Spain' no longer seemed to apply. Even the Whigs could scarcely argue that Habsburg Charles, who had succeeded his brother as Holy Roman Emperor, should be given the whole Spanish Empire. The most urgent problem was to prevent Philip v from wearing two crowns and now, with his renunciation of the French throne, even that thorny question had been resolved.

The desire for peace was so widespread that Oxford was able to write to his cousin: 'The bent of the Nation is so strong for the Queen's Measures that there is scarce one in a thousand against them.'[49]

Nevertheless, at the end of the debate on 6 June a protest was registered by a number of lords, including Marlborough, Godolphin, Cowper, Somerset and Nottingham. Marlborough declared

that the measures pursued in England for a year past were directly contrary to her Majesty's engagements with the allies, sullied the triumphs and glories of her reign and would render the English name odious to all other nations.[50]

Odious to all other nations? As things turned out this was scarcely an exaggeration. At the end of June, Ormonde announced to the Allies that Britain had signed an armistice with France, and on 28 June, three days before the surrender of Quesnoy, sent written orders to all the generals of foreign troops in British pay to hold themselves in readiness to march. 'A storm of anger swept through the Allied camp and the veterans of twenty nations cursed England, her Ministers and her General.'[51] Apart from a handful of battalions, the commanders replied in unison that they could not separate themselves from Eugene without express orders from their princes. Although the armistice agreement that St John had made with Torcy promised that Ormonde would leave the battlefield with 40,000 soldiers, giving Villars a large superiority over the Allies, the foreign troops flatly refused to follow him, sacrificing the British half of their pay to stay with their comrades. Many of them did not search for polite excuses. General von Bulow of Hanover said that nothing in the world would induce him to behave so dishonourably. The same line was taken by Prince Leopold of Anhalt-Dessau, acting on orders from the King of Prussia; Prince Carl Rudolph of Württemberg, who commanded the Dutch troops; General Bielke of Saxony and the Crown Prince of Hesse-Cassell. St John was furious and referred to Eugene as a 'beggarly German general' who had insulted the English Queen.[52] Ormonde struck a blow at his former allies by insisting that the British pontoon-bridges over the Scheldt, near Denain, should be removed despite the probability of a major French attack.

So Ormonde left the field with his 12,000 British-born troops. The soldiers, once so proud of being 'Marlborough's men', some of them veterans of ten campaigns, were almost sick with embarrassment. Strict orders had been issued against recriminations so their comrades parted from them with exchanges of glum looks and mute reproaches. When they broke ranks at the end of the march, Captain Parker and Sergeant Millner relate that many of them wept and broke their muskets, cursing the Queen and her ministers for forcing them into such an ignominious position. Not all were entirely altruistic. Some were disappointed at missing the rich plunder of France which they reckoned they had dearly earned after a decade of fighting.

Meanwhile the French fulfilled their part of the bargain by turning over Dunkirk to an English force headed by Abigail's brother, the Jack Hill who had failed so miserably in the expedition to Quebec. This time he had nothing to do but settle down in the biggest house in town as governor, while demolition was carried out to destroy it as a pirate stronghold. However, Abigail was delighted and Swift wrote her a flowery letter complimenting her as 'the governess of Dunkirk'. Mr St John was rewarded for the crucial part he had played in these disreputable episodes by being made a viscount. He considered this an insult as he had asked for an earldom in order to revive the Bolingbroke title which had lapsed in the older branch of his family. Lord Oxford, however, was not sorry to thwart his one-time friend as he resented St John's growing arrogance; but his action merely turned the arrogance into open antagonism.

It is sad to record what happened next. Eugene was subjected to a series of shattering defeats. This was an astonishing development as the opposite had been expected. When the Duke of Ormonde joined the Allied army in the spring, Eugene had not only 25,000 more troops, but also far better equipment than the French. Seventy-five-year-old Louis was so apprehensive that he instructed Villars that if he were threatened by disaster he must 'risk a last effort determined to perish or save the state.' Lord Bolingbroke was aware of how close the French were to defeat when he issued his Restraining Orders. He wrote exultantly to a friend: 'I do not say this order saved their army [the French] from being beat but I think in my conscience it did.'[53] A modern American historian, Professor Edward Gregg, has expressed it even more succinctly: 'Together, the Queen and the Lord Treasurer, aided and abetted by St John, saved France as surely, though scarcely as nobly, as Jeanne d'Arc.'[54]

Eugene still had a numerical superiority over Villars despite the British withdrawal; but the very fact of the desertion combined with the absence of the magical Duke of Marlborough, who never lost a battle, played their part in destroying Allied morale. As well as this, Eugene had made the mistake of investing Landrecies, exposing his communications to an enemy flank attack along a sixty-mile front. Villars was not slow to grasp his opportunity and at the end of July defeated the Prince at the battle of Denain (where Ormonde had removed the pontoon-bridges), the only French victory in the Netherlands during the previous ten years. But this was only the beginning. By the autumn Villars had swept the Allies out of Douai, Quesnoy and Bouchain, nullifying Marlborough's achievement for 1710 and 1711.

No comment remains from the Duke of Marlborough on these distressing happenings. However, it is certain that his love and respect for Eugene never flagged or faltered, for at the end of the disastrous summer he sent the Prince the sword that he, Marlborough, had worn in battle. Eugene held it up and kissed the hilt, saying: '*Voila l'épée que j'ai suivie par toute cette longue guerre.*'[55]

Blenheim Palace was still uninhabitable – the roof was not even on – and the building had been stopped again on Oxford's orders. The Marlboroughs therefore divided their time between Marlborough House and St Albans. Sarah was so busy writing her 'vindication' with the help of Arthur Maynwaring that the weeks sped past. The Duke had his dear friend Sidney Godolphin, who was a permanent house-guest, as a companion. On Blenheim Day he put up his campaign tent on the bowling-green of Holywell House and gave a feast which was attended by Walpole, Cowper and many others. The press reported spitefully that the avaricious Duke charged the public sixpence to inspect the tent, a wonderful creation made of 'Arras-work and very curious of its kind', but no doubt that was done to limit the number of sightseers.

When Sarah finally finished her writing she submitted it to Robert Walpole who, like Marlborough, had been subjected to a trumped-up charge of misusing public funds and, unlike Marlborough, had spent some weeks in the Tower. Sarah regarded him as 'extreamly her friend' but was disappointed by his reaction to her memoirs. He was favourably impressed, he said, but advised her not to publish them at the present time as the Ministry would employ 'all the pens of the most scurrilous people whom they had in their pay to write against her.' Maynwaring protested, as he had spent many hours working on the manuscript and thought Walpole's argument was ridiculous since all the lies about her 'that malice could invent' had already been told. However, the Duchess heeded Walpole's advice and laid the work aside to await a more receptive climate.

Godolphin was in poor health all summer, suffering from a stone in the kidney. Sarah nursed him devotedly, but he grew steadily worse and, in September, to the Marlboroughs' great grief, he died. 'The best man that ever lived,' Sarah wrote on the fly-leaf of her Bible. Even Godolphin's enemies praised his unblemished record of faithfulness and incorruptibility. He had served four sovereigns and the fact that he died a poor man showed, Sarah asserted, 'that he had been indeed the nation's treasurer and not his own.'[56]

Poor Sarah; yet another blow was in store for her. In September Arthur Maynwaring caught a chill in the garden at St Albans and two months later followed Godolphin to the grave. Sarah wept inconsolably at the death of this gay, witty, forty-four-year-old writer and politician who had been her only close intellectual friend – a man who discussed books and personalities with her, each making the other laugh by mutually irreverent observations. Now, within eight weeks, Sarah had lost her two closest friends.

Meanwhile, Marlborough's political enemies did not slacken their attacks. He was still the greatest man in Europe and they were well aware that at any moment capricious fortune might return him to power. Indeed, if the Queen died and a Hanoverian sovereign came to the throne, where would the Tories be? As a result, every malicious slander their inventive minds could conjure up was hurled against him. Lord Bolingbroke's scurrilous paper, the *Examiner*, declared that thousands of soldiers had died on the battlefield because Marlborough had appropriated the money intended for medicine. Another article cried out that the Duke was 'a very great coward' and so confounded by every little happening that he would cry in confusion to those about him: 'What shall we do now?' 'Had I not read those very words,' commented Captain Robert Parker, 'I should never have believed that any man could have the face to publish so notorious a falsehood.'[57]

Other falsehoods, just as outrageous, led to crucial developments. In June 1712 a debate took place in the House of Lords in which the new Captain-General, the Duke of Ormonde, was criticized for preventing British troops from taking part in the fighting. Lord Poulett rose from his seat and flung at Marlborough a monstrous accusation that was going the rounds. Ormonde, he said, 'was not like a certain general who led troops to slaughter . . . in order to fill his pockets by disposing of their commissions.'[58] As soon as the debate was over Marlborough sent his friend, Lord Mohun, to challenge Poulett to a duel. Poulett had not expected politics to take such a nasty turn and, although he was twelve years younger than the Duke, saw death staring him in the face. He bemoaned his fate to his wife, who promptly took up her pen and wrote no fewer than five letters to the Secretary of State, Lord Dartmouth, imploring him to intervene. Dartmouth placed two sentries outside the Pouletts' house and personally requested Marlborough 'not to stir abroad'. The Queen was then informed and sent the Duke a royal command that 'this might go no further'. When Poulett apologized, Marlborough had no alternative but to let the matter drop.

Though the Duke remained unperturbed by the slander that swirled around him, his Olympian calm was shattered when he learned that the Attorney General was toying with the idea of suing him for repayment of all the money he had spent on the army intelligence service for the last ten years – in other words the $2\frac{1}{2}$ per cent deducted from the pay of foreign troops (despite the Queen's Warrant countersigned by Mr Secretary Hedges) and the commissions paid by Medina for the bread contracts. And this was not all; another suit was pending over the 'monument of national gratitude'. When the Crown ordered the work on Blenheim to be suspended in June 1712, a total of £233,000 had been swallowed up and another £44,000 was owing to workmen and suppliers. This money had nothing to do with Marlborough; yet the Crown now alleged that the Duke had written from the front (at a time when payments were in arrears) to keep the workmen in employment and therefore was liable to meet some of the costs. This, they estimated, came to the staggering sum of £30,000. Altogether Marlborough might be confronted with judgements exceeding a quarter of a million sterling.

The Duke was advised that if he left England the processes on foot against him might be dropped. He was indignant to think that his persecutors might wrest his fortune from him and immediately set about making plans for an extensive stay abroad. To take care of his needs on the Continent he transferred £50,000 to General Cadogan at The Hague with instructions to invest the money in Dutch securities. He applied for a passport on the grounds of health and gave his ultimate destination as Naples.[59]

Marlborough travelled to Dover on 24 November 1712. Sarah promised to join him as soon as she could shut up her house and attend to children, servants, agents and dogs. The Duke had to wait a week for a favourable wind, but on 1 December he boarded an ordinary packet-boat accompanied by two servants. No ceremony of any kind was accorded him as he took his leave from the island whose prestige he had raised so high.

Marlborough's sudden departure caused a flurry of speculation. Was he really leaving because of his health? Or to escape from the threat of legal proceedings? Or, as some people contended, because Lord Oxford had been given incriminating evidence that Marlborough had asked Versailles for two million crowns to make a peace? None of Marlborough's correspondence for this period has survived, and for years historians have brooded over these questions and been forced to draw their own conclusions. Winston Churchill, for instance, believes that Marlborough left England primarily to escape the threat of an impeachment. Undoubtedly, he was tired of being a target for Tory abuse and longed for the fame and admiration that shone so willingly upon him from foreign skies. However, there is evidence, slight but tantalizing, to show us that Marlborough's sojourn was laced with more heady stuff than a desire to retreat. For a brief and impulsive moment he was seeking the ships and the men to break up the Queen's ministry and put an end to the Utrecht peace treaty.

Fourteen

Plots and Counter-plots Abroad

As the packet-boat approached Ostend, the captain raised the ensign on the top mast as a signal that the celebrated Duke of Marlborough was aboard. General William Cadogan was waiting on the quayside to serve his master during his self-imposed exile. Cadogan had been obliged to ask the Lord Treasurer for leave from the army. 'The Duke of Marlborough's ill health,' he had written to Lord Oxford, '. . . and his being without one friend to accompany him, makes the requesting leave to wait on him an indispensable duty to me who . . . owe all I have in the world to his favour.'[1] The Queen's permission was forthcoming, but three months later Cadogan was relieved of all his military appointments for making it plain where his loyalties lay. Luckily his action did not do him permanent harm for eventually he himself became Captain-General of the British army.

John met Sarah at Maestricht. 'I did not know', she wrote later, 'whether I should ever see my own country again.'[2] Everything was dangerously uncertain – the animosity of England's political leaders, even the successor to Anne's throne. Although Dr Hare referred to the Marlboroughs' travels as 'a sort of pilgrimage', Sarah came equipped for a long stay. She brought 120 parcels with her, containing everything from wigs and candlesticks to 'a vast quantity of linen'; a tea-kettle to hold five pints, a 'blew bagg' lined with fox-skins, a powder-puff, seven leopard-skin muffs, and forty coats. Accompanied by Cadogan and a sufficient number of servants to handle Sarah's belongings, they made a leisurely journey along the Rhine. They had no intention of going to Italy, which had been specified merely to mislead Oxford. Sarah had only been abroad once before and was as enthusiastic as a schoolgirl. At Frankfurt she wrote a good many letters to Mrs Clayton, the agent's wife at Woodstock, and Mr

Robert Jennings, her relation and lawyer, who had escorted her to Dover. She commented on 'the pretty green hedges' and the stoves that were so hot they made her 'uneasy'. She was impressed by the politeness of the people, distressed by the poverty and hated the disagreeable 'sand that goes over one's shoes'. Quite naturally she was enraptured by the 'civilities' shown to her husband. 'I am come just now', she wrote home from Frankfurt in May,

> from a Window from which I saw a great many troops pass that were under the Command of Prince Eugène. They paid all the Respects as they went by to the D. of Marlborough as if he had been in his old Post . . . to see so many brave men marching was a very fine Sight, it gave me Melancholy Reflections, and made me weep; but at the same time I was so animated that I wished I had been a Man then I might have ventured my Life a Thousand Times in the glorious Cause of Liberty. . . .[3]

Sarah recovered from her despondency by singing, for the amusement of her husband, the ballad of Queen Anne's 'dark deeds at night', set to the rollicking tune of 'Lillibulero'.* Very little is known about the Marlboroughs' social life at this time; they probably had a steady flow of people passing through their house, but Sarah seldom mentions names. What interested her far more than guests and well-wishers was the 'monstrous iniquities' of the Catholic Church. She talks about 'the poor deluded people' and the 'mony they must pay to the priests for the forgiveness of their Sins.' In visiting 'Nunnerys' she had seen 'such rediculous things as would appear to you incredible.'[4] However, she had a few things to say for the misguided populace:

> Although the Generality of them I have seen are Roman Catholics they fear the power of France so much that they drink to the Protestant Succession, and the Honours they have don me in all Places upon the Duke of Marlborough's account is not to be imagined, which is not disagreeable now, because as it cannot proceed from Power, it shows that he has made a right use of it when he was a General.[5]

Judging from Sarah's breathless letters one might have imagined that the Marlboroughs were on a pleasure-trip, avidly drinking in new sights and impressions. Yet it would have been difficult to assemble a more politically conscious group than the Duke and Duchess of Marlborough, General Cadogan and the two confederates in England – Lord Sunderland and James Craggs Senior. Cadogan was hoping to enter Parliament as the Member for Woodstock, the village

---

* 'Lillibulero' was an anti-Papist, anti-Irish song that swept England in the 1680s.

near Blenheim Palace. On the Continent he was received everywhere as the famous Quartermater-General of Marlborough's army, and this made it easy for him to act as the Duke's 'eyes and ears'. Sunderland was not only Marlborough's son-in-law but the most energetic of the Whig leaders, and Craggs was Marlborough's business manager. These four men kept each other well-informed by weekly letters, using as intermediaries Jean de Robethon, head of the Hanoverian chancery, and the Baron von Bothmar, the Hanoverian envoy at The Hague.

The Marquis de Torcy, the French Minister of State, was alarmed to learn that Marlborough was travelling abroad. Torcy knew the Duke better than his own countrymen: Marlborough was not a man to accept defeat tamely and the Frenchman began to speculate wildly as to what he could be up to. Would he try to subvert the British regiments in the Southern Netherlands? Or might he go so far as to consent to lead the Imperial armies against France? Torcy worked himself up to such a state that Oxford was driven to comfort him by insisting that Marlborough had not gone abroad of his own volition but had been forced into exile by the ministry. This, of course, was not wholly true, and Torcy was too shrewd to believe it.

On the other hand, he was right to fear Marlborough, as the Duke's ideas were even more dangerous than the Frenchman imagined. On this occasion, however, Marlborough's proposal was less of a plan than a dream – a dream of retribution so impractical that it did not have the slightest chance of support or success. His aim was both original and startling: to launch an Allied invasion of England that would break up the Queen's ministry, put an end to the Utrecht peace conference and secure the Protestant succession.

Soon after arriving in Antwerp (20 December 1712) Marlborough wrote to Prince Eugene that 'everyone will agree that England must be detached from France for the well-being of Europe'. If England completed the Utrecht Treaty and had time to bring in the Pretender they would 'not only destroy the Liberty of England but that of Europe as well.' The only remedy, he stressed, was '*une revolution*' forcing Anne to accept a government which sincerely embraced the Allied cause.[6]

Everything depended on Holland, so early in January 1713 Marlborough sent Cadogan to unfold his scheme at The Hague.

Under the pretense of establishing a Mediterranean fleet, the emperor should lease ten or twelve Dutch warships, which would be retained at Ostend and Nieuport. From there, with Cadogan acting as logistical director, Hanoverian troops hired by the States and the emperor (ostensibly to garrison the southern Netherlands) would be dispatched into England, where Sunderland and General James Stanhope had been left in charge of arrangements.[7]

Meanwhile, Sunderland had written to Bothmar in Hanover assuring him that only a very small force would be needed as England was ready for an 'anti-ministerial revolution'. This, he emphasized, 'was the only thing that would be able to save Europe.'[8]

All Marlborough's proposals were imaginative, but this one seemed peculiarly lacking in common sense. To overthrow the Queen's Government would be tantamount to deposing the Queen, for how could any sovereign continue to reign after such a humiliation? And considering the vote in Parliament in favour of the Utrecht settlement, what made the conspirators think that only a small invasion force would be necessary? We know that the Marlboroughs felt strongly that England's freedom depended on keeping Louis XIV at bay and in ensuring the Hanoverian succession. And in fairness to them, it should be kept in mind that many people believed that when Queen Anne died, mighty France, free of the burden of war, would launch an invasion to put the Pretender on the throne. Lord Bolingbroke's activities did nothing to calm these fears. For months he had been promoting Jacobites to prominent positions, both in civil and military posts. The Whig Earl of Dorset had been ejected from Dover Castle; a Jacobite controlled Edinburgh; and the man who had succeeded Marlborough, the Duke of Ormonde (a strong adherent of 'James III'), had been appointed Warden of the Cinque Ports. The Irish regiments in the French service had been moved towards the coastal towns and Abigail's brother, Brigadier Jack Hill, the Governor of Dunkirk, recommended his port as an advantageous embarkation port for a cross-Channel fleet.

Despite these threats and anxieties all three of Marlborough's former Allies rejected his proposals out of hand.* The Dutch were almost bankrupt and totally opposed to a venture that, if it went wrong, could lead to another conflict; furthermore, they were pinning their hopes on the Barrier Treaty that Bolingbroke was negotiating for them. As for the Hanoverians, only the aged Electress Sophia showed any interest in the plan. Her son, the Elector George, who was in charge of foreign affairs, was appalled by the idea of a revolution that might cost him the throne. He was willing to take up arms after Queen Anne's death, if and when the occasion warranted

---

* Marlborough destroyed all correspondence to do with this plan, but the details cited above found their way into the Hanoverian archives where they were unearthed by Professor Edward Gregg in 1972.

it, but nothing would induce him to put his future needlessly at risk. (He was too tactful to say this to Marlborough and gave Holland's withdrawal as his excuse.) The Emperor took his cue from this and also slid out gracefully, simply by pointing to the refusals of the other two.

By the time the Treaty of Utrecht was signed in April 1713, all hope of Marlborough's 'preventative invasion' had crumbled away. Roughly speaking, the Treaty divided the Spanish Empire in the way that William III had suggested. Philip V was left in possession of Spain and the Indies, and Charles got the Spanish Netherlands and all the Spanish territory in Italy except for Sicily, which went to the Duke of Savoy. The Elector Max Emmanuel was obliged to content himself with his ancestral lands in Bavaria. The Dutch were given a good barrier, not as fulsome as the one drawn for them by Lord Townshend in 1709 but certainly not niggardly. The outer line included such important strongholds as Ypres, Menins, Tournai, Mons, Charleroi and Namur. Prussia secured Guelderland at the expense of the Dutch, and France was delighted to be given back her fortresses in the Low Countries below the Barrier, particularly the great city of Lille.

England emerged from the war as the dominant force, not only because of Lord Bolingbroke's skilful negotiations but because the Bank of England's credit system enabled her to bear the burden of war without undue strain. The Treaty made her mistress of the Mediterranean by giving her the naval bases of Gibraltar and Minorca. Across the Atlantic she took possession of St Kitts island and Acadia, Newfoundland and Hudson Bay, opening the doors to a New World empire. And she was accorded by Spain the thirty-year-monopoly of the South American slave trade. Finally, Louis XIV agreed to recognize Queen Anne, to acknowledge the Protestant succession and to banish the Pretender to the Duchy of Lorraine.

To understand Marlborough's feelings, it must be realized that the Treaty of Utrecht seemed to him a near-disaster. He argued that England, by letting France off the hook, had restored her confidence and encouraged her to return to her bad old ways. Soon she might be just as aggressive as she had been ten years earlier. Although French expansion had been halted temporarily, Marlborough had put so much emphasis on 'No Peace Without Spain' that England's failure to achieve it almost seemed to nullify the effect of his victories. In April 1713, Sarah wrote to Lady Mohun that she had seen the terms of the Treaty of Utrecht in a French paper and referred to Lord Oxford as the villain 'that ruined his country to sett himself up.' Two months later, in a letter to James Craggs, apparently referring to the return of the Low Countries fortresses to France, she wrote: 'In noe place there ever was such a farse as in England where men seem to be giving up with joy and thanks what they preserved at soe much expense for soe many years.'⁹

Not everyone was as angry as the Marlboroughs. The Dutch, although disappointed not to have exactly the barrier they had wanted, finally admitted that they had been given a satisfactory peace, and put their signature to the Treaty. But the Imperialists and the Hanoverians were so indignant at the 'betrayal' over Spain that they refused to sign and went on fighting for another twelve months.

Although Marlborough's desire to invade England before the Treaty of Utrecht had come into being had foundered, he was determined to fight if France tried to put the Pretender on the throne. Sarah was convinced that such an attempt would be made. According to Lord Bolingbroke, who was anxious to believe that Anne was a Jacobite, the Queen was wearing a packet of letters around her neck, which she never took off even at night. It was rumoured to be Anne's secret instructions in case of her sudden death, urging the Tories to restore her half-brother, the Pretender, to the throne. And as Lord Bolingbroke could hope for nothing if George of Hanover mounted the throne, it was obvious that he, too, would favour a Stuart restoration. 'Be sure', Sarah wrote to Craggs, 'nothing can stand before the King of France long, if England continues to assist him. . . .'¹⁰

Marlborough did not express himself as dramatically as his wife, but agreed with her assessment. Although Louis xiv had promised to support 'the Protestant succession' no one took him seriously. Their suspicions were well-founded, as he had secretly instructed his Foreign Minister Torcy to make a Jacobite restoration his primary objective. Not surprisingly Oxford and Bolingbroke were already conniving for the same end. Using Torcy and Abbé Gaultier as intermediaries the two English ministers put themselves in touch with 'the Prince of Wales' as soon as the Utrecht agreement was out of the way. Oxford assured young James that he had his interests at heart and was 'trying to bring the Queen around'.

However, in September 1713 an event took place which distracted Marlborough's attention from the main struggle. A general election was held in England which gave the Tories – the peace party – a massive majority. Marlborough was deeply worried that, on the strength of this, Oxford might start impeachment proceedings against him which would strip him of his fortune. 'The villainy and malice of my Enemys are such', he had written to James Craggs in June 1713, 'that were I even at Constantinople they would indeavour to vex me.'[11] Sarah was even more vehement about Oxford and Bolingbroke: 'Nay, for the good of the Publick no Death could bee so cruell for such villains.'[12]

This brings us to a strange incident which does nothing to endear us to Marlborough. It was triggered off by a message from James II's widow, the once-beautiful Mary of Modena. The ex-Queen and her son, the Old Pretender, had been banished to Lorraine by the Treaty of Utrecht and Mary wanted to know if the Duke was prepared to do anything to help them. Marlborough had been in touch with the exiled Stuarts intermittently for twenty-five years. As he never put anything in writing, information about this is based on the unreliable reports of Jacobite agents who claim that the Duke always talked of 'repaying his debt' to the Stuarts, whatever that was supposed to mean. On this occasion he informed Mary of Modena's agent, Mr Turnstal, that there was nothing he could do for them unless they could intervene to ensure that the fortune he had left in England remained intact. Otherwise, he explained, he would be obliged to come to an arrangement with Oxford that would prevent him from acting as a free agent. Everything would be different, he stressed, if the 'Prince of Wales' could prevail on Louis XIV to make a joint appeal to Lord Oxford resulting in a promise from him not to instigate impeachment proceedings. Marlborough would then be at liberty to take an independent line. The French Foreign Minister, Torcy, recognized this proposal as a masterpiece of unscrupulous self-interest and invited the Duke of Berwick to handle the affair.

Berwick knew his uncle very well, and told him flatly that the Prince of Wales could not assist him unless he, Marlborough, came out publicly in support of the Stuarts. As might be expected, Marlborough slid away from the ultimatum and began arguing about irrelevant details. No one can accuse the Great Duke of diffidence; nevertheless, to invite the King of France, against whom he had been waging war for ten years, to intervene to save his personal fortune surpassed the normal bounds of audacity and bordered on the bizarre.

This rather discreditable episode came to an end at Christmas 1713 when Queen Anne was taken ill at Windsor and nearly died. Lord Oxford and Lord Bolingbroke had not come to any arrangement with the Pretender and suddenly went into a frenzy of fear that the House of Hanover would seize the throne before anything could be done to stop it. As this would spell disaster for the sovereign's chief ministers, it was not surprising that Lord Bolingbroke stood by the Queen's bed wringing his hands and praying: 'God in his Mercy to these Kingdoms preserve her.' When rumours swept the town that she was dead, the Whig chiefs hurried around in their sedan-chairs, calling on one another in a buzz of anticipation. The Tories were very glum; but when Anne recovered, they angrily accused their Whig opponents of unnatural levity at a time of national stress.[13] Meanwhile, Lord Oxford had panicked; he suddenly saw a very bleak future stretching out for himself, and without more ado, sent Marlborough a cheque for £10,000 for back salary, long overdue, and assured him that no impeachment proceedings would be started against him.

When the Queen recovered, Oxford and Bolingbroke sighed with relief and decided that they must come to an immediate arrangement with the Pretender. However, the Queen's illness had demonstrated that a change had taken place in England. The Tories were no longer the fervent Jacobites they had been a generation earlier; they were no longer willing to accept a Stuart King no matter what his religious faith. They would support James III enthusiastically if he would embrace the Protestant faith. But so, for that matter, would the Whigs. Indeed, if the Pretender would agree to change his religion, the whole British people would acclaim him wildly. Oxford therefore sent James an ultimatum demanding that he announce his intention of joining the Anglican Church. The Abbé Gaultier carried the message and, as he saw in James's succession a chance of bringing England back into the French orbit, he did everything in his power to persuade James to accede. In his letter of 6 February, the Abbé advised the young man to 'ask God to enlighten you as to the part you should take.' James would never sit on the English throne, he added, unless he changed his religion or dissimulated it (as Charles II had done) and he would never retain the throne unless he 'kept his word better than the King his father had kept his.'[14]

If James had agreed, there is not a shadow of a doubt that a Stuart restoration would have taken place. Then Sarah's warnings would have come true as later he might have come under the influence of priests – as did his father, James II – and tried to introduce Popery. However, the Pretender refused indignantly to change his religion and Oxford and Bolingbroke were at a loss what to do next. The problem seemed insoluble as both Ministers recognized the Catholic religion as an insurmountable stumbling-block. Bolingbroke told the French envoy: 'People would rather have a Turk than a Catholic.'[15] Oxford began to make feeble overtures to Hanover; but Bolingbroke was resilient enough to convince himself that the Queen might survive much longer than people thought and the Pretender, whatever he said now, might eventually change his mind.

The Duke of Marlborough knew nothing of these developments. Nevertheless he, too, had a fright when Anne lay at death's door and decided that there could be no harm in insuring himself against further contingencies by asking James for a pardon. When the request came, the Duke of Berwick warned the Pretender not to expect any good from his uncle, but advised him to keep on good terms with him. He explained contemptuously:

> One may give to those sort of people as good as they bring, that is to say words for words, for I see nothing else in all M. Malbranch [Marlborough] says and indeed he has never behaved himself otherwise; however one must not seem not to believe him.[16]

Marlborough took care to conceal his Jacobite contacts from his wife, as Sarah's nature had no room for compromise. Indeed, when a Roman Catholic gentleman in Frankfurt assured her that a Stuart restoration was a certainty, and advised her to protect herself by bringing Marlborough into the project 'now ripening', she gave him short shrift. 'I would rather', she wrote, 'have [the Duke] suffer upon that account than to change Sides, for that would look as if what he did at the Revolution was not for Justice, as it really was, but to comply with the Times. . . .'[17] This was putting it mildly. If Marlborough had ever been tempted to return to his old allegiance with the Stuarts (which he never was), Sarah would have fought him tooth and nail. Liberty was her watchword, and liberty meant 'No Popery' and 'No Interference from France'. 'If I were a man,' she often proclaimed, 'I should struggle to the last moment in the glorious cause of liberty.'[18]

The House of Hanover was well aware of Marlborough's contacts with the Pretender (the Duke's enemies saw to that); nevertheless, they retained complete confidence in him. Despite his dealings with the Stuarts, he never failed to oppose Louis XIV or to come down on the side of the Protestant succession – these were the great causes of his life. Although he was a born dissembler who liked to play with words, his acts were always prompt and reliable. Indeed, the innermost feelings of both Marlboroughs can be gauged by the fact that although neither of them liked to part with money, they loaned the Elector George £20,000 to meet pressing demands.

Meanwhile, the growing tension was having an effect on the Elector's mother, the eighty-four-year-old Electress Sophia, who was praying that she would not die before 'Queen of England' could be inscribed on her tombstone. Without consulting her son, who was in charge of all Hanoverian diplomacy, she allowed her London envoy, Herr Schultz, to apply to the Lord Chancellor for a writ of summons so that the Electoral Prince (the Elector's son) could take his seat in the House of Lords as Duke of Cambridge.

The gossip which had been circulating for years that Anne refused to allow her German heirs to visit England because she harboured a particular aversion for the Elector George – or a particular fondness for her half-brother James – still persisted; yet later it became clear that Anne suffered from a violent neurosis about death. Anything related to her own demise created a trauma which she could not control. To be asked to receive a member of the family who would mount the throne as she was being lowered into her grave was the part of the plan that she found unbearable. (Indeed, she even refused to sign her will and died intestate; as a result, her favourite, Abigail, got nothing.) Lord Oxford – or possibly Lord Bolingbroke – drafted the vehement reply that was sent to Hanover. Poor Sophia was deeply upset by the tone of the letter which again emphasized that, although the writ of summons had been issued, members of the Hanover family were not welcome in England in the Queen's lifetime. Three days later, when Sophia was walking in the garden, she dropped dead of a heart attack. Everyone, of course, put the blame on Anne.

The Elector George was now the Heir Apparent. Although he had refused to contemplate Marlborough's invasion scheme, he came up with a plan of his own suggested by his foreign affairs adviser, Count Bernstorf. To enable George to seize control within hours of the Queen's death, Marlborough must become Captain-General and try to secure the allegiance of the British troops at Bruges, Ghent and Dunkirk; the Electoral Prince must take charge of the troops in the Southern Netherlands; General Cadogan must go to London, seize the Tower and administer the oath of allegiance to the soldiers serving in the home forces.

In order to make sure that there were no difficulties in the case of an emergency, George issued undated commissions to Marlborough and Cadogan so that they could take command at a moment's notice. Marlborough wrote to Herr Robethon asking him to thank the Elector for his confidence and promising 'to hazard both life and fortune' in serving him.

Marlborough divided his time between Frankfurt and Antwerp for over a year, waiting to see what developments would take place. But when, in the summer of 1714, the Duke of Berwick left France for Spain, he became convinced that no invasion attempt would be made in the immediate future and decided to return to England. French intelligence got wind of his intention long before he made a public announcement and communicated it to Oxford and Bolingbroke who, by this time, were at daggers drawn with each other. Torcy had always been impressed by Marlborough's tenacity and was certain he was returning home to destroy 'the Tory ministry'. He prophesied a civil war, while Matthew Prior, one of Bolingbroke's special envoys, wrote from Paris, 'We are all frightened out of our wits.'[19]

They had every reason for anxiety as the Duke was still worshipped by the army that he no longer commanded. The Marlboroughs left for Ostend on 21 July, and when they were in the neighbourhood of Ghent the chief magistrates met them on the road and said that they had prepared a handsome breakfast for them in a nearby village. Accompanying the magistrates were a great many officers from the Royal Irish Regiment – ultra-Protestants from Northern Ireland – who had come to pay their respects. 'I was so much surprised and touched', Sarah wrote to Charlotte Clayton, her friend at Woodstock,

> that I could not speak to the officers without a good deal of concern saying that I was sorry for what they did fearing that it might hurt them, to which they replied very pollitickly or ignorantly, I don't know which, 'that it was not possible for them to suffer for having done their duty'.[20]

The Marlboroughs were at Ostend for ten days hoping for 'a fair wind', as Sarah declared that it was 'intolerable to go to bed in those boats' and insisted on waiting for weather that would enable them to cross the Channel in daylight. Meanwhile, during those days of delay, the enmity between Lord Oxford and Lord Bolingbroke was nearing breaking-point. For some time Bolingbroke had been determined to oust Oxford from the Lord Treasurership and take over himself. Oxford, on the other hand, was equally determined to stay where he was and busied himself compiling a list of Bolingbroke's financial irregularities. While making this scrutiny he discovered that large sums of money had been removed from the South Sea Company which controlled the Asiento contract, and had been split three ways between the Trade Commissioner, Arthur Moore, Bolingbroke and Abigail.

Abigail's friendship with Oxford foundered on this rock. Swift wrote that the Lord Treasurer had refused her 'a job of some money out of the Asiento contract'. Added to this, Oxford threatened to inform Parliament of the malpractices of her brother Jack as Governor of Dunkirk. She told Oxford heatedly that she would 'carry no more messages to the Queen nor medle nor carry', and later assailed him saying: 'You never did the Queen any service, nor are you capable of doing her any.'[21] Perhaps this is the moment when the Duke of Buckingham exclaimed:

> Good God! How this poor Nation has been governed in my time! During the reign of King Charles the Second we were governed by a parcel of French whores; in King James the Second's time by a parcel of Popish priests; in King William's time by a parcel of Dutch Footmen; and now we are governed by a dirty chambermaid, a Welsh attorney and a profligate wretch that has neither honour nor honesty.[22]

During the Marlboroughs' ten days of waiting, 'the dirty chambermaid' triumphed over 'the Welsh attorney'. By 27 July the Queen had bent to the relentless pressure on her to get rid of Oxford. He knew of her decision when he attended the Cabinet Council that day; according to most historians a horrifying scene took place, with Oxford denouncing the man who was trying to supplant him. He called him a rogue and a liar, enumerating the occasions on which he had swindled the Government, beginning with the Quebec expedition and ending with the Asiento contract. Anne was appalled by the scene. She was in such bad health she could not stand or walk, and after the violent interchange was carried out of the room, half-dead, in her sedan-chair. She received Oxford that night and accepted the White Staff from him. 'They say the Queen was loath to part with the Treasurer,' wrote a Tory peer, 'but was teased into it. . . .' However, Oxford's close friend, Erasmus Lewis, wrote to Swift that the Queen had dismissed him because

> he neglected all business, that he was seldom to be understood, that when he did explain himself, she could not depend on the truth of what he said; that he never came to her at the time she appointed; that he often came drunk, that lastly to crown all he beh'd himself toward her with ill manner, indecency and disrespect.[23]

This seems a fairly solid list of grievances. At his final meeting with the Queen, Oxford warned her against trusting Marlborough, saying that the Duke was returning to England for the sole purpose of creating civil unrest. Apparently she made no answer. Although the Queen had dismissed Oxford, she could not bring herself to give the Treasury to a man as corrupt as Bolingbroke; so she let the matter slide.

Nevertheless, even without the White Staff, Bolingbroke had emerged the victor and was in a position – at least until a new Treasurer was appointed – to take decisive action. But he was not of the stuff that heroes are made. Despite all his boasts and threats, he had no plan and was incapable of forming one. On 28 July he gave an astonishing dinner-party composed of his enemies – the young Whigs who were Marlborough's friends and admirers and were destined to lead England: Stanhope, Craggs, Pulteney and Cadogan. Only Walpole, who was out of London in the country, was absent. Bolingbroke amazed the company by announcing his devotion to the House of Hanover and declaring that all present would be offered jobs in his Cabinet if he became Lord Treasurer. His guests soon realized that he was merely 'testing the temperature of the water'. Stanhope did not beat about the bush; if Bolingbroke would restore Marlborough to his command in the army and put the fleet into hands loyal to the Hanoverian succession, they would not cross swords with him during the remainder of the Queen's life. But even now he could not make up his mind what course to follow and the dinner broke up inconclusively.

On 29 July, the gout that had attacked the Queen's body was said to have moved to her brain, and the doctors declared that her end was approaching. Apparently at this point the dying Queen even toyed with the notion of sending for Marlborough. A report in an unsigned newsletter sent to the French Ambassador stated that she asked repeatedly whether the Duke had yet reached London; and the answer, of course, was in the negative.[24] On the 30th, the Cabinet Council met, hoping that the Queen would have moments of consciousness when she would be able to accept their recommendation for a Lord Treasurer. If no one was appointed, the law stipulated that Oxford would be within his rights to pick up the White Staff himself. This was too much for Bolingbroke, so he proposed that the office be given to Lord Shrewsbury, the one-time 'King of Hearts' and one of the 'immortal seven' who had summoned William III to England. 'From near noon', Dr Malthus recounted later, 'Her Majesty had her understanding perfect, but from that time answered nothing but ay or no.'[25] The Lord Chancellor and several members of the Council entered her bedchamber, read out their request and received her assent. Lord Chancellor Harcourt placed her hand on the White Staff and guided it to Shrewsbury. The Queen then sank into a coma. She died two days later, on 1 August, at seven in the morning.

The mystery surrounding the packet of letters that the Queen wore around her neck, and that had inspired so many pro-Jacobite rumours, followed her into the grave. The envelope bore written instructions in her own hand to destroy the contents without reading. Her orders were carried out but, when the papers were burning, witnesses saw that they were written in French. As the Pretender always addressed his sister, Anne, in English, Count von Bothmar accepted the likely view that they were early love letters from Prince George.

Marlborough did not land in Dover until 2 August. The succession of George I had been announced by the heralds twenty-four hours earlier and had been received with perfect calm. The upheaval that had been feared had not taken place. To avoid unnecessarily offending the Tories, none of the important opposition leaders – Marlborough, Sunderland, Somers, Wharton – were appointed to the Council of Regency which would rule the country until the new King arrived. Thus, the Protestant succession which underpinned English freedom and English independence – and for which Marlborough had fought so long – was now an established fact.

George I landed on 18 September at Greenwich where England's greatest nobles gathered to greet him. He did not speak a word of English but he greeted the Duke of Marlborough with noticeable warmth. 'My Lord Duke,' he exclaimed (through an interpreter), 'I hope your troubles are now all over.' The King immediately granted the Duke an hour's audience and the first warrant signed by the sovereign reinstated him as Captain-General, Master-General of the Ordnance, and Colonel of the 1st Guards.

Once again the Duke of Marlborough basked in the sunlight of royal favour. George I was not very likeable and despised his new subjects for conniving with the enemy in 1712 and deserting the field of battle. For a while he even toyed with the idea of repudiating the Treaty of Utrecht and starting the war again, but this notion was too fanciful to be entertained for long. Soon, all the lords of the Whig Junto were established in Cabinet posts. Lord Shrewsbury willingly yielded the Treasurer's Staff, resuming his former position as Lord Chamberlain, while the Treasury was placed in commission under the presidency of Lord Halifax. The three men who emerged as the force that really ran the Government were from a younger generation and all special friends of Marlborough: Lord Townshend, who had served with him at The Hague as a peace negotiator in 1709, and General James Stanhope, whom he had sent to Spain in 1711, were Secretaries of State, while the forceful Robert Walpole was given the lucrative post of Paymaster of the Forces. Marlborough's son-in-law, Lord Sunderland, was disappointed to receive no more than the Lord Lieutenancy of Ireland, but his career was in the ascendancy, and before long he was called upon to head a government.

This was not all. Marlborough believed in making use of his opportunities and pushed his good fortune to the limit. He secured for his daughter, the Duchess of Montagu, an appointment as Lady-in-Waiting to the Princess of Wales, and for his two rather undistinguished sons-in-law, Lord Godolphin and the Earl of Bridgwater, Cofferer of the Household and Lord Chamberlain to the Prince of Wales's Household. Sarah was disdainful of these honours. Although she was thrilled to be home again ('Tis better to be dead than live out of England' she had decided when abroad), she had had enough of Court life and seldom accompanied her husband to royal soirées. 'I think', she wrote to Lady Cowper, 'anyone that has common sense must needs be very weary of everything that one meets with in Courts.'[26] Nevertheless, to please her husband she gave the first large reception for the King at Marlborough House.

The two men who had turned Queen Anne against Marlborough, depriving him of his command and preventing his march to Paris, waited uneasily to see what Fate had in store for them. Bolingbroke built an enormous bonfire in front of his house to celebrate George's coronation, but it did not alter the sovereign's view of him. In March 1715, a newly elected Whig Parliament established a Committee of Secrecy to investigate the Utrecht negotiations, and possible Jacobite plots on the part of the ministers involved. Bolingbroke had the audacity to go to Marlborough and ask for advice on what to do. Marlborough invented an alarming story; with a perfectly straight face he told him that plans were afoot to accuse him of high treason and send him to the scaffold. Bolingbroke was so frightened that he crossed the Channel disguised as the valet of a Frenchman, M. de La Vigne, and went hot-foot to throw in his lot with the Pretender in Lorraine. There he became Secretary of State. Three months later he was joined by another prominent Jacobite, the Duke of Ormonde.

Oxford, on the other hand, played a more dignified part. He faced his approaching impeachment with imperturbability saying that he would 'neither flee the country nor conceal himself'. He was confined in the Tower for two years, but the impeachment proceedings were finally dropped because of a procedural dispute between the two Houses. When this announcement was made in the House of Lords, the Duke broke down and wept – Oxford was the only man in the world whom he truly hated. However, he found some satisfaction in the fact that the ex-Lord President played no further part in the affairs of the country. Abigail Masham also disappeared into the shadows: she slipped off to her estate at Langley Marsh near Windsor and lived so quietly with her husband and children that no one heard of her again. When Queen Anne was dying she played very little part as the Duchess of Somerset took over the sick-room. All sorts of tales circulated about Abigail's behaviour. 'The town tells a world of stories,' Peter Wentworth wrote to his brother, '. . . as at a Friday she left the Queen for three hours to go and ransack in St James's. I can't say if this is true or false.' A few days later he decided that it was only too true and wrote that Lady Masham and her sister, Mrs Hill, 'Tho they roar'd and cry'd enough while there was life as soon as there was none they took care of themselves.'[27] Abigail died in obscurity in 1734.

Marlborough was not only Captain-General of the army but a member of the Cabinet. Throughout 1715 he was reputed to be a member of a small inner circle consisting of two Hanoverians and two Englishmen including himself. 'Under cover of darkness', wrote Hoffmann, the Imperial resident in London, 'Marlborough, Townshend and Bernstorf meet every night at Bothmar's house.' 'This quadrumvirate settles everything,' confirmed the Prussian envoy.[28] During that year the Duke's most agreeable task was to reinstate the gallant officers who had served him in the field, and been purged from the army by Lord Bolingbroke. He protected his foreign recruits, particularly the French Huguenots who were usually overlooked, and modernized the board responsible for the army's heavy guns. This led to the creation of the Royal Regiment of Artillery.

That September Marlborough's great adversary, seventy-five-year-old Louis xiv, died. The Duke of Orléans was appointed Regent until five-year-old Louis xv would be old enough to rule. This changed things for the Stuarts. No longer was the French Court interested in their claim to the English throne. 'James iii' was well aware of his dimming prestige and decided to have one more try for the Crown across the channel. He was encouraged to mount an invasion by the violent Tory reaction against the new Whig Government. Bolingbroke and Ormonde predicted that James would have no difficulty in landing in Scotland – which proved correct – and for a few days the Scottish Jacobites treated the young man as their sovereign. But all this came to an end when Marlborough sent the Duke of Argyll (with whom he had become reconciled) to put down the revolt. Before long the Pretender, sad and chastened, was wending his way back to Lorraine; and a few weeks later he moved his Court to Rome at the invitation of the Pope.

With the passing of these events, Marlborough's professional life came to a close. Many historians describe the great Duke as 'a secret man'. This is because he never explained any of his actions. At every crucial turning-point in his life the biographer is left to form his own deductions. We do not know what future Marlborough saw for himself when he deserted James. Did he hope to play the role of a General Monck? Nor do we know for certain why he was dismissed by William III. Was he conniving to put Anne on the throne? Nor what he had in mind when he kept pressing for the Queen to make him Captain-General for life; nor why he did not try harder to make a world peace in 1709; nor why he thought it worthwhile to ask 'James III' for a pardon in 1714. Marlborough left posterity to form its own verdict. 'I am persuaded that an honest man', he wrote in 1706, 'must be justified by his own actions and not by the pen of a writer. . . .'[29] It is perfectly true that when we judge this great man by his actions, and his actions alone, he becomes much easier to understand. From the day he deserted James he never wavered from his determination to free Europe from France's hegemony and to ensure that a Protestant prince would succeed Anne.

The Marlboroughs spent at least half the year in the country as the Duke only felt well if he could ride out for several hours each day. They divided their time between Holywell House – 'the dear clean haus' that Sarah had thought about so much when she was abroad – and Windsor Lodge which she had enlarged and made wonderfully attractive. However, the Duke's greatest interest was in the place where he still hoped to live, the unfinished palace at Woodstock.

Work on the edifice had stopped in 1712. When he went abroad that year he had left the estate in the care of a twenty-one-year-old draughtsman, Mr Joynes, and one of the gardeners, Mr Robart. There was nothing these two could do to advance the three acres of building or, for that matter, to keep the 2,000 acres of park and gardens in good order. So they made hay and went fishing. Not surprisingly, when the Marlboroughs visited Blenheim upon their return to England, they were dismayed by the general disarray. Even Woodstock Manor, which Sarah regarded as an eyesore because it spoiled the view from the palace windows, was still standing. Although Vanbrugh had been instructed to pull it down, he had moved into it instead. Sarah was outraged because he had even built on the roof 'a closet as though he intended to study the planets' – but apparently he went there to study 'the cast and turn of the House'.

In 1714 Parliament voted to pay the huge arrears still owing to Vanbrugh's workmen and eighteen months later building began again. Although over a quarter of a million pounds had already been spent on the construction, not even the private apartments were ready for occupation. Nevertheless, throughout 1715 Sarah spent most of her time planning and commissioning furniture for the palace. 'I am employing every morning at least four hours in cutting out, and ordering furniture for Woodstock,' she wrote to her lawyer, Mr Jennings. 'My next bed will be for the room you chose, where I hope to see you often, and dear Mrs Jennings.' In another letter she specifies that she will want 'a vast number of feather-beds and quilts. I wish you would take this opportunity to know the prices of all such things as will be wanted in that wild, unmercifull house. I would have some of the feather-beds swansdown, all good and sweet feathers, even for the servants.'[30]

For a while Marlborough (encouraged by Sarah) toyed with the idea of dismissing Vanbrugh and finishing the work himself. But the playwright-architect was not easy to discard. He had influential friends at the Kit Kat Club; he was agreeable and witty, and quite capable of kicking up a tremendous fuss if his patrons quarrelled with him. At this point the problem was left in abeyance, over-shadowed by several sad events. In April 1716, Marlborough's thirty-two-year-old daughter Anne, the wife of Lord Sunderland, died of pleuritic fever, another name for tuberculosis. She was the second daughter that John and Sarah had lost within two years. When they were abroad the next to youngest of their four children, twenty-five-year-old Elizabeth, wife of the Earl of Bridgwater, had succumbed to smallpox. The Duke was so deeply stricken when he heard the news that he is said to have fainted. Now the blow was even more severe, as Anne was the delight and favourite of both parents. She was the Queen's god-daughter, the 'golden girl' who was always toasted at the Kit Kat Club as 'the little Whig'. She was, Sarah wrote of her, 'everything that was good and everything that was charming.' Anne, in turn, had always adored her mother and as a child could not bear to be in her bad books. Once, when Sarah censured her, she had cried herself to sleep every night for two weeks; another time she had called out miserably, 'What have I done that you think so ill of poor me who loves you so passionately?'[31] Anne always had a presentiment that her life would be short and in 1713 had written a letter to her husband not to be opened until after her death. In it she asked Sunderland to enlist her mother's help in caring for her two daughters, Anne and Diana Spencer, and ended with the words: 'We must all die but 'tis hard to part with one so much belov'd and in whom there was so much happiness as you, my dearest, ever were to me. . . .'[32]

A month after his daughter's death, in the spring of 1716, Marlborough suffered the first of the strokes that ended his public life. The result was paralysis and loss of speech; however, by the summer he was walking about slowly and could talk again. Accompanied by Dr Garth, Sarah took him to Bath for the waters. She commented on the Duke's 'want of spirits' adding that on some days he could be 'pritty chairfull' and occasionally even took a hand at ombre. She was always looking for new remedies. 'I am told today', she wrote to the elder Craggs,

> that vipors boyl'd in the Duke of Marlborough's broath is an Admerable thing & will mend his blood & take off the lowness of his spirits. . . . An apothecary here told me hee had known severall take it with good success but the Duchess of Shrewsbury says there is non good in England & that I must sent into France. . . . She talks of having them come alive in boxes with holes fill'd with bran, but I fancy they have a more easy way of sending them. . . .[33]

Apparently the Duke rejected viper broth so forcefully that Sarah was forced to search for other remedies.

In the autumn she went to Woodstock to see how the palace was getting on, and found that Sir John Vanbrugh (Marlborough had got him a knighthood), instead of finishing the private apartments so that she and the Duke could move in, had begun building a bridge to span the valley. This creation, he decided, must be on a grandiose scale, worthy of a Roman conqueror; at the same time it would have a touch of informality about it, with delightful towers and an arched superstructure. Sarah fumed that a skilled mason and dozens of workmen should be employed on this astonishing creation and wrote angrily to Mr Craggs:

> I have no mind to fall out with Sir John & much less to vex the D. of Marl at a time when his health is so bad. At the same time I think I owe it to him & to my family to prevent if I can having a great estate thrown away in levelling of hills, filling up precipices and making bridges in the air for no reason that I or anybody else can see but to have it said hereafter that Sir John Vanbrugh did that thing which was never done before.[34]

Now that Marlborough was ill and no longer able to control his wife, Sarah gave full vent to her spleen. She did not mean to have an irreconcilable quarrel with Vanbrugh; but what made her even angrier than the altercation over the bridge was the fact that, after offering to arrange a match between his friend, the Duke of Newcastle and Sarah's grand-daughter Harriet, nothing had come of it.

Sarah talked about Vanbrugh's ineptitude and engaged a professional matchmaker to try and bring the matter to a conclusion. At
the same time she sent Sir John a list of Blenheim grievances. Later,
she said she thought he would laugh about it 'over a bottle of wine';
instead he resigned on the spot. He was mortified at being excluded
from the matchmaking, and even angrier over the rumours that
Sarah intended to use in his place James Moore, the cabinet-maker,
whom she now alluded to as her 'oracle'. Vanbrugh sent her a
blistering letter:

> These Papers, Madam, are so full of far-fetch'd labour'd Accusations,
> mistaken Facts, wrong Inferences, groundless Jealousies and strain'd
> Constructions that I should put a very great affront upon your under-
> standing if I suppos'd it possible you cou'd mean any thing in earnest by
> them. But to put a Stop to my Troubling you any more, you have your
> end, Madam, for I will never trouble you more unless the Duke of Marl-
> borough recovers so far as to shelter me from such intolerable
> Treatment.
>
> I shall in the meantime have only this Concern on his account (for
> whom I shall ever retain the greatest Veneration) that your Grace having
> like the Queen thought fit to get rid of a faithful servant, the Torys will
> have the pleasure to see your Glassmaker, Moor, make just such an end
> of the Duke's Building as her Minister Harley did of his victories for
> which it was erected.
>
> I am,
Your Grace's Most Obedient Servant[35]

The Marlboroughs were staying in High Lodge, a small house in
Woodstock, when Sarah received Vanbrugh's letter. Two days later
the Duke suffered a second, and even more severe stroke. Sarah
thought his end was approaching and in a panic sent for three
doctors and summoned her two daughters.

> The doctors came faster than it was possible for the children to come and
> before they could come a Doctor from Oxford had given him something
> that had very much relieved him and upon that I writ another letter to
> tell my Lady Godolphin and the Duchess of Montagu that their father
> was so much better that I hope he would be able to come to town soon,
> that the roads were very bad (it was November) and we were in a very
> small lodge where there were but three rooms to lye in and garrets, and
> the house being prodigious full with Doctors and servants I knew it
> would be very uneasy and therefore I desired them not to come. For I had
> bred them up to be such fine ladies that they could not shift, and I knew
> that they and their servants must go to bed and mine that were harrassed
> must sit up.[36]

However, Sarah had another fright and in the end Henrietta Godolphin arrived, but not Mary, who was ill. Once again Marlborough defied the grim reaper and before many weeks had passed was once again regaining control of his faculties. Soon he was riding each day; but although his mind was clear, he slurred some of his words and became increasingly silent in the presence of strangers. He tried to resign his post as Captain-General, but George I refused to hear of it as he feared he would have to give the command to his son and heir whom he cordially hated. Marlborough looked old and frail and although he frequently attended the debates in the House of Lords where he was treated with great deference, he rarely stopped to talk to anyone. The only person with whom he was completely at ease was his beloved Sarah.

Sarah, of course, lived for her lord, watching, comforting him, protecting him and battling to bring him the pleasure for which he still hankered: Blenheim. Now that Vanbrugh was gone, she personally masterminded the completion of the work. 'It is impossible for me to be at this place', she wrote to Lord Sunderland in 1717,

> without being very melancholy, which has already cost £315,000 without one room in a condition to put a bed in; but the vast bridge in the air, without so much as a possibility to have water, and the prodigious cavitys, as the workmen call them, which all the hills in the park cannot fill up, is such a picture of maddnesse and folly as no person can describe. . . .

The only bright note in her letter was that Marlborough had benefited greatly from the waters of Tunbridge, 'and is so strong that yesterday, after being at the building in the morning, he went . . . to the old manor-house where he went up a vast number of steps while I was glad to take my ease at the bottom. . . .'[37]

Sarah worked hard, directing every move, counting every penny, and making innumerable trips to the site. The private apartments were completed; the manor-house pulled down; the arcades intended for the bridge discarded; much-disputed frescoes painted in the salon. Finally work was begun on the 'attick' where the guests were to sleep. Vanbrugh's concern had been the great state-rooms and apparently he had given very little thought to the bedrooms, which induced an unknown lampoonist to scribble the following verse on the back of one of Sir John Thornhill's sketches:

> 'See, sir, here's the grand approach
> This way is for his Grace's coach;
> There lies the bridge and here's the clock
> Observe the lion and the cock,

The spacious court, the colonnade,
And mark how wide the hall is made!
The chimneys are so well design'd
They never smoke in any wind.
The Gallery's contrived for walking,
The window's to retire and talk in;
The council chamber for debate,
And all the rest are rooms of state.'

'Thanks, sir,' cried I, 'tis very fine,
But where d'ye sleep, or where d'ye dine?
I find by all you have been telling
That 'tis a house, but not a dwelling.'[38]

Although Sarah was deeply enmeshed in the problems of Blenheim, she still had time to quarrel. Some time in the middle of the year she discovered that General Cadogan had mishandled the £50,000 that Marlborough had entrusted to him when he went abroad in 1712. The Duke had asked Cadogan to invest the money in Dutch government bonds which were paying $2\frac{1}{2}$ per cent. Some time later, the General had switched the money to Austrian funds which were paying 8 per cent, but of course at a commensurate risk. By the time that Sarah discovered what Cadogan had done, the capital had shrunk to only half its value. Although Cadogan was Marlborough's closest friend, Sarah suspected that he had switched the original investment in an attempt to speculate with the money to his own advantage. He had, she wrote, 'a passion for money that is beyond anything that I ever knew.'[39] She was determined to recover every penny, both of capital and interest, and started a suit against him, unbeknown to Marlborough. 'The letters come three hours before he [Marlborough] reads or sees anything,' she explained to Craggs, 'so that I can easily take anything out that would be peevish to see.'[40] In the end Cadogan was obliged to pay in full, at great hardship to himself, and his hatred for Marlborough's Duchess burned fiercely for the rest of his life.

Sarah did not seem to mind. Without Marlborough's restraining hand, she began to cross swords with almost everyone with whom she had dealings. Her next target was Lord Sunderland, who in 1717 announced his intention of marrying the fifteen-year-old Miss Judith Tichborne, described by Sarah as 'a woman unknown, without a shilling and without a name'.[41] Sarah told Sunderland that it was odd of a wise man of forty-five to marry 'a kitten' whose conversation 'could not be agreeable to him'. However, her main objection to the proposal was that the marriage settlement seemed to prejudice the interest of her daughter Anne's five children. After two years of alter-cation the settlement was finally amended and the wedding took place; but Sarah had lost another friend.

In 1719 the embittered one-time friend hit back. That was the year that the Marlboroughs at last moved into Blenheim; the work was not yet finished, but at least they could live in the private apartments and receive friends and relations in the salon and the Long Gallery. Furthermore Sarah had plenty of money for pictures and furnishings as she had netted a cool £100,000 from the spectacular rise in South Sea Company stock. This concern had been started by Lord Oxford in 1710 to provide the Tories with the same credit that the Bank of England, controlled by the Whigs, had raised for Marlborough's campaigns. When the shares began to rocket to unimagined heights, Sarah quickly sold them, explaining:

> Every mortal that has common sense or that knows anything of figures sees that 'tis not possible by all the arts and tricks upon earth to carry £400,000,000 of paper credit with £15,000,000 of specie. This makes me think that this project must burst in a little while and fall to nothing.[42]

When the bubble burst in 1720 Sarah urged all the 'parliament men' she knew to punish the directors of the company. As Sunderland was then First Minister, and not only had been deeply involved in the doings of the company but had lost a great deal of money he could ill afford to part with, he was furious.

Marlborough's ex-chaplain, Francis Hare, who had tutored their son and heir who had died in 1702, and later accompanied the Duke on many campaigns, spoke out fearlessly to Sarah. 'You seem to think nothing ought to be censured as evil speaking,' he told her, 'if it be speaking truth, but . . . if people were at liberty to vent in all places all the ill they thought true of others, it would destroy Society and there would be no living in the world. . . .'[43] But he warned her that Lord Sunderland had been driven to fury by 'continued provocations' and that Lord Cadogan was dangerous. 'With submission I would not tell everybody I was robbed on the highway,' he wrote, 'and describe the man if I thought it would expose me to be robb'd again and perhaps murder'd by him.'[44]

Unfortunately, this warning came too late. Cadogan and Sunder-land got together and attacked the Duchess as a secret Jacobite, claiming that she had carried on a treasonable correspondence with the Pretender and transmitted a great sum of money to him. Nothing was calculated to put Sarah, the life-long Whig and opponent of Catholicism, into more of a temper, and no doubt this was what they were after. Nevertheless it became more than a joke and she was forced to seek an audience with the King to 'vindicate herself'. However, the King did not seem quite sure what the trouble was all about, and finally allowed his First Minister – Sunderland himself – to handle the matter by drafting a short, sharp letter to Sarah to which he put the royal signature.

The Marlboroughs lived at Holywell House and Windsor Lodge and spent only a few months a year at Blenheim where the building was still going on. There the grandchildren gathered and occasionally entertained the Duke with theatricals. They performed Dryden's *All for Love*, which was carefully vetted by Sarah for unsuitable passages. Sometimes Marlborough took his hand at his favourite game, ombre; often he wandered through the Long Gallery looking at the pictures he had bought in Holland and Belgium, a wonderful collection including Madonnas by Raphael, Rubens and Van Dyck, and the huge Van Dyck of Charles I on horseback. Once he stood before a painting of himself done by Kneller. Contemplating the handsome young man in armour, he was heard to murmur: 'That was once a man!'

The Duke had always been devoted to his children and was deeply upset to see that his only surviving daughters, Henrietta and Mary, were becoming increasingly estranged from their mother. For once it was not entirely Sarah's doing. The troublemaker was the youngest daughter, Mary, who from childhood had always been short-tempered and disagreeable. Now that she was Duchess of Montagu she had grown even more hard-hearted, 'just like her mother', people said. As soon as the quarrel over 'curtseying' was repaired, another disagreement arose; and after that another, and then another. It was not always Sarah's fault as she had a capacity for affection and a devotion to duty entirely lacking in Mary, but the characteristic they had in common was an amazing pettiness, a willingness to allow an inconsequential development to shatter the friendship of a lifetime.

Mary's grudge against her mother probably sprang from childhood jealousy. 'I know you can't be enough alone when Papa is with you to care for me,' she had once declared. However, when Sarah went abroad in 1712 she was not estranged from her daughters, although before long she was complaining that Mary

very seldom writ to me, and upon my reproaching her and complaining to her sisters of her want of kindness she writ very odd letters – upon which her father writ a very moving letter to the present Earl of Godolphin – desiring him who was so responsible a man to convince the Duchess of Montagu how much she was in the wrong not to live kindly with so good a mother.[45]

Godolphin, however, turned the task over to his wife, Henrietta, who had no influence with her sister and was scarcely a model of good behaviour. Henrietta's marriage was not happy and for many years she had been the mistress of the playwright, Congreve. Much to Sarah's disapproval Henrietta flaunted her love affair, travelling about openly with her lover, and patronizing what Sarah regarded as 'the lowest circles' which were composed of writers and actors. Instead of Henrietta making an impression on Mary, Mary brought Henrietta to her own way of thinking.

It was tragic that the two daughters who had loved Sarah had died, leaving the two rebels who took pleasure in treating their mother with studied rudeness. When Marlborough was ill in November 1716 and Sarah sent for Henrietta, the latter behaved outrageously. She brushed past her mother without a word of commiseration and went straight to the bedside. 'She took no more notice of me', wrote Sarah, 'than if I had been the nurse to snuff the candles.'[46] It was particularly wounding as this was the very time that Sarah was doing everything in her power to arrange a great match for Henrietta's extremely plain daughter, Harriet. In the end she succeeded in capturing the Duke of Newcastle by providing the girl with a dowry of £20,000 – a large sum even for a ducal conquest. Even this did not melt Henrietta's heart, and when she and her sister Mary went to see their father at Blenheim they took pleasure in snubbing their mother. They would not even nod to her as they went around the room greeting the guests.

On one occasion Mary had the audacity to write to her father urging him to come alone to her house for cards and amusement. Marlborough refused to allow this invitation to pass without a reprimand which he sent on New Year's Day, 1721:

> I thank you for your letter my dear child but I observe that you take no notice of your mother; and certainly when you consider of that, you can't imagine that any company can be agreeable to me, who have not a right behaviour to her. I know she has been a very kind mother to all her children; and if you would please me you would show that duty which becomes you to her. This is doing what is right to yourself as well as to your affectionate father,
>
> Marlborough.

In a second letter sent the next day, he wrote the following postscript in his own hand:

> I am not well enough to write so long a letter with my own hand; and I believe I am the worse to see my children live so ill with a Mother for whom I must have the greatest tenderness and regard.[47]

But even this pathetic appeal did not move Mary's cold heart. Although she replied politely to her poor father, she did not change her ways.

Marlborough was attacked by further paroxysms when he was staying at Windsor Lodge in June 1722. His strength began to fail rapidly and the doctors knew that the end was near. Sarah summoned her two daughters which cast a macabre light on the death-bed scene.

> I am sure it is impossible [wrote Sarah] for any tongue to express what I felt at that time; but I believe anybody that ever loved another so tenderly as I did the Duke of Marlborough may have some feeling of what it was to have one's children come in, in those last hours who I knew did not come to comfort me but like enemies that would report to others whatever I did in a wrong way. However at the time I thought that my soul was tearing from my body and that I could not say many things before them, yet I could not refuse them to come in, for fear I should repent of it. Upon which I desired Mrs Kingdom to go to them and tell them that I did not know what disorder it might give their father to go to him now, but I desired they would judge themselves and do as they liked, but I begged of them that they would not stay long in the room because I could not come in while they were there, being in so much affliction. Mrs Kingdom delivered this message and she told me that the Duchess of Montagu answered that she did not understand her but that if she meant that they were not to see their mother they were very well used to that.
>
> They staid a great while and not being able to be out of the room longer from him I went in though they were there and kneel'd down beside him. They rose up when I came in and made curtsys but did not speak to me and after some time I called for prayers. When they were over I asked the Duke of Marlborough if he heard them well and he answered Yes and he had joined in them. After that he took several things and when it was almost deark the ladies being all the time present, I said I believed he would be easier in his bed, his couch being too narrow and ask'd him if he liked to go to bed. He said Yes, so we carried him upon the couch to his own room.[48]

For some hours Marlborough lay in a coma but, as dawn broke, he died. The date was 16 June 1722, and the Duke was in his seventy-third year.

The funeral was a splendid scene of martial pomp. Eight Dukes walked behind the chief mourner, the Duke of Montagu, as he followed the gun-carriage bearing the coffin through huge crowds to Westminster Abbey. General William Cadogan, now an earl and Commander-in-Chief of the British army, led a procession of high officers who had fought in the Duke's campaigns. Marlborough's coffin was lowered into the vault of Henry VII's Chapel and rested there until 1744 when it was transferred to the tomb at Blenheim.

Soldiers all over England and in many of the towns of Europe learned of Marlborough's death with deep emotion. In their minds' eye they could see their 'incomparable chief' riding with his aides-de-camp along his noisy smoke-laden battle-lines, oblivious to the cannon-balls that sometimes landed close enough to cover him with mud. Hawklike, he watched the ebb and flow of the conflict, sending his aides off with a sheaf of orders. His soldiers still chuckled at the way he had fooled poor old Villars in crossing the latter's impenetrable *Ne Plus Ultra* lines; but the most cherished memory was that wonderful moment at Elixem in 1705 when the Duke had ridden up and taken his place for the first time in the front line of troopers, awaiting the order for the cavalry charge. 'His successes were so great', wrote Captain Robert Parker, who had served in most of the Duke's campaigns, 'that he became the terror of France (who were but the other day the bullies of Europe) the Ornament of Britain and admired by all the world, except a villainous faction at home.'[49] Parker went on to pay his Chief a moving tribute that still glows through the centuries:

> It was allowed by all men, nay even by France itself that he [Marlborough] was more than a match for all the generals of that nation. This he made appear beyond contradiction in the ten campaigns he made against them; during all which time it cannot be said that he even slipped an opportunity of fighting when there was any probability of his coming to the enemy. And upon all occasions he concerted matters with so much judgement and forecast that he never fought a battle which he did not gain nor laid siege to a town which he did not take. . . . He was peculiarly happy in an invincible calmness of temper and serenity of mind and had a surprising readiness of thought even in the heat of battle.[50]

When the peace of Utrecht was signed in 1713, Louis XIV was so delighted that he sent Queen Anne six beautiful gowns and 2,000 bottles of champagne. Many people – the Marlboroughs included – felt that the Duke's last campaigns had been fought in vain. After all, France had clawed back large portions of the territory she had lost, and retained a Bourbon prince on the throne of Spain. But as the years passed, Marlborough's contribution became increasingly significant. By breaking France's domination of Europe he not only had raised Britain to the forefront of the world's nations and secured her Protestant faith, but had opened the door to two centuries of imperial power and glory. No British soldier ever did more than this.

Yet Marlborough has never received the acclaim from posterity that is his due. The English (and particularly the Victorian English) do not like heroes with blemishes. Even his famous descendant, Winston Churchill, admitted that Marlborough was 'a greater do-er than he was a man'. However, in our age and our day the Duke's faults tend to increase rather than diminish his attractions. A genius on the battle-field, a remarkably patient and successful diplomat, it is comforting to know that he possessed the human frailties of lesser men. He was self-seeking, sometimes amazingly deceitful and occasionally unkind; at the same time he was one of the few men of his era and his class to marry a penniless girl; he performed many acts of generosity for humble people; he had long and faithful friendships; and he has come down in history as the most humane of all army commanders. The contra-dictions in his character, however, often make it difficult for bio-graphers to determine the motives for his actions. Probably he was a much simpler man that he was made out to be. His lifelong use of dis-simulation and his tendency to maintain a foothold in opposing camps stemmed from the dangers of a boyhood spent in the fierce aftermath of a civil war.

Marlborough was not a statesman in the true sense of the word as some historians suggest. His efforts in this sphere were mainly con-cerned in strengthening the Grand Alliance and, above all, in working with Sidney Godolphin to keep the guns and supplies rolling out from England. Although no one could equal Marlborough's record as a mili-tary commander (no defeats, only victories), one of the reasons for his success is often overlooked: his astonishing capacity to retain in his mind's eye the whole panorama of a vast and shifting battlefield. As his lines of combat often stretched for four miles across the countryside, a steady stream of aides-de-camp kept him in touch with all parts of the front. Yet it was his ability to make lightning calculations and re-adjustments throughout the heat and smoke of battle that enabled him to form his final assessments with computor-like accuracy. 'I have five horse to four!' he would suddenly exclaim, and this would presage the order for the decisive assault.

Marlborough was not, as some of his spiteful contemporaries de-clared, 'a bad great man', but a great and good man with a fierce com-pulsion to bring glory to his country and to himself. His faults sprang from ambition. They were magnified because of his prominence, yet even his enemies were forced to admit that he was cast in a heroic mould.

Fifteen

Sarah Alone

The Duchess of Marlborough survived her husband by twenty-two years. She was sixty-two years old when he died and still beautiful, although she refers ruefully to her 'shape' as being 'of the fattest'. She had the reputation of being the richest woman in Europe, worth nearly £2,000,000 and enjoying an income of £40,000 in the commanding currency of the day. The Duke had been in his grave barely five months before Sarah received her first proposal of marriage. It came from one of her oldest friends, Lord Coningsby, a good-natured but foolish Irish peer who had a farm not far from Woodstock and who had always been a great admirer of Marlborough. He called on Sarah at Blenheim on 8 October 1722 and was concerned to find her in poor health. But two months later his thoughts were on very different things:

> I live in hopes [he wrote] that the Great & Glorious Creater of ye World who dos & must direct all things will direct you to make mee ye happyest man upon ye face of the Earth and Enable mee to make my dearest dearest lady Marlborough as she is ye wisest and ye Best, ye happyest of all Women. I am Yr Grace knows I am with ye Truest, ye Sincerest & ye most faithfull hart Yr Graces most dutifull most obedient humble servant.[1]

Tacked to the end of this letter was an unromantic postscript informing his lady love that the sheep she wanted for Blenheim would not be available until July. It was not surprising that Sarah politely fobbed off her suitor and made excuses not to see him again.

Her second offer of marriage came from a man that no one could call a fortune hunter. He was the Duke of Somerset, owner of Petworth House in Sussex and Syon House on the outskirts of London, and one of the wealthiest peers in England. It was Somerset who, in

1708, had prevented a ministerial upheaval when Godolphin and Marlborough handed in their resignations in protest at Harley's behaviour. Somerset had broken up a Cabinet meeting by pointing to Harley and asking why 'that fellow' was treating 'affairs of the war' without the advice of Marlborough? He had saved the day but later fell into Sarah's bad books by joining Harley against Marlborough, dazzled by promises of becoming first Minister himself. His wife, the Percy heiress, had died in 1722. Upon Sarah's dismissal she had been given the latter's Gold Key and become the Queen's companion, which was enough to make the Duchess of Marlborough hate both her and her husband.

But vanity is a powerful emotion and, now that Somerset was clamouring for Sarah's hand, she took a more favourable view of him. His attention was flattering, as he was the grandest and the most arrogant of all eighteenth-century oligarchs. Nicknamed 'the Sovereign', his *hauteur* had become a byword in fashionable London. Everyone knew how he had disinherited a daughter because she had sat down in his presence; and how the roads were always scoured by outriders before his progresses to prevent the vulgar gaze of the *hoi polloi* from falling on him.

However, he was not a stupid man. He proved to be a distinguished Chancellor of Cambridge University, and was a great patron of the arts, adding to the beauty of his wonderful houses by superb taste in decorations. David Green paints an agreeable picture of this great aristocrat setting forth to press his suit with Sarah in the summer of 1723:

> The outriders sped from Petworth to clear the lanes for the glorious equipage emblazoned with bull and unicorn, heading for Blenheim. And what a sight that must have been for those bold enough to gaze upon it! The gleaming coach-and-six between the green hedgerows, the horn calling and winding in the clear air over the unpoisoned fields; and within the coach Lord Foppington in full splendour, the periwigged beau, the ardent, impatient lover, heaving huge sighs, at sixty-five, for the woman he already called his *souveraine*, now sixty-three.[2]

Somerset was an ardent lover and there was no nonsense about farm business tacked to the end of his letters:

> I will not have a thought but what shall bee to make you Happy & Easy in all things whatever. Your Grace shall command and make your Tearmes and Conditions. Give mee but your most charming Person, I neither covert nor desire more nor greater riches, for that is the onely & most valuble Treasure to mee. . . . Apoynt mee an hour when I may lay my selfe at your ffeett. . . .[3]

Sarah did not reply in the famous words cited by Horace Walpole, which have been repeated in many subsequent biographies:

> If I were young and handsome as I was, instead of old and faded as I am, and you should lay the Empire of the world at my feet, you should never share the heart and hand that once belonged to John Duke of Marlborough.

Instead she wrote back in the graceful style of the day, giving her answer firmly but with proper regard for the honour paid to her:

> My lord,
> I am at a great loss to know how to express myself upon the subject of your Grace's letter of yesterday. There cannot possibly bee a greater mark given of your esteem than in the offers which you have been pleased to make to me and I am confydent that there is very few women (if any) that would not bee extreamly pleased with what your Grace proposes to me; but I am resolved never to change my condition and if I know anything of myself I would not marry the Emperor of the world tho I were but thirty years old.
> I hope your Grace will not dislike my truth in this declaration and that you will reward it by giving me the honour of your friendship, which I am extreamly desirous of, and I assure you that I will never do the least thing to forfeit it as long as I live, but I will endeavour upon all occasions to deserve it as much as I can by shewing that I am with all the respect imaginable,
> > Your Grace's most faithfull and
> > most humble servant.[4]

The Duke was not easy to shake off. He called her his *souveraine* and showered her with ardent letters:

> You are the woman, the very woman, the only woman I doe love, I doe value, I doe adore the most & that I doe and will forever seek for all occasions to give Prooffes and Demonstrations of it to you & to the wholle world, my most Dear Dear Dear charming Souveraine.[5]

Sarah was delighted to have such a fulsome admirer, particularly one who gave the appearance of taking an interest in her personal troubles and who always made the right comments. After reading her Brown Book, containing Queen Anne's letters, he declared 'that the late Queen's treatment of Your Grace was the very reverse of the expressions in most of her letters to you. . . .'; and when he read her Green Book, describing the behaviour of her children, he exclaimed that they seemed 'to affect a most unnaturall & most Barbarous part to the best of mothers & the very best of women.'[6]

In the end Sarah wearied of Somerset's courtship and saw that the only way to put a stop to it was to find him a wife. This she did in the person of Lady Charlotte Finch, daughter of the Duke of Newcastle. Somerset was pleased with her choice, but begged her not to withdraw her friendship, insisting that 'noe change in the way of life or of fortune shall ever change me from being the same man I have many years professed to be.'[7] His marriage with Lady Charlotte was happy and she bore him two daughters. Only once did the bride's imposing husband find it necessary to reprimand her. That was when she tapped him on the shoulder with her fan. 'Madam,' he exclaimed, 'my first Duchess was a Percy and she never took such a liberty.'

Sarah now turned her attention back to finishing Blenheim. By act of Parliament the Marlborough dukedom, in the absence of a male heir, descended to the eldest female. So Henrietta, Lady Godolphin, had become Duchess of Marlborough in her own right. However, the Duke had taken care to leave the estate to Sarah during her lifetime, which was just as well as the rift between mother and daughter was wider than ever and, if Henrietta had moved into the palace, it would never have been finished.

The Duke had earmarked £50,000 in his will for the completion of the work, and Sarah was so thrifty and vigilant that she had money to spare. Nevertheless, the cost was high in exasperation and anxiety. Although liability for the building belonged to the Crown, the workmen filed a suit against the Marlboroughs which dragged on long after the Duke's death. Sir John Vanbrugh's loathing of Sarah led him to withhold testimony as to the Crown's legal obligation for the outstanding debts; and in the end the Duchess was compelled to pay nearly £10,000 of her own money to meet the settlement.

Even Sir John himself managed to extract £1,700 from the Duchess for what he claimed were 'expenses'. He did this with the help of Sir Robert Walpole who was also at loggerheads with Sarah. Vanbrugh was overjoyed by his success and wrote exuberantly:

> Being forced into Chancery by that B.B.B.B. old B. the Duchess of Marlborough and her getting an injunction upon me by her friend the late good Chancellor who declared I never was employed by the Duke of Marlborough and therefore had no demand upon his estate for my services at Blenheim, since my hands were tied up from trying by law to recover my arrears, I have prevailed with Sir Robert Walpole to help me in a scheme I proposed to him, by which I have got my money in spite of the hussy's teeth. . . .[8]

Sarah got her own back in 1725 when Vanbrugh invited Lord and

Lady Carlisle, the owners of Castle Howard which he had built for them, on a tour of Blenheim. Sarah got wind of the expedition and sent word that the Carlisles were more than welcome but that Sir John Vanbrugh was not to be admitted.

> And lest that shou'd not mortify me enough [wrote Vanbrugh] She having somehow learn'd that my wife was of the Company, sent an Express the night before we came there with orders, if she came with the Castle Howard Ladys, the Servants shou'd not Suffer her to see either House, Garden or even to enter the Park, which was obey'd accordingly and She was forc'd to sit all day and keep me company at the Inn.[9]

Five months later Vanbrugh died at the age of sixty-two. Although his witty plays are still being performed on the London stage, the only visible reminder of his presence at Blenheim is an enormous 'V' which is carved on a sealed-off window on the bridge.

Sarah tells us that she worked 'like a packhorse' for ten years to finish and furnish the house and to put the final touches to gardens and park. Her most agreeable task was to erect a Victory Column that rose to a height of 130 feet, with a colossal figure of Marlborough on top in Roman dress. The approach to this Pillar, as Sarah called it, was through a triumphal arch designed by Nicholas Hawksmoor, at the Woodstock entrance to the park. It bore the inscription:

> This gate was built the year after the death of the most illustrious John, Duke of Marlborough, by order of Sarah, his most beloved wife, to whom he left the sole direction of the many things that remained unfinished of this fabric. The services of this gallant man to his country the Pillar will tell which the Duchess has erected for a lasting monument to his glory and her affection for him.

However, to find the right words and the right style to describe the Duke's military achievements on the pedestal of the Pillar caused the Duchess many sleepless nights. Pope was approached but declined the honour; Dr Hare tried and failed.

Eventually a friend sent the Duchess some words that Lord Bolingbroke had written. This man had done more than any other being, with the exception of Oxford, to bring about Marlborough's downfall. He had been living in exile in France since the advent of the Hanovers, but in 1723 had managed to obtain a pardon from George I and two years later was allowed to return to England. Sarah wept over Bolingbroke's masterly summary of the Duke's ten campaigns. Its sharp, staccato sentences, more like the style of the twentieth century than the eighteenth, seemed to ring out as decisively as a battle command. 'When I first read it', she wrote, 'I thought it the finest thing that it was possible for any man to write and as often as I have read it I still wet the paper.'[10] To her it was heroic prose and she then and there decided to overlook the fact that Bolingbroke was a scoundrel and gladly accepted his gift. 'The Battle was bloody: the Event decisive. The Woods were pierced: the Fortifications trampled down. The Enemy fled. The Town was taken. . . .'

Sarah only spent a few weeks a year at Blenheim – 'that wild, unmercifull house' as she called it – and scarcely more time at Holywell House in St Albans because it was so full of memories of her husband that it made her sad. Instead, she divided her time between Marlborough House and Windsor Lodge, which she had made 'extream pritty' and which had every convenience including that of being close to London.

Sarah's old age was very exacting because of the time demanded in caring for her large fortune. For some years she invested her money in government funds, but the interest was low and, much worse, the bonds had a way of falling sharply when there was a decline in trade or a hint of war. She came to the conclusion that property and land were the safest investments and during the last fifteen years of her life bought thirty estates in ten separate counties. On one slip of paper she lists twenty-two properties purchased for a total of £236,092. These estates brought in an annual rent of nearly £12,000 per annum, approximately 5 per cent. One of her best known purchases was the Wimbledon estate of Sir Theodore Jansen, one of the directors of the South Sea Company who had lost everything in the crash. She considered it

> a very cheap purchase. The wood was valued but at £2,000 I was offer'd between four and five thousand for it just after I bought it. I have sold some of the worst that I was oblig'd to sell by Mr Cole's lease, and I have cut wood for the building but altogether that and what I sold was not worth more than £1,000. Mr Cole's lease when 'tis out will let for a great deal more than he gives for it.[11]

Sarah was a superb business woman and undoubtedly increased the value of the Marlborough estate by many thousands of pounds. Unfortunately, the famous story about how she saved Childs Bank from bankruptcy is apocryphal. She was reputed to have drawn a cheque on the Bank of England, which was threatening to foreclose the smaller bank and simply passed it onto Childs. This tale is so much in keeping with Sarah's character that it is sad to have to part with it. Another uncorroborated story claims that she once lent a huge sum of money to the British Government, and that she did it in a manner to cause Sir Robert Walpole the maximum inconvenience. Later she complained loudly of the low interest rate which she had received.

Not everything in the Duchess's life had to do with money. Sarah was generous, particularly when she saw hardship with her own eyes. She gave a good deal of money to the poor in the villages near her country estates. Once, when she was ill, a chimney-sweep was summoned to clear the fireplace in her bedroom. The little boy who arrived was in rags and Sarah was so upset that she not only paid the child handsomely, but gave instructions that he was to be reclothed from head to foot. Altogether, Sarah was reputed to have given £300,000 to charity in her widowhood. Her greatest single contribution were the alms-houses in St Albans. These were built for soldiers who had fought in Marlborough's wars and their dependants. The houses are still standing today and are used by the local council for public work.

The tragedy of Sarah's old age were the fierce animosities that often flared up over the most trivial incidents. Quarrelling had always been one of her greatest failings but when Marlborough was alive he often managed to subdue her wrath and to smooth things over. Francis Hare, now Bishop of Chichester, often begged Sarah to change her ways. In a letter written in 1726 he points to Marlborough and the equable Sidney Godolphin as masters of tact and diplomacy and wishes that she could profit from their example. At the same time, he realized how ridiculous it was to expect the vibrant Sarah to pattern herself on these quiet, controlled men. Godolphin's example, he admitted, 'would not become your Grace. It would destroy the pleasure you give your friends by saying perpetually things which are extremely diverting and agreeable.' However, the Bishop felt on safer ground when he referred to the Duke who always managed to suppress 'whatever resentments he had'.[12]

But, alas, Sarah was not the Duke but the Duchess of Marlborough, and in the end the Bishop gave up trying to reform her. 'It's as impossible for your Grace to converse without warmth and force', he finally concluded, 'as it is for you to be dull and ugly, but to whom God has given so fine an understanding and so much beauty.'[13] Unfortunately Sarah became increasingly undisciplined, and with old age allowed ludicrous incidents to create lasting hatreds. Sir Robert Walpole was her *bête noire* because he taxed the £5,000 a year that constituted the Marlborough Grant and because he refused to prevent the Duke of St

Albans from driving through Windsor Park and disturbing her peace at Windsor Lodge. Furthermore, she claimed that Walpole, who at one time was in charge of the Post Office, deliberately gave instructions to cause trouble by mixing up letters between herself and Henrietta, the young Duchess of Marlborough – a suspicion that was pathetically far-fetched.

Nevertheless, the hatred was very real and when Walpole became First Minister and Princess Caroline, wife of the Heir Apparent, became Queen, Sarah included her, too, in her list of 'detestables'. This was sad because Caroline had been a favourite of Sarah when she first arrived in England. She was a clever, charming woman who had been educated by the Electress Sophia. She read the works of Bacon, was a friend of the celebrated philosopher, Leibnitz, and, when her husband succeeded to the throne, exerted a strong influence over him. In the early days Sarah greatly admired Caroline and when she became Queen invited her to pay a visit to Blenheim which never materialized. On the day of George II's coronation, Sarah joined the procession and, in her flowing robes and resplendent jewels, walked all the way from St James's Palace to Westminster. By the time she reached Palace Yard she was so tired she borrowed a drum from the band-master and, to the delight of the crowd, made herself a seat.

Since that day many things had happened. The fact that Queen Caroline supported Walpole through thick and thin was enough to make Sarah despise her. Furthermore they had a disagreement over Sarah's Wimbledon property. The Queen wished to use the road that ran across the land and agreed to donate a specific sum of money to the poor for the privilege. Apparently Caroline did not stick to her bargain and Sarah went to law, forcing her to make financial amends. The Queen then avenged herself by persuading Walpole to stop the grant of £500 a year which Sarah was paid as Ranger of Windsor Park. Sarah was so angry that she began to talk of the virtues of Queen Anne compared to the 'upstart German' now on the throne. Indeed, she went to the celebrated sculptor Rysbrack and commissioned a full-length statue of Anne that stands today in the Long Library at Blenheim and bears the inscription:

> To the memory of Queen Anne under whose auspices John, Duke of Marlborough conquered and to whose munificence he and his posterity with gratitude owe the possession of Blenheim.

Sarah's worst quarrels, however, were reserved for her own kith and kin. 'The most vindictive Highland chief', wrote Lady Mary Wortley Montagu, 'never had so many feuds but her deadliest were in the bosom of her own family.'[14] The trouble was triggered by the rift between herself and her daughters, Henrietta and Mary. After her husband's funeral she never saw them again. This was not her doing, for deep down she loved them both. ''Tis not to be expressed', she wrote years later, 'how much I suffered before I could overcome the tenderness I had in my heart for them.'[15] But the fine ladies, as she called them, were too unimaginative to see that their mother was one of the great originals of history and to forgive her idiosyncracies. Of course, she was outrageously outspoken and infuriatingly self-righteous, but despite her faults she had a warm heart and would have gladly made peace if the girls had been willing. Henrietta was weak and flighty and might have relented, but she was under Mary's influence and Mary was made of steel. 'An ill wife,' pronounced Sarah, 'a cruel daughter and mother, and a very harsh mistress – must have a bad heart.'[16] It was a pity that Mary was so diverting!

Henrietta had plenty of reason to dislike her mother. Sarah called her Congreve's 'moll' and talked about the 'vile company' that he threw her into. This was scarcely a valid complaint as Congreve's inseparable companions were John Gay, author of *The Beggar's Opera*, and the irrepressible Sir John Vanbrugh. Considering that Henrietta's marriage had always been a failure (her husband only liked horses and stable-boys) and that Congreve had given her the only happiness she had ever known, it is not surprising that she resented her mother's jibes.

In 1722, shortly after Marlborough's funeral, Henrietta settled down in Bath with her lover. Congreve was fifty-two and suffered from gout and a complaint known as 'cataract'. Although Henrietta was forty-one and had not had a baby for twenty years, shortly after her return from the spa she gave birth to a daughter who was named Mary. Lord Godolphin accepted the child with pleasure; but if there was any doubt about the baby's paternity, Congreve dispelled it when he died in 1729. In his will he left £10,000 to the already rich Henrietta; and Henrietta in turn left to Mary 'all Mr Congreve's personal estate that he left to me.' Henrietta's grief was so excessive that she set a good many tongues wagging. She was said to have had a wax figure made of her lover which she kept at the dining-room table, except at night when she moved it into her bedroom. She erected a monument in Westminster Abbey, which stands at the right of the west door, with the inscription:

Set up by Henrietta, Duchess of Marlborough, as a mark how dearly she remembered the happiness and honour she enjoyed in the friendship of so worthy and honest a man.

'Happiness perhaps,' commented Sarah, 'but not honour.'

As Sarah was on bad terms with Henrietta she made a point of being on good terms with Henrietta's only son, Willigo, the heir to the Marlborough title and estate. Willigo drank too much and hated his mother. Sarah quite wrongly gave him an income of £3,000 a year which made him independent of Henrietta and quite ungovernable. However, he did not survive long; in 1731 he attended a gala at Balliol College, Oxford, and apparently drank himself to death. Although Sarah had never held him in much esteem she was so shocked by his death that she had a brief period of acute regret, probably prompted by remorse. 'I should have given half my estate to have saved him,' she cried. 'I hope the Devil is picking that man's bones who taught him to drink.'[17]

Henrietta's heir was now Charles Spencer, the eldest surviving son of her sister, Anne. Sarah had taken Charles, Diana and John Spencer under her wing when Anne died in 1716. She was very fond of Johnny, and Diana became the apple of her eye, but Charles was a stupid boy who was always wild. 'Extremely like his father, violent and ill-natured,' wrote Sarah. 'But his understanding is infinitely worse.'[18] The only one of her Spencer grandchildren that she had little to do with was Anne, a wilful, disagreeable girl, who in 1720 married Viscount Bateman.

Anne Bateman exerted a strong influence over her brother Charles and decided to marry him off to one of her friends. She introduced him to Elizabeth Trevor, a grand-daughter of the Lord Trevor who had been one of the twelve peers created by Queen Anne to pass the peace of Utrecht. When Sarah learned that Charles was actually plann-ing to marry into the family of this arch-traitor she was enraged. Lady Bateman, with the help of the Trevors, had drawn up a marriage settlement which assumed that Charles would inherit both Blenheim and Althorp, the Spencer estate. Sarah had other plans. She intended dear little Johnny to have Althorp and was taking steps to make him financially independent. However, she had to go to Court to get her way and she never spoke to Lady Bateman again. She blackened the latter's portrait at Blenheim and wrote underneath: 'She is more black within.'[19] 'Your brother will find to his cost,' she wrote to Johnny in 1732 when Charles married Miss Trevor,

> what a disagreeable mean Family he has married into, where there is nothing but beggars and odd people. Which a man might be willing to pass over for the sake of a Woman, if he had a passion for her. But the present case is very different from that if what I am told is true, that the Woman

don't know how to behave on any occasion has a very indifferent Person and very bad Teeth.[20]

A year after Charles's wedding Henrietta died and he became Duke of Marlborough. He saw the letter quoted above after Sarah's death and inserted the words 'All Lies' over the last two sentences and signed the initial 'M'.

As Blenheim belonged to Charles's grandmother for life, and as Althorp was earmarked for Johnny,* the new Duke was without a roof of his own for many years. This was just as well, as he had become an inveterate gambler. 'I hear the Duke of Marlborough', wrote Lord Hervey in 1726, 'is ruining himself at play at the Bath, though he won £4,600 on one card at Basset.'[21] Sarah made the great mistake of giving Charles her husband's diamond-studded sword (a gift from the Emperor Charles) to make amends for her attack on his wife; but when she learned how rapidly his debts were mounting and that he was borrowing heavily, she became alarmed. She went to Court to ensure that he would not be allowed to part with such an heirloom. 'That sword my lord would have carried to the gates of Paris,' she said. 'Am I to live to see the diamonds picked off one by one and lodged at the pawn-brokers.'[22] She won her case and the sword is still in the possession of his descendants.

Lady Diana Spencer was the joy of Sarah's old age, the last person whom she truly loved and who warmly returned her affection. Diana was an unusually charming and attractive girl who revelled in the company of her amazing grandmother. She laughed at 'Mama Duch-ess' and her irreverent remarks, and promised to let the old lady choose a husband for her. This was a rash promise for at one moment Sarah nearly married her off to Frederick, Prince of Wales, a mon-strous cad whom even the most ardent royalists found difficult to defend. Clearly Sarah's aim was to annoy Queen Caroline, who found it impossible to control her wilful son. Sarah told the young man that if he married her grand-daughter she would endow Diana with the staggering sum of £100,000. Not surprisingly, the Prince accepted with alacrity. The wedding was arranged to take place at Windsor, but at the eleventh hour Robert Walpole got wind of the arrangement and put a stop to it. As there was no Marriage Act in those days, it is not known what he said. Perhaps the whole story was an invention, for although a number of biographers relate the event, no reliable authority is cited. In the end, Diana married Lord John Russell who became Duke of Bedford in 1732.

---

* John Spencer's son became the first Earl Spencer and is a direct ancestor of the present Earl.

The Duchess of Marlborough's most exasperating quality was her belief that everything she did was right. This irritating trait became apparent in her dealings with Queen Anne, but as she grew older, it became even more pronounced. She did not mind breaking off relations with the most powerful people in England; she did not mind baiting them, insulting them, suing them. But she clamoured for the approbation of the spectators who watched her gladiatorial contests. They must confirm her belief that she was right, absolutely *right*!

This obsession gave birth to her famous Green Book. After the Duke of Marlborough's death, rumours spread that Sarah had been unkind to her daughters when they came to their father's sick-bed. Sarah gave her own account of what happened in a green book with the subtitle: *An Account of the Cruell Usage of My Children*. The work extended far beyond the incidents surrounding her husband's last hours. She described her daughters as children and moved on to their unkindness to her in adult life, focussing on ridiculously petty incidents. She encouraged friends and acquaintances to read her composition and was delighted by their reactions. 'My lord – cr'd out P. Monsterus! O Vile Wretches!' wrote Lady Bristol; 'Folly & undutifulness,' pronounced Robert Jennings; 'Young as I was it shocked me, . . .' rasped Lady Blayney. 'Not only despicable but detestable,' wrote Mrs Boscawen.[23] Sarah kept these letters neatly filed away. As she had secured the satisfaction she craved, she then tried to heal the rift with her daughters, but by this time it had grown too wide and she finally was forced to abandon the idea. 'Thank God I am now at ease as to that matter,' she wrote some years later, 'and if I have done anything wrong I am sorry for it . . . and if there is any mother that has had more patience I wish I could see her, for I have yet met with no such person.'[24]

At the age of seventy-five the Duchess of Marlborough was suffering increasingly from gout and rheumatism. She was so crippled she could only walk with sticks, and finally could not walk at all but had to ride about in sedan-chairs as her one-time friend, Queen Anne, had done. Her grand-daughter, Lady Diana Spencer, now the wife of the Duke of Bedford, continued to be her greatest joy. Sarah loved music, and when she was at Windsor Lodge often sat in a high-backed chair listening to the wonderful chamber-organ which she had bought at Handel's recommendation. When she was in London, Diana tried to cheer her up by offering to take her to the opera. 'It would please me', Sarah replied, a thousand times more than any musick that can be perform'd but I fear I shall never be able to go . . . because I can't get out of my chair without two people to help me & when I am got out I can't stand nor goe one step without two chairmen to hold me up.[25]

That summer – 1735 – the Duchess forgot her own infirmities in her growing concern for Diana. The girl suffered from congestion of the lungs and, despite the attendance of five doctors, her health did not improve. Sarah sent her the Duke of Marlborough's campaigning tent, which was set up on the lawn of Woburn, so that she could rest there during the day and get plenty of fresh air. But in September 1735 the incomparable Diana died of consumption. Sarah was so distraught that she shut herself up in Windsor Lodge and refused to see anyone for many weeks.

Eventually, the old Duchess recaptured her spirit. She was a born fighter and, although life's tragedies frequently laid her low, she was never defeated by them. Despite her age and infirmities her mind was as sharp and clear as ever, and once again she began to attend to the many demands imposed by her wealth and position. In the evening, when the curtains were drawn, she spent hours rearranging her letters by candle-light, often annotating them with caustic comment and no doubt destroying anything that might be prejudicial to the Duke. She had decided at long last to give the public the memoirs about her service with Queen Anne that Walpole had persuaded her not to publish in 1712.

But first they must be edited. When Voltaire visited Blenheim in 1727 and asked to see her manuscript, she refused. 'Wait a little,' she told him. 'I am altering my account of Queen Anne's characters. I have begun to love her again since the present lot have become our governors.'[26] Eventually she showed the Frenchman her work and asked him to collaborate with her. According to Oliver Goldsmith, he not only declined but remonstrated with her for the bitterness of her observations. 'I thought the man had sense,' she is said to have remarked. 'But at bottom he is a fool or a philosopher.' This observation is so unlike Sarah that it must have been invented; in fact she actually liked philosophers!

In 1735 the Duchess asked Alexander Pope to edit the work, but he too was wary of the task and suggested Nathaniel Hooke. Hooke had lost everything in the South Sea Bubble and was delighted to be employed, particularly as the Duchess paid him £5,000 – a huge sum for the day. Nevertheless, he had to work hard for his money, for although Sarah was bedridden she sometimes dictated to him for six hours at a stretch. Hooke was conscientious and hard working and

Sarah was delighted with the final result. The memoirs were published in 1742 with the full title: *Account of the Conduct of the Dowager Duchess of Marlborough from her First Coming to Court to the Year 1710.*

The work did not create the same sensation that it would have done in 1712. Nevertheless it certainly was not overlooked, and as the years rolled on it provided historians with raw materials for Queen Anne's reign. Horace Walpole, a son of Robert Walpole whom Sarah particularly loathed, took up the family feud and made a point of being disobliging. 'Old Marlborough has at last published her Memoirs,' he wrote scathingly. 'They are digested by one Hooke who wrote a Roman History; but from her materials which are so womanish that I am sure the man might have made a gown and petticoats with them.'[27] But later in his review he had to admit that the work contained 'curious anecdotes and a few of those sallies of wit which fourscore years of arrogance could not fail to produce in so fantastic an understanding.'

However, the Duchess had more than one champion – Henry Fielding, the father of the English novel, came galloping to her rescue with a pamphlet entitled *Fulle Vindication of the Dowager Duchess.* He could recognize a great woman when he saw one and tells us that he 'never contemplated the character of that Glorious Woman but with admiration.'[28] Another champion, this one nameless, goes too far perhaps even for Sarah, when he asserts that the 'vivacity, freedom and contempt for dignatories . . . set it beyond comparison with any other of its kind, except it be the Lord Clarendon's History.'[29]

The Duchess had one final literary duty to perform: to find the right person to write the life of the Duke of Marlborough. It is not known why she took so little notice of the excellent three-volume life written by Thomas Lediard and published in 1736. Lediard had been secretary to the British envoy at Hamburg and had accompanied Marlborough on his visit to Charles XII of Sweden in 1707. The Duchess did not give Lediard access to the Duke's private papers, but he produced a reliable and scholarly account based on public documents and foreign sources and personal detail from eye-witness reports. Perhaps the Duchess did not recognize Lediard's work because she had no authority over it. As early as 1714, when the Duke was still alive, Richard Steele had asked to undertake a book entitled *The War in Flanders.* Many papers had been handed over to him but the years passed and nothing appeared. After the Duke's death the indignant Duchess had retrieved the documents and decided to pursue the matter no further until a reliable writer crossed her path.

Her instructions, however, were so dictatorial and such common knowledge that no one stepped forward. 'Painters, poets and builders have very high flights, but they must be kept down,' she often said.[30] As far as her husband's biography was concerned, she wrote out what she expected in a paper entitled: *Instructions to the Historians for Beginning the Duke of Marlborough's History*. She even told them the style in which they were to write. It was to begin: 'I write the history of the Duke of Marlborough' and it would continue in this staccato manner as it would require 'no Flourishes to set it off, but short plain facts'.[31] They must say how cheaply he had managed the war; how generous he had been with pensions; how truly sad he had been to leave King James II; and how he would have benefited far more if he had stayed with James and helped him to establish Popery (this was to show that he had not left for personal advantage!). Furthermore she was not prepared to hand over the original documents until she had read and annotated them. As there were thousands of them, the task would take months – if not years.

When Sarah was over eighty she finally settled on two reputable but undistinguished historians to undertake the biography: David Mallet, Lord Bolingbroke's literary executor, and Richard Glover, Member of Parliament for Weymouth and an enemy of Walpole, which, of course, recommended him to Sarah. She told them that she would give them each £500 for their work which would be supervised by Lord Chesterfield and her executors. 'And I desire', she stated firmly, 'that no part of the said History may be in verse, and that it may not begin in the usual Forms of writing Histories, but only from the Revolution.'[32] Mr Glover thanked the Duchess but threw in his hand. He was not prepared to work under such onerous restrictions. Mr Mallet, on the other hand, persisted, and a month before the Duchess died wrote that as he was so sensible of the dignity of his undertaking, 'I will throw all other business aside, even the work I have so long been engaged in, that I may enter into this with my whole attention and application.'[33] For years Mr Mallet went about talking of his great undertaking, but he never had anything to submit and, as Dr Samuel Johnson pointed out: 'Mallet, I believe, never wrote a single line of his projected life of the Duke of Marlborough but groped for material and thought of it till he had exhausted his mind.'[34] Nevertheless he pocketed the £500 that the Duchess left him in her will.

Three years before the Duchess breathed her last she was critically ill. She was eighty-one years old, an amazing performance for the eighteenth century, and the doctors held a consultation at the foot of her bed. 'She must be blistered or she will die,' one of them whispered. Sarah immediately sat up. 'I won't be blistered and I won't die.'[35] A year later she again fell ill and Horace Walpole wrote warily, 'Old Marlborough is dying – but who can tell?' Who indeed! She recovered once more 'to spite her enemies' and continued on her tempestuous journey for two more years.

She was not a religious woman, yet in her old age she frequently contemplated the imponderables. 'I do firmly believe in the immortality of the soul,' she wrote to Lord Marchmont in 1742, '. . . though I am not learned enough to have found out what it is like.'[36] She made preparations for her death with characteristic efficiency, reconsidering her beneficiaries and revising her will for the twenty-sixth time. She even gave explicit orders for her funeral – 'only decent, without Plumes or Escutcheons'. She was not sorry that Death was drawing near. She was crippled and weary and, even worse, cruelly bored. 'If I could have walked out of this world I would have departed long ago,' she sometimes sighed. At other times she expostulated, 'I think the generality of people in England are rediculous and I had rather be shut up between four walls than converse with them.'[37] She was even sharper in her criticism of royalty. In her old age she looked back on the long line of sovereigns whom her husband had served – Charles II, James II, William III, Anne, George I. 'Were I a man,' she wrote,

I freely own that I would not venture anything that I could avoid for any King that I know or that I have heard of. As princes are not the best judges of right and wrong, from the flattery they are used to, not to say worse of them, I think the best thing for them and the whole nation is not to let them have power to hurt themselves or anybody else.[38]

Sarah was always *avant garde*, so it is not surprising to catch a preview of the rebellious sentiments that one day would manifest themselves across the Atlantic.

In the summer of 1744, when the Duchess was in her eighty-fifth year, she felt sure that her end was approaching. 'I am going out of the world', she wrote to Johnny, 'and am packing up.'[39] She died at Marlborough House on 18 October, forty years after her husband's famous victory at Blenheim. No member of her family was with her, only her devoted servants.

John Spencer was the main beneficiary of the Duchess's will, not the spendthrift Charles, Duke of Marlborough, who was said to be in debt to the tune of half a million pounds. Charles, of course, inherited Blenheim Palace and an enormous income from the Marlborough Trust. Sarah, therefore, left very little to him, but she made a point of giving him the diamond-studded sword that she had gone to law to save from the money-lenders. Attached to this gift was Sarah's parting jibe at Charles's sister, the hated Lady Bateman. 'What makes me more uneasy about the diamond sword', she wrote, 'is that I do think Lady Bateman is capable of getting it to make buckles for stays.'[40]

The Duchess did not forget any of her servants, from the humble chairmen who carried her about, to the Porter – an educated man who 'copied her papers' and delivered her messages. Grace Ridley, the parson's daughter who had attended her all her life as a glorified housekeeper and jack-of-all-trades, was left £16,000 plus an additional annuity of £300 a year. There were several surprises in the Duchess's will. For one thing she mentioned with kindness her daughter, Mary, whom she had not seen for twenty-two years:

I give to my daughter Mary Dutchess of Montague my Gold Snuff Box that has in it two pictures of her Father the Duke of Marlborough when he was a Youth. Also a Picture of her Father covered with a large Diamond & hung to a string of small Pearls for a Bracelet. And two enamelled Pictures for a Bracelet of her Sister Sunderland and her Sister Bridgwater.[41]

There was another surprise. The Duchess made a bequest to a Member of Parliament whom she had never met, because he opposed the hated Walpole, and she therefore wished to make him independent of Court or Cabinet favour. So £10,000 went to William Pitt, 'upon Account of his Merit in the noble Defense he has made for the Support of the Laws of England and to prevent the Ruin of his Country.'[42] It is an extraordinary fact, observed Winston Churchill, that the Duchess's instinct 'in the bloom of youth and in extreme old age . . . discerned undiscovered genius in the two greatest builders of British imperial power.'[43]

When we think of the Duchess of Marlborough we should forget her quarrelsome old age and remember the pert young miss of fifteen who captured the dashing John Churchill; the sophisticated twenty-five-year-old married lady who cast a magic spell over Princess Anne; the thirty-five-year-old Countess who visited her husband in the Tower, who defied Queen Mary and who refused to patch up her feud with King William; the forty-five-year-old Duchess who drove with Queen Anne to St Paul's to offer thanks for the victory of Blenheim which had changed the face of Europe. Above all, we must remember the witty, high-spirited beauty who kept her husband enthralled for a lifetime. This was the tempestuous Sarah who cut off her wonderful blond hair to punish 'Lord Marl', but at the same time fought for him with the ferocity of a tigress. However much she lambasted her contemporaries, or railed against her own fair daughters, not one word of criticism about her husband ever reached the public. She had many glaring faults and it is not easy to forget her outrageous behaviour in demanding huge financial 'back payments' from Queen Anne for monetary gifts originally declined; nor is it easy to overlook the embarrassment of her grovelling letter to the sovereign in a futile effort to retain her Court appointments. Nevertheless, if we set the dross of her character against the gold, she emerges as a fearless, outspoken, liberty-loving woman two centuries ahead of her time.

On 21 October, two days after the Duchess's death, the coffin of the Duke of Marlborough was sent from Westminster Abbey to the Chapel at Blenheim Palace. There, John Churchill was laid to rest beside his wife for all eternity.

Select Bibliography

The list that follows is limited to books of particular value to the author in gaining an understanding of the period, and to works cited in the text. The author's most indispensable sources are Winston Churchill's wonderful biography of his ancestor; G.M.Trevelyan's masterly survey of the age of Queen Anne; John Wolf's *Louis XIV*; David Chandler's military books on Marlborough's campaigns; David Green's study of Sarah, Duchess of Marlborough; and the superb biography of Queen Anne by the American historian, Edward Gregg.

Archival Sources
    The Blenheim Papers. Now in the British Library
    The British Museum Additional Manuscripts

Reports of the Historical Manuscript Commission
    Rutland Papers, Report XII, Appendix Part V, 1889
    Dartmouth Papers, Report XI, Appendix V, 1887
    Northumberland Papers, Report III and Appendix, 1872
    Portland Papers, Report XV, Vols IV and V, 1897
    Hare Papers, Report XIV (Appendix), Part IX, 1895
    Atholl Papers, Report XII, Appendix, Part VIII, 1891
    Marlborough Papers, Report VIII, Part I, 1881
    Bath Papers, Report XV, Vols I and II, 1881
    Stuart Papers, Vol. I, 1902
    Downshire Papers, Vols I and II, 1924
    HMC Second Report

Ailesbury, Thomas Bruce, Earl of, *Memoirs* (2 vols), Roxburgh Society, London 1890
Arneth, Ritter von, *Prince Eugene von Savoyan*, Vienna 1884
Ashley, Maurice, *Charles II, The Man & The Statesman*, Weidenfeld, London 1971

Ashley, Maurice, *James II*, J.M.Dent & Sons, London 1977
Atkinson, C.T., *Marlborough and the Rise of the British Army*, G.P.Putnam & Sons, London 1921
Bathurst, Lieutenant-Colonel Benjamin *Letters of Two Queens*, London 1924
Baxter, Stephen, *William III*, Longmans, London 1966
Berwick, James Fitzjames, Duke of, *Memoirs* (2 vols), English trs. 1779
Bishop, Matthew, *Life and Adventures of Matthew Bishop from 1702–1711*, London 1774
Burnet, Gilbert, *History of His Own Time*, 1660–1685 (6 vols), London 1823
Burnet, Gilbert, *Supplement to History of His Own Time*, ed. H. Foxcroft, Oxford 1902
Butler, Iris, *The Rule of Three*, Hodder & Stoughton, London 1967
Chandler, David, *Marlborough as Military Commander*, Batsford, London 1973
Chandler, David, *The Art of War in the Age of Marlborough*, Batsford, London 1976
Churchill, Winston S., *Marlborough: His Life and Times* (4 vols), Harrap & Co., London 1933–8
Cibber, Colley, *An Apology for His Life*, London 1740
Clarendon, Henry Hyde, Earl of, *The Correspondence of the Earl of Clarendon and his brother the Earl of Rochester; and Lord Clarendon's Diary* (2 vols), ed. S.W.Singer, London 1828
Corbett, J.S., *England in the Mediterranean*, London 1904
Cowper, William First Earl, *Private Diary of William, First Earl Cowper*, Roxburgh Club, London 1846
Coxe, William, *Memoirs of John Duke of Marlborough* (6 vols), London 1820
Curtis, Brown, Beatrice, *The Letters and Diplomatic Instructions of Queen Anne*, Cassell & Co., London 1935
Dalrymple, Sir John, *Memoirs of Great Britain and Ireland*, 1790
Deane, Pvt John, *A Journal of the Campaign in Flanders*, London 1840
Dickinson, H.T., *Bolingbroke*, Constable, London 1970
Dugdale, George, *Whitehall Through the Centuries*, Phoenix House, London 1950
Dutems & Madgett, *Histoire de Jean Churchill*, Paris 1806
Evelyn, John, *Diary*, ed. H.Wheatley, London 1906
Falkus, Christopher, *Charles II*, Weidenfeld, London 1972
Feiling, Keith, *History of the Tory Party 1640 to 1714*, The Clarendon Press, Oxford 1924
Fox, Charles James, *James II*, London 1808
Foxcroft, H., *Life and Letters of George Saville, Marquis of Halifax*, London 1898
Fuller, Major-General J.F.C., *Decisive Battles of the World* (2 vols), Methuen, London 1939
Green, David, *Blenheim Palace*, Country Life, London 1951
Green, David, *Sarah, Duchess of Marlborough*, Collins, London 1967
Greene, Graham, *Lord Rochester's Monkey*, Bodley Head, London 1974
Gregg, Edward, 'Marlborough in Exile', *Historical Journal* xv, Cambridge University Press 1972
Gregg, Edward, 'Was Queen Anne a Jacobite?', *History*, Vol. 57, London 1972
Gregg, Edward, *Queen Anne*, Routledge and Kegan Paul, London 1980
Hamilton, Anthony, *Memoirs of the Count de Grammont*, London 1811

Hamilton, David, *The Diary of Sir David Hamilton 1709–1714*, ed. Philip Roberts, The Clarendon Press, Oxford 1975

Hamilton, F.W., *History of the Grenadier Guards*, London 1877

Hare, Dr Francis, *Hare's Journal*, HMC Report IV, Part IX

Hare Journal: *see* Coxe, Vol. I, and Marlborough, John, Duke of, *Letters and Dispatches*, Vol. I

Henderson, Nicholas, *Prince Eugene of Savoy*, Weidenfeld, London 1964

Holmes, Geoffrey, *British Politics in the Age of Queen Anne*, Macmillan, London 1967

Howard, Michael, *War in European History*, Oxford University Press 1976

Kane, Brigadier-General Richard, *Campaigns of King William and Queen Anne*, London 1745

La Colonie, Jean Martin de, *The Chronicles of an Old Campaigner 1692–1717*, trs. Walter Horsley, London 1904

Lediard, Thomas, *Life of John, Duke of Marlborough* (3 vols), London 1736

Legrelle, A., *La Diplomatie Française et la Succession d'Espagne*, Paris 1892

Lever, Sir Tresham, *Godolphin, His Life and Times*, John Murray, London 1952

Macpherson, James, *Original Papers*, London 1775

Marlborough, John, Duke of, *Letters and Dispatches* (5 vols), ed. General Sir George Murray, London 1845

Marlborough, John, Duke of, *The Correspondence of Marlborough and Heinsius*, ed. B. Van T'Hoff, The Hague 1951

Marlborough, Sarah, Duchess of (and Nathaniel Hooke), *Account of the Conduct of the Dowager Duchess of Marlborough from her First Coming to Court to the Year 1710*, London 1742

Marlborough, Sarah, Duchess of, *Memoirs* (including Conduct) *together with her Character of her Contemporaries & Her Opinions*, ed. William King, London 1930
    (a)   *Letters from Madresfield Court*, London 1875
    (b)   *Private Correspondence* (2 vols), ed. Lord John Jessell, London 1838

Mayor, J.E.B., *Cambridge Under Queen Anne*, Cambridge Antiquarian Society 1911

McInnes, Angus, *Robert Harley*, Gollancz, London 1970

Mérode-Westerloo, Comte de, *Mémoires . . . publie par le Comte (HMC) de Mérode-Westerloo*, Paris 1840

Millner, Sergeant John, *A Compendious Journal 1701–1712*, London 1733

Mitford, Nancy, *The Sun King*, Hamish Hamilton, London 1966

Montague, Lady Mary, *Letters*, ed. Lord Wharncliffe & W.M. Thomas, London 1887

Ogg, David, *Europe in the 17th Century*, London 1925

Orme, W., *Remarkable Passages in the Life of William Kiffin*, London 1925

Parker, Captain Robert, *Memoirs of Military Transactions, 1683–1718*, London 1747

Pelet, J.J.G., & F.E. de Vault, *Mémoires militaires relatifs à la succession d'Espagne sous Louis XIV*, Paris 1850

Pepys, Samuel, *The Diary of Samuel Pepys* (8 vols), ed. H. Wheatley, London 1893

Ranke, Leopold von, *History of England*, English trs. Oxford 1875

Reid, Stuart J., *John and Sarah, Duke and Duchess of Marlborough*, John Murray, London 1914

Robb, Nesca A., *William of Orange*, Heinemann, London 1966

Rowse, A.L., *The Early Churchills*, Macmillan, London 1956

Russell, Lady, *Letters of Rachel, Lady Russell* (2 vols), ed. Lord John Russell, Camden Society, London 1853

Saint-Simon, Louis de Rouvroy, Duc de, *Mémoires* (23 vols), ed. Churuel & Regnier, Paris 1881–1907

Seward, W., *Anecdotes*, London 1820

Shrewsbury, Charles Talbot, Duke of, *Shrewsbury Correspondence, Private and Original*, ed. William Coxe, London 1821

Snyder, Henry L., 'The Duke of Marlborough's Request of the Captain Generalcy for Life', *Journal of the Society for Army Historical Research*, xLV, 1967, pp. 67–83

Snyder, Henry L. (ed.), *The Marlborough–Godolphin Correspondence*, Oxford University Press 1975

Strickland, Agnes, *Lives of the Queens of England since the Norman Conquest*, Vol. VII, London 1852

The Works of Jonathan Swift (20 vols), ed. Sir Walter Scott, London 1824

Swift, Jonathan, *The Journal to Stella*, ed. Harold Williams, Clarendon Press, Oxford 1948

Torcy, Jean-Baptiste Colbert, Marquis de, *Mémoires*, ed. Michaud & Pouljat, Paris 1850

Trevelyan, G.M., *England Under Queen Anne* (3 vols), Longmans, London 1930–4

Turner, E.S., *The Court of St James's*, Michael Joseph, London 1959

Turner, F.C., *James II*, Eyre & Spottiswoode, London 1948

Vanbrugh, Sir John, *Correspondence* (4 vols), ed. Geoffrey Webb, Nonesuch Press, London 1927–8

Verney, Lady, *Memoirs of the Verney Family during the 17th Century*, London 1899

The Wentworth Papers 1703–1739, ed. J.J. Cartright, London 1882

Wolf, John, *Louis XIV*, Victor Gollancz, London 1968

Wolseley, General Viscount, *Life of Marlborough* (2 vols), London 1894

Source Notes

Chapter One
The Restoration

1 Christopher Falkus, *Charles II*, p. 54
2 George Dugdale, *Whitehall Through the Centuries*, p. 22
3 E.S. Turner, *The Court of St James's*, p. 157
4 *The Diary of Samuel Pepys*, Vol. II, p. 83 (16 August 1661)
5 Anthony Hamilton, *Memoirs of the Count de Grammont*, p. 107
6 Pepys, Vol. III, p. 302
7 Turner, *The Court of St James's*, p. 163
8 Pepys, Vol. II, p. 123
9 Gilbert Burnet, *History of His Own Time*, Vol. I, p. 171
10 F.C. Turner, *James II*, p. 60
11 Ibid, p. 14
12 Ibid, p. 61
13 Falkus, *Charles II*, p. 80
14 Pepys, 27 January 1666
15 Hamilton, *Memoirs of the Count de Grammont*, Vol. I, p. 149 and Vol. II, pp. 115, 117
16 Ibid, Vol. II, p. 127
17 Ibid, Vol. II, p. 235
18 Ibid, Vol. II, p. 221
19 Turner, *James II*, p. 191
20 Winston S. Churchill, *Marlborough: His Life and Times*, Vol. I, p. 51
21 John Wolf, *Louis XIV*, p. 182
22 Ibid, p. 204
23 Graham Greene, *Lord Rochester's Monkey*, p. 85
24 Count de Grammont, *The Personal History of Charles II*, ed. Sir Walter Scott (1864), p. 450
25 Churchill, *Marlborough*, Vol. I, p. 59
26 Ibid, p. 61 (Spencer Mss, Duchess of Marlborough in a letter to David Mallet, 1744)
27 Hamilton, *Memoirs of the Count de Grammont*, Vol. II, p. 285

Chapter Two
Arms and the Man

1 Wolf, *Louis XIV*, p. 198
2 Ibid, p. 213
3 Churchill, *Marlborough*, Vol. I, p. 89
4 Ibid, p. 97
5 Wolf, *Louis XIV*, p. 237
6 Churchill, *Marlborough*, Vol. I, p. 112
7 Ibid, p. 111
8 Ibid, p. 112
9 General Viscount Wolseley, *Life of Marlborough*, Vol. I, p. 146
10 Turner, *James II*, p. 112

11 Rutland Papers, HMC XII, Appendix v, Vol. II, pp. 32, 34
12 Ibid
13 David Green, *Sarah, Duchess of Marlborough*, p. 31
14 Ibid, p. 31
15 Iris Butler, *The Rule of Three*, p. 171
16 Wolseley, *Marlborough*, Vol. I, pp. 183–4
17 Ibid, p. 183
18 All the love letters in the chapter (of which only extracts are given) may be found among the Blenheim Papers in the British Library, ref. 61427 ff. 31–66. Almost all have been published by Archdeacon Coxe and all by Winston Churchill.
19 *Letters of Lord Chesterfield*, ed. Manon (1853), p. 221
20 Churchill, *Marlborough*, Vol. I, p. 125
21 Ibid, p. 129
22 Butler, *Rule of Three*, p. 35
23 *Saville Correspondence* (Camden Society), p. 49
24 Churchill, *Marlborough*, Vol. I, p. 126
25 Ibid, p. 137

Chapter Three
Lady-in-Waiting

1 Churchill, *Marlborough*, Vol. I, Appendix, p. 564
2 Stuart Reid, *John and Sarah, Duke and Duchess of Marlborough*, p. 31
3 Churchill, *Marlborough*, Vol. I, pp. 162–3
4 Ibid, p. 11
5 Wolseley, *Marlborough*, Vol. I, pp. 202–3
6 Burnet, *History*, Vol. II, p. 245
7 Wolseley, *Marlborough*, Vol. I, p. 207
8 Churchill, *Marlborough*, Vol. I, p. 151
9 Turner, *James II*, p. 141
10 Churchill, *Marlborough*, Vol. I, p. 153
11 Turner, *James II*, p. 165
12 Churchill, *Marlborough*, Vol. I, p. 156
13 *Clarendon Correspondence*, Vol. I, p. 45
14 Churchill, *Marlborough*, Vol. I, p. 162
15 Ibid, p. 164
16 Ibid, p. 165
17 *Clarendon Correspondence*, Vol. I, p. 51
18 Burnet, *History*, Vol. I, p. 304
19 Anon., *The Lives of Two Illustrious Generals* (London 1713), p. 15
20 Churchill, *Marlborough*, Vol. I, p. 172
21 Dartmouth Papers, HMC XI, Appendix v, pp. 67–8
22 Turner, *James II*, p. 215
23 Churchill, *Marlborough*, Vol. I, pp. 176–7
24 Rutland Papers, HMC Part II, p. 282
25 Nathaniel Hooke, *An Account of the Conduct of the Dowager Duchess of Marlborough . . .*, pp. 9–10
26 Lt-Colonel Benjamin Bathurst, *Letters of Two Queens*, pp. 108–9
27 Edward Gregg, *Queen Anne*, p. 27
28 Ibid, p. 28
29 Butler, *Rule of Three*, p. 55
30 William Coxe, *Memoirs of John Duke of Marlborough*, Vol. I, p. 27
31 *Sarah's Conduct*, pp. 13–14

32 Wolseley, *Marlborough*, Vol. I,
   pp. 252–3
33 *Sarah's Conduct*, pp. 10–11
34 Churchill, *Marlborough*, Vol. I,
   p. 191
35 *Sarah's Conduct*, pp. 10–11
36 Coxe, *Memoirs of John Duke of
   Marlborough*, Vol. I, p. 25
37 Butler, *Rule of Three*, p. 59

Chapter Four
The Conspiracy

1 Turner, *James II*, p. 243
2 Leopoldd von Ranke, *History of
   England*, Vol. IV, p. 215
3 Charles James Fox, *James II*,
   p. 88
4 Burnet, *History*, Vol. III, p. 269
5 Churchill, *Marlborough*, Vol. I,
   p. 209
6 Agnes Strickland, *Lives of the
   Queens of England*, Vol. VII,
   p. 91
7 Ibid, p. 98
8 Northumberland Papers, HMC
   Third Report (Appendix), p. 99
9 Wolseley, *Marlborough*, Vol. I,
   p. 292
10 *Clarendon Correspondence*, Vol.
   I, p. 141
11 Wolseley, *Marlborough*, Vol. I,
   p. 336
12 Ibid, p. 340
13 Turner, *James II*, p. 281
14 Wolseley, *Marlborough*, Vol. I,
   p. 345
15 Churchill, *Marlborough*, Vol. I,
   p. 225
16 Turner, *James II*, p. 235
17 Gilbert Burnet, *Supplement to
   History of His Own Time*, ed.
   Foxcroft, p. 293
18 Churchill, *Marlborough*, Vol. I,
   p. 190

19 Sarah, Duchess of Marlborough,
   Memoirs, ed. King, p. 230
20 Historical Manuscript
   Commission 8th Report, p. 52a
21 Burnet, *Supplement to History*,
   pp. 207–8
22 Curtis Brown, *The
   Letters and Diplomatic
   Instructions of Queen Anne*,
   p. 43
23 *Lives of Two Illustrious
   Generals*, pp. 19–21
24 Lady Verney, *Memoirs of the
   Verney Family*, Vol. IV, p. 413
25 Curtis Brown, *Letters
   and Diplomatic Instructions*,
   p. 43
26 *Russell Letters*, Vol. I, p. 204
27 Churchill, *Marlborough*, Vol. I,
   pp. 236–7
28 Curtis Brown, *Letters
   and Diplomatic Instructions*,
   p. 31
29 Ibid, pp. 30–31
30 Burnet, *History*, Vol. IV,
   pp. 291–2
31 Churchill, *Marlborough*, Vol. I,
   p. 240
32 Burnet, *History*, Vol. III, p. 181
33 Ibid, p. 279
34 Burnet, *Supplement to History*,
   pp. 29–32
35 Strickland, *Lives of the Queens
   of England*, Vol. VII, pp. 130,
   134
36 Martin Haile, *Mary of Modena*
   (London 1905), p. 173
37 Curtis Brown, *Letters
   and Diplomatic Instructions*,
   p. 34
38 Ibid, p. 35
39 *Lives of Two Illustrious
   Generals*, p. 22
40 Burnet, *History*, Vol. III, p. 324n
41 Curtis Brown, *Letters
   and Diplomatic Instructions*,
   p. 37

42 Churchill, *Marlborough*, Vol. I,
p. 272
43 Gregg, *Queen Anne*, p. 60
44 Turner, *James II*, Vol. II, p. 218
45 Churchill, *Marlborough*, Vol. I,
pp. 299–300
46 'Instructions to Historians from
Sarah Duchess of Marlborough',
reprinted in Churchill,
Marlborough, Vol. I,
pp. 569–70
47 *Sarah's Conduct*, p. 16
48 Colley Cibber, *An Apology for
His Life*, pp. 57–9

Chapter Five
William and Mary
1 Nesca A. Robb, *William of
Orange*, Vol. II, pp. 274–5
2 *Sarah's Conduct*, p. 20
3 *Life and Letters of George Saville,
Marquis of Halifax*, Vol. II,
p. 203
4 *Sarah's Conduct*, p. 21
5 Gregg, *Queen Anne*, p. 69
6 Lord Ailesbury, *Memoirs*, Vol. I,
p. 245
7 Ibid
8 Ibid
9 Burnet, *History*, Vol. IV, p. 2
10 Strickland, *Lives of the Queens
of England*, Vol. VII, p. 201
11 Macpherson, *Original Papers*,
Vol. I, p. 284
12 Ibid
13 Churchill, *Marlborough*, Vol. I,
p. 341
14 Ibid, p. 319
15 Ibid
16 Ibid
17 *Sarah's Conduct*, p. 25
18 Strickland, *Lives of the Queens
of England*, Vol. VII, p. 231
19 *Sarah's Conduct*, p. 29
20 Sir John Dalrymple, *Memoirs of

Great Britain and Ireland*, Vol.
III, p. 107 (QA p. 28)
21 *Memoirs of Mary, Queen of
England*, ed. Richard Doebner
(London 1886), pp. 17–18
22 Gregg, *Queen Anne*, p. 79
23 C.T. Atkinson, *Marlborough
and the Rise of the British Army*,
p. 110
24 Churchill, *Marlborough*, Vol. I,
p. 324
25 Butler, *Rule of Three*, p. 93
26 Wolseley, *Marlborough*, Vol. II,
p. 216
27 Churchill, *Marlborough*, Vol. I,
p. 334
28 Ernest Law, *History of Hampton
Court Palace* (London 1888),
Vol. III, p. 13
29 *Sarah's Conduct*, p. 38
30 Churchill, *Marlborough*, Vol. I,
p. 350
31 *Lives of Two Illustrious
Generals*, p. 30
32 Churchill, *Marlborough*, Vol. I,
p. 381
33 Strickland, *Lives of the Queens
of England*, Vol. VII, pp. 352–3
34 Burnet, *Supplement to History*,
pp. 373–4
35 Wolseley, *Marlborough*, Vol. II,
p. 263
36 Ibid
37 Curtis Brown, *Letters
and Diplomatic Instructions*,
pp. 52–3
38 *Sarah's Conduct*, pp. 43–4
39 Strickland, *Lives of the Queens
of England*, Vol. VII, p. 345
40 Ibid, p. 347
41 Gregg, *Queen Anne*, p. 88
42 Ibid, p. 89
43 Sarah's unpublished 'Conduct
1704', Blenheim Papers, British
Library, ref. f. 61421, ff.
71–136, f. 90
44 Ibid, f. 95

45 Curtis Brown, *Letters and Diplomatic Instructions*, p. 58
46 *Sarah's Conduct*, pp. 75–6
47 Butler, *Rule of Three*, p. 108
48 Churchill, *Marlborough*, Vol. I, Appendix, p. 568
49 Ibid, Vol. II, p. 75
50 Ibid, Vol. I, p. 565
51 Reid, *John and Sarah*, p. 422
52 Green, *Sarah*, p. 231
53 B.M. Additional Mss 35853, f. 17
54 Churchill, *Marlborough*, Vol. I, p. 46
55 Duke of Berwick, *Memoirs*, p. 113
56 Burnet, *History*, Vol. V, p. 453
57 *Shrewsbury Correspondence*, p. 47
58 Ibid, p. 53
59 Churchill, *Marlborough*, Vol. I, p. 362
60 Ibid, p. 449
61 Ailesbury, *Memoirs*, Vol. II, p. 391
62 Gregg, *Queen Anne*, p. 98
63 *Sarah's Conduct*, pp. 105–6

**Chapter Six
The Grand Alliance**

1 Lewis Jenkin, *Memoirs of Prince William Henry of Gloucester* (London 1784), p. 42
2 *Sarah's Conduct*, p. 100
3 *Shrewsbury Correspondence*, p. 220
4 Sarah's unpublished 'Conduct 1704', Blenheim Papers, British Library, ref. 61421, ff. 71–136, f. 128
5 Strickland, *Lives of the Queens of England*, Vol. VII, p. 129
6 Berwick, *Memoirs*, p. 132
7 Additional Mss 17677, QQ f. 626, Letter from Dublin envoy in London, M. L'Hermitage to the States-General
8 Wolf, *Louis XIV*, p. 487
9 Gregg, *Queen Anne*, p. 100
10 *Private Correspondence*, Vol. II, pp. 66, 120
11 Green, *Sarah*, p. 100
12 Ibid, p. 101
13 Ibid, p. 100
14 Ibid, p. 101
15 Churchill, *Marlborough*, Vol. I, p. 495
16 *Sarah's Conduct*, p. 180
17 Ibid, pp. 177–81
18 Sarah's unpublished 'Conduct 1704', Blenheim Papers, British Library, ref. 61421, ff. 71–136 (fair copy made in Duchess's life-time probably by her steward Christopher Loft), f. 127
19 Gregg, *Queen Anne*, p. 121
20 *Shrewsbury Correspondence*, p. 573
21 Gregg, *Queen Anne*, p. 117
22 Ibid
23 Ibid, p. 120
24 Ibid, p. 121
25 Churchill, *Marlborough*, Vol. I, p. 525
26 G.M. Trevelyan, *England Under Queen Anne*, Vol. I, p. 144
27 Wolf, *Louis XIV*, p. 516
28 Churchill, *Marlborough*, Vol. I, p. 545
29 Curtis Brown, *Letters and Diplomatic Instructions*, pp. 67–8
30 Churchill, *Marlborough*, Vol. I, p. 549

**Chapter Seven
The Sunshine Day**

1 Sarah, Duchess of Marlborough, *Memoirs* p. 235

2 Portland Papers, HMC Report xv, Vol. IV, p. 34

3 HMC Second Report, p. 242, Sir Robert Southwell to William King, 14 March 1702

4 Burnet, *History*, Vol. III, pp. 280–1, Dartmouth's note

5 *The Marlborough–Godolphin Correspondence*, ed. Henry L. Snyder, Vol. I, p. 67

6 John, Duke of Marlborough, *Letters and Dispatches*, ed. Murray, Vol. I, p. 4

7 Ibid, p. 127

8 Trevelyan, *England Under Queen Anne*, Vol. I, p. 239

9 Berwick, *Memoirs*, Vol. I, p. 170

10 Churchill, *Marlborough*, Vol. II, p. 135

11 Ailesbury, *Memoirs*, Vol. II, p. 535

12 Ibid, p. 541

13 W.Seward, *Anecdotes*, Vol. II, p. 259

14 Ailesbury, *Memoirs*, Vol. v, pp. 541–2

15 Ibid

16 David Chandler, *Marlborough as Military Commander*, p. 140

17 Ailesbury, *Memoirs*, Vol. v, p. 540

18 Churchill, *Marlborough*, Vol. II, p. 138

19 Wolf, *Louis XIV*, pp. 521–2

20 Ibid

21 Ibid, p. 522

22 Trevelyan, *England Under Queen Anne*, Vol. I, p. 180

23 Churchill, *Marlborough*, Vol. II, p. 156

24 Coxe, *Marlborough*, Vol. I, p. 147 (Trev. 238)

25 Churchill, *Marlborough*, Vol. II, p. 158

26 Coxe, *Marlborough*, Vol. I, p. 194

27 *Sarah's Conduct*, p. 86

28 Ibid, p. 87

29 Ibid, pp. 90–1

30 Trevelyan, *England Under Queen Anne*, Vol. I, p. 175

31 Churchill, *Marlborough*, Vol. II, p. 166

32 Gregg, *Queen Anne*, p. 169

33 Sir Tresham Lever, *Godolphin, His Life and Times*, p. 129

34 Ibid, p. 130

35 Ibid

36 Gregg, *Queen Anne*, p. 168

37 Ibid, p. 170

38 HMC Portland Report XV, IV, p. 59

39 Trevelyan, *England Under Queen Anne*, Vol. I, p. 313

40 Ailesbury, *Memoirs*, Vol. II, p. 558

41 Trevelyan, *England Under Queen Anne*, Vol. I, pp. 313–14

42 Ibid, p. 314

43 Sarah, Duchess of Marlborough, *Letters from Madresfield Court*, p. 143

44 Churchill, *Marlborough*, Vol. II, p. 236

45 Gregg, *Queen Anne*, p. 182

46 Ibid

47 J.E.B. Mayer, *Cambridge Under Queen Anne*, p. 372

48 Gregg, *Queen Anne*, p. 174

49 Ibid

50 Ibid, p. 176

51 *Marlborough–Godolphin Correspondence*, p. 237

52 Churchill, *Marlborough*, Vol. II, p. 245

53 Wolf, *Louis XIV*, p. 528

54 Coxe, *Marlborough*, Vol. I, pp. 23–4

55 Trevelyan, *England Under Queen Anne*, Vol. I, p. 16

56 Churchill, *Marlborough*, Vol. II, p. 78

57 Trevelyan, *England Under Queen Anne*, Vol. I, p. 282

58 Gregg, *Queen Anne*, p. 177
59 Churchill, *Marlborough*, Vol. II,
pp. 245–6
60 Ibid, pp. 294–5

Chapter Eight
The Blenheim Gamble

1 Trevelyan, *England Under
Queen Anne*, Vol. II, p. 344
2 Churchill, *Marlborough*, Vol. II,
p. 302
3 Ibid, p. 308
4 Ibid, p. 309
5 Captain Parker, *Memoirs of
Military Transactions*, p. 94
6 Churchill, *Marlborough*, Vol. II,
p. 335
7 Trevelyan, *Selected Documents*,
p. 100
8 Parker, *Memoirs*, pp. 94–5
9 Chandler, *Marlborough as
Military Commander*, p. 72
10 Trevelyan, *England Under
Queen Anne*, Vol. I, p. 351
11 Thomas Lediard, *Life of John,
Duke of Marlborough*, Vol. I, xx
12 John, Duke of Marlborough,
Letters and Dispatches, Vol. I,
pp. 299–301
13 Ibid, p. 320
14 Trevelyan, *England Under
Queen Anne*, Vol. II, p. 350
15 Churchill, *Marlborough*, Vol. II,
p. 336
16 Dutems & Madgett, *Histoire de
Jean Churchill*, Vol. I, p. 293
(quoting from Hare's Journal)
17 Churchill, *Marlborough*, Vol. II,
p. 343
18 Ibid, p. 360
19 Ibid, p. 354
20 Ibid, p. 354 (quoting Hare's
Journal)
21 Coxe, *Marlborough*, Vol. I,
p. 346
22 La Colonie, *Chronicles*, p. 185
23 Trevelyan, *England Under
Queen Anne*, Vol. II, p. 368
24 Coxe, *Marlborough*, Vol. I,
pp. 375–6
25 Churchill, *Marlborough*, Vol. II,
p. 408
26 La Colonie, *Chronicles*,
p. 207
27 Churchill, *Marlborough*, Vol. II,
p. 406
28 Ibid
29 Trevelyan, *England Under
Queen Anne*, Vol. I, p. 373
30 Ibid, p. 376
31 Comte de Mérode-Westerloo,
Mémoires, p. 298
32 Ibid, p. 299
33 Churchill, *Marlborough*, Vol. II,
p. 437
34 'Marlborough's letter to the
States-General says he had 166
squadrons and 64 battalions;
Kane puts the Allies at 181
squadrons and 67 battalions;
Hare at 160 and 66, Orkney at
170 and 66; Millner at 188 and
66.... The Franco–Bavarians
are put by Kane at 163 squadrons
and 82 battalions; by Millner at
160 and 87; by Marlborough at
147 and 82; by Tallard at 123
squadrons and 78 battalions and
all accounts agree making them
stronger in infantry and weaker
in cavalry.' *See* Atkinson,
*Marlborough and the British
Army*, p. 215
35 Churchill, *Marlborough*, Vol. II,
pp. 441–3
36 Portland Papers, HMC Vol. IV,
p. 503
37 John Millner, *A Compendium
Journal*, p. 115
38 Parker, *Memoirs*, p. 105
39 Brig.-General Kane, *Campaigns*
(1745 edition), p. 52

40 Pelet & de Vault, *Mémoires*, Vol. IV, p. 586
41 'The Letters of Lord Orkney', *English Historical Review*, April 1904, p. 308
42 Mérode-Westerloo, *Mémoires*, p. 309
43 *Lives of Two Illustrious Generals*, p. 72
44 Maj.-General J.F.C. Fuller, *Decisive Battles of the World*, p. 419
45 Parker, *Memoirs*, p. 110
46 Mérode-Westerloo, *Mémoires*, pp. 310–11
47 Churchill, *Marlborough*, Vol. I, p. 459
48 Hare's Journal, B.M. Additional Mss 9114 (quoted by Trevelyan, *England under Queen Anne*, Vol. I, p. 398)
49 Atholl Papers, HMC Report XII, Part VIII, p. 62
50 Hare's Journal (quoted by Trevelyan, *England Under Queen Anne*, Vol. I, p. 398)
51 Coxe, *Marlborough*, Vol. I, pp. 213–14, 313
52 Wolf, *Louis XIV*, p. 538
53 Parker, *Memoirs*, p. 112
54 Gregg, *Queen Anne*, p. 187
55 Coxe, *Marlborough*, Vol. II, p. 27
56 Saint-Simon, *Mémoires*, Vol. IV, p. 130
57 Lediard, *Marlborough*, Vol. I, p. 464

Chapter Nine
The Duke Triumphant
1 Russell Letters, Vol. II, p. 169
2 John Evelyn, *Diary*, 7 September 1704
3 Wolf, *Louis XIV*, p. 539
4 Trevelyan, *England Under Queen Anne*, Vol. I, p. 420

5 Green, *Sarah*, p. 105
6 Evelyn, *Diary*, 9 February 1704–5
7 Chandler, *The Art of War in the Age of Marlborough*, p. 7
8 Wolf, *Louis XIV*, p. 540
9 Churchill, *Marlborough*, Vol. II, p. 524
10 John, Duke of Marlborough, *Letters and Dispatches*, Vol. II, p. 82
11 Pelet & de Vault, *Mémoires*, Vol. V, p. 451
12 Dutems & Madgett, *Histoire de Jean Churchill*, Vol. II, p. 83
13 Coxe, *Marlborough*, Vol. II, p. 122
14 'I can refuse you nothing', quote by Trevelyan, *England Under Queen Anne*, Vol. II, p. 5; the other excerpts are from Churchill, *Marlborough*, Vol. II, pp. 213, 220, 530, 532, 577
15 Hare Papers, HMC Report XIV, Part IX, p. 202
16 'Letters of the First Lord Orkney', *English Historical Review*, April 1904, p. 312
17 Trevelyan, *England Under Queen Anne*, Vol. II, p. 53
18 Coxe, *Marlborough*, Vol. II, p. 144
19 Churchill, *Marlborough*, Vol. I, p. 143
20 Parker, *Memoirs*, pp. 126–7
21 Churchill, *Marlborough*, Vol. II, p. 586
22 Coxe, *Marlborough*, Vol. II, p. 170
23 Wolf, *Louis XIV*, p. 542
24 Pelet & de Vault, *Mémoires*, Vol. V, p. 90
25 Trevelyan, *England Under Queen Anne*, Vol. II, p. 409
26 *Shrewsbury Correspondence*, p. 57

27 Ailesbury, *Memoirs*, Vol. II,
   pp. 586–7
28 Trevelyan, *England Under
   Queen Anne*, Vol. II, p. 59
29 Parker, *Memoirs*, p. 128
30 Trevelyan, *England Under Queen
   Anne*, Vol. II, p. 102
31 Pelet & de Vault, *Mémoires*,
   Vol. VI, p. 18
32 La Colonie, *Chronicles*, p. 305
33 Ibid, p. 309
34 Pelet & de Vault, *Mémoires*,
   Vol. VI, p. 19
35 'Letters of the First Lord
   Orkney', *English Historical
   Review*, April 1904, p. 315
36 Ibid
37 Chandler, *Marlborough as
   Military Commander*, p. 178
38 Saint-Simon, *Mémoires*, Vol. IV,
   p. 427
39 Coxe, *Marlborough*, Vol. II,
   p. 366
40 Churchill, *Marlborough*, Vol.
   III, pp. 137–8
41 Ibid, p. 138
42 Pelet & de Vault, *Mémoires*,
   Vol. VI, p. 41
43 Churchill, *Marlborough*, Vol.
   III, p. 144
44 Pelet & de Vault, *Mémoires*,
   Vol. VI, p. 94
45 Saint-Simon, *Mémoires*, Vol. IV,
   p. 427
46 Trevelyan, *England Under
   Queen Anne*, Vol. II, p. 144
47 Churchill, *Marlborough*, Vol.
   III, p. 89
48 Reid, *John and Sarah*, p. 228

**Chapter Ten
Abigail**

1 *Memoirs of the Life of Sir John
   Clerk* (Roxburgh Club, London
   1895), p. 62
2 Curtis Brown, *Letters
   and Diplomatic Instructions*,
   p. 188
3 *The Correspondence of
   Marlborough and Heinsius*,
   p. 259
4 *Marlborough–Godolphin
   Correspondence*, Vol. II, p. 663
5 Gregg, *Queen Anne*, p. 217
6 Churchill, *Marlborough*, Vol.
   III, p. 198
7 Trevelyan, *England Under
   Queen Anne*, Vol. II, p. 130
8 John, Duke of Marlborough,
   Letters and Dispatches, Vol. III,
   p. 166
9 *Letter Books of John Hervey, 1st
   Earl of Bristol* (3 vols, London
   1894), Vol. I, p. 205
10 Green, *Sarah*, p. 80
11 Gregg, *Queen Anne*, p. 223
12 Curtis Brown, *Letters
   and Diplomatic Instructions*,
   p. 196
13 Gregg, *Queen Anne*, p. 223
14 Ibid, p. 217
15 Churchill, *Marlborough*, Vol.
   III, p. 240
16 David Green, *Blenheim Palace*,
   p. 67
17 Ibid, p. 83
18 Coxe, *Marlborough*, Vol. III,
   p. 302
19 Ibid, p. 198
20 Green, *Sarah*, p. 101
21 Letters to and from Henrietta,
   Countess of Suffolk and the
   Hon. George Berkeley, Vol. I,
   pp. 292–3
22 Gregg, *Queen Anne*, p. 112
23 *Jonathan Swift's Political Tracts
   1713–1717*, ed. Herbert Davis
   (Oxford 1951), p. 153
24 Burnet, *History*, Vol. VI, p. 27
25 Butler, *Rule of Three*, p. 191
26 *Sarah's Conduct*, pp. 183–4
27 Gregg, *Queen Anne*, p. 235

28 *Sarah's Conduct*, pp. 185–6
29 Ibid, p. 183
30 Ibid
31 *Sarah's Conduct*, pp. 205–6
32 Gregg, *Queene Anne*, p. 244
33 Curtis Brown, *Letters and Diplomatic Instructions*, p. 227
34 HMC Portland Report XV, Vol. IV, p. 454
35 Curtis Brown, *Letters and Diplomatic Instructions*, p. 229
36 Green, *Sarah*, p. 126
37 William Cowper, 1st Earl, *Private Diary*, p. 33
38 *Sarah's Conduct*, p. 261
39 Atkinson, *Marlborough and the Rise of the British Army*, p. 323
40 Churchill, *Marlborough*, Vol. III, p. 339
41 Gregg, *Queen Anne*, p. 259
42 *The Works of Jonathan Swift*, Vol. XV, p. 297
43 HMC Portland Report XV, Vol. IV, p. 496
44 Gregg, *Queen Anne*, p. 262
45 Ibid
46 Reid, *John and Sarah*, p. 275
47 Curtis Brown, *Letters and Diplomatic Instructions*, p. 270
48 Ibid, p. 355
49 Churchill, *Marlborough*, Vol. III, pp. 397–8
50 Nancy Mitford, *The Sun King*, p. 218
51 Ibid
52 Chandler, *Marlborough as Military Commander*, p. 215
53 Trevelyan, *England Under Queen Anne*, Vol. II, p. 362
54 Saint-Simon, *Mémoires*, Vol. VI, p. 56
55 Ibid, p. 57
56 Chandler, *Marlborough as Military Commander*, p. 222
57 Churchill, *Marlborough*, Vol. III, p. 431
58 Coxe, *Marlborough*, Vol. IV, p. 154
59 Atkinson, *Marlborough and the Rise of the British Army*, p. 343
60 Saint-Simon, *Mémoires*, Vol. VI, p. 64
61 Coxe, *Marlborough*, Vol. IV, pp. 152–3
62 Ibid, pp. 194–5
63 Ibid, p. 188
64 Curtis Brown, *Letters and Diplomatic Instructions*, pp. 255–6
65 Green, *Sarah*, p. 133
66 Ibid, p. 168
67 Gregg, *Queen Anne*, p. 275
68 Green, *Sarah*, p. 318
69 Ibid, p. 320
70 *Marlborough–Godolphin Correspondence*, Vol. II, p. 1073
71 Gregg, *Queen Anne*, p. 276

**Chapter Eleven
The Lost Peace**

1 *Sarah's Conduct*, p. 219
2 Curtis Brown, *Letters and Diplomatic Instructions*, p. 258
3 Gregg, *Queen Anne*, p. 278
4 Burnet, *History*, Vol. V, p. 454
5 Gregg, *Queen Anne*, p. 280
6 Ibid, p. 283
7 Ibid
8 Coxe, *Marlborough*, Vol. IV, p. 168
9 John, Duke of Marlborough, *Letters and Dispatches*, Vol. IV, p. 127
10 Atkinson, *Marlborough and the Rise of the British Army*, p. 343
11 Berwick, *Memoirs*, Vol. II, p. 406

12 HMC Portland Report XV, Vol. IV, p. 510
13 Chandler, *Marlborough as Military Commander*, p. 225
14 John, Duke of Marlborough, *Letters and Dispatches*, Vol. IV, p. 144
15 Ibid, p. 165
16 Atkinson, *Marlborough and the Rise of the British Army*, pp. 355–6
17 Ibid
18 Coxe, *Marlborough*, Vol. IV, pp. 238–9
19 Ibid, p. 235
20 Ibid
21 Churchill, *Marlborough*, Vol. IV, p. 24
22 A.Legrelle, *La Diplomatie Française et la Succession d'Espagne*, p. 387
23 Ibid, p. 385
24 Ibid, pp. 390–1
25 Berwick, *Memoirs*, Vol. II, pp. 51–3
26 Atkinson, *Marlborough and the Rise of the British Army*, p. 364
27 Churchill, *Marlborough*, Vol. III, p. 532
28 *The Complete Works of John Vanbrugh*, ed. Geoffrey Webb, Vol. IV, p. 23
29 Green, *Blenheim Palace*, p. 95
30 Sarah, Duchess of, *Private Correspondence*, Vol. I, p. 58
31 Ibid, pp. 118–19
32 Churchill, *Marlborough*, Vol. III, p. 386
33 Green, *Blenheim Palace*, p. 106
34 Wolf, *Louis XIV*, pp. 557–8
35 Torcy, Marquis de, *Mémoires*, Vol. II, p. 592
36 Churchill, *Marlborough*, Vol. IV, pp. 63–4
37 Torcy, *Mémoires*, Vol. II, p. 606
38 Ibid, p. 605
39 Churchill, *Marlborough*, Vol. IV, p. 75

40 A. Geoffrey, *Lettres Authentiques*, Vol. II, p. 207 (*see* Reid, *John and Sarah*, p. 293)
41 Reid, *John and Sarah*, p. 295
42 Coxe, *Marlborough*, Vol. IV, p. 393
43 Churchill, *Marlborough*, Vol. IV, p. 87
44 *The Correspondence of Marlborough and Heinsius*, p. 445
45 Gregg, *Queen Anne*, p. 288
46 Wolf, *Louis XIV*, p. 566
47 Ibid, p. 567
48 Ibid
49 Ibid, p. 568
50 Trevelyan, *England Under Queen Anne*, Vol. III, p. 13
51 Ibid, p. 14
52 Chandler, *Marlborough as Military Commander*, pp. 264–5
53 Coxe, *Marlborough*, Vol. V, p. 70
54 Ritter von Arneth, *Prince Eugene von Savoyan*, Vol. II, p. 88
55 Reid, *John and Sarah*, p. 299
56 Trevelyan, *England Under Queen Anne*, Vol. III, p. 18
57 Churchill, *Marlborough*, Vol. IV, p. 181
58 Sarah, Duchess of Marlborough, *Private Correspondence*, Vol. II, p. 293
59 Ibid, p. 401

**Chapter Twelve
Sarah's Dismissal**

1 *See* H.L. Snyder, 'The Duke of Marlborough's Request for a Captain Generalcy for Life', *Journal of the Society for Army Historical Research*, XLV, 1967, pp. 73–4

2 Curtis Brown, *Letters and Diplomatic Instructions*, pp. 285–6

3 Coxe, *Marlborough*, Vol. v, pp. 110–11

4 Gregg, *Queen Anne*, p. 292

5 Sarah, Duchess of Marlborough, *Private Correspondence*, Vol. I, p. 129

6 Green, *Sarah*, p. 147

7 Gregg, *Queen Anne*, p. 294

8 Green, *Sarah*, p. 148

9 Gregg, *Queen Anne*, p. 302

10 Ibid

11 *Marlborough–Godolphin Correspondence*, Vol. III, p. 1346 (QA 303)

12 Geoffrey Holmes, *British Politics in the Age of Queen Anne*, p. 209

13 Lever, *Godolphin*, p. 225

14 Sarah, Duchess of Marlborough, *Private Correspondence*, pp. 391–2

15 B. M. Additional Mss 41178

16 Hare Journal, HMC Report XIV, p. 228

17 Legrelle, *La Diplomatie Française*, Vol. v, p. 486

18 Wolf, *Louis XIV*, p. 568

19 Lever, *Godolphin*, p. 225

20 Churchill, *Marlborough*, Vol. IV, pp. 235–6

21 Ibid, p. 90

22 Green, *Sarah*, p. 150

23 Churchill, *Marlborough*, Vol. IV, p. 210

24 Coxe, *Marlborough*, Vol. v, p. 156

25 Green, *Sarah*, p. 150

26 Gregg, *Queen Anne*, p. 307

27 Blenheim Papers, British Library, ref. 61422, 'an Account of a Conversation with the Queen upon Good Friday, 1710', ff. 72–7

28 Ibid

29 Coxe, *Marlborough*, Vol. v, p. 278

30 Curtis Brown, *Letters and Diplomatic Instructions*, p. 303

31 Churchill, *Marlborough*, Vol. IV, pp. 275–6

32 Hamilton, *Diary*, p. 9 (QA)

33 Ibid (QA 315)

34 Ibid

35 Churchill, *Marlborough*, Vol. IV, p. 252

36 Parker, *Memoirs*, p. 91

37 *The Correspondence of Marlborough and Heinsius*, p. 280

38 Green, *Sarah*, p. 160

39 Ibid

40 *Marlborough–Godolphin Correspondence*, Vol. III, pp. 1513–14

41 Ibid, p. 1575

42 Coxe, *Marlborough*, Vol. v, pp. 321–2

43 Chandler, *Marlborough as Military Commander*, p. 281

44 Gregg, *Queen Anne*, p. 324

45 Churchill, *Marlborough*, Vol. IV, p. 318

46 Reid, *John and Sarah*, p. 345

47 *The Prose Works of Jonathan Swift*, ed. Temple Scott (12 vols, G. Bell & Sons, London 1922), Vol. IX, p. 97

48 Hamilton, *Diary*, p. 20 (QA p. 326)

49 Ibid, p. 12

50 Ibid

51 Ibid, p. 23

52 Ibid, p. 26

53 Ibid, p. 22

54 Gregg, *Queen Anne*, p. 326

55 Hamilton, *Diary*, p. 21

56 Sarah, Duchess of Marlborough, *Private Correspondence*, p. 106

57 Churchill, *Marlborough*, Vol. IV, p. 370

58 Ibid, p. 340

59 Hamilton, *Diary*, p. 24

60 Ibid, p. 23

61 Ibid, p. 29
62 Ibid, p. 29
63 Green, *Sarah*, p. 172

Chapter Thirteen
Marlborough's Last Campaign

1 Sarah, Duchess of Marlborough, *Memoirs*, p. 227
2 Coxe, *Marlborough*, Vol. v, p. 312
3 Churchill, *Marlborough*, Vol. iv, p. 416
4 Wolf, *Louis XIV*, p. 579
5 Chandler, *Marlborough as Military Commander*, p. 287
6 Ibid, p. 288, Footnote
7 Ibid, p. 179
8 Lediard, *Marlborough*, Vol. iii, p. 149
9 Parker, *Memoirs*, pp. 181–2
10 Ibid, p. 184
11 B.M. Stowe Mss 751, f.10, from the camp before Bouchain, 11 September 1711
12 Parker, *Memoirs*, pp. 191–2
13 Churchill, *Marlborough*, Vol. iv, p. 455
14 Gregg, *Queen Anne*, p. 339
15 Churchill, *Marlborough*, Vol. iv, p. 466
16 Ibid, p. 468
17 Gregg, *Queen Anne*, p. 335
18 Wolf, *Louis XIV*, p. 578
19 Marlborough Papers, HMC p. 39 (Wolf, *Louis XIV*, p. 578)
20 Churchill, *Marlborough*, Vol. iv, p. 479
21 Macpherson, *Original Papers*, Vol. ii, p. 347
22 HMC Bath, Vol. i, p. 213
23 Ibid, p. 217
24 Gregg, *Queen Anne*, p. 345
25 *Parliamentary History*, ed. William Cobbett (London 1810), Vol. vi, p. 1037–8
26 Coxe, *Marlborough*, Vol. vi, p. 153
27 Churchill, *Marlborough*, Vol. iv, p. 505
28 Matthew Bishop, *Life and Adventures*, pp. 235–6 (SC 511)
29 Churchill, *Marlborough*, Vol. iv, p. 511
30 Kane, *Campaigns of King William and Queen Anne*, p. 102
31 Jonathan Swift, *The Journal to Stella*, Vol. ii, p. 453
32 Burnet, *History*, Vol. vi, pp. 36–7
33 Churchill, *Marlborough*, Vol. iv, p. 515
34 Ibid, p. 517
35 Swift, *The Journal to Stella*, Vol. ii, p. 481
36 Burnet, *History*, p. 103 (WC 52)
37 Coxe, *Marlborough*, Vol. vi, p. 24
38 Burnet, *History*, Vol. vi, p. 34
39 Green, *Sarah*, p. 171
40 Churchill, *Marlborough*, Vol. iv, p. 532
41 Ibid, Vol. i, Appendix, p. 569
42 Trevelyan, *England Under Queen Anne*, Vol. iii, p. 211
43 Portland Papers, HMC Vol. v, p. 157
44 *Bolingbroke Correspondence, Letters and Correspondence of Henry St John Viscount Bolingbroke*, ed. Gilbert Parke (4 vols, London 1798), Vol. ii, p. 320
45 Churchill, *Marlborough*, Vol. iv, pp. 541–2
46 *Parliamentary History*, Vol. vi, pp. 1135–8 (QA 357)
47 *Bolingbroke Correspondence*, Vol. ii, p. 403
48 Trevelyan, *England Under Queen Anne*, Vol. iii, p. 211
49 Gregg, *Queen Anne*, p. 358
50 *Parliamentary History*, Vol. vi, p. 1146

51 Trevelyan, *England Under Queen Anne*, Vol. III, p. 219
52 Coxe, *Marlborough*, Vol. VI, p. 186
53 *Bolingbroke Correspondence*, Vol. II, p. 403
54 Gregg, *Queen Anne*, p. 356
55 Reid, *John and Sarah*, p. 437
56 Sarah, Duchess of Marlborough, *Private Correspondence*, Vol. II, pp. 125–6
57 Parker, *Memoirs*, p. 200
58 *Parliamentary History*, Vol. VI, p. 1131 (WC 548)
59 Gregg, 'Marlborough in Exile', p. 596

Chapter Fourteen
Plots and Counter-plots Abroad
1 *Parliamentary History*, Vol. VI, p. 1131
2 Green, *Sarah*, p. 182
3 Sarah, Duchess of Marlborough, *Letters from Madresfield Court*, p. 32
4 Ibid, p. 28
5 Ibid, p. 26
6 Gregg, 'Marlborough in Exile', p. 599
7 Ibid
8 Ibid
9 Green, *Sarah*, p. 185
10 Sarah, Duchess of Marlborough, *Letters from Madresfield Court*, p. 68
11 Gregg, 'Marlborough in Exile', p. 603 (from B.M. Stowe Mss 751, fos 67–8)
12 Ibid (from B.M. Stowe Mss 751, fos 48–51)
13 Portland Papers, HMC Vol. V, p. 374
14 Trevelyan, *England Under Queen Anne*, Vol. III, pp. 266–8
15 Churchill, *Marlborough*, Vol. IV, p. 605
16 Stuart Papers, Vol. I, p. 308
17 Sarah, Duchess of Marlborough, *Letters from Madresfield Court*, p. 69
18 Ibid, p. 41
19 *Bolingbroke Correspondence*, Vol. IV, p. 579
20 Churchill, *Marlborough*, Vol. IV, p. 610
21 *The Works of Jonathan Swift*, Vol. XVI, p. 149
22 Parker, *Memoirs*, p. 219
23 *The Correspondence of Jonathan Swift*, ed. Harold Williams (5 vols, London 1963–5), Vol. II, p. 86
24 Gregg, 'Marlborough in Exile', pp. 615–16
25 Downshire Papers, HMC Vol. III, Part II, p. 902
26 *Diary of Mary, Countess of Cowper* (London 1864), p. 196
27 *The Wentworth Papers*, p. 408
28 Churchill, *Marlborough*, Vol. IV, p. 635
29 Coxe, *Marlborough*, Vol. I, p. 365
30 A.L. Rowse, *The Early Churchills*, p. 349
31 Green, *Sarah*, p. 199
32 Ibid, p. 200
33 B.M. Stowe Mss 751, f. 146
34 Ibid, f. 152
35 Sir John Vanbrugh, *Correspondence*, Vol. IV, p. 85
36 Butler, *Rule of Three*, p. 294
37 Green, *Sarah*, p. 210
38 Ibid, pp. 213–14 (attributed to Dr Abel Evans)
39 B.M. Stowe Mss 751, f. 131
40 Ibid, f. 134
41 Green, *Sarah*, p. 208
42 Butler, *Rule of Three*, p. 296
43 Blenheim Papers, British Library, ref. 61464, f. 84
44 Ibid, f. 87
45 Reid, *John and Sarah*, p. 229

46 Green, *Sarah*, p. 207
47 Churchill, *Marlborough*, Vol. IV,
   pp. 646–7 (from Blenheim
   Papers, British Library, Sarah's
   Green Book, ref. 61451, f. 116)
48 Ibid, pp. 648–9 (from Sarah's
   Green Book, ref. 61451, f. 117)
49 Parker, *Memoirs*, p. 197
50 Ibid, pp. 201–2

Chapter Fifteen
Sarah Alone

1 to 7 Green, *Sarah*, pp. 240–5. The
   letters between Sarah and the
   Duke of Somerset can also be
   found in the Blenheim Papers,
   British Library, ref. 61458
8 Vanbrugh, *Correspondence*, Vol. IV,
   p. 170
9 Ibid, pp. 170–1
10 Butler, *Rule of Three*, p. 319
11 Ibid, p. 117
12 Green, *Sarah*, p. 253
13 Ibid
14 Green, *Sarah*, p. 304
15 Blenheim Papers, British Library,
   Sarah's Green Book, ref. 61451, f. 50
16 *Letters of a Grandmother*, ed. Gladys
   Scott Thomson (Jonathan Cape,
   London 1943), p. 96
17 Reid, *John and Sarah*, p. 435
18 *Lord Hervey and His Friends*, ed.
   Lord Ilchester, John Murray,
   London 1950, Appendix

19 Butler, *Rule of Three*, p. 327
20 Ibid, p. 328
21 *Lord Hervey and His Friends*, p. 258
22 Reid, *John and Sarah*, p. 437
23 Green, *Sarah*, p. 237
24 Blenheim Papers, British Library,
   Sarah's Green Book, ref. 61451, f. 50
25 Green, *Sarah*, pp. 271–2
26 Rowse, *The Early Churchills*, p. 397
27 *The Letters of Horace Walpole*, ed.
   Mrs Paget Toynbee (16 vols, The
   Clarendon Press, London 1903),
   Vol. I, p. 139
28 G.M. Godden, *Henry Fielding*,
   (London 1910), p. 137
29 Rowse, *The Early Churchills*, p. 401
30 *Letters of a Grandmother*, p. 134
31 Churchill, *Marlborough*, Vol. I,
   Appendix
32 Ibid
33 Blenheim Papers, British Library,
   ref. 61451, 23 September 1744
34 Green, *Sarah*, p. 298
35 *The Letters of Horace Walpole*, Vol.
   I, p. 140
36 Green, *Sarah*, p. 306
37 Ibid, p. 303
38 Sarah, Duchess of Marlborough,
   Memoirs, p. 301
39 Green, *Sarah*, p. 307
40 B.M. Additional Mss 29549
41 Burnet, *History*, Vol. VI, p. 30
42 Rowse, *The Early Churchills*, p. 403
43 Churchill, *Marlborough*, Vol. IV,
   p. 652

Index